Teaching Reading & Writing
Combining Skills, Strategies, & Literature

Second Edition

D0705613

John F. Savage
Boston College

Boston, Massachusetts Burr Ridge, Illinois Dubuque, Iowa
Madison, Wisconsin New York, New York San Francisco, California St. Louis, Missouri

WCB/McGraw-Hill

A Division of The McGraw·Hill Companies

TEACHING READING AND WRITING: COMBINING SKILLS, STRATEGIES, AND LITERATURE

 This book is printed on recycled paper containing 10% postconsumer waste.

1 2 3 4 5 6 7 8 9 0 QPF/QPF 9 0 9 8 7

ISBN 0–697–24437–7

Publisher: *Jane E. Vaicunas*
Sponsoring editor: *Beth Kaufmann*
Marketing manager: *Daniel M. Loch*
Project manager: *Gloria G. Schiesl*
Production supervisor: *Sandy Ludovissy*
Cover designer: *LuAnn Schrandt*
Photo research coordinator: *Carrie K. Burger*
Art editor: *Jodi K. Banowetz*
Compositor: *Shepherd, Inc.*
Typeface: *10/12 Palatino*
Printer: *Quebecor Printing Group/Fairfield*

Library of Congress Cataloging-in Publication Data
Savage, John F., 1938-
     Teaching reading and writing: combining skills, strategies, and literature/John F. Savage.–2nd ed.
          p.   cm.
     Rev. ed. of: Teaching reading using literature. c1994
     Includes bibliographical references and index.
     ISBN 0–697–24437–7
     1. Reading (Elementary).   2. Children's literature—Study and teaching (Elementary)   I. Savage, John F., 1938-   Teaching reading using literature.   II. Title.
LB1573.S245   1998
372.4–dc21   97–8708
                                                       CIP

http://www.mhhe.com

Contents

Preface

Mrs. Chris Zajak, the elementary school teacher who is the "star" of Tracy Kidder's book *Among Schoolchildren,* was interviewed in 1989 by *The Boston Globe.* When the reporter asked Mrs. Zajak, "What teaching methods have you changed since you started teaching 17 years ago?" the teacher replied, "I use a lot more literature now to teach reading."

She went on to explain how she had discovered the power of children's literature as a means of helping her pupils come to love reading and to become lifelong readers.

Thus began the preface to the first edition of this book, *Teaching Reading Using Literature.* In the few short years that have elapsed since Chris Zajak's interview, three major movements have risen in reading and writing instruction in the elementary grades:

1. The use of children's literature has become firmly established. Literature-based instruction is no longer a "new and different" approach to teaching reading and writing; it is becoming the norm. The vast majority of elementary school teachers now use trade books for instructional purposes.
2. Basal readers have become more literature based. Every newly published basal reading series is saturated with authentic literature produced by noted authors. Trade books have become integral parts of the text series designed to teach reading.
3. Some have become worried that we've lost our focus on skills. They wonder what has happened to phonics, and they worry that we will lose some of the positive features of the skills-based approach that dominated reading instruction for a hundred years or more.

Second Editon

This second edition—*Teaching Reading and Writing: Combining Skills, Strategies, and Literature*—is designed for Chris Zajak and the thousands of teachers like her in today's elementary classrooms—teachers who have adopted literature as the primary vehicle for reading and writing instruction. While this edition continues to treat literature as the centerpiece of the classroom literacy program, it is focused on the balance children need in learning to read and write.

While the orientation and organization of the book are unchanged, the content has been updated to reflect changes that have occurred in literacy instruction. Overall, you will find an increased focus on combining instruction in reading skills and strategies with the use of children's literature, a change reflected in the revised title of the text. Professional references have been updated in all chapters, and newly published children's trade books are included.

In addition to updated content, many chapters contain specific changes in other areas. In the chapter on children's literature, science fiction has been added and the discussion of censorship has been expanded. Throughout the book you will see a greater emphasis on the use of technology in teaching reading and writing. New features have been added on decoding, multiple intelligence, integrated units, and other topics. The chapter on atypical learners has been revised to discuss the practice of inclusion, and the chapter on assessment has been expanded to provide more options and ideas for alternative assessment—including running records, retelling, portfolios, and other techniques. Caldecott and Newbery Award winners are listed in the appendix. And throughout, this edition provides an increased number of practical, classroom-tested ideas.

Teaching Reading and Writing: Combining Skills, Strategies, and Literature continues to deal with the whys and hows of using trade books in the classroom. The book is not primarily about children's literature; it is about planning and implementing a reading and writing program that uses literature as a major component in teaching children how to read.

What is literature-based reading? Like love, literature-based reading means different things to different people. For some teachers, it means abandoning conventional instructional materials for reading and writing and using only children's trade books for literacy instruction. For others, it means following a literature-based basal program and supplementing that program with trade books. For still others, it means retaining features of conventional instruction but increasing the use of trade books for instructional purposes. Whether trade books are used alone or in close combination with other instructional materials, literature is an integral part of promoting literacy in the classroom.

In a literature-based approach, teachers use literature as the starting point for teaching children how to read. Reading instruction starts with story and not with skills. Teachers begin with stories and poems, folktales and fairy tales, biographies and realistic fiction, and other genres that make up the rich montage of literature for children. From this base, teachers lead children to discover the joys of effective reading and writing, and to develop a lifelong love of reading.

Does literature-based instruction mean that skills and strategies are abandoned altogether? *Absolutely not!* Do children need to learn phonics? Of course they do! It's impossible to learn to read and write an alphabetic language like English without a knowledge of the orthographic system of sounds and symbols that written language is based upon. Do children need strategies? Of course they do! We all need to know how to figure out an unfamiliar word we encounter as we read and how to determine how to write a word that we're not sure how to spell. And we need the best and most efficient ways of making meaning of what we read.

But do children also need literature? You bet they do! Literature is as essential to their education as it is to their lives. It enriches their experiences, stimulates their imaginations, fosters their personal growth, and educates their hearts as well as their heads. *Teaching Reading and Writing: Combining Skills, Strategies, and Literature* focuses throughout on the balanced instruction that characterizes the teaching of competent teachers as they integrate important skills and strategies into instruction using children's books.

How successful is literature-based instruction? Very. A growing body of evidence indicates that using children's literature is a very effective way of teaching children how to read. Anecdotal accounts from teachers and empirical studies from researchers show that literature-based instruction produces positive results with a range of pupils—with those who learn easily as well as with those who do not.

What does a literature-based program look like in action? Read on. There is no single, simple definition of a literature-based instructional program, but the chapters that follow present the basic philosophy of using literature as the instructional centerpiece of language arts in the classroom, along with practical suggestions on how this program can be put to work in a balanced, efficient manner in the classroom.

A Word about Organization

Teaching Reading and Writing: Combining Skills, Strategies, and Literature is divided into thirteen chapters. The first three chapters are largely foundational. The opening chapter briefly presents literature-based reading, discusses how it differs from more conventional approaches, and explains how to achieve a balanced program with literature at the core. Chapter 2 presents an overview of the field of children's literature, a quick review for those who have had a course in this important area and a brief introduction for those who have not yet studied the topic. Chapter 3 deals with how to organize and manage a literature-based reading and writing program in the classroom.

The next seven chapters deal with the content of developmental literacy instruction—the day-to-day topics related to teaching reading and writing in the elementary school classroom. Chapter 4 focuses on emergent literacy, emphasizing how literature contributes to the developing reading and writing competencies of young children in the early years of their school lives. Chapter 5 focuses on words—how instruction in phonics and other decoding strategies can be integrated with vocabulary development within the context of literature-based instruction.

The next two chapters explore reading comprehension. Chapter 6 examines narrative text, discussing how teachers can help pupils develop broader and deeper understanding of the stories they read. Chapter 7 extends the topic of comprehension to expository text—that is, understanding and producing text written to present information rather than to tell stories. Chapter 8 is a brief chapter that focuses on the library, a central resource for children's literature and other materials used as tools for teaching reading and writing. The next chapter is about oral reading, a perennial classroom practice that has taken on new importance in light of literature-based instruction. And chapter 10 examines reading-writing connections, since both dimensions of literacy are integrally connected in the instructional process.

The final three chapters round out the book with topics of special importance in classroom reading and writing instruction. Chapter 11 focuses on adapting literature-based instruction to meet the needs of the full spectrum of children typically found in any classroom, including children with special learning needs. With a focus on multicultural literature, chapter 12 explains how to make the best use of literature with children who come from diverse cultural and linguistic backgrounds. The final chapter is about assessment; it explores the tools and techniques teachers use to measure the success of their efforts in teaching reading with literature.

An honest attempt has been made throughout the book to balance theory and practice. It is important that teachers know how to use literature to teach reading, but even more important that they understand how literature contributes to the development of pupils' abilities and attitudes in learning to read and write. Every chapter features boxed sections with practical suggestions for applying theory to practice, along with resources such as book lists. Suggestions for in-class and field-based assignments follow each chapter.

The Audience

This book is written for teachers—those preparing to enter the teaching profession as well as current professionals trying to stay abreast of the field and adapt their teaching strategies to reflect current research and trends in teaching reading. The book is basic enough to be appropriate for undergraduates or graduate students who may be taking their first course in teaching reading. At the same time, the content is contemporary enough to be appropriate for experienced teachers who are seeking a sound theoretical base and usable, practical ideas for using literature for instructional purposes in their classrooms.

The book was written in the belief that of all the forces that have an impact on education—administrative pressures, organizational patterns, materials, facilities, policies, and everything else that touches the lives of teachers and students—the teacher is at the heart of the instructional process. The competent professional in the classroom is the one who makes things happen.

Ancillaries

An Instructor's Manual is available for teachers using this text. The manual includes a chapter overview, instructional suggestions, test items, and resources and references for each chapter. It also includes transparency masters and an appendix that shows a sample course syllabus.

To access more information about children's literature, use *Children's Literature Database.* This database was created by Barbara Kiefer, coauthor of *Children's Literature in the Elementary School* (6th ed.), by Huck, Hepler, Hickman, and Kiefer. The database includes over 2,000 titles and can be sorted by many different criteria, including genre, reading level, interest, and more. It is available in both Macintosh and Windows (IBM compatible) versions.

Acknowledgments

The appreciation expressed to those who help an author is often a professional courtesy. The thanks I offer to the people who helped shape this book are heartfelt expressions of gratitude. Sections of this book belong to them as much as to me (although I'll take responsibility for misinterpretations of any of their ideas).

Teachers in whose classrooms I have worked—professionals like Deborah Davies, Annmarie White-Hunter, Ann Carmola, Pam Amster, and others—helped me grasp firsthand the practical realities of using literature with children. Literally hundreds of teacher-colleagues whom I encountered in classes, at in-service workshops, and at conferences provided ideas and suggestions that I begged, borrowed, or stole from them. A number of graduate students—Patricia Heimgartner, Suzanne Bresnahan, Keri Consiglio, Christine Beard, Christine Daly, and Amy Selden—provided practical assistance. My friend and colleague Audrey Friedman provided creative ideas and conceptual input.

I would also like to thank those reviewers whose invaluable suggestions guided me throughout the development of this second edition: Dolores P. Dickerson, Howard University; Dr. Jann James, Troy State University; Ann D. Rainsford, University of South Carolina-Aiken; Delores E. Heiden, University of Wisconsin-La Crosse; Marilyn Wikstrom, Buena Vista University; Janis E. Schmoll, University of Rio Grande; and Deborah H. Strevy, Samford University.

The interest and help of Sue Pulvermacher-Alt, Suzanne Guinn, Sarah Dermody, Amy Halloran, Gloria Schiesl, LuAnn Schrandt, and Laura Fuller kept me going when my get-up-and-go occasionally got up and went.

More personally, thanks are due to Stacey, Jay, and Donna, my three children, whose accomplishments are testimony to the power of literature in their lives, and to Mary Jane, my wife, whose love has never diminished.

Each of these people contributed time and talent to help make this book a tool for teachers to use in making literature part of children's instructional lives in the classroom. I thank them all.

John F. Savage

*L*iterature and Literacy in the Elementary Classroom

James L. Shaffer

Chapter 1 Outline

Features

Key Concepts in This Chapter

Children's literature has inundated the language arts curriculum in today's schools. Literature-based instruction emphasizes the use of trade books in teaching children to read and write.

In contrast to conventional skills-based instruction, a literature-based approach places primary emphasis on story and meaning instead of on development of specific reading skills.

A literature-based approach offers compelling advantages in helping pupils learn to read and write.

Trade books can be used alone or in combination with other instructional materials to create an inspired, effective instructional program.

Introduction

*L*earning to read and write has long been at the heart of education. In any literate society, the issue of how best to teach reading is a concern, and reading instruction is a major part of the educational enterprise. Reading is the central focus of primary grade instruction, and "readin' and writin'" continue to constitute two-thirds of the 3 R's in our schools.

Methods and materials for teaching reading have evolved through the ages. Young schoolboys in ancient Greece and Rome practiced drills on letters and syllables while studying the works of the masters. These practices continued through the Middle Ages for those fortunate enough to enjoy the opportunity to gain an education. When Johannes Gutenberg invented the printing press in the mid-15th century, books previously copied by hand and available to a select few became mechanically producible and available to many. Learning to read assumed a more important role in the lives of more people.

In early America, Pilgrim children studied the *New England Primer*—

> A In Adam's Fall
> we sinned all.
> B Thy Life to mend,
> This Book attend.

—learning the alphabet so that they could read the Bible and other religious materials. After the American Revolution, children used the Noah Webster *Readers* and the *New American Spelling Book,* programs that taught the same alphabetic method with content that stressed moral principles and patriotic values. In the mid-1800s, the famous *McGuffey Eclectic Readers,* the first graded reading series, appeared, filled with prayers, psalms, and stories about children and animals that reflected the values and experiences of society at the time.

In the early years of the 20th century, an intense interest in reading instruction resulted in several new programs. These new reading series were significantly different from earlier programs—they stressed learning whole words rather than letters and syllables; they emphasized reading comprehension rather than oral reading; they contained stories that reflected the experiences of middle-class children, featuring characters like the legendary Dick and Jane; they were written with the expressed purpose of helping pupils develop the skills needed to learn to read. As the instructional pendulum swung from whole word reading to phonics and linguistics, and then back again to a more eclectic approach, the content of reading books changed to reflect both social and educational trends.

As schools enter the 21st century, a new approach to literacy instruction has emerged, an approach that uses children's literature as the major vehicle for teaching children how to read and write. Increasingly, schools use real books by real authors as part of the reading program. Pupils use

1.1 Putting Ideas to Work
What Is a Trade Book?

A trade book is a book that is published for sale to the general public, as opposed to a textbook that is published specifically for instructional purposes. Trade books are the picture books, storybooks, novels, and informational books found in bookstores and on library shelves. Although written for sale to the general public and not designed primarily for school use, trade books are being used more and more in classrooms, both as independent entities and as part of literature-based programs.

Trade books may be written primarily:

To entertain, as Ludwig Bemelmans's wonderful stories about *Madeline* do.

To inform, as do the science books by Franklyn Branley in the Let's-Read-and-Find-Out series, such as *Sunshine Makes the Seasons*.

To both entertain and inform, as do Jean Fritz's many humorous but historically accurate accounts of American history, such as *And Then What Happened, Paul Revere?*

Trade books are the essential elements in literature-based reading programs.

trade books (see Putting Ideas to Work 1.1) as a major tool in developing their reading ability. A new generation of basal readers—programs designed to serve as the main vehicles of reading instruction—has been infused with quality literature written for children. In short, a tidal wave of literature-based reading has hit our schools.

Educators have widely promoted and adopted the move toward literature-based reading instruction. "At the 1987 Coalition of English conference—a kind of summit meeting of language arts educators from all levels of schooling—literature was the most widely discussed topic of the entire meeting" (Teale, 1990; p. 808). Programs at teachers' conventions continue to offer numerous workshops on how to use literature to teach reading and writing; journals are full of articles on the topic; catalogues bulge with literature-related classroom materials; and professional books about literature in the classroom flood the educational marketplace. A survey of state reading and language arts directors indicates that statewide initiatives and literacy programs that hinge on literature exist in many states. In short, in the past decade or so, schools have experienced what McGee (1992) has called "a literature-based reading revolution."

Standards for the English Language Arts, developed jointly by the International Reading Association and the National Council of Teachers of English (1996), call for students to read "a wide range of literature from many periods in many genres to build an understanding of the many dimensions (e.g., philosophical, ethical, aesthetic) of human experience." These national standards call for the inclusion of both classic and contemporary works of poetry, short stories, novels, plays, essays, biographies, and autobiographies, not only as a vehicle for learning to read and write, but also to experience other times and places in human culture and to discover the relevance of literature to their own lives.

Local initiatives toward literature-based instruction are pervasive; curriculum guides published in the past ten years reflect the trend. Data from the 1992 National Reading Assessment (Mullis, Campbell, and Farstrup, 1993) indicate that 88 percent of children in fourth grade are in classrooms with a heavy or moderate emphasis on literature-based teaching, and that "students whose teachers reported a heavy emphasis on literature-based reading instruction had a higher average proficiency than students who received little or no such emphasis" (p. 10).

Literature will continue to shape language arts instruction into the 21st century. When preeminent researchers were asked to project research questions regarding a curriculum that would equip children for the future, literature-based instruction was one of the major topics that emerged from their responses (Purcell-Gates, 1995). The tidal wave of literature has swept with it the conventional basal reader. Conventional basals were designed to be skill-development tools, containing stories written with a tightly controlled vocabulary for the specific purpose of helping children develop particular reading skills. Today's basals abound with quality children's stories, stories written by well-known and well-respected children's authors (Reutzel and Larsen, 1995).

What Is a Literature-Based Program?

Literature-based reading is a program that uses children's literature as the central core for language arts instruction. It is a program in which literature is an integral (rather than incidental) part of teaching pupils how to read and write. Such programs extensively use trade books as instructional tools. They center teaching on authentic texts written for meaningful purposes.

Children's literature is used in different ways for different purposes at different levels in literature-based programs. All these programs, however, use literature to help pupils develop the ability and inclination to read. There is no designated set of trade books to be used in a prescribed fashion at a particular grade level. Programs consist of lessons and activities using a wealth of children's books and stories—picture books, fiction, informational books, folktales, poetry, fantasy, and other literary forms—to promote pupils' language development and literacy competency.

Characteristics of Literature-Based Instruction

Certain qualities or characteristics mark programs that make literature the heart of the language curriculum.

Trade books constitute the centerpiece of the curriculum. Stories and poems serve as major vehicles of instruction in the language arts, and literature is related to other components of the school program. Activities related to literature are a regular part of each day's activities. Pupils have time to

share books, to discuss what they have read, to write and react to stories, to talk with visitors about what they are reading, and to show their enthusiasm about reading not only as a school subject but as part of their lives.

Trade books are primary vehicles in the instructional process. In the early stages, predictable books like Pat Hutchins's *Good Night, Owl* and simple children's classics such as Wanda Gag's *Millions of Cats* are used to involve pupils in their initial reading experiences. In the upper grades, books such as Lois Lowry's *The Giver* and *Number the Stars* or Robert Lawson's *Rabbit Hill* are used for directed reading lessons in small groups. At all levels, pupils receive time and encouragement to read and respond to literature all day long.

Reader response is an integral feature of literature-based instruction. Response is part of the meaning-making process pupils engage in as they read. Students respond in a variety of ways—through discussion, the arts, and writing in its many forms—to the literature they experience. They laugh with Harry in Cathy Dumbrowski's *Cave Boy*, cry with Jemmy in Sid Fleischman's *The Whipping Boy,* and share Chibi's pride and satisfaction in Taro Yashima's *Crow Boy.* Through response, they share the unique meaning and significance they derive from their interaction with the stories and poems they read.

"Read alouds" are part of the daily reading diet in a literature-based program. Teachers at all levels share a steady flow of stories and poems with pupils throughout the day. They open the world of literature by sharing stories in anthologies by famous writers—for example, Rudyard Kipling's *Just*

So Stories, or Carl Sandburg's *Rootabaga Stories*. They also use reading aloud as a means of sharing popular chapter books—Roald Dahl's *Danny, Champion of the World* or Natalie Babbitt's *Tuck Everlasting*. From kindergarten through sixth grade and beyond, reading aloud to pupils is an essential feature of literature-based instruction.

Sustained silent reading is another daily activity, a time set aside when pupils and teachers read books of their own choosing. In the lower grades, children spend this special reading time engaged in old favorites like Arlene Mosel's *Tikki, Tikki, Tembo* and Maurice Sendak's *Where the Wild Things Are*, or getting to know newer books such as Ralph Manheim's translation of the Grimm fairy tale *Dear Mili* or Angela Johnson's *Tell Me a Story, Mama*. As their independence in reading grows, pupils spend sustained silent reading time getting acquainted with Amelia Bedelia, Paddington Bear, the Boxcar children and the kids from the Polk Street School, Curious George, Anastasia Krupnik, Henry Huggins, Pippi Longstocking, and the rest of the wonderful cast of characters who inhabit the world of children's books. In the upper grades, they become part of the family in Mildred Taylor's *The Gold Cadillac* and part of the circle of friends in Barthe DeClements' *The Fourth Grade Wizards*. Sustained silent reading is a time to truly enjoy reading. It is also a time when teachers enjoy their own recreational novels, becoming models for students.

Thematic units are a regular feature of literature-based instruction. Sometimes, these units are focused around a theme or topic in science or social studies, as when children use books like Byrd Baylor's *The Desert Is Theirs* or Steven Krensky's *Children of the Earth and Sky* to learn about Native Americans in the Southwest. At other times, thematic units are cross-curricular; math, science, social studies, and the arts are integrated with reading and writing as children study dinosaurs with books like Jim Murphy's *The Last Dinosaur* and Aliki's *My Visit to the Dinosaurs*. Collections of informational trade books provide depth, breadth, and currency to the full range of topics that occupy pupils' interests and their curriculum needs.

Classroom libraries are provided to put a selection of trade books at children's fingertips. Where budgetary restrictions limit possibilities for providing extensive classroom collections of trade books, teachers use the school or public library as a source of trade books in the classroom.

A learning environment trumpets the place of literature in the classroom lives of pupils and their teacher. *Author study* engages students in learning about people who produce the literature they enjoy and learn from to become literate. *Displays* document pupils' engagement with literature, with samples of their artistic and written responses to the books they are reading. Book covers and posters students design to share their favorite books decorate display areas in the reading corner. Pupils' original poems and responses to books they have read adorn bulletin boards. Trade books on topics such as leaves or rocks are part of the science display in the corner. Posters of poems that children have enjoyed cover the wall. In short, there is a print-rich environment built around literature.

Teachers who are "plugged into" literature are the key to the success of the program. The teacher is the most important element in any reading program. Literature-based programs need teachers who are committed to offering pupils the best in children's books, who are enthusiastic about literature, and who see themselves as readers. Guice and Allington (1994) recognize the centrality of teachers in implementing literature-based programs. While the overall design and implementation of the concept of literature-based instruction may be diverse, all programs need teachers who are tuned into books, who recognize the importance of generating a love of literature in children, and who are skillful enough to build in lessons on word recognition and meaning strategies as needed.

Teachers are different, of course, and so not all programs will have the characteristics identified here implemented in the same way in every classroom. Some teachers integrate these elements with a literature-based basal program; others won't use basals at all and rely entirely on trade books; and still others will use a combination of basals and individual trade books. All these features, however, are part of literature-based reading and, taken together, constitute what might be called a literature-based program.

In sum, a literature-based program is one in which children are immersed in literature and where literature permeates literacy instruction. Children's literature forms the core of the program and trade books are used as primary vehicles for teaching children how to read and write. But any program is more than the sum of its parts. McGee and Tompkins (1995) describe literature-based reading in light of theoretical perspectives that teachers take. Using models and case studies, they describe how literature-based processes fit into teachers' beliefs about reading. These beliefs move

1.2 Putting Ideas to Work
Research-Based Qualities of Literature-Based Programs

*F*rom their research on literature-based reading, Tunnell and Jacobs (1989) list these basic elements of literature-based programs:

Natural reading, which involves the acquisition of reading skills in much the same way as speaking skills. "Learning to read naturally begins when parents read to young children and let them handle books, and that process is continued with the teacher reading aloud and including books naturally in the classroom" (p. 474).

Use of natural text, reading material written in language unencumbered by the controls basals impose.

Neurological impress, in which pupils follow lines of text and read along as the teacher or another pupil reads aloud. Reading along (another term for neurological impress) from enjoyable trade books is a key to unlocking literacy growth.

Sustained silent reading, in which pupils and teachers read material of their choosing without interruption.

Teacher modeling, with teachers showing themselves as enthusiastic readers.

Improving pupils' attitudes, with an emphasis on the affective dimensions of helping pupils appreciate literature and enjoy reading.

Self-selection of materials, allowing pupils a large measure of choice in what they read.

Meaning orientation, with skills taught in the meaningful context of real books and pupils' own writing.

Writing as an "output activity" consistently occurring along with reading.

the teachers into a theory-based stage of implementing a literature-based program. Heald-Taylor (1996) also describes programs from different theoretical perspectives. She describes how literature-based activities build from more teacher-directed, traditional approaches to those that involve children in more self-initiated, open-ended activities using trade books.

Why Literature-Based Reading?

The first ripples from using literature in reading and writing instruction in schools began in the 1970s, and the wave began to build toward a peak in the 1980s. Educators began to examine critically the notion of a conventional skill-development approach to literacy instruction, an approach that emphasized mastery of a collection of discrete skills in order to learn to read. Criticism of basal reading instruction that relied primarily on a skill-development model mounted. In fact, basal bashing became something of a professional pastime during the 1980s. Whole language philosophy lent momentum to the wider use of literature in teaching children how to read. The appeal of using authentic text from real books by real authors instead of contrived stories built around particular reading skills became apparent, and children's literature began to achieve greater prominence as part of literacy instruction.

Whole Language

The whole language movement had its beginnings in the work of people like Frank Smith (1988), Kenneth Goodman (1988), and others who recognized that it was psycholinguistically naive to attempt to divide language into so many discrete and isolated components in teaching children to read and write. Whole language advocates suggested that pupils be taught to read and write in a more integrated, holistic fashion. Rather than teaching children to read by helping them master separate and isolated units, an approach emerged that emphasized the close interrelationship of language components. Whole language practice did not ignore instruction in skills and strategies, as some critics maintain; rather, teachers integrated skills instruction into a more holistic context using literature.

Despite the popular use of the expression, "whole language" is not an easy term to define. In search of a definition, Bergeron (1990) reviewed 64 articles pertaining to whole language. She found it variously described as an approach, a belief, a method, a philosophy, an orientation, a theory, a theoretical orientation, a program, a curriculum, a perspective on education, and an attitude of mind. Bergeron even found the same expert defining whole language differently in different sources. Walmsley and Adams (1993) found that classroom practitioners, even though they considered themselves "whole language teachers" and could describe what they did in the classroom, could not articulate a clear definition of whole language itself. Taken together, the attempts to define the concept of whole language reflect what Newman (1985) calls a "state of mind" and what Watson (1989) calls "the spirit" of whole language.

In explaining the theory of whole language, Cambourne (1988, 1995) examines the process of learning to read and write in light of the process of learning to speak. Cambourne points out that learning to talk is a stunning intellectual achievement, a task children with extremely immature brains have been learning successfully for thousands of years. He proposes that the human brain can "learn to process oral and written forms of language in much the same way, provided the conditions under which each is learned are also much the same" (1988; p. 30). What are these conditions?

Immersion. When children learn spoken language, they are immersed in a total language environment. In the classroom, this translates into a constant focus on reading and writing activities. Pupils are surrounded and bombarded with what they are supposed to learn—printed language.

Demonstration. In learning to talk, children are constantly exposed to models of others using language in different ways for different purposes. In school, teachers and pupils see each other as language models using print for the same variety of purposes.

Engagement.   Learners are actively engaged in learning to talk. In the classroom, they engage in reading and writing as meaningful, holistic activities, not as empty exercises.

Expectations.   Young learners receive the message that they are expected to learn to talk. Similar expectations of success are expressed regarding the ability to learn to read and write.

Responsibility.   "When learning to talk, learner-talkers are permitted to make some decisions (i.e., take responsibility) about what they'll engage in and what they'll ignore" (Cambourne, 1995; p. 185). Choice is part of the learning environment in the classroom as well.

Approximations.   In learning to talk, children are not afraid to experiment with language; they are not expected to talk as adults do from the beginning. Processes like guessing at words, role-play reading, and invented spelling are encouraged in learning to read and write.

Employment.   Children learning spoken language have plenty of opportunity for practice. Active practice of reading and writing in the classroom is important as well.

Response.   Children's initial attempts at spoken language typically produce positive, encouraging responses from parents and others. Similar responses with expectations of success in reading and writing is part of the whole language philosophy.

Of these eight conditions, research suggests that engagement is the key. Cambourne has found that children are more likely to engage in learning to read and write if they believe that they are capable of success, if they believe that what they are learning is of some use to them, if they're free from anxiety, and if they're engaged with someone they admire and trust (Cambourne, 1995).

Classroom instruction in reading and writing has changed dramatically as whole language teaching has gained attention. Even those teachers who do not consider themselves "whole language teachers" are being splashed, if not doused, by the wave of whole language. More writing is taught. More trade books are used. Language arts is becoming an integral part of instruction in content areas of the curriculum. Basal reading series are full of authentic text. As a result of these cumulative changes, literacy instruction will never be the same.

Part of the spirit of whole language is the increased use of literature in the classroom. In the very early grades, students learn easy-to-read stories with repeated language patterns. Children use their language skills to build stories around wordless books such as Jan Omerod's *Moonlight* and Mitsumasa Anno's many picture books such as *Anno's Journey* and *Anno's Flea Market*. In the primary grades, children enjoy old favorite picture books such

1.3 Putting Ideas to Work
Contrasting Whole Language Theory

*T*he following chart (Reutzel and Hollingsworth, 1988) summarizes major differences between whole language theory and conventional theories of language instruction in the classroom.

What it is . . .	What it isn't . . .
Philosophical Views about Children and Language	
1. Humanism is the philosophical base.	1. Essentialism is the philosophical base.
2. Children already know how to learn.	2. Teachers must teach children how to learn.
3. Process is most important.	3. Product is most important.
4. Language is indivisible.	4. Language is divisible.
Research Support	
1. Ethnographic and qualitative research methods predominate.	1. Experimental and quantitative research methods predominate.
2. Instruction is based on language acquisition and development research.	2. Instruction is based on scientific analysis of learning research.
How Children Learn Language	
1. Whole-to-parts learning is emphasized.	1. Parts-to-whole learning is emphasized.
2. Learning begins with the concrete and moves to the abstract.	2. Learning begins with the abstract and moves to the concrete.
3. Instruction is based on transactional/ transformational theories in reading.	3. Instruction is based on transmission/interactive theories in reading.
4. Instruction is associated with theories of gestalt psychology.	4. Instruction is associated with theories of cognitive and behavioristic psychology.
5. Language learning is based on personal relevance and experience.	5. Language learning is based on a hierarchy of skills.
6. Learners use language for personal purposes.	6. Learners use language to satisfy others.
7. Inward forces motivate learning.	7. Outward forces motivate learning.
8. No extrinsic rewards are given for behavior.	8. Extrinsic rewards are given for learning and behavior.
9. Language is learned through immersion.	9. Language is learned through imitation and shaping.
Classroom Environment	
1. School learning is like home.	1. School learning is different from home.
2. Environment is "littered" with children's and teacher's printed language.	2. Environment is often characterized by teacher-made, professional bulletin boards or exhibits of children's perfect papers.
3. Centers focus on a topic or theme; for example, kites, karate, etc.	3. Centers focus on skill acquisition.
4. Groups are flexible and often formed by interest.	4. Groups are inflexible and often formed by achievement.
5. Classroom fosters cooperation and collaboration.	5. Classroom fosters competitiveness and isolation.

Source: D. Ray Reutzel and Paul M. Hollingsworth. (1988). Whole Language and the Practitioner. *Academic Therapy* 23:(4)405–416.
Copyright © 1988 by PRO-ED, Inc. Reprinted by permission.

	What it is . . .		**What it isn't . . .**

What it is . . .

Teacher Behavior

1. Teachers facilitate learning.
2. Teachers do not label or categorize children.

3. Instruction is informal and discovery-based.
4. Teachers give children choices.
5. Teachers emphasize trying and taking risks.
6. Teachers emphasize the meaning of language.

7. Instruction takes place in sentence-level or larger language units.
8. Phonics principles are taught through known sight words using the analytic approach.
9. Teachers instruct with whole stories, books, or poems.
10. Brainstorming is used to build background experiences for instruction.
11. Teachers are always teaching by example.
12. Teachers participate with students in reading and writing.

Child Behavior

1. Children often plan their own learning.
2. Children often choose their own topics/purposes for writing.
3. Children often assist one another in reading and writing.
4. Children use language to learn about their language.
5. Children participate more often in discussion and cooperative learning.

Evaluation

1. Evaluation is informal—kid-watching, tapes, samples.

What it isn't . . .

1. Teachers direct learning.
2. Teachers often label children; for example, dyslexic, buzzards, weeds, etc.
3. Instruction is formal, direct, and systematic.
4. Teachers do not often give children choices.
5. Teachers emphasize correctness and accuracy.
6. Teachers often emphasize the isolated parts of language.
7. Instruction focuses on small steps in skill acquisition.
8. Phonics principles are often taught in isolation using the synthetic approach.
9. Teachers instruct with learning letter names/ sounds and basal readers.
10. Advanced organizers are used to build background for instruction.
11. Teachers often teach only by precept.
12. Teachers seldom participate in reading assigned tasks on an equal basis with children.

1. Children follow the plan the teacher sets.
2. Children follow the assigned purposes for writing.
3. Children often compete with one another in reading and writing.
4. Children learn language conventions to use language.
5. Children often work privately and quietly at their desks.

1. Evaluation is formal—standardized or criterion referenced.

as Esphyr Slobodkina's *Caps for Sale* and Ludwig Bemelmans's *Madeline*, along with newer titles that have quickly become favorites such as Pamela Allen's *Who Sank the Boat?* and Nancy Van Laan's *Possum Come A-Knockin'*. Throughout their school lives, pupils come to enjoy the people, places, adventures, emotions, and other experiences books introduce to them. They recognize the genius in the language and imagination of authors like Arnold Lobel, Roald Dahl, Maurice Sendak, Virginia Hamilton, Katherine Patterson, and the hundreds of other writers and illustrators who produce quality literature for children. Encounters with literature are a vital part of their daily lives in the classroom.

Whole language is much more than literature, of course. It recognizes that children come to school with three cueing systems built into their language:

an awareness of the sounds of spoken language, which letters of the alphabet can represent (*graphophonic* system);

an awareness of how language units are strung together to produce meaning (*syntactic* system); and

an awareness of the meaning of thousands of words (*semantic* system).

In the context of authentic reading and writing, children learn to use the three cueing systems in relation to one another to construct meaning from print. But whole language does not ignore skills. Word recognition, phonics, and the other components of conventional skill instruction are taught and used in whole language classrooms.

Consistent with whole language practice, literature is used to cement the reading-writing connection, and informational trade books are used in thematic units at all grade levels. In short, more and more classrooms have moved closer to literature-based programs.

Advantages of Using Literature

The enormous advantages of using children's literature at the heart of a classroom language program have become apparent with widespread use. Literature has a powerful impact not only on children's reading ability, but also on their inclination to read. Literature offers many advantages, including the following.

Affective Response. Literature generates enjoyment. Trade books address the affective side of reading by promoting positive attitudes. When the names of a beloved character or favorite book are mentioned, people typically respond, "I *love* that character," or "Isn't that book *wonderful?*" Words like *love* and *wonderful* reflect the affective side of reading. Literature generates a positive attitude—a love of reading—that is the ultimate goal of teaching children to read. The purpose of education is to create learners. The purpose of reading instruction is to create readers—not only people who *can* read but people who *will* read. Literature promotes the inclination to read by producing an affective response.

Involvement in Reading. Trade books involve pupils in the act of learning to read by reading. In skill-development programs, pupils spend lots of time doing skill-related exercises. A national survey of reading practices indicates that pupils spend as much as 70 percent of their reading instructional time doing seatwork; they spend considerably more time with their workbooks than they do with their teachers (Anderson et al., 1985). Literature involves reading, not filling out worksheets. Popular author Jim Trelease's (1995) observations to parents apply in the classroom as well: children's literature arouses children's imaginations, emotions, and sympathies, awakening their desire to read and providing them with a sense of purpose and identity. With trade books at the heart of the program, children learn to read by reading.

Content. The content of trade books is generally appealing to children. Educational book publishers need to be careful about content in reading material because they have to respond to a variety of easily offended pressure groups. School books do not have to please everybody, but they cannot offend anyone; thus, publishers of school texts tend to shy away from topics that might offend. It is difficult—some say impossible—to provide an interesting diet of reading material with such constraints. Censorship and parent pressure can sometimes be an issue in selecting trade books for literature-based instruction, but literature offers a far broader range of appealing reading material.

Language. Authors of quality children's books—people like Robert McCluskey and Betsy Byars, Mildred Taylor and Chris Van Allsberg—give pupils the best that language has to offer. The language of literature is rich and appealing, written for meaning without tight vocabulary control. Before publication, a trade book comes under the critical scrutiny of an editor, so quality control is paramount, rather than vocabulary control. In literature, the best children's authors produce the best language for pupils.

Skills and Strategies. A literature-based program incorporates skills and strategies that children need to become competent readers and writers. "Essential reading skills can be taught through a literature-based curriculum in a subtle, efficient manner within the context of material each child is reading" (Fuhler, 1990; p. 314). Effective vocabulary lessons on synonyms and antonyms, for example, can be spun off from Judith Viorst's wonderful *Alexander and the Terrible, Horrible, No Good, Very Bad Day*. Folktales, fairy tales, animal stories, legends, fantasy, realistic fiction, poetry, and all the other literary genres can be potent vehicles for developing the critical and creative thinking that reading comprehension requires. As pupils read trade books, they apply skills and develop strategies as they enjoy stories. As long as skill-development does not get in the way of story enjoyment, teachers can "find" lessons to improve skills as pupils use trade books in learning to read. Literature is no less powerful in providing models for writing and material to write about.

1.4 Putting Ideas to Work
Describing a Literature-Based Program

*H*epler (1989) poses the question, "How does a year look when you have a full-blown literature program?" and answers it for teachers in this way:

> You would have set aside time for reading aloud, Sustained Silent Reading, and group work, whether reading with you, working independently, or working in small purposeful groups. You would have decided on an author or two to study and a thematic unit or two to develop in concert with another teacher. You would have in place some form of record keeping that would include what children have read, heard read, and have made in response to books. And you would have a repertoire of experiences you would wish children to have—delight in rhyme and repetition of Mother Goose and discovery of cumulative pattern in folktales for kindergartners, or appreciation of figurative language both in poetry and in the books of Byars for fifth graders.
>
> Your classroom would show that children love books. There would be a reading corner, displays of books currently being worked on, perhaps a chart of books read aloud so far this year with stars by the ones most favored by the class, and bulletin boards not of canned and preprinted posters but of children's work. Of course, there would be no book report forms. Instead, writing in many modes—explanations, first-person accounts, letters, "next chapters," poetry—as well as a variety of projects would reflect the teacher's understanding of how to help children organize their literary experiences.
>
> Most importantly, children would be brimming with enthusiasm to tell visitors to the classroom or each other about the books they are enjoying and what they are discovering. Their ability to discuss what they read would be expanding with practice so that literary terms and patterns would be an easy part of their vocabulary. They would know and love some authors and illustrators. And they would see themselves as readers. So would you. (pp. 218–219)

Classroom displays related to trade books document the idea that literature is an important part of the reading program.

© Michael Weisbrot/The Image Works

Extracted with permission from S. Hepler (1989), "A Literature Program: Getting It Together, Keeping It Going" in *Children's Literature in the Classroom: Weaving Charlotte's Web*. Janet Hickman and Bernice E. Cullinan (eds.) Copyright © 1989 by Christopher-Gordon Publishers, Inc. Reprinted with permission of Christopher-Gordon Publishers, Inc, Norwood, MA.

Effectiveness.   A substantial research base is growing to support the effectiveness of literature-based reading instruction in the classroom. Anecdotal evidence and empirical studies indicate that children's literature is a viable means of teaching children how to read.

Teachers who have implemented literature-based reading programs in their classrooms repeatedly report positive results. Vida Welsh (1985), for example, describes a program in which literature was used as the core of instruction rather than as a supplement to the basal. After strong initial resistance, her opinion changed. "I could see before my eyes a wonderful thing happening. The teachers were enthused, the kids were extremely happy and productive, and best of all, students were becoming more and more involved in their own education" (p. 7). Carol J. Fuhler (1990), a junior high school teacher, reports similar results: "I teach a literature-based reading program to a group of learning disabled boys who revel in the absence of worksheets and tests. Two of them showed a three-year growth in reading this year while another improved a year and a half. For students who used to dislike and distrust books, that's exciting" (p. 315). Scharer and Detwiler (1992) report not only on the positive effects of a shift to literature-based emphasis, but on some of the steps involved in making the transitions from basals to trade books.

Beyond anecdotal accounts, research studies have also shown that using literature is an effective way to help pupils improve their reading abilities. Tunnell and Jacobs (1989) reviewed research studies on literature-based reading instruction with different ages and different types of pupils. Their conclusion: "The success for literature-based programs is well documented" (p. 476). Savage (1992) reviewed research on using literature with "regular" and "at-risk" students. The conclusion: "The evidence suggests that using trade books as an integral part of the reading instructional program has a strong and positive impact on increasing pupils' reading ability, even when this ability is measured by conventional skill-oriented reading achievement tests" (p. 30). In reviewing the growing body of research on literature-based techniques, McGee (1992) concluded that "children can take responsibility for critical reading, displaying enormously creative and critical thinking. . . . In addition, knowledge about literature itself, not just about reading, is an important outcome of instruction in a literature-based classroom" (p. 534). Children in classrooms using literature read more as well. Mervar and Hiebert (1989) found that children in literature-based programs read far more than their counterparts in traditional classrooms.

Research also indicates that literature has positive effects on pupils' writing abilities. Based on a summary of this research, Noyce and Christie (1989) conclude, "Children who read large amounts of children's literature are exposed to models of elaborated structures and tend to write more naturally than children whose reading diet consists mainly of basal reader stories" (p. 5).

In sum, children's literature is continuing to have a powerful influence on the development of pupils' reading and writing abilities in the elementary grades, and the increased use of trade books promises to impact instruction in the years ahead.

How Is Literature-Based Reading Different from Conventional Reading Instruction?

Literature-based reading has enormous advantages over conventional approaches, and direct instruction in skills and strategies can be made part of literature-based instruction. But the contemporary literature-based approach to reading does differ from the conventional skill-development view prevalent for so long in our schools.

Skill-Development versus Literature-Based Instruction

For decades, the view that dominated reading instruction was a skill-development view. Reading was seen as a series of discrete components or skills, and instruction consisted of helping children develop these skills. "The skills-based curriculum is based on the idea that written language is learned through teacher-directed lessons and practices as discrete skills that are taught sequentially. It uses specific reading and writing tasks as vehicles for skills acquisition" (Dahl and Freppon, 1995; p. 53). In reading, the two broad skills areas were vocabulary and comprehension. Each of these was broken into categories and subcategories, so that learning to read involved extensive practice on long inventories of isolated skills and subskills. Pupils spent time doing worksheets and exercises to learn vowels and consonants, synonyms and antonyms, prefixes and suffixes, main ideas and details, and other components that would, it was presumed, "add up" to reading. So much time, effort, and attention were devoted to learning these subskills that the bigger picture of reading tended to get lost.

This view of reading came about in large measure as a result of the spirit of the early 20th century, an age of great confidence and expectation in the power of science and technology. Scientific information spread rapidly. People in all walks of life experienced the benefits of science. Medical science was advancing. Scientific management principles were applied to business, producing assembly lines that made the United States an industrial giant. Science was perceived as "the wave of the future."

In this spirit, people became interested in a "science" of education, invoking science in an attempt to discover laws of learning. Principles of scientific management and production were applied to school administration. Experts conducted "scientific investigations" to validate classroom practices. Standardized tests were designed to measure learning "scientifically." In this scientific approach, each activity was analyzed according to its discrete parts, and each element was further analyzed. Reading was analyzed and divided into its component parts, and the skill-development view of reading was born.

This skill-development framework dominated reading instruction in the decades that followed. Reading was taught as a combination of skills. Competency was measured in terms of skill mastery, and pupils who failed were given more practice in skills. This constellation of individual skills, it was believed, would come together to produce competent readers.

In contrast to the skill-development view, literature-based instruction starts with story rather than with skills. Total meaning, not mastery of a set of discrete and isolated skills, is the goal of instruction. Reading is viewed as a holistic activity. Conventional skills are not ignored, since readers need to know the meanings of words and be able to figure out words they do not recognize in order to build meaning. But with a literature-based approach, the primary emphasis in teaching reading is on understanding story, and the major means of helping pupils achieve this understanding is literature.

Basal Readers

The skill-development view of reading was implemented largely through the use of basal reading programs. The basal system became the technology that applied scientific principles to reading instruction. "Basal reading materials met the expectations of a public and profession enthralled with business, science, and psychology" (Goodman et al., 1988; p. 19). The aura of scientific authority surrounding basals persisted, as many educators came to see basals as embodying scientific truth when it comes to teaching reading (Shannon, 1983).

Many teachers still rely heavily on basals as teaching tools in the classroom. Basals have been used to teach reading in as many as 90 percent of the classrooms in the United States, and these "reading schemes" have been used widely in English-speaking countries, such as Great Britain (Arnold, 1982) and Australia (Winch, 1982) as well. They remain among the most widely used instructional tools on the educational landscape, and their popularity makes them powerful in shaping the way reading is taught in schools.

An important part of any basal program is its scope and sequence of skills. A scope and sequence chart presents a comprehensive overview of the skills component of the series. It deals with every skill at every level and constitutes the blueprint a basal program is built upon.

Pros and Cons of a Basal Program

Basal programs offer attractive benefits for teaching reading, particularly for the beginning teacher. Basals have not, however, escaped their share of criticism.

On the positive side, basals provide comprehensive, structured tools to use in teaching reading. They contain carefully chosen reading materials, with directions on how to present this material in an orderly and sequenced manner. They address many dimensions of learning to read—oral and silent reading, narrative and expository text, and strategies for developing a full range of reading competencies.

Basals help the teacher relate theory to practice. "Basal series play a critical role in reading instruction in part because of the difficulties associated with translating research findings and theory into practice" (McCallum, 1988; p. 204). Designed by reputable experts in the field of reading instruction, basals offer ready-made tools to translate current theory into instructional practice. They provide decision-making tools for teachers, with suggestions on how to present materials and extend ideas.

Basals facilitate organization because each part contributes to the organization and management of a classroom reading program. They provide teachers with a sense of security, and they give administrators confidence that teachers are following a well-designed plan. Basals give pupils the sense of progression as they move from one level of a program to the next. In addition, today's basals give children a rich diet of literature.

On the negative side, some heavy criticism has been leveled against traditional basal programs. Criticism has focused on:

Content that was unexciting and uninspiring.

Language that was stilted and controlled to conform to the vocabulary or skill being taught.

Scope and sequence that emphasized isolated skills over real reading.

Workbooks that contained tedious skill-development exercises that "distort children's view of language. Huffing and puffing at letters, marking whether vowels are glided or unglided, deciding whether *b* or *d* goes at the beginning or ending of the tattered remnant of a mutilated word rendered meaningless in its isolation—these merely leave children puzzled about what it's all about. Such Kafka-esque activities are not likely to motivate the learner, nor will they provide promise of the best repertoire of pleasure and increased social power that literacy provides" (Johnson and Louis, 1987; p. 3).

Teachers editions with scripted lessons that tended to ritualize instruction and offered such a wealth of suggestions that they proved to be "a quagmire from which the floundering teacher must dig her own way out or sink" (Yatvin, 1980; p. 13).

Perhaps the greatest concern or criticism expressed about traditional basal programs is that teachers overrelied on these instructional tools. Many teachers saw the basal as the only reading material they needed to provide for students. They were reluctant to abandon the basal even for a short time, for fear that their pupils would somehow lose out if they missed a workbook page or skipped a story. Many felt compelled to finish the program, so pupils were exposed to very little reading material beyond the basal. In short, "the roles of teachers and the textbook seem to be reversed . . . whereby teachers become a support system for the textbook rather than the other way around" (Shannon, 1989; p. xiv).

1.5 Putting Ideas to Work
What Is a Basal Series?

A basal reading program is an instructional materials package designed specifically for teaching reading from kindergarten through sixth (and sometimes eighth) grade. The series consists of:

Readers, graded textbooks containing stories, poems, an occasional play, riddles, and other material for children to read. A series will typically contain 15 or 20 of these reading textbooks—several preprimers for the very early stages of reading and two books at each grade level.

Workbooks containing exercises and activities related to the stories in the readers themselves. These worksheets are designed to help pupils develop or review the material presented in the program; the exercises are often directly related to the content of particular stories in the pupils' texts.

Teacher's editions, manuals that contain detailed lesson plans, questions, teaching suggestions, activities, background information, answers to exercises, and other materials designed to direct the teacher on how to use the program.

Tests to assess reading development and to monitor pupils' progress through the program.

While the readers, workbooks, teacher's editions and tests constitute the four essential components of a basal series, these programs typically have additional components as well, including:

Additional assessment components of various kinds—placement tests, level tests, skills-mastery tests, and informal assessment devices designed to indicate where a student should begin in a program and/or how well a student has learned the skills that the program is designed to teach.

Supplementary workbooks in addition to those that are part of the basic program—reinforcement workbooks with additional exercises for pupils who need additional practice; enrichment workbooks to address or extend material that the basic part of the program may not address; ESL (English as a Second Language) exercises; skill sheets to be done at home; and other skill-development components.

Parent materials such as newsletters, sample correspondence, and other information designed to explain the program to parents.

Record-keeping tools such as charts, forms, folders, and other devices to provide a system for recording pupils' scores and progress.

Literature-related materials such as trade books, activity cards, read-aloud libraries, and other materials that reflect the increased use of literature in the reading curriculum.

CD-ROMs and other software related to the series.

Other materials that might include Big Books, wall charts, card sets, tapes, and other materials designed to reinforce or extend the instruction in the basal.

Wiggins (1994) suggests that "the problems associated with basals do not stem from the materials but from our mindset about reading instruction" (p. 454). Instead of adjusting the level of reading material for poor readers, he suggests maintaining the level but adjusting instructional strategies in light of the needs of these children.

Newer Basal Programs

More recent basal series have responded to many of these concerns and criticisms. While the idea of a comprehensive graded series remains the same, most contemporary basal programs include far fewer subskills. Model lessons and teaching suggestions are less didactic and reflect updated research and theories on learning to read. Assessment components have expanded (Valencia, 1992). Workbooks contain more open-ended activities and exercises that encourage pupils to write instead of merely filling in blanks or underlining items in isolated skills-based exercises. But perhaps the most striking change that has occurred in basal programs today is the increased inclusion of literature.

Basals have been caught up in the tidal wave of literature that has swept literacy instruction. Conventional programs contained occasional selections from popular children's stories, but these stories often underwent some procrustean alterations before becoming part of the series. Language was altered to conform to the intended grade level of the book, adjustments were made to bring the story in line with the skill being taught, and content was changed to eliminate possible objections to the story.

Contemporary programs have far more literature than their predecessors, and while publishers still make some minor adjustments in stories (Reutzel and Larsen, 1995), the literature is largely unexpurgated. "Freshly revised textbook series reflect a concerted effort to include recognized children's authors, a variety of literary genre, excerpts, and complete stories from award winning books" (Fuhler, 1990; p. 312). In addition to simple repetitive stories such as *The Gingerbread Man* at the kindergarten level, today's basals include folktales and fairy tales, selections from contemporary fiction, expository selections, more poetry than before, and the full range of material that constitutes the world of literature for children. Given the extent to which basals dictate the reading curriculum in schools (Langer and Allington, 1992), the shift to a literature-based orientation is a significant shift indeed.

Beyond the inclusion of more literary selections in the readers themselves, newer basal programs reflect other qualities of literature-based instruction. They pay more attention to author awareness and to helping pupils understand the qualities of good literature rather than merely developing skills. Teachers are encouraged to move children beyond the pages of the basal text and into books containing original versions of the stories. Some basals offer a collection of trade books as an ancillary feature. Reflecting the growing emphasis on the use of literature, even the ubiquitous basal has adopted a literature-based approach to teaching reading.

Newer basals still include skills, but in a different way than before. Reading skills and strategies are taught within the context of the literary content of the stories. Isolated skills practice has diminished. Skills are addressed after reading stories, not before, as in old programs (Hoffman et al., 1994). The effect has been reading materials that are more engaging to

1.6 Putting Ideas to Work
Approaches to Teaching Reading

A variety of ideas and programs for helping pupils learn to read have been used in schools in the recent past. Aukerman (1984) has identified 165 different approaches or programs designed to teach children how to read. Each of these systems, and scores of others, has enjoyed a measure of popularity among devotees, and many are still found in schools today. Some of these include:

Color-coded programs that utilize colors as additional visual clues to help pupils remember sound-symbol relationships.

Picture-writing aids that use simple drawings or rebus symbols in place of words and letters.

Reformed alphabet approaches that add symbols to augment or supplement the 26 letters of our alphabet.

Computer programs that present pupils with letters, words, sentences, and longer passages to help them develop basic reading competency.

---

children. Basals remain a widely used reading instruction tool in schools, but Dick and Jane would hardly recognize them today.

Achieving a Synthesis

How best to teach children to read has been an ongoing argument in literate societies for centuries (Mathews, 1966), an argument sometimes fought with religious intensity. Eminent literacy educators have engaged in what Allington describes as "oppositional polemics and politics, us-versus-them groupings, good-guys-versus-bad-guys characterizations" (Adams, Allington et al., 1991; p. 373). Chall (1996) has called the controversy "The Great Debate." Kantrowitz (1990) has termed it "The Reading Wars."

What is this debate all about? The issues take different forms, and not everybody on one side of the question is in complete agreement with everyone else in the same camp. Cheek (1989) summarizes the issue as a basic difference between skills-based and holistic philosophies, and he describes the impact that the debate has had on preparing teachers to teach reading and on reading programs in schools.

These arguments trace their origins to one's view of language or conceptions of the reading process. Through colonial and later periods in schools, reading instruction emphasized decoding skills. Teachers taught children to memorize sounds and syllables, and then read by attaching the correct sounds to the symbols they encountered on the page. In the second half of the 19th century, Horace Mann questioned what he termed the "torturous practice of subjecting young children to the tedious task of first learning letters and sounds." When Mann visited Germany, he found Prussian educators teaching

1.7 Putting Ideas to Work
The Language Experience Approach

One approach to reading that fits well in a literature-based environment is the Language Experience Approach (LEA). Developed and researched largely by Roach Van Allen (Allen, 1976), LEA integrates listening, speaking, reading, and writing. The approach involves:

Dictation.   Children dictate stories or accounts of their own experiences.

Transcription.   The children's stories are transcribed on a *language experience chart.*

Reading.   The dictated material becomes the vehicle for reading instruction.

As the teacher transcribes and the children read their dictated stories, pupils begin to recognize familiar words, develop new vocabulary, note how letters are formed and what sounds they represent, discover the structure of language and how it affects meaning, learn the conventions of punctuation, and focus on elements of language that will support their independent reading and writing.

The Language Experience Approach is very appropriate in a literature-based program. While children's dictated messages are often based on shared experiences such as baking cookies or going on a field trip, their accounts can also focus on trade books they have experienced. For example, after reading a story such as Allen Say's *Grandfather's Journey,* the class can retell the story in their own words, dictate stories about their own grandparents, make up a sequel about what might have happened to the narrator when he became a grandfather, or dictate their own collective response to the story.

Sampson, Allen, and Sampson (1991) discuss LEA in light of today's educational environment. They suggest that the approach is especially appropriate for a diverse student population, and they detail how computer technology can be used with language experience activities.

children to read whole words at a time, and he ardently promoted the use of this "new revolutionary" method of teaching reading when he returned home. Mann's ideas caught on, and basal reading programs published through the middle of the 20th century adopted this technique.

During the 1960s, the pendulum swung back to code-emphasis approaches that stressed making sound-symbol associations as the key to learning to read. Linguistic programs were prevalent, programs in which vocabulary was controlled by consistent spelling patterns, producing sentences such as "Flick the tick off the chick with a thick stick, Nick." The pendulum subsequently swung back to a more eclectic approach, and literature-based instruction began to emerge.

Basals and Trade Books

A major part of the current debate about reading instruction relates to questions regarding skills-based versus whole language programs. Basal reading series have been used so widely for so many years to deliver a skills model to pupils, and schools have for so long viewed reading primarily as a skill-development process, that any departure from this still occasionally meets with suspicion or uneasiness. Now that holistic techniques and trade books are so widely and firmly established in schools, some parents (and educators) are concerned that the new approaches ignore skills altogether. Teachers are urged from some quarters to hit hard on skills, to emphasize phonics, and to provide reading comprehension drills as part of their instructional regimen. Does the decision to use a whole language or a skills-based model, or to use basal readers or trade books as primary vehicles for reading instruction, have to be an either/or proposition? Some researchers insist that the two views are so theoretically at odds with each other that they constitute "conflicting educational paradigms" that cannot be reconciled (Edelsky, 1990); others suggest that a consensus model makes practical sense. Spiegel (1992) calls for building bridges between traditional, direct instruction and more holistic, literature-based programs by blending "the best of both in order to help every child reach his or her full literacy potential" (p. 43). Strickland (1995) suggests balance in the search for "bridges between the conventional wisdom of the past and the need to take advantage of new research and wisdom" (p. 295). Rather than focusing on incompatibilities and points of conflict, teachers need to see how direct teaching of reading skills and strategies can be part of literature-based instruction.

Different theories tend to dichotomize, and teachers are led to believe that any deviation from a single theory compromises quality instruction and intellectual integrity. Instead, quality instruction comes from inspired teaching. "Inspired teaching does not originate in a particular philosophy, theory approach, or program. It originates in the creativity of teachers" (Duffy, 1992). In the practical reality of most classrooms, creative teachers skillfully synthesize skill-development and the literature-based approaches into a reading and writing program that makes sense for pupils while it helps them achieve competence as literate users of language.

How to Synthesize

The different theoretical models can work together as part of reading and writing instruction. Strategies conventionally associated with the skill-development approach can be effectively integrated into instructional activities using literature. Trade books and basals can complement each other in well-planned instructional segments.

Integration of reading strategies with literature occurs as teachers use trade books to illustrate and apply sound reading techniques. For example, Lapp, Flood, and Farnan (1992) illustrate how teachers can model such techniques as setting purposes, making predictions, building vocabulary, and checking for understanding—all components of a typical basal reader lesson—while using a biography that pupils are reading.

Synthesis occurs through integrated speaking/listening/reading/writing activities that start with literature. The teacher shares a story and pupils dictate their own account of the story, which the teacher transcribes onto a chart. As the group reads the story on the chart, the teacher covers certain words and asks students to predict what the words might be (context), to suggest other words that might be used (vocabulary), or to call attention to certain sound-symbol relationships in the words (phonics). The teacher can also help the children see how the story progresses (story structure), the relationship between ideas in the story (cause-effect relationships, for example), or how the story might have ended differently (creative thinking). In activities such as these, literature is the starting point and strategies are modeled and applied within the context of the material, always keeping enjoyment of the story paramount.

Thematic units also integrate direct skills approaches using literature. In a science unit on insects, for example, children read stories like Julie Brinckloe's *Fireflies,* the humorous verses in Nancy Winslow Parker and Joan Richards Wright's *Bugs,* and Eric Carle's *The Very Lonely Firefly.* Pupils write factual accounts of what they learn and imaginative stories based on information about insects. They do paintings of insects and compile lists of what bugs eat. All the while, the teacher is providing lessons on how language works, how readers and writers communicate, how to make predictions and monitor meaning while reading, how to use context and phonics when students meet words they do not know, and how to reflect on what they have learned.

Used side by side, trade books and basals provide balance in a reading program. Basals provide literature selected and presented by the publisher; trade books provide literature selected by the teacher and the children. The two can complement each other in a number of ways. The basal may be used part of the week, while trade books are the focus of instruction the rest of the time. Weekly units can be planned, with a two-week basal unit followed by a three-week unit on fantasy, biography, or folklore that uses both trade books and appropriate selections from basals at different levels. One group may read from the basal while another is using a trade book in directed reading lessons.

Advantages of a Combined Program

Duffy (1992) identifies three advantages of combining literature-based instruction with more structured approaches. First, with trade books and authentic reading-writing opportunities, skills and strategies are learned within the context of practical experiences. The focus is on teaching and learning for understanding, not on completing a workbook page or passing a test. Second, direct instruction does take place, with the teacher playing a direct role and the pupils applying what they have learned in realistic ways. Third, students "do what literate people do in real life—use reading to complete genuine and useful tasks successfully" (p. 445).

A combined or synthesized program is geared to individual differences in teachers. Teachers differ from one another. Some, while they recognize the importance and value of literature, are more confident with the support that the structure of a basal program offers. Other teachers chafe at the bondage of a scope-and-sequenced program; they prefer to put basals aside in favor of the exclusive use of trade books. Most of us are somewhere between these two extremes, and synthesized instructional programs provide a comfortable middle ground.

1.8 Putting Ideas to Work
A Continuum

The use of trade books and basal readers for reading instruction might be viewed as two extremes on a continuum. At one extreme are teachers who see reading primarily as a skill-development activity and who rely so heavily on basal programs that they have little time to use trade books in their language arts programs. At the other extreme are teachers who view reading as a holistic activity and who rely exclusively on trade books to teach reading and writing.

Along this continuum is a considerable middle ground where teachers find an overlap between both views. It is within these areas that synthesis occurs. The synthesis model is a dynamic view adapted to the human nature of teachers.

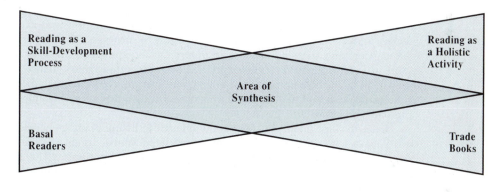

As humans, we change. It is possible for teachers to move from a skills-based view to a language-based view as they gain more confidence with experience. Synthesizing instruction from different approaches suggests the possibility that a teacher can change and adapt according to the levels and needs of a particular class.

Teaching is a uniquely human enterprise. Having comprehensively reviewed 165 programs designed to teach reading, Aukerman (1984) concluded, "the answer [to which is the best method for teaching reading] lies neither in the materials or the methods, but in the commitment that a practitioner is willing to make" (p. 607). While recognizing human variability, today's education demands that all teachers use literature as an integral component of literacy instruction in the classroom.

What follows in this book is a further description of literature-based instruction. The ideas presented are based on the belief that, while direct teaching of skills and strategies may be appropriate, children's literature belongs as the centerpiece of the language arts curriculum—the heart and soul of the classroom program—and trade books can serve as primary vehicles for helping children develop both the ability and the inclination to read and write.

Summary and Conclusions

Literature has become a powerful force in language arts instruction in schools. Increasingly, children's literature serves as the centerpiece of reading and writing instruction in the elementary grades.

Teachers and researchers have long sought to determine the best way to teach children how to read and write, and over the years, different approaches and philosophies have evolved. Throughout most of the 20th century, basal programs dominated instruction—programs consisting of reading books and related materials designed to provide a total instructional diet for students. Although the instructional emphasis of these programs differed from time to time, the nature and purpose of basals generally remained the same: namely, to help children learn to read by providing them with a structured program of skills to learn.

As schools enter the 21st century, the view that suggests reading is best learned as a holistic entity rather than as a set of discrete and isolated skills has brought about the widespread use of trade books as tools for teaching reading and writing. This tidal wave of literature has swept schools, transforming instructional programs in the elementary grades. Basals have also changed to include an exclusive diet of children's literature. More and more schools are instituting a literature-based approach as the advantages of this approach become apparent. Sometimes trade books are used exclusively in an instructional program; at other times, they are combined with more conventional methods and materials in a synthesized system that keeps literature at the heart of the program.

Even the best literature alone is not enough to assure reading success, however. Success comes from the efforts of inspired and knowledgeable teachers who can analyze the needs of their pupils and adapt instruction accordingly. That is what this text aims to help teachers learn. Inspired teachers using good literature make a strong combination for tomorrow's readers.

Discussion Questions and Activities

1. What was your favorite trade book as a child? What made it your favorite? If you were to share this book with a child today, how would you share it?
2. Research the topic of whole language. (Finding references should not be difficult.) Based on your research, write a two- or three-paragraph description of what whole language involves in the classroom.
3. In your school's Curriculum Library or Educational Resource Center, review a set of basal readers. Select a sample that includes the reader, workbook, and teacher's edition from the same grade level. Note how much literature is used in the material. If possible, compare this series to materials published ten or more years ago. Write a brief critique of each set of materials as instructional tools, telling why you would or would not use them as part of your reading instructional program.
4. How does the use of literature relate to what you know about whole language theory? With a partner or in a group, make a list of ways that trade books can be used as instructional tools in the reading program.
5. Respond to the following statement: "My teacher uses a literature-based approach to teaching reading. Last week, she put away the basal and gave the class a book on Helen Keller with 17 worksheets to complete. This is using literature to teach reading, isn't it?"

1. Survey the classroom you are working in as part of your field placement. Using the descriptive characteristics listed in Putting Ideas to Work 1.4, how would you rate your classroom as a literature-based environment? Why?

2. Observe as an experienced teacher presents a reading lesson. Note the type of material the teacher chooses, how he or she prepares the pupils, guides their reading, and checks comprehension. What might you do differently?

3. Interview teachers about the topic of whole language and the use of children's literature to teach reading. What advantages do these teachers see? What are some of their concerns?

4. Talk to the children in your class about the trade books they are reading. Which ones are their favorites? Why? What might you do to build an instructional component around some of these books?

5. As a teacher, you are forming your own model or view of reading. Place yourself on the basal/trade book continuum in Putting Ideas to Work 1.8. Tell why you place yourself at that point. Describe the implications your position would have if you were in charge of teaching reading in your field placement.

Children's Trade Books Cited in This Chapter

Aliki. *My Visit to the Dinosaurs.* New York: Crowell, 1985.
Allen, Pamela. *Who Sank the Boat?* New York: Coward, 1983.
Anno, Mitsumasa. *Anno's Flea Market.* New York: Philomel, 1984.
Anno, Mitsumasa. *Anno's Journey.* New York: Philomel, 1978.
Babbitt, Natalie. *Tuck Everlasting.* New York: Farrar, Straus & Giroux, 1976.
Baylor, Byrd. *The Desert Is Theirs.* New York: Simon and Schuster, 1987.
Bemelmans, Ludwig. *Madeline.* New York: Viking, 1962.
Branley, Franklyn. *Sunshine Makes the Seasons.* New York: Harper and Row, 1985.
Brincklow, Julie. *Fireflies.* New York: Macmillan, 1985.
Carle, Eric. *The Very Lonely Firefly.* New York: Putnam, 1995.
Dahl, Roald. *Danny, Champion of the World.* New York: Knopf, 1975.
DeClements, Barthe. *The Fourth Grade Wizards.* New York: Viking, 1989.
Dumbrowski, Cathy. *Cave Boy.* New York: Random House, 1989.
Fleischman, Sid. *The Whipping Boy.* New York: Greenwillow, 1986.
Fritz, Jean. *And Then What Happened, Paul Revere?* New York: Putnam, 1973.
Gag, Wanda. *Millions of Cats.* New York: Coward, 1928.
Grimm, Wilhelm (translated by Ralph Manheim). *Dear Mili.* New York: Farrar, Straus & Giroux, 1989.
Hutchins, Pat. *Good Night, Owl.* New York: Macmillan, 1972.
Johnson, Angela. *Tell Me A Story, Mama.* New York: Orchard Books, 1989.
Kipling, Rudyard. *Just So Stories.* New York: Viking, 1902.
Krensky, Steven. *Children of the Earth and Sky.* New York: Scholastic, 1992.
Lawson, Robert. *Rabbit Hill.* New York: Viking, 1941.
Lowrey, Lois. *The Giver.* Boston: Houghton Mifflin, 1994.
Lowrey, Lois. *Number the Stars.* Boston: Houghton Mifflin, 1989.
Mosel, Arlene. *Tikki, Tikki, Tembo.* New York: Holt, 1968.
Murphy, Jim. *The Last Dinosaur.* New York: Scholastic, 1988.
Omerod, Jan. *Moonlight.* New York: Lothrop, Lee & Shepard, 1982.
Parker, Nancy Winslow, and Joan Richards Wright. *Bugs.* New York: Greenwillow, 1987.
Sandburg, Carl. *The Rootabaga Stories.* New York: Odyssey, 1968.
Say, Allen. *Grandfather's Journey.* Boston: Houghton Mifflin, 1993.

Sendak, Maurice. *Where The Wild Things Are.* New York: Harper and Row, 1963.
Slobodkina, Esphyr. *Caps for Sale.* New York: Harper and Row, 1947.
Taylor, Mildred. *The Gold Cadillac.* New York: Bantam, 1987.
Van Laan, Nancy. *Possum Come A-Knockin'.* New York: Knopf, 1990.
Viorst, Judith. *Alexander and the Terrible, Horrible, No Good, Very Bad Day.* New York: Macmillan, 1971.
Yashima, Taro. *Crow Boy.* New York: Viking, 1955.

References

Adams, M. J., Allington, R. L., et al. (1991). Beginning to Read: A Critique by Literacy Professionals and a Response from Marilyn Jager Adams. *The Reading Teacher* 44:370–395.

Allen, R. V. (1976). *Language Experiences in Communication.* Boston: Houghton Mifflin.

Anderson, R. C., et al. (1985). *Becoming a Nation of Readers.* Washington, DC: National Institute of Education.

Arnold, H. (1982). *Listening to Children Read.* London: United Kingdom Reading Association.

Aukerman, R. C. (1984). *Approaches To Beginning Reading* (2nd ed.). New York: John Wiley and Sons.

Bergeron, B. S. (1990). What Does the Term Whole Language Mean? Constructing a Definition from the Literature. *Journal of Reading Behavior* 22:301–329.

Cambourne, B. (1988). *The Whole Story: Natural Learning and the Acquisition in the Classroom.* New York: Ashton-Scholastic.

Cambourne, B. (1995). Toward an Educationally Revelant Theory of Literacy Learning: Twenty Years of Inquiry. *The Reading Teacher* 49:182–190.

Chall, J. (1996). *Learning To Read: The Great Debate* (3rd ed.). Boston: Houghton Mifflin.

Cheek, E. H., Jr. (1989). Skills-Based vs. Holistic Philosophies: The Debate among Teacher Educators in Reading. *Teacher Education Quarterly* 16:15–20.

Cullinan, B. E. (1989). Latching onto Literature: Reading Initiatives Take Hold. *School Library Journal* 35:27–31.

Dahl, K. L., & Freppon, P. A. (1995). A Comparison of Inner City Children's Interpretation of Reading and Writing Instruction in the Early Grades in Skills-Based and Whole Language Classrooms. *Reading Research Quarterly* 30:50–74.

Duffy, G. G. (1992). Let's Free Teachers to Be Inspired. *Phi Delta Kappan* 73:442–447.

Edelsky, C. (1990). Whose Agenda Is This Anyway? A Response to McKenna, Robinson, and Miller. *Educational Researcher* 19:7–11.

Fuhler, C. J. (1990). Let's Move toward Literature-Based Reading Instruction. *The Reading Teacher* 44:312–315.

Goodman, K. (1988). *What's Whole in Whole Language?* Richmond Hill, ONT: Scholastic-TAB.

Goodman, K. S., Shannon, P., Freeman, Y. S., and Murphy, S. (1988). *Report Card on Basal Readers.* Katonah, NY: Richard C. Owens Publishers.

Guice, S., and Allington, R. (1994). It's More than Reading Real Books! Ten Ways to Enhance the Implementation of Literature-Based Instruction. *Literature Update.* Albany, NY: National Research Center on Literature Teaching and Learning, SUNY Albany.

Heald-Taylor, B. G. (1996). Three Paradigms for Literature Instruction in Grades 3–6. *The Reading Teacher* 49:456–466.

Hepler, S. (1989). A Literature Program: Getting It Together, Keeping It Going. In J. Hickman and B. E. Cullinan (eds.), *Children's Literature in the Classroom: Weaving Charlotte's Web.* Norwood, MA: Christopher-Gordon Publishers.

Hoffman, J. V., McCarthy, S. J., Abbott, J., Christian, C., Carman, L., Curry, C., Dressner, M., Elliot, B., Matherne, D., and Stabile, D. (1994). So What's New in the New Basals? A Focus on First Grade. *Journal of Reading Behavior* 26:47–73.

International Reading Association and National Council of Teachers of English. (1996). *Standards for the English Language Arts.* Newark, DE and Urbana, IL: IRA and NCTE.

Johnson, T. D., and Louis, D. R. (1987). *Literacy through Literature.* Portsmouth, NH: Heinemann.

Kantrowitz, B. (1990). The Reading Wars. *Newsweek Special Edition: Education, A Consumer's Handbook* 64:8–14.

Langer, J. A., and Allington, R. L. (1992). Curriculum Research in Writing and Reading. In Philip W. Jackson (ed.), *Handbook of Research on Curriculum.* New York: Macmillan.

Lapp, D., Flood, J., and Farnan, N. (1992). Basal Readers and Literature: A Tight Fit or a Mismatch? In K. D. Wood and A. Moss (eds.), *Exploring Literature in the Classroom: Content and Methods.* Norwood, MA: Christopher-Gordon Publishers.

Mathews, M. M. (1966). *Teaching to Read Historically Considered.* Chicago: University of Chicago Press.

McCallum, R. D. (1988). Don't Throw the Basals Out with the Bath Water. *The Reading Teacher* 42:204–208.

McGee, L. M. (1992). Focus on Research: Exploring the Literature-Based Reading Revolution. *Language Arts* 69:529–537.

McGee, L. M., and Tompkins, G. E. (1995). Literature-Based Reading Instruction: What's Guiding the Instruction? *Language Arts* 72:19–28.

Mervar, K., and Hiebert, E. (1989). Literature Selection Strategies and Amount of Reading in Two Literacy Approaches. In S. McCormick and Z. Zutell (eds.), *Thirty-Eighth Yearbook of the National Reading Conference.* Rochester, NY: National Reading Conference.

Mullis, I. V. S., Campbell, J. R., and Farstrup, A. E. (1993). *NAEP 1992 Reading Report Card for the Nation and the States.* Washington, DC: U.S. Department of Education.

Newman, J., ed. (1985). *Whole Language: Theory in Use.* Portsmouth, NH: Heinemann.

Noyce, R. M., and Christie, J. F. (1989). *Integrating Reading and Writing Instruction in Grades K–8.* Boston: Allyn and Bacon.

Purcell-Gates, V. (1995). Language Arts Research for the 21st Century: A Diversity of Perspectives among Researchers. *Language Arts* 72:56–65.

Reutzel, D. R., and Hollingsworth, P. M. (1988). Whole Language and the Practitioner. *Academic Therapy* 23:405–415.

Reutzel, D. R, and Larsen, N. S. (1995). Look What They've Done to Real Children's Books in the New Basal Readers. *Language Arts* 72:495–507.

Sampson, M., Allen, R. V., and Sampson, M. (1991). *Pathways to Literacy: A Meaning-Centered Approach.* San Antonio: Holt, Rinehart and Winston.

Savage, J. F. (1992). Literature-Based Reading Instruction: It Works! *The New England Reading Association Journal* 28: 28–31.

Scharer, P. L., and Detwiler, D. B. (1992). Changing As Teachers: Perils and Possibilities of Literature-Based Language Arts Instruction. *Language Arts* 69:186–192.

Shannon, P. (1989). *Broken Promises: Reading Instruction in Twentieth Century America.* Granby, MA: Bergin and Garvey Publishers.

Shannon, P. (1983). The Use of Commercial Reading Materials in American Elementary Schools. *Reading Research Quarterly* 19:68–85.

Smith, F. (1988). *Understanding Reading* (4th ed.). Hillsdale, NJ: Lawrence Erlbaum Associates.

Spiegel, D. L. (1992). Blending Whole Language and Systematic Direct Instruction. *The Reading Teacher* 46:39–44.

Strickland, D. S. (1995). Reinventing Our Literacy Programs: Books, Basics, Balance. *The Reading Teacher* 48: 294–302.

Sumara, D., and Walker, L. (1991). The Teacher's Role in Whole Language. *Language Arts* 68:276–285.

Teale, W. (1990). Dear Readers. *Language Arts* 67:808–810.

Trelease, J. (1995). *The Read-Aloud Handbook.* (4th ed.). New York: Penguin.

Tunnell, M. O., and Jacobs, J. S. (1989). Using "Real" Books: Research Findings on Literature-Based Reading Instruction. *The Reading Teacher* 42:470–477.

Valencia, S. (1992). Basal Assessment Systems: "It's Not the Shoes." *The Reading Teacher* 45:650–652.

Walmsley, S. A., and Adams, E. L. (1993). Realities of "Whole Language." *Language Arts* 70:272–280.

Watson, D. J. (1989). Defining and Describing Whole Language. *The Elementary School Journal* 90:129–141.

Welsh, V. (1985). *Why Change? A Teacher's Perspective.* Paper presented at the 1985 Spring Conference of National Council of Teachers of English, Houston. ERIC Document ED 255 868.

Wiggins, R. A. (1994). Large Group Lesson/Small Group Follow-up: Flexible Grouping in a Basal Reading Program. *The Reading Teacher* 47:450–463.

Winch, G. (1982). The Use of Reading Schemes: A Comparative Study. In D. Burnes, A. Campbell, and R. Jones (eds.), *Reading, Writing, and Multiculturalism.* Sydney: Australian Reading Association.

Yatvin, J. (1980). *Trade Books or Basals? Two Programs Measured against the Standard of What a Reading Program Should Be.* Urbana, IL: ERIC Clearinghouse on Reading and Communications Skills, ED 215 336.

*T*he World of Children's Literature

Chapter

2

© Ewing Galloway

Chapter 2 Outline

Features

2.1 **Picture Books about Teachers to Tickle the Funnybone**
2.2 **Sharing Folk Literature through Storytelling**
2.3 **Award-Winning Books**
2.4 **Poetry Anthologies for the Classroom Bookshelf**
2.5 **Censorship**
2.6 **Story Maps: Roadmaps to Understanding**
2.7 **Author/Illustrator of the Week/Month**
2.8 **Where To Find Information about Children's Authors?**

Key Concepts in This Chapter

Apart from being a vehicle in the development of literacy, children's literature belongs as a major part of the elementary school curriculum because it is part of children's heritage.

Children's literature has a history and tradition leading up to the explosion in the publication of books for young readers in the past decade.

Students can experience a variety of literary forms—picture books, folktales and fairy tales, fantasy, realistic fiction, historical fiction, and poetry—as part of their school experiences.

Although literary analysis is not the primary purpose of using literature in the elementary grades, pupils can become aware of important literary elements such as plot, setting, characterization, and theme as they begin to comprehend the stories they read.

An important avenue for helping children come to know and appreciate literature is an awareness of the people who create this literature.

Introduction

*T*his chapter is about literature for children. It is no substitute for a good course in children's literature, a course that is becoming more and more essential for teachers working in today's elementary and middle schools. However, given the scope of the task at hand, this brief overview will have to suffice. Those who have already taken a course in children's literature should be able to move fairly quickly through this chapter. Those who haven't will need to read more carefully.

Children's Literature: What and Why

Children's literature is the body of prose and poetry written specifically for young people. Although designed primarily for children, this body of literature appeals to readers beyond the childhood years. Children's literature also includes works that, although not originally written specifically for children, have proved to be popular with younger readers. For example, Jonathan Swift's *Gulliver's Travels* was written as a critique of humanity addressed to the mature imagination, but it became a glamorous children's adventure story.

Some of the special advantages of using literature to teach reading were presented in the previous chapter, but literature for children has values that extend well beyond those related to developing literacy. Literature is part of children's cultural heritage, the human attempt to record, communicate, and control experience from ancient to present times.

Literature is a rich source for feeding and enriching children's language, adding to their store of vocabulary and sharpening their sense of style. It stimulates their intellectual and emotional lives, generating both cognitive and affective responses to ideas. It nurtures children's imaginations by providing them with vicarious experiences—from exploring the depths of the ocean in times long gone to reaching the remote regions of outer space in times yet to come. Books afford unlimited opportunities to foster children's personal growth, while providing a window through which children can examine their own emotions and experiences. Literature offers children a chance to weigh their lives against a wide human spectrum and helps them develop ethical values and insights. Charlotte Huck (1982) talks about the power of literature to make us "more human (and) more humane." She also identifies literature's power to educate children's hearts as well as their heads, to develop their imaginations, and to provide a lifetime of reading pleasure.

In short, children's literature offers what Maurice Saxby (1987) calls "The Journey to Joy": hours of entertainment, satisfaction, and renewal found through the pages of books. Literature is as essential to children's education as it is to their lives.

A Brief History of Literature for Children

The field of children's literature, as all literature, grows out of the oral tradition. Preliterate peoples gathered around the fire to hear storytellers spin tales that would teach and entertain. Many of these storytellers had priest-like powers, as they were charged with keeping an exact account of history within their minds and passing it along to succeeding generations.

A classroom library is important to a literature-based reading program.
© James L. Shaffer

The oral tradition continued in the courts and cottages of the Middle Ages, as minstrels and balladeers roamed the countryside sharing popular tales that the Brothers Grimm later recorded. Even after William Caxton established a printing press in England in 1476, the oral tradition continued, with its emphasis on both entertainment and instruction. The first children's books were published solely with instructional intent, and the content was usually religious. Many had horribly didactic titles such as *A Token for Children of New England, or Some Examples of Children in Whom the Fear of God Was Remarkably Budding before They Died.*

Among the first nonreligious books published for children were chapbooks, small and crudely printed books that 17th- and 18th-century street vendors sold. These roughly illustrated, eight-page books contained stories about the adventures of Robin Hood and other popular tales with appeal to a young audience. Mother Goose rhymes and fairy tales also found their way into print in the 1700s.

The birth of "children's literature" took place in 1744 with the publication of *A Pretty Little Pocketbook* by John Newbery, the man for whom the Newbery Medal is named (See Putting Ideas to Work 2.3, p. 43). Newbery's book was the first specifically written and published to entertain and amuse young children. Other books designed for children followed, and while a didactic focus persisted, a body of literature designed for a young audience began to emerge.

The 19th century saw tremendous growth in the number of books written for children. Jacob and Wilhelm Grimm recorded the old stories that had been popular in Europe for so long. Hans Christian Andersen wrote his

famous fairy tales. American authors like Washington Irving and Nathaniel Hawthorne wrote stories that were popular with youngsters. Although the moralistic trend continued in many books, a growing number of stories with no didactic or moralistic intent were written solely to entertain. Louisa May Alcott's *Little Women* and Mark Twain's *The Adventures of Huckleberry Finn* appeared toward the end of the century. Jules Verne introduced his popular science fiction stories; Rudyard Kipling wrote his famous animal stories; Lewis Carroll wrote the fantasy *Alice's Adventures in Wonderland;* Edward Lear produced his humorous limericks. These and other authors wrote solely to entertain their readers, young and old alike.

In the 1800s, color printing was introduced, and illustrators began to gain recognition. Pictures were transformed from rough woodcuts and sketches to works of art capturing the mood and tone of the stories and the storytellers. Among the best known of these 19th-century illustrators is Randolph Caldecott, for whom the Caldecott Medal, the award for the most distinguished American picture book, is named (See Putting Ideas to Work 2.3, p. 43).

In the 20th century, the field of children's literature has truly come into its own. Authors have produced a proliferation of books for children, and these books have come to be valued and respected. In the early decades of the 20th century, picture books became exceedingly popular, while stories like L.M. Montgomery's *Anne of the Green Gables* and Kate Douglas Wiggin's

Rebecca of Sunnybrook Farm provided reading for older children. Series books introducing Tom Swift, the Hardy Boys, and Nancy Drew were widely read. Animal fantasies like Beatrix Potter's *The Tale of Peter Rabbit* and A. A. Milne's *Winnie-the-Pooh* arrived on the literary landscape. Special collections of poetry for children appeared. Books for children took their places in classroom instruction.

Today's teachers are witnesses and beneficiaries of the more recent history of children's literature. The production and distribution of juvenile books is big business. Thousands of books for young readers are published annually. Sales of juvenile paperback books for 1995 were over half a billion dollars, up almost 30 percent from the previous year (Bogart, 1996). Authors like Dr. Seuss have become household names. Books like E. B. White's *Charlotte's Web* and Maurice Sendak's *Where the Wild Things Are* have sold well over one million copies. Children's trade books have come to be an integral part of reading instruction in schools.

Literary Genres

In a literature-based reading program, children encounter a range of literary genres—picture books; fairy tales, folktales, and other forms of traditional literature; fantasy, including animal stories; realistic fiction; historical fiction; and poetry. Some types of books will be more prevalent at one particular grade level (picture books in the primary grades, for example); some (like poetry) will be appropriate at all grade levels.

Picture Books

From the very early years, pupils are exposed to picture books, books in which illustrations are essential complements to the text in telling the story. In these books, the visual and the verbal work together; words and images interact to create a story, an impression, an experience. "Picture books present the reader with a succession of images, some in the presence of written text, some alone, which taken together provide an aesthetic experience which is more than the sum of the parts" (Kiefer, 1988; p. 261).

Some experts in children's literature distinguish between a picture book and a picture storybook. The former may be an alphabet or counting book that merely synchronizes words and pictures without developing a story line. The latter uses words and illustrations to develop a story with setting, plot, theme, and characters. Although an awareness of this distinction may be important in using these respective books to teach reading, the terms *picture books* and *picture storybooks* are typically used interchangeably.

As the name suggests, illustration is essential in picture books. Illustrations keep the story moving, excite children's imaginations, and enhance the text. In some picture books, the pictures themselves carry the entire meaning. In wordless books, for example, illustrations alone, without any text, fully develop the characters and actions. (Actually, the expression *wordless book* is a misnomer; since a word or two may appear in the book itself and since children provide words as they read these books, these books are more properly referred to as *textless books*.) Even when words are featured in picture books, illustrations are essential to telling the story. In a book such as Pat Hutchins's *Rosie's Walk*, for example, the entire story centers on the misadventures of an unfortunate fox who follows Rosie the hen around the barnyard, yet the fox is never once mentioned in the text. Although the book uses words, the pictures really tell the story. In *Black and White* by David Macaulay, a mystery story is creatively integrated with the illustrations.

Artists use a variety of visual media in illustrating picture books—woodcuts, collages, paints and oils, pen and ink, watercolors, crayons, and photographs. Their style and choice of color convey the mood and action of the story. Robert McCloskey's changing colors in *Time of Wonder*, for example, reflect the various moods of the changing seasons and weather conditions on the coast of Maine. By contrast, Chris Van Allsburg's dark and almost haunting drawings in *Polar Express* reflect the mystery of the mood of Christmas Eve night, as do David Diaz's illustrations in *Smoky Night* by Eve Bunting, a picture book suggested by the Los Angeles riots of the early 1990s.

Picture books cover the gamut of children's real and imagined experiences. Animals and objects come to life in William Steig's *Doctor DeSoto*, the story of a mouse dentist who outwits a foxy patient, and in Hardie Gramatky's tale of the gutsy tugboat *Little Toot*, who saves an ocean liner in a storm. Children explore their feelings through stories like Ezra Jack Keats's *Peter's Chair*, the story of a boy who worries about the arrival of a new baby in the family, and Judith Viorst's *The Tenth Good Thing about Barney*, the story of how a boy copes with grief when his pet cat dies. Children enjoy the incongruity of the concept and the hilarity of the illustrations in Judi Barrett's *Animals Definitely Should Not Wear Clothes* and cry at the end of Sally Wittman's *A Special Trade*, the simple but sensitive story of a friendship between a young man and a little girl that develops into a friendship between an old man and a young woman. Through picture books, children appreciate the colorful details of everyday reality in Ezra Jack Keats's *The Snowy Day* and the vivid fantasy of Faith Ringgold's *Tar Beach*.

The artistic styles found in picture books represent a range of art forms—from simple line drawings to intricate illustrations, from actual photographs to metaphorical representations, from watercolors to woodcuts. These books stimulate the senses as they stimulate the imaginations and the language of children.

Folktales and Fairy Tales

"Folktale is an inclusive term, referring to all kinds of narrative that has its origin in the oral tradition" (Bosma, 1987; p. 4). The roots of folk literature trace back to the stories that were part of the myths and legends, folktales and fairy tales, ancient peoples shared. Groups would gather in caves, castles, cottages, temples, and clearings to hear storytellers spin their yarns, some of which are as popular with children today as they were centuries ago.

2.1 Putting Ideas to Work

Picture Books about Teachers to Tickle the Funnybone

Children love picture books that make them laugh, silly stories such as Babette Cole's *Princess Smarty Pants* and Robert Munsch's *Mud Puddle.* Stories that seem to especially delight children, however, are those in which teachers find themselves in outrageously impossible situations. Here are six picture books in this category:

Miss Nelson Is Missing by Harry Allard. Miss Nelson is a wonderful teacher with an obnoxious class. When the disgusting Viola Swamp "replaces" her, strange things happen. (Two Miss Nelson sequels are available, but they cannot match the original.)

The Day the Teacher Went Bananas by James Howe. Children learn a lot of strange things when their teacher is supposed to be in the zoo.

A Hippopotamus Ate the Teacher by Mike Thaler. Instruction still goes on, even after a hippopotamus eats the teacher on a field trip to the zoo.

The Teacher from the Black Lagoon by Mike Thaler. Miss Green is green, and she breathes fire and zaps kids, too.

Thomas' Snowsuit by Robert Munsch. Efforts by the teacher and the principal to get Thomas into his snowsuit result in some bizarre wardrobe combinations.

John Patrick Norman McHennessey by John Burningham. The teacher doesn't believe John's fascinating accounts of his activities until one becomes a reality.

Folktales originated in the oral tradition. Part of the popularity of these traditional stories stems from the way they deal with universal human themes—good and evil, cruelty and kindness, honesty and deceit, life and death. Virtue is always rewarded; wickedness is always punished. Cinderella lives happily ever after, as does Tattercoats in Joseph Jacobs's version of the rejected-and-impoverished-girl-meets-and-marries-prince story. The universal themes in folktales account for the equivalent African, Near Eastern, Far Eastern, and American Indian versions, with each version reflecting the unique flavor of the culture from which it comes. Rafe Martin's *The Rough-Faced Girl* is an Algonquin version of Cinderella, for example, and Robert San Souci's *Sootface* is an Ojibwa Cinderella story. Literature indeed provides a human link among peoples of different cultures.

The first comprehensive compendium of European folktales was recorded by the Brothers Grimm, Jacob and Wilhelm. Ironically, the Grimms' primary intent was not to entertain; they were linguistic scholars who recorded the stories in order to analyze the language used to tell the tales. The Grimms' work, however, has left a literary rather than a linguistic legacy, though the brothers did make their impact in linguistics as well.

Fairy tales have the qualities of folktales, but they originated in written rather than oral form. Stories like Hans Christian Andersen's *The Princess* and the Pea and Rudyard Kipling's *Just So Stories* (such as "How the Elephant Got His Trunk") followed the folk tradition and remain popular long after they were written. The appeal of traditional literature transcends the boundaries of continents and centuries. Tomorrow's generations of children will enjoy traditional stories as much as the children of earlier times. For example, they are likely to delight in the French tale *Stone Soup*, retold by Marcia Brown, which tells of the trickster who cons an old woman into adding a series of delicious ingredients to a pot with a rock in it to create "stone soup." And stories like Esphyr Slobodkina's retelling of the Slavic folktale *Caps for Sale*—the story of the hapless peddler who recovers his caps from a band of mischievous monkeys—will continue to delight new readers. The appeal of folktales and fairy tales is ageless.

The field of traditional literature also includes fables, myths, legends, and tall tales. *Fables* are stories in which animals behave like humans and which present a moral. The oft-told children's stories of "The Hare and the Tortoise" or "The Boy Who Cried Wolf" are good examples of fables with lessons that children are expected to absorb. Several contemporary editions of Aesop's fables are available to be enjoyed in school and at home, as are modern renditions of traditional fables, such as Marcia Brown's *Once a Mouse*.

Myths are an ancient story form, typically told to explain natural phenomena and usually containing larger-than-life characters. Different cultures had their own accounts of why the sun and moon are in the sky, where the mountains came from, and how the world was born. Stories of gods and goddesses passed down from the ancient Greeks and Romans are still popular today. Books such as Doris Gates's *Mightiest of Mortals: Heracles* or *Heroes and Monsters of Greek Myth* by Bernard Evslin, Dorothy Evslin, and Ned Hoopes tell stories of ancient heroes that today's children still enjoy.

Legends are historical tales handed from generation to generation, first by word of mouth and later in written form. Like myths, legends involve larger-than-life figures—sometimes supernatural beings—who perform heroic deeds in keeping with the traditions of their cultures. The Arthurian legends, for example, which chronicle the great deeds of King Arthur and his knights, still capture the imaginations of children. T. H. White's *The Sword in the Stone* and Margaret Hodges's *The Kitchen Knight: A Tale of King Arthur* retell the old legends.

Finally, tall tales have long been a popular form of literature for children. *Tall tales* are exaggerated accounts of people and events told in a realistic manner, often with heavy doses of humor. Perhaps the best known stories of this type feature the American legendary hero, Paul Bunyan. Children enjoy the fantastic accounts of this giant of a man from picture books like Steven Kellogg's *Paul Bunyan* and from longer accounts like Glen O. Rounds's *Ol' Paul, The Mighty Logger*. Well-known characters like Pecos Bill and Mike Fink enrich a child's view of the world, as does Anna Isaacs's *Swamp Angel*, the greatest woodswoman in Tennessee, who saves settlers from the "Thundering Tarnation." Children delight in Adrien Stoutenburg's

2.2 Putting Ideas to Work

Sharing Folk Literature through Storytelling

The same qualities that made folk literature appealing fare for the ancient storyteller sitting by the fire make this genre appealing to the modern pupil sitting in the classroom—clearly defined plots, basic characters, and fast action. Folktales and fairy tales begin quickly, move rapidly, and conclude happily. Good is rewarded; evil, punished. Storytelling provides an ideal way to share this literature, while at the same time helping students develop oral language skills.

Five steps in planning and carrying out storytelling activities with folk literature include:

1. *Choosing the story.* Folktales make good subjects, but any story children can enjoy is a good choice.
2. *Preparing the story.* To become familiar with a story, it is necessary to read it two or three times beforehand.
3. *Selecting simple props.* Although props are not absolutely necessary to telling a good story, simple devices like wearing a cap, holding up an object such as a stuffed animal, or using simple drawings or flannel-board figures can bring the story alive for an audience.
4. *Practicing the story.* Stories are practiced with an eye to involving the audience on certain phrases or lines, stressing particular parts, using hand gestures or sound effects, and employing other devices to help the story come alive. Students can use a tape recorder as they practice telling favorite tales.
5. *Telling the story.* As pupils relate the story, they can focus on expression and other oral language qualities that make the story more enjoyable to the audience.

After the storytelling activity, children can read copies of the story, since the oral language activity provides a background for comprehension. Storytelling can be extended into dramatics and puppet activities as well. Older pupils can prepare stories to tell to children in the lower grades.

American Tall Tales and in Mary Pope Osborne's *American Tall Tales,* which introduces tales about female heroes as well.

The heroes found in traditional literature often represent the nature of the society the literature comes from. The epic hero Odysseus represents the ideals of intelligence and the virtues the ancient Greeks valued. Robin Hood embodies the goodness and bravery the downtrodden English peasants admired. Paul Bunyan represents the brashness and resourcefulness required for opening the American wilderness. But beyond their symbolic and cultural significance, these characters from traditional literature entertain children of all ages from one generation to the next.

Fantasy

Fantasy is another form of literature long popular with children. Fantasies are highly fanciful stories about people and places that, though sometimes believable, do not really exist. The ancients sought answers to natural and supernatural phenomena in witches and warlocks, in magic and mysteries. Modern fantasy traces its roots to these sources, and many of these stories still delight children today.

2.3 Putting Ideas to Work
Award-Winning Books

*E*ach year, various organizations and agencies award a number of prizes for children's books. Among the most notable are:

The Newbery Award.   The John Newbery Medal is awarded annually by the American Library Association to the author of the most distinguished contribution to American literature for children.

The Caldecott Medal.   Also awarded by the American Library Association, the Caldecott Award is presented each year to the artist of the most distinguished American picture book for children.

The Laura Ingalls Wilder Award.   Named after the famous *Little House* author, this award is given every three years for substantial and lasting contributions to literature for children.

The Hans Christian Andersen Prize.   This international award is given every two years to one author and one illustrator who have made contributions to children's literature the world over.

Children's Choice.   While adults select the other award-winning books, the Children's Choice Award, sponsored by the International Reading Association, is based on books that children recommend. The October issue of *The Reading Teacher* reviews these books annually.

Literally hundreds of other awards and prizes go to quality children's books. These awards signal the type of literature teachers can bring into the classroom for their pupils.

A list of Newbery and Caldecott Award-winning books appears in the Appendix.

Fantasy is not only an important part of children's reading experiences; it is an important part of their lives. According to psychologists, fantasy provides a way to help pupils deal with their emotions, their dreams, their fears, their conflicts, and their worlds (Bettelheim, 1978). "Fantasy helps the child develop imagination. The ability to imagine, to conceive of alternative ways of life, to entertain new ideas, to create strange new worlds, to dream dreams are all skills vital to the survival of humankind" (Huck, Hepler, and Hickman, 1987; p. 337). Fantasy opens the world of wonder to students of all ages.

Children have long been fascinated by the world of kings and queens. Just as Jacob and Wilhelm Grimm recorded the actions of royalty in such popular traditional tales as *Cinderella,* so Hans Christian Andersen created entertaining stories about the nobility in *The Princess and the Pea* and *The Emperor's New Clothes.* More modern writers place royal characters in their fantasy tales as well. The young princess in Jane Yolen's *The Emperor and the Kite,* for example, rescues her father, the emperor. Dr. Seuss's hilarious *The 500 Hats of Bartholomew Cubbins* tells of a vain and angry king who insists that young Bartholomew remove his hat. A popular modern fairy tale involving royalty is Antoine de Saint-Exupéry's *The Little Prince,* a lovely story full of symbolism and written with several levels of meaning. And the illustrated re-creation of Oscar Wilde's *The Happy Prince* is a moving story about traditional values.

Animals, too, have long played an important part in the world of fantasy literature. Writers bring animal characters to life by making them act, feel, talk, and think like humans. Beatrix Potter's Peter Rabbit, Michael Bond's Paddington Bear, and H. A. and Margaret Rey's Curious George have become as well known as they are well loved as animal fantasy characters. One of the most popular children's books ever written—E. B. White's *Charlotte's Web*—is an animal fantasy. The rabbits who inhabit the Connecticut farm in Robert Lawson's *Rabbit Hill* or the incredibly intelligent rats who create a whole culture in Robert C. O'Brien's *Mrs. Frisby and the Rats of NIMH* take on real-life qualities that make them entirely engaging and believable.

In the world of children's fantasy, authors also anthropomorphize toys and other objects, giving them human qualities. A. A. Milne's Winnie-the-Pooh seems so real that we tend to forget he is a stuffed animal. Authors like Hardie Gramatky and Virginia Lee Burton have created such delightfully believable characters as Gramatky's Little Toot, the irresponsible little tugboat who eventually saves an ocean liner in a storm, and Burton's Katy, the snow plow who singlehandedly plows out the town in *Katy and the Big Snow*. In Lynne Reid Banks's more recently popular *The Indian in the Cupboard*, a plastic toy Indian comes to life to the delight and consternation of his nine-year-old owner. These objects not only delight children (and adults); they often teach valuable lessons.

Fantasy feeds on the preposterous. Children delight in reading about miniaturized characters like John Peterson's the Littles or Mary Norton's the Borrowers, both in books of the same name, characters who exist unbeknown to the people whose houses they inhabit. Astrid Lindgren's Pippi Longstocking is an outrageously funny character in a series of stories that children have loved for a long time. Characters like James in Roald Dahl's *James and the Giant Peach* tickle children's fancy, as do the events recounted by such authors as Norton Juster in *The Phantom Tollbooth* and Judi Barrett in *Cloudy with a Chance of Meatballs*. Characters with magic powers, settings that transcend the world of reality, stories that reach back in time, tales that project into the future—all fill children's imaginations and extend their worlds.

A more serious type of fantasy popular with many older children is high fantasy. These complex tales deal with ultimate values of good and evil and are often enjoyed by adults as well as upper elementary-grade pupils. Madeleine L'Engle's *A Wrinkle in Time* leads readers beyond the bounds of time and space as children search for their scientist-father; C. S. Lewis's *The Lion, the Witch, and the Wardrobe*, perhaps the most popular of the Narnia chronicles, sends children into a world of ancient creatures and into a battle for the forces of good; and J. R. R. Tolkien's *The Hobbit* sends its title character to battle the evil creatures of Middle Earth. All are classic fantasies that provide compelling reading for children.

Science Fiction

Just as historical fiction deals with the past, science fiction deals with the future. Science fiction is an imaginative form of literature based on hypothesized scientific advancements and imagined technologies. The continuing popularity of the Star Trek television, book, and movie series continues to fan the interest of today's children.

Science fiction is not new. Jules Verne's imaginative works from the 1800s, books like *Twenty Thousand Leagues Under the Sea* and *Journey to the Center of the Earth*, still fascinate today's readers—in part, perhaps, because we have seen some of these fantastic events become reality. Young children are introduced to this genre through books like *The Wonderful Flight to the Mushroom Planet* by Eleanor Cameron. Later books like Madeleine L'Engle's Newbery Award-winning *A Wrinkle in Time* and Michael Crichton's enormously popular *Jurassic Park* move science fiction to the present and into the future.

Science fiction recounts fantastic events, but the characters, setting, and plot are scientifically plausible and, at least theoretically, technically possible. Settings and events are extensions of existing technologies that may be familiar to readers. An internal consistency exists between what the characters do and the worlds they live in.

Science fiction doesn't deal only with futuristic technology, the gimmicks and gadgets of space travel, and new worlds. A story like Lois Lowry's compelling *The Giver* explores human interaction with science and poses deep and complex questions regarding the impact of future advances on human lives.

Stories that offer a more imaginative leap into the unknown by mixing elements of mythology or traditional fantasy with scientific concepts fall into the *science fantasy* genre. The distinction between science fiction and science fantasy is neither clearly defined nor universally acceptable (Tomlinson and Lynch-Brown, 1996). It may be said that while science fantasy creates a world that never was and never could be, science fiction speculates on events that one day may be possible.

In a world in which cybertechnology has made what was previously unthinkable a reality in daily life, it's not surprising that science fiction is growing in popularity with a generation moving toward the 21st century.

Realistic Fiction

At the other end of the literary spectrum from fantasy and science fiction is reality, represented in children's literature by realistic fiction. Realistic fiction consists of stories that attempt to portray people and events as they are in real life. It mirrors children's experiences. It often explores the problems and conflicts that children face as they grow up, and it sometimes gives them insights and outlets in dealing with these issues and concerns.

Although it is a form of fiction (and therefore imaginative in nature), contemporary realistic works reflect the realities of life—death, divorce, abandonment, hostility, school failure, and disabilities. But these stories also reflect the joys of life—love, happiness, friendship, satisfaction, and laughter. It is little wonder that contemporary realistic fiction tends to be the most popular story choice among children in the upper elementary and middle grades.

One of the more common themes of contemporary realistic fiction is living as part of a family. Beverly Cleary's books about Ramona Quimby and Lois Lowry's stories about the often irascible Anastasia Krupnik are stories that mirror life's problems as they entertain. More serious complexities of family relationships are revealed in other books; for example, Katherine Patterson's *Jacob Have I Loved*, the story of serious sibling rivalry between two sisters; Betsy Byars's *The Animal, the Vegetable, and John D. Jones*, the story of two sisters who find that their vacation with their divorced father is to be shared with his girlfriend's son; and Beverly Cleary's *Dear Mr. Henshaw*, a story told in an ingenious manner about the feelings of a boy living in a single-parent household. But not all realistic fiction about family relationships is sad and poignant. In books like the popular *Tales of a Fourth Grade Nothing* and the sequel *Superfudge*, Judy Blume depicts family relationships with humor and delight.

Getting along in school is important to children and is a popular theme in contemporary realistic fiction. Patricia Reilly Griff's Polk Street School series consists of relatively easy-to-read books on a variety of school-related topics (including problems in learning to read). Judy Blume's *Blubber*, a story about an overweight girl; Johanna Hurwitz's *Aldo Applesauce*, the story of a boy who acquires a nickname he hates; and Barthe DeClements's *Nothing's Fair in Fifth Grade*, the story of a girl who has problems entering a new school all recount incidents children can usually relate to and stories they can enjoy.

Compelling works of realistic fiction examine such tender topics as coping with physical and developmental disabilities and facing emotional problems associated with death and dying. Ivan Southall's *Let the Balloon Go* is about a physically handicapped 12-year-old who strives for—and achieves—independence. Betsy Byars's *Summer of the Swans* is a Newbery Award-winning story about an adolescent girl and her mentally retarded brother. Rose Blue's *Grandma Didn't Wave Back* is the touching story of a girl who watches her beloved grandmother grow old. Katherine Patterson's deeply moving *Bridge To Terabithia*, one of the most widely read stories in the elementary grades, deals with the grief of a child facing the death of a friend.

Obviously, an author is not restricted to writing about a single theme in a work of contemporary realistic fiction. Cynthia Voigt's *Dicey's Song* is a compelling story that involves the loss of a parent, some of the difficulties of living in an extended family, the problems of poverty, the struggles of having learning disabilities, an adolescent's search for independence, and friendship, all woven into a warm and beautiful story. Nor is contemporary realistic fiction restricted to portraying hardship and crises. Beverly Cleary's stories about Henry Huggins, Thomas Rockwell's *How to Eat Fried Worms*, and Barbara Robinson's story about *The Best Christmas Pageant Ever* are examples of contemporary realistic fiction that constitute some of the funniest selections in the field of literature for children.

A classic in literature is a work that continues to appeal to readers long after it is written. *Peter Rabbit* is a classic of children's literature. So is *Alice in*

Wonderland. Most books of contemporary realistic fiction have not been around long enough to have stood the test of time. But the popularity of books like *Bridge to Terabithia* and other works of contemporary realistic fiction indicate that some of the recent books in this burgeoning field will likely earn the designation of classic in generations to come.

Historical Fiction

Just as contemporary realistic fiction reflects life as it is (or might be) lived today, historical fiction reflects life as it was (or may have been) lived in the past. Historical fiction draws on both fact and imagination to allow children to learn about and to appreciate what life was like long ago.

Historical fiction leads children into the past in a way no history textbook can. *My Brother Sam Is Dead* by James and Christopher Collier enables children to experience the real emotion of choosing sides in the American Revolution, and *Johnny Tremain* by Esther Forbes allows them to feel the excitement and tension in the streets of Revolutionary Boston. Historical fiction is based on fact, but an author's imagination brings the facts to life.

Historical fiction reaches as far back as prehistoric times. It paints pictures of the life of a slave girl in ancient Egypt, a warrior among the early Celtic tribes, a boy in ancient Rome, and seafaring Vikings. Tales of heroes long gone and stories of life in medieval Europe capture the imaginations of today's children.

Among the most popular works of historical fiction for children are those based on American history. *The Thanksgiving Story* by Alice Dalgliesh details the life of an early Pilgrim family, and *The Courage of Sarah Noble,* by the same author, tells about a young child in the wilderness. Another popular story about life in early America is Elizabeth Speare's *The Witch of Blackbird Pond,* the story of a lively girl forced to make a new life for herself in a dour Puritan village.

Subsequent periods and events in American history—the Revolution, the expansion to the West, the Civil War, immigration, World War II, and the 20th Century—are all chronicled by works of historical fiction for children. Historical fiction stories that give children a glimpse into times and places past include Jean Fritz's *And Then What Happened, Paul Revere?* and her other books about famous historical figures; Scott O'Dell's *Sing Down the Moon,* the story of how white settlers helped destroy the lives of Native Americans; Laura Ingalls Wilder's *Little House on the Prairie* and her other books telling about life on the American frontier; Irene Hunt's *Across Five Aprils,* the moving story of the devastating personal effects the Civil War had on one family; Katherine Patterson's *Lyddie,* the story of a girl's experience in the mills in Lowell, Massachusetts during the Industrial Revolution; Beth Bao Lord's *In the Year of the Boar and Jackie Robinson,* the story of a young immigrant's early experiences in the United States; and Yoshiko Uchida's *Journey to Topaz,* a disturbing story about Japanese internment during the second World War. Historical fiction is history that touches children's lives.

Biography

Biographies are nonfiction stories about people who really lived. While the author of historical fiction has the freedom to invent characters and events, the biographer must be concerned with accuracy. Biography is rooted in reality. The elements of the story must be real; the details of the setting must describe real times and places; the events in the plot must have really happened; the characters must be developed to reflect their real personalities.

Biographies enrich children's lives by helping them peek through literary windows into the lives of famous people. Often, a biography makes a statement about humanity. Young readers discover human qualities that make people special (for better or for worse).

Biographies have a special place in multicultural literature, since textbooks have sometimes omitted or limited coverage of people of color (Harris, 1992). Biographies such as *Rosa Parks* by Eloise Greenfield or *José Marti* by Ted Appel help dispel stereotypes and help children learn about people who greatly influenced the experiences of others.

Informational Books

While not traditionally considered a genre of children's literature, books that present information are popular with children and often play a role in literature-based reading programs. Nonfiction children's trade books are gaining more and more attention as the quality of their language and illustrations improves and as they generate increasing enthusiasm in children.

Informational trade books present materials of interest to pupils of all ages and enhance the curriculum at all levels. Nonfiction books present information in many forms: in sophisticated ABC books like Jerry Pallotta's *The Yucky Reptile Alphabet Book;* in detailed picture books like Aliki's *A Medieval Feast;* in photo essays like Russell Freedman's *Lincoln: A Photobiography;* in a ribbon of narrative like David Macaulay's *Cathedral;* or in a straightforward presentation of information like Simon Seymour's *Our Solar System.* Nonfiction books are popular with children, and they constitute up to 70 percent of the collection in a school library.

Poetry

Poetry has a major place in children's literature. Poetry is the expression of language in metrical form to convey ideas or create images. Eleanor Farjeon defined the essence of poetry in this way:

Poetry

What is poetry? Who knows?
Not the rose, but the scent of the rose;
Not the sky, but the light from the sky;
Not the fly, but the gleam of the fly;
Not the sea, but the sound of the sea;
Not myself, but something that makes me
See, hear, and feel something that prose
Cannot. What is it? Who knows?[1]

1. From *Poems for Children* by Eleanor Farjeon, 1966. Reprinted by permission of the author and the Watkins\Loomis Agency.

As Farjeon so eloquently reveals, poetry reflects not only an object or idea or experience; it captures the essence of that object or idea or experience.

Poetry is designed to delight. It reaches into both the hearts and the heads of children, appealing to both emotions and intelligence. When poetry is a part of children's literature in the classroom, the emphasis is usually on enjoyment rather than analysis, as children naturally delight in the poet's language.

Why does poetry appeal to children? First, the rhythm delights the ear. The beat of a line such as "To market, to market to buy a fat pig," attracts and entertains even a very young child. The rhythmic patterns David McCord uses in his anthology *Every Time I Climb a Tree* maintain this appeal beyond the early years. Rhythm is the primary feature that distinguishes poetry from prose.

Rhyme is another feature children find appealing. Not all poetry has end-line rhyme, but the strong rhyming patterns of Mother Goose— *pig-jig, hog-jog, diddle-fiddle, dock-clock*—tickle the eardrums and help children enjoy poetry. Strong rhyming patterns appeal to the ears of children and adults alike.

The language of poetry is uniquely appealing as well. In addition to the qualities of rhythm and rhyme, poetry is marked by an efficiency of language, an economy of words. Poetry captures the essence of a scene, an idea, or an emotion with a single phrase or line. The language is subtle. Words are often used in special ways. Images are often (although not always) conveyed through symbolism and figurative language. "The reason a successful poem works is not easy to sum up. There is a perfection in the selection of words and word order, an effective matching of the mood to the metre; a certain balance; a reaching out with language; a wholeness. To achieve this success, the poet-craftsman works hard with language" (Winch, 1987; p. 126).

The imagery of poetry often appeals to children. The poet tends to see common, everyday objects and experiences in new ways, expressing his or her vision in metaphors that appeal to children's imagination and creativity. A tall apartment building becomes "a filing cabinet of human lives"; a toaster is a fire-breathing dragon; a steam shovel becomes a latter-day dinosaur. The images of poetry appeal to all the senses—sight, sound, smell, and even touch and taste (not to mention the emotion)—of readers of all ages.

Literature for children is filled with an enormous variety of poems that pupils can enjoy:

Narrative poems tell a story. A good example is Clement Moore's " 'Twas the Night Before Christmas," recreated in a beautiful picture book illustrated by Tomie de Paola and entitled *The Night Before Christmas.*

Lyric poems are melodic poetry that creates an impression and evokes an emotion through the rhythmic use of language. This type of poetry is represented by poems like Robert Louis Stevenson's "The Wind" and "The Swing."

Free verse is poetry that is free of the traditional elements of stress, meter, and rhyme. Beautiful examples appear in Richard Lewis's collection *Miracles: Poems by Children of the English-Speaking World.*

2.4 Putting Ideas to Work
Poetry Anthologies for the Classroom Bookshelf

A good anthology of children's poems should never be far from the teacher's fingertips. Among hundreds of good poetry collections available for use in the classroom, the following anthologies have proved to be particularly popular with teachers and pupils in the elementary grades:

The Random House Book of Poetry for Children, with poems selected by Jack Prelutsky, is a collection of poems on a variety of topics appropriate for virtually every classroom occasion.

Where the Sidewalk Ends, by Shel Silverstein, is a collection of humorous poems that seem everlastingly popular with students in the elementary and middle grades (and their teachers, too!).

A Light in the Attic, another collection by Shel Silverstein, reflects the same absurd humor and insight that children in succeeding generations continually enjoy.

Sing a Song of Popcorn: Every Child's Book of Poems, edited by Beatrice Schenk de Regniers, is a more contemporary collection of poems arranged thematically. This book has outstanding illustrations.

Other poetry collections will depend on teacher preference and purpose. For example:

Hailstones and Halibut Bones: Adventures in Color, by Mary O'Neill, is an appealing anthology of poems that describe and define colors.

Talking Like the Rain is a collection of poems by several well-known poets, selected especially for the youngest child by X. J. Kennedy and Dorothy M. Kennedy.

Nathaniel Talking, by Eloise Greenfield, is the poetry of a nine-year-old boy who raps and rhymes about the people in his world.

If You're Not Here, Please Raise Your Hand: Poems about School, a delightfully humorous collection of poems by Kalli Dakos, celebrates the joys and heartaches of life in an elementary school.

Animals, Animals, a collection of animal poems edited by Laura Whipple and brilliantly illustrated by Eric Carle, can be used in conjunction with animal studies.

A Basketful of White Eggs is a book of riddle-poems gathered by Brian Swann from all over the world.

Circle of Seasons, by Myra Cohn Livingston, is a dazzling book of seasonal poems brilliantly illustrated by Leonard Everett Fisher.

Finally, no early-level classroom should be without one of the many finely illustrated collections of *Mother Goose.*

Teachers who especially enjoy the work of particular poets—Aileen Fisher or Eleanor Farjeon or John Ciardi, for example—are sure to have collections by these poets to share as treasures with pupils. Any classroom bookshelf should have as wide a selection of poetry as possible so that children can enjoy poems throughout their school experience.

Haiku is an ancient but currently popular Japanese verse form. It contains three lines consisting of seventeen total syllables, and it usually focuses on nature. Another Richard Lewis collection, called *In a Spring Garden* and illustrated by Ezra Jack Keats, features haiku.

Limericks are a highly structured verse form that children enjoy. Edward Lear's *The Complete Nonsense Book* includes original limericks, as does the more contemporary *The Hopeful Trout and Other Limericks* by John Ciardi.

These and other forms of poetry—including the five-line verse form, cinquain; concrete poems, shaped to reflect the topic of the poem; and ballads, which are part of traditional folk literature—open a whole new world of experiences to children. Topics of children's poetry vary from the sublime (in poems such as Robert Frost's "Stopping By Woods on A Snowy Evening") to the ridiculous (in works like Shel Silverstein's "They've Put a Brassiere on the Camel"). The world of children's poetry is a wide world, indeed, and a world that enriches our lives.

Helping children happily enter this world is an important job for teachers. Taste in poetry is an individual matter. A poem that appeals to one child (or adult) may have no appeal for another. Perhaps the best way to kill a child's interest in poetry is to attempt to force appreciation. Providing a smorgasbord of poetry which children can sample and share every day will likely lead them to develop an appreciation that will endure all their lives.

Literary Elements

As children learn to read through exposure to and practice with literature, they will become aware of literary elements inherent in the stories they read. Recognizing these elements and how they contribute to story comprehension and appreciation is an essential part of literature-based reading instruction. The four major literary elements found in children's stories are: *setting*—the time and place in which a story takes place; *characterization*—the way the story portrays the characters; *plot*—the structure of the action in a story; and *theme*—the major idea the story or poem presents.

Other literary elements include mood, tone, irony, figurative language, style, and point of view, but the four that receive the most attention are setting, characterization, plot, and theme. Becoming aware of these four elements is important for both reading and writing. Understanding these elements in stories is an essential part of reading comprehension, and consciously including these elements improves pupils' writing.

Setting

Setting provides the "story stage." It involves the time in which a story takes place, from the past of historical fiction to the future of science fiction. It also involves the place in which the action occurs, from as specific a locale as the New York subway tunnels to as generic a setting as a nameless suburban middle school.

Setting is a vitally important literary element because a story derives its credibility and authenticity from time and place. The entire plot of Elizabeth Speare's *The Witch of Blackbird Pond*, for example, revolves around the

2.5 Putting Ideas to Work
Censorship

*A*n issue that many teachers face in selecting and recommending reading material for their pupils is censorship. Censorship is the attempt to limit the accessibility of certain books, films, drama, magazines, or other forms of media. It impacts schools when people deem certain books inappropriate for the library or for classroom use. Throughout history, people have repeatedly tried to ban certain books from schools. Efforts to exclude books whose content or language offends some segment of the population continue in the 1990s.

Community groups or school boards have attempted to censor books on a number of different grounds. Some object to artwork. Maurice Sendak's drawing of Mickey, the little boy who "falls out of his sleeper" in the highly imaginative **fantasy** *In the Night Kitchen,* generated a swarm of controversy because the boy is nude, even though the cartoonish nature of the artwork makes the illustration inoffensive to most. Some object to content. Judy Blume's popular *Are You There God? It's Me, Margaret,* the story of a girl concerned with some of the bodily changes involved in approaching puberty, has generated controversy for more than 20 years. Some object to language, as children's authors occasionally use words like *damn* and *jerk* (in reference to another person). And some object to books like Trina Schart Hyman's *Little Red Riding Hood.* In this version, Red Riding Hood brings her grandmother a bottle of wine, which granny enjoys in an illustration suggesting that she's a bit tipsy. Books have been attacked on a variety of grounds, indeed.

Censorship is a volatile and two-sided issue. While some people insist that books should be scrutinized and selected to conform to community standards, these standards can vary considerably. And while citizens in a democracy have the right to question the inclusion of certain books in public libraries or schools, censorship has been viewed as a violation of the personal right to read what one chooses and a threat to the professionalism and autonomy of teachers and librarians. By limiting access to print, censorship poses a threat to literacy.

Censorship impacts children, parents, teachers, librarians, and school administrators. It diminishes children's access to a wide variety of literature. It denies students the opportunity to enjoy a particular book and to exercise critical judgment about the content of reading material.

While parents certainly have the right to monitor and restrict what their children are reading, they hardly have the right to restrict what *all* children in a community read. When objections are raised to particular book titles, parents on both sides of the issue—not just those who object to the book—ought to engage in the discussion.

mood and attitudes of the people living in Puritan New England. Authors of good children's stories carefully craft time and place so that the stories, even if they are fantasies, will be truly believable. Illustrators carefully design their artwork to faithfully and realistically reflect the settings they represent.

Characterization

The author places characters, those who drive the action and the story, into the story setting. Character development is a complex process. Authors create characters in very specific ways: through description in the text, through the characters' thoughts, words, and actions, and through the comments other characters in the story make about them.

Teachers and librarians are most directly impacted by censorship in a professional sense. It poses a threat to their professional judgment and places limitations on their ability to do their best job. Teachers and librarians are those most often caught in the crossfire of controversy when censorship arises.

Censorship can be exercised at a broad level, as when a book such as Michael Willhoite's *Daddy's Roommate,* a book which depicts the homosexual lifestyle of two males, is banned from a school or community library. Or censorship can be exercised at the classroom level, as when a parent objects to the use of the enormously popular *The Great Gilly Hopkins* by Katherine Patterson because of the realistic language of the main character. Sometimes, a parent's objection can be based on a short passage or even a single word.

How does the classroom teacher deal with censorship? First, teachers should be prepared to justify the choice of a trade book to a parent who questions its use. They need to be ready to counter criticisms with sound reasons for using a particular book based on its literary or instructional merit. While teachers need to be sensitive to parents' concerns, they also need to be sensitive to the educational and psychosocial needs of all children in their classrooms. Sometimes a teacher can take a proactive stance by sending a list of books home at the beginning of the year and inviting parents to respond if they wish. If a parent objects to a particular book, the teacher can provide alternatives for that particular child or for the class from what parents consider appropriate titles.

School administrators play an essential role in supporting teachers and librarians. And administrators can exercise leadership in formulating a policy and procedures on censorship issues.

A policy is essential. Collaboration among administrators, teachers, librarians, and parents is important in formulating a policy statement. Policies indicate that a district has thoroughly considered the significance of controversial books and has considered alternatives. Policies should govern not only procedures for selecting books, but also for filing and resolving formal complaints. The American Library Association and the National Council of Teachers of English have issued guideline policies and strategies regarding censorship and the right of free access to books.

In the final analysis, censorship is a matter of professional judgment. "In responding to censorship, one should first recognize that teachers are professionals who develop curricula based on sound judgments and select print and nonprint teaching materials that will enable them to do their best to teach every child. While input from the community might be desirable, final decisions about selection of methods and materials to be used should lie with professionals" (Weiss, 1995; p. 29).

Characterization is a crucial dimension of literature for children. Folktales and fairy tales tend to include stock figures whose characters are "flat" and who simply symbolize good and evil: the cruel stepmother, for example, or the generous king. Other forms of literature, however, require characters that are well rounded, believable, and realistic. These are the people (or animals or objects) whom children come to love or hate, admire or pity, laugh at or cry with. Children often form special relationships with characters they meet in the stories they read.

Just as the story's setting must be realistic, well-developed story characters must behave with consistency and authenticity. Their words, thoughts, and actions must be consistent with the personalities the author breathes into them. Even animals and objects take on personalities that children remember long after they have outgrown childhood literary favorites: readers long remember the disarming charm of Winnie-the-Pooh, for example, or the loyal bond of friendship between Frog and Toad. Characters like Madeline and Henry Huggins remain our friends forever.

Plot

Plot, the action of the story, is an essential literary element. A children's book may have beautiful illustrations, attractive characters, a noble theme, a fascinating setting, and all the other qualities that characterize good literature. But to the child, one question is paramount: does the book tell an exciting, interesting, or entertaining story?

Narrative stories usually follow a fairly well-defined plot structure. The story's beginning sets the scene and introduces the characters. Characters develop and action rises through the middle of the plot. The plot reaches its climax as conflict between the protagonist and the antagonist peaks. The conflict may be between the main character and other people, between the character and nature, between the character and social values, or between the character and him or herself. In most children's stories, the plot concludes with the successful resolution of the conflict and a speedy tidying up of loose details. In most children's stories, the plot proceeds in this fairly linear fashion, although some authors use flashbacks effectively to develop action, as Robert C. O'Brien does in *Mrs. Frisby and the Rats of NIMH*.

Plot is more than a simple linear series of events, however. It is a structured plan that dynamically develops the relationship between events that occur as part of the story. The events in the plot may also reinforce the other literary aspects of setting, characterization, and theme. Plot is the literary element that keeps the story moving. The setting might shift and the characters change, but a good plot makes the reader want to continue reading. Good plots, even in simple stories, maintain a suspense that makes the reader wonder what will happen next.

Theme

Theme reaches beyond the other literary elements and reveals the author's purpose in writing a story. Theme may be described as the author's interpretation of the events he or she is writing about; the "focal point" for the setting, characters, and the episodes that make up the plot; "the interconnecting thread that brings all the elements together in wholeness and harmony" (Saxby, 1987; p. 11); or the ultimate outcome that emerges from the literary experience. In sum, theme involves the essential meaning of a piece of literature.

Children's books can have more than one layer of meaning. On one level, E. B. White's enormously popular *Charlotte's Web* is an animal fantasy about a spider who saves the life of a pig; on another, it is a strong statement about friendship; on yet a third level, it is a commentary on the cycle of life and death. C. S. Lewis's *The Lion, the Witch, and the Wardrobe* is an allegorical tale with deep religious meaning, but even without ascribing any spiritual

2.6 Putting Ideas to Work

Story Maps: Roadmaps to Understanding

When readers understand the elements contained in a story, they have a better chance of comprehending and appreciating what they read. Davis and McPherson (1989) describe the effective use of story maps as a strategy to help students understand story elements. A story map is a graphic representation of story elements and their relationship to one another.

Story maps can take many forms, from the simple linear plot design to more elaborate text diagrams.

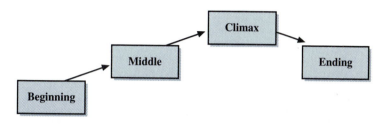

Children can prepare story maps before reading, discuss them during prereading, and complete them as students actually read the story. Teachers can use maps to guide questions during reading, or to enhance postreading activities as pupils look back at story elements.

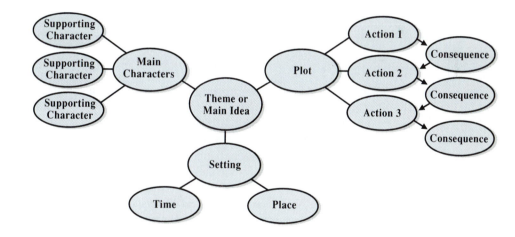

Continued on next page.

meaning to the story, one can enjoy it as a highly imaginative and philosophical adventure.

A single story can have more than one theme. "The theme may be a moral one, involving acceptance of others. It may be psychological, an observation about a personality that forbids traits unlike its own. It may be

2.6 Putting Ideas to Work—Continued

Story Maps: Roadmaps to Understanding

Although story maps have proved to be effective instructional devices, they should never intrude so much that they interfere with children's enjoyment of the literature they read.

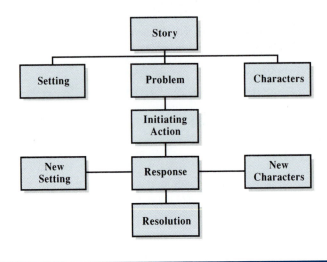

sociological, an observation about peer group behavior in a suburban neighborhood. The theme may unify all these fields of inquiry, as well as some others" (Sebesta and Iverson, 1975; p. 60).

Many children's stories have a moral. Traditional folk literature celebrates virtues such as kindness, patience, and perseverance. Much contemporary children's literature also focuses on ethical or social values. But in good literature, the moral is understated; the theme emerges naturally from the story. In Evaline Ness' *Sam, Bangs, and Moonshine,* for example, it is not hard to recognize the message that it is dangerous to confuse reality and fantasy and to mislead others based on this confusion, but the story suggests the lesson rather than driving it home with undue emphasis. As in all good literature, the moral emerges from the context of the story and is not merely a tacked-on sermon.

In addition to the four elements of setting, character, plot, and theme, other literary devices appear in quality works of literature for children, including irony, tone, style, and point of view.

Irony is the technique of suggesting an underlying message very different from, and incongruous with, the message the text seems to present. For example, in Ellen Raskin's *Nothing Ever Happens on My Block,* a boy sits on

the curb and complains of boredom as all kinds of exciting events take place behind him.

Mood is the emotional atmosphere an author creates with language or an illustrator creates with art; the mood of a story can be lighthearted or somber, poignant or silly. In *Sounder,* William Armstrong uses setting and figurative language to create a mood of hostility and sadness.

Tone, so closely related to mood that the terms are sometimes used interchangeably, reflects the author's attitude toward a topic; a story can be told as a personal experience shared with a peer (á la Judy Blume) or as an outrageous joke an adult tells to a child (á la Roald Dahl).

Style is the author's way of writing, the unique way he or she uses language to depict setting, create characters, or describe action. Father Rabbit speaks in an aristocratic style in Robert Lawson's *Rabbit Hill,* for example, while Jill speaks in the adolescent vernacular in Judy Blume's *Blubber.*

Point of view reflects the "eyes" through which the author presents the story. Although most stories are told from an omniscient or all-knowing point of view, we see some stories through the eyes of one of the characters observing or participating in the action. Jon Scieszka's *The True Story of the 3 Little Pigs!* and *The Frog Prince Continued* are clever variations of the traditional stories (the former told by the wolf, and the latter by the princess who married the frog). These two books can be used to teach point of view from the earliest years through the upper grades. In a more serious vein, Jane Yolen's *Encounter* recounts the arrival of Columbus in the New World through the eyes of a native named Taino.

Because authors use language to create both the major and minor literary elements, tone, mood, style, point of view, setting, characterization, plot, and theme are closely woven together in a good story. The time and place of the setting shape the characters and direct their actions. As they perform the actions in the plot, characters achieve a depth of personality. All four major elements create story unity. By synthesizing these elements, skilled authors create the stories that make a lasting mark on the field of literature for children.

By taking these literary elements into account, teachers can gain a "set of eyes" for examining children's stories. As teachers select books for classroom libraries or recommend books for children to read, they can use their knowledge of literary elements to judge the quality and characteristics of various books. Librarians and reading resource specialists are usually available to help teachers make judgments and recommendations about children's books as well. Knowledge of setting, character, plot, and theme are also important for formulating questions and discussing text in instructional situations, either in reading groups or in individual conferences. These elements can suggest guidelines for questions and discussion, whether the teacher is using basal stories or trade books.

How important is it for children in the classroom to learn about literary elements? Clearly, an awareness of who (character) is doing what (plot) where (setting) and for what purpose (theme) is basic to the most literal comprehension of a story. The more a reader understands the personality and motives of a character or the details of the time and place in which the story occurs, the more complete the reader's understanding and appreciation of the story will be. And recognizing the contrasting themes and moods of different stories comes with critical thinking and understanding at the higher levels.

Helping pupils recognize these literary elements, however, does not mean overanalyzing the story. The point of introducing literature to a child is enjoyment. Good books for children are like fine wine for adults—they ought to be savored. The adult does not need to know the chemical composition of the wine or the way it was produced to enjoy it, and a child does not need to be consciously aware of the nature of the conflict or the techniques an author uses for character development to enjoy reading a good story. In-depth knowledge should enhance appreciation, not kill interest.

Children's literature can be an effective vehicle for helping students develop reading competency in the classroom, but analysis should never get in the way of enjoyment.

Getting to Know Authors

When a child (or an adult) reads a book, he or she and the author enter into a relationship with each other. The story becomes the medium that forms the bond between the two. Knowing a little about the person who wrote the book helps enhance the relationship between writer and reader; it helps the child to know and appreciate the book a little more. This awareness is part of the reading-writing connection.

2.7 Putting Ideas to Work
Author/Illustrator of the Week/Month

One way to develop author awareness is to feature a bulletin board display of an author or an illustrator students especially enjoy. For example:

Author/Illustrator of the Month

BERNARD WABER

Education
University of Pennsylvania
Philadelphia College of Art

Facts about Mr. Waber
The youngest of four children in his family
Married, with three children
Served in the Army
Worked as an artist in New York City

Some of His Books
Ira Sleeps Over (1972)
Lyle, Lyle, Crocodile (1965)
The Snake: A Very Long Story (1978)
An Anteater Named Arthur (1967)
Bernard (1982)

What We Think about Bernard Waber's Books
(Pupils tack index cards with comments and reactions to books by Waber that they have read.)

Courtesy of Houghton Mifflin Company

Born
September 27, 1924, in Philadelphia, PA

With each display, the teacher can set up a collection of the books the author has written. A new author or illustrator may be featured every few weeks. (Teachers who do this typically report that pupils read the books so quickly the display has to be changed more frequently.) Teachers of young children can enlist the help of parent volunteers in collecting information for the bulletin board. In the upper grades, student teams can gather information as part of a library-research assignment.

Where do you find information on authors for these displays? See Putting Ideas to Work 2.8, p. 61.

A reader does not need to know an author's life story in order to read and enjoy a book. But bits and pieces of information about an author can enhance the reader's understanding and appreciation of a piece of literature. For example, the book *And to Think That I Saw It on Mulberry Street* by Dr. Seuss, an imaginative account of what a child sees on his way to and from school, can be enjoyed without ever knowing who wrote it. But to know that Theodore Geisel (Dr. Seuss's real name) wrote the book on a boring ocean voyage as he tried to put words to the rhythm of the ship's engine gives us insight into the language he used. For aspiring authors, it is reassuring to know that this book, Geisel's first attempt at writing for children, was rejected by more than twenty-five publishers. In the early days, experts in children's literature did not acknowledge Seuss's work as worthy of mention. Ignorant of the experts' opinions, children made him a powerful force in the field.

It is interesting for children to know there is a real person behind the books that they read—to learn, for example, that Beverly Cleary writes stories about topics she wanted to read about when she was a child, humorous stories about problems that seem small to adults but loom large for children (like Ellen Tebbits's worry that she is the only one who has to wear long underwear). When children learn that Beverly Cleary writes "for the little girl within her," they can understand the charm of all the wonderful characters she has created.

Beyond the element of interest, author awareness actually affects how children learn to read. Madura (1995) describes how studying authors and illustrators can enable primary grade children to develop insight, improve responses, and heighten understanding. Author awareness also improves the choices children make about books outside the classroom (Hiebert, Mervar, and Person, 1990). In the upper grades, Krieger (1988) found that developing her students' author awareness—"a sense of *who* wrote the story, *how,* and *why*"—increased their interest, improved their comprehension, and enhanced their writing abilities.

Author awareness develops in stages, from a knowledge that real people write the books to more sophisticated understandings about the relationship between an author/illustrator and his or her work. Awareness does not develop automatically; it requires teacher direction, careful questioning, and well-planned classroom activities. Focusing on multicultural literature, Zarrillo (1994) describes how to set up whole units of author study, including book selection, activities, projects, and lessons related to the works of a particular author. Wepner (1993) describes how to tie computer technology into author study as well.

Connecting with authors can also be an aspect of the critical analysis that contributes to reading comprehension. In judging the accuracy or authenticity of a piece of writing, the child may need to know about the author's qualifications or background in writing about a topic.

Children and teachers can come into contact with authors in a variety of ways. Obviously, face-to-face meetings are best. Popular children's authors

2.8 Putting Ideas to Work
Where To Find Information about Children's Authors

*I*nformation about authors and illustrators of children's literature is available from a number of reference sources.

Books Are By People (1969) and *More Books By More People* (1974), two books by Lee Bennett Hopkins, contain interesting, brief biographical sketches of well-known children's authors. *Once Upon a Time: An Encyclopedia for Successfully Using Children's Literature with Young Children* by Carol Otis Hurst (1990) contains biographical items related to authors and illustrators, along with teaching suggestions for using their books. *An Author a Month* by Sharron McElmeel (1988) also has some interesting biographical information about authors of children's literature.

Books of Junior Authors and Illustrators are published periodically by the H. W. Wilson Company, and the Gale Publishing Company produces annual volumes of *Something about the Author*. Both sources contain a wealth of information. Most children's librarians can help teachers and pupils find other references like these.

Some well-known children's authors have written interesting autobiographies. Pupils can use these accounts to discover the thoughts and writing techniques of the real people whose work they enjoy, and to discover that famous authors were once young, too. A sampling of these autobiographies includes:

Bill Peet: An Autobiography, simply written and delightfully illustrated by the author in his own style;

A Girl from Yamhill, Beverly Cleary's story of her childhood, which shaped her as a writer;

How I Came to Be a Writer, Phyllis Reynolds Naylor's account of her experiences as a young person;

Boy, Roald Dahl's fascinating and personal account of growing up, told in the author's inimitable style; and

Homesick: My Own Story, Jean Fritz's account of her world as a child.

Biographies such as Beverly Gherman's *E. B. White: Some Writer!* are also available.

Finally, some professional magazines regularly profile children's authors:

Language Arts, the journal published by the National Council of Teachers of English for teachers in the elementary grades;

The Horn Book Magazine, a bimonthly publication devoted exclusively to literature for children; and

The New Advocate, another excellent magazine "for those involved with young people and their literature."

All these sources provide children and teachers with enlightening information about their favorite writers and illustrators.

often appear at professional conferences, bookstores, libraries, or meetings. Some even make a regular practice of visiting schools to meet children.

Movies, videos, or CD-ROMs of authors and illustrators commenting on their work bring children into indirect contact and are available for classrooms. The Weston Woods Company (Weston, CT) has films of authors and illustrators such as Maurice Sendak explaining where he gets his wonderfully imaginative ideas, Ezra Jack Keats discussing his work, and Robert McCloskey talking about experiences that have shaped his writing. Teachers sometimes have children write letters to authors. Although many authors discourage this practice, some make an honest effort to answer their "fan mail." Some popular authors, like Judy Blume and Eric Carle, have home pages on the World Wide Web.

Summary and Conclusions

This chapter presents a brief overview of a very extensive field, the world of children's literature. It mentions some of the significant historical developments, identifies the types of literature elementary school students most often encounter, describes some of the elements of literature, and suggests how to help children learn more about authors.

This chapter is a microcosmic view, at best. It does not address many important issues related to children's literature—sexism, racism, or stereotyping, for example. Nor does it discuss in any detail how to "teach" literature, or use instructional activities or devices to help children respond to books in the classroom. Given the limited scope of the chapter, these important topics must be left for another time and place.

In the final analysis, it is impossible to take a crash course in children's literature, to find a shortcut through the world of children's books. To know and appreciate the field, one must read a wide range of stories and poems. But the challenge of becoming familiar with children's literature is hardly a formidable task. Most children's books are relatively short and can be read in a reasonably brief period of time. Besides, those who get to know children's books are rewarded by the pleasure and enjoyment they derive from the search. The journey through the world of children's books is, for children and adults alike, "a journey of joy."

Discussion Questions and Activities

1. Think back to your own early experiences with children's literature. What books do you remember most vividly from your childhood? Why do they stand out in your mind? Make a list of what you might do to make these stories memorable to the children you will teach.
2. Review four or five picture books for the primary grades. Note how text and illustrations complement each other, the illustrators' styles, how the authors tell a story with an economy of language. Make a chart summarizing your comparisons. Or review several chapter books popular with pupils in the intermediate grades. What elements do they share that might account for their appeal to children at this level?
3. Classic children's books such as *Peter Rabbit* have stood the test of time. Other books don't make it beyond the first printing. What do you think makes a book everlastingly appealing to children?
4. Review some children's poetry anthologies and make a list of six or eight poems you might use with children in the elementary grades. The poems can focus on a particular theme (such as weather or patriotism) or cover a wide range of topics that would appeal to children.
5. Research your favorite children's author, selecting an author whose work you loved as a child. Use the references listed in Putting Ideas to Work 2.8 and other sources of information the librarian suggests. Write a brief biographical sketch of your favorite children's author and share this with a group of fellow students.

1. What do your pupils think of children's literature? Conduct a quick, informal survey of the books they most enjoy and why they like these books. Chart the results of the survey and try to find other books that have the children's favorite qualities.
2. Identify a theme your class is studying in science or social studies. Find as many trade books as you can on that topic and prepare a display of books related to the theme. Don't forget to include some poetry selections.
3. Review the literary elements the chapter describes. In an informal discussion with a small group of students, determine their awareness of these elements in stories. Make a list of teaching suggestions you could use to make them more aware of setting, characters, and other literary elements.
4. Interview a teacher or a librarian to see whether and how they use award-winning books. How do you think the librarian can serve more effectively as a resource person in your school?
5. Who is the favorite author of the pupils in your classroom? With help from the children and the librarian, locate some biographical information about that author and prepare a display similar to the one Putting Ideas to Work 2.7 shows.

Children's Trade Books Cited in This Chapter

Aliki. (1983). *A Medieval Feast.* New York: HarperCollins.

Alcott, Louisa May. (1981). *Little Women.* New York: Putnam. (Other editions available.)

Allard, Harry. (1977). *Miss Nelson is Missing.* Boston: Houghton Mifflin.

Andersen, Hans Christian. (1982). *The Emperor's New Clothes.* New York: Harper & Row. (Many other editions available.)

Andersen, Hans Christian. *The Princess and The Pea.* (1979). Boston: Houghton Mifflin. (Many other editions available.)

Appel, Ted. (1993). *José Marti.* New York: Chelsea House.

Armstrong, William. (1969). *Sounder.* New York: Harper & Row.

Banks, Lynne Reid. (1985). *The Indian in the Cupboard.* New York: Doubleday.

Barrett, Judi. (1980). *Animals Definitely Should Not Wear Clothes.* New York: Atheneum.

Barrett, Judi. (1978). *Cloudy with a Chance of Meatballs.* New York: Macmillan.

Blue, Rose. (1972). *Grandma Didn't Wave Back.* New York: Franklin Watts.

Blume, Judy. (1972). *Are You There, God? It's Me, Margaret.* New York: Dell.

Blume, Judy. (1974). *Blubber.* New York: Dell.

Blume, Judy. (1980). *Superfudge.* New York: Dutton.

Blume, Judy. (1972). *Tales of a Fourth Grade Nothing.* New York: Dutton.

Brown, Marcia. (1961). *Once a Mouse.* New York: Scribner.

Brown, Marcia. (1947). *Stone Soup.* New York: Scribner.

Bunting, Eve. (1994). *Smokey Night.* San Diego: Harcourt Brace.

Burningham, John. (1987). *John Patrick Norman McHennessey.* New York: Crown.

Burton, Virginia Lee. (1943). *Katy and the Big Snow.* Boston: Houghton Mifflin.

Byars, Betsy. (1982). *The Animal, the Vegetable, and John D. Jones.* New York: Dellacourt.

Byars, Betsy. (1970). *Summer of the Swans.* New York: Viking.

Cameron, Eleanor. (1954). *The Wonderful Flight to the Mushroom Planet.* Boston: Little, Brown.

Ciardi, John. (1989). *The Hopeful Trout and Other Limericks.* Boston: Houghton Mifflin.

Cleary, Beverly. (1983). *Dear Mr. Henshaw.* New York: Morrow.

Cleary, Beverly. (1988). *A Girl from Yamhill*. New York: Morrow.

Clemens, Samuel L. (Mark Twain). (1973). *Huckleberry Finn*. West Haven, CT: Pendulum. (Other editions available.)

Cole, Babette. (1987). *Princess Smartypants*. New York: Putnam.

Collier, James and Christopher. (1974). *My Brother Sam Is Dead*. New York: Four Winds Press.

Crichton, Michael. (1993). *Jurassic Park*. New York: Putnam.

Dahl, Roald. (1984). *Boy*. New York: Farrar, Straus and Giroux.

Dahl, Roald. (1962). *James and the Giant Peach*. New York: Knopf.

Dakos, Kalli. (1991). *If You're Not Here, Raise Your Hand: Poems About School*. New York: Four Winds Press.

Dalgliesh, Alice. (1954). *The Courage of Sarah Noble*. New York: Scribner.

Dalgliesh, Alice. (1954). *The Thanksgiving Story*. New York: Scribner.

DeClements, Barthe. (1981). *Nothing's Fair in Fifth Grade*. New York: Viking.

de Paola, Tomie. (1980). *The Night Before Christmas*. New York: Holiday House.

de Regniers, Beatrice Schenk. (1988). *Sing a Song of Popcorn: Every Child's Book of Poems*. New York: Scholastic.

de Saint-Exupéry, Antoine. (1943). *The Little Prince*. New York: Harcourt.

Evslin, B., Evslin, D., and Hoopes, N. (1975). *Heroes and Monsters of Greek Myth*. New York: Viking.

Forbes, Esther. (1945). *Johnny Tremain*. Boston: Houghton Mifflin.

Freedman, Russell. (1987). *Lincoln: A Photobiography*. New York: Clarion.

Fritz, Jean. (1973). *And Then What Happened, Paul Revere?* New York: Coward, McCann and Geoghegan.

Fritz, Jean. (1982). *Homesick: My Own Story*. New York: Dell.

Gates, Doris. (1967). *Mightiest of Mortals: Heracles*. New York: Scholastic.

Gramatky, Hardie. (1939). *Little Toot*. New York: Putnam.

Greenfield, Eloise. (1989). *Nathaniel Talking*. New York: Writers and Readers.

Greenfield, Eloise. (1996). *Rosa Parks*. New York: HarperCollins.

Hodges, Margaret. (1990). *The Kitchen Knight: A Tale of King Arthur*. New York: Holiday House.

Howe, James. (1984). *The Day the Teacher Went Bananas*. New York: Dutton.

Hunt, Irene. (1964). *Across Five Aprils*. Chicago: Follett.

Hurwitz, Johanna. (1979). *Aldo Applesauce*. New York: Morrow.

Hutchins, Pat. (1968). *Rosie's Walk*. New York: Macmillan.

Hyman, Trina Schart. (1983). *Little Red Riding Hood*. New York: Holiday House.

Isaacs, Anna. (1994). *Swamp Angel*. New York: Dutton.

Jacobs, Joseph. (1989). *Tattercoats*. New York: Putnam.

Juster, Norton. (1961). *The Phantom Tollbooth*. New York: Random House.

Keats, Ezra Jack. (1965). *In A Spring Garden*. New York: Dial.

Keats, Ezra Jack. (1967). *Peter's Chair*. New York: Harper & Row.

Keats, Ezra Jack. (1962). *The Snowy Day*. New York: Viking.

Kellogg, Steven. (1984). *Paul Bunyan*. New York: Morrow.

Kennedy, Dorothy M., and Kennedy, X. J. (eds.). (1992). *Talking Like the Rain*. New York: Little, Brown.

Kipling, Rudyard. (1982). *Just So Stories*. New York: Macmillan. (Other editions available.)

Lawson, Robert. (1944). *Rabbit Hill*. New York: Viking.

Lear, Edward. (1946). *The Complete Nonsense Book*. New York: Dodd Mead.

L'Engle, Madeleine. (1962). *A Wrinkle in Time*. New York: Farrar, Straus and Giroux.

Lewis, C. S. (1961). *The Lion, the Witch, and the Wardrobe*. New York: Macmillan.

Lewis, Richard (ed.). (1989). *In a Spring Garden*. New York: Dial.

Lewis, Richard (ed.). (1966). *Miracles: Poems by Children of the English-Speaking World*. New York: Simon & Schuster.

Lindgren, Astrid. (1950). *Pippi Longstocking*. New York: Viking.

Livingston, Myra Cohn. (1982). *Circle of Seasons.* New York: Holiday House.

Lord, Beth Bao. (1984). *In the Year of the Boar and Jackie Robinson.* New York: Harper & Row.

Lowry, Lois. (1994). *The Giver.* Boston: Houghton Mifflin.

Macaulay, David. (1990). *Black and White.* Boston: Houghton Mifflin.

Macaulay, David. (1981). *Cathedral.* Boston: Houghton Mifflin.

Martin, Rafe. (1992). *The Rough-Face Girl.* New York: Putnam.

McCloskey, Robert. (1957). *Time of Wonder.* New York: Viking.

McCord, David. (1967). *Every Time I Climb a Tree.* Boston: Little, Brown.

Milne, A. A. (1981). *Winnie-the-Pooh.* New York: Dell. (Other editions available.)

Montgomery, Lucy M. (1976). *Anne of the Green Gables.* New York: Bantam.

Munsch, Robert. (1982). *Mud Puddle.* Willowdale, ON: Firefly Books.

Munsch, Robert. (1985). *Thomas' Snowsuit.* Willowdale, ON: Firefly Books.

Naylor, Phyllis Reynolds. (1988). *How I Came to Be a Writer.* New York: Morrow.

Ness, Evaline. (1966). *Sam, Bangs, and Moonshine.* New York: Holt.

Norton, Mary. (1953). *The Borrowers.* New York: Harcourt Brace.

O'Brien, Robert C. (1971). *Mrs. Frisby and the Rats of NIMH.* New York: Macmillan.

O'Dell, Scott. (1970). *Sing Down the Moon.* Boston: Houghton Mifflin.

O'Neill, Mary. (1961). *Hailstones and Halibut Bones: Adventures in Color.* Garden City, NY: Doubleday.

Osborne, Mary Pope. (1991). *American Tall Tales.* New York: Knopf.

Palotta, Jerry. (1990). *The Yucky Reptile Alphabet Book.* Watertown, MA: Charlesbank.

Paterson, Katherine. (1977). *Bridge to Terabithia.* New York: Crowell.

Paterson, Katherine. (1980). *Jacob Have I Loved.* New York: Crowell.

Paterson, Katherine. (1991). *Lyddie.* New York: Dutton.

Paterson, Katherine. (1978). *The Great Gilly Hopkins.* New York: Harper & Row.

Peet, Bill. (1989). *Bill Peet: An Autobiography.* Boston: Houghton Mifflin.

Peterson, John. (1967). *The Littles.* New York: Scholastic.

Potter, Beatrix. (1903). *The Tale of Peter Rabbit.* New York: Dover. (Other editions available.)

Prelutsky, Jack (ed.). (1983). *The Random House Book of Poetry for Children.* New York: Random House.

Raskin, Ellen. (1966). *Nothing Ever Happens on My Block.* New York: Atheneum.

Ringgold, Faith. (1991). *Tar Beach.* New York: Crown.

Robinson, Barbara. (1972). *The Best Christmas Pageant Ever.* New York: Harper.

Rockwell, Thomas. (1973). *How to Eat Fried Worms.* New York: Franklin Watts.

Rounds, Glen O. (1976). *Ol' Paul, The Mighty Logger.* New York: Holiday House.

San Souci, Robert. (1994). *Sootface: An Ojibwa Indian Tale.* New York: Doubleday.

Scieszka, Jon. (1991). *The Frog Prince Continued.* New York: Viking.

Scieszka, Jon. (1989). *The True Story of the 3 Little Pigs!* New York: Viking.

Sendak, Maurice. (1970). *In the Night Kitchen.* New York: Harper & Row.

Sendak, Maurice. (1963). *Where the Wild Things Are.* New York: Harper & Row.

Seuss, Dr. (Theodore Geisel). (1937). *And to Think That I Saw It on Mulberry Street.* New York: Vanguard.

Seuss, Dr. (Theodore Geisel). (1938). *The 500 Hats of Bartholomew Cubbins.* New York: Vanguard.

Seymour, Simon. (1992). *Our Solar System.* New York: Morrow.

Silverstein, Shel. (1981). *A Light in the Attic.* New York: Harper.

Silverstein, Shel. (1974). *Where the Sidewalk Ends.* New York: Harper.

Slobodkina, Esphyr. (1947). *Caps for Sale.* New York: Harper & Row.

Southall, Ivan. (1968). *Let the Balloon Go.* New York: St. Martin.

Speare, Elizabeth George. (1958). *The Witch of Blackbird Pond.* Boston: Houghton Mifflin.

Steig, William. (1982). *Doctor DeSoto.* New York: Farrar, Straus and Giroux.

Stoutenburg, Adrien. (1966). *American Tall Tales.* New York: Viking.

Swann, Brian. (1988). *A Basketful of White Eggs*. New York: Orchard Books.
Swift, Jonathan. (1947). *Gulliver's Travels*. New York: Putnam. (Other editions available.)
Thaler, Mike. (1989). *The Teacher from the Black Lagoon*. New York: Scholastic.
Thaler, Mike. (1981). *A Hippopotamus Ate the Teacher*. New York: Avon.
Tolkien, J. R. R. (1938). *The Hobbit*. Boston: Houghton Mifflin.
Uchida, Yoshiko. (1971). *Journey to Topaz*. New York: Scribner.
Van Allsburg, Chris. (1985). *Polar Express*. Boston: Houghton Mifflin.
Viorst, Judith. (1971). *The Tenth Good Thing about Barney*. New York: Atheneum.
Voigt, Cynthia. (1982). *Dicey's Song*. New York: Atheneum.
Whipple, Laura. (1989). *Animals, Animals*. New York: Putnam.
White, E. B. (1952). *Charlotte's Web*. New York: Harper & Row.
White, T. H. (1939). *The Sword in the Stone*. New York: Putnam.
Wiggin, Kate D. (1986). *Rebecca of Sunnybrook Farm*. New York: Puffin. (Other editions available.)
Wilde, Oscar. (1989). *The Happy Prince*. New York: Simon & Schuster.
Wilder, Laura Ingalls. (1953). *Little House on the Prairie*. New York: Harper.
Willhoite, Michael. (1991). *Daddy's Roommate*. Boston: Alyson.
Wittman, Sally. (1978). *A Special Trade*. New York: Harper & Row.
Yates, Elizabeth. (1989). *Amos Fortune, Free Man*. New York: Dutton.
Yolen, Jane. (1967). *The Emperor and the Kite*. Cleveland: World.
Yolen, Jane. (1992). *Encounter*. San Diego: Harcourt Brace Jovanovich.

References

Bettelheim, B. (1978). *The Uses of Enchantment*. New York: Knopf.
Bogart, D., ed. (1996). *Bowker Annual of Library Book and Trade Information* (41st ed.). New Providence, NJ: R. R. Bowker.
Bosma, B. (1987). *Fairy Tales, Fables, Legends and Myths: Using Folk Literature in Your Classroom*. New York: Teachers College Press.
Davis, Z. T., and McPherson, M. D. (1989). Story Map Instruction: A Road Map for Reading. *The Reading Teacher* 43:232–240.
Harris, V. J. (1992). *Teaching Multicultural Literature in Grades K–8*. Norwood, MA: Christopher-Gordon Publishers.
Hiebert, E. H., Mervar, K. B., and Person, D. (1990). Children's Selections of Trade Books in Libraries and Classrooms. *Language Arts* 67:758–763.
Hopkins, L. B. (1969). *Books Are By People*. New York: Citation.
Hopkins, L. B. (1974). *More Books By More People*. New York: Citation.
Huck, C. S. (1982). I Give You the End of a Golden String. *Theory into Practice* 21:315–321.
Huck, C. S., Hepler, S., and Hickman, J. (1987). *Children's Literature in the Elementary School*. New York: Holt, Rinehart and Winston.
Hurst, C. O. (1990). *Once Upon a Time: An Encyclopedia for Successfully Using Children's Literature with Young Children*. Allen, TX: DLM.
Kiefer, B. (1988). Picture Books as Contexts for Literary, Aesthetic, and Real World Understandings. *Language Arts* 65:260–270.
Krieger, E. (1988). *Developing Reading Comprehension through Author Awareness*. Unpublished report, Newton, MA.
Madura, S. (1995). The Line and Textures of Aesthetic Responses: Primary Children Study Authors and Illustrators. *The Reading Teacher* 49:110–118.
McElmeel, S. (1988). *An Author A Month*. Englewood, CO: Libraries Unlimited.
Prelutsky, J. (1983). *The Random House Book of Poetry for Children*. New York: Random House.

Saxby, M. (1987). The Gift of Wings: The Value of Literature to Children. In M. Saxby and G. Winch, eds., *Give Them Wings: The Experience of Children's Literature.* Melbourne: Macmillan of Australia.

Sebesta, S. L., and Iverson, W. J. (1975). *Literature for Thursday's Child.* Chicago: Science Research Associates.

Tomlinson, C. M., and Lynch-Brown, C. (1996). *Essentials of Children's Literature* (2nd ed.). Boston: Allyn & Bacon.

Weiss, M. J. (1995). Censorship: Rage and Outrage. In T. L. Harris and R. E. Hodges, eds., *The Literacy Dictionary.* Newark: International Reading Association.

Wepner, S. B. (1993). Technology and Author Studies. *The Reading Teacher* 46:616–619.

Winch, G. (1987). The Supreme Fiction: On Poetry and Children. In M. Saxby and G. Winch, eds., *Give Them Wings: The Experience of Children's Literature.* Melbourne: Macmillan of Australia.

Zarrillo, J. (1994). *Multicultural Literature, Multicultural Teaching: Units for the Elementary Grades.* Fort Worth: Harcourt Brace.

*O*rganizing and Managing a Literature-Based Reading Program

© Robert Finken/Photo Researchers, Inc.

Chapter 3 Outline

Features

3.1   **A Daily Classroom Schedule**

3.2   **Word Board**

3.3   **Sample Classroom Floor Plan**

3.4   **Patterns of Selecting and Using Reading Materials**

3.5   **Guide for Selecting Literacy CD-ROM Technology**

3.6   **Grouping**

3.7   **Using Literature in Heterogeneous Reading Groups**

3.8   **Cooperative Learning Using Literature**

3.9   **Cooperative Integrated Reading and Composition**

3.10 **Grouping in the Elementary Classroom**

Key Concepts in This Chapter

Organizing and managing a literature-based reading program involves the manipulation of four major variables: time, space, materials, and pupils.

Instructional time must be carefully planned so that pupils can enjoy maximum time for reading and writing.

The learning environment should reflect a commitment to making literature the centerpiece of literacy instruction.

Trade books constitute the mainstay of a literature-based reading program, but a range of other instructional materials may be appropriate as well.

Children need to be grouped in a variety of ways to achieve different purposes in reading and writing instruction.

Introduction

Gretchen Treacher, first-year teacher, sat in her third-grade classroom and stared nervously at the door. School would open in three days. Gretchen knew that in 72 hours, 23 eager 8- and 9-year-olds would come charging through the classroom door. She hadn't met any of her pupils yet, but she had reviewed their portfolios and related records from the previous year. She knew that 13 were boys and 10 were girls. Their reading levels, measured on the previous April's achievement test, ranged from first grade through seventh grade. Three of the children were from the nearby housing project, four were from the affluent Rocky Hill section of town, and the rest were from surrounding neighborhoods. One child would be repeating third grade. Four had been diagnosed as having special needs. Five had received extra reading help from the Title I teacher the previous year.

All Gretchen had to do was to set up a reading program for these students. Her emotions ran the gamut from heady excitement to raw terror.

One of the initial decisions any teacher has to make each year is how to organize and manage a classroom reading program. There is no such thing as a "typical" reading program, just as there is no such thing as an "average" third-grade class; the average class remains a statistical abstraction. Teachers place special marks on their own unique programs. A classroom reading program depends on a range of factors—the teacher's beliefs about the best way to foster pupils' growing competency in literacy; the expectations and resources of the school and community; the physical environment the teacher must work in; the teacher's own level of energy and creativity; individual style; and the like.

Gretchen's principal expected her to use the basal reading program the school district had adopted two years before. All teachers were expected to "cover" this program. Gretchen had no objections to the basal series. As a first-year teacher she was in no position to object; she had used the program during her student teaching and liked it. It was full of quality children's stories by well-recognized children's authors. Besides, the basal would provide the structure she felt she needed as she began her professional career. The basal would be a fine place to start.

But Gretchen wanted to move well beyond the basal. She was determined to give her pupils a rich diet of literature beyond the selection the basal program offered. She remembered her own school experience and, more recently, her experience as a student teacher when she discovered how excited her pupils became about the books she shared with them. The basal might indeed be a fine place to start, but Gretchen fully intended to make children's trade books the centerpiece of her language arts program.

Three days before the children showed up, Gretchen began to make plans for her reading program. Like veteran teachers and tyros alike, Gretchen had to take four factors into account in organizing and managing the reading program in her classroom:

Time

Space

Materials

Pupils

Although administrative and related constraints (for example, the number of children in the class, size of the room, resources available, and school scheduling) may place some of these variables beyond the direct influence of the classroom teacher, teachers must consider the elements of time, space, materials, and pupils as factors that they can control in organizing and managing a classroom reading program.

Time

Time—no one ever has enough. Yet it is a very important part of reading instruction. In reviewing research and descriptive reports of effective reading programs, Wolf (1977) concluded that "one of the most effective tools for teaching reading may be the simplest and most ignored: time" (p. 76). Time consistently emerges as a crucial variable in successful reading instruction.

Usually, teachers devote much time in a school day to reading, writing, and language instruction. Reading permeates the entire curriculum. In addition to learning to read through direct instruction, students learn and practice reading through incidental vocabulary work, written language activities, recreational and content reading, integrated units, discussion and other oral-language activities, and all the other activities that support literacy development.

Time alone is not enough, of course, to promote reading success. *Becoming a Nation of Readers* (Anderson et al., 1985), a study on the state of reading instruction in the United States, reported the alarming information that silent reading time in a typical primary classroom consisted of only seven or eight minutes per day, less than 10 percent of the total time devoted to reading. Concern over such figures led to the increasing practice of allowing students to read quality children's books in place of completing workbook exercises to help them learn to read.

In addition to the amount of time, the quality of time—engaged versus nonengaged time, for example—is very important. Educators often assess quality by measuring how much time children spend directly involved in tasks

3.1 Putting Ideas to Work
A Daily Classroom Schedule

*P*lanning a schedule for the most effective use of time is usually an early step in organizing a reading program. All teachers use time differently, but a typical classroom schedule might look something like this:

9:00–9:20	Whole class work
9:20–10:20	Small group work
10:20–10:45	Snack and recess
10:45–11:00	Story time (read aloud)
11:00–11:45	Math
11:45–12:15	Lunch
12:15–1:00	Specialist (art, music, physical education)
1:00–1:20	Sustained Silent Reading
1:20–2:45	Integrated learning units
2:45–3:00	Cleanup and dismissal

No schedule is ever cast in stone, as daily variations occur according to classroom activities. Although schoolwide schedules often demand that certain activities be "locked in" (for example, lunch or library time), teachers ordinarily have opportunities to revise their schedules according to needs and activities that vary on a day-to-day basis.

related to learning to read (time on task) as opposed to how much time they spend lining up to move from one activity to another, preparing for and cleaning up after an activity, sharpening pencils, passing out papers, collecting work, or doing other noninstructional tasks necessary in a classroom. Although a certain amount of "down time" may be part of the job of working with young children, achievement increases when pupils spend more time directly and actively engaged in appropriate learning activities. It stands to reason that pupils who pay attention—who are on task—are more likely to learn.

No matter how the teacher organizes blocks of classroom time, literature-based reading programs normally include whole class work, small group work, story time, theme projects, math, and specialists' assistance.

Whole Class Work

Whole class work, typically planned at the beginning of the day, differs according to the age and grade level of pupils. It might involve talking about books or other topics, organizing daily activities, discussing current events, viewing a filmstrip or a video of a popular book, or planning class projects. The teacher might demonstrate a particular reading or writing strategy, or the class might engage in some other activity that provides for the exchange of language and stimulates reading and writing experiences.

Small Group Activities

Small group activities "engage pupils in a range of elective and compulsory activities that have been carefully designed according to principles that ensure plenty of social interaction and collaborative learning. During this time, the teacher played the role of 'consultant,' interacting with and supporting as many pupils as possible as she roved and 'hit base' with children engaged in different activities" (Cambourne and Turbill, 1990; p. 341). During this time, pupils read to one another, work independently or collaboratively on writing, receive extra help as needed, practice a play they may be preparing, complete literature journals and other reader-response activities, engage in literature circles or reading workshops, work together on the computer, meet in groups for booktalk or directed reading lessons, and engage in a variety of other activities that constitute language- and literature-rich classrooms.

Story Time

During story time, the teacher reads a story, a chapter from a longer book, or some poetry to the class, or the students read aloud some of their original writing. Reading aloud is vital at any level, because "the sharing of literature aloud anchors the sounds of the language of literature in the minds of the students. Children of all ages absorb the language they hear" (Peterson and Eeds, 1990; p. 9).

Sustained Silent Reading

Sustained silent reading (SSR) is inviolable in literature-based programs. Sustained silent reading involves setting a period of time aside each day in which everybody in the classroom (pupils and teacher) reads. SSR involves planned, uninterrupted time with books and is another means of injecting literature directly into the reading program. Sometimes known by other names, such as Drop Everything and Read (DEAR), the practice has proved to effectively promote interest in reading.

SSR involves free reading; all involved choose the books and other materials they want to read. "Opportunities to read self-selected books may be considered among the most authentic of literacy activities that can be given to children in their classrooms" (Pinnell et al., 1995; p. 28). No formal comprehension checks, questions, exercises, or other assignments are attached to sustained silent reading, although students may informally interact with one another about books they have read. Some schools have schoolwide SSR programs in which everyone in the school—principal, secretaries, cafeteria workers, and custodians, along with teachers and pupils—puts aside assigned tasks and reads for 20 or 30 minutes. This creates a community of readers important to a young child's literacy development.

The teacher's role in SSR is especially important. This is not a time to correct pupils' work or to put the finishing touches on report cards. By participating in SSR, teachers model that reading is an important and enjoyable activity.

Pupils can enjoy Sustained Silent Reading any place in the classroom.
© Elizabeth Crews/The Image Works

Integrated Thematic Units

Integrated thematic units extend literacy education across the curriculum. Through these units, teachers can help pupils read and comprehend expository writing in textbooks and informational trade books, while also helping them develop research and related study skills. Thematic units integrate math, science, social studies, and other subjects with reading and writing. At the same time, they allow pupils to engage in authentic, integrated learning experiences as they explore curriculum topics in depth.

Gretchen Treacher decided that her first theme unit would be about her favorite pets—cats. She had already gathered trade books students would enjoy on the topic—books such as Mary Calhoun's *Cross Country Cat*, about a cat who learned to ski, and David McPhail's *Great Cat*, a fantasy about an oversized kitten. Gretchen had also gathered informational books such as Don Estep's *Cats and Kittens* and Simon Seymour's *Big Cats*. She planned to set up an attractive display of these books, with a poster of the cartoon cat Garfield overlooking them, to capture pupils' attention from the first day of school. Gretchen would begin by reading Beverly Cleary's delightful *Socks* to the class and initiating a discussion about cats before asking pupils to work cooperatively in exploring topics related to the care and feeding of cats, species of wild cats, and other cat-related topics. Through all these activities, students would engage in authentic reading and writing practices that would integrate science and social studies as well.

Theme teaching is based on the idea of integration. Children develop and apply skills and strategies more effectively within the context of a central learning experience than when they learn these strategies in isolation. "Use of thematic units makes sense in light of what we know about the value of background knowledge—the more ideas are connected, the more likely they are to make sense, be understood and remembered" (Raphael and Hiebert, 1996; p. 220). By presenting opportunities to develop literacy in authentic learning contexts, theme units give pupils the sense that reading and writing are more than "school subjects" to be learned from 9:00 to 10:00 in the morning and then dropped. Thematic units make learning useful and personal and help children discover the relationships between learning in the classroom and their lives outside of school (Bergeron and Rudenga, 1996).

Math

Because of its sequential nature, math is usually scheduled in its own time slot during the school day. Nevertheless, a lot of language learning occurs during math time. *The Curriculum and Evaluation Standards* of the National Council of Teachers of Mathematics (1989) emphasizes the role that reading and writing play in developing math competency. Trade books involving mathematics abound. Writing about math reinforces understanding, provides feedback, and helps students organize their ideas. "In writing about math problems or activities, students become familiar with analytical writing while gaining and displaying a deeper understanding of the math concept" (Fortescue, 1994; p. 576). Learning mathematics extends beyond computation and into the reasoning process involved in logical and critical thinking. Ample opportunities occur to integrate math into a wide variety of language learning activities.

Specialists

Special instruction in areas such as music, art, and physical education is often scheduled separately, although classroom teachers are becoming more and more responsible for teaching these subjects.

It is often necessary and sometimes advantageous to rotate a classroom schedule—that is, to plan the same activities at different times on different days. Formal reading instruction is usually scheduled first thing in the morning, on the assumption that students are more alert and ready to learn best at that time. Some children, however, may learn better at another time during the school day. Moreover, new curriculum projects or the introduction of a new topic in another curriculum area may suggest beginning the day or week with that subject. Finally, in most classrooms, some children receive help from specialists outside the classroom—speech therapists, counselors, special education resource teachers, or Title I teachers provide extra help inside or outside the classroom. A rotating schedule ensures these students will not miss the same activity at the same time every day.

Some teachers, when they hear about literature-based reading programs, think of literature as something extra tacked on to use up their already limited time. But literature does not need to be an addition to a crowded classroom schedule. Planning and implementing literature-based reading instruction does not require more time; it involves the use of time in a different way. Activities like sustained silent reading and story time are already part of most sound elementary classroom programs. Inaugurating a literature-based program involves using literature as a vehicle in already scheduled learning—using trade books for instructional purposes, centering oral language activities on literature, including appropriate novels or informational trade books to enrich learning in social studies and science, building art and drama activities around books that pupils have enjoyed—in short, integrating literature into many dimensions of an ongoing classroom program.

In the final analysis, the amount of time available for reading instruction in the classroom is finite. The time must be scheduled and managed so that all children enjoy the maximum time for reading and related language activities during the day. Economy and efficiency are the crucial elements in managing classroom time.

Space

The arrangement of space is another practical classroom management concern for the teacher, a dimension over which the teacher maintains maximum control. A teacher's classroom is like an artist's studio; it reflects the type of activity going on within.

The classroom environment is an important dimension to learning. "The environments within which students learn will affect what they learn, how they learn, and how they feel about learning" (Rhodes and Dudley-Marling, 1988; p. 95). Morrow and Rand (1991) have demonstrated how classroom environment can affect literacy development in the early school years. Learning areas filled with samples of print—menus and recipes in the restaurant corner, a store with labels and signs, a post office with writing materials, a gas station with posters and maps—give young children a chance to develop their emerging reading and writing abilities. Neuman and Roskos (1992) found that the presence of literacy objects—books, paper, posters, signs, writing implements, and the like—in the early learning environment increased the quality and quantity of children's literacy activities.

The environment of the classroom at any grade level should be lively and attractive, with displays documenting the children's interests and learning. Displays should extend beyond lists of spelling words written in columns on half sheets of paper or perfect math worksheets adorned with happy-face stickers. Displays should include student artwork, stories and poems, and a range of creative products that reflect the students' responses to the literature they have experienced.

Other classroom displays can document the important role literature plays in the classroom. A bulletin board might focus on the life and work of

3.2 Putting Ideas to Work
Word Board

*O*ne effective display is a word board, a small area in which a new "Word for the Day" is displayed. The teacher writes the word on a colorful oak tag card and mounts it on the board, along with a sentence illustrating its meaning in context. For example:

soporific

It is said that the effect of eating too much lettuce is soporific. (This is the opening sentence from Beatrix Potter's *The Tale of the Flopsy Bunnies*, illustrated with a delightful picture of overstuffed bunnies sleeping in the lettuce patch.)

Every couple of days, the word can be replaced with words like *obstreperous, scintillating,* or *supercilious* that pupils encounter in their reading and other language activities. Words like these pique students' interest in language, enrich their vocabularies, and make them aware of the power of our lexicon. After the first week or so, the pupils themselves can take responsibility for supplying the Word for the Day.

When taken from the word board, word cards may be placed in a word file for continuing practice and review.

a particular author; pupil-designed book covers might hang from the ceiling; a *book review* board might exhibit children's responses to books they have read; a tree-shaped display labeled *poet tree* might display poems that students have written hanging from its branches; or favorite story scenes, illustrated and described, might adorn the walls just outside the classroom. All these help create a classroom atmosphere that conveys a simple message: literature is well loved and well used within these walls.

A lively classroom environment also usually includes plants, pictures, charts, pets, and other objects that stimulate language development, percolate interest, and promote learning. Pets become the focus of scientific observation and reporting. Mobiles made in art may be based on the characters children meet in books. The environment reflects the pupils' interests and addresses their needs, and displays enhance their ownership of the environment and promote self-empowerment in their learning.

A flexible teaching program demands the flexible arrangement and use of space. Pupils generally need an individual desk or station, a place they can call their own. Other space should be used flexibly enough that it suits the variety of activities and multiple learning opportunities that characterize a lively classroom. In addition to the necessary conventional arrangement of desks and chairs, special areas can be set up to facilitate the range of reading and related activities that characterize the literature-rich classroom. Special areas can include a reading corner, writing center, computer and interest centers, and study carrels.

Reading Corner

A *reading corner* may be as simple as a rug on the floor and a couple of comfortable chairs or large pillows pupils can relax on as they enjoy reading. The classroom library is located here. Posters, student-designed displays of book jackets, reports, and other materials that stimulate an interest in and love of reading are part of this area as well. Some teachers have incorporated a boat, a bathtub, a tent, or some other appealing and imaginative structure into their reading corner.

Writing Center

A *writing center* includes dictionaries, a thesaurus, and other aids children might need in their writing. The center is supplied with an ample supply of pens, pencils, markers, and other writing implements, along with plenty of paper (including chart paper for producing Big Books in the early grades). A typewriter or word processor can be part of the center, too. Student writing is on display—the books they have produced are placed on tables, and individual files of their own writing are housed here as well.

Computer Center

In a *computer center* students can engage in drill and practice tutorials, work on stories on the word processor, search the Internet for information about a topic related to a thematic unit, or enjoy interacting with a favorite storybook presented on CD-ROM.

Interest Centers

Interest centers display science materials (such as rocks, plants, magnets, or collections of other artifacts) or other materials related to the curriculum. These centers should be full of books, magazine articles, pupil-written reports, and other fiction and nonfiction materials related to particular topics. They should be more than storage areas for supplies and equipment. They should be activity centers, areas where pupils can go to engage in reading, writing, and other language-learning activities.

Individual Reading-Study Carrels

Individual reading-study carrels provide a place where pupils who need quiet and privacy can go for independent work.

The idea that teachers designate different areas for different purposes does not imply inflexibility. Quiet reading during SSR can be done in a study carrel or in the reading corner, just as well as at one's desk. And writing activities need not—in fact, should not—be limited to the writing center. When groups of students are moving around the classroom, however, spatial organization helps maintain efficient management of a classroom program.

Rules must be established for learning centers. The teacher may need to limit the number of pupils permitted in a given center at a specific time. Since groups or individuals often use centers for independent or small

3.3 Putting Ideas to Work
Sample Classroom Floor Plan

*H*ow a teacher arranges classroom space depends on the number of children in a class, whether classroom walls are fixed or movable, the proportion of wall-to-window area, bulletin board and chalkboard space, the amount of material and equipment in the room, type of furniture, and a number of other physical factors. This diagram is merely a suggestion of how classroom space might be used for different purposes.

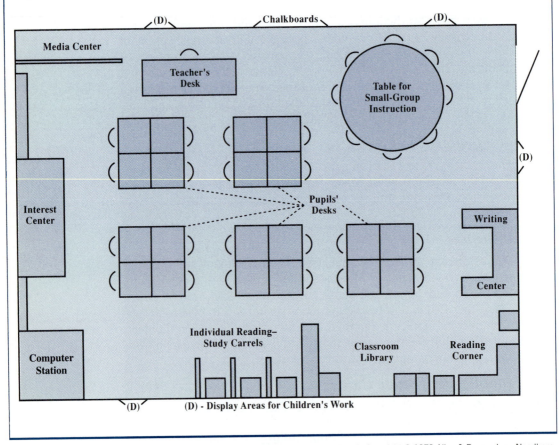

From John F. Savage and Jean F. Mooney, *Teaching Reading to Children with Special Needs.* Copyright © 1979 Allyn & Bacon, Inc., Needham Heights, MA. Reprinted by permission of the authors.

group learning, the teacher may need to give specific instructions in the use of each area. Centers should be located so that quiet areas and noisy areas are far enough apart.

Setting up a learning environment involves the imaginative arrangement of bookcases, file cabinets, portable dividers, and maybe some "cardboard carpentry." One teacher, for example, joined two cardboard refrigerator cartons to make a media center for her classroom so that pupils could enjoy videos and tapes of favorite stories without disturbing the rest of the class.

Since children spend hundreds of hours in classrooms, teachers owe it to them to make their learning environment as pleasant and exciting as possible. An effective classroom atmosphere is one that promotes the notion that literacy is central to classroom life and that reading and writing are important, authentic, enjoyable activities.

Materials

Ever since the days of the New England *Primer*, materials have been an essential factor in reading instruction in our schools. Materials are important because they provide the vehicles through which children learn to read. When a particular reading program is followed to the letter, materials may even dictate the approach used to teach reading.

In many instances, educators falsely assume that materials will do the teaching. Shannon (1983) demonstrated that many teachers and principals believe the basal program is the crucial element in teaching children how to read. They believe that we can "plug pupils in" to a particular published program and expect the materials to do the teaching. Nothing could be further from the truth!

Despite their unquestioned importance, materials are merely tools of the trade in teaching reading. And like any tools, they are only as good as the craftsperson using them. It is the teacher and the students, not the materials, that make learning come alive.

A balanced and flexible reading program requires balance and flexibility in the choice and use of instructional materials. In a literature-based program, trade books obviously play a crucial role. Basal materials may be part of this program as well. Among the other materials used for reading instruction in the classroom are supplementary, literature-related enrichment materials, supplementary skill-building materials, computers, and other devices.

Trade Books

Obviously, a literature-based reading program requires a plentiful supply of trade books in the classroom. A well-stocked classroom library will contain books at different levels. In the very early grades, wordless/textless books and picture storybooks will dominate the collection, although plenty of books for children who develop early independent reading skills should be included as well. Simple reading textbooks that are easy to decode—containing sentences such as *Nat the fat cat sits on the mat*—may also be a part of this collection. Decoding these simple texts can provide basic practice for beginning readers, and their success in decoding these texts can produce a positive affective response.

In the upper grades, the classroom library must be widened to accommodate students' expanding interests and increasing reading abilities. Sources like Regie Routman's *Transitions from Literature to Literacy* (1988), Jim

Trelease's well-known *The Read-Aloud Handbook* (1989), Margaret Mary Kimmel and Elizabeth Segal's *For Reading Out Loud! A Guide to Sharing Books with Children* (1983), and Beverly Korbin's *Eye Openers: Choosing Books for Kids* (1988) recommend books for various grade levels. Magazines such as *The Reading Teacher, Language Arts*, and *The Horn Book* provide monthly reviews that suggest good leads in selecting books. Teachers use the selection guides and reviews of children's literature that appear in these magazines to stay abreast of recently published books for use in their reading programs and to expand their own children's literature horizons.

Displays of books related to various themes the class is studying (for example, football, winter, or Booker T. Washington) supplement the regular classroom collection. The teacher may also establish a special collection of books for reading aloud, along with some poetry anthologies. A classroom environment where literature is treasured will naturally be filled with all kinds of books.

Librarians are usually enormously helpful to teachers in assembling a classroom collection of books. Most libraries have policies allowing the long-term loan of books for classroom use. With reasonable advance notice, librarians can put together topic-related lists and provide titles that will ensure freshness and variety in children's reading fare.

Permanent classroom libraries are becoming more common. As administrators in more and more school districts make a stronger commitment to literature-based reading instruction, more funds are becoming available for the purchase of trade books for classroom use. Some of the money traditionally used for buying workbooks is now used to purchase "real books." State departments of education sometimes provide grants to teachers to establish classroom libraries, and parent-teacher organizations are often more than happy to provide funds for classroom book collections. In some schools, instead of sending cupcakes for a child's birthday or other special occasion, parents donate a book to the classroom library. Commercial book clubs can be another source used to supply a classroom collection; teachers can use book club "bonus points" to obtain free copies of favorite titles. Energetic teachers leave no stone unturned in garnering a collection of books that grows impressively over the years.

A practical management matter is the circulation of books in the classroom library. Classroom collections are typically housed on simple shelving or inexpensive wire racks in the reading corner. Usually, a simple sign-out honor system works to keep track of books, or a student helper or parent volunteer may act as class librarian. Computers can also help keep track of books. Whatever system a teacher chooses to use, he or she should provide pupils easy access to the books in the classroom library.

Basal Readers

For many years, basal reading materials were the staple of reading instruction in most classrooms. Basals reached this position of preeminence for a number of reasons, not the least of which was that they helped facilitate

3.4 Putting Ideas to Work
Patterns of Selecting and Using Reading Materials

*H*iebert and Colt (1989) suggest three patterns for selecting and using trade books for instructional purposes in the classroom.

Pattern 1: *Teacher-selected literature in teacher-led groups.* In this pattern, the teacher chooses a book for instructional purposes. For example, a teacher might read a fable, conduct a large group lesson about the structure of fables, and ask students to write fables on their own. In this pattern, pupils discuss the books or stories the teacher selects.

Pattern 2: *Teacher- and student-selected literature in teacher- and student-led small groups.* The teacher recommends several books on a topic of interest and pupils choose different titles from the list. They then meet in small groups to share their interpretations of what they have read, to describe their favorite books, and to talk about strategies they use in reading.

Pattern 3: *Student-selected literature read independently.* Independent reading is the ultimate test of an effective literacy program. Students need many opportunities to participate in authentic reading situations. This occurs when they read on their own for Sustained Silent Reading or for individual conferences with the teacher.

All three patterns may work in concert with one another. Classroom programs should include both teacher and student interaction and literature selection to create thoughtful, proficient readers.

classroom organization and management. Basals are well-designed packages that provide teachers with the tools they need to run a classroom program. The scope and sequence charts constitute a grand scheme for instruction. The reading books themselves provide a common core of literature selections for all children. The teacher's editions contain detailed plans for carrying out lessons, and the workbooks provide materials for students to use when they are not working directly with the teacher. Although basal programs can help in classroom organization and structure, few today would suggest that these teaching tools should constitute an exclusive reading diet in school.

Supplementary Literature-Based Materials

The increased use of literature as part of reading instruction has resulted in a plethora of supplementary programs designed for classroom use. "The publication of lessons and worksheets to be used with children's novels has become something of a cottage industry" (Zarrillo, 1989; pp. 23–24). These programs provide both enrichment and skill-development activities related to popular children's books. Some programs provide hands-on, consumable activity sheets for pupils to use as they read the books; others supply guides for teachers, with suggestions on how to use the book as a learning aid.

These supplementary literature-related programs have become popular for a number of reasons. On the one hand, programs such as *LEAP* or *LIFT* (Sundance Publishers), *Portals to Reading* (Perfection Form), and *Novel-ties* (Learning Links) provide hands-on activities for students working independently. On the other hand, some packages provide a skills orientation that allows the teacher to supplement literature-based instruction of certain reading skills. But a real danger arises in using this literature/skills mix: the danger that pupils will come to see literature as something to work on rather than to enjoy. Critics call this the basalization of good children's literature.

These materials also invite the danger of overkill. Some teaching guides are longer than the books they supplement. If pupils have to complete an interminable series of uninteresting exercises related to a book they have read, their enjoyment and enthusiasm for the book will be tempered. This is contrary to the central purpose of literature-based reading instruction.

Supplementary literature-based programs can have a positive impact if they bring literature into the reading curriculum. When used judiciously, they can help organize the reading program by providing pupils with independent activities that extend their understanding and deepen their appreciation of a well-liked book. As with any classroom reading materials, however, teachers should use them with thought and purpose.

Audiovisual Devices

Traditionally, we have viewed reading as a book-oriented activity; however, audiovisual devices have long played a role in reading instruction and remain useful in literature-based reading programs. "Audio and visual technologies and their respective media can make a significant contribution to a literature-based reading curriculum." Besides enhancing "the already provocative appeal of children's literature," an audiovisual activity with literature "solidifies children's concept of story, encourages the use of prediction strategies, expands receptive vocabularies, captures the imagination, and most importantly, promotes further literary involvement" (Rickelman and Henk, 1990; p. 682).

Electronic media provide an effective means of sharing literature with pupils. Auditory media such as tape recorders and CD players allow students (especially young children or pupils with reading difficulties) to enjoy stories read to them. Having children follow a line of print as they listen to a story has proved to be effective in helping them learn to read. Sound effects can enhance comprehension and enjoyment, and the technology allows for repeated review of the selection. A number of cassette-and-book packages are available for home and classroom use. Some of these feature well-known entertainment personalities: Meryl Streep reading *Peter Rabbit*, for example, or Robin Williams reading *Pecos Bill* (Saxonville, MA: Picture Book Studio). Tape recorders can also help children develop important auditory skills associated with learning to read.

Visual media provide opportunities for a variety of "screen reading" activities in the classroom. Filmstrips of favorite stories like *Paul Bunyan* can

Although it is a technological device, the computer can enhance student interaction in reading and writing.

© David M. Grossman/ Photo Researchers, Inc.

project illustrations as the teacher reads to the class, making it easier for all students to see the pictures (and relieving the teacher from holding up the book and hearing complaints like, "Susan's head is in my way!").

Audiovisual devices—those that combine visual images with auditory input—can be used to present stories to students and to help them develop reading competency. Videotapes bring stories to life, although the overuse of videos could deprive pupils of the inclination to enjoy these stories in print. Many literature-related videotapes feature the author or illustrator commenting on and explaining the story. An impressive collection of these films and videos is available from Weston Woods in Weston, Connecticut.

Other Technology

Computers and telecommunication are becoming more and more a part of literacy instruction from the very early grades. As schools move into the 21st century, technology will assume a more integral part in teaching reading and writing. "Cybertechnology is not something that some people will choose to adopt; it is already part of our literacy practices regardless of what we do" (Bruce, 1995; p. 10). Emerging technologies are expanding so rapidly that teachers are often dazzled by what's available.

Computers can contribute in a variety of ways to literature-based reading and writing instruction. In reading:

Drill and practice programs—often in game format—help reinforce phonics, word recognition, and other conventional basic skills. Sometimes called electronic workbooks, these materials motivate pupils to engage in otherwise tedious practice. Some of these programs focus directly on strategies in content area reading of expository text. Others focus on specific skills such as punctuation or spelling, making them ideal independent tutorials in writing skills

Popular children's trade books presented in electronic formats include CD-ROM presentations of stories that allow the child to hear the story aloud (sometimes in several languages). Some have features that allow the child to read the story and receive help on difficult or unfamiliar words. Many have animation that brings illustrations alive; some allow children to alter or interact with the story in interesting ways.

Electronic encyclopedias provide rich sources of information, as do CD-ROMs in science and social studies, that can be used as part of the reading program.

Software of various other types allows students to monitor their comprehension, to develop semantic maps and an awareness of story structure, to create and solve crossword and other puzzles focused on language and thinking, and to otherwise stimulate and challenge themselves in literature-based reading experiences.

Computerized management systems, such as *The Accelerated Reader,* test children on the trade books they have read and record the results.

Programs that aid literacy are also available for home use, so many children will be used to learning through computers when they enter the classroom for the first time.

Computers also benefit students in other areas of learning. In writing:

Word processing programs have revolutionized writing in (and outside) the classroom. Children work independently and cooperatively in producing, editing, and revising stories, reports, poems, and other written products.

Integrated presentation programs (such as *ClarisWorks*) contain word processing along with drawing, painting, and graphics components to enable pupils to illustrate their stories and build charts and graphs into their reports. With the use of simple desktop publishing programs, children's classroom publications take on an almost professional quality that often gratifies and excites them and motivates them to produce more.

The World Wide Web provides a powerful means to improve teaching and learning as well. Telecommunications networks such as Kidsnet allow children to share their writing with children around the globe and reach real audiences who can provide feedback. The Web is also a source of up-to-the-minute information that students can use for research projects and for exploring topics of personal interest. Thousands of websites are available for students—for example, Cyberkids (http://www.mtlake.com/cyberkids), an online source of puzzles, stories, articles, and material created by other children; and Kidding Around (http://alexia.lisuius.edu/watts/diddin.html) which includes children's literature web pages. More web pages for school use come online daily. A useful reference for teachers is *The Best Web Sites for Teachers* by Vicki F. Sharp, Martin G. Levine, and Richard M. Sharp.

In sum, from drill and practice on letter-sound relationships to sharing folk literature with children in classrooms half a world away, technology provides classroom tools that touch every aspect of literacy learning. "Thousands of programs support reading, language arts, and composition. Availability is not an issue; appropriateness is. When you consider any computer software, . . . the appropriate software must 'fit' in several different ways" (Willis, Stephens, and Matthew, 1996, p. 90).

Along with providing valuable instructional tools for children, technology provides a powerful source of support and information for teachers. An expanding array of technological devices is available to support teachers in organizing and managing a classroom reading program:

Electronic grade books provide tools to compute grades and record data. Some of the types of integrated tools children use in writing and illustrating stories (such as in *ClarisWorks*) help teachers keep and organize class records as well.

Electronic portfolios provide an alternative to bulky folders in storing papers, tapes, videotapes, and other materials used to track pupil progress.

Presentation programs, such as *Persuasion,* enable teachers to improve classroom presentations by producing attractive and colorful instructional materials such as overhead projectuals. Authoring systems (such as *HyperCard*) can also help create instructional materials, as Heller and McLellan (1993) found in making materials to help children learn story structure.

Lesson plans can be downloaded from the Internet, and electronic lesson planning programs are available to help teachers create and schedule daily lessons.

E-mail is available to reduce the flow of paper, and web sites allow teachers to share ideas and questions with other professionals that have similar interests and concerns.

The World Wide Web puts teachers in touch with colleagues across the globe. It gives them the chance to interact with mathematicians, scientists, and other experts in different fields of knowledge. It enables teachers to seek advice on everything from teaching phonics to improving educational opportunities for children with disabilities, gives them immediate access to ERIC and other educational databases, and links them to an incredible variety of resources for teaching reading and writing.

3.5 Putting Ideas to Work
Guide for Selecting Literacy CD-ROM Technology

Reutzel (1996) has developed a checklist to assist teachers in selecting and rating CD-ROM technology for use in teaching reading and writing.

International Reading Association Conference New Orleans—1996,
D. Ray Reutzel, Ph.D., Brigham Young University, Literacy CD-ROM Technology: Instruction or Diversion?

Instructional Criteria	Excellent	Very Good	Fair	Poor	Not Available	Comment
1. Variety of engaging literature						
2. Variety of literary genre						
3. High quality, time recognized literature						
4. Provides storage and practice on sight words						
5. Encourages word play/building						
6. Uses onset/rime for word building						
7. Provides pronunciation/blending help						
8. Provides spelling practice						
9. Encourages and supports the writing process						
10. Integrates reading and writing						
11. Provides for cross-discipline responses to text (transmediation)						
12. Provides for repeated readings						
13. Demonstrates one-to-one correspondence						
14. Provides a variety of supported practice						
15. Asks children to self assess progress						
16. Helps students to monitor their own reading						
17. Helps students toward independence						
18. Provides for fluency practice						
19. Provides models of fluent, expressive reading						
20. Models appropriate strategy use						
21. Encourages student choice						
22. Incorporates parental involvement						
23. Multiple language options						
24. Multi-cultural literature						
25. Provides for storage of reading/writing samples						
26. Provides storage for oral retellings						
27. Provides storage for written summaries						
28. Encourages a variety of personal responses						
29. Provides for assessment management						
30. Assesses skill knowledge and application						
31. Adequate structure and options to support all learners						
32. Authentic sharing options						

Reprinted with permission of Dr. D. Ray Reutzel.

Key: 5 = Excellent, 4 = Very Good, 3 = Fair, 2 = Poor, and 1 = Not Available

Scoring: 140–160 Excellent   120–139 Very Good   100–119 Fair
              80–99   Poor   Below 80 Do Not Purchase

For teachers using the Internet and other online services, the monthly magazine *Classroom Connect* (P. O. Box 10488, Lancaster, PA 10488/URL: mailto:connect@classroom.net) is an extremely useful resource that contains news, information, lesson plans, resources, classroom projects, teaching suggestions, and other materials for using telecommunications in and for the classroom.

Technology has transformed our lives, and we can expect it to continue to affect the teacher's role as a professional in the classroom and the way we teach children to read and write. The choice of materials for reading instruction is almost limitless. Choosing the right materials in terms of student interests, backgrounds, and learning needs—and scheduling the use of these materials in a sane and orderly fashion—is a major task in managing reading instruction in the classroom. No matter what materials a teacher chooses, however, real books remain central to instruction in a literature-based reading program.

Pupils

At the heart of all classroom organization and management—including the allocation of time, the use of furniture and space, and the selection and assignment of materials—are the pupils. They are the ones we make choices and arrangements for, and the success of our schools must be judged in terms of how well management decisions meet their needs. Ever since teachers have entered a room filled with 25 or so children of unequal ability, they have confronted the task of providing a reasonable and orderly scheme for teaching all these children to the best of their ability.

As they learn to read and write, students are organized or grouped in a variety of ways. Some activities are carried on with the whole class. At other times, pupils are assigned to small groups for either teacher-directed or independent learning activities. And at still other times, children are expected to complete literacy-related tasks on their own.

The key to any grouping pattern is flexibility. Different types of groups create a balanced program that meets curriculum requirements and at the same time meets the children's reading needs and interests. In any type of grouping pattern, literature plays an important role as the vehicle of instruction.

Large Group Instruction

In any classroom, the realities of school life and the nature of the curriculum will make large group or whole class instruction appropriate at times. These occasions arise when all pupils in a class can profit from the same instruction at the same time. Large group or whole class sessions may be appropriate for such activities as:

> *literature-based language* activities like storytelling, booksharing, creative dramatics or choral reading;
>
> *sharing stories* by reading aloud or by viewing a filmstrip or video;

3.6 Putting Ideas to Work
Grouping

*T*here are a variety of options for grouping pupils for reading and writing activities, including:

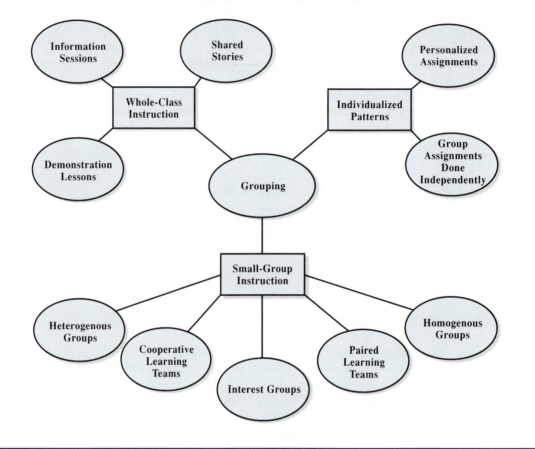

introducing a new reading strategy such as using context clues, map reading, or dictionary use;

teaching a mini-lesson on an item of common need, such as recognizing and using similes and metaphors in reading and writing;

art activities like making book posters or illustrating and describing scenes from novels.

The same text can be used to demonstrate effective reading strategies to an entire class. "With one copy of a highly interesting book with fine illustrations, the teacher can effectively demonstrate and promote reading strategies with the whole class at one time. Students have opportunities to predict text and vocabulary, integrate phonics with meaning clues, use oral and written cloze (in which pupils supply missing words in text) to predict words in context, predict and confirm events, and read orally and silently in a supportive group situation. . . . (The) emphasis is on enjoying a story together" (Routman, 1988; p. 144). Routman describes a typical whole class reading lesson. The teacher introduces the story aloud, asking appropriate high-level questions. The overhead projector displays selected pages that pupils read aloud together, read silently, or use for large group vocabulary and context exercises. The whole class is involved in a group reading experience.

Sometimes whole class instruction can be coordinated with small group activity. Student teams may work on assignments that spring from large group presentations. For example, the teacher can introduce a single story to an entire class by presenting key vocabulary, directing a prereading discussion, and setting purposes for reading. Then one group may listen to a version of the story on the tape recorder, another group may read under the teacher's direction, and a third group may read the story independently. Afterward the whole class works together in postreading discussion of the theme, in comparing the taped version to other versions, or in planning follow-up activities such as choral reading or creative dramatizations based on the story. This is an example of the flexibility that characterizes effective grouping practices.

In large group instructional situations, the teacher still needs to be aware of individual differences within the group. A group of 23 children is not one child 23 times; rather, it is 23 children "one time each." Thus, different parts of large group instruction must be directed at individual pupils, and differentiated follow-up is vital.

While whole class instruction may be appropriate at times, most of the reading instruction that goes on in any classroom occurs in small groups.

Small-Group Instruction

For a long time, teachers have divided their classes into smaller, more manageable organizational units for reading instruction. Research supports the idea that small group organization enhances reading instruction. "Teachers who group their students for instruction tend to have more academically engaged time and higher reading achievement. . . . Grouping students for instruction allows for more teacher-led demonstrations and practice. It also gives the students more opportunities to practice new skills under the teacher's guidance and to receive feedback concerning their performance. Grouping also makes it much easier for teachers to monitor the students' behavior, to keep them on task, and to avoid major classroom management problems" (Rosenshine and Stevens, 1984; p. 787).

Grouping involves more than gathering pupils together; it requires students to interact as they work toward a goal. "Often, so-called 'groups' are nothing more than aggregations. . . . When a few students meet with the teacher, and each communicates only with the teacher, then they are not functioning as a group. When each student communicates with the others as well as with the teacher, a true group is functioning" (Hittleman, 1988; p. 390). Just because children are in a group does not mean that they are functioning as a group.

Traditionally, reading instruction groups have been formed on the basis of perceived ability or achievement. More recently, other criteria have been used to form these groups.

Homogeneous Grouping.
The most common basis for grouping students for reading instruction has been reading level. Pupils are grouped according to their ability or reading achievement, creating instructional groups as homogeneous as possible. This "Robins, Bluebirds, Sparrows" arrangement was introduced and widely accepted in the 1920s, and it continued as a mainstay in grouping patterns for decades.

These ability/achievement groups typically place children according to their standardized reading achievement test scores, their observed reading ability (from informal measures), the recommendation of their teacher from the previous year or the reading specialist, and/or the pupil's measured reading performance in previous grades. The class may be divided into as few as two or as many as five reading groups, but the major criterion is the same—the pupils' measured or perceived reading level.

The intent of ability grouping is to gear instruction as closely as possible to children's reading levels. The teacher usually meets with each group separately every day, using materials (basal readers or trade books) at appropriate levels. Instruction focuses on the range of strategies and techniques needed for reading competency. More often than not, all children in any one group receive the same instruction.

Grouping pupils by ability or achievement is commonly viewed as a way to manage instruction. It makes it easier to choose materials, enables the teacher to pace instruction more appropriately, and provides guided interaction and feedback. Homogeneous grouping aims to promote instructional efficiency. All six or eight pupils in a group can work from the same book, providing a common basis of discussion and academic learning.

However, the practice of ability grouping has been challenged as problems with this practice have become apparent. Being in the "low" group year after year can have a disastrous effect on a child's self-concept. Placement in the slow group "clearly sends negative messages to struggling readers—messages of limited potential and low expectations. As a result, remedial readers are often isolated from the literature-based activities of more accomplished classmates" (Schumaker and Schumaker, 1989; p. 546).

The nature of instruction differs from group to group as well. Pupils on the fast track tend to receive more favorable treatment from teachers (Wuthrick, 1990). Pupils in the slower group receive a different quality of reading instruction, with less time, less emphasis on meaning, and less interesting reading materials (Allington, 1983). Research indicates that grouping pupils by their reading ability levels does *not* promote better reading achievement.

Paratore et al. (1991) summarize major research findings on grouping pupils for reading instruction. They conclude that grouping pupils according to achievement or ability does not enhance reading achievement, that assignment to permanent groups based on ability affects pupils' perceptions of themselves and others, that alternative grouping arrangements (such as cooperative learning or peer tutoring groups) lead to significant increases in literacy, and that "heterogeneous groups supplemented by smaller 'needs-based' groups for providing additional help surpass homogeneous groups in reading achievement" (p. 8).

Although there may be times when it is appropriate to group pupils of similar ability in a flexible grouping pattern, sole reliance on this practice is highly questionable. The intent may be positive, but the negative effects of reduced expectations, differing instructional practices, damaged self-concepts, and lower reading achievement levels have caused educators to reexamine the practice of homogeneous grouping. Alternative grouping patterns are increasingly used for reading instruction in the classroom.

Heterogeneous Grouping.   Any teacher who engages in whole class instruction is necessarily dealing with a heterogeneous group. But opportunities abound for using smaller, mixed-ability groups in reading instruction.

Activities involving multi-ability groups usually begin with teacher direction—the teacher reads part of a story demonstrating effective reading strategies, or conducts a mini-lesson on a component such as identifying character traits. Following this, groups that each reflect different ability levels focus on targeted skills or apply the thinking processes and reading strategies the teacher modeled for them.

Literature can be the basis for forming heterogeneous groups (see Putting Ideas to Work 3.7). Trade books provide a vehicle for developing and applying reading strategies as different groups read different books. No matter what level the book, students of varying abilities can discuss their reactions, their reflections, and their reading development based on what they have read. Interest (not achievement) is a major factor in forming groups.

In fact, children can be grouped heterogeneously on the basis of shared interest. Mixed-ability groups can read and discuss materials related to sports, hobbies, occupations, or curriculum-related topics. Stories, poems, magazine articles, and sometimes basal stories at different levels explore these topics.

Schools are moving away from a reliance on ability and achievement as the prime criterion for grouping pupils and using a variety of more heterogeneous grouping patterns. Two practical ways of forming heterogeneous groups in the classroom are cooperative learning teams and mixed-ability peer-tutoring teams.

Cooperative Learning.   Cooperative learning is one of the most promising and popular instructional practices in today's schools. Cooperative learning involves students in pairs or small groups that work together to promote one another's learning. The idea behind cooperative learning is simple: children often learn more working with one another than they do

3.7 Putting Ideas to Work
Using Literature in Heterogeneous Reading Groups

*T*rade books lend themselves especially well to activities in which pupils at different reading levels work together. For example:

Literature Study Groups. Grouping pupils according to trade books they are reading is an essential practice in a literature-based reading program. At any grade level, the teacher selects several books sure to appeal to children. The books range from easy to more challenging to read. The teacher briefly introduces each book, students indicate which titles appeal to them, and the class forms heterogeneous groups based on their selections.

Peterson and Eeds (1990) describe in some detail the rationale behind and procedures for organizing literature study groups. They detail what goes into the organization, management, and instruction of these groups, including:

parent involvement to "get literature going at home";

reading aloud to make connections with authors and books;

extensive reading of appealing trade books in the classroom;

intensive reading, in which children are invited to extend themselves more deeply into the world of literature; and

dialogue that encourages interpretation and active involvement in the story.

Groups form in two phases. First, pupils read the book for fun with brief (five-to-seven minutes) daily meetings to check progress and share meanings. Phase 2 involves critical interpretation, personal response, focus on literary elements, and generating involvement through a "conscious connection" to the literature. For evaluation, Peterson and Eeds suggest checklists, daily reading records, and reading response journals.

The type of activity that takes place in literature study groups is very different from that which occurs in the traditional reading group. The teacher does not ask questions with predetermined correct answers. "Instead, the teacher is a participant, a fellow reader who shares the joys and difficulties, insights and speculations, and asks only those questions he or she genuinely wonders about" (Eeds and Peterson, 1991; p. 119). Discussions include reflection and dialogue, as pupils reflect in unique ways on the stories they have read (Keegen and Sharke, 1991).

working on their own. Cooperative learning gives pupils opportunities to work collaboratively in seeking additional information, discussing ideas, practicing skills, finding solutions to problems, or extending learning from teacher-directed activities.

Cooperative learning can take many forms in the literature-based classroom. For example, it might involve:

two or three pupils reading together, sharing a story, taking turns reading, figuring out words together, or just browsing through books;

a team of pupils working together on reading-related strategies, such as using context clues to determine the meaning of unfamiliar words or seeing how details support the main idea in a story;

groups of pupils searching for creative solutions to problems suggested through class discussion;

Theme Groups. The teacher selects books at different levels centered on a theme. A selection of survival books, for example, might include:

> Jean Craighead George's *My Side of the Mountain*, the story of a boy who survives by living off the land in the Catskill Mountains;
>
> Jean Craighead George's *Julie of the Wolves*, a story about a girl who survives with the help of wolves on the Alaskan tundra;
>
> Felice Holman's *Slake's Limbo*, a book about a boy who survives in the subway tunnels of New York City;
>
> Cynthia Voigt's *The Homecoming*, an account of four children who walk from Connecticut to their grandmother's home in Maryland;
>
> Armstrong Sperry's *Call It Courage*, an adventure story about a boy who has to prove his manhood in the South Pacific; and
>
> Gary Paulsen's *Hatchet*, the story of a boy who survives in the Canadian wilderness after his plane crashes.

Each student reads a tale of survival at his or her reading level. Instruction focuses on vocabulary (survival-related or descriptive words), literary elements (the effect of the setting or characterization on the action), comprehension (main idea or cause-effect relationships), critical thinking (how personal traits have an impact on the main character's survival), and the like.

Author Groups. Pupils of differing ability may group to read books by the same author. For example, Val is reading a more sophisticated Judy Blume title such as *Are You There God? It's Me, Margaret*, while Attila is reading the easier *Freckle Juice*. They meet to share facts they have researched about the author's life and writing style, and to discuss similarities and differences in the books.

teams working on alternative endings to stories, additional chapters to favorite books, or any number of literature-based writing activities.

Cooperative learning involves more than group work; it involves teamwork, genuine cooperation, and peer interaction. Baloche and Platt (1993) describe a literacy project that demonstrated many of the values of cooperative learning: genuine interdependence, so that one pupil's success is linked to the success of his or her partners; face-to-face interaction of various types; individual accountability; and group processing.

At times, cooperative learning groups are formed according to similar performance levels, and at other times, they are formed without regard to members' reading abilities. In any cooperative learning arrangement, students take responsibility for checking each other's work and making sure that the final product reflects the group's collective knowledge. Individuals are rewarded on the basis of the group's accomplishments.

3.8 Putting Ideas to Work
Cooperative Learning Using Literature

Nancy Whisler and Judy Williams (1990) provided a plethora of ideas and suggestions for using children's literature for cooperative learning activities, including:

> *group prediction strategies,* in which small groups brainstorm ideas related to a topic or theme before reading;
>
> *collaborative word webbing,* in which cooperative learning groups construct webs related to key words or characters in the story;
>
> *Venn diagrams* that pupils cooperatively construct for comparing story elements with their personal experiences;
>
> *literature report cards,* in which groups of children evaluate and "grade" story characters on various qualities; for example, they might grade Barbara Cooney's wonderful *Miss Rumphius* on her imagination and thoughtfulness.

Whisler and Williams also include cooperative learning activities using a variety of prediction and anticipation strategies, vocabulary activities, creative thinking experiences, classification exercises, listening activities, paired reading, story mapping, writing, discussion, and other activities that encourage students to interact as they read books.

In synthesizing research related to cooperative learning, Slavin (1991) reports that the most successful approaches incorporate two elements: group goals and individual accountability; that is, "groups must be working to achieve some goal or to earn rewards or recognition, and the success of the group must depend on the individual learning of every group member" (p. 76). When group goals and individual accountability are built in, achievement is consistently positive. Slavin also reports positive effects from cooperative learning across grade levels, across subject areas, and in many of the affective dimensions of learning (such as self-esteem, social skills, attitude toward school, and the ability to work with others). Cooperative learning has also been shown to work effectively to help students develop and apply high-level reading-comprehension skills (Flynn, 1989), enhance interpersonal reading strategies (Bergk, 1988), improve comprehension of reading material (Uttero, 1988), and improve reading attitudes (Madden, 1988).

Cooperative learning, when carefully planned and skillfully implemented, is a promising alternative to teacher-directed ability groups. Beyond the feelings of belonging, acceptance, and support that the practice can generate, it can improve reading and writing performance. Moreover, a teacher can effectively integrate it with traditional practices in a flexible grouping plan.

Paired Learning. Another popular technique for cooperative work in the classroom is paired learning. Paired learning occurs when two pupils of similar ability work together, acting as teachers and learners simultaneously.

Cooperative learning promotes interdependency and social skills essential in today's world.
© James L. Shaffer

This can also occur as peer tutoring, in which a more capable pupil works with one who needs help.

There are plenty of opportunities for teams of students to work together in literature-based reading and writing activities. Equal-ability pairs can work together in previewing a story and making predictions before reading, in listening to one another read aloud to confirm hypotheses or answer questions, and in helping one another with a discussion or writing assignment following reading. The teacher evaluates the pupils jointly after they complete an assignment.

Mixed-ability pairs can engage in cooperative learning activities such as comparing literary elements in different stories they have read or using different print sources to locate information and find answers to questions. Research has documented the effectiveness of peer tutoring. "Peer tutoring correlates with significant gains among both tutors and tutees" (Paratore et al., 1991; p. 7).

The effects of peer tutoring are especially impressive when low-achieving older readers tutor pupils in the lower grades. Reading aloud to younger children gives the poor reader, even a seriously at-risk student (Top and Osguthorpe, 1987), a sense of purpose, along with authentic opportunities to develop vocabulary and comprehension. The practice gives the younger students an opportunity to hear new stories and to talk about books, and it provides them with reading models they can readily relate to.

The various small group organizational patterns this section describes are certainly not mutually exclusive; in fact, they complement one another. They provide the flexibility of allowing the best readers to work alongside the less able, at least some of the time—providing true mainstreaming for the child with special needs.

3.9 Putting Ideas to Work
Cooperative Integrated Reading and Composition

Stevens et al. (1987) have demonstrated that cooperative learning practices help elementary students develop literacy. In a program called Cooperative Integrated Reading and Composition (CIRC), third and fourth graders worked in heterogeneous learning teams for a variety of reading and writing activities. Research showed impressive results.

The cycle of instruction begins when the teacher presents a new skill or introduces the story to the reading group. Next comes teacher-guided practice with the group, with pairs of students working cooperatively to answer questions. Pupils work in mixed-ability learning groups on activities coordinated with their group instruction. The teacher monitors their work and provides feedback and reteaching as necessary. When children show that they understand the work, they engage in team practice and preassessment activities. At the end of the cycle, the students take quizzes to assess understanding and mastery.

In comparison to pupils taught in the conventional manner (meeting in reading groups and then working independently on worksheets), standardized test results favored the CIRC pupils on a variety of measures—reading comprehension, vocabulary, writing mechanics, language expression, spelling, oral reading, and general writing ability.

Jenkins et al. (1994) tested CIRC with regular, remedial, and special education students. They found that the procedure had significant positive effects on reading vocabulary, total reading, and language scores.

More important than the grouping arrangements themselves, however, is the type of instruction the groups receive and the activities the groups carry on. Directed lessons, lively discussions, and exciting supplementary work are the keys to using books for reading and writing activities in various small group patterns in the classroom.

Individualized Patterns

Literature-based reading instruction also offers ample opportunities for individual work. Individualized instruction has historical roots. "From the very beginning, Americans have been inclined to value the individual student and to seek ways to accommodate the needs and aspirations of individuals in the practice of schooling" (Otto, Wolf, and Eldridge, 1984; p. 800). Schools today are no less concerned with the growth and development of the individual pupil. Even as they participate in a variety of small groups, pupils need activities that are *individual* and/or *individualized*. These two terms have different meanings.

Individual activities are carried out by each pupil in the class working alone. Students might perform a variety of individual activities related to trade books they have read—using a map to trace the movements of the animals in Robert Lawson's *Rabbit Hill*, for example. In individual activities, pupils work independently on teacher-directed tasks. These tasks may or may not relate to a larger group effort.

Individualized activities are prescribed for or chosen by the child according to his or her individual interests and needs. A good example is working on a personal literature journal. Individualized activities are often part of a literature-based reading program.

In most classrooms, students are expected to work independently for a considerable amount of time completing seatwork, using supplementary literature-related materials, engaging in independent reading and research projects, and doing other learning activities. All the pupils might be working on the same assignment, but each is doing it on his or her own.

Independent activities help children learn to function on their own and to take responsibility for their learning. These activities also provide personalized learning opportunities, with assignments tailored to individual interests and needs; however, when pupils are functioning on their own, the teacher must carefully plan and monitor the work. Independent work time (and in some cases, group time) provides ample opportunities for doodling, daydreaming, socializing, or just plain fooling around, so time on task is an important objective when pupils work on their own. That is why independent work requires teacher supervision and feedback, just as group work often does. The more time teachers (or other adults) spend supervising pupils during independent assignments, the more pupils seem to achieve in these assignments. Also, pupils need to be held accountable for the completion of independent work.

Teachers must also take practical considerations into account as students work on their own. Work should be within each child's ability to complete it. It makes little sense to ask pupils to research a topic from an encyclopedia two or three grade levels beyond their reading ability or to let them struggle with a trade book so difficult that it is frustrating. Some students may need a "buddy" to seek direction from, because they quickly forget teacher directions given at the beginning of an independent work period. Students who have trouble attending to a task while classmates are working around them may need quiet work areas. Computers can sometimes help pace independent instruction and provide feedback.

Accommodations for each individual's learning habits, along with teacher planning and supervision, make the individually oriented component of a classroom program run smoothly.

Flexibility in Grouping

Should a teacher concentrate on whole class or individualized teaching? Homogeneous or heterogeneous grouping? Large group instruction or paired learning? The answer is all of the above.

The key to effective grouping is flexibility. One of the problems with the traditional practice of ability/achievement grouping is that pupils were locked into one group for their entire school lives. The cliché, "Once a wombat, always a wombat," too often rang true. This type of grouping contributed to an educational caste system.

3.10 Putting Ideas to Work

Grouping in the Elementary Classroom

*B*erghoff and Egawe (1991) describe alternatives to ability grouping in the following chart. The authors caution, however, that these grouping patterns "work because they are connected with our understandings of literacy, learning, and community. They are not simply logistical mechanisms that can be plugged into any classroom. They are thoughtful choices of organizational patterns that support learning and the creating of meaning in the way we theorize it can best be accomplished" (p. 537).

Grouping in the Elementary Classroom

	Whole Group	Small Group	Pairs	Independent
Why?	Develops the learning community; time to share culture and literacy.	Common interests; strategy instructions; opportunities to plan, think, work toward a goal.	More intimate group requires less negotiation about agenda; more opportunity to construct.	Allows sustained reading and writing; allows personal choice; time for personal reflection.
How?	Possibilities include sitting in a circle, having a special chair for authors or report givers, musical signals to call the group together.	Groups of three or four self-chosen for interest; teacher-planned, considering social relationships, expertise, or needed language support.	Self-chosen partner; teacher-assigned partner to assure success—stronger/ weaker, expert/ novice; teacher- or self-chosen to encourage new friendships.	Teacher specifies time for independent work; children separate to work alone.
When?	Decision making—class rules, plans; problem solving—playground issues; listening to stories; choral reading; teacher or expert demonstrations; shared experiences— cooking, science experiments, art activities; celebrating— completion of a major project, individual accomplishments; sharing individual scholarship.	Discussion groups; literature study; content area explorations; writing support groups; instruction groups; any inquiry project.	Shared reading; study partners; cross-age tutors; letter exchanges; skill pairings—author/ illustrator, reader/ actor.	Sustained reading and writing; personal investigation; journal writing; alternative sign system response; gathering personally inviting resources; time for personal reflection.

	Whole Group	Small Group	Pairs	Independent
How does it foster literacy?	Provides a meaning-rich context where language is used to share meaning and students' individuality is explored and supported.	Opportunity to use oral language in social context to construct meaning; functional reasons to read and write; allows students to shape their own development of personal literacy.	Opportunities to practice making personal meanings public in face-to-face interaction with a peer; "two heads are better than one"—learning can go farther with two.	Allows the child to set a personal pace for thinking; allows the child to make personal connections to the class learning; time to savor language; time to use written language.
How does it support students with diverse language, cultural, ability, or experience backgrounds?	Shared experiences give the class a shared vocabulary and practice in social meaning making. Exposes differences and similarities of all students so that they are expected and accepted.	Develops awareness of multiple perspectives; peers provide support and language opportunities.	Opportunities to make connections with all class members; reasons to relate in spite of differences.	Allows time for the child to do what he or she enjoys without pressure to negotiate with the larger community; time to practice, to own new learning; time to work in the child's first language.
What does the teacher learn from the students?	What the children value; what energizes the group; which children need more help in making their meanings public.	How the children try out different perspectives and roles; how the children's personal sense of power is evolving; what knowledge is constructed.	What the child can do with support; what kind of support the child needs; how the child accepts or rejects different perspectives.	What the child's interests are; what the child thinks about; what aspects of reading and writing make sense to the child and can be used for her or his own purposes.

A balanced literacy program provides opportunities for students to work in various types of groups as they learn to read and write. In a given day, children might share stories with small groups of friends who are at the same reading level, participate in whole class lessons on topics of common need, work on reading-related projects with classmates who have varying abilities, participate in writing conferences and editing sessions with one other classmate, and complete individual assignments tailored to their needs and interests.

Unsworth (1984) has suggested a set of principles to guide flexible grouping in the classroom. As an alternative to permanent groups, he suggests that the teacher periodically create new groups to meet new needs as they arise. Group size can vary from two members to the whole class. The composition of each group changes according to its task. The purpose of the group's task should be clear, students should know how their work relates to the overall program, and the teacher should use group assessment.

To answer the question, "Am I allowed to group?" Flood et al. (1992) identify the variables in using flexible grouping patterns and describe how different groups can work in a single, literature-based lesson using Verna Aardema's *Why Mosquitoes Buzz in People's Ears*. Pupils can be grouped according to several criteria, depending on the activity. Group size can vary from two pupils to a whole class. Every group can use the same material, or each group can use its own resources.

Flexible grouping patterns require flexibility on the part of the teacher. Rather than setting a classroom atmosphere that some children "just don't fit into," teachers need to design literacy experiences that allow students to work together in an environment marked by enthusiasm, support, respect, and recognition that everyone has something to contribute to the class and to the reading program.

Parents in the Classroom

Parents are a potential source of help in organizing and managing an efficient classroom reading program. By extending their considerable influence beyond the home and by providing extra sets of hands in the classroom, parent volunteers can help make literature-based reading programs run more smoothly.

Involving parents in classroom reading programs helps build strong home-school relationships. It allows parents to learn about their children's reading and writing development, enables parents to better understand what literature-based instruction is all about (and why few worksheets come home), and encourages them to carry classroom learning experiences over into their homes.

Parents—and grandparents, too—can do a number of jobs to help students in the classroom: they can listen to children read; answer the inevitable "What do I do next?" and other procedural questions; help pupils spell unfamiliar words as they write; help them edit their writing, with guidance from the teacher to do so sensitively and skillfully; read stories to small groups of students; assist pupils who are having trouble with assignments; research

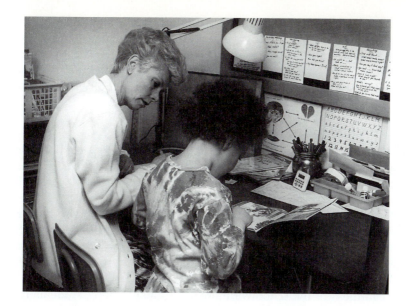

Classroom volunteers can play many roles in helping pupils with literature-based reading and writing instruction.
© James L. Shaffer

information for author-awareness displays; keep track of books in the classroom library; work on putting student-written books together; and otherwise contribute unique skills in their own unique ways.

Large doses of sensitivity and common sense are needed when parents work in classrooms. Often, parents need to know about school or district policies they must follow. Training and orientation are essential so that parents clearly understand their roles and functions. They must be prepared to keep student records absolutely confidential.

The first parent-teacher conference or PTA meeting of the year is an effective time to recruit parent volunteers. The invitation may also be extended in an opening-of-school letter to pupils' homes. Since many parents do not have time for this type of activity, other community resources (such as senior citizen centers) might also help recruit volunteers.

Some teachers find it hard to involve parents in the classroom. Teachers who use volunteers effectively, however, find that parents become an essential part of their classroom reading programs.

Schoolwide Organizational Patterns

Other organizational patterns—such as departmentalization, team teaching, and other alternatives to self-contained classrooms—may affect reading and writing instruction.

Departmentalization

Departmentalization is a teacher-oriented organizational pattern sometimes used in the upper elementary grades. Different teachers specialize in certain academic areas (science, social studies, math, or language arts) through the day. One teacher, for example, might be responsible for reading instruction for several classes. The lower grades sometimes adopt a modified version of departmentalization, as when two second-grade teachers trade classes so that one teaches all the math and science and the other teaches language arts. Although this arrangement offers teachers with particular interest and expertise in specific areas, it hardly promotes the idea of wholeness or the integration of language arts into all areas of the curriculum.

Team Teaching

Team teaching involves teachers with different subject specialties working together in a coordinated effort. Team teaching is characterized by careful, close planning, which increases the chances that language will permeate the students' experiences in other areas of the curriculum.

Each of these organizational patterns—and others used over the years—reflects a different philosophy or approach to education. Each has advantages and disadvantages and can represent the best or worst of educational practices. None has been shown conclusively to have a significant effect on pupils' achievement in reading.

Regardless of the schoolwide organizational pattern, students need a balance between large group, small group, and independent activities as they learn how to read and write. And though these organizational patterns may decrease the flexibility inherent in a self-contained classroom, none preclude the extensive use of literature in the reading instructional program.

Summary and Conclusions

When all is said and done, a well-run classroom is conducive to student achievement. Efficient and effective reading instruction is the goal of organization and management. Organization and management are not ends in themselves; they are a means to an end—and the end is to provide the best reading instruction possible.

Teachers must make managerial decisions and adjustments to ensure that children receive the best possible reading instruction. These decisions involve scheduling time, arranging space, choosing and assigning materials, and keeping records of pupils' progress. Of course, teachers must also establish a "traffic pattern" for children who leave the room to work with specialists, keep the milk money separate from the picture money, and assume all the other noninstructional administrative responsibilities that go with the job of teaching. Managing classroom reading instruction effectively is indeed a many-splendored thing!

Organizing and managing a literature-based reading program involves the same variables involved in any instructional program. It requires the commitment to make literature a frequent part of the classroom experience, access to many trade books at various levels, and flexibility in grouping pupils on something other than a basal reading placement. It involves using every opportunity possible to use trade books to help students become readers and writers.

In the final analysis, no ideal organizational pattern exists. No amount of grouping eliminates the individual differences that children carry into the classroom. No technology generates a love of reading or real writing competency in children. Although time, space, materials, and pupils influence the type of classroom program needed to teach reading, the teacher remains the mightiest force of all. Notwithstanding the advantages and disadvantages of one organizational pattern over another, reading achievement depends largely on the activities the teacher implements in the classroom.

Teachers have different personalities and different teaching styles. Teachers' styles determine in large measure their ability to work in one organizational system or another. Some teachers work best in a highly structured and orderly classroom, while others are more comfortable working in a freewheeling classroom atmosphere. A set of materials that appeals to one teacher might have little or no appeal to another. Human diversity is, paradoxically, one of the most beautiful strengths and, at the same time, one of the greatest challenges of the educational process.

Establishing and maintaining a literature-based classroom program involves more than merely using occasional, isolated activities based on children's books. It involves a commitment to using literature as the primary basis for developing students' literacy and designing a structured set of experiences that will put this commitment to work in the classroom. To this end, Johnson and Louis (1987) offer step-by-step suggestions to teachers who want to progress from following the traditional plan using the basal, an unrelated writing program, and only the occasional use of literature:

1. Maintain your basal and writing programs. Develop literature-based routines for your literature program.
2. Use literature-based routines with the contents of the basal reader. Eliminate less useful workbook activities. Develop some writing activities around the literature program.
3. Increase the number of literature-based routines applied to the basal reader. Reserve workbook activities for remedial work. Increase the number of writing activities that focus on good books.
4. Eliminate the use of basal readers for your more competent children. Eliminate writing exercises and focus all writing on functional classroom activities, content areas, and literature.
5. Eliminate the use of the basal for less competent children. Fuse reading, writing, speaking, and listening activities into an information- and literature-centered literacy program.
6. Maintain your literature-based literacy program. Experience less stress, more joy, greater progress, and more satisfaction for your children. Receive approval from administration and parents. Give workshops to colleagues. Rest on your laurels! (Johnson and Louis, 1987; p. 150)[1]

The last few sentences may sound facetious, but the steps in the process are basically sound!

Discussion Questions and Activities

1. List some of the ramifications that literature-based instruction has for organizing and managing a classroom reading program in terms of time, space, materials, and pupils.
2. Design a word board similar to that suggested in Putting Ideas to Work 3.2. Select words from children's books. What other displays related to reading, writing, and literature would you plan for your classroom?

[1]From J. D. Johnson and D. R. Louis, *Literacy Through Literature*, Thomas Nelson Australia, 1987. Reprinted with permission.

3. Which of the four major aspects of organization and management described in this chapter (time, space, materials, and pupils) do you consider most important? Research the topic you consider most vital and report your findings.
4. From your educational resources center or curriculum library, select a piece of computer software related to children's literature. What is the focus of the program? How is it to be used in promoting student interest or competency in reading or writing? What is your opinion of the material?
5. When you were in elementary school, what reading group were you in? How did you feel about being in that group? How did it affect your reading? How will these experiences influence your grouping practices as a teacher?

School-Based Assignments

1. Carefully observe the reading program in your classroom in terms of the four variables identified in this chapter: time, space, materials, and pupils. How much time is scheduled for reading each day? How is this time spent? How is the classroom arranged? What types of reading materials are available? What types do students use most often? How are pupils grouped for instruction? What changes would you make if you were in charge of the classroom?
2. As you observe pupils in your classroom, note how they spend their time during reading instruction. How much time do they spend in whole class work? In small groups? Working independently? Focus your attention on one child and note that student's time on task. How do you think the teacher could use instructional time more effectively?
3. A teacher's classroom is something like an artist's studio. Describe the "teaching studio" in which you work. Which parts of the environment emphasize literacy instruction? What signs tell you that reading is alive and well in the classroom?
4. Select a children's book, and plan a reading activity using this book with a heterogeneous group of pupils. Describe the results of your efforts.
5. What record-keeping system does the teacher or school use to keep track of student progress, the books they have read and heard read, and other aspects of literacy development? Briefly describe the system and the changes you would make to improve it.

Children's Trade Books Cited in This Chapter

Aardema, Verna. (1975*). Why Mosquitoes Buzz in People's Ears: A West African Folk Tale*. New York: Dial.
Blume, Judy. (1972). *Are You There God? It's Me, Margaret*. New York: Dell.
Blume, Judy. (1978). *Freckle Juice*. New York: Dell.
Calhoun, Mary. (1979). *Cross Country Cat*. New York: Morrow.
Cleary, Beverly. (1979). *Socks*. New York: Morrow.
Cooney, Barbara. (1985). *Miss Rumphius*. New York: Penguin.
Estep, Don. (1990). *Cats and Kittens*. New York: Checkerboard Press.
George, Jean Craighead. (1972). *Julie of the Wolves*. New York: Harper & Row.
George, Jean Craighead. (1959). *My Side of the Mountain*. New York: Dutton.
Holman, Felice. (1974). *Slake's Limbo*. New York: Macmillan.
Lawson, Robert. (1994). *Rabbit Hill*. New York: Viking.
McPhail, David. (1982). *Great Cat*. New York: Dutton.
Paulsen, Gary. (1987). *Hatchet*. New York: Macmillan.
Potter, Beatrix. (1903). *The Tale of the Flopsy Bunnies*. New York: Dover.

Seymour, Simon. (1991). *Big Cats.* New York: HarperCollins.
Sperry, Armstrong. (1940). *Call It Courage.* New York: Macmillan.
Voigt, Cynthia. (1981). *Homecoming.* New York: Macmillan.

References

Allington, R. L. (1983). The Reading Instruction Provided Readers of Differing Ability. *Elementary School Journal* 83:548–559.

Anderson, R. C., Hiebert, E. H., Scott, J. A., and Wilkinson, A. G. (1985). *Becoming a Nation of Readers.* Washington: National Institute of Education.

Baloche, L., and Platt, T. J. (1993). Sprouting Magic Beans: Exploring Literature through Creative Questioning and Cooperative Learning. *Language Arts* 70:264–272.

Bergeron, B. S., and Rudenga, E. A. (1996). Seeming Authenticity: What is "Real" about Thematic Literacy Instruction? *The Reading Teacher* 49:544–551.

Berghoff, B., and Egawe, K. (1991). No More "Rocks": Grouping To Give Students Control of Their Learning. *The Reading Teacher* 44:536–541.

Bergk, M. (1988). Fostering Interpersonal Forms of Reading. *The Reading Teacher* 40:210–218.

Bruce, B. C. (1995). *Twenty-First Century Literacy.* Technical Report No. 624, Center for the Study of Reading. Champaign: University of Illinois at Champaign-Urbana.

Cambourne, B., and Turbill, J. (1990). Assessment in Whole-Language Classrooms: Theory into Practice. *The Elementary School Journal* 90:338–349.

Eeds, M., and Peterson, R. (1991). Teacher as Curator: Learning to Talk about Literature. *The Reading Teacher* 45:118–126.

Flood, J., Lapp, D., Flood, S., and Nagel, G. (1992). Am I Allowed to Group? Using Flexible Patterns for Effective Instruction. *The Reading Teacher* 45:608–615.

Flynn, L. L. (1989). Developing Critical Reading Skills through Cooperative Problem Solving. *The Reading Teacher* 43:664–668.

Fortescue, C. M. (1994). Using Oral and Written Language to Increase Understanding of Math Concepts. *Language Arts* 71:576–580.

Heller, M., and McLellan, H. (1993). Dancing with the Wind: Understanding Narrative Text Structure through Response to Multicultural Children's Literature (with an assist from HyperCard). *Reading Psychology* 14:285–310.

Hiebert, E. H., and Colt, J. (1989). Patterns of Literature-Based Reading Instruction. *The Reading Teacher* 43:14–20.

Hittleman, D. (1988). *Developmental Reading, K–8: Teaching from a Whole Language Perspective.* Columbus, OH: Merrill Publishing.

Jenkins, J. R., Jewell, M., Leicester, N., O'Connor, R. E., Jenkins, L. M., and Troutner, N. M. (1994). Accommodations for Individual Differences Without Classroom Ability Groups: An Experiment in School Restructuring. *Exceptional Children* 60:344–358.

Johnson, T. D., and Louis, D. R. (1987). *Literacy through Literature.* Portsmouth, NH: Heinemann.

Keegan, S., and Sharke, K. (1991). Literature Study Groups: An Alternative to Ability Grouping. *The Reading Teacher* 44:542–547.

Kimmel, M. M., and Segal, E. (1983). *For Reading Out Loud! A Guide to Sharing Books with Children.* New York: Delacourte Press.

Korbin, B. (1988). *Eye Openers: Choosing Books for Kids.* New York: Viking.

Madden, L. (1988). Improve Reading Attitude of Poor Readers through Cooperative Reading Teams. *The Reading Teacher* 42:194–199.

Morrow, L. M., and Rand, M. K. (1991). Promoting Literacy during Play by Designing Early Childhood Classroom Environments. *The Reading Teacher* 44:396–402.

National Council of Teachers of Mathematics. (1989). *Curriculum and Evaluation Standards for School Mathematics.* Reston, VA: NCTM.

Neuman, S. B., and Roskos, K. (1992). Literacy Objects as Cultural Tools: Effects on Children's Literacy Behaviors in Play. *Reading Research Quarterly* 27:203–225.

Otto, W., Wolf, A., and Eldridge, R. G. (1984). Managing Instruction. In P. D. Pearson et al., eds., *Handbook of Reading Research*. New York: Longmans.

Paratore, J. R., Fountas, I. C., Jenkins, C. A., Mathers, M. E., Oulette, J. M., and Sheehan, N. M. (1991). *Grouping Students for Literacy Learning: What Works*. Boston: Massachusetts Reading Association.

Peterson, R., and Eeds, M. (1990). *Grand Conversations: Literature Groups in Action*. New York: Scholastic.

Pinnell, G. S., Pikulski, J. J., Wixon, K. K., Campbell, J. R., Gough, P. B., and Beatty, A. S. (1995). *Listening To Children Read*. Washington, DC: U. S. Department of Education.

Raphael, T. E., and Hiebert, E. H. (1996). *Creating an Integrated Approach to Literacy Instruction*. Fort Worth: Harcourt Brace.

Reutzel, D. R. (1996). *Literacy CD-ROM Technology: Instruction or Diversion?* Paper presented at the International Reading Association Convention, New Orleans, LA.

Rhodes, L. K., and Dudley-Marling, C. (1988). *Readers and Writers with a Difference: A Holistic Approach to Teaching Learning Disabled and Remedial Students*. Portsmouth, NH: Heinemann.

Rickelman, R. J., and Henk, W. A. (1990). Children's Literature and Audio/Visual Technologies. *The Reading Teacher* 43:182–184.

Rosenshine, B., and Stevens, R. (1984). Classroom Instruction in Reading. In P. D. Pearson et al., eds., *Handbook of Reading Research*. New York: Longmans.

Routman, R. (1988). *Transitions from Literature to Literacy*. Portsmouth, NH: Heinemann.

Schumaker, M. P., and Schumaker, R. L. (1989). 3000 Paper Cranes: Children's Literature for the Remedial Reader. *The Reading Teacher* 42:544–559.

Shannon, P. (1983). The Use of Commercial Reading Materials in American Elementary Schools. *Reading Research Quarterly* 19:68–85.

Sharp, V. F., Levine, M. G., and Sharp, R. M. (1996). *The Best Web Sites for Teachers*. Eugene, OR: International Society for Technology in Education.

Slavin, R. E. (1991). Synthesis of Research on Cooperative Learning. *Educational Leadership* 47:71–82.

Stevens, R. J., Madden, N. A., Slavin, R. E., and Farnish, A. M. (1987). Cooperative Integrated Reading and Composition: Two Field Experiments. *Reading Research Quarterly* 22:433–445.

Top, B. L., and Osguthorpe, R. T. (1987). Reverse Role Tutoring: The Effects of Handicapped Students Tutoring Regular Class Students. *The Elementary School Journal* 87:413–423.

Trelease, J. (1989). *The Read-Aloud Handbook*. New York: Penguin Books.

Unsworth, L. (1984). Meeting Individual Needs through Flexible Whole Class Grouping of Pupils. *The Reading Teacher* 38:298–304.

Uttero, D. A. (1988). Activating Comprehension through Cooperative Learning. *The Reading Teacher* 42:390–395.

Whisler, N., and Williams, J. (1990). *Literature and Cooperative Learning: Pathway to Literacy*. Sacramento, CA: Literature Co-op.

Willis, J. W., Stephens, E. C., and Matthew, K. I. (1996). *Technology, Reading, and Language Arts*. Boston: Allyn & Bacon.

Wolf, A. (1977). Reading Instruction: Time Will Tell. *Learning* 5:76–81.

Wuthrick, J. A. (1990). Blue Jays Win! Crows Go Down in Defeat! *Phi Delta Kappan* 71:553–556.

Zarrillo, J. (1989). Teachers' Interpretations of Literature-Based Reading. *The Reading Teacher* 43:22–28.

*E*arly Literacy

© David M. Grossman/Photo Researchers, Inc.

Chapter 4 Outline

3. Literature in Kindergarten
   a. Wordless Books
   b. Big Books
4. Phonetic Awareness and Alphabet Training
   a. Alphabet Training
   b. Phonemic Awareness
5. Writing
   C. Beginning Reading and Writing Instruction
   V. The Parents' Role: Home Support for Emergent Literacy
   A. Parents in the Preschool Years
   B. The Parents' Role When Children Come to School
   VI. Summary and Conclusions
Discussion Questions and Activities
School-Based Assignments
Children's Trade Books Cited in This Chapter
References

Features

4.1   Child's Schema of a Birthday Party
4.2   The First Three Years
4.3   Emergent Literacy and Reading Readiness
4.4   A Selected Sample of Concept Books
4.5   A Sampler of Alphabet Books
4.6   NAEYC Position Statement on Developmentally Appropriate Practice
4.7   Using Literature in Kindergarten
4.8   A Cross-Grade Library Assignment
4.9   Developing a Reading Lesson with a Wordless Book
4.10 Authors Who Write Stories Without Words
4.11 Steps in a Shared Reading Lesson with a Big Book
4.12 Books to Develop Phonemic Awareness
4.13 First Day in First Grade
4.14 Beginning First Grade with a Literature-Based Program
4.15 Ten Ways Parents Can Help Children Become Better Readers
4.16 What Parents Can Do to Promote Literacy for Preschoolers
4.17 A Hierarchy of Home-School Relationships
4.18 A Note to Parents
4.19 Useful References for Parents about Reading in the Home

Key Concepts in This Chapter

A child does not gain the ability to read and write all at once. Literacy develops and emerges over time. Much of what happens during the early literacy process will continue to influence the child as a learner for years to come.

The concept of emergent literacy and the conventional notion of reading readiness are two different ideas. The emergent literacy perspective holds that a child learns to read and write as a gradual developmental process involving all forms of language learning; readiness emphasizes teaching specific skills to prepare a child to read.

Literature-based programs can encourage and enhance children's early literacy in nursery school, kindergarten, and first grade. Although they obviously may differ in

110   Chapter 4

many respects, these programs share an emphasis on language learning and children's literature, as well as the integration of instruction in reading and writing.

Parents are crucial to the child's emerging literacy. Parents can provide a variety of literacy-related experiences in the home before, during, and following their children's entrance into an early childhood instructional program.

Introduction

*T*he process of learning to read and write begins long before a child first enters a classroom. In some ways, it begins the moment the child is born. The range of experiences children encounter during their early years will have a significant impact on their literacy development. While some experiences may influence children's literacy development more than others, all early experiences potentially influence the child as a learner.

Childhood Development and Early Literacy

For most children, literacy begins to emerge during the early years of life. The expressions "the early years" or "early childhood education" normally refer to the years from birth through age eight, from preschool through the early years of school.

Early childhood is a time of dramatic growth and development. Children proceed through stages of physical and cognitive development that facilitate different types of learning. Through their early experiences, children construct their first view of the world and build the foundation for later learning. They acquire language; in fact, children learn more language during the preschool years than they will learn for the rest of their lives. Part of this language learning includes their initial encounters with print. Each area contributes to the child's later development in learning to read and write.

Physical and Mental Development

The early childhood years are important to the child's physical development. Children reach milestones at individual times, but most learn to sit, crawl, and walk during the first year of life. By age 2, children are running, climbing up and down stairs, and gaining more control of their large and small muscles. By age 3, they have reached approximately half their adult height and can run easily, ride a tricycle, and perform many physical functions independently. Their physical growth continues throughout the preschool years, into their school-aged years and beyond.

As children's bodies develop, so do their minds (although their mental development is less easily observed). Working from an initial concrete base of experiences, children learn to confront increasingly complex intellectual tasks.

Knowledge grows as children glean information from their immediate environments through their senses. They construct their initial knowledge of reality by sensing and manipulating the objects they encounter. With repeated and expanding contact with their immediate worlds, children begin to discriminate important features of objects and relationships from the vast flow of sensory information, and thus they begin to form concepts. To the child, a "doggie" is everything from a favorite stuffed animal to the deer she sees on a trip to a petting zoo. But she learns to differentiate between stuffed toys and real animals when she tries to pull the hair on a neighbor's puppy.

A child's attention span increases dramatically over the early years. The immediate aspects of a stimulus control an infant's attention, and a child this young can sustain attention for only short periods of time. As they grow, young children develop longer attention spans, and they attend to learning-related tasks for longer periods of time and at finer levels of detail. Memory improves as well, in part because of neurological changes and in part because children develop methods or strategies that help them remember things.

As they grow, children separate their thinking from the immediate physical environment. They become capable of symbolic thought and abstract reasoning. They can mobilize perception, attention, and memory in problem solving, and they begin to develop organized plans or systematic strategies to solve problems. As they interact with others and with their environment, they begin to take an active role in selecting, organizing, and interpreting information that will help them deal with the problems they encounter. They are developing their schemata.

Schemata

A *schema* (plural = *schemata*) is an abstract concept of how humans organize and store information, an organized plan or conceptual system for arranging knowledge in our minds. The schemata children develop during the preschool years form the foundation for much of their later learning. Later experiences modify and expand these schemata.

For many years, theoreticians viewed the young child's mind as a *tabula rasa*, a blank slate not yet affected by the knowledge gained from experience. This theory held that as children grow, they acquire knowledge that is "written" on the "blank slate" of their minds. Today, rather than viewing the child's mind as a clean slate, cognitive psychologists see it as a set of empty shelves or slots, which are filled, modified, or expanded by learning. These "slots" constitute the schemata by which the child organizes information. They are modified and expanded, and verbal labels are attached, as the child grows and learns.

How does schema theory relate to the way young children learn to read and write? Here are two examples:

1. After attending several birthday parties, the preschooler builds a knowledge base that might be called a "birthday party schema" (see Putting Ideas to Work 4.1). Various parts of this schema include other

4.1 Putting Ideas to Work

Child's Schema of a Birthday Party

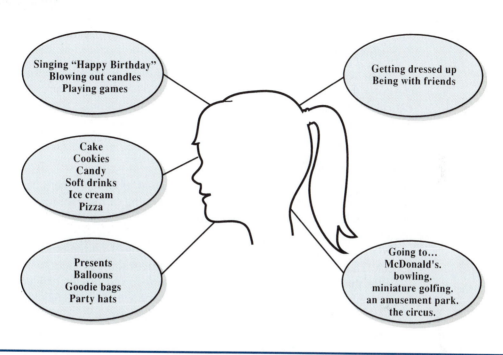

children, candy and cake, singing "Happy Birthday," blowing out candles, playing games and winning prizes, bringing presents for the birthday boy or girl, and remembering to say "thank you" when leaving. When the child subsequently reads a simple story about a birthday party, his or her comprehension of the story is affected by his or her schema. The child will be able to understand, anticipate, confirm, and relate to the story according to the information he or she already has. As the child grows and acquires more information, this birthday party schema may expand to include dancing, drinks, gag gifts, and other elements that are sometimes part of adult birthday parties. The schema will also likely be incorporated into a more generalized party schema, which might include going-away parties, office parties, wedding parties, and the like. The more schemata the child brings to early encounters with literature, the better he or she will likely understand the story.

2. In the preschool years, children encounter stories through television and through books. These stories become part of the schemata they will use when they learn to read. If a preschooler's experience includes

classic children's fairy tales such as *Hansel and Gretel, Little Red Riding Hood*, and *The Three Pigs*, the child will make them part of a "fairy tale schema," and the child's comprehension and appreciation will be more complete when he or she hears these stories in an early childhood educational setting. When children achieve a measure of independence in literacy, they will likely be able to read these stories on their own. Previous knowledge will be activated when they see the familiar words in print.

The schemata children build as a result of their preschool experiences can color their view of the world. Children who have many interesting experiences during the preschool years, who have opportunities for verbal interaction with others, and who see print regularly will have a different set of schemata and view of reading when they start to learn to read.

Language Development

Language development is one of the major areas of development in the process of gaining literacy. As the babbling and cooing of early infancy turn into vocal sounds that elicit a response from others, language acquisition is well under way. By the time they reach their first birthdays, most children have spoken their first words and shown definite signs of understanding others' speech. They have begun to use language to meet some of their basic needs.

By the age of 18 months, children's new-found power of locomotion has brought them into greater contact with the world, and they develop a repertoire of words and expressions in response. By age 3, vocabulary has expanded dramatically and most of what the child says is intelligible, even (at times) to strangers.

More remarkable, by age 3, most children have mastered syntax, the pattern of word order that allows the child to express meaning in phrases, clauses, and sentences. Although they cannot define an adjective or diagram a sentence, they can intuitively apply the intricate system of English grammar to arrange words in ways that meet a variety of needs. The one- or two-word utterances of holophrastic speech (the use of single words to represent whole classes of objects, such as referring to all adult males as "daddy") have progressed through the key-word combinations of telegraphic speech ("Mommy go bye-bye") to a form of language that comes close to adult sentences. Children this young still overgeneralize grammatical rules, making statements such as "Three mans comed here" or "I cutted my finger and it bleeded," but they can manipulate language to meet a full range of communication purposes.

During the next two years of life, children's language is well established. The child is able to communicate within the family and other social groups, has acquired a vocabulary of thousands of words, and has developed a basic competency in language. By kindergarten, most children have learned 90 percent of the phonology (sounds), morphology (meaning units), and syntax (grammatical structure) they will use as adults.

How children develop language is a subject of speculation and debate among the experts. Behaviorists explain language acquisition in terms of stimulus-response. Children hear sound and respond by imitation. Meaningful sounds are reinforced; parents show delight when the child says the sounds ma-ma and da-da, so the child learns to repeat these sounds. Although this type of classical conditioning explains some of what takes place, it cannot account for the many language forms children invent and use.

The nativist theory suggests that children are born with an innate capacity to produce language. Children have an internalized set of rules that allow them to generate, refine, and expand language. This inborn ability is triggered by what the child hears in his or her language environment.

Cognitive psychologists link language development with mental development. Although theoreticians in this field do not always agree—some say that language development enables thought to take place, and others hold that language develops to allow the expression of thought—all link language development to the thinking process.

No theory fully explains what goes on inside young children's minds as they develop the wondrous ability to communicate. And language learning never stops; we learn new words all the time, and we continue to gain skill in learning the language we speak and write. But humans never again learn as much language as they do during the early childhood years.

Early Experiences with Print

Throughout their early years, children are surrounded by environmental print. Their first encounters with print help them develop the concept of reading and writing. They see print in advertisements flashed on television and splashed on billboards. They see it on cereal boxes and milk cartons in the kitchen. They come to associate print with words that have pleasant associations for them—for example, to recognize the McDonald's logo. If they are lucky, they see print in the books their parents buy for them and hear it translated into speech as parents and others read to them. Through encounters with print, children acquire concepts of letters, words, and sentences; they come to understand what books are and what they contain; they gain the awareness that print conveys meaning.

Early encounters with print not only develop young children's knowledge about reading and writing, they also shape children's attitudes about literacy. When books have been a satisfying part of their preschool experiences, children are more likely to develop an interest and success in learning to read. If reading and writing are absent, or if books cause criticism or unpleasantness, the child may feel less positive about his or her prospects of learning to read and write.

Oral language is an essential part of the physical, mental, emotional, and social development that children experience in the preschool years. So, in many instances, is print. The nature of a child's interaction with print will influence emerging literacy.

4.2 Putting Ideas to Work
The First Three Years

*A*s children grow physically, they also develop . . .

. . . print awareness through contact with written language in the world around them.

. . . language ability, from babbling and cooing to language that meets their daily communication needs.

. . . concepts and ideas gleaned from their immediate environments.

At no stage of the child's life will growth be as dramatic as it is in the first three years.
Photos: © Elizabeth Crews/The Image Works

Reading Readiness and Emergent Literacy

The term educators traditionally used to refer to reading and writing experiences in the preschool years was *reading readiness*. *Readiness* has been defined as "preparedness to cope with a learning task" and reading readiness as "the readiness to profit from beginning reading instruction" (Harris and Hodges, 1995; p. 206, p. 212). The concept of readiness was based on the child's sense of general maturity, state of preparedness, and predisposition for reading, as well as on the time when formal reading instruction would be productive for that child. Experts believed that a child's readiness was determined by physical factors (such as adequate vision and hearing), social qualities (such as the ability to relate to others), emotional elements (like the ability to work independently), and psychological factors, especially general intelligence.

Readiness instruction consisted of drills and exercises designed to help children "get ready" to profit from formal reading instruction. Activities focused on classifying different shapes and sounds and on developing the fine motor control needed for writing. Children learned to recognize letters and match letters to sounds.

Reading readiness tests were constructed to assess children's state of readiness for reading according to these factors. Checklists on cognition, language, interest in reading, and knowledge of the alphabet were designed to determine a child's state of readiness. Preschool screening programs were carried out to determine a child's potential placement in kindergarten and to ascertain specific areas in which the child might need help. Early childhood educators designed and carried out reading readiness programs to develop the factors that would help the child get ready to learn to read when the time came.

Emergent literacy has replaced the concept of reading readiness. Rather than suggesting that a child learns to read at a precise point in time, and that he or she can be "readied" to cross the line and become a reader, emergent literacy implies that literacy develops gradually over time. In other words, it emerges. The term *emergent literacy* reflects a shift in how we view reading and writing development in young children (Teale and Sulzby, 1986).

Emergent literacy stems from research on the psychological, social, and linguistic aspects of reading and is rooted in whole language philosophy. In this view, the acquisition of literacy is analogous to the acquisition of speech. Rather than viewing the preschool years as a period of "getting ready" to read, the emergent literacy perspective views the young child's preschool experiences with print as part of the actual process of learning to read and write. When a young child can repeat the lines of a favorite story she has heard again and again, she is learning to read. When a young child independently recognizes his name in print, he is reading. These are authentic literacy experiences for the very young child.

According to the emergent literacy perspective, young children's attempts to read and write are important, viable, age-appropriate efforts to deal with print. We cannot judge the attempts according to the standards of

4.3 Putting Ideas to Work

Emergent Literacy and Reading Readiness

Vacca, Vacca, and Gove (1991) provide the following comparison between emergent literacy and reading readiness.

Comparison Between Emergent Literacy and Reading Readiness

	Emergent Literacy	Reading Readiness
Theoretical Perspective	Children are in the process of becoming literate from birth and are capable of learning what it means to use written language before entering school.	Children must master a set of basic skills before they can learn to read. Learning to read is an outcome of school-based instruction.
Acquisition of Literacy Skills and Strategies	Children learn to use written language and develop as readers and writers through active engagement with their world. Literacy develops in purposeful ways in real-life settings.	Children learn to read by mastering skills arranged in a hierarchy according to level of difficulty.
Relationship of Reading to Writing	Children progress as readers and writers. Reading and writing (as well as speaking and listening) are interrelated and develop concurrently.	Children learn to read first. Reading skills must be developed before introducing written composition.
Functional-Formal Learning	Children learn informally through interaction with and modeling from literate significant others and explorations with written language.	Children learn through formal teaching and monitoring (i.e., periodic assessment) of skills.
Individual Development	Children learn to be literate in different ways and at different rates of development.	Children progress as readers by moving through a "scope and sequence" of skills.

adult correctness. When children recite stories that they have heard read, they are not merely being "cute"; these are authentic and important efforts by the child to recreate meaning from written language.

While the readiness concept views learning to read as a two-step operation, with separate "prereading" and "reading" categories, emergent literacy views learning to read (and write) as a continuous process.

In conventional readiness programs, reading and writing are generally taught separately, the former preceding the latter. In emergent literacy, reading and writing are closely related and taught as connected operations. Young children write (though it may be a scribble unintelligible to adults at the early stages) and then read what they have written (or ask someone else to "tell me what this says"). Children learn about reading and writing simultaneously.

Freeman and Hatch (1989) summarize the differences between the traditional concept of reading readiness and the more contemporary perspective of emergent literacy:

> Reading readiness assumes the existence of a set of skills that are necessary prerequisites to formal reading instruction. Reading is viewed as a process distinct from writing. Writing should not be "taught" until children can read and spell. These reading skills, which are charted sequentially, can be learned through direct instruction. . . .
>
> An emergent literacy perspective recognizes that children begin literacy development long before school entry as they interact in their home and community. Young children develop as readers/writers; the two processes should not be taught in isolation from each other. Instead of following a preset adult-imposed sequence of skills, children are in the process of becoming literate from a very young age and therefore are not "getting ready to do it." They are actively engaged as constructors of their written language system. (p. 22)[*]

McGee and Richgels (1996) identify five assumptions about children's literacy that underlie the emergent literacy perspective: "(1) even young children are knowledgeable of written language; (2) young children's reading and writing are as important as adults' reading and writing; (3) reading and writing are interrelated and are also related to talking, drawing, and playing; (4) children acquire literacy knowledge by participating in meaningful activities; (5) children acquire literacy knowledge as they interact with others" (pp. 31–32). Most reading and writing activities in today's early childhood settings are based on these contemporary assumptions about how young children develop literacy.

Early Childhood Programs

Between the ages of 2 and 8, children often participate in programs designed to promote their growth and development. They may attend a day-care center, a play group or other home-care program, a preschool, a Head Start program, or a community program designed to provide a range of learning experiences and to lay a firm foundation for success in school. These early childhood education programs, formerly available to only a fortunate few, have become accessible to an increasingly large number of preschoolers.

Early childhood education also includes kindergarten, although kindergarten programs are now normally included as part of children's formal compulsory education. And since reading and writing skills are still generally acquired during the first couple of years of a child's formal school life, early childhood education extends into the primary grades as well.

[*]From E. B. Freeman and J. A. Hatch. (1989). "Emergent Literacy: Reconceptualizing Kindergarten Practice" in *Childhood Education*, 66:21–24. Reprinted with permission of Association for Childhood Education International.

The focus of programs offered to promote emergent literacy differs from one level to the next. In prekindergarten programs such as day care and preschool, the typical focus is global and informal. In kindergarten, the exploration of literature and the focus on literacy development usually become more immediate and specific. By first grade, formal structured programs for teaching reading and writing begin.

Nevertheless, these programs often promote literacy development in much the same way. The materials—wordless books or magnetized plastic letters, for example—are no less applicable for use in nursery school than for use in first grade. The prekindergarten teacher may engage in the same literacy-related activities as the first grade teacher—sharing stories such as Esphyr Slobodkina's *Caps for Sale*, for example. While the input for these types of activities may be similar, the output varies considerably from one level to another. The 3-year-old in preschool can hardly be expected to respond in the same way as the 6-year-old first grader. The preschooler might be expected to react to *Caps for Sale* by retelling or acting out the story. The first grader, on the other hand, might be able to independently recognize some of the more familiar words, to recall the story events in sequence, to think of alternative elements in the plot (how else the peddler might have retrieved his caps, for example), to explain why the story is humorous, and/or to read the story independently.

Although prekindergarten, kindergarten, and first grade programs are treated in different sections of this chapter, all three have a lot in common. They are developmental settings that can be designed to address children's emergent literacy. A rich environment that stimulates language development is common to all three. All are designed to develop children's awareness of, and competency in, reading and writing. Each uses children's literature as the basis for promoting literacy development. "More and more early childhood teachers are choosing literature as the core of their literacy program, and administrators at local and state levels are supporting this choice" (Salinger, 1996; p. 258).

Prekindergarten Programs

Prekindergarten (Pre-K) programs provide many children with their first organized, large-group learning experience. These programs focus on the development of the physical, emotional, intellectual, and aesthetic aspects of the whole child, with an emphasis on social and language development. Most programs try to help the child get along independently in the milieu of a group experience.

Language development receives the lion's share of attention, in part because language is an important vehicle for social interaction, and in part because language development is so essential to the learning of young children. "Studies of early readers strongly support the connection between language development and literacy development" (Thomas, 1985; p. 469). Pre-K programs are full of language experiences that promote fluent speaking, accurate listening, and overall competency in using oral language.

Language experiences typically permeate organized Pre-K programs. The constant verbal bombardment of the usually busy Pre-K school environment provides countless opportunities for children to develop and extend language. As children observe nature in science, they focus on words that can describe the rocks, plants, and small animals they see. Adults record the children's language as they learn about their relationship to the community in social studies. Simple stories and poems help the children learn basic number concepts ("One, two, buckle my shoe . . ."). Reading and writing are viewed as extensions of speaking and listening. Play is obviously important, but whether the play is aimed at large muscle development on the playground or at socialization in the housekeeping corner, language is central to the activity.

Pre-K programs that promote emergent literacy are saturated with literature. A library or reading corner—a "book nook"—is part of the learning environment. Children have many opportunities to handle books, not only to enjoy the illustrations and other contents, but also to learn how to hold a book, open it, turn its pages, and take care of it. Children's book experiences usually begin with shared stories such as Margaret Wise Brown's *Goodnight, Moon* and Wanda Gag's *Millions of Cats*, which the teacher might read a number of times during the day. Stories are read in an informal, secure atmosphere, often using Big Book versions. The atmosphere during shared stories is similar to that surrounding a bedtime story, when children usually want to hear favorites again and again. Teachers also share books one-to-one and in small group settings.

As stories are read to the children, something interesting often happens in Pre-K programs. Children pick up favorite books and begin to read these books on their own. Their reading does not involve verbatim repetition of the text or word-by-word memorization, but it does capture and recreate story meaning and often story structure. "Quite early this reading-like play becomes story-complete, page-matched, and picture-stimulated. The story tends to be reexperienced as complete semantic units transcending sentence limits" (Holdaway, 1982; p. 295). This process is particularly important to the child's emergent literacy.

In addition to a rich variety of picture storybooks, three types of books especially appropriate in Pre-K programs (as well as in kindergarten and first grade classrooms) are concept books, alphabet books, and wordless books.

Concept books are a potential source of enjoyment and learning. "A concept book is one that describes various dimensions of an object, a class of objects, or an abstract idea" (Huck, Hepler, and Hickman, 1987; p. 172). During the preschool years, children develop concepts primarily from direct experiences. Concept books support these experiences with illustrations and simple text. Concept books discuss color, size, shape, animals, opposites, travel and transportation, tools, and other topics of interest and importance to young children (see Putting Ideas to Work 4.4). One concept book especially appropriate for this level is Harlow Rockwell's *My Nursery School.* In it, the author describes activities in a nursery school and the good feeling that comes with being picked up at the end of the morning.

Concept books can stimulate oral language, sharpen perception, enhance children's growing understanding of the world around them, and provide pleasurable experiences. They allow children to see relationships between different objects and to grasp abstract ideas.

Books that invite participation are also popular with children of nursery school age. One such book that has gained enormous popularity is Eric Carle's *The Very Hungry Caterpillar,* the story of a voracious caterpillar who eats holes in the book's pages as he devours the food pictured. What makes this book so much fun for children—apart from the outrageous diet that the caterpillar enjoys—is that children can poke their fingers through the die-cut holes in the pages. The book can also provide the basis for focusing on many important concepts: days of the week, colors, fruits, life cycle of a caterpillar to a butterfly, prediction, and the like. Another long-time favorite in this category is Dorothy Hunhardt's *Pat the Bunny.* This book has tactile surfaces (a fuzzy bunny, sandpaper for Daddy's unshaven face) that extend reading beyond sight and sound.

Alphabet books have a number of potential uses in Pre-K programs. They help children focus on letters and awaken their awareness of the sounds the letters represent. Depending on the content of the pictures, ABC books help children learn to identify objects, animals, and concepts. With limited text on the page and plenty of picture clues to help with word identification, alphabet books often provide young children with their first independent reading experience.

The plethora of alphabet books available ranges from books simply illustrated with single objects on a page to books with incredible levels of detail and abstraction in their illustrations. Some ABC books are designed

4.4 Putting Ideas to Work

A Selected Sample of Concept Books

*H*ere is a limited sample of concept books that young children can enjoy and use for informational purposes in the preschool years:

> Byron Barton's *Airport*, a concept book showing details of a place that children find interesting.
> Donald Crews's *Freight Train*, a fascinating description of a journey that illustrates color, movement, and opposites, among other concepts.
> Tana Hoban's *Is It Red? Is It Yellow? Is It Blue?* in which colors are brightly illustrated with photographs of common objects. Ms. Hoban has written a number of other concept books popular with nursery school children.
> John Reiss's *Shapes*, with colored pictures of shapes you can find in common objects.
> Anne Rockwell's *First Comes Spring*, which illustrates the concept of the seasons of the year.
> Harlow Rockwell's *My Kitchen*, with pictures of everyday objects that children can find in their environment.
> Peter Spier's *Fast-Slow, High-Low: A Book of Opposites*, which illustrates the concept of opposites in an interesting, often sophisticated, way.

These titles represent only a small sampling of the range of topics concept books discuss. The books can be used for pleasure and for learning experiences in preschools.

for the simple purpose of identification and naming; others incorporate themes, simple narratives, puzzles, and other informational material. Still others come with records or tapes that encourage pupils to sing along. Most are fascinating vehicles for children and parents to enjoy together.

In addition to providing enjoyment and awakening early alphabet awareness, ABC books can help develop vocabulary and stimulate language use.

Counting books, which are related to ABC books, integrate illustrations and numerals to develop various number concepts. Books such as Tana Hoban's *Count and See* and Nancy Tafuri's *Who's Counting* illustrate number-symbol relationships and help young children become aware of numbers. In addition, counting books extend knowledge beyond number awareness. Counting books can be effective devices for literacy-related learning in early childhood settings.

Wordless books, described more fully in the section on kindergarten programs, are also good books to use in Pre-K settings. Because these books contain no words, very young children have no trouble reading them. Books without words can be used to stimulate language development and to let the children handle books. Children learn to respond to the pictures depicting the story line, dictate stories based on the books, and enjoy the experiences the books provide.

4.5 Putting Ideas to Work
A Sampler of Alphabet Books

*H*undreds of alphabet books are available for use with young learners. Here are a handful of highly regarded widely used ABC books, though some may be a bit sophisticated for very young children:

Mitsumasa Anno's *Anno's Alphabet*, an ingeniously illustrated book full of intriguing visual illusions.

Jane Bayer's *A, My Name Is Alice*, in which the words of the popular old jumprope rhyme are delightfully illustrated by Stephen Kellogg.

Burt Kitchen's *Animal Alphabet*, a simple alphabet book with large block letters and striking animal pictures.

Anita Lobel's *Alison's Zinnia*, an entertaining walk through a garden of flowers from A to Z.

Arnold and Anita Lobel's *On Market Street*, an account of a boy who lavishly "shops" his way through the alphabet.

Bill Martin, Jr., and John Archambault's *Chicka Chicka Boom Boom*, an alphabet book with a lively, jazzy rhythm and a delightful style that children love to read.

Margaret Musgrove's *Ashanti to Zulu: African Traditions*, the only alphabet book ever to win the Caldecott Medal, focusing on objects and ideas from African culture.

Helen Oxenbury's *ABC of Things*, with entertaining illustrations.

Stephen T. Johnson's *Alphabet City*, a book in which letter forms are embedded in photographs of city scenes.

Laura Rankin's *The Handiwork Alphabet*, a striking presentation of finger-spelled letters used in sign language.

Jerry Pallotta's *The Icky Bug Alphabet Book*, one of several Palotta ABC books that introduce content as well as letters of the alphabet.

Brian Wildsmith's *ABC*, an old favorite with brilliant illustrations by a famous illustrator.

Cathi Hepworth's *Antics! An Alphabet Anthology*, a rather sophisticated but fascinating set of alphabet entries.

Literally hundreds of other alphabet books are available for use in schools and homes, including books that extend learning in curriculum areas in the upper grades, such as Ann Whitford Paul's *Eight Hands Round: A Patchwork Alphabet*, which presents a history lesson by illustrating various types of patchwork quilts, and Anne Doubilet's *Under The Sea from A to Z*, a science alphabet book featuring aquatic creatures from anemone to zebrafish.

Books with a multicultural perspective are important in preschool programs. From their earliest years, children need the chance to enjoy literature that reflects the rich cultural diversity of our society. Part of the diet of literature shared in the early years should be books like Virginia Grossman's *Ten Little Rabbits*, which depicts the activities of ten tribes of Native Americans from all regions of the United States. Another good addition is Muriel Feelings's *Moja Means One: A Swahili Counting Book,* which relates number concepts to African cultures.

Books reflecting language diversity should also be part of children's Pre-K experiences. Bilingual versions of popular titles such as Eric Carle's *The Very Hungry Caterpillar* can be enjoyed along with the original. Some books have non-English and English text side by side on each page. These books are especially important in classrooms with non-English-speaking children. Moreover, bilingual books provide Pre-K children with early exposure to other languages.

Writing in pre-K programs usually takes the form of dictation, as teachers transcribe what the children say about pictures they have drawn or write down stories the children tell. Children's writing can also be part of their play activity as they compile grocery lists or recreate signs. At this level, children's "free writing" will involve scribbling and other experimental forms. Their spelling will likely use random letters and reflect their prephonetic stage, but such activities help children become aware of the functions of writing. Large sheets of paper (newspaper rolls work well) and writing implements (large markers, crayons, paints, and pencils) are available for children's independent attempts at writing.

Although preschool programs are by nature informal, they offer many opportunities for children to develop awareness and competency that will help them when they enter a more formal program in kindergarten.

Kindergarten

For some children, kindergarten is their first experience with directed learning in a large group setting. For others, it is another step in a series of early educational experiences. For all children, kindergarten is a time of more intensive literacy-related activities. Children bring a developing form of literacy when they enter kindergarten, and the number of activities directly related to reading and writing increases.

Like prekindergarten programs, kindergarten programs typically stress the development of the whole child, with a special emphasis on socialization. For decades, in fact, conventional wisdom suggested that no reading instruction at all should take place in kindergarten. This belief was the result of a well-publicized and widely accepted 1931 research study which concluded that children must reach a mental age of 6.5 before they learn to read (Morphett and Washburne, 1931). The conclusion that it was safer not to try to teach children to read before they reached the mental age of 6.5 "gained almost universal acceptance and probably influenced educational programs as much as any single research investigation" (Gentile, 1983; p. 171). This conclusion was quickly disproved (Gates, 1937), as other researchers showed that instructional factors were more crucial than mental age to success in beginning reading. Nevertheless, the myth persisted that any reading instruction attempted before the magic mental age of 6.5 was at best useless and at worst harmful.

4.6 Putting Ideas to Work
NAEYC Position Statement on Developmentally Appropriate Practice

*T*he position statement of the National Association for the Education of Young Children (NAEYC) on developmentally appropriate curriculum and instructional practices for young children includes the following section on literacy instruction:

Appropriate Practice

The goals of the language and literacy program are for children to expand their ability to communicate orally and through reading and writing, and to enjoy these activities. Technical skills and subskills are taught as needed to accomplish these larger goals, not as the goal itself. Teachers provide generous amounts of time and a variety of interesting activities for children to develop language, writing, spelling, and reading ability, such as: looking through, reading, or being read high-quality children's literature and nonfiction for pleasure and information; drawing, dictating, and writing about their activities or fantasies; planning and implementing projects that involve research at suitable levels of difficulty; creating teacher-made or child-written lists of steps to follow to accomplish a project; discussing what was read; preparing a weekly class newspaper; interviewing various people to obtain information for projects; making books of various kinds (riddle books, books about pets); listening to recordings or viewing high-quality films of children's books; being read at least one high-quality book or part of a book each day by adults or older children; using the school library and the library area of the classroom regularly. Some children read aloud daily to the teacher, another child, or a small group of children, while others do so weekly. Subskills such as learning letters, phonics, and word recognition are taught as needed to individual children and small groups through enjoyable games and activities. Teachers use the teacher's edition of the basal reader series as a guide to plan projects and hands-on activities

relevant to what is read and to structure learning situations. Teachers accept children's invented spelling with minimal reliance on teacher-prescribed spelling lists. Teachers also teach literacy as the need arises when working on science, social studies, and other content areas.

Inappropriate Practice

The goal of the reading program is for each child to pass the standardized tests given throughout the year at or near grade level. Reading is taught as the acquisition of skills and subskills. Teachers teach reading only as a discrete subject. When teaching other subjects, they do not feel that they are teaching reading. A sign of excellent teaching is considered to be silence in the classroom and so conversation is allowed infrequently during select times. Language, writing, and spelling instruction are focused on workbooks. Writing is taught as grammar and penmanship. The focus of the reading program is the basal reader, used only in reading groups and accompanying workbooks and worksheets. The teacher's role is to prepare and implement the reading lesson in the teacher's guidebook for each group each day and to see that other children have enough seatwork to keep them busy throughout the reading group time. Phonics instruction stresses learning rules rather than developing understanding of systematic relationships between letters and sounds. Children are required to complete worksheets or to complete the basal reader although they are capable of reading at a higher level. Everyone knows which children are in the lowest reading group. Children's writing efforts are rejected if correct spelling and standard English are not used.

National Association for the Education of Young Children. (1988). NAEYC Position Statement on Developmentally Appropriate Practice in the Primary Grades, Serving 5- through 8-Year-Olds. *Young Children* 43:64–84. Reprinted by permission of the National Association for the Education of Young Children, 1834 Connecticut Avenue NW, Washington, DC 20009.

Today's situation has certainly changed. Well-balanced kindergarten programs continue to attend to the full range of children's needs, but programs now provide a rich variety of experiences to promote children's growing competency in reading and writing. Most children arrive in kindergarten with some knowledge of reading and writing. As they try to make sense of their world, most have learned that print has a place in that world. Kindergarten literacy training is designed to build on this knowledge.

Metalinguistic Awareness. Among the essential concepts of emergent literacy is metalinguistic awareness. Metalinguistic awareness involves the ability to reflect upon, and talk about, language concepts. At the early learning stage, this involves such concepts as what a book is, what it contains, how we use it, what a word is, the function and content of the signs children see all around them, what a letter is, the correspondence between speech and print, the correspondence between sentence units in speech and similar units in print, and the relationship between a reader's eyes and a writer's pencil as they move from left to right in a line of print, as well as other concepts about the written word. This metalinguistic knowledge about language develops as part of emergent literacy. Teachers support and extend an understanding of literature by talking about books, authors, illustrators, and what is contained on the title page. Later, as independence develops, children can locate this information themselves.

Many children entering school have developed considerable metalinguistic awareness in the home because their parents regularly share and talk about books, casually but deliberately call attention to letters and sounds ("There's the M in milk, the same as in Mommy and McDonalds"), and demonstrate reading for functional purposes ("Let's look in the cookbook to see if we can find a recipe for muffins").

In more formal school settings, the same kind of informal teaching can occur. Every encounter with print provides opportunities for teachers to promote metalinguistic awareness. For example, as teachers share stories in Big Books or favorite nursery rhymes written on charts, they can sweep their hands over the lines of print, maintaining the rhythm of the language as they point to key words. When children are familiar with these stories and poems, the children can do the pointing, indicating a general awareness of the correspondence between the markings on the line and the words they are saying. The ability to match words or phrases written on cards to the same words or phrases in the text is another indication of the young child's awareness of the speech-to-print relationship in language. Each time a teacher transcribes children's language, either in group or individual settings, the opportunity is there to develop metalinguistic awareness in children.

Language Development. Continual attention to children's language development through speaking and listening is a vital part of literacy instruction in kindergarten, as it is in Pre-K programs. Large- and small-group oral language activities—show and tell, flannel-board stories, creative dramatics, choral speaking, conversation and discussion, puppetry, and other activities—help children increase their vocabularies, build sentence structures, expand their competency in listening and speaking, and generally improve their ability to manipulate verbal concepts.

In the language-rich classroom, print is everywhere—in displays of children's books, on word lists related to areas of interest, on charts of stories that children have dictated, on signs and posters. There are directions about keeping the housekeeping corner clean and a note pad next to the phone for "taking messages." The classroom features an "I Can Read Board," which posts everything that children can read, from bubble-gum wrappers to restaurant placemats.

Label words are a feature of many early learning environments. These words are written on cards and attached to common objects in the classroom: *door, window, chair, desk*, and so on. Label words serve a number of functions. They clearly establish the object-symbol relationship, they often become basic sight words that children can instantly recognize, and they can help teach letter recognition and other literacy-related concepts. Some teachers place single label words in sentence context—*I sit in my **chair**. The sun shines through the **window**.*—with the target word written in a color different from the rest of the sentence. Children help make these label words on the first day of school as they learn their way around the classroom.

Literature in Kindergarten.

Much of the direct literacy-related instruction in kindergarten is literature based. The classroom library is full of books appropriate for reading in kindergarten, books like Bill Martin, Jr.'s *Brown Bear, Brown Bear, What Do You See?* and Pat Hutchins's *Rosie's Walk*. Children hear about the people who wrote these stories. Children read these stories to one another in pairs and small groups. They hear good stories read to them several times a day. Children in kindergarten are regular visitors to the school library, in search of books both for enjoyment and for information. They share stories they have read and act out stories they have heard. They begin to write and dictate their own versions of favorite stories. They use trade books to find out more about topics like dinosaurs and stars. In short, encounters with books permeate their classroom lives, and these books become the vehicles for learning to read and write.

Reading and writing in kindergarten focuses on both narrative and expository text. Narrative text tells the stories that children traditionally enjoy—stories that have a beginning, a middle, and an end. Expository text, reading material that conveys information rather than tells a story, also has a place in the kindergarten program. Informational picture books about a variety of topics can expand children's developing knowledge of their world, along with their emerging literacy competencies. Pupils can do many of the same activities with informational books that they do with storybooks. Putnam (1991) describes how dramatizing nonfiction books stimulates language development and builds important concepts for emergent readers and writers.

Wordless books are valuable teaching tools in kindergarten (and in the years beyond). As the name suggests, wordless books contain virtually no

4.7 Putting Ideas to Work
Using Literature in Kindergarten

*F*ollowing is an example of some ways in which trade books can be used for literacy and related learning activities in kindergarten:

The teacher selects Maurice Sendak's *Chicken Soup with Rice*, a whimsical and imaginative poem about a boy who drinks chicken soup all year long.

The teacher reads the poem aloud in a large group setting at the beginning of the school day, sharing Sendak's delightful illustrations. Because children love this poem, the children will probably ask the teacher to repeat the reading several times and will join in the refrain after the second or third reading.

The teacher will read the poem several times during the same day (or on subsequent days) so that the children become thoroughly familiar with the text and learn to relate the spoken form of the poem to the written form.

Since Carole King recorded a lively version of *Chicken Soup With Rice* in song as part of the musical *Really Rosie,* the children can follow along the lines of the poem as they listen to the words sung on tape. Even without the music, children can read the book on their own using the illustrations.

There is a strong element of rhyming in this poem. Building on rhyming elements like *rice/ice/nice, door/floor/more,* and *peep/deep/cheap*, children develop additional rhymes or substitute alternative rhyming words in the poem.

Since each verse begins with a month of the year, the teacher might make a list of the names of each month to be used while the poem is read. Children certainly are not required to memorize these as sight words, but they do gain an awareness of the names of the months in order. Words associated with the various months can provide a direct spin-off vocabulary activity.

Sendak has filled this poem with an array of sensory images, so pupils can talk about the tastes, smells, and touches portrayed in the poem.

As an extension of the poem itself, the teacher writes on a chart and reads with the students a recipe for chicken soup. The teacher may even bring the ingredients in and guide children in making a pot of chicken soup in the classroom. Now children become aware of the differences between the fanciful language of the poem and the practical language of expository text.

Based on their repeated exposure to the poem, children write or dictate and illustrate their own imaginative stanzas for *Chicken Soup with Rice* or other poems that strike their fancy.

These and hundreds of other ideas can help children make the jump from spoken to printed language, using text that they genuinely enjoy.

text; the entire story is presented through illustrations. Not only do the illustrations carry the story idea or plot; they also develop characterization, portray setting, convey theme, and deliver other literary qualities that characterize stories told in text. Some wordless books contain detailed information in their illustrations; for example, John Goodall's *The Story of an English Village* portrays changes that occurred in an English village from the 14th through 20th centuries.

Wordless books offer several unique advantages as instructional tools in the kindergarten classroom. First, they serve as a powerful stimulus for

4.8 Putting Ideas to Work
A Cross-Grade Library Assignment

*D*uring the week, the teacher had read a number of stories about the moon—Maurice Sendak's fantasy *In the Night Kitchen; Why the Sun and Moon Live in the Sky,* an African folk tale retold by Elphinstone Dayrell; Laura Jane Coates's *Marcella and the Moon;* Jane Yolen's *Owl Moon;* and others. As a result, the kindergarten students had generated a number of questions about the moon: *Why does the moon change shape? What makes the moon shine? What is the moon made of?* The teacher made a list of the research questions the children had generated, wrote them on slips of paper, and gave them to a group of five kindergartners. These children then went to the library to find answers to the questions.

When they arrived at the library, five fifth graders assigned to help find the answers met their younger counterparts. With the help of a library aide (who had been notified in advance), the pupils formed pairs and researched the information together. Then the kindergartners reported the answers back to the class. In this cross-grade cooperative learning activity, the fifth graders had a purposeful, authentic assignment in library research, while the younger children saw print used for information-gathering purposes and learned that the library is a place to find answers to their questions.

language development. Having children tell the story the pictures portray is a natural language experience. The illustrations provide a focus that allows children to suggest words to describe the people, places, and actions depicted, and the books provide a structure that children can fashion their own stories around. The children can dictate stories on a tape recorder, and different versions of these transcribed stories can encourage discussion, critical thinking, and early reading experiences. In the later grades, wordless books can be used for book reports since, as one teacher joked, "The kids can't just copy words from the book for their report."

Wordless books foster positive attitudes in young children because they provide a fail-safe reading experience: there are no words to get "right" or "wrong." As a kindergarten pupil once explained to a curious classmate, the black lines on the page of a book are "for people who have not learned to read pictures yet."

A group lesson with a wordless book can engage children in the full range of reading/thinking strategies that they will use when they encounter text as part of their reading (see Putting Ideas to Work 4.9). These books can stimulate critical and creative thinking, as children suggest solutions to problems or think of alternative endings to stories. Illustrations in informational wordless books can clarify abstract concepts and add information to the young child's developing schemata. Wordless books may even serve as cross-age tutoring devices for fifth graders working with first graders (Ellis and Preston, 1984).

Wordless books are popular at various levels of early childhood education. Obviously, the level of sophistication in response will vary according to

4.9 Putting Ideas to Work

Developing a Reading Lesson with a Wordless Book

Wordless books are effective in helping young children develop reading techniques before they can recognize a single word of print. In *Bobo's Dream*, Martha Alexander uses pictures alone to tell an amusing and captivating story about a boy and his dog. The boy buys his small dachshund a bone and takes him to the park, where a larger dog takes the bone away. The boy retrieves the bone for his pet. The little dog sleeps and dreams about returning the favor by retrieving his master's football from a group of older bullies. Through his dream, the little dog finds the courage to intimidate his tormentor.

 Without a word of print, this story can be used to generate a lesson involving a full range of comprehension skills that can be applied to print. With careful questioning about the pictures, the teacher can develop a lesson that helps children focus on:

Setting a purpose. "See if you can tell how Bobo's dream changed his attitude."

Following the literal sequence of events. "What happens after the big dog takes Bobo's bone away?"

Forming and confirming hypotheses. "What do you think the boy will do now?"

Inferring actions and feelings. "How does Bobo feel when . . . ?"

Recognizing elements of humor and irony. "Why do you think Martha Alexander makes Bobo look so large in this picture?"

Seeing cause-effect relationships. "Why did Bobo bark at the big dog near the end of the story?"

Recognizing theme. "What lesson can you learn from this story?"

Relating the story to the pupils' own experiences. "Can you tell about a time when you were brave?"

 Wordless books provide rich language experiences as children generate the text. When they recount the story based on the pictures, students have the opportunity to use a variety of words to describe the actions and scenes depicted, to use sentences that relate the story in sequence, and to tell about their reactions to what is happening.

 Beyond these speaking, thinking, and reading experiences are opportunities to develop writing skills. For each simply illustrated page, children can dictate or write sentences to describe the action and produce their own versions of *Bobo's Dream*.

---

the age of the child. In prekindergarten, for example, wordless books might be used to encourage children to describe feelings. In the primary grades, they might be used for full-blown lessons on story structure. At any level, these books can serve as valuable tools to enhance children's developing literacy.

 Big Books are also popular devices used for literature-based reading instruction in kindergarten (as well as in Pre-K settings and first grade classrooms). The introduction of Big Books in the early 1980s greatly strengthened the use of literature in school programs for helping young children become competent in beginning reading skills. Big Books spread with incredible rapidity, so that now they are used widely in early childhood reading programs, both to share literature with children and to foster fluent reading.

4.10 Putting Ideas to Work

Authors Who Write Stories without Words

Rather than a list containing scores of wordless books that can be used in kindergarten, here is a list of well-known authors/illustrators of these books. Look for these authors in selecting wordless books for the classroom.

- Martha Alexander, who wrote *Bobo's Dream* and *Out, Out, Out!*
- Mitsumasa Anno, whose brilliantly designed series of wordless books are among the most fascinating and popular available.
- Alexandra Day, who wrote the hilarious and popular accounts of Carl, the caring rottweiler in such books as *Good Dog, Carl* and *Carl's Christmas*.
- Tomie de Paola, whose *Pancakes for Breakfast* is one of the most widely enjoyed wordless books.
- John S. Goodall, whose wordless books delight young children. Some, like *The Story of An English Village*, entertain and inform even older readers.
- Pat Hutchins, who designed the fascinating *Changes, Changes*.
- Ezra Jack Keats, who illustrated *Clementine's Cactus*.
- Fernando Krahn, whose clever illustrations contribute to lively action in a number of wordless books.
- Mercer Mayer, whose series and other wordless books are hilarious.
- Jan Omerod, whose works represent some of the best examples of wordless books available.
- Peter Spier, who consistently entertains and informs with his books.
- David Wiesner, who authored the enormously engaging, Caldecott-award-winning *Tuesday*.

Some of these authors—such as Mitsumasa Anno and Jan Omerod—specialize in picture books alone; others—such as Pat Hutchins and Ezra Jack Keats—are authors of award-winning picture storybooks as well.

This list of names is a starting point. Children's libraries are full of quality wordless books written by other authors for use in the kindergarten classroom and beyond.

In the simplest sense, Big Books are oversized copies of children's books, with enlarged print and illustrations. The size of Big Books varies slightly, but the books are large enough so that all children in a group can see them clearly when they are mounted on an easel. When they can see the print and illustrations, children in groups can participate actively in early reading experiences. Related in theory and practice to the idea of family storybook reading, "enlarged texts allow groups of children to see and react to the printed page as it is being read aloud, a factor considered key to the effectiveness of shared reading between parent and child. . . . Fundamental concepts are acquired through actual participation in a nonthreatening, joyful manner" (Strickland and Morrow, 1990; p. 342).

Stories that lend themselves especially well to Big Book presentation have repetitive language, stories that feature "strong rhythm and rhyme, repeated patterns, refrains, logical sequences, supportive illustrations, and traditional story structure that provide emergent readers support in gaining meaning from text" (Heald-Taylor, 1987; p. 6). Examples of such stories include:

Brown Bear, Brown Bear, What Do You See? by Bill Martin, Jr. (Brown bear, brown bear, what do you see?)

The Gingerbread Man (Run, run as fast as you can. You can't catch me, I'm the Gingerbread Man!)

The Little Red Hen ("Not I," said the cat. "Not I," said the dog. "Not I," said the pig. "Then I'll do it myself," said the Little Red Hen.)

Good Night Owl, by Pat Hutchins (And owl tried to sleep.)

I Know an Old Lady (I know an old lady who swallowed a fly. I don't know why she swallowed a fly. Perhaps she'll die.)

This is the House That Jack Built (This is the cat that swallowed the rat that lives in the house that Jack built.)

These books contain predictable, patterned language that enables readers to make educated guesses about what the author is saying and how he or she will say it. Children use context clues to determine what the next word will be. Seeing and repeating high-frequency words and phrases in dependable contexts helps children build a sight vocabulary, a store of words they can recognize independently in other contexts. Patterned books based on rhyme—such as Barbara Emberley's *Drummer Hoff*—can help children learn word families and phonetic elements as well. Even pupils who are having difficulty with beginning reading can participate successfully in the shared reading of a Big Book as they chime in on the oft-repeated refrains.

Publishing Big Books has become big business. Publishers' catalogs are full of lists of Big Books available for use in classrooms, and enlarged editions of popular stories are on the shelves in supermarkets and discount stores. But Big Books need not be purchased. With chart paper, pupils frequently make their own Big Books in the classroom, versions of popular stories as well as their own creations.

Strickland (1989) provides a number of suggestions for reading-related activities to do with Big Books. They include tracking print (to develop left-to-right directionality), thinking aloud (to demonstrate thinking strategies while reading), cloze activities in which pupils fill in missing words (to promote the use of context clues), examining text features (including punctuation and other features of print), and others.

Apart from enjoying smaller editions of the book independently, numerous opportunities exist for follow-up experiences to Big Book lessons. Perhaps the most common follow-up is writing, as children dictate or write and illustrate their own versions of predictable stories using the language model of the text. For example, Pat Hutchins's *Good Night, Owl*, which contains strong predictable language patterns accounting for why owl could not sleep, provides a language model for Halloween stories ("Ghost tried to

4.11 Putting Ideas to Work

Steps in a Shared Reading Lesson with a Big Book

1. *Introduce the book,* reading the title and the author's and illustrator's names, calling attention to the illustration on the cover and asking pupils to predict what the story might be about. Set a listening/reading purpose: "Let's read this book to see how. . . ."
2. *Read the book aloud* to the group, pointing to the lines of print to reinforce the writing-reading connection. Stop periodically (not so often as to disrupt the rhythm or enjoyment of the story) to ask such questions as, "What do you think will happen next? Why? How does (the character) feel? How do you know?" Use subsequent parts of the story to confirm hypotheses.
3. *Read the book again,* this time inviting children to join in on predictable parts to involve them actively in the reading. Children can read predictable parts in unison, or different groups can read different lines ("Not I," said the fox.). After reading, talk about the story. Ask pupils what they liked about it, what problem the main character had, how he or she solved the problem, other ways he or she might have solved the problem. But be careful about killing interest through overanalysis.
4. *Extend participation* by giving the students cards containing words, phrases, or sentences from the story. Let individual children hold up their cards as their words occur in the story or match their words with the written words in the text.
5. *Extend the lesson* by having students read the story on their own during free time, make puppets based on story characters, write their own versions of the story, note words that begin with the same letter or sound, use sentences from the story written on oaktag strips to reconstruct the story, role play, or engage in other story-related activities that will promote their emergent literacy. Not all Big Books ought to be treated in the same way. Some can simply be read in unison for the pleasure of participation and the enjoyment of the story. At other times, the teacher may plan different lessons to develop reading strategies.

sleep"), stories about winter animals ("Bear tried to sleep"), and creative adaptations about machines ("Computer couldn't sleep").

While designed primarily for early literacy experiences, Big Books can be used in different and creative ways from Pre-K through the upper elementary years. Ideas for writing based on the content of Big Books are virtually limitless.

Phonemic Awareness and Alphabet Training. While children often become aware of letters and sounds in their prekindergarten encounters with print, they become more directly involved with these elements of written language through kindergarten literacy experiences. These experience help develop alphabet and phonemic awareness as part of their emerging literacy.

Alphabet training involves recognition of the 26 symbols that make up all the words we read and write. For many years, learning letter names and sounds has been an indispensable element for success in beginning reading, since alphabet knowledge is important to skilled reading and ranks among the best predictors of reading achievement (Bond and Dykstra, 1967; Durrell, 1980; Adams, 1990).

Alphabet awareness is part of the metalinguistic knowledge that characterizes the child's emerging literacy. In kindergarten, alphabet training aims to build the basic decoding skills children will need to learn to read.

Alphabet awareness includes more than the ability to say or sing the alphabet from A to Z. It includes:

knowing the names of the letters when the teacher points to them in random order;

matching uppercase (capital) letters with their lowercase equivalents;

being able to write the letters of the alphabet; and

knowing basic letter sounds; that is, being able to identify the first letter in a word based on the initial sound of the word.

Activities centered on alphabet awareness often provide practice in visual and auditory perception. For example, matching letters with the same shape requires visual awareness; identifying rhyming elements in Maurice Sendak's *Chicken Soup with Rice* involves auditory discrimination and letter-sound recognition; and tracing and writing letters requires visual-motor skills. Children can develop much alphabet knowledge through writing. As teachers transcribe dictated stories and as children begin to write independently, the questions "What sound do you hear?" and "What letter do I need to use to make this sound?" help develop awareness of sound-symbol relationships.

Alphabet books are made to order for helping children learn letter names and sounds. Beyond using these books in the classroom, kindergarten children can create their own alphabet books by drawing or cutting out pictures for each letter. Student-created ABC books can focus on a number of themes—ABC and Me, The ABC of Jobs, The ABC of Transportation, or The ABC of Animals, for example (Jones, 1983). These books can extend into a whole range of related learning beyond mastery of the symbols of written language. Joan Walsh Anglund's *In a Pumpkin Shell* is a Mother Goose alphabet book that contains letters for key words in popular nursery rhymes: C for *clock* in "Hickory, Dickory, Dock"; D for *dog* in "Old Mother Hubbard"; E for *early* in "Early to Bed." Many children come to school without ever having met Mother Goose, and this book can be used effectively with the rich language and sound patterns of popular nursery rhymes.

Phonemic awareness involves paying conscious attention to the phonemes that make up the basic sound elements in words. Children come to school automatically blending individual phonemes in the words they speak. They need to become more conscious of these discrete sound elements as they learn to read and write.

Phonemic awareness is essential in learning to read. "A substantial body of literature has provided evidence of the importance of phonemic awareness . . . in producing later reading success" (Williams, 1995; p. 185). Whether it's a prerequisite to or a consequence of learning to read (it's probably both), phonemic awareness is closely linked to success in beginning reading.

Phonemic awareness involves:

Matching words by sounds. "Which two words begin with the same sound: *bat, bell, rock*?" or "Which two words rhyme: *door, book, look*?" The emphasis in these activities is on the sound, not the letter that represents it.

Isolating the sounds in a word. "Which sound do you hear at the beginning of these words: *road, run, rip*?" or "Which sound do you hear at the end of these three names: *Dirk, Rick, Clark*?" Again, the emphasis is on the sound and not the letter.

Blending or combining individual speech sounds to form a word. "Here are three separate sounds: /r/, /a/, /t/; can you put these words together to form a word?" This raises to a conscious level the notion that spoken words are made up of individual sounds.

Adding, deleting, or substituting sounds in words. "If you take the /m/ sound away from *meat*, what word do you hear?" or "If I take the /r/ sound from *rat* and replace it with a /b/ sound, what new word do I have?" This lends itself to rhyming activities.

Segmenting a word into its constituent sounds. "See if you can put these three sounds together into a word: /r/, /u/, and /n/." Segmentation is one of the more difficult tasks for the young child to perform.

Often, phonemic awareness activities are part of direct instruction in the kindergarten classroom. However, they can be made part of games, songs, word play, and other oral language activities that promote verbal development in a rich learning environment. "The objective of any phonemic awareness activity should be to facilitate children's ability to perceive that their speech is made up of a series of sounds" (Yopp, 1992; p. 699).

How does instruction in phonemic awareness fit into a literature-based program in kindergarten? Trade books that play with sound through rhyme, alliteration, and other sound elements are normally part of literature-based instruction in the early years (see Putting Ideas to Work 4.12 for a list of these books). The rhyming schemes of Mother Goose provide a mother lode of material for phonetic awareness. Books such as Barbara Emberley's *Drummer Hoff* offer many opportunities for phonemic awareness activities. Richgels, Poremba, and McGee (1996) describe a classroom process which makes alphabetic awareness part of the shared reading of simple children's books in the context of everyday, functional literacy activities.

It is indisputable that knowledge of letter names and phonemic elements in words is important to successful reading and writing (Adams, 1990). But knowing letter names and becoming aware of phonemes in words are not ends in themselves. These are parts of children's emergent literacy that will help them achieve independence in decoding and encoding printed language. Children do not learn one isolated speech sound at a time when learning to talk; they learn language in its entirety. Focusing on letters and sounds should not divert children from focusing on meaning. To the extent

4.12 Putting Ideas to Work
Books to Develop Phonemic Awareness

Yopp (1995a) has developed an annotated list of books that draw attention to language sounds—books that are useful to teachers who are helping young children become aware of phonemes. Criteria for selecting the books included: 1. the play with language is an explicit, dominant feature of the book; 2. the books are appropriate for young children; and 3. they lend themselves to language play. Yopp's list includes:

Brown, M. W. (1993). *Four Fur Feet*. New York: Doubleday.

Buller, J., and Schade, S. (1988). *I Love You, Good Night*. New York: Simon & Schuster.

Cameron, P. (1961). *"I Can't," Said the Ant*. New York: Coward-McCann.

Carle, E. (1974). *All about Arthur* (an absolutely absurd ape). New York: Franklin Watts.

Carter, D. (1990). *More Bugs in Boxes*. New York: Simon & Schuster.

Deming, A. G. (1994). *Who is Tapping at My Window?* New York: Penguin.

de Regniers, B., Moore, E., White, M., and Carr, J. (1988). *Sing a Song of Popcorn*. New York: Scholastic.

Ehlert, L. (1988). *Eating the Alphabet: Fruits and Vegetables from A to Z*. San Diego: Harcourt Brace Jovanovich.

Emberley, B. (1992). *One Wide River to Cross*. Boston: Little, Brown.

Fortunata. (1968). *Catch a Little Fox*. New York: Scholastic.

Galdone, P. (1968). *Henny Penny*. New York: Scholastic.

Geraghty, P. (1992). *Stop that Noise!* New York: Crown.

Gordon, J. (1991). *Six Sleepy Sheep*. New York: Puffin Books.

Hague, K. (1984). *Alphabears*. New York: Henry Holt.

Hawkins, C., and Hawkins, J. (1986). *Tog the Dog*. New York: G. P. Putnam's Sons.

Hymes, L., and Hymes, J. (1964). *Oodles of Noodles*. New York: Young Scott Books.

Kraus, R. (1985). *I Can Fly*. New York: Golden Press.

Kuskin, K. (1990). *Roar and More*. New York: Harper Trophy.

Lewison, W. (1992). *Buzz Said the Bee*. New York: Scholastic.

Martin, B. (1974). *Sounds of a Powwow*. New York: Holt, Rinehart, & Winston.

Marzollo, J. (1989). *The Teddy Bear Book*. New York: Dial.

Obligado, L. (1983). *Faint Frogs Feeling Feverish and Other Terrifically Tantalizing Tongue Twisters*. New York: Viking.

Ochs, C. P. (1991). *Moose on the Loose*. Minneapolis: Carolrhoda Books.

Otto, C. (1991). *Dinosaur Chase*. New York: Harper Trophy.

Parry, C. (1991). *Zoomerang-a-Boomerang: Poems to Make Your Belly Laugh*. New York: Puffin Books.

Patz, N. (1983). *Moses Supposes his Toeses Are Roses*. San Diego: Harcourt Brace Jovanovich.

Pomerantz, C. (1993). *If I Had a Paka*. New York: Mulberry.

Prelutsky, J. (1982). *The Baby Uggs Are Hatching*. New York: Mulberry.

Prelutsky, J. (1989). *Poems of A. Nonny Mouse*. New York: Alfred A. Knopf.

Continued on next page.

Adapted from Yopp, H. K. (1995). Read-Aloud Books for Developing Phonemic Awareness: An Annotated Bibliography. *The Reading Teacher* 48:538–542.

Provenson, A., and Provenson, M. (1977). *Old Mother Hubbard*. New York: Random House.
Raffi. (1987). *Down by the Bay*. New York: Crown.
Raffi. (1989). *Tingalayo*. New York: Crown.
Sendak, M. (1990). *Alligators All Around: An Alphabet*. New York: Harper Trophy.
Seuss, Dr. (Theodore Geisel). (1963). *Dr. Seuss's ABC*. New York: Random House.
Seuss, Dr. (Theodore Geisel). (1965). *Fox in Socks*. New York. Random House.
Seuss, Dr. (Theodore Geisel). (1974). *There's a Wocket in My Pocket*. New York: Random House.
Shaw, N. (1989). *Sheep on a Ship*. Boston: Houghton Mifflin.
Showers, P. (1991). *The Listening Walk*. New York: Harper Trophy.
Silverstein, S. (1964). *A Giraffe and a Half*. New York: HarperCollins.
Staines, B. (1989). *All God's Critters Got a Place in the Choir*. New York: Penguin.
Tallon, R. (1979). *Zoophabets*. New York: Scholastic.
VanAllsburg, C. (1992). *The Z was Zapped*. Boston: Houghton Mifflin.
Winthrop, E. (1986). *Shoes*. New York: Harper Trophy.
Zmach, M. (1976). *Hush, Little Baby*. New York: Dutton.

This list is by no means exhaustive. Teachers familiar with children's literature can expand this list for their own purposes.

Yopp (1995b) has also developed a test for assessing phonemic awareness in young children. The instrument itself—*The Yopp-Singer Test of Phonemic Segmentation*—along with data related to the test appears in the September 1995 issue of *The Reading Teacher*.

possible, learning letter names and sounds should be part of a larger focus on language learning in the kindergarten classroom.

Writing.   Building on children's emerging writing abilities is an integral part of today's kindergarten program as well. Traditionally, writing instruction was delayed until reading ability was well established. Currently, schools heavily emphasize writing as part of emergent literacy in kindergarten. The reading-writing connection begins in the early stages of emergent literacy.

Children's early attempts at writing convey little meaning to most adults; they appear to be little more than jagged scribbles on the page. But there is usually more to these attempts than meets the adult eye. When we ask children to read what they have written and when we view the experience as the child's early attempt to create meaning, the significance of these scribbles becomes apparent.

It is important to take young children's writing seriously, since respect provides a foundation for further growth. "If we are not afraid of children's errors, if we give them plenty of opportunity for writing, and if their classrooms provide rich, literate environments, the children will learn quickly. By the end of kindergarten, many children are writing long stories" (Calkins, 1986; p. 43).

The author's chair is a special place to share stories in the literature-based classroom.
© Elizabeth Crews/The Image Works

As literacy emerges and children gain a greater sense of the alphabetic nature of our writing system, they begin to use alphabet symbols to represent sound and meaning. As they develop phonemic awareness, they use invented spelling, approximations of the correctly spelled or orthographic forms of words; for example, they may write *Once upon a time* as *Wns pn a tim*. This "temporary spelling" will progress from only one or two letters per word to rough approximations of the actual spellings. What is important at this stage is not that children spell all words correctly, but that they get their thoughts down on paper in as meaningful a way as they can.

The *writing center* belongs in a kindergarten classroom, just as it belongs in the learning environment of the upper elementary grades. This learning area is filled with pencils, markers, and other writing implements, as well as large, unlined pads of paper and other notepads on which children can record their thoughts. Interesting photographs, old greeting cards, unusual objects, toy figures, and other visual devices can help stimulate writing. This learning area provides incentive and encouragement for young children to develop their growing ability to deal with language in print.

The *author's chair* has become a prominent feature in many classrooms, from kindergarten through the upper grades. Originated by Donald Graves and Jane Hansen (1983), this special chair is reserved for reading aloud to the group. The teacher sits in the author's chair when sharing a trade book, and children sit there when they want to read a piece they have written aloud to classmates. Thus, from the very beginning, the child begins to experience the gratification of authorship.

Writing is an important part of emergent literacy at the kindergarten level. The teacher's role is to provide time, materials, and opportunities to write within the context of a language- and literature-rich learning environ-ment. Teachers who provide many functional opportunities for writing, who encourage writing activities, and who take children's initial efforts seriously are encouraging development of this important dimension of literacy.

Beginning Reading and Writing Instruction

After kindergarten, children enter first grade, when all children are expected to learn to read. Although people commonly accept that children learn to walk and talk at different ages, parents and educators alike are anxious when a child does not learn to read at exactly the "right" time. First grade is the year when most children acquire considerable independence in reading and writing.

Perhaps no year of teaching is as challenging or as rewarding as first grade. First grade teachers meet a group of children, most of whom cannot read or write at the beginning of the year, and send most of them on largely literate at the end of the year. No other level of education evidences such dramatic progress.

Although first grade programs continue to address the physical, social, and emotional development of children, the emphasis on content gradually expands according to the curriculum demands of the school and the expec-tations of the community. This is the year when reading and writing instruc-tion becomes more formal.

Children will likely encounter skill-development exercises in first grade—word recognition (with sight words presented on flash cards), phonics practice (with specific attention to letter-sound relationships), and reading comprehension activities (with exercises aimed at developing and testing ability to comprehend meaning in printed text). The inclusion of these skills is not inappropriate nor entirely inconsistent with a literature-based program. Children need to be aware of sound-symbol relationships as a backup to context when they analyze unfamiliar words they encounter in print and when they learn to write. Teachers in the second grade may well expect children to be familiar with all the basic skills, but first graders should not be given the impression that these skills are all-important for their own sakes. The emphasis in first grade reading instruction needs to be on meaning and enjoyment, since at this stage it is especially important to develop a positive attitude toward reading. Literature offers ample opportu-nities to maintain that focus.

Children's literature is as important in first grade as it is in the earlier stages of emergent literacy. All of the trade books used in preschool and kindergarten—picture storybooks, simple informational books, wordless books, predictable stories presented in Big Books, poems and nursery rhymes, concepts books, and all the rest—can be appropriate in the first grade classroom, too. In addition, most first graders are ready to enjoy "chapter books" teachers read to them, books such as the ever-popular E. B. White's *Charlotte's Web* and Janwillem van de Wetering's *Hugh Pine*, the delightful story of a porcupine who tries to pass himself off as a human.

4.13 Putting Ideas to Work
First Day in First Grade

Children (not to mention their parents) enter first grade expecting to learn to read. And children can learn to read something on day one.

A good book to read on the first day of school is Miriam Cohen's *When Will I Read?*, a story about a first grader impatient to begin reading. This story has some interesting child's-eye insights on reading.

As part of the first day's activities, share with students a short segment of familiar text—a nursery rhyme such as "Jack and Jill," the refrain from a song that all children might know, or some other sample of familiar material that is easy to read. Write the material on a chart or on the chalkboard and share it with pupils as you would share a Big Book story. When the children are thoroughly familiar with the words, give individual copies to each and have them practice reading their own copies.

Have students write their names on their sheets (some may need help) and send the sheets home for the children to read to their parents. It is only the first day and already the children are reading!

Easy-to-read books are especially appropriate as pupils gain more competency and independence in first grade. Designed for readers with a minimal level of reading ability, these books give children the satisfaction of independently reading a whole book, and they allow children to enjoy their new reading capabilities. Even though not all easy-to-read books meet the standards of quality literature, these books do meet the needs of the first grader. Books such as Arnold Lobel's *Frog and Toad* stories and *Mouse Tails*, along with stories like Crosby Bonsall's *Mine's the Best*, have enormous appeal to children, while their vocabulary loads and sentence structure are manageable for beginning readers. Dr. Seuss is a perennial favorite in the field of easy-to-read books. Many of Seuss's books are too difficult for a first grader to read independently, but others like *The Cat in the Hat*, *Green Eggs and Ham*, and *Hop on Pop* are appropriate for use in the first grade classroom to help children exercise their ever-developing reading skills.

There is no precise moment at which we can say, "Emergent literacy stops here." Literacy is a developmental process, and teachers continue to teach vocabulary, comprehension, study skills, and all other dimensions of reading throughout first grade and beyond.

The Parents' Role: Home Support for Emergent Literacy

Parents play a vital role in their children's emerging literacy. The traditional attitude of "keep the parents at arm's length" is dissipating as educators realize how important parents are in helping their children develop literacy. Educators have learned that parents are vital in supporting and extending the school's mission. As the child's first and most important teachers in the

4.14 Putting Ideas to Work

Beginning First Grade with a Literature-Based Program

Pam Amster, a first grade teacher at the Plymouth River School in Hingham, Massachusetts, explains how she launches her literature-based reading/writing program every year.

Starting first grade, some children are not ready to leap right into a formal program, so we make heavy use of predictable trade books, along with selected stories from the basal, during our first couple of weeks of school. We start with a unit on color. Our reading group instructional sessions consist of shared reading of books like:

Bill Martin, Jr.'s Brown *Bear, Brown Bear, What Do You See?,* a popular book with patterned
   language;
Joy Cowley's *Houses,* a little book portraying different-color houses;
Ellen Stoll Walsh's *Mouse Paint,* the story of three white mice who change colors all the time;
Kathleen Sullivan Carroll's *One Red Rooster,* a story about a bright red rooster;
Dr. Seuss's *Green Eggs and Ham,* with Sam-I-Am (we also play a tape of an operatic rendition of this
   book, and the kids love it!).

A flexible grouping model for reading instruction is used to present, read, and discuss stories.

Our basal reading program is literature based. The books are anthologies filled with wonderful stories by recognized children's authors. From the basal we read *Monster and the Baby* by Virginia Mueller and *I Need a Lunch Box* by Jeanette Caines, stories that children enjoy and that have lots of color words and concepts. We also **read** *How To Hide a Polar Bear and Other Mammals.* It's difficult for the children to read that story at any time in the year, so we use a shared reading approach to read the story with repeated readings done in small groups and in pairs.

My read-alouds also involve color. Every day, I read a different poem from *Hailstones and Halibut Bones,* Mary O'Neill's book of color poems. Some of the other trade books that I read to the class include:

Lois Ehlert's *Color Farm,* a book that creates animals with colorful shapes;
Sam Swope's *The Araboolies of Liberty Street,* a very funny story about a boisterous family who
   enliven their neighborhood;

preschool years, parents are crucial to the awakening of children's literacy. And educators are involving parents more and more in school-based efforts to promote children's literacy.

Many schools and community organizations are establishing family literacy programs. One of the "Goals 2000" of the Educate America Act, a set of goals schools are trying to achieve by the end of the century, is for schools to promote partnerships that will increase parental participation in the academic growth of their children. To actively engage parents in family literacy, many schools have begun outreach efforts that teach parents (and

Alan Baker's *White Rabbit's Color Book,* the story about a rabbit who changes colors by falling into paint pots with primary colors;

Ed Emberley's *Go Away, Big Green Monster,* which creates a monster with cut-away pages;

Ed Young's *Seven Blind Mice,* a colorful adaptation of the old folk tale about seven blind men and the elephant;

Daniel Manus Pinkwater's *The Big Orange Splot,* a simple story about Mr. Plumbean as he creates a colorful street;

Robert McCloskey's *Burt Dow, Deep-Water Man,* who paints his boat many colors;

John Burningham's Colors, a simple book with a color word on every page.

Many of these read-aloud books are easy enough that some of the more capable readers can read them independently once they've heard the stories read.

Children respond in writing to each selection that they read and are encouraged to share their written responses in small groups or with the whole class. In addition to written responses, children are encouraged to take response questions and extend the questions to their writing in math and science.

The unit extends across the curriculum. Our math program—Math Land (Creative Publications, 1995)—has lots of colorful manipulatives, shapes, pattern blocks, and the like, so the carryover is natural.

In science, we study how light creates color in a rainbow, and kids learn technical vocabulary like *prism* and *spectrum* (along with lots of incidental phonics). We also do minilessons on how the eye works in perceiving colors, colors that change (changing leaves), the color of life (green), and animal camouflage.

In social studies, we talk about the color of people's skin (which leads us toward our Thanksgiving study of the Pilgrims and their Native American friends). Since many of the trade books we use involve people painting houses, we extend the theme to the neighborhood.

Art naturally involves colors, and children draw rainbows, learning how to mix colors to produce indigo and violet. They also focus on color in their other art activities.

Using color as a theme for beginning readers and writers provides a foundation for much of what they do as first graders. In addition, children are introduced to the world of literacy with activities that are meaningful to them and that promote learning and communication across the curriculum.

grandparents) and children together (France and Hager, 1993; Unwin, 1995; Come and Fredericks, 1995). To expand literacy into the home, for example, Neuman (1995) and her associates have designed literacy "prop boxes" containing objects, toys, storybooks, and writing books, along with suggestions for working on literacy activities, to be used at home by parents and children in economically distressed areas. These efforts are bound to grow as multiservice and community schools expand their focus and as schools recognize that strengthening family resources is essential to their own success with children.

Reading forms an important bond between parent and child and promotes interest and ability in literacy.
© Elizabeth Crews/The Image Works

Parents in the Preschool Years

From the time a child is born, parents have a role to play in the emerging literacy of their offspring. It has been well documented that children can learn to read before they come to school. Researchers report numerous cases of children whose parents have helped them learn to read before kindergarten (Durkin, 1966; Bissex, 1980; Lass, 1982, 1983). These studies have helped us better understand how young children develop competency in reading and writing and what parents can do to support and encourage the process.

Relatively few parents actively set out to teach their children how to read. Instead, they provide a stimulating environment, read frequently to their children, engage in conversation and word play, respond to their children's requests for information, and help their children begin to understand how literacy fits into their lives. These parents create an environment conducive to reading achievement—an environment full of verbal interaction, where reading is valued and pursued as a worthwhile activity, where children have access to reading material, where opportunities for leisure reading are provided, and where adults frequently read to children. These are the factors that research shows are important to early reading development (Greaney, 1986; Meyer, Hastings, and Linn, 1990; Neuman and Roskos, 1992). Parents who create this type of environment and who respond to their children's requests for help are strongly supporting the beginnings of literacy, even though they have not set out to teach their children how to read.

Making books accessible to children in the home is important. For very young children, publishers produce books with pages made of heavy cardboard, cloth, or plastic to withstand the wear and tear a toddler can inflict on a well-loved object. Books can be gifts for birthdays, holidays, and other occasions. The library can be a regular stop on the weekly shopping

4.15 Putting Ideas to Work

Ten Ways Parents Can Help Children Become Better Readers

Becoming A Nation of Readers, the Report of the National Commission on Reading (Anderson et al., 1985) presents ten suggestions on how parents can help their children become better readers:

1. Help children acquire a wide range of knowledge.
2. Talk with children about their experiences.
3. Encourage children to think about events.
4. Read aloud to children.
5. Provide preschool children with writing materials.
6. Encourage children to watch TV programs that have educational value.
7. Monitor how much TV children watch.
8. Monitor children's school performance.
9. Encourage children to read independently.
10. Continue to be personally involved in children's continuing growth as readers.

trip. Putting books in children's hands is an important step in their emergent literacy.

In addition to providing books and creating conditions that foster literacy development, specific aspects of parent-child interaction relate directly to learning to read and write.

One of the first things parents can do in encouraging early literacy is to help their children develop print awareness. This is part of the metalinguistic knowledge that includes learning why people read and what people do when they read. Parents can develop this awareness at home in a number of ways, both directly and incidentally: by talking about books, by casually mentioning something they have read, by reading to children every day, by naming books by their titles while calling their children's attention to the words on the cover, and by creating innumerable experiences with print in the home.

Everyday occasions can become literacy-related activities. While bathing or dressing a young child, the parent can recite playful poems about parts of the body. While putting away the dinner dishes, parent and child can sort the utensils according to size, shape, and function. Telling stories or playing word games such as "I Spy" can fill casual moments with verbal interaction. There is hardly a moment of the day that could not potentially be used to engage in some sort of literacy-related activity, however informal.

Parents can view educational television programs such as "Sesame Street," "Long Ago and Far Away," or "Reading Rainbow" with their young children. Shows like these are specifically designed to promote learning and to provide a foundation in school-related areas. What they lack is what all television lacks: the important element of feedback. Parents or other caregivers can enhance learning when they follow the show with activities that reinforce the concepts the program presented, saying, for example:

"Let's see how many S-words we can find in the kitchen."
"Can you remember what a *lullaby* is?"
"Let's look for things that are *empty* and things that are *full*."
"Tell me what's *above* the TV and what's *below* the TV."
"Can you remember three things that the girl said about monkeys?"
"Think of all the things you know that come in *pairs*."

Follow-up questions and activities are essential to reinforce the language and cognitive lessons the television show presents. These activities also demonstrate a parent's interest in the child's learning and make the child feel successful and important.

Parents can introduce children to the alphabet at home through thousands of planned and spontaneous activities that arise all the time. Saying the alphabet a letter at a time as children climb the stairs is a routine that helps them learn the alphabet in sequence. Calling attention to letters in the environment—"Can you see the *K* in K-Mart?" "Show me the *M* on the milk carton,"—reinforces the child's awareness of letter names.

ABC books directly introduce young children to letter names and sounds, and at the same time provide enjoyable early encounters with literature. As parents and children share these books in the informal setting of the home, the child can begin to develop alphabet awareness, learn new concepts, have successful independent reading experiences, and learn to enjoy literature.

Sharing books at home is likely the best way to help children develop an interest in and success with reading. Reading stimulates a child's interest, imagination, and emotional and linguistic development. It introduces children to literature that invites them to read for pleasure. Sharing books extends beyond simply reading them; it includes asking questions (though not so many as to kill the child's interest), talking about the pictures, discussing feelings, and enjoying the delight that good stories offer.

When preschool children choose favorite and familiar books, parents can practice paired reading, a technique in which parents and children read together. They can read simultaneously, they can read alternate pages, they can "echo read" (with parent reading and child repeating), or they can read different parts of books ("You read what the giant says."). However they do it, paired reading actively involves young children in their emerging reading. Even as children enter school and achieve more reading competency and gain independence, the practice can be continued.

In the preschool years, parents can also be effective models for reading. When impressionable children see their parents reading books and magazines for information and pleasure, they get the message early in their lives that reading is important and enjoyable.

Parents can also foster children's development as writers in the preschool years. Parents who respond enthusiastically to their children's early

4.16 Putting Ideas to Work
What Parents Can Do to Promote Literacy for Preschoolers

*H*ardly a moment goes by that does not afford opportunities for parents and other caregivers to foster the emergent literacy of young children. They can do so by:

1. Talking to them, encouraging them to talk, exchanging accounts of events, and patiently answering their interminable *why* questions.
2. Reading to them every day, several times a day—every chance they get.
3. Having books around, and letting even very young children experience and enjoy sturdy cardboard books as toys.
4. Developing routines for learning the alphabet, naming parts of the body, and playing games with sounds and words.
5. Calling attention to print in the environment—words in the supermarket, on street signs and billboards, in magazines and in books.
6. Watching "Sesame Street" and other instructional TV programs, while asking questions and providing information to extend the concepts the programs are designed to develop.
7. Copying stories and simple messages that children dictate, and encouraging children to write their own stories.
8. Being models by reading for information and enjoyment and by calling attention to their reading.

attempts to scribble stories and messages help their youngsters gain both awareness and confidence as writers. When parents respond, children see a purpose to writing. Transcribing stories that children dictate encourages children to attempt to write, and at the same time develops important elements of print awareness.

Parents are children's first teachers. Before children ever enter a preschool program, parents can do much to encourage and promote emergent literacy in the home.

The Parents' Role When Children Come to School

Throughout the early years, the home provides a significant foundation for a child's emerging literacy. When a child enters kindergarten, the school becomes the second major influence in the child's language learning, and the home continues to support reading growth. More and more schools recognize the importance of having parents play a continuing role as their children learn to read and write. Parents and teachers become partners in the emerging literacy of the young child.

When a child enters school, parents can reinforce and extend literacy development in the home in an unlimited variety of ways, just as they can provide support for emergent literacy in the preschool years. Through verbal interaction, parents promote their children's continuing language development. They provide access to print by continuing to make books and magazines available to their children. By reading to children, parents provide both a cognitive and emotional "shot in the arm" for literacy development. By listening to their children read, they convey the message that reading is important. In short, the home continues to exert a powerful influence in a child's emerging literacy.

More often than not, parents are more than happy to provide help at home for children learning to read, but many parents are not sure what to do. During their children's preschool years, parents seem to have an intuitive sense of how to foster language learning. But their confidence seems to diminish once a child enters school and is under the direction of a trained and expert teacher. Often, they feel that they are "on the outside looking in." The confidence built while reading to their children and answering their children's questions about print dissipates a little when their child brings home the first phonics worksheet or word list. Feeling they do not possess "teaching skills," they often draw back and become less involved in their children's literacy development.

Not all home environments are conducive to maximum literacy development in the early years. For many children, home is a crowded place where emotional and intellectual neglect is a fact of life. Many parents struggle with the challenge of meeting the family's most basic needs. Time and material resources may be at a premium. Parents may be unaware of the importance of verbal interaction, and their own level of literacy may be limited. The role the school plays is essential in compensating for much of what these children missed during their preschool years.

Schools can take the initiative to help parents promote reading and writing in the home. Rasinski and Fredericks (1989) suggest a model or plan for creating parent-teacher cooperation in promoting emergent literacy (see Putting Ideas to Work 4.17). At the most basic level, teacher and parents monitor the children's learning. The second level involves communication, when a two-way, home-school line of communication is established through the regular, positive sharing of information. At the next level, participation, parents become engaged in the school lives of their children by serving as classroom volunteers and schools participate by offering special programs for parents. The highest level of mutual involvement is empowerment, in which parents and teachers achieve an almost collegial relationship of trust and commitment.

Even without a formal program or plan, parents can remain a vital part of their children's emergent literacy during the primary school years. Rare indeed are parents who are not interested in their children's success as readers and writers, but they often need help and guidance to most effectively help their children. To encourage parents to be involved in their children's ongoing literacy development, a teacher might compile a list of suggestions like the one in Putting Ideas to Work 4.18, sending it home early in the year or distributing it at an open house or parents' night at school. It is important that these suggestions be practical and not require an unreasonable investment of time or money.

4.17 Putting Ideas to Work

A Hierarchy of Home-School Relationships

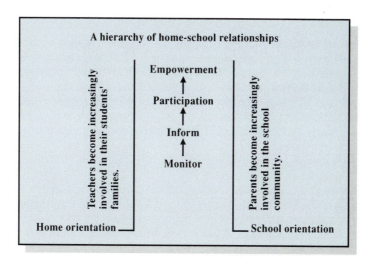

A hierarchy of home-school relationships

Teachers become increasingly involved in their students' families.

Parents become increasingly involved in the school community.

Empowerment
↑
Participation
↑
Inform
↑
Monitor

Home orientation   School orientation

Figure from Timothy V. Rasinski and Anthony D. Fredericks, (1989, November) "Dimensions of Parent Involvement," *The Reading Teacher* 43:(2),180–182. Copyright © 1989 International Reading Association. Reprinted with permission of Timothy Rasinski and the International Reading Association.

School-initiated lines of communication with parents are important. When parents initiate contact with schools, those contacts are apt to be antagonistic because parents tend to approach the school only when a problem arises. Believing that communication is the key to building a better understanding of, and support for, emergent learning programs, Enz (1995) suggests setting up newsletters and parent workshops to provide relevant information about the school's emergent literacy perspective and its instructional implications. Some schools are experimenting with electronic mail, fax machines, and other telecommunications techniques that may help bridge the gap between home and school.

Once communication is established, how can schools help parents reinforce reading at home? Informal reading instruction in the home requires no special materials. Home-based reading and writing experiences can emanate from reading the labels on soup cans and cereal boxes, checking the listings of television shows, reading the comic section of the Sunday newspaper, making out weekly grocery lists, and looking at billboards and other signs from the car window.

Some schools offer workshops or special programs to help parents of kindergarten pupils become more aware of what they can do to promote literacy at home. In these programs, parents learn about the type of literature

4.18 Putting Ideas to Work
A Note to Parents

*H*ere are ten steps that parents can take to help children improve their reading:

1. Turn off the television for half an hour each evening. Use this time to read to your children or to listen to them read to you. Some children begin to prefer reading good stories to watching television.
2. Have children's books from the library or inexpensive books from the supermarket available. Share these books as often as possible. Let your children select some of these books.
3. Let your child help you look up numbers in the telephone book, read recipes in the cookbook, or read directions on the backs of food containers.
4. Put a note with a "happy message" in your child's lunch box and exchange simple notes with him or her at home.
5. Play games involving reading and writing; for example, play "restaurant," in which you and your child read menus and write orders.
6. Cut pictures from magazines. Label them; describe them; classify objects; and make up captions.
7. Help your children realize that reading is important to you; let them see you reading books, newspapers, and magazines as sources of information and enjoyment.
8. Share *Mother Goose* rhymes and other simple poems; emphasize the sounds and the rhythm of the language.
9. After a shared experience—a family vacation, a birthday party, a trip to the grocery store—talk about the occasion and keep a family diary; copy down what your child has to say and read the story back to him or her.
10. Encourage your child to read to you; be a good listener and don't ask too many questions; praise your child for his or her best efforts.

Each activity takes only a few minutes yet can give your child a head start in becoming a successful reader and writer. Remember, the greatest gifts you can give your child are time and love.

appropriate for young children and where to find it; how to share books with children, not only by reading them but also by talking about books and sharing feelings about what they read; how to create a home reading environment; how to help children develop as writers; and how to listen to children as they read. When parents have a meaningful decision-making role in planning and implementing these programs, the effort is more successful. In some cases, programs like these spur parents to volunteer in the classroom, work as library aides, or become actively involved members of the school community.

Teachers can also inform parents about the many sources of information available to help them learn more about reading- and literacy-related activities they can engage in with their children (see Putting Ideas to Work 4.19). Since many of these brochures and booklets are available free or at a minimal cost, schools can easily make them available to parents. These resources can be available for parents to examine when they come to teacher conferences or open house.

4.19 Putting Ideas to Work
Useful References for Parents about Reading in the Home

*T*he following is a sampling of materials available for parents interested in supporting literacy in the home.

Brochures

"Choosing a Child's Book"—The Children's Book Council (67 Irving Place, New York, NY 10003).

"How to Help Your Child Become a Better Writer"—National Council of Teachers of English (1111 Kenyon Road, Urbana, IL 61801).

"Good Books Make Reading Fun for Your Child," "Your Home Is Your Child's First School," "You Can Use Television to Stimulate Your Child's Reading Habits," and others—International Reading Association (P.O. Box 8139, 800 Barksdale Road, Newark, DE 19714–8139).

"Helping Children Learn about Reading"—National Association for Education of Young Children (1834 Connecticut Ave. NW, Washington, DC 20009–5780).

"Children's Classics: A Book List for Parents"—*The Horn Book Magazine* (14 Beacon Street, Boston, MA 02108).

Booklets

"Getting Involved: Your Child and Reading" and "Getting Involved: Your Child and Writing"—Government Printing Office (1511 K Street NW, Suite 740, Washington, DC 20005).

"How Can I Encourage My Primary-Grade Child to Read?" "Why Read Aloud to Children?" "Helping Your Child Become A Reader," "How Can I Help My Young Child Prepare for Reading?" and others—International Reading Association (P.O. Box 8139, 800 Barksdale Road, Newark, DE 19714–8139).

"Parents and Children Together," a series of audio journals containing a read-along booklet with a cassette tape—ERIC Clearinghouse on Reading and Communications Skills, Indiana University (2805 East 10th Street, Bloomington, IN 47408–2698).

Books

A Parent's Guide to Children's Reading (5th ed.) by Nancy Larrick. New York: Bantam Books, 1982.

The New Read-Aloud Handbook by Jim Trelease. New York: Penguin, 1995.

Home: Where Reading and Writing Begin by Mary W. Hill. Portsmouth, NH: Heinemann Educational Books, 1989.

Choosing Books for Children: A Commonsense Guide by Betsy Hearne. New York: Dellacourt, 1990.

These titles and other books about reading in the home are generally available in bookstores.

As children are introduced to writing instruction in the classroom, parents can also continue to foster their youngsters' developing competency as writers at home. Often, parents need to realize that the primary focus of a child's early attempts to write is the thought the child is trying to express, not how accurately he or she spells or punctuates. While the child will ultimately have to learn the conventions and mechanics of writing, the initial focus should be on the child's willingness to attempt to express meaning. Parents need to respond to the message, not to how neatly or correctly the message is written.

Summary and Conclusions

The early years are vitally important to a child's development as a reader and writer. What goes on during these years, both at home and in school, will influence the child's success in developing the power of literacy.

Under ideal circumstances, a child's early meaningful exposure to reading and writing begins in the home. The child owns books, hears stories read, and develops an awareness of the role print plays in the environment.

Emergent literacy continues to develop through prekindergarten programs that foster language and allow children to interact with a variety of books and to engage in early writing activities.

In kindergarten, the emphasis on language development and exposure to print continues, but instruction takes on a more formal dimension. The teacher introduces specific aspects of learning directly related to reading and writing.

In first grade, the instructional program becomes even more formalized. The child is expected to begin the road to independence in reading and writing.

Even after the child begins school, parents play an important role. Parents provide support for their children's literacy development and extend the efforts of the school in teaching the child to read and write.

Discussion Questions and Activities

1. Think about your preschool years. What experiences with reading and writing stand out in your mind? What were your favorite stories? In what ways did your preschool experiences affect you when you went to school?
2. Interview the parent of a young child or, if possible, observe the child in action. Note the type of language the child uses, how he or she reacts to books, the type of activities he or she enjoys most. Given the child's stage of emergent literacy, what types of activities might you suggest to foster the child's interest in reading and writing?
3. Watch an episode of "Sesame Street." Which aspects of literacy does the program try to develop? Make a list of follow-up activities that could reinforce or extend the learning of a child who watched the program.
4. Make a list of ten trade books you might use with young children in an emergent literacy setting. Include a balance of concept books, picture storybooks, and other literature appropriate to this level. Make sure your list contains books that reflect multicultural perspectives. Describe how you might use these books with children.
5. Examine the preprimer, primer, or first grade textbook from a basal reading series. What literature selections does it include? What instructional suggestions does it provide? How might you integrate the use of the basal reading text with the literature you select?

School-Based Assignments

1. Visit a Pre-K setting, kindergarten, or first grade classroom. Make a list of print found in the learning environment, print produced by both adults and children. How are children using print? What kinds of books are available and how are they used?
2. Following the guidelines presented in Putting Ideas to Work 4.11, plan a reading lesson based on a predictable story in a Big Book. Teach the lesson to a

group of children in an early childhood education setting. Prepare a brief report on the pupils' reactions.

3. Prepare a letter about reading that might be sent home to parents the first week of school. What are the five most essential pieces of information you might include? Get opinions from colleagues and administrators on your letter.

4. Select a picture storybook, a wordless book, a concept book, an alphabet book, or other trade book that might be used with young children. If possible, share the book with children at different stages of emergent literacy. Explain what type of input you would provide at each level and what kind of output you might expect from the children.

5. Examine the NAEYC statement regarding appropriate and inappropriate practices (Putting Ideas to Work 4.6). Using these standards as your guide, observe instruction in a first grade classroom over a period of time. Give the class an "appropriateness rating" based on these standards.

Children's Trade Books Cited in This Chapter

Alexander, Martha. (1970). *Bobo's Dream*. New York: Dial.
Alexander, Martha. (1970). *Out, Out, Out!* New York: Dial.
Anglund, Joan Walsh. (1960). *In a Pumpkin Shell*. New York: Harcourt Brace.
Anno, Mitsumasa. (1975). *Anno's Alphabet*. New York: Crowell.
Baker, Alan. (1994). *White Rabbit's Color Book*. New York: Kingfisher.
Barton, Byron. (1982). *Airport*. New York: Harper & Row.
Bayer, Jane. (1984). *A, My Name Is Alice*. New York: Dial.
Bonsall, Crosby. (1973). *Mine's the Best*. New York: Harper & Row.
Brown, Margaret Wise. (1947). *Goodnight, Moon*. New York: Harper & Row.
Burningham, John. (1985). *John Burningham's Colors*. New York: Crown.
Caines, Jeanette. (1988). *I Need a Lunch Box*. New York: HarperCollins.
Carle, Eric. (1969). *The Very Hungry Caterpillar*. New York: Philomel.
Carroll, Kathleen Sullivan. (1992). *One Red Rooster*. Boston: Houghton Mifflin.
Coates, Laura Jane. (1986). *Marcella and the Moon*. New York: Macmillan.
Cohen, Miriam. (1977). *When Will I Read?* New York: Greenwillow.
Cowley, Joy. (1992). *Houses*. New York: Scholastic.
Crews, Donald. (1978). *Freight Train*. New York: Greenwillow.
Day, Alexandra. (1990). *Carl's Christmas*. New York: Farrar, Straus and Giroux.
Day, Alexandra. (1985). *Good Dog, Carl*. San Marcos, CA: Green Tiger Press.
Dayrell, Elphinstone. (1968). *Why The Sun and Moon Live in the Sky*. Boston: Houghton Mifflin.
de Paola, Tomie. (1978). *Pancakes for Breakfast*. New York: Harcourt Brace.
de Wetering, Janwillem van. (1980). *Hugh Pine*. Boston: Houghton Mifflin.
Doubilet, Anne. (1991). *Under the Sea from A to Z*. New York: Crown.
Ehlert, Lois. (1990). *Color Farm*. New York: HarperCollins.
Emberley, Barbara. (1967). *Drummer Hoff*. Englewood Cliffs, NJ: Prentice-Hall.
Emberley, Ed. (1992). *Go Away, Big Green Monster*. Boston: Little, Brown.
Feeling, Muriel. (1971). *Moja Means One: A Swahili Counting Book*. New York: Dial.
Gag, Wanda. (1928). *Millions of Cats*. New York: Putnam.
Galdone, Paul. (1961). *This Is The House That Jack Built*. New York: McGraw Hill.
Galdone, Paul. (1975). *The Gingerbread Man*. New York: Clarion.
Galdone, Paul. (1973). *The Little Red Hen*. New York: Scholastic.
Goodall, John. (1972). *Jacko*. New York: Harcourt Brace.
Goodall, John. (1979). *The Story of an English Village*. New York: Macmillan.
Grossman, Virginia. (1991). *Ten Little Rabbits*. San Francisco: Chronicle Books.

Hepworth, Cathi. (1992). *Antics! An Alphabetical Anthology*. New York: Putnam.

Hoban, Tana. (1972). *Count and See*. New York: Macmillan.

Hoban, Tana. (1978). *Is It Red? Is It Yellow? Is It Blue?* New York: Greenwillow.

Hunhardt, Dorothy. (1942). *Pat the Bunny*. New York: Western.

Hutchins, Pat. (1971). *Changes, Changes*. New York: Macmillan.

Hutchins, Pat. (1972). *Good Night Owl*. New York: Macmillan.

Hutchins, Pat. (1968). *Rosie's Walk*. New York: Macmillan.

Johnson, Stephen T. (1995). *Alphabet City*. New York: Viking.

Keats, Ezra Jack. (1982). *Clementine's Cactus*. New York: Viking.

Kitchen, Burt. (1984). *Animal Alphabet*. New York: Dial.

Lobel, Anita. (1990). *Alison's Zinnia*. New York: Greenwillow.

Lobel, Arnold. (1970). *Frog and Toad Are Friends*. New York: Harper & Row.

Lobel, Arnold. (1972). *Mouse Tails*. New York: Harper & Row.

Lobel, Arnold, and Lobel, Anita. (1981). *On Market Street*. New York: Greenwillow.

Martin, Bill Jr. (1983). *Brown Bear, Brown Bear, What Do You See?* New York: Holt.

Martin, Bill Jr., and Archambault, John. (1989). *Chicka Chicka Boom Boom*. New York: Simon & Schuster.

McCloskey, Robert. (1963). *Burt Dow, Deep-Water Man*. New York: Penguin.

Musgrove, Margaret. (1976). *Ashanti to Zulu: African Traditions*. New York: Dial.

Omerod, Jan. (1982). *Moonlight*. New York: Lothrop.

Omerod, Jan. (1981). *Sunshine*. New York: Lothrop, Lee & Shepard.

O'Neill, Mary. (1961). *Hailstones and Halibut Bones: Adventures in Color*. Garden City, NY: Doubleday.

Oxenbury, Helen. (1983). *Helen Oxenbury's ABC of Things*. New York: Dellacort.

Palotta, Jerry. (1989). *The Icky Bug Alphabet Book*. Watertown, MA: Charlesbridge.

Paul, Ann Whitford. (1991). *Eight Hands Round: A Patchwork Alphabet*. New York: HarperCollins.

Pinkwater, Daniel Manus. (1977). *The Big Orange Splot*. New York: Scholastic.

Rankin, Laura. (1991). *The Handiwork Alphabet*. New York: Dell.

Reiss, John J. (1974). *Shapes*. New York: Macmillan.

Rockwell, Anne. (1985). *First Comes Spring*. New York: Harper & Row.

Rockwell, Harlow. (1980). *My Kitchen*. New York: Greenwillow.

Rockwell, Harlow. (1976). *My Nursery School*. New York: Greenwillow.

Sendak, Maurice. (1962). *Chicken Soup with Rice*. New York: Harper & Row.

Sendak, Maurice. (1970). *In the Night Kitchen*. New York: Harper & Row.

Sendak, Maurice. (1981). *Outside Over There*. New York: Harper & Row.

Sendak, Maurice. (1963). *Where The Wild Things Are*. New York: Harper & Row.

Seuss, Dr. (Theodore Geisel). (1957). *The Cat in the Hat*. New York: Random House.

Seuss, Dr. (Theodore Geisel). (1960). *Green Eggs and Ham*. New York: Random House.

Seuss, Dr. (Theodore Geisel). (1960). *Hop on Pop*. New York: Random House.

Slobodkina, Esphyr. (1947). *Caps for Sale*. New York: Harper & Row.

Spier, Peter. (1972). *Fast-Slow, High-Low: A Book of Opposites*. New York: Doubleday.

Swope, Sam. *The Araboolies of Liberty Street*. New York: Crown.

Tafuri, Nancy. (1986). *Who's Counting?* New York: Greenwillow.

Walsh, Ellen Stoll. (1987). *Mouse Paint*. Fort Worth: Harcourt Brace.

Wescott, Nadine Bernard. (1980). *I Know an Old Lady Who Swallowed a Fly*. Boston: Little, Brown.

White, E. B. (1952). *Charlotte's Web*. New York: Harper & Row.

Wiesner, David. (1991). *Tuesday*. New York: Clarion.

Wildsmith, Brian. (1962). *Brian Wildsmith's ABC*. New York: Watts.

Yolen, Jane. (1987). *Owl Moon*. New York: Scholastic.

Young, Ed. (1992). *Seven Blind Mice*. New York: Philomel.

References

Adams, M. J. (1990). *Beginning to Read: Thinking and Learning about Print*. Cambridge, MA: MIT Press.

Anderson, R. C., Hiebert, F. H., Scott, J. A., and Wilkinson, A. G. (1985). *Becoming a Nation of Readers*. Washington, DC: National Institute of Education.

Bissex, G. L. (1980). *GNYS AT WRK: A Child Learns to Write and Read*. Cambridge, MA: Harvard University Press.

Bond, G. L., and Dysktra, R. (1967). The Cooperative Research Program in First-Grade Reading Instruction. *Reading Research Quarterly* 2:5–142.

Calkins, L. M. (1986). *The Art of Teaching Writing*. Portsmouth, NH: Heinemann.

Come, B., and Fredericks, A. D. (1995). Family Literacy in Urban Schools: Meeting the Needs of At-Risk Children. *The Reading Teacher* 48:566–570.

Durkin, D. (1966). *Children Who Read Early*. New York: Teachers College Press.

Durrell, D. D. (1980). Letter-Name Value in Reading and Spelling. *Reading Research Quarterly* 16:159–163.

Ellis, D. W., and Preston, F. W. (1984). Enhancing Beginning Reading Using Wordless Picture Books. *The Reading Teacher* 37:692–698.

Enz, B. J. (1995). Strategies for Promoting Parental Support for Emergent Literacy Programs. *The Reading Teacher* 49:168–170.

France, M. G., and Hager, J. M. (1993). Recruit, Respect, Respond: A Model for Working with Low-Income Families and Their Preschoolers. *The Reading Teacher* 46:568–572.

Freeman E. B., and Hatch, J. A. (1989). Emergent Literacy: Reconceptualizing Kindergarten Practice. *Childhood Education* 66:21–24.

Gates, A. (1937). The Necessary Mental Age for Beginning Reading. *Elementary School Journal* 37:497–508.

Gentile, L. M. (1983). "A Critique of Mabel V. Morphett and Carleton Washburne's Study: When Should Children Begin to Read?" In L. M. Gentile, M. L. Kamil, and J. S. Blanchard, eds., *Reading Research Revisited*. Columbus, OH: Merrill.

Graves, D., and Hansen, J. (1983). The Author's Chair. *Language Arts* 60:176–183.

Greaney, V. (1986). Parental Influences on Reading. *The Reading Teacher* 39:813–818.

Harris, T. L., and Hodges, R. E. (1995). *The Literacy Dictionary*. Newark, DE: International Reading Association.

Heald-Taylor, G. (1987). Predictable Literature Selections and Activities for Language Arts Instruction. *The Reading Teacher* 41:6–12.

Holdaway, D. (1982). Shared Book Experience: Teaching Reading Using Favorite Books. *Theory into Practice* 21:293–300.

Huck, C. S., Hepler, S., and Hickman, J. (1987). *Children's Literature in the Elementary School* (4th ed.). New York: Holt, Rinehart & Winston.

Jones, M. (1983). AB(by)C Means Alphabet Books by Children. *The Reading Teacher* 36:646–648.

Lass, B. (1982). Portrait of My Son as an Early Reader. *The Reading Teacher* 36:20–28.

Lass, B. (1983). Portrait of My Son as an Early Reader II. *The Reading Teacher* 36:508–515.

McGee, L. M., and Richgels, D. J. (1996). *Literacy's Beginnings: Supporting Young Readers and Writers* (2nd ed.). Boston: Allyn & Bacon.

Meyer, L. A., Hastings, C. N., and Linn, R. L. (1990). *Home Support for Emerging Literacy: What Parents Do that Correlates with Early Reading Achievement*. Center for the Study of Reading Technical Report No. 518. Champaign: University of Illinois at Urbana-Champaign.

Morphett, M. V., and Washburne, C. (1931). When Should Children Begin to Read? *Elementary School Journal* 31:496–503.

National Association for the Education of Young Children. (1988). NAEYC Position Statement on Developmentally Appropriate Practice in the Primary Grades, Serving 5- through 8-Year-Olds. *Young Children* 43:64–84.

Neuman, S. B. (1995). Reading Together: A Community-Supported Parent Tutoring Program. *The Reading Teacher* 49:120–129.

Neuman, S. B., and Roskos, K. (1992). Literacy Objects as Cultural Tools: Effects on Children's Literacy Behaviors in Play. *Reading Research Quarterly* 27:202–225.

Putnam, C. (1991). Dramatizing Nonfiction with Emergent Readers. *Language Arts* 68:463–469.

Rasinski, T. V., and Fredericks, A. D. (1989). Dimensions of Parent Involvement. *The Reading Teacher* 43:180–182.

Richgels, D. J., Poremba, K. J., and McGee, L. M. (1996). Kindergarteners Talk about Print: Phonemic Awareness in Meaningful Contexts. *The Reading Teacher* 49:632–642.

Salinger, T. S. (1996). *Literacy for Young Children* (2nd ed.). Columbus, OH: Merrill.

Strickland, D. S. (1989). Some Tips for Using Big Books. *The Reading Teacher* 41:966–968.

Strickland, D. S., and Morrow, L. M. (1990). Sharing Big Books. *The Reading Teacher* 43:342–343.

Teale, W. H., and Sulzby, E. (1986). *Emergent Literacy: Writing and Reading*. Norwood, NJ: Ablex.

Thomas, K. F. (1985). Early Reading as a Social Interaction Process. *Language Arts* 62:469–475.

Unwin, C. G. (1995). Elizabeth's Story: The Potential of Home-Based Family Literacy Intervention. *The Reading Teacher* 48:552–557.

Vacca, J. L., Vacca, R. T., and Gove, M. K. (1991). *Reading and Learning to Read* (2nd ed.). New York: HarperCollins.

Williams, J. (1995). Phonemic Awareness. In T. L. Harris and R. E. Hodges, eds., *The Literacy Dictionary*. Newark, DE: International Reading Association.

Yopp, H. K. (1992). Developing Phonemic Awareness in Young Children. *The Reading Teacher* 45:696–703.

Yopp, H. K. (1995a). Read-Aloud Books for Developing Phonemic Awareness: An Annotated Bibliography. *The Reading Teacher* 48:538–542.

Yopp, H. K. (1995b). A Test for Assessing Phonemic Awareness in Young Children. *The Reading Teacher* 49:20–29.

Recognizing and Decoding Words: Vocabulary Study in a Literature-Based Program

© James L. Shaffer

Chapter 5 Outline

Features

5.1   **Three Related Areas of Word Study**
5.2   **What Does It Mean to "Know" a Word?**
5.3   **Semantic Maps**
5.4   **Word for the Day**
5.5   **Literature-Based Activities for Promoting Word Knowledge**
5.6   **Nothing Need Ever Be Boring Again!**
5.7   **Books about Words**
5.8   **Bookwords: High-Frequency Words in Storybooks for Beginning Readers**
5.9   **Personal Words**
5.10 **Teaching Sight Words**
5.11 **Context Clues Exercise**
5.12 **Using Cloze**
5.13 **Point-Counterpoint on Phonics**
5.14 **The Language of Phonics**
5.15 **Phonics Lessons Using Trade Books**
5.16 **Trade Books That Repeat Phonics Elements**
5.17 **Word Building as an Approach to Phonics**
5.18 **Guidelines for Exemplary Phonics Instruction**
5.19 **Phonics Programs**
5.20 **Teaching Morphemic Elements through Literature**

Key Concepts in This Chapter

Word knowledge is essential to reading success in literature-based reading programs. The more words pupils know, the better the chances they will understand what they read.

Reading requires the recognition of words in print, the ability to say a word and know what it means. Pupils can recognize words instantly by sight or through context.

Words students cannot immediately recognize need to be analyzed. Children learn to recognize words phonetically (by letters and sounds) or structurally (by larger meaning-bearing parts). Phonics is an important part of literature-based instruction.

To recognize words in print, students must use a combination of strategies. Their ultimate purpose in using these strategies is to arrive at meaning.

Introduction

Words are the currency of communication, the main medium in the exchange of ideas through language. Words are essential to any spoken or written language experience. For this reason, vocabulary development is an essential part of language arts throughout the school years.

Vocabulary development begins long before formal reading instruction. Learning new words is part of the language acquisition process that takes place through the emergent literacy stage, and vocabulary growth is rapid in the early years of a child's life.

The exact size of a person's vocabulary is impossible to measure, so the number of words most children know when they come to school is a matter of debate. Vocabulary size is not as easy to measure as height or weight, and the best researchers can do is to estimate the number of words a young child knows. Although estimates of children's vocabulary size vary considerably, it is reasonable to assume that most first graders have a listening/speaking vocabulary of about 5,000 words, and that this number will grow to about 50,000 by the time these pupils enter college (Just and Carpenter, 1987).

We can be confident that, whatever the exact size of their vocabularies, children bring to school a vast lexicon, the total set of words they have in their heads. This repertoire of words provides the meaning pupils bring to print and underlies their understanding of the trade books and other materials they read in literature-based programs.

Three aspects of vocabulary study are part of the typical classroom program: word knowledge, recognition, and analysis. The first area, word knowledge, focuses on helping children build a store of words they can use to meet a full range of communication needs. But in order to read, pupils not only need to "know" words, they also need to be able to identify these words in print and understand their meaning. Thus, instruction focuses on two other areas: word recognition, or the ability to know what a word is and what it means; and word analysis, or the ability to figure out the pronunciations and meanings of words that students do not immediately recognize in print.

As literature-based instruction has grown more popular, some parents and educators worry that phonics has been lost from the process of learning to read and write. Literature-based instruction does *not* ignore phonics. It's impossible to learn to read and write an alphabetic orthographic system (like English) without a knowledge of the sounds and symbols that make up

5.1 Putting Ideas to Work

Three Related Areas of Word Study

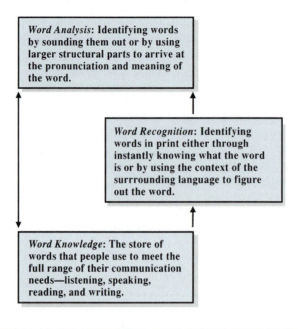

Word Analysis: Identifying words by sounding them out or by using larger structural parts to arrive at the pronunciation and meaning of the word.

Word Recognition: Identifying words in print either through instantly knowing what the word is or by using the context of the surrrounding language to figure out the word.

Word Knowledge: The store of words that people use to meet the full range of their communication needs—listening, speaking, reading, and writing.

this system. Phonics remains an important part of literature-based instruction and word study.

The three dimensions of word study—knowledge, recognition, and analysis—are related. All are rooted in the need to understand meaning; all aim to help pupils derive meaning from what they read and express meaning in what they write.

Word Knowledge

Word knowledge is essential to reading and writing competency. Ultimately, students demonstrate success at reading by understanding what they read, and they display effectiveness in writing by using words appropriately in written discourse. Word knowledge does not stand alone within the language arts curriculum; it is related to the broader context of meaning. And knowing the meaning of individual language units (words) is essential to creating meaning in reading and writing.

"Without a doubt, there exists a strong relationship between vocabulary knowledge and reading comprehension" (Tierney, Readence, and Dishner, 1995; p. 302). Research has consistently shown the importance of vocabulary and word knowledge as a fundamental factor in understanding what one reads. Researchers such as Davis (1972), Anderson and Freebody (1985), and Blachowicz (1985) have found that knowledge of word meaning is an important factor in reading comprehension . Devine (1986) summarized research on the vocabulary-comprehension link: "Of all aspects of prior knowledge, word knowledge seems to be the most important for reading comprehension" (p. 29). Based on his research, Pearson (1985) concluded that knowledge of key vocabulary words predicts comprehension better than any other test of reading ability or achievement. William Nagy (1988) writes, "A wealth of research has documented the strength of the relationship between vocabulary and comprehension . . . a reader's vocabulary knowledge is the single best predictor of how well that reader can understand text" (p. 1).

In sum, the more words a reader knows, the better he or she will understand what he or she reads. That is why vocabulary study is such an important part of language arts instruction.

As pupils encounter words in print, they develop knowledge of the subject matter and competency in literacy.
© Pedrick/The Image Works

Words and Concepts

Children progress through different stages or steps in coming to know a word (see Putting Ideas to Work 5.2). Klein (1988) describes the stages of word knowledge as three categories or "dictionaries": "the ownership dictionary, the mid-level dictionary (accessible with contextual assistance), and the low-level dictionary (marginal; possible, but with increased risk of error). . . . Each of us possesses all three dictionaries in our heads" (Klein, 1988; p. 62). As students encounter new words, they enter each word into one of these mental "dictionaries." Words normally enter at the low- or mid-level and work up to full ownership through repeated use.

Ultimately, to "know" a word means to understand the concept the word represents, not just to be able to quote its dictionary definition. Vocabulary development and concept development are intimately related. Words represent objects, events, experiences, emotions, and ideas in the world around us. Attaching a word label to the objects and ideas we encounter is the final step in the process of cognition. At the same time, understanding the meaning of a word is a way of acquiring new knowledge. Within the classroom (and outside it, too), every new learning experience presents the opportunity to learn new words.

Literature is essential to continued vocabulary growth throughout the school years. The language children encounter in trade books extends their knowledge of words and their ability to use this knowledge in various contexts. Peterson and Eeds (1990) use an example from William Steig's *Sylvester and the Magic Pebble*, the story of a donkey who temporarily turned into a rock. When pupils hear or read the words *confused, perplexed, puzzled,* and *bewildered* to describe the hungry lion who circles the donkey-suddenly-turned-boulder, there is little need to teach what these words mean.

Words take on credence, worth, and accuracy in relationship to the concepts they represent. The more abstract a concept is, the harder it is to conceptualize. People can easily agree that a *doll,* a *shirt,* and a *chair* fall into

5.2 Putting Ideas to Work
What Does It Mean to "Know" a Word?

Do pupils know a word when they can simply pronounce it? Do they know the word when they can give a synonym or dictionary definition for it? Or do they need to use the word in a number of contexts before they really know it?

Edgar Dale (1965) has produced a useful definition of what it means to know a word. Dale suggests five stages of word knowledge:

1. *I never saw/heard the word before.* These are totally unfamiliar words completely outside the pupil's vocabulary.
2. *I know there's such a word, but I don't know what it means.* For many adults, a word like *antidisestablishmentarianism* would fall into this category; we know that the word exists, but we don't know its meaning.
3. *I have a vague contextual placement of the word.* Words like *zither* or *beguile* would fit into this category for many adults. They are familiar with the words, but not familiar enough to define them in isolation.
4. *I know the word. I will be able to recognize the word again if I see it and I am likely to use it.* These are words we can be sure are becoming part of a student's vocabulary.
5. *I know the word well. I can make fine and precise distinctions in its meaning.* At this stage, the person can distinguish between the meanings of closely related words—between *satire* and *irony*, for example.

the categories of *toys, clothing,* and *furniture,* respectively. But they do not agree as readily on whether Tom, Dick, and Harry are *conservative, moderate,* and *liberal,* respectively. Abstract concepts are more difficult to grasp because we cannot sense them in the way we can touch and feel and see concrete objects. We cannot touch love or happiness, so we try to describe these concepts in concrete terms: *Love is a warm puppy,* or *Happiness is Friday afternoon when all the children have gone home.*

Words represent concepts, and concepts are tied to experiences. A student who has never seen the ocean still learns the meaning of the word *ocean* by hearing about it, reading about it, or seeing it on TV. But this child's concept of ocean will be thin in comparison to the child who has been to the beach, seen the fury of an ocean storm, enjoyed the ocean's calm at sunset, tasted its salty brine, or felt its seaweed while swimming in its cool water. Simply experiencing a concept or object does not assure vocabulary growth, however; children must attach language to all the direct and vicarious experiences they have in and out of school. As they develop new concepts, their vocabulary will broaden and deepen as well. One of the most effective ways for promoting concept/vocabulary growth is to use literature in the classroom.

Vocabulary Development in the Classroom

A literature-based program needs to be saturated with planned and incidental opportunities to learn about language, to learn about words. Nagy (1988) identifies three qualities of effective vocabulary instruction in the classroom: integration, repetition, and meaningful use.

Integration.   Integration means teaching vocabulary in relation to what pupils already know, connecting the meanings of new words to familiar concepts and experiences. Rather than teaching new words as isolated items, the teacher introduces and develops the meaning of new terms by relating them to familiar concepts and experiences. As the students encounter new words, they integrate those words with words they already know.

Semantic mapping is one effective technique for integrating vocabulary instruction with known concepts. A semantic map is a web or scheme that focuses vocabulary instruction on a central object or concept. It is a visual representation of the relationships among words and concepts associated with a particular topic. New vocabulary items connect to words and ideas that pupils are already familiar with. The teacher begins by writing the key concept on the chalkboard or on a chart (see Putting Ideas to Work 5.3). Students brainstorm, and the teacher writes the words they suggest, adding new words he or she wants to teach and perhaps categorizing the various classes of words. Pupils see new words in relationship to those they already know.

Besides the format presented in Putting Ideas to Work 5.3, other visual designs have been used for semantic mapping, including:

Venn diagrams, intersecting circles that allow the classification of words according to concepts;

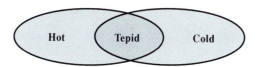

hierarchical arrays, with "branching tree" formats showing the relationships among words;

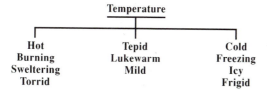

linear arrays, which allow pupils to show degrees of relationship between words and ideas.

Chilly ⟶ Cool ⟶ Frosty ⟶ Icy ⟶ Frigid

Whichever form is used, semantic maps provide integrated vocabulary instruction by presenting new words in relationship to familiar concepts,

5.3 Putting Ideas to Work
Semantic Maps

A semantic map can be used to develop vocabulary related to a single trade book or to several trade books centered on a theme or concept. For example:

1. The following semantic map may be constructed to introduce Miska Miles's *Annie and the Old One*, the touching story of a young Navajo girl whose efforts to forestall her grandmother's death help her to understand more about the cycle of life:

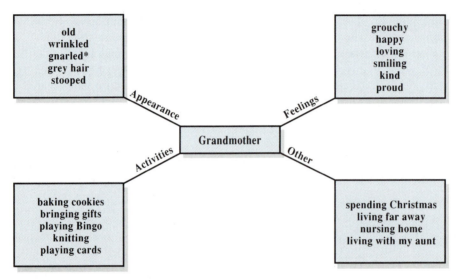

* word suggested by the teacher

and not as isolated entities. These tools emphasize concept development as well as vocabulary development, and they have proved very effective in promoting vocabulary growth.

Analogies also make use of the principle of integration in vocabulary study. Analogies focus not only on words, but also on the conceptual relationships between words—for example, *shower:hurricane :: fire:conflagration*. Pupils can create their own analogies for new vocabulary items. Analogies require higher-level thinking and help pupils develop and extend word meanings. They also help measure a child's language and cognitive functioning.

This integrated type of activity serves several purposes. While introducing new words, it also relates the story to the students' backgrounds and activates their motivation before reading. It is diagnostic, because the teacher can anticipate from the children's responses what problems they might encounter in comprehending the story. It also provides experience in creative thinking (brainstorming) as well as a format for follow-up activities.

2. As pupils read books related to a common theme—for example, Marjorie Weinman Sharmat's *Mitchell Is Moving*, Barbara Cooney's *Miss Rumphius*, and Wendy Kesselman's *Emma*, all of which deal with loneliness—the teacher can design a semantic map like the following:

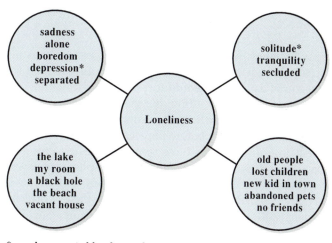

* words suggested by the teacher

Similar semantic maps can be constructed around other themes in children's books—themes such as courage, belonging, friendship, and success.

Semantic maps, analogies, and other activities provide integration by linking the meanings of new words to words and concepts pupils already know. These activities can carry over into the second characteristic of word study in the classroom: repetition.

Repetition. A second quality of effective vocabulary instruction is repetition. Encountering a word once or twice will not guarantee that the word will become part of a student's mental "ownership dictionary." The child needs to use the word a number of times in order to "own" it.

5.4 Putting Ideas to Work
Word for the Day

A daily starting point for word study can be a class "Word for the Day." The daily word can be a new and interesting word pupils have encountered in trade books or other reading material or a key word the teacher suggests from a content area. Students can quickly take responsibility for suggesting words.

The Word for the Day can be written on a card and placed in a special location in the classroom. (A year's worth of multicolored word cards makes a more interesting display than the traditional alphabet cards tacked above the chalkboard in most classrooms.) The word becomes the subject of day-long attention as pupils use it as often as they can. It also becomes a focus for word study: Where did the word come from? What other meanings does it have? What other words are related to it? Using and reusing the daily word in as many contexts as possible makes the word familiar to students.

Although we sometimes think of vocabulary as a single entity, pupils actually have four vocabularies corresponding to the four major areas of language arts: listening, the auditory receptive function; speaking, the auditory expressive function; reading, the visual receptive function; and writing, the visual expressive function. Students may, for example, understand a word the teacher says orally before they learn how to write that word. In literature-based programs, pupils have opportunities all day long to engage in language activities in all these modes. As pupils hear new words as they listen to stories or participate in literature circles, as they try using new words to describe books they have read, as they see these words in print and use them in their writing, they quickly claim ownership. This is why it is important for teachers to serve as models, to create "word alerts," to call attention to interesting uses of words in read-aloud stories, and to use new words repeatedly in classroom activities. Repetition of new words in a variety of situations extends vocabulary.

Word study and vocabulary development elements of literature-based programs constantly make children aware of the richness of their language through literature. Some of these elements may include etymology, curiosity about language, word games, and computer programs.

Etymology, the study of the origins and development of words, is a fruitful source for exploring word meanings. Pupils often get excited about word study as they question, "Where did this word come from?"

Curiosity about how words enter the language can also stimulate understanding. Most of our words are borrowed from other languages, of course; there are few languages spoken on the face of the earth that have not made a contribution to our word stock. We also build our own new words, adding prefixes or suffixes to familiar stems (*deplane, **empower***) or combining units in new ways (***astronaut, aquanaut***). We sometimes drop meaning units from the original forms of words: *creation* becomes *create* and *denotation* becomes *denote*

5.5 Putting Ideas to Work
Literature-Based Activities for Promoting Word Knowledge

*T*here are an endless number of possible classroom activities that can increase pupils' vocabulary knowledge and use in a literature-based classroom. For example:

Synonym searches provide repeated encounters with words. Students can learn about synonyms early in their school lives. After reading Margery Williams's classic *The Velveteen Rabbit* to the class, the teacher might ask how the rabbit felt when the boy abandoned him and the rabbit was condemned to be burned. The children's typical initial response—"sad" can expand to include other words that describe the rabbit's feelings: *unhappy, miserable, melancholic, woeful,* and *heartbroken*, to name a few. (In planning this activity ahead of time, the teacher might choose one of these words as the class Word for the Day or develop a semantic web based on the concept.)

Antonym searches are natural extensions of synonym searches. The title of Judith Viorst's *Alexander and the Terrible, Horrible, No Good, Very Bad Day* already suggests an extension of words. To learn about antonyms, children might list "happy words" to form a title like *Alexander and the Wonderful, Terrific, Marvelous, Stupendous, Very Good Day*. (And this title might suggest ideas for a story pupils could write about their own experiences.)

A thesaurus is a valuable reference in working with synonyms and antonyms. Some available for use in the elementary grades are: *The Clear and Simple Thesaurus Dictionary,* Harriet Wittels and Jon Greisman, eds., Putman Publishing Group, 1971 (for grades 2–7); *The Doubleday Children's Thesaurus*, Pete Stevenson, ed., Doubleday, 1987 (for grades 3–8); and *In Other Words: A Beginning Thesaurus*, Andrew Schiller and William Jenkins, eds., Scott Foresman, 1987 (for grades 3–4).

Semantic study is an important part of literature-based instruction. Semantics, the formal study of word meaning, involves denotative meanings (the literal, direct, explicit dictionary definitions) as well as connotative meanings (the implied, suggested, associated meanings) of words. Some words—for example, *peppermint*—have positive associations for children; others—for example, *homework*—have less positive associations. Studying these associated meanings in language is what semantics is all about. As lower-grade pupils talk about books like *Too Short Fred*, Susan Meddaugh's story of the cat who is a hero despite his diminutive stature, or upper-grade pupils discuss *Blubber*, Judy Blume's story about a girl who is overweight, words and their associated meanings can provide a focus for discussion. For example, *diminutive, dwarf, runt*, and *petite* are words that might describe Too Short Fred; *obese, rotund, corpulent*, and *stout* are synonyms for *fat*. Yet all have different connotations or associated meanings.

In sum, literature-based instruction provides opportunities for wide reading—the quintessential element in fostering vocabulary growth.

(which, when it was coined, was called "an American barbarism"). We shorten words in other ways: *examination* becomes *exam; dormitory* becomes *dorm*. And we do the same with acronyms: a child with learning disabilities is "an LD kid." We also blend elements to create new words: *motel* from *motor* and *hotel; chortle* from *chuckle* and *snort*. We use proper names to represent ordinary concepts: *sandwich* and *pasteurize*. In short, our language is a vibrant, dynamic entity that adapts its lexicon to the needs of its users.

5.6 Putting Ideas to Work

Nothing Need Ever Be Boring Again!

*A*n overused word among pupils at all levels is the word *boring*. With the help of a thesaurus, it is easy to find alternatives to this overworked term: *vapid, tedious, uninteresting, banal, wearisome,* or *dull*, for example. With practice, pupils can expunge the "b-word" and use alternatives:

"Mr. Savage, this is the most vapid book I've ever read."
"This exercise is tedious. Do we have to do it?"

Vapid? Perhaps. *Tedious?* Maybe. But *boring?* Never!

Word games bring out the fun of language; for example, in the game "The Minister's Cat," students add adjectives in alphabetical order ("The minister's cat is an *affable* cat, a *brave* cat," and so on). In "Hinky Pinky," riddles ask for pairs of rhyming words ("What's a smooth young hen?" *"A slick chick."* "What tale is told in a horror movie?" *"A gory story."*). In "Swifties," an action word or adverb is matched to the context of a sentence to create a pun ("There goes Moby Dick!" Tom *wailed*. "I'm losing my hair," the man *bawled*.). In the "Alliteration Game," pupils supply alliterative adjectives (*aggravating* alligators, *bashful* baboons). In "Meaning Shifts," they make up questions like, "If lawyers are *disbarred*, can electricians be *delighted*? Can cowboys be *deranged*? And can dry cleaners be *depressed*?" Games like these, which children frequently play outside of school, too, can spring from encounters with literature in the classroom.

Computer programs are also available to reinforce vocabulary activities in the classroom. While some of these programs are drill-and-practice—designed to provide practice with words the teacher has already "taught"—other programs give students the opportunity to explore language through synonyms, antonyms, analogies, and other types of encounters with words.

In sum, repeated word use in a variety of forms will help pupils expand their awareness and knowledge of vocabulary. "For enhancement of children's vocabulary growth and development, there can be no substitute for voluminous experience with rich, natural language" (Anderson and Nagy, 1991; p. 722). Word knowledge builds through planned and spontaneous opportunities to set children on the road to finding (in the words of Mark Twain) *just the right word* instead of *almost the right word*.

Meaningful Use. A third characteristic of effective vocabulary instruction, one closely related to repetition, is meaningful use. Asking students to "look up the dictionary meanings of the words on this list and write a sentence using each word" is not an especially effective approach. Words have meanings, and students learn those meanings as they use the words in meaningful contexts.

5.7 Putting Ideas to Work
Books about Words

A classroom with a constant attention to word study will contain many books about words, such as:

Fun with Words by Maxwell Nuinberg, which relates the origins and history of selected words.

The Weighty Word Book by Paul M. Levitt, Douglas Burger, and Elissa Gurlnick, which contains stories about words form *abasement* to *zealot*.

Many Luscious Lollipops by Ruth Keller, one of a brilliantly illustrated series of word books with a grammatical focus as well.

A Little Pigeon Toad, A Chocolate Moose for Dinner, The King Who Rained, and other books by Fred Gwynne, with delightful plays on words.

These are only a few of the hundreds of interesting trade books that will both spark and satisfy pupils' interest in learning about words.

Vocabulary development is rooted in meaning. Experience with words is at the heart of any language arts program, since words are essential to any language activity—expressive or receptive, oral or written. Writing a letter to a favorite author; preparing a travel brochure based on France Lessac's *My Little Island;* writing an advertisement for Betsy Byars's book *The Not-Just-Anybody Family;* recreating a ghost story using Mary Downing's *The Doll in the Garden* as a model; persuading parents or teachers to agree to one's plans as in Judith Viorst's *Earrings*, the story of a girl who wants her ears pierced—all provide occasions for reinforcing words in meaningful contexts. The teacher in a literature-based classroom must look for opportunities to explore words and their meanings in as many ways as possible to ensure that vocabulary development will be a constant focus.

Two other elements are essential to rich vocabulary development in a reading instructional program: the teacher's active involvement and wide student reading.

Teacher involvement is key in creating a rich vocabulary diet in the classroom. The teacher's curiosity and excitement about the world of words will be contagious. Teachers need to use new words that the pupils are learning, using as rich a vocabulary as possible without losing the students. "A significant factor for helping students develop and extend their vocabularies seems to be the excitement teachers generate about words. When teachers demonstrate enthusiasm for words and transfer this excitement to students, all instructional activities seem to be equally effective" (Hittleman, 1988; p. 166). As in other aspects of reading instruction, teacher modeling is essential to help children become independent word learners.

Wide reading—
wherever that reading
is enjoyed—is a key to
growing literacy.
© Michael Siluk/
The Image Works

Wide reading is the main idea behind literature-based instruction, one of the major reasons why trade books have become so prominent in classroom literacy programs. Reading itself is an excellent means of acquiring word knowledge. The relationship between reading success and word meaning is reciprocal. Knowledge of word meaning contributes greatly to reading ability, and wide reading contributes significantly to vocabulary development. The amount of free reading pupils do has been shown to be the best predictor of vocabulary growth in the elementary grades (Fielding, Wilson, and Anderson, 1986). Word knowledge may be both a cause and an effect of reading success. "Given the number of words to be learned and the number of encounters it takes to learn them thoroughly, reading is necessarily the major avenue of large-scale vocabulary growth" (Nagy, 1988; p. 31). The road that leads to reading achievement is paved with the words students know.

Reading competency is rooted in understanding the meanings of words in print, but to arrive at these meanings, the reader must first be able to identify what the words are. For pupils learning to read, word recognition and analysis strategies must be integrated into literature-based reading instruction.

Word Recognition

Word recognition is the identification of the form, pronunciation, and meaning of a word in print. It involves an awareness of what the word is and what it means in context. As they are learning to read, pupils learn to recognize words by sight and through context.

Sight Words

Instruction in word recognition focuses on sight words, words that children recognize quickly and accurately as entire units on visual contact. "When reading sight words, the reader goes directly from the written word to its meaning" (Groff, 1995; p. 2) It stands to reason that the more words a student can recognize instantly, the smoother and more efficient his or her reading will be.

The goal of instruction in word recognition is to help pupils recognize printed words as quickly and easily as possible. Readers recognize sight words as single, holistic units. They establish a direct connection between the word in print and its meaning (Ehri, 1992).

Word recognition separates good readers from poor readers. Some wonder if the relationship is "a chicken and egg" situation; in other words, do people read well because they have good word recognition skills, or do they recognize words because they have good general reading ability? Whatever the nature of the relationship, word recognition is related to reading competency. The initial processing of a word depends on recognition of its visual form, and word recognition provides the basis for reading comprehension.

Selecting Vocabulary.

Selecting sight words is an early decision in the instructional process. Traditionally, commercial programs selected these words and provided suggestions on how to teach them. Stories were often written with the specific purpose of teaching a sight word through repeated use (resulting in the stereotypical *Run, Dick, run. Run, run, run*). More authentic reading materials require that teachers decide which words they should teach for instant recognition.

Meaning is an important criterion in the selection process. "Intensive instruction is most worthwhile when words to be covered are important, in either of two senses: important to the understanding of the selection or important because of their general utility in the language" (Nagy, 1988; p. 33). Children should know the words that are crucial to understanding a text before they are expected to read that particular text.

Word frequency is another criterion for selecting sight words. Experts have compiled lists of frequently used words. One of the earliest and best known lists is the Dolch Basic Sight Vocabulary List (1939), which contains 220 of the words that most frequently appear in beginning basal readers. A number of other sight-word lists have been compiled with the same idea in mind. For literature-based instruction, Durr (1973) and Eeds (1985) have compiled lists of high-frequency words used in trade books for children. The former list was compiled from books that children in the upper primary and intermediate grades generally read. The Eeds list was compiled from K–3 children's books.

Many of the words contained on sight-word lists are what structural linguists call function words. Syntactically, words may be designated as *form* words or *function* words. Form words correspond roughly to the four major parts of speech: nouns, verbs, adjectives, and adverbs. Function words make up all the other word classes: prepositions, conjunctions, auxiliary verbs, pronouns, and the like. Form words convey most of the meaning in language; function words indicate the relationships between form words. Form and function words may be compared to a brick wall. Form words are like bricks, providing the form and substance of the wall; function words are like mortar, "cementing" the unit together as a whole entity.

What do form and function words have to do with word recognition? In the English lexicon, there are relatively few function words—only about 150—but these words constitute 30 to 50 percent of running words in text. In Pamela Allen's genuinely funny *Who Sank the Boat?*, the opening sentence— *Beside the sea, on Mr. Peffer's place, there lived a cow, a donkey, a sheep, a pig, and a tiny little mouse.*—contains a total of 22 words, ten (or 45 percent) of them function words. The pupil who can recognize function words instantly will be well on the way to smooth and meaningful reading.

Students also learn function words as they use these words in their own writing. From simple captions to cohesive stories, function words are used so frequently that children quickly come to realize the importance of being able to recognize and spell them.

In the final analysis, the teacher must select sight words based on meaning and function. The reason children need to learn to recognize words instantaneously by sight is so they can quickly and easily arrive at meaning in what they read. The words that most directly serve this purpose should become part of the pupils' sight vocabularies.

Deciding How to Teach. Traditionally, teachers provided repeated exposure to sight words by using flash cards. Pupils practiced reading the words for rapid and accurate recognition. (Some modern programs flash the words on computer screens.) At times, isolated practice with words on cards may be appropriate—as when label words are attached to objects in kindergarten classrooms to develop print awareness and to help students recognize common words in print. At most times, however, sight words are best taught in the context of connected text. In other words, instead of introducing sight words isolated on flash cards, new sight words should be part of a semantic web that uncovers meaning by relating the sight words to known ideas. The efficacy of presenting a list of unfamiliar words prior to reading a story has also been questioned (Anderson and Nagy, 1991). While at times it may be important to make sure students understand the meanings of essential words before reading, the gist of a story is likely to assist them in learning the meanings of unfamiliar words. Presenting words *within the context* of stories, poems, and informational trade books preserves the meaning while helping children build a store of words that they can recognize instantly by sight.

Since function words are used so frequently, teachers may need to teach them as sight words; yet because they have no concrete meaning, they are difficult to define in isolation. These words should be learned in the context of larger segments of text. For example, as young children share the popular finger rhyme "Eensy, Weensy Spider," and as they learn to associate

5.8 Putting Ideas to Work

Bookwords: High-Frequency Words in Storybooks for Beginning Readers

**Bookwords: Final List of 227 Words from 400 Storybooks
for Beginning Readers and Number of Times Each Word Appears**

the	1,334	good	90	think	47	next	28
and	985	this	90	new	46	only	28
a	831	don't	89	know	46	• am	27
I	757	little	89	help	46	began	27
to	746	if	87	grand	46	head	27
said	688	just	87	boy	46	keep	27
you	638	• baby	86	take	45	• teacher	27
he	488	way	85	eat	44	• sure	27
it	345	there	83	• body	43	• says	27
in	311	every	83	school	43	• ride	27
was	294	went	82	house	42	• pet	27
she	250	father	80	morning	42	• hurry	26
for	235	had	79	• yes	41	hand	26
that	232	see	79	after	41	hard	26
is	230	dog	78	never	41	• push	26
his	226	home	77	or	40	our	26
but	224	down	76	• self	40	their	26
they	218	got	73	try	40	• watch	26
my	214	would	73	has	38	• because	25
of	204	time	71	• always	38	door	25
on	192	• love	70	over	38	us	25
me	187	walk	70	again	37	• should	25
all	179	• came	69	side	37	• room	25
be	176	were	68	• thank	37	• pull	25
go	171	ask	67	why	37	• great	24
can	162	back	67	who	36	gave	24
with	158	now	66	saw	36	• does	24
one	157	friend	65	• mom	35	• car	24
her	156	cry	64	• kid	35	• ball	24
what	152	oh	64	give	35	• sat	24
we	151	Mr.	63	around	34	• stay	24
him	144	• bed	63	by	34	• each	23
no	143	an	62	Mrs.	34	• ever	23
so	141	very	62	off	33	• until	23
out	140	where	60	• sister	33	• shout	23

Continued on next page.

Bookwords: Final List of 227 Words from 400 Storybooks for Beginning Readers and Number of Times Each Word Appears

up	137	play	59	find	32	• mama	22
are	133	let	59	• fun	32	• use	22
will	127	long	58	more	32	turn	22
look	126	here	58	while	32	thought	22
some	123	how	57	tell	32	• papa	22
day	123	make	57	• sleep	32	• lot	21
at	122	big	56	made	31	• blue	21
have	121	from	55	first	31	• bath	21
your	121	put	55	say	31	• mean	21
mother	119	• read	55	took	31	• sit	21
come	118	them	55	• dad	30	• together	21
not	115	as	54	found	30	• best	20
like	112	• Miss	53	• lady	30	• brother	20
then	108	any	52	soon	30	• feel	20
get	103	right	52	ran	30	• floor	20
when	101	• nice	50	• dear	29	wait	20
thing	100	other	50	man	29	• tomorrow	20
do	99	well	48	• better	29	• surprise	20
too	91	old	48	• through	29	• shop	20
want	91	• night	48	stop	29	run	20
did	91	may	48	still	29	• own	20
could	90	about	47	• fast	28		

• Indicates words *not* on Durr list

Since this list was first published, Eeds has done extensive research in holistic classrooms where children are acquiring written language. She now believes that children acquire high-frequency words naturally as a teacher demonstrates their use in the daily life of the classroom (recording plans, learning, and so on) and as the children, steeped in literature, use them in their daily writing.

printed words with the familiar spoken words of the poem, the teacher can introduce phrase cards with such predictable expressions as *Up the water spout, Down came the rain,* and *Out came the sun.* As children say or sing the poem in unison, the teacher can point to each card as the familiar phrases are spoken. The cards place common function words such as *up, down,* and *out* into context as the students learn to recognize these words in print.

5.9 Putting Ideas to Work
Personal Words

One way to build sight vocabulary is to adopt Sylvia Ashton-Warner's idea of "organic words" (1963) and have pupils choose their own special sight words. On the very first day of school, the teacher asks students, "What word would you really like to learn today?" The words are personal choices, taken from each child's own experience, words that (for whatever reason) are of immense importance to the child: *watermelon, skeleton, birthday.*

The pupil sits next to the teacher and observes the teacher writing the word on a card. The child then must do something with the word—illustrate it, read it to a classmate, or use it in a story. The words usually become sight words fairly quickly because the child has chosen words loaded with personal meaning and is motivated to learn them.

Over time, the student builds up a collection of personal sight-word cards, which may be gathered on a ring and hung at the pupil's desk. These personal word cards have multiple uses all year long: in writing sentences and stories, in practicing word analysis ("See how many words in your stack have this sound," or "Do you have a compound word on your ring?"), as well as in vocabulary enrichment activities ("Can you find a synonym for your word?").

Research supports the efficacy of using literature to help pupils build a store of sight words. Bridge, Winograd, and Haley (1983) found that predictable books were especially effective for promoting early word recognition. Moe (1989) suggests a plan for using trade books to help beginning readers increase their sight vocabularies. Noting that most of the words in early picture books are already part of the young child's listening/speaking vocabulary, Moe suggests the extensive use of trade books in early reading instruction. With a very limited sight vocabulary, pupils can independently read beginning trade books such as Nancy Tafuri's *Have You Seen My Duckling?*, Pat Hutchins's *Rosie's Walk*, or Linda Bancheck's *Snake In, Snake Out*, all of which contain a very limited number of words. By reading simple books like these, beginning readers are exposed repeatedly to words in the meaningful reading of connected text.

Word lists can be a useful inventory of words that appear frequently in children's books, but the payoff occurs when students recognize and use these words in their own reading and writing. Words carry meaning and worth as they are used in the context of authentic language. The teacher can post chart poetry, language experience stories, songs, and chants around the classroom to help pupils build sight vocabulary quickly and easily, with meaning intact.

Practice in word recognition needs to be saturated with meaning. It makes little sense for a child to recognize a word without knowing the meaning of that word in context.

5.10 Putting Ideas to Work
Teaching Sight Words

*E*eds (1985), who compiled the list of 227 high-frequency words from children's trade books that appears in Putting Ideas to Work 5.8, recommends that the teacher avoid presenting these words in isolation, since "it is hard to envision a less meaningful situation than subjecting children to flash card drill or to lists of words to be memorized" (p. 421). Instead, she suggests an integrated technique for teaching the words on her list:

1. Using a Big Book or projected page, begin by focusing on words that are most irregular and most frequent, using a masking technique.
2. Cover the target word and let the children predict from context which word from Eed's list is missing.
3. Uncover the masked word to show the actual target word. Was it the one they identified? If not, students can match an isolated word from the list back into a standing context.

Context Clues

Context clues are another strategy readers rely on as they interact with print, and learning to use these clues is an important part of learning to read. Context clues consist of information presented in the surrounding passage that helps the reader recognize the meaning (and occasionally the pronunciation) of a word. The meaning of a word often depends on the context the word is in, and children acquire much of their vocabulary knowledge through context (Nagy, 1995).

Syntactic and Semantic Clues. Pupils use both the syntactic and semantic components of their knowledge of language when they seek context clues. Syntactic context clues provide information about the grammatical *function* of a word in a sentence. For example, consider the sentence, *In the old Soviet Union, Lenin's face used to be **ubiquitous.*** It is not difficult to recognize that the final word is an adjective. The way it is used and its position in the sentence fits a familiar pattern and provides a syntactic clue about the function of the word.

But syntactic clues provide only limited information about unknown words. For example, in the sentence, *When Susan goes to the beach, she runs through the sand and **waves**, waves* may be a noun or a verb; the syntactic context is ambiguous because either would fit. In this case, contextual analysis demands the use of semantic clues.

Semantic context clues provide information about the *meaning* of a word. In the expanded sentence, *In the old Soviet Union, Lenin's face used to be ubiquitous; it gazed from statues in public places, looked down from banners on the sides of buildings, appeared on stamps and medals, and adorned pictures in every classroom,* the meaning of *ubiquitous* is more clearly defined from the added information. Although syntactic clues are helpful, semantic clues are far more useful in figuring out unknown words in print.

5.11 Putting Ideas to Work
Context Clues Exercise

*T*o see how context helps in word identification, do the following exercise. Try to jot a synonym or a brief definition for each of the following five words:

1. cynosure _____
2. polysemous _____
3. effulgent _____
4. obsequious _____
5. tyro _____

Now read the following sentences to see if you can get a better idea of the meaning of each of these words:

1. Jamie was a shy and retiring person who didn't want to be noticed; his brother, on the other hand, wanted to be the *cynosure* of the group.
2. *Polysemous* words have more than one meaning.
3. Sarita's *effulgent* smile and manner are a sharp contrast to her sister's dour personality.
4. The *obsequious* waiter bowed to the host and fawned on the guest as he served the meal.
5. You could tell by the way Jared looked nervously at the dashboard as he sat behind the wheel for the first time that he was a *tyro* when it came to driving.

Although these sentences do not provide full and complete definitions, the context in each sentence gives clues to what the italicized words mean.

1. cynosure—center of attention; 2. polysemous—diversity of meaning; 3. effulgent—radiant or shining; 4. obsequious—submissive or servile; 5. tyro—beginner, novice.

Among the different types of context clues that can be found in text are:

definitions, in which a synonym for or description of a potentially difficult word is provided right in the text itself. This often appears as an appositive expression: *The rider gripped the* **pommel**, *the rounded hump on the front of the saddle, as the horse galloped out of control.*

comparison/contrast, which unlocks the meaning of a word by comparing it with another key word: *My father is* **parsimonious**, *but he's not nearly as cheap as my uncle.*

summaries or examples, which provide cues needed for identification: *They took all the* **paraphernalia** *they would need for a camping trip—a tent, sleeping bags, cooking utensils, and a first aid kit.*

experience, or aspects of a child's life and background that might suggest the meaning of an unfamiliar word: *Rosa's favorite part of the party was when her grandmother brought the* **piñata** *out.*

Using context requires a student to form a hypothesis or make an educated guess about the meaning of an unfamiliar word. The ability to use contextual analysis depends partly on the semantic and syntactic information the author provides. It also depends on qualities the reader brings to print—a certain level of competency in decoding, grammatical knowledge, semantic awareness, experiential background, and reasoning ability.

Although clues to the pronunciation and meaning of an unknown word may appear in a single sentence, such neatly defined clues are not always easy to find in trade books and other forms of narrative text. Pupils may need to search for clues in other sentences in the surrounding passage. They must get used to the idea of searching for the clues they need, and cloze exercises have proved extremely useful for this practice.

Cloze Exercises. Cloze involves the systematic deletion of words from a text. Every fifth, eighth, or tenth word in a passage is deleted and the reader fills in the missing element. Originally designed as a text readability measure and as a means of determining reader comprehension, cloze is an effective way to help students practice contextual analysis because it forces them to figure out what the word might be by looking for information in the surrounding text. Initially the teacher should discuss (not just check) the students' responses so that pupils learn how to use this word-identification strategy. Children can be introduced to cloze in emergent literacy settings by deleting words in familiar text, as in:

> To market, to _____, to buy a fat pig.
> Home again, _____ again, jiggedy jig.
> To market, _____ market, to buy a fat hog.
> Home _____, home again, jiggedy jog.

As students become more proficient, they can try longer cloze passages to practice using context clues as a word recognition technique (see Putting Ideas to Work 5.12).

Cloze procedure can be modified by providing pupils with multiple choices for missing words, or by consistently deleting particular word classes—for example, adjectives. This type of modified cloze gives students clues to help them determine which words might fit.

In addition to cloze exercises, teacher modeling can effectively demonstrate how to use context clues as a word recognition strategy. When teachers explain how they use context to determine the pronunciation and meaning of a new word they meet in their own reading, pupils gain insight into the process.

Beyond providing an effective word-recognition strategy for individual vocabulary items, context clues play a broader role in the process of learning to read. Direct instruction could never account for the incredible vocabulary growth—from an estimated 5,000 words to an estimated 50,000—that occurs in a child's school life. Research indicates that students learn much of this vocabulary through context (Nagy, Herman, and Anderson, 1985). Learning from context through independent reading is the major mode of vocabulary

5.12 Putting Ideas to Work
Using Cloze

*T*he following cloze exercise is based on the story *Sarah, Plain and Tall*, Patricia MacLachlan's beautiful Newbery Award winner:

> Anna and Caleb lived with their father in a farmhouse on the prairie. Their mother had died _(1)_ their father wrote a _(2)_ to see if he _(3)_ find a wife. Sarah, _(4)_ woman from Maine who _(5)_ that she was plain _(6)_ tall, answered his letter. _(7)_ came to live with _(8)_ family. Although she missed _(9)_ brother in Maine, she _(10)_ the children and their _(11)_, so she decided to _(12)_. Sarah was happy because the prairie reminded Sarah of the ocean back in Maine.

> *Answers:* 1. and; 2. letter; 3. could; 4. a; 5. wrote; 6. and; 7. Sarah; 8. the; 9. her; 10. loved; 11. father; 12. stay.

> In this passage, every fifth word was deleted. Children will probably need fewer deletions until they become adept at using cloze techniques for practice in using context clues.

> Passages like this can be used not only to help pupils develop skill in using context clues; they can also be used to determine how appropriate a book is for a student's reading level.

acquisition during the school years, and this accounts for the relationship between wide reading and vocabulary size. Learning from context while reading is a major factor in a student's reading development.

Proficient readers rely heavily on context to determine the meanings of unfamiliar words. Helping pupils learn to use context clues helps them interact more effectively with print.

Word Analysis

In a literature-based program, students will encounter millions of words in their experiences with books. For example, experts have estimated that an average middle grade child encounters about a million words in print each year (Nagy, Herman, and Anderson, 1985). The typical pupil will instantly recognize many of these words and will be able to determine what other words mean through context. Some words will be entirely unfamiliar, however, and the student will have to develop word analysis strategies to determine the pronunciations and meanings of these unfamiliar words.

Word analysis (or word attack) involves the identification of an unknown word by its constituent parts, either by analyzing letter-sound relationships or by analyzing larger meaning-bearing units (roots, prefixes, and suffixes). Using letter-sound relationships is known as *phonetic analysis;* using larger meaning-bearing elements is known as *structural analysis.* Both areas are major components of the reading instructional program in the elementary grades.

Phonetic Analysis

Phonics—the conscious study of letter-sound relationships for the purpose of learning to read and spell—has long been an integral part of literacy instruction in American schools. Phonics is an essential part of beginning reading instruction and it remains an important part of reading throughout the grades.

The code or communication system of written language is the connection between printed symbols and their equivalent spoken sounds. You can pronounce a word that you have never seen—a nonsense word like *infractaneous*, for example—by "sounding it out"; that is, by using graphophonic (writing-sound related) information in attaching the appropriate sounds to the letters in the word. This is a form of decoding, or the process of applying phonics in reading.

The Great Debate. Phonics and its role in reading instruction has been a hotly debated issue for centuries (Mathews, 1966). The debate centers on both theoretical and practical issues. One's view of the importance of phonics is often related to one's view of the reading process. Those who view reading as a "bottom-up" process believe reading involves building parts (individual sounds and symbols) into a whole (the larger meaning conveyed via print). Those who see reading as a "top-down" or holistic process place less importance on explicit instruction in sound-symbol relationships. Skills-based advocates tend to favor a heavy emphasis on direct, systematic phonics instruction. Holistic advocates tend to place a different type of emphasis on sound-symbol relationships.

There is certainly no shortage of research and expert opinion to support arguments both pro and con. Rudolph Flesch's *Why Johnny Can't Read* (1955) blamed illiteracy on the absence of phonics in reading instruction, while Bruno Bettelhiem and Karen Zelan's *On Learning to Read* (1982) blamed poor reading performance on overemphasizing phonics. Researchers like Marilyn Jager Adams (1990) and Jeanne Chall (1996) cite research evidence that strongly supports phonics; researchers like Kenneth Goodman (1976) suggest that phonics is less useful in leading children toward meaning as they read.

Code-emphasis advocates argue on behalf of phonics, asking how anyone can read the bumper sticker *I LOVE LAKE WOLOMOLOPOAG* without sounding out the name of the lake. Opponents point to the idiosyncrasies of our spelling system and argue against learning to read by "huffing and puffing at letters, marking whether vowels are glided or unglided, deciding whether *b* or *d* goes at the beginning or ending of the tattered remnant of a mutilated word rendered meaningless in isolation" (Johnson and Louis, 1987; p. 3). The debate about phonics has raged in the professional literature (see Chall, 1989a, 1989b and Carbo 1988, 1989), in teacher's rooms, and in the popular press.

In practical terms, neither school of thought denies that learning phonics is essential to learning to read. Phonics advocates see decoding as an important, foundational step along the road to deriving meaning from

5.13 Putting Ideas to Work
Point-Counterpoint on Phonics

Aunt Millie

I'll tell you what's wrong with schools today. They don't teach enough about phonics.

How can you read without phonics? You *have* to sound out words you don't know.

Yes, but you have to use some phonics in reading new words, don't you?

But phonics opens the door so that children *can* read more!

I read a book not long ago about how important phonics was in reading.

But look at cousin Alphie. He failed first grade, but once he got a teacher who taught him phonics, he quickly learned to read.

I think **you're** wrong.

Uncle Max

Hogwash! Phonics is old fashioned and out of date. Besides, nobody taught me phonics and I can read.

Not really. There are often more words that are exceptions than words that follow the rules. Phonics can be misleading for a kid trying to learn to read.

I agree, but that doesn't mean that teachers should spend all their time teaching phonics. They should have children read more.

The kids will be so tired of books with sentences like "Flick the tick off the chick with a thick stick, Nick" that they'll be turned off by the time they get to read anything interesting.

And I read one that said that phonics is not as important as everyone once thought it was.

Yes, and what about cousin Rosie? The whole family thought she was stupid because she couldn't learn to read. Once they got her away from that phonics stuff, she really bloomed. No pun intended!

I think *you're* wrong.

To get a better idea of some of the deep research-based issues in "the great debate," and to get a sense of the intensity with which professionals carry on the debate, see the exchange of articles between Marie Carbo (1988, 1989) and Jeanne Chall (1989a, 1989b) in the highly respected professional journal *Phi Delta Kappan.*

print; those who favor literature-based instruction believe that deriving meaning is paramount and phonics is a useful tool for learning to read new words and uncover meaning. Thus, the debate is less a "phonics or no phonics" question and more of a controversy over how much emphasis should be placed on phonics and how phonics should be taught.

Despite the controversy surrounding phonics and its place in the process of teaching reading, decades of research support the importance of graphophonic knowledge, or a knowledge of the relationship between sound and written symbol, in the early stages of learning to read. Phonemic awareness is a better predictor than IQ of future reading achievement. Knowledge of phonics is vital not only to identifying unknown words in print, but to fluent reading and comprehension. In updating the research on her classic book *Learning to Read: The Great Debate*, Chall (1996) continued to find that code-emphasis (or phonics) programs offer an advantage.

In her comprehensive review of reading research, Adams (1990) also emphasized the importance of phonics. Stahl, Osborn, and Lehr (1990) summarized this research:

> Explicit, systematic phonics is a singularly successful mode of teaching young or slow learners to read (p. 38).
>
> Knowledge of letters and phonemic awareness have been found to bear a strong and direct relationship to success and ease of reading acquisition (p. 54).
>
> Children's levels of phonemic awareness on entering school may be the single most powerful determinant of their success—or failure—in learning to read (p. 54).
>
> Activities requiring children to attend to the individual letters of words, their sequencing, and their phonological translations should be included in any beginning reading program (p. 73).
>
> Sounding out words is a way of teaching children what they need to know to comprehend text. The only reason for learning to read words is to understand text (p. 88).
>
> Good readers decode rapidly and automatically (p. 92).
>
> Phonics is of inescapable importance to both skillful reading and its acquisition (p. 117).[*]

Cunningham (1995) not only reviews research on the types of phonics we should teach, but provides a wealth of practical suggestions for phonics activities.

Phonics instruction is not an end in itself. The goal is to help pupils acquire the ability to read connected text fluently and with understanding. An awareness of phonics is a means to that larger end.

Phonics in a Literature-Based Program.

Phonics as an aid to word analysis is an important part of literature-based reading programs. Literature-based approaches and phonics instruction are not inconsistent. Plenty of references show how phonics can be effectively integrated into literature-based instruction (Mills, O'Keefe, and Stephens, 1990; Freppon and Headings, 1996). Literature-based instruction involves giving children strategies and skills for effective, independent reading and writing, and phonics is part of gaining control over written language.

In debunking the myths associated with whole language, Newman and Church (1990) assert that phonics is part of holistic instruction, but not as something isolated from authentic reading and writing. Literature-based advocates "have no argument with the claim that children must . . . have an understanding of phonics. It is just that we disagree with much traditional

---

[*]Excerpted from Marilyn Jager Adams, "Beginning to Read: A Summary," prepared by S. A. Stahl, J. Osborn, & F. Lehr, 1980. Reprinted by permission of the Center for the Study of Reading, University of Illinois at Champaign, Urbana.

practice in the manner of (its) acquisition" (Johnson and Louis, 1987; p. 13). The disagreement with traditional practice lies in two areas:

1. Literature-based instruction starts with text intended primarily to express meaning rather than text designed primarily to illustrate phonetic principles; and
2. Literature-based instruction proceeds from whole-to-part rather than part-to-whole.

The phonics knowledge children need to learn does not change in a literature-based program. What changes is the way in which the teacher presents this knowledge to pupils. Direct, explicit instruction in phonics occurs, but it takes place primarily within the context of reading authentic text.

Connected, meaningful discourse is the starting point for instruction when literature is used as a vehicle for developing phonetic awareness. Instead of learning isolated sounds and practicing them with stacks of worksheets containing sentences like *Can a big cat tap a tan pan?*, pupils learn phonetic elements as they encounter them within the context of familiar stories, poems, and songs written to inform or entertain, and as they learn to write in response to what they read. Freppon and Dahl (1991) suggest principles to apply to phonics instruction in a literature-based context. Phonics instruction:

focuses on the needs of the learner rather than on a predetermined sequence of phonics concepts;

is learned in the context of reading and writing activities;

builds upon pupils' basic knowledge of written language;

is tied to communication goals and purposes and integrated with other language activities;

involves teacher demonstration;

uses multiple information sources—books the students read, stories they write, print around the room, other children, and the teacher.

The world of children's literature offers unlimited opportunities for helping students acquire the phonics knowledge that will enable them to decode print successfully. Learning letter names and sounds is an important part of emergent literacy. Yopp (1995) has suggested a list of books that can be used to develop phonemic awareness at the beginning reading stage. Shared Big Books allow pupils to learn about the basic sound-symbol relationships that lie at the heart of phonics.

Children become aware of the relationship between spoken language and its written representation as they are exposed to literature. Directed activities during shared stories help them understand concepts related to phonics: the relationship between letters and sounds, the ordered sequence of sounds and letters, the relationship between the length of spoken words and the length of their written equivalents, and the like. Writing down their dictated stories also helps them attend to sound-symbol relationships. This is where instruction in phonics begins.

5.14 Putting Ideas to Work
The Language of Phonics

*I*ncluded here are some of the concepts and some of the terminology you may encounter as part of phonics instruction in the classroom.

English has an *alphabetic* writing system; that is, individual letters represent individual speech sounds. The sounds are called **phonemes;** the letters are called **graphemes.**

Consonants and **vowels** are the two classes of sounds. American English has approximately 24 consonant phonemes, with 21 letters to represent these sounds. The language also has 20 vowel phonemes, with only five letters to represent these sounds. The mismatch between letters and sounds leads to the graphophonic irregularity one finds in spelling English words.

Vowel letters include *a, e, i, o, u,* sometimes *y* and sometimes *w. Y* is a vowel when it is the only letter in a syllable representing a vowel sound (as in the word *by*) or when it immediately follows a vowel (as in *boy*). *W* is considered a vowel letter only when it immediately follows another vowel (as in *cow*).

Vowels can be either "short" or "long." Short vowel sounds are represented in the words *pat, pet, pit, pot,* and *putt.* The letter name can be heard as a long vowel is pronounced: *rate, Pete, ride, robe,* and *rude* all contain long vowels.

Double vowels occur in combination as digraphs and diphthongs. **Digraphs** consist of two vowels that together represent a single sound: the *oa* in *boat,* the *ea* in *seat,* and the *ie* in *chief* are digraphs. **Diphthongs** are letter combinations that together represent a "blended" sound: the *ou* in *mouse* and the *oi* in *noise* are diphthongs.

Consonant letters are all the letters besides *a, e, i, o,* and *u.* Consonants occur in blends and digraphs as well. **Blends** are two or three consonant letters with closely related but separate sounds: **b**room, **d**roop, and **s**tream contain consonant blends. Consonant digraphs, like vowel digraphs, consist of two letters that represent a single phoneme, as in **sh**ip, **th**in, and **ch**op.

Silent letters are graphemes that have no phonetic correspondence—in other words, letters that in a particular word make no sound: for example, **k**nee, lam**b**, and **p**sychology.

Syllables are divisions of speech sounds within words: *syl.la.ble* or *com.bin.a.tion.* The nucleus of a syllable is a vowel. Syllables are *open* when they end with a vowel (as in **ho**.tel or **be**.cause) or *closed* when they end with a consonant sound (as in ho.**tel** or **jus**.tice).

Onsets and **rimes** are parts of syllables or words. An *onset* is the part of a syllable preceding the vowel: **str**um. A rime is a vowel and any of the consonants that follow it in a syllable: b**ook**.

Generalizations are statements that apply to most sound-symbol relationships, such as "When two vowels go walking, the first one does the talking" or "Magic e makes the sound of the previous vowel long." The term *generalization* rather than *rule* is used to convey the idea that these principles do not apply in all cases. In fact, some of these generalizations apply in fewer than 50 percent of English words (Clymer, 1963).

Whole-to-part instruction is another feature of teaching phonics in a literature-based approach to reading. Synthetic approaches to phonics (sometimes called "explicit" or "direct" phonics instruction) focus on learning sound-symbol relationships and blending these elements to sound out words. By contrast, analytic approaches (sometimes called "implicit" or "indirect" methods) start with larger units of language. A literature-based approach begins with whole words in whole stories to help children develop the graphophonic awareness that will enable them to decode unknown words.

5.15 Putting Ideas to Work
Phonics Lessons Using Trade Books

Phonics can be made part of the fabric of literature-based reading lessons in a number of different ways:

Direct Teaching. Each time children encounter a problem word, the teacher can demonstrate and explain decoding strategies and teach sound-symbol combinations that will enable children to decode words.

Nursery Rhymes. As children hear and see familiar Mother Goose rhymes such as "Hickory, Dickory, Dock," they can experiment with creating new words by substituting initial consonants and blends, maintaining the rhyming element: *The mouse ran up the clock (rock, sock, block, crock, lock,* and so forth).

Shared Reading. As the teacher extends a shared reading lesson with a book such as Pat Hutchins's *Rosie's Walk,* the expression "past the mill" can be extended into a direct mini-lesson on the rime *-ill (hill, bill, thrill,* and so on).

Basal Stories. In teaching a basal lesson on Arnold Lobel's *Bumps in the Night,* the key words *owl* and *down* can help a group of readers generate a list of words in which the *ow* combination represents the vowel sound.

Experiences with Books. The predictable patterns found in the language of many trade books make these stories ideal vehicles for instruction in sound-symbol relationships. The patterned, predictable lines of Barbara Emberley's *Drummer Hoff,* which rhyme people's names to their actions; the more subtle rhymes of Ludwig Bemelmans's *Madeline* and subsequent stories; the unforgettable rhyming names (Foxy Loxy, Henny Penny, and so on) in Stephen Kellogg's popular "updated" version of *Chicken Little;* Deborah Guarin's rhyming story *Is Your Mama a Llama?;* the lines of Rosemary Wells's warm and touching *Noisy Nora*—these and hundreds of other names and lines from stories can be used for explicit instruction in phonics that will help pupils learn to decode words in print.

In integrating phonics instruction into early exposure to literature, teachers need to remember that the primary purposes of reading are meaning and enjoyment.

Trachtenburg (1990) explains the whole-part-whole approach that integrates phonics instruction with quality children's literature:

1. *Whole*: Read, comprehend, and enjoy a quality literature selection.
2. *Part*: Provide instruction in a phonic element by drawing from or extending the literature selection.
3. *Whole*: Apply the new phonic skill when reading (and enjoying) another high-quality literature selection (p. 649).

This whole-part-whole approach makes sense, because it connects phonics instruction with authentic reading experiences, which is the ultimate purpose of phonics instruction in the first place. The purpose of reading is to understand and appreciate what is read. The purpose of phonics is to help readers achieve understanding and appreciation. Teaching phonics through meaningful text makes sense in achieving both goals.

5.16 Putting Ideas to Work
Trade Books That Repeat Phonics Elements

*T*rachtenberg (1990) suggests the following list of books that repeat common phonic elements in their text.

Short *a*

Flack, Marjorie. (1931). *Angus and the Cat.* New York: Doubleday.

Griffith, Helen. (1982). *Alex and the Cat.* New York: Greenwillow.

Kent, Jack. (1971). *The Fat Cat.* New York: Scholastic.

Most, Bernard. (1980). *There's an Ant in Anthony.* New York: Morrow.

Nodset, Joan. (1963). *Who Took the Farmer's Hat?* New York: Harper & Row.

Robins, Joan. (1985). *Addie Meets Max.* New York: Harper & Row.

Schmidt, Karen. (1985). *The Gingerbread Man.* New York: Scholastic.

Seuss, Dr. (Theodore Geisel). (1957). *The Cat in the Hat.* New York: Random House.

Long *a*

Aardema, Verna. (1981). *Bringing the Rain to Kapiti Plain.* New York: Dial.

Bang, Molly. (1985). *The Paper Crane.* New York: Greenwillow.

Blume, Judy. (1974). *The Pain and the Great One.* New York: Bradbury.

Byars, Betsy. (1975). *The Lace Snail.* New York: Viking.

Henkes, Kevin. (1987). *Sheila Rae, the Brave.* New York: Greenwillow.

Hines, Anna G. (1983). *Taste the Raindrops.* New York: Greenwillow.

Short and Long *a*

Aliki. (1986). *Jack and Jake.* New York: Greenwillow.

Slobodkina, Esphyr. (1940). *Caps for Sale.* Reading, MA: Addison-Wesley.

Short *e*

Ets, Marie Hall. (1972). *Elephant in a Well.* New York: Viking.

Galdone, Paul. (1973). *The Little Red Hen.* New York: Scholastic.

Ness, Evaline. (1974). *Yeck, Eck.* New York: Dutton.

Shecter, Ben. (1977). *Hester the Jester.* New York: Harper & Row.

Thayer, Jane. (1975). *I Don't Believe in Elves.* New York: Morrow.

Wing, Henry Ritchet. (1963). *Ten Pennies for Candy.* New York: Holt, Rinehart & Winston.

Long *e*

Galdone, Paul. (1986). *Little Bo-Peep.* New York: Clarion/Ticknor & Fields.

Keller, Holly. (1983). *Ten Sleepy Sheep.* New York: Greenwillow.

Martin, Bill, Jr. (1967). *Brown Bear, Brown Bear, What Do You See?* New York: Henry Holt.

Oppenheim, Joanne. (1967). *Have You Seen Trees?* New York: Young Scott Books.

Soule, Jean C. (1964). *Never Tease a Weasel.* New York: Parents' Magazine Press.

Thomas, Patricia. (1971). *"Stand Back," said the Elephant, "I'm Going to Sneeze!"* New York: Lothrop, Lee & Shepard.

Short *i*

Browne, Anthony. (1984). *Willy the Wimp.* New York: Knopf.

Ets, Marie Hall. (1966). *Gilberto and the Wind.* New York: Viking.

Hutchins, Pat. (1971). *Titch.* New York: Macmillan.

Keats, Ezra Jack. (1964). *Whistle for Willie.* New York: Viking.

Lewis, Thomas P. (1981). *Call for Mr. Sniff.* New York: Harper & Row.

Lobel, Arnold. (1969). *Small Pig*. New York: Harper & Row.

McPhail, David. (1984). *Fix-It*. New York: Dutton.

Patrick, Gloria. (1970). *This Is . . .* New York: Carolrhoda.

Robins, Joan. (1986). *My Brother, Will*. New York: Greenwillow.

Long *i*

Berenstain, Stan and Jan. (1964). *The Bike Lesson*. Random House.

Cameron, John. (1979). *If Mice Could Fly*. New York: Atheneum.

Cole, Sheila. (1985). *When the Tide Is Low*. New York: Lothrop, Lee & Shepard.

Gelman, Rita. (1976). *Why Can't I Fly?* New York: Scholastic.

Hazen, Barbara S. (1979). *Tight Times*. New York: Viking.

Short *o*

Benchley, Nathaniel. (1966). *Oscar Otter*. New York: Harper & Row.

Dunrea, Olivier. (1985). *Mogwogs on the March!* New York: Holiday House.

Emberley, Barbara. (1967). *Drummer Hoff*. Englewood Cliffs, NJ: Prentice-Hall.

McKissack, Patricia C. (1986). *Flossie & the Fox*. New York: Dial.

Miller, Patricia, and Seligman, Ira. (1963). *Big Frogs, Little Frogs*. New York: Holt, Rinehart & Winston.

Rice, Eve. (1979). "The Frog and the Ox" from *Once in a Wood*. New York: Greenwillow.

Seuss, Dr. (Theodore Geisel). (1965). *Fox in Socks*. New York: Random House.

Long *o*

Cole, Brock. (1986). *The Giant's Toe*. New York: Farrar, Straus & Giroux.

Gerstein, Mordicai. (1984). *Roll Over!* New York: Crown.

Johnston, Tony. (1972). *The Adventures of Mole and Troll*. New York: Putnam.

Johnston, Tony. (1977). *Night Noises and Other Mole and Troll Stories*. New York: Putnam.

Shulevitz, Uri. (1967). *One Monday Morning*. New York: Scribner.

Tresselt, Alvin. (1947). *White Snow, Bright Snow*. New York: Lothrop, Lee & Shepard.

Short *u*

Carroll, Ruth. (1950). *Where's the Bunny?* New York: Henry Z. Walck.

Cooney, Nancy E. (1987). *Donald Says Thumbs Down*. New York: Putnam.

Friskey, Margaret. (1940). *Seven Little Ducks*. New York: Children's Press.

Lorenz, Lee. (1982). *Big Gus and Little Gus*. Englewood Cliffs, NJ: Prentice-Hall.

Marshall, James.(1984). *The Cut-Ups*. New York: Viking Kestrel.

Udry, Janice May.(1981). *Thump and Plunk*. New York: Harper & Row.

Yashima, Taro. (1958). *Umbrella*. New York: Viking Penguin.

Long *u*

Lobel, Anita. (1966). *The Troll Music*. New York: Harper & Row.

Segal, Lore. (1977). *Tell Me a Trudy*. New York: Farrar, Straus & Giroux.

Slobodkin, Louis. (1959). *"Excuse Me—Certainly!"* New York: Vanguard.

Although these trade books repeat phonics elements, they should not be used primarily to teach phonics. To use *Caps for Sale*, for example, merely "because it has a short and a long vowel in the title" is unconscionable—it's a wonderful story in itself.

5.17 Putting Ideas to Work
Word Building as an Approach to Phonics

Gunning (1995) suggests word building as an approach to helping children learn phonics. The strategy is based on research that shows that novice readers use pronounceable word parts to reconstruct entire words; that is, "A student encountering the word *branch* might read it as *bran-ch-branch* or *ran-bran-branch* or *an-ran-bran-branch*." Gunning suggests teaching children to seek out pronounceable word parts as a strategy in sounding out unknown words.

While word building doesn't always work (the known word part *have* is a distraction in trying to sound out *shave*), there are enough high frequency rimes and syllables to make the technique useful in helping children learn to use phonic elements to decode difficult words.

High-Frequency Rimes and Syllables

-ab	cab	-e	me	-ice	mice	-o	no	-op	mop
-ack	tack	-ea	sea	-id	lid	-oad	toad	-ope	rope
-ad	sad	-eak	beak	-ide	ride	-oak	oak	-ot	pot
-ade	made	-eal	seal	-ie	pie	-oat	goat	-ound	round
-ag	bag	-ean	bean	-ig	pig	-ob	Bob	-out	shout
-age	page	-ear	ear	-ight	night	-ock	lock	-ow	cow
-ail	nail	-eat	eat	-ike	bike	-od	rod	-ow	crow
-ain	train	-ed	bed	-ill	hill	-og	dog	-own	clown
-ait	wait	-ee	bee	-im	him	-oice	voice	-oy	toy
-ake	cake	-eed	seed	-ime	time	-oil	boil		
-al(l)	ball	-eel	wheel	-in	pin	-oin	coin	-ub	sub
-ale	whale	-een	green	-ine	nine	-oke	joke	-uck	duck
-am	ham	-eep	jeep	-ing	ring	-old	gold	-ug	rug
-ame	name	-eet	feet	-ink	pink	-ole	mole	-um	gum
-an	pan	-ell	bell	-tion	action	-oll	roll	-un	sun
-and	sand	-en	ten	-ip	ship	-one	bone	-ture	future
-ap	map	-end	send	-ish	fish	-ong	song	-us(s)	bus
-at	cat	-ent	went	-it	hit	-ook	book	-ut	nut
-ate	gate	-et	net	-ite	kite	-ool	school		
-aw	saw			-ive	five	-oom	broom	-y	cry
-ay	hay			-ive	give	-oon	moon	-y	sunny

Phonics and Writing. Phonics is just as necessary in learning to write as in learning to read. An understanding of letter-sound relationships is essential to encoding written language. From a sound-symbol perspective, writing is the flip side of reading; that is, the reader goes from symbol to sound, and the writer goes from sound to symbol. At the early stages of writing, pupils apply their knowledge of phoneme-grapheme (sound-

5.18 Putting Ideas to Work
Guidelines for Exemplary Phonics Instruction

Stahl (1992) suggests the following nine principles of exemplary phonics instruction. Such instruction:

1. *Builds on a child's rich concepts about how print functions;* that is, is grounded on children's knowledge of words and experiences with reading.
2. *Builds on a foundation of phonemic awareness,* or pupils' awareness of sounds in spoken words.
3. *Is clear and direct,* avoiding ambiguity and focusing specifically on the phonetic elements to be learned.
4. *Is integrated into a total reading program,* not taught as an isolated entity.
5. *Focuses on reading words,* not learning rules, since mature readers don't think about the rules governing open and closed syllables, for example, when they are trying to figure out how to read an unfamiliar word.
6. *May include onsets* (the part of the syllable preceding the vowel) and *rimes* (the part of the syllable following the vowel), using spelling patterns to help decode words.
7. *May include invented spelling practice,* since invented spelling necessitates and reinforces an awareness of sound-symbol relationships.
8. *Develops independent word-recognition strategies,* focusing attention on the internal structure in words and looking at larger spelling patterns as an aid to decoding.
9. *Develops automatic word-recognition skills* so that students can devote their attention to comprehension, not words, placing phonics in its proper perspective.

symbol) relationships in inventive spellings. Mastery grows as children learn to express themselves more extensively in writing. Phonics remains part of the reading-writing connection that chapter 10 addresses.

Structural Analysis

Once pupils can use their graphophonic knowledge to sound out an unfamiliar word they encounter in print, they can come a step closer to the meaning of the word through structural or morphemic analysis. Morphemes, the basic and indivisible units of meaning, are the building blocks of words. The word *untidiness*, for example, is built from three morphemes:

> the free morpheme *tidy*, meaning "neat" or "clean" (a free morpheme is a meaning unit that can stand alone);

> the bound morpheme *un-*, meaning in this case "not" (a bound morpheme is a meaning unit that must be joined to another morpheme);

> the bound morpheme *-ness*, meaning "a quality or state."

5.19 Putting Ideas to Work
Phonics Programs

A number of decoding programs have been designed for direct, systematic phonics instruction. While many of these programs are intended to help children who have severe reading disabilities, some are usable in the classroom. Here are capsule descriptions of a representative sample of these programs, along with sources of additional information.

Orton-Gillingham Program. Designed for one-on-one instruction, the Orton-Gillingham method has provided a model other programs have built on. The approach uses auditory, visual, and kinesthetic aspects of learning in teaching letter sounds and blending these sounds into words. Carefully sequenced letters and phonograms are featured on cards. When the child has a secure knowledge of letter names and sounds, formal reading instruction begins. For more information, contact The Orton Dyslexia Society, 8600 LaSalle Road, Baltimore, MD 21204–6020

Slingerland Approach. The Slingerland method is an adaptation of Orton-Gillingham that uses multisensory instruction on letters and sounds in a large group setting. Instruction begins with handwriting, as pupils trace and later write letters. After they master individual letters and sounds, children move to decoding words. For more information, contact the Slingerland Institute, 1 Bellevue Center, 411 108th Ave, N.E., Bellevue WA 98004.

Alphabetic Phonics. This program also builds upon the Orton theory and also uses a multisensory approach to learning letter sounds and letters. In addition, the curriculum covers aspects of language acquisition and listening skills. Letters and letter combinations are marked with diacritical marks and presented on cards. Structured lessons include drill on letters and sounds, spelling, reading with phonetically controlled text, verbal expression, and cursive writing. For more information, contact Texas Scottish Rite Hospital for Children, 2222 Welborn St., Room 425, Dallas, TX 75219–3993.

Recipe for Reading. This tutorial program is a synthetic phonics approach that teaches letter sounds in isolation before combining them in syllables and words. As in Orton-Gillingham, multisensory techniques using visual, auditory, and kinesthetic reinforcements are used. Spelling precedes reading as children learn the forms and sounds of letters. For more information, contact Recipe for Reading, 323 Concord Street, Dix Hills, NY 11746.

Just as phonetic analysis involves decoding unfamiliar words by their phonetic (sound) units, structural analysis involves trying to determine word meaning by analyzing their morphemic (meaning) units.

The major classes of morphemes in English are roots and affixes (prefixes and suffixes). The root (base or stem) carries the essence of word meaning. Prefixes—morphemes attached to the beginnings of root words—and suffixes—morphemes attached to the end of root words—modify meaning by creating new words. When readers can recognize these morphemic elements, they can attempt to determine the meanings of the words they read.

Children come to school with an intuitive knowledge of morphemic elements in words. Children will say, for example, "I runned and catched the ball,"

Project READ.   Developed as a classroom program of direct phonics instruction for the lower-achieving children in the primary grades, Project READ is now used throughout the grades. The three-phase curriculum focuses on phonics, reading comprehension and vocabulary development, and written expression. Structured lessons provide specific techniques that involve multisensory activities. For more information, contact The Language Circle, P.O. Box 20631, Bloomington, MN 55420.

Wilson Reading System.   Based on Orton-Gillingham principles, the Wilson program was originally developed for adults and adolescents with dyslexia. It is designed for use in a tutorial setting, although it has been adapted for small and large group settings. The program is sequenced in 12 steps that instruct the student about patterns of consonant and vowel combinations in syllables. Lessons are structured with work on sound cards, word cards, sentence and story reading, and writing. For more information, contact Wilson Language Training, 162 W. Main Street, Millbury, MA 01527.

The Stephenson Program.   This program is a synthetic phonics approach that relies heavily on learning by association. Phonetic patterns are presented in the context of images children are familiar with (layer cakes, for example, and peanut butter and jelly sandwiches). The carefully sequenced three-level instructional program includes a beginning level with essential decoding elements; a basic level, which extends to comprehension work, along with the introduction of new letter patterns; and an intermediate level, which introduces compound words, prefixes and suffixes, and the like. Students read controlled text at all three levels. For more information, contact Stevenson Learning Skills, Inc., 8 Commonwealth Ave., Attleboro Falls, MA 02763–1014

These seven programs are by no means the only ones used in schools and clinical settings. Other formal programs also focus on direct, systematic, intensive phonics instruction as an essential tool for teaching children—particularly children with reading difficulties—how to read and spell.

adding the common tense-forming suffix -ed to the words they know. A good example of this type of overgeneralization using morphemes is the statement of the kindergartner who complained to her teacher, "Jack *tookened* my crayons." The child began with the verb *take*, made it past tense (*took*), generalized from *taken* to *tooken*, and added -ed just for good measure! Students begin to consciously apply their knowledge of structural elements as they learn to read.

Learning about structural analysis typically begins when children encounter compound words, words consisting of two free morphemes, such as *afternoon* or *football*. The component parts of such words are easily identifiable. This is not to say, however, that the meaning of the word is derived

5.20 Putting Ideas to Work
Teaching Morphemic Elements through Literature

*U*sing structural analysis as a word attack strategy starts, as with phonics, with whole texts and not with lists of prefixes, suffixes, and roots. Instruction in structural analysis is thus part of a broader base of reading.

Morphemic elements can be taught both directly and incidentally. For example, the compound words that appear on the first page of Jean Craighead George's *My Side of the Mountain* (snowstorm, knothole, deerskin) can be the focus of a discussion on compounds. Similarly, when pupils read that Andrew turns "greenish" after he drinks a concoction to rid him of freckles in Judy Blume's *Freckle Juice*, the teacher can take the opportunity to talk about the meaning and function of the suffix *-ish*, and pupils can brainstorm other words containing this element.

Although literature provides real language for real instruction on morphemes, the focus of a literature-based program is always on understanding and enjoyment. Reading a story to find all the compound words, or all the words containing the suffix *-tion*, is a tedious practice that detracts from the purposes of reading to understand and enjoy literature.

from the sum of its two parts. The compound word *understand* does not mean "to stand under," nor is a *fireman* "a man made out of fire," though a *snowman* is "a man made out of snow." Once they can identify a compound word, pupils can probably grasp the meaning from their prior language experiences. As they come across compound words in the stories they read, the relationship between the two free morphemes can spur some interesting discussions about word meaning.

Structural analysis also includes learning about contractions. A contraction is a verbal convention combining separate elements into a single unit: *I am* becomes *I'm*, *can not* becomes *can't*, *it is* becomes *it's*. In writing, the apostrophe is used to indicate the deleted letters; when learning to read, students certainly need to become aware of the written forms of contractions. However, contractions are usually regular parts of even young children's spoken language; children use contractions like, "*I'm* three years old" "*That's* my cookie," and "*He's* my brother" relatively early in the language acquisition process. When contractions appear in trade books and other materials pupils are reading, it makes sense to move from the known to the unknown, to refer to their spoken language to help them understand contractions in print.

Since many words are structured with morphemic units, the ability to break words down or analyze them by their structural elements is an important word-identification skill. Moreover, as students learn to do this, they expand their vocabularies and discover new word meanings on their own.

The Dictionary: "Look It Up"

Susan has just read and enjoyed E. L. Konigsburg's *From the Mixed-Up Files of Mrs. Basil E. Frankweiler*. Now she wants to read another book by the same author. On the library shelf, she finds Konigsburg's *Father's Arcane Daughter*.

As she reads the title, she gets stuck on the second word. It is not in her sight vocabulary. From syntactic context, she knows it is an adjective, but there are no semantic context clues to help her out. She uses phonics to sound out the word, but there are no structural units to help her figure out what *arcane* means. Susan has four choices.

1. She can ask a classmate, her teacher, or the librarian what *arcane* means.
2. She can put the book back on the shelf and forget about it.
3. She can ignore the fact that she does not completely understand the title and begin to read the book anyway.
4. She can look up *arcane* in the dictionary (to find that it means "mysterious" or "obscure").

The final choice—looking it up in the dictionary—is typically a last resort. As the ultimate word book of our language, the dictionary is an important and reliable aid to reading. Writers rely on the dictionary for spelling, and readers use it to learn the pronunciations and meanings of unknown words. Like other aspects of a reading instructional program, the dictionary needs to be viewed—and used—in proper perspective.

Traditionally, the dictionary was often used as a starting point for students to expand their vocabularies and learn word meanings. Pupils received lists of new words and were assigned to look up their meanings in the dictionary and write a sentence containing each word. Apart from the fact that such assignments are tedious and time-consuming, the technique has proved not to be especially effective in promoting word knowledge or vocabulary growth (Just and Carpenter, 1987; Nagy, 1988). Based on their research, Anderson and Nagy conclude, "If we are correct and word meanings are context sensitive, a dictionary is a questionable aid for an inexpert language learner" (in finding the meanings of isolated words) (Anderson and Nagy, 1991; p. 722).

A number of problems arise in beginning with this definitional approach to vocabulary study. Elementary school dictionaries often do not include many of the more interesting and challenging words pupils encounter in their reading. Dictionary definitions can be sparse, confusing, or inadequate for helping pupils discover meaning, and the definitions themselves often contain new words that may be difficult for the child to comprehend. Moreover, since words often have multiple meanings, the pupil needs to know the context to find the appropriate definition. "Definition-based learning typically involves memorizing (or attempting to memorize) brief definitions representing only a single meaning of the word to be learned, and hence leads to only a shallow level of word knowledge. Reviews of research clearly indicate that instruction relying on definitions alone does not increase comprehension of text containing the instructed words" (Nagy, 1995, p. 11).

Even when the student finds the appropriate definition of a word, the dictionary tells what a word means without indicating how to use it. A third grader who looked up the word *pregnant*, for example, found that it meant "carrying a child," and wrote the sentence, *The fireman climbed up the ladder and came down pregnant.*

Where, then, does the dictionary fit into literature-based reading instruction? The dictionary is a valuable tool pupils can consult after they have exhausted other strategies for attempting to determine what a word is and what it means. Because it contains a lot of interesting information about words, the dictionary is a fruitful reference for exploring and extending word meanings, but it ought not be overused as a vocabulary tool in the classroom.

As students learn to use the dictionary to check word meanings, they acquire several skills required for using the dictionary as a reference tool: awareness of alphabetical order, use of guide words, interpretation of the symbols that indicate pronunciation, and the ability to select the correct meaning. These skills can be developed through both direct and incidental instruction as children use the dictionary as a word-finding tool in the classroom.

Dictionary use requires not only knowledge and skill but also a certain attitude. Pupils must determine whether it's necessary to disrupt the flow of reading to check the meaning of an unfamiliar word, and they must care enough to spend the time looking the word up. They must also know enough to recognize which words are crucial to understanding, since the redundancy of a text allows readers to tolerate a certain proportion of unknown words (perhaps as many as 15 percent of the words in a passage) without interfering with comprehension (Nagy, Herman, and Anderson, 1985; Nagy, 1988).

The dictionary might be considered the ultimate resource in vocabulary study. However, the teacher needs to enhance and enrich dictionary approach and to explore other avenues in helping pupils learn new words and new meanings for familiar words as part of a classroom reading instructional program.

A Combination of Word-Identification Skills

Five ways of identifying words in print have been presented in this chapter:

1. Immediate recognition by sight;
2. Using context clues to determine what the word is and what it means;
3. Analyzing the word phonetically, using sound-symbol relationships;
4. Analyzing the word structurally, using the morphemic building blocks of the word;
5. Referring to the dictionary to determine pronunciation and meaning.

Each of these word-identification strategies is an important part of learning to read. None, however, is an end in itself; none can be used alone to identify all the words children encounter as they read. Any of the strategies may be used in flexible combination with the others, and all aim at the broader purpose of reading for meaning. Imagine that Jack sees the sentence, *The circus featured a clown dressed as a police chief.* He recognizes all the words up to the final one. A knowledge of phonics enables Jack to eliminate words such as *car* or *station,* words that make sense within the context of the sentence. But if he follows the "two vowels go walking" rule of phonics, the word would rhyme with *life.* So context clues or phonics alone will not help

Jack much; he must rely on word knowledge and experience or turn to the dictionary to identify the pronunciation and meaning of the word.

In conventional programs, each word-identification skill is taught as a separate, isolated entity. Word recognition begins with a list of sight words. Phonics and structural analysis start with an inventory of elements the student must learn. Context and dictionary use involve separate sets of practice materials. The practical effect is that pupils spend inordinate amounts of time alphabetizing interminable lists of words or marking the accent patterns of syllables in words that they already know how to pronounce. Instruction begins and ends with the specific component the teacher emphasizes, and the skill becomes more important than the larger purpose of reading.

In literature-based programs, the act of reading itself is the starting point and ultimate aim of word identification. The instruction focuses on the ability to sound out words, to recognize words instantly upon visual contact, to learn the meaning of the prefix *un-*, and to understand the correct accent pattern of a word in a dictionary. These skills and techniques are important only insofar as they contribute to the ultimate goal: helping children recognize words so that they can understand and enjoy what they read.

Summary and Conclusions

While the world of words is important to reading, words are merely vehicles for expressing and arriving at meaning. To recognize words in print—to know what they are and what they mean—is the purpose for learning vocabulary as part of literature-based reading and writing instruction.

Word knowledge is reciprocally related to reading comprehension. On the one hand, a large vocabulary contributes to reading success. At the same time, wide reading is one of the primary ways a reader can increase word knowledge. Accordingly, vocabulary development and constant interaction with all kinds of print are two essential components of classroom reading instruction. When a teacher makes literature the centerpiece of the program, he or she addresses both dimensions.

Readers must not only know what words mean, they must be able to identify words quickly and easily in print. Efficient readers identify words by sight and by using clues they find in the language in the surrounding text. When they encounter words they do not know immediately, they sound the words out phonetically, analyze them structurally, and/or look up the troublesome words in the dictionary.

Pupils need to apply these strategies flexibly as they read. It is unrealistic to memorize each of the more than 600,000 words in our lexicon, impossible to find context clues for each unfamiliar word, unthinkable to seek meaning by sounding out every new word encountered in print, impractical to rely on morphemic elements to derive meaning from all words, and unfeasible to look up every new word in the dictionary. No single strategy will suffice. We need them all in learning to read, and all play a part in literature-based reading instruction in the classroom.

Discussion Questions and Activities

1. Make a list of interesting, challenging words you might introduce to upper elementary students, words such as *effulgent, lugubrious, cantankerous*, and *scintillating*. Design some activities to help pupils develop "ownership" of

these words. Keep the qualities of integration, repetition, and meaningful use in mind as you plan.

2. In a magazine, you read this sentence: *The creeping kudzu spread across the hills.* Assuming you don't know what *kudzu* is, describe some strategies you could use to figure out the meaning of the word.

3. What are some important factors to keep in mind in helping primary grade pupils develop word knowledge and word-identification skills? How would these factors differ for upper elementary students?

4. Read the exchange of opinion between Aunt Millie and Uncle Max in Putting Ideas to Work 5.13. Choose a side in the debate and defend your position.

5. Examine a trade book appropriate for use in the elementary grades. Choose words you might use as vehicles for vocabulary instruction and decide how you would help children learn these words. Design a phonics lesson to use with this book.

School-Based Assignments

1. Review a reading lesson from the teacher's edition of a literature-based basal reading series used in your school. How much emphasis does the lesson place on developing vocabulary? What words are identified for instruction? What suggestions are made for teaching these words? What alternative strategies would you use?

2. Working with a group of three or four pupils, develop a semantic map centered on a theme from a book they are reading or a curriculum topic they are studying.

3. Observe an experienced teacher teaching a reading lesson. How much time does he or she spend on developing word meaning? Does the teacher emphasize the use of context clues or phonetic analysis as strategies for figuring out unknown words? What other techniques does the teacher use to teach vocabulary?

4. Using words you have selected from student stories or trade books used in the classroom, plan and teach a small group lesson in phonetic or structural analysis. First, determine what pupils already know about the words you select. Develop your lesson in light of this.

5. Design a bulletin board display focusing on vocabulary. Consider making a display on words with multiple meanings, a semantic web, or a word board related to a particular topic. If possible, involve students in planning your display.

Children's Trade Books Cited in This Chapter

Allen, Pamela. (1983). *Who Sank the Boat?* New York: Coward.
Bancheck, Linda. (1978). *Snake In, Snake Out*. New York: Crowell.
Bemelmans, Ludwig. (1939). *Madeline*. New York: Viking.
Blume, Judy. (1974). *Blubber*. New York: Dell.
Blume, Judy. (1978). *Freckle Juice*. New York: Dell.
Byars, Betsy. (1986). *The Not-Just-Anybody Family*. New York: Dell.
Cooney, Barbara. (1985). *Miss Rumphius*. New York: Viking.
Downing, Mary. (1990). *The Doll in the Garden: A Ghost Story*. New York: Clarion.
Emberley, Barbara. (1967). *Drummer Hoff*. Englewood Cliffs, NJ: Prentice-Hall.
George, Jean Craighead. (1959). *My Side of the Mountain*. New York: Dutton.
Guarin, Deborah. (1989). *Is Your Mama a Llama?* New York: Scholastic.

Gwynne, Fred. (1988). *A Chocolate Moose for Dinner*. New York: Simon & Schuster.
Gwynne, Fred. (1988). *The King Who Rained*. New York: Simon & Schuster.
Gwynne, Fred. (1988). *A Little Pigeon Toad*. New York: Simon & Schuster.
Hutchins, Pat. (1968). *Rosie's Walk*. New York: Macmillan.
Keller, Ruth. (1989). *Many Luscious Lollipops*. New York: Grossett & Dunlop.
Kellogg, Steven. (1989). *Chicken Little*. Boston: Houghton Mifflin.
Kesselman, Wendy. (1985). *Emma*. New York: Harper & Row.
Konigsburg, E. L. (1986). *Father's Arcane Daughter*. New York: Dell.
Konigsburg, E. L. (1967). *From the Mixed-up Files of Mrs. Basil E. Frankweiler*. New York: Atheneum.
Lessac, France. (1984). *My Little Island*. New York: Harper & Row.
Levitt, Paul M., Burger, Douglas, and Gurlnick, Elissa. (1985). *The Weighty Word Book*. Longmont, CO: Bookmaker's Guild.
Lobel, Arnold. (1984). *Bumps in the Night*. New York: Bantam.
MacLachlan, Patricia. (1985). *Sarah, Plain and Tall*. New York: Harper & Row.
Meddaugh, Susan. (1978). *Too Short Fred*. Boston: Houghton Mifflin.
Miles, Miska. (1971). *Annie and the Old One*. Boston: Little, Brown.
Nuinberg, Maxwell. (1970). *Fun with Words*. Englewood Cliffs, NJ: Prentice Hall.
Sharmat, Marjorie Weinman. (1985). *Mitchell Is Moving*. New York: Macmillan.
Steig, William. (1969). *Sylvester and the Magic Pebble*. New York: Simon & Schuster.
Tafuri, Nancy. (1986). *Have You Seen My Duckling?* New York: Puffin Books.
Viorst, Judith. (1972). *Alexander and the Terrible, Horrible, No Good, Very Bad Day*. New York: Atheneum.
Viorst, Judith. (1990). *Earrings*. New York: Atheneum.
Wells, Rosemary. (1973). *Noisy Nora*. New York: Scholastic.
Williams, Margery. (1984). *The Velveteen Rabbit*. New York: Doubleday.
Other children's trade books are listed in Putting Ideas to Work 5.16 (p. 186).

References

Adams, M. J. (1990). *Beginning to Read: Thinking and Learning about Print*. Cambridge, MA: MIT Press.
Anderson, R. C., and Freebody, P. (1985). Vocabulary Knowledge. In H. Singer and R. B. Ruddell, eds., *Theoretical Models and Processes of Reading* (3rd ed.). Newark, DE: International Reading Association.
Anderson, R. C., and Nagy, W. E. (1991). Word Meanings. In R. Barr, M. L. Kamil, P. Mosenthal, and P. D. Pearson, eds. *Handbook of Reading Research*, Vol. II. New York: Longman.
Ashton-Warner, S. (1963). *Teacher*. New York: Simon & Schuster.
Bettelheim, B., and Zelan, K. (1982). *On Learning to Read: A Child's Fascination with Meaning*. New York: Alfred Knopf.
Blachowicz, C. L. (1985). Vocabulary Development and Reading: From Research to Instruction. *The Reading Teacher* 38:876–881.
Bridge, C. A., Winograd, P. N., and Haley, D. (1983). Using Predictable Materials vs. Preprimers to Teach Beginning Sight Words. *The Reading Teacher* 36:884–891.
Carbo, M. (1988). Debunking the Great Phonics Myth. *Phi Delta Kappan* 70:226–240.
Carbo, M. (1989). An Evaluation of Jeanne Chall's Response to "Debunking the Great Phonics Myth." *Phi Delta Kappan* 71:152–157.
Chall, J. S. (1989a). Learning to Read: The Great Debate 20 Years Later—A Response to "Debunking the Great Phonics Myth." *Phi Delta Kappan* 70:521–538.
Chall, J. S. (1989b). The Uses of Educational Research: Comments on Carbo. *Phi Delta Kappan* 71:158–160.
Chall, J. S. (1996). *Learning to Read: The Great Debate.* (3rd ed.). Fort Worth: Harcourt Brace.

Clymer, T. (1963). The Utility of Phonics Generalizations. *The Reading Teacher* 16:252–258.

Cunningham, P. M. (1995). *Phonics They Use* (2nd ed.). New York: HarperCollins.

Dale, E. (1965). Vocabulary Measurement: Techniques and Major Findings. *Elementary English* 42:895–901.

Davis, F. B. (1972). Psychometric Research on Comprehension in Reading. *Reading Research Quarterly* 7:628–678.

Devine, T. G. (1986). *Teaching Reading Comprehension: From Theory to Practice.* Boston: Allyn & Bacon.

Dolch, E. (1939). *A Manual for Remedial Readers.* Champaign, IL: Garrard.

Durr, W. R. (1973). Computer Study of High-Frequency Words in Popular Trade Juveniles. *The Reading Teacher* 27:37–42.

Eeds, M. (1985). Bookwords: Using a Beginning Word List of High-Frequency Words from Children's Literature K–3. *The Reading Teacher* 39:418–423.

Ehri, L. C. (1992). Reconceptualizing the Development of Sight Word Reading and Its Relationship to Reading. In P. B. Gough, L. C. Ehri, and R. Treiman, eds., *Reading Acquisition,* Hillsdale, NJ: Erlbaum.

Fielding, L. G., Wilson, P. T., and Anderson, R. C. (1986). A New Focus on Free Reading: The Role of Trade Books in Reading Instruction. In T. Raphael, ed., *The Contexts of School-Based Literacy.* New York: Random House.

Flesch, R. (1955). *Why Johnny Can't Read.* New York: Harper & Row.

Freppon, P. A., and Dahl, K. C. (1991). Learning about Phonics in a Whole Language Classroom. *Language Arts* 68:190–197.

Freppon, P. A., and Headings, L. (1996). Keeping It Whole in Whole Language: A First Grade Teacher's Phonics Instruction in an Urban Whole Language Classroom. In E. McIntyre and M. Pressley, eds. *Balanced Instruction: Strategies and Skills in Whole Language.* Norwood, MA: Christopher-Gordon Publishers.

Goodman, K. S. (1976). The Reading Process: A Psycholinguistic View. In E. B. Smith, K. S. Goodman, and R. Meredith, eds., *Language and Thinking in School.* New York: Holt, Rinehart & Winston.

Groff P. (1995). A Serviceable Definition of Sight Words. *The New England Reading Association Journal* 31:2–9.

Gunning, T. G. (1995). Word Building: A Strategic Approach to the Teaching of Phonics. *The Reading Teacher* 48:484–488.

Hittleman, D. R. (1988). *Developmental Reading, K–8: Teaching from a Whole-Language Perspective* (3rd ed.). Columbus, OH: Merrill.

Johnson, T. D., and Louis, D. R. (1987). *Literacy through Literature.* Portsmouth, NH: Heinemann.

Just, M. S., and Carpenter, P. A. (1987). *The Psychology of Reading and Language Comprehension.* Boston: Allyn & Bacon.

Klein, M. L. (1988*). Teaching Reading Comprehension and Vocabulary: A Guide for Teachers.* Englewood Cliffs, NJ: Prentice-Hall.

Mathews, M. M. (1966). *Teaching to Read, Historically Considered.* Chicago: University of Chicago Press.

Mills, H., O'Keefe, T., and Stephens, D. (1990). *Looking Closely—Exploring the Role of Phonics in One Whole Language Classroom.* Portsmouth, NH: Heinemann.

Moe, A. J. (1989). Using Picture Books for Reading Vocabulary Development. In J. W. Stewig and S. L. Sebasta, eds., *Using Literature in the Elementary Classroom* (2nd ed.). Urbana, IL: National Council of Teachers of English.

Nagy, W. E. (1988). *Teaching Vocabulary to Improve Reading Comprehension.* Urbana, IL: National Council of Teachers of English.

Nagy, W. E. (1995). *On the Role of Context in First- and Second-Language Vocabulary Learning.* Technical Report No. 627, Center for the Study of Reading. Champaign: University of Illinois at Urbana-Champaign.

Nagy, W. E., Herman, P. A., and Anderson, R. C. (1985). Learning Words from Context. *Reading Research Quarterly* 20:233–253.

Newman, J. M., and Church, S. M. (1990). Commentary: The Myths of Whole Language. *The Reading Teacher* 44:20–27.

Pearson, P. D. (1985). Changing the Face of Reading Comprehension. *The Reading Teacher* 38:724–728.

Peterson, R., and Eeds, M. (1990). *Grand Conversations: Literature Groups in Action.* New York: Scholastic.

Stahl, S. A. (1992). Saying the "P" Word: Nine Guidelines for Exemplary Phonics Instruction. *The Reading Teacher* 45:618–625.

Stahl, S. A., Osborn, J., and Lehr, F. (1990). *Beginning to Read: Thinking and Learning about Print by Marilyn Jager Adams; A Summary Prepared by Steven A. Stahl, Jean Osborn, and Fran Lehr.* Urbana: Center for the Study of Reading, University of Illinois at Urbana-Champaign.

Tierney, R. J., Readence, J. E., and Dishner, E. K. (1995*). Reading Strategies and Practices: A Compendium* (4th ed.). Boston: Allyn & Bacon.

Trachtenburg, P. (1990). Using Children's Literature to Enhance Phonics Instruction. *The Reading Teacher* 43:648–652.

Yopp, H. K. (1995) Read-Aloud Books for Developing Phonemic Awareness: An Annotated Bibliography. *The Reading Teacher* 48:538–542.

Reading Comprehension: Understanding Narrative Text

© Michael Siluk/The Image Works

Chapter 6 Outline

Features

Key Concepts in This Chapter

Understanding what one reads is essential to reading. Comprehension results when a reader interacts with a piece of print in a certain context.

Text-based features such as the level of text, the structure of text, and its content can help or hinder reading comprehension.

What the reader brings to print has a powerful influence on his or her understanding. Reader-based factors such as language background, cognitive processing, schemata, and metacognition have a strong impact on comprehension.

Teacher questioning is key in helping pupils learn to comprehend trade books and other materials they read in a literature-based classroom.

Introduction

Comprehension is the consummation of the reading process; if a person does not understand what he/she reads, that person is not really reading. All aspects of reading instruction should therefore lead to the ultimate goal of comprehension.

Simply defined, reading comprehension is the process of determining meaning. In this process, readers construct an author's intended message in their own minds. In a broad sense, comprehension means understanding the full meaning of any communication, from interpreting the significance of a casual wave or a flirtatious glance to unraveling the plot of a Victorian novel or deciphering a complicated set of written directions. In reading, comprehension means understanding the meaning of a printed passage by reconstructing the message the author intended to send.

In literature-based instruction, we can make a distinction between comprehension and interpretation. Comprehension involves understanding what a story text contains. Interpretation is an individual reaction or response to that content. Comprehension and interpretation are closely related, and both are essential to literature-based reading instruction.

Before the early 1900s, educators did not pay much attention to reading comprehension or interpretation. They took it for granted that a student comprehended a passage if the student could adequately read the passage aloud. According to one story, a famous educator once visited a high school classroom and asked a student to read the front page of a newspaper. The student read the same line across all the columns, jumping from story to story, but nobody worried because the pupil's reading of the words was "accurate." Since the early part of the 20th century, however, comprehension has become the primary, fundamental goal of reading instruction.

A Renewed Emphasis on Comprehension

As schools move into the 21st century, there is an intensely renewed emphasis on comprehension, "an atmosphere in which the psychic energy of the reading field has been unleashed toward the study of comprehension" (Pearson, 1985a; p. 724). This emphasis on comprehension has had several effects: educators are more aware of the varying demands of different types of text; they are placing more emphasis on the process (rather than the product) of comprehension; and they have developed an interactive model of reading comprehension that takes both text-based and reader-based features into account.

Narrative and Expository Text

Even though all writing shares communicative intent and the features of written language, different types of texts require varying kinds of mental processing. Reading a newspaper ad to find out what time a movie is playing at the local theater involves cognitive demands that differ from those required when reading a critical review of that movie. Reading a recipe calls for a type of comprehension that differs from the comprehension required when reading a love letter. And reading a novel for pleasure during Sustained Silent Reading requires a type of comprehension that differs from that required when reading an informational trade book for a thematic report in science.

Comprehension differs according to the nature of the material and the reader's purpose in reading it. In each case, readers assume what Rosenblatt (1978, 1989) calls a stance, which is predominantly efferent or predominantly aesthetic. The reader takes an *efferent* stance when he or she wants to retain (or carry away) information after reading. The reader takes an *aesthetic* stance when focusing attention on what he or she is experiencing during the reading event. While neither stance is mutually exclusive, the predominant stance a reader takes differs depending on the type of text.

In this chapter, we will focus on comprehending narrative text, since most of the text children encounter for the purpose of learning to read—and much of the literature that they enjoy in the elementary grades—is narrative in nature. Narrative text is a form of writing that tells a story. Its primary purpose is to relate a series of episodes that unfold as a plot. Narrative text includes settings, characters, and a particular structure.

Product and Process

Reading comprehension involves both product and process. For many years, schools dealt primarily with the products of comprehension. Although the end product of comprehension is important, schools are now focusing more and more on the comprehension process.

The *product* is the result of comprehension. In the classroom, for example, teachers typically make statements such as, "Ramona recognized the main idea of the paragraph and stated two of the five details supporting that main idea," or "After reading the newspaper article, Joe could tell us what happened at the conference, but he didn't seem to understand the more subtle implications of the article." These statements relate to the measured results or outcomes of comprehension. These are the products.

Questions or tests measure the products of comprehension. The reader's ability to tell who the characters were, what they did, when, and why are indicators of basic understanding and recall.

The *process* of comprehension is more difficult to get at because it occurs inside the reader's head; it is not readily observable. We can tell, for example, that Ramona remembered two of five details in a paragraph (product); now we want to find out why she remembered those two and not the other three (process). We can say that Joe could basically understand what he read in the newspaper (product); now we want to find out why he couldn't understand the implied information (process).

A focus on the comprehension process is vital to teaching children how to read. It shifts the instructional emphasis from trying to determine what a pupil has understood to helping the child become aware of what goes into understanding written text. Studying the comprehension process help us understand how people comprehend written discourse. It has led educators to develop an interactive model of reading comprehension.

An Interactive Model

Recently, research-based theories of reading comprehension have emphasized the interactive nature of the comprehension process. This view suggests that comprehension depends on three factors: reader, text, and context. Reader and text *combine* within a social context to produce meaning. In other words, comprehension results when a reader processes printed text using the experiences and expectations that he or she brings to the text.

The interactive model of reading comprehension (see Putting Ideas to Work 6.1) reflects the communication between a writer and a reader. "Meaning does not reside ready-made in the text or in the reader; it happens during the transaction between reader and text" (Rosenblatt, 1989; p. 157).

Comprehension comes from the integration of two types of information: information in the text itself—which is "in front of the eye"—and information in the reader's head—which is "behind the eye." Reading is an active process; the reader uses clues found in the text to construct meaning in his or her head.

What are the factors that influence a person's reading comprehension? What enables you to understand what you are reading right now? Your understanding depends on a constellation of factors, some within the print you are looking at and some of which you bring to the act of reading.

6.1 Putting Ideas to Work
Interactive Model of Reading Comprehension

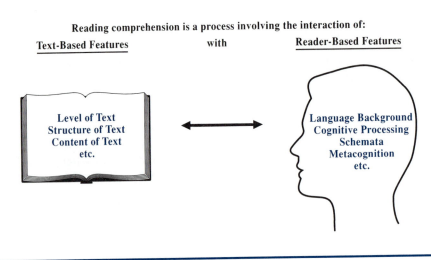

Reading comprehension is a process involving the interaction of:

Text-Based Features   with   **Reader-Based Features**

Level of Text
Structure of Text
Content of Text
etc.

Language Background
Cognitive Processing
Schemata
Metacognition
etc.

Text-based factors, those "in front of the eye," include:

the level of text, or the relative difficulty of the language the author uses to present the ideas;

the structure of text, or the organizational scheme or pattern the author uses to present the information;

content, or the level of sophistication or familiarity of the material; and

other factors, including the arrangement of type and the use of graphic aids (such as the diagram that appears in Putting Ideas to Work 6.1).

Reader-based factors, those "behind the eye," include:

language background, or the ability to recognize words, grasp sentence meaning, and deal effectively with language in larger segments of text;

cognitive processing, or the ability to apply the appropriate type of comprehension and level of thinking;

schemata, or the background and knowledge the reader already possesses;

metacognition, or one's awareness and control over one's mental functioning; and

other factors, such as one's state of mind, level of comfort, and the like.

In a literature-based program, the teacher must take these text- and reader-based factors into account to help pupils build reading competency as they interact with stories, poems, plays, informational trade books, and other materials. This involves explaining and modeling strategies that have proven effective in helping readers build meaning as they read.

Text-Based Features

Meaning does not reside in text alone; it depends to a great extent on what readers bring to the printed page from their backgrounds and experiences. Nevertheless, certain features of the text can greatly influence a reader's ability to comprehend. "Although contemporary research seems more interested in the reader than in the text, most authorities would still concur that text, its forms and structures, represents an important aspect of reading and of reading instruction" (Klein, 1988; p. 17). Features in the text that may affect reading comprehension include the difficulty of the writing, the structure the author uses to organize the information, and the content of the information or ideas in the text.

Level of Text

The level of text refers to the relative difficulty a person can expect to experience in reading. Level of text is commonly referred to as "readability."

Readability involves the estimated ease with which a reader can read and understand a piece of print. Readability is normally computed with a formula that calculates the relationship between sentence length and word length or difficulty, yielding an index of how "easy" or "difficult" a text is expected to be. Most formulas express estimated readability by grade level; that is, a book is measured at a "third-grade readability level" or at an "eighth-grade level of difficulty." At times, a year/month distinction is made; that is, the readability is indicated to be "at the "5.8 grade level."

Teachers, reading specialists, and publishers traditionally have put a great deal of faith in readability. One can still find readability figures for popular children's books, but much of the confidence in the absolute accuracy of these numbers is beginning to dissipate. Formulas include only measurable aspects of language. They do not take into account the reader's background, familiarity with the material, interest, or other factors "behind the eye." Moreover, different formulas often yield different readability estimates for the same material. And readability figures can be arbitrary and misleading. For example, the readability level of Florence and Richard Atwater's humorous *Mr. Popper's Penguins* is listed as sixth grade; yet third graders typically read and enjoy this book, and most sixth graders would reject it as "too babyish." For these reasons, schools are adhering less strictly to the guidelines these readability formulas suggest, especially for narrative material.

Concerns about overreliance on readability figures notwithstanding, a text's level of difficulty will influence a reader's ability to comprehend it.

Beginning readers find books with familiar words, natural language, and repeated sentence patterns easier to understand. Traditionally, textbook authors have controlled vocabulary tightly and have artificially manipulated sentence patterns for the sole purpose of achieving a certain readability level.

Easy-to-read trade books such as Crosby Bonsall's *Mine's The Best*, Arnold Lobel's *Frog and Toad* stories, and some of Dr. Seuss's books, such as *Green Eggs and Ham*, are appropriate instructional fare for young children. The repeated and predictable language patterns of books like Pat Hutchins's *Good Night, Owl* and Barbara Emberley's *Drummer Hoff* make these books eminently readable as well. Giving pupils books that they can read more easily will improve their chances of comprehending what they read and boost their confidence for reading more difficult text later on.

Teachers need to be cautious, however, about assigning books on the basis of a single readability figure alone. What the teacher does with a story—relating the child's background to the story, activating prior knowledge, setting purposes, asking directed questions, introducing vocabulary, carefully guiding the reading—will do more to enhance a child's comprehension than selecting a book based primarily on a single readability figure.

Structure of Text

Text has structure. When authors write, they tell their stories or present their ideas in an organized pattern. This organization has been called "the text-in-the-head of the author." When the "text-in-the-head of the reader" corresponds to this text, comprehension occurs.

Authors structure different types of discourse in different ways. Recognizing the genre or type of reading material one is about to delve into can be an important initial step to comprehension. Students must recognize the nature of the text—whether it is designed to move or to entertain (as a narrative story, poem, or play), to inform (as an informational trade book about machines), or to persuade (as an editorial or advertisement). The nature of the material often determines the structure of the writing, so recognizing the form of a piece of writing increases one's chances of understanding.

Even narrative text contains a structure, a "grammar" or set of rules for creating a story. The elements of this structure consist of setting, plot, character, conflict, and the like. As children learn to recognize and understand these elements of story grammar or text structure, they will be better able to understand and recall stories.

The organization of narrative text follows a pattern that runs from the beginning of the story (*Little Red Riding Hood sets out to see her grandmother*), through the middle (*she meets the wolf, who races ahead to Grandma's house*), to a conflict or crisis (*the wolf devours Granny*), to a solution (*the woodsman arrives and saves the day*). Children who are exposed to stories begin to develop a sense of story structure from a very early age. From "Once upon a time . . ." to ". . . and they all lived happily ever after," children become aware that stories move in a predictable manner, and this awareness helps them comprehend the story.

In guided reading, the teacher can build on pupils' backgrounds, set purposes, and design questions to help students better comprehend what they read.

© Stuart Spates

For children who arrive at school without this awareness, developing a sense of story structure is an early step in reading comprehension. Among the techniques most frequently suggested for helping students develop an awareness of story structure are story maps and graphic devices that show the relationships between the major elements of story structure.

Pupils who are aware of the elements of story structure and are able to follow a plot through its stages are in a much better position to comprehend narrative text. Expository text is structured differently from narrative text, because the emphasis in expository writing is on presenting information and not on telling a story.

Content of Text

The content or subject matter of a text also has an impact on comprehension; however, understanding of a text depends in large measure on one's familiarity with the topic. For example, a business major reading a text on the stock market is likely to comprehend it better than a music major unfamiliar with stocks who is reading the same book. Similarly, pupils who already know the story of "The Three Little Pigs" will understand it better in print than children totally unfamiliar with the story.

Most children find that the stories they encounter contain familiar content. Even when some aspects of the story structure may be new, themes and experiences often fit comfortably with the child's base of knowledge. For

6.2 Putting Ideas to Work
Teaching Story Structure

Among the techniques for helping pupils develop an awareness of story structure are:

Direct questioning that focuses specifically on story elements: *Where does this story take place?* (setting). *Who are the main characters? What does the author say about them?* (characterization). *What problem does the main character face?* (conflict). *What does the character decide to do?* (resolution). These questions may expand depending on the nature of the story, the teacher's purposes, and student reading levels.

Literature discussions, dialogues about stories that occur in literature study groups. These discussions focus on pupils' responses to various literary elements in what they read.

Flow charts that pupils follow—as they might follow a road map—to chart the structure of a story. Students can create these charts (see figure 6.A).

Figure 6.A

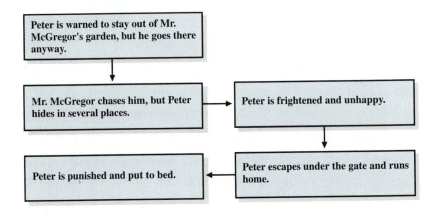

example, Patrick Skene Catling's *John Midas in the Dreamtime* is a story set in the Australian outback about a boy who meets a group of prehistoric aboriginal people. Although pupils may be unfamiliar with the setting and supporting characters, many will have met new people unlike themselves, and some may have experienced their own imagined trips back in time.

Part of the appeal of children's literature is the familiarity of the themes the stories contain. Harry Allard's goofy ghost story *Bumps in the Night* or Barbara Robinson's humorous *The Best Christmas Pageant Ever* are

Plot diagrams that visually represent story action. These diagrams are similar in nature and intent to a flow chart. The one in figure 6.B is only one of many forms that can be used.

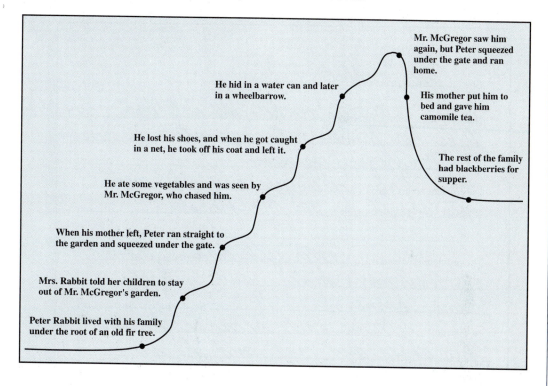

Figure 6.B

Continued on next page.

easily understood because the situations they present have been part of most children's experiences—at least their imagined if not their real experiences.

In addressing content, teachers need to consider both the subject matter and the knowledge and background of their pupils. Teachers can help students comprehend a story's content by activating their prior knowledge of the subject, by clarifying concepts, by providing background information essential to understanding the story, by making sure pupils understand key vocabulary before they read, and by guiding reading through skillful questioning.

Story frames, suggested by Fowler (1982), which are skeletal paragraphs with sequential spaces tied together by signal words and/or transitional phrases (see figure 6.C).

Title *Peter Rabbit*

The story starts when *Peter's mother goes out but tells her family not to go into Mr. McGregor's garden.*

The problem occurs when *Peter goes anyway and gets chased by Mr. McGregor.*

The problem is solved when *Peter gets away from Mr. McGregor, hides, and finally runs home.*

At the end, *Peter is sad because he lost his shoes and coat and he is put to bed.*

Figure 6.C

These are only a few of the many devices teachers can use to help pupils develop an awareness of story structure. Understanding structure will help them better comprehend the literature they encounter as they learn to read.

Other Text-Based Features

Other features of text that can hinder or enhance comprehension are design and illustration. Research has "demonstrated that nonprint aspects of text such as illustrations influence comprehension and response, particularly among children" (Beach and Hynds, 1991; p. 469). These features enhance understanding when they provide a visual dimension that clarifies the content of the text.

Design includes the size, amount, and arrangement of type on a page. Printed lines that are difficult to follow or large blocks of uninterrupted text might be detrimental to understanding, especially for the less capable or reluctant reader. For this reason, design is a crucial element in children's books.

Illustrations can also help pupils understand what they read. Although illustrations may be more important in expository writing, pictures in narrative material help children form mental images of the settings and characters in stories. The type of illustration also helps shape the reader's perceptions and create the mood or tone for the story.

Reader-Based Features

Text features have a powerful influence on pupils' ability to comprehend what they read. Comprehension, however, is not dependent solely on text; readers inject meaning into the verbal symbols on the page. Text is the vehicle for conveying an author's intended meaning, but that meaning is recreated or constructed in the mind of the reader. Helping pupils comprehend what they read involves addressing characteristics or qualities "behind the reader's eye," features such as language background, cognitive processing, schemata, and metacognition.

Language Background

An obvious prerequisite to reading comprehension is the reader's ability to understand language. Reading is one of the language arts. Printed language conveys meaning, and the ability to comprehend facts or ideas in print depends on the ability to understand the language used.

Metalinguistic Awareness. The language background necessary for reading begins with the metalinguistic awareness that is developed with Big Books, language experience stories, and other reading-writing activities that are part of emergent literacy. Metalinguistic awareness involves understanding the nature of language as a tool of communication; learning the meaning and function of letters, words, and sentences; recognizing the connection between spoken and written language; and understanding the nature of reading itself.

Decoding Ability. Language background also includes the child's ability to decode with ease and fluency. Decoding ability is a "behind the eye" factor that the reader brings to the printed page, and it influences what the reader takes away from the printed page. The relationship between decoding ability and comprehension is well documented (Adams, 1990).

More specific and extended reading comprehension requires the understanding of expanding units of language—from words and sentences to paragraphs and longer selections. Complete comprehension demands the recognition of appropriate meanings for each of these language units.

Vocabulary. Words are the building blocks to meaning. Understanding the meanings of words in their proper contexts is essential to comprehension. Without knowing the meanings of words, attempts at further understanding are largely futile.

Sentences. Sentences carry the essence of meaning in language; that is, basic ideas are expressed at the sentence level. In any language, words are not simply strung together like beads on a string; rather, they are arranged in syntactic patterns so that their relationship to one another conveys meaning. The individual words in the sentences *Norman ate the fish* and *The fish ate Norman* are exactly the same; however, the meanings of the sentences are very different (especially for Norman!). The ability to understand these syntactic relationships is essential to understanding meaning in print.

When a student exhibits comprehension problems, it often makes sense for the teacher to look at the way the child understands sentences. Working on expressing and extracting meaning in sentences also helps cement the reading-writing relationship.

Anaphoric relationships can be important to understanding sentence meaning. *Anaphora* refers to the use of one word as a substitute for another word or group of words. For example, to understand the meaning of the second sentence in this pair

Ralph took the motorcycle to the wastebasket. He decided to hide it there.

the reader must understand the anaphoric references *Ralph = he, it = motorcycle,* and *there = wastebasket.*

Anaphora is also involved in elliptical sentences, such as:

The mouse saw Keith riding the motorcycle. He wanted to try, too.

The reader needs to supply the invisible anaphoric element:

He wanted to try (to ride the motorcycle), too.

Recognizing this type of anaphoric relationship requires inferential thinking.

Devine (1986) suggests the following strategies for helping students understand anaphoric relationships: (1) direct questioning, (2) matching the terms with their antecedents, (3) encouraging pupils to make their own rules to explain anaphora, and (4) heightening their awareness by directing their attention to anaphoric references in text.

6.3 Putting Ideas to Work
Sentence Comprehension

*T*he teacher can focus on comprehension of sentence units by engaging students in such activities as:

locating key sentences and asking children to discuss their meaning.

asking pupils to determine the deep structure of a sentence by identifying pairs of sentences with the same meaning:

There was a mouse in Keith's motel room.
Keith knew about mice in motel rooms.
A mouse was in the motel room where Keith stayed.

asking pupils to change the structural patterns of sentences; for example, having them change sentences from the active voice *(Keith saw the mouse)* to the passive voice *(The mouse was seen by Keith)*.

asking students to break long and difficult sentences apart, especially sentences with relative clauses that add multiple elements of meaning into a sentence.

having children rephrase sentences in their own words.

Each of these activities focuses on the pupil's ability to understand language at the sentence level. (The sentences are based on the content of Beverly Cleary's delightful fantasy, *The Mouse and the Motorcycle*.)

Since anaphora is a stylistic device that authors use for organizational purposes, helping pupils understand these relationships is part of helping them understand text structure.

Paragraphs. Groups of related sentences form paragraphs. Understanding the relationship among the various sentences is the key to understanding the paragraph. Comprehending sentence relationships may also involve understanding the relationship among ideas that the author expresses, main ideas and details, sequence of ideas, cause-effect relationships, or the other relationships the next section describes.

In narrative text, paragraphs may not have a clear or specific central focus that ideas are organized around. Paragraphs may provide details about the character or setting, or add elements to the plot that keep the story moving. Understanding the meaning of narrative paragraphs often requires the ability to recognize and recall paragraph content, to understand the paragraph in relation to the rest of the narrative, and to determine the paragraph's importance to the text (as, for example, when conflict is introduced or particularly important information about a character is presented).

What we can say about language understanding through the paragraph unit also applies to comprehending poetry. Word meanings may be figurative and sentence structures unconventional, but comprehending the meanings of the words and seeing the relationships among the various syntactic elements the poet uses enables the reader to understand the meaning and import the poem expresses.

Selections. Larger selections consist of chapters, stories, whole books, and other segments of text with multiple paragraphs. Comprehension of these larger segments of language requires not only an understanding of the meanings of smaller segments but also long-term recall and cognitive processing. It is in understanding these larger segments that comprehension really occurs.

Readers bring their language backgrounds to the printed page. When problems in reading comprehension become apparent, the succeeding segments of language—from words to sentences to paragraphs—provide the teacher with focal points for diagnosing and addressing broader problems of reading comprehension. Instruction in how to approach these elements of language to build understanding is part of the process of developing reading comprehension.

Cognitive Processing

Reading is a cognitive operation; mental processing is essential to comprehending written text. This mental processing includes both the type of comprehension and the level of comprehension involved in reading a particular piece of text.

Types of Comprehension. Under the heading of *Comprehension*, the scope and sequence charts of conventional basal programs, school curriculum guides, and skills-management systems typically contain lists of items such as recognizing main ideas and details, identifying cause-effect relationships, making comparisons and contrasts, following sequence, distinguishing fact from fancy, separating fact from opinion, determining the author's purpose, predicting outcomes, judging the validity or relevancy of material, making generalizations, and other processes, numbering over 100 in some inventories. Comprehension is seen as the sum total or combination of all of these elements.

These inventories often refer to specific factors as "comprehension skills and subskills." Calling these components "skills" implies that children can develop and improve them through isolated, repeated drill and practice. In conventional programs, skills are the starting point and primary focus in reading instruction. The result has been a plethora of instructional materials containing hundreds of exercises designed to develop one or another of these skills, largely separated from other factors or components of the total comprehension process.

Many problems arise when we view reading comprehension primarily as a series of discrete, specific factors. The distinction between certain factors

Teaching reading comprehension involves more than having children master a set of discrete skills.
© James L. Shaffer

is not always clear; for example, factors such as *summarizing* and *drawing conclusions* can be more alike than different. Some factors are general *(interpreting the meaning of sentences*, for example); others are more specific *(recognizing the anaphoric relationship between a pronoun and its antecedent)*. Moreover, the skill-development approach often places more emphasis on mastering individual skills than on the larger act of reading.

Careful analysis of the research on the distinctiveness of these skills has led to the conclusion that "there is simply no clear evidence to support the naming of discrete skills in reading comprehension" (Rosenshine, 1980; p. 552). These supposedly separate factors may all relate to one generalized element that we could call "reasoning while reading." Even basal programs have considerably reduced the number of separate skills they include in their scope and sequence charts.

Despite the dangers in trying to teach comprehension "skills" as discrete and separate entities, it is important to recognize that different reading materials place varying demands on the reader. Reading the cooking directions on the back of a frozen pizza box, for example, requires a type of comprehension that differs from the mental processing needed to read a romantic novel or a newspaper editorial on the dangers of acid rain. The nature and purpose of each of these reading acts is quite different. Texts are organized differently, and the types of material that children (and adults) encounter impose different demands upon them as readers. And though the skill itself is not the starting point in literature-based instruction, teachers can emphasize different aspects of reasoning as they use literature to develop pupils' reading competency.

What are the different types of comprehension teachers commonly address as they teach reading? When we examine lists from different sources, the lists are typically characterized by some commonality but great diversity. If we itemized all the different "skills and subskills" on published lists, the inventory of factors would extend into the hundreds. However, eight major factors seem to emerge as most often included in most sources: (1) determining the meaning of words in context, (2) getting the main idea, (3) identifying details that support the main idea, (4) following the sequence, (5) drawing conclusions, (6) identifying cause-effect relationships, (7) making inferences, and (8) critical reading/interpretation. Other components appear on some lists: predicting outcomes, identifying a character's motives, summarizing, and the like. But the eight just identified seem to be most commonly addressed by instructional programs.

Understanding words in context is recognized as an important vocabulary element. This chapter will discuss making inferences and critical reading later. The other five factors—identifying main ideas, details, sequence, conclusions, and cause-effect relationships—draw the focus of reading instruction in the literature-based classroom.

Main ideas are the central thoughts or major topics a paragraph or longer segment of text is organized around. Since reading is a form of communication, it is obviously important for the reader to be able to understand the main idea an author is trying to convey.

Some teachers make a distinction between main topics and main ideas. The main *topic* is a word or a phrase that summarizes the central point; the main *idea* is a sentence about the major thought. This may be a moot distinction; no matter how it is expressed, understanding the main idea involves comprehending the major point the author is making.

The main idea is sometimes—although not always—contained in a topic sentence. When the author uses them, topic sentences usually appear as the first or last sentence of a paragraph. The opening paragraph of Judy Blume's *Freckle Juice* contains a topic sentence that sets the tone and purpose of the book: "Andrew Markus wanted freckles." Clear, clean topic sentences like this do not always exist, however, especially in narrative stories.

The main idea may not be directly stated in a paragraph or story. When it is unstated, the main idea must be inferred, often from details. Getting the main idea from implied information is closely related to drawing conclusions.

Details are the less important pieces of information related to the main idea. In any well-written paragraph or story, the main idea is supported by details. Details help clarify concepts, complete a picture that constitutes the setting for a story, provide evidence to support a conclusion, show how to apply an idea, fill in gaps to make a plot or character more understandable, or otherwise provide information to enhance the reader's understanding. Good readers are skilled at identifying details that lead to a full and accurate understanding of the main idea.

Details should always be considered in light of their contribution to the main idea. Teachers are often criticized for spending too much time quizzing children on unimportant and trivial bits of information that have little significance in a story. Those small facts that collectively support the main idea should be the subject of a teacher's questioning and discussion.

Distinguishing between main ideas and details involves reasoning and selecting as one reads. It requires the ability to see the difference between ideas of greater and lesser importance. This is important not only so that children will not become awash in an ocean of trivial facts, but also so that they can distinguish what is relevant when seeking information in expository text.

Main ideas and details can be the focus of instruction for both paragraphs and longer selections of narrative text. By definition, a paragraph is one or more sentences clustered around a single topic or idea. To understand and write effective paragraphs, pupils need to recognize the main idea as a tool authors use to organize their ideas.

Not all paragraphs have an explicit main idea, but all are focused around some kind of unifying element. As students read paragraphs, they can identify topic sentences (if they are present) that contain the main idea, or identify details that suggest the unifying thought or idea of the paragraph.

Paragraphs are part of longer discourse. In narrative stories, individual paragraphs carry the flow of main concepts or actions the author wants to convey. In much children's literature, main ideas are not directly stated, so students need to identify them through discussion. The main idea of a story may be the conflict a protagonist faces and how he or she resolves it. Pupils may determine the main idea for a chapter by suggesting possible chapter titles. They may be able to capture the main idea of a whole book by writing a 25-word summary of its plot.

Finding the main idea in a piece of poetry nearly always requires inferential comprehension. The central thought of a poem may be a simple metaphor, like Carl Sandburg's beautiful image of fog creeping in "on little cat's feet," or it may be an action, as in Shel Silverstein's ludicrous image of putting a bra on a camel. Whatever the thought, image, or metaphor expressed, to comprehend the main idea and details of a poem it is almost always necessary for children to go beyond the literal meaning of the lines.

As teachers use literature to help pupils learn to read, they need to be aware of opportunities to help children recognize main ideas and details as they read and discuss trade books.

Questions that teachers ask before, during, and after a story will help students focus on main ideas. Questions help focus the pupils' attention on the main point of the story throughout. Obviously, the nature of the story will largely determine the main idea questions the teacher might ask. One would not ask the same types of questions when discussing a story like Evaline Ness's *Sam, Bangs, and Moonshine* as one would ask when reading a book like Dr. Seuss's *Green Eggs and Ham*.

There's a big difference between using trade books and using more conventional skill-oriented materials in helping children to identify main ideas and details (as well as other components of comprehension). Conventional programs first identify the skill they wish to develop and then provide

6.4 Putting Ideas to Work
Graphic Organizers for Main Ideas

Graphic organizers can help children see the relationship between main ideas and details in paragraphs. The following is an example of a graphic device that shows the relationships between the main idea and details in Arnold Lobel's *Frog and Toad Are Friends*:

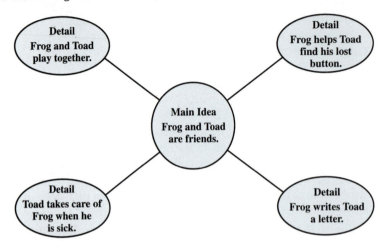

This graphic organizer focuses on the element of setting, using Sheila Burnford's *Incredible Journey*:

The Nurmi farm was neat and attractive. (main idea)
A small cabin stood near the bank of a river.
The door was bright blue.
Scarlet geraniums grew in window boxes.
The vegetable gardens and fields were neatly fenced.

This example from Lynne Reid Banks's *Indian in the Cupboard* focuses on the element of plot:

Little Bear and Boone had a fierce fight. (main idea)
The two men rolled on the ground.
They grabbed and punched at one another.
Boone tried to bite the Indian.
They groaned and screamed.

Pupils can construct these visual devices based on what they read. Graphic organizers can summarize whole stories as well.

6.5 Putting Ideas to Work

Questioning for Main Ideas and Details

*I*n using literature to help children learn to read, the teacher needs to watch for opportunities to help them learn to recognize main ideas and details as they read. Questions that teachers ask before, during, and after a story can help students focus on the main ideas. For example, a teacher could pose questions like the following to students reading Evaline Ness's haunting *Sam, Bangs, and Moonshine*, the story of a little girl whose difficulty in separating fact from imagination gets a friend in trouble:

> *Before*—Why do you think it's important for a person to see the difference between what's real and what's made up?
> *During*—What do you think might happen to Thomas when he goes looking for Sam's imaginary baby kangaroo?
> *After*—What do you think Sam learned from her experiences?

Questions like these help focus pupils' attention on the main points of the story as they read.

Main ideas can also be the focus of questions about literary elements in a story. For example, as children discuss the literary elements in E. L. Konigsburg's mystery *From the Mixed-Up Files of Mrs. Basil E. Frankweiler*, they can focus on the main ideas and details of:

> *character*—the details that make Jamie such a good companion for his sister Claudia;
> *setting*—the details of the museum in which the characters spend their time; and
> *plot*—the details of what the children do in trying to solve the mystery of the statue.

materials that specifically illustrate the skill. The skill comes first; the text comes second. For example, a paragraph such as the following might be designed to teach the concept of a main idea:

Spring came. The snow melted. The grass grew green.
Buds appeared on the trees. Furry animals began to appear.
The best title for this story is:
A. Spring came.
B. Furry animals are important.
C. Spring is the best season of the year.

Trade books are not so tidy and contrived. A children's author starts with an idea and a story. In literature, text comes first; it's up to the teacher to "tease out" the skills from the story. In Jean Craighead George's *My Side of the Mountain*, one can find text with ideas similar to the main idea exercise about spring. Teachers need to adapt their teaching techniques and questioning strategies to the nature of the text the students are reading.

Finally, it is important to keep in mind that many pieces of children's literature do not have a "main idea and details" in the conventional sense. Asking children to find the main idea in one of Peggy Parrish's *Amelia Bedelia*

6.6 Putting Ideas to Work

Teaching Sequence

To teach children how to follow the flow of events in a story, teachers can use a number of devices:

Story maps and *flow charts* like those in Putting Ideas to Work 6.2 involve sequence. Children focus on the sequence of events as they follow the plot line of a story.

Time lines can also be used to teach sequence. Students can construct these devices for the stories they read.

Sentence strips, each listing an event in the story, may be arranged in order.

Specific trade books may lend themselves to teaching sequence:

Karla Kuskin's *The Philharmonic Gets Dressed* is a carefully sequenced account of how members of an orchestra prepare for a performance.

Donald Hall's *The Ox-Cart Man*, strikingly illustrated by Barbara Cooney, follows the sequence of the seasons.

Robert Munsch's *Mortimer* is a hilarious account of a series of people who try to get the obstreperous Mortimer to quiet down after he goes to bed.

Creative teachers will spot many other opportunities to help children learn sequence in the books they read in the classroom.

books, for example, would be counterproductive. The way children smile and giggle as they read these books provides ample evidence they are getting the main idea!

Sequence, the order in which events or ideas occur in text, is another element frequently included in lists of comprehension components, included in instructional programs, and assessed in reading tests. Sequence is sometimes referred to as the "chaining" of events or ideas. Anyone who has attempted to put together an item marked with the innocuous warning "Some Assembly Required" recognizes the importance of understanding sequence in text.

In narrative text, sequence can be indicated in sentences, in paragraphs, or in longer segments of text. At the sentence level, the sequential order can be stated explicitly *(After Miss Nelson left, Viola Swamp arrived)* or implied *(Miss Nelson left and Viola Swamp arrived)*. Whether stated or implied, understanding sequential order in sentences is essential to comprehending whole texts.

In paragraphs, the order of events is usually expressed in separate sentences, and signal words such as *now, before, afterward, then,* and *finally* frequently connect the transitions between sentences.

In narrative text, the sequence of events in a story constitutes the literary element of plot. Sequencing requires pupils to understand the action of a story as it leads from the beginning to the conclusion or resolution.

As with main ideas, sequence in a story can be either stated or implied. Inferring the sequence of events leads to predicting outcomes—that is, forecasting the events to follow based on the order of events that have already happened. A popular instructional technique for this component is asking children to tell or write a subsequent event for a story they have enjoyed.

In selecting trade books to teach about sequencing, it is important that sequence be essential to the plot. It makes little sense, for example, to try to teach sequencing with a book like Peggy Parrish's *Amelia Bedelia*, since the sequence in which this literal-minded maid draws the drapes (with paper and pencil), dusts the furniture (with dusting powder), and trims the steak (with ribbons) makes little difference in the story.

Usually, events in a narrative story flow chronologically. There are occasions, however, when it becomes important for the reader to understand flashbacks to fully comprehend a story. A *flashback* is a literary device that authors sometimes use to present important story information by returning to an earlier time. For example, understanding details about how the Tillerman children arrived at their grandmother's house in Maryland is important to comprehending Cynthia Voigt's Newbery Award-winning *Dicey's Song*. A specific exercise that involves rearranging events according to the order in which they happened may help pupils comprehend the story.

When appropriate, prereading questions and postreading discussions can focus on the sequence of events in a story. The purpose of these questions is not merely to have pupils recall what happened when, but to focus their attention on sequential elements that are important to the full comprehension of significant events in the story and the relation of these events to one another.

The purpose of focusing on sequence of events in teaching reading through trade books is not to develop this "skill" as an end in itself. Rather, its purpose is to help students see the order of events as part of understanding and appreciating stories in literature-based programs.

Drawing conclusions is another frequent focus of reading comprehension in the classroom. Drawing conclusions involves the ability to deduce or infer ideas from evidence presented in a piece of print. As they read, pupils piece together facts to arrive at a conclusion—that is, to recognize a conclusion that the text may state or to infer their own conclusion based on what they read. Drawing conclusions is closely associated with the ability to determine main ideas; both involve using information (details) to arrive at a conclusion (main idea).

Drawing conclusions is not a "reading skill" alone; it is a cognitive activity children need to exercise in all their school subjects and in their out-of-school lives as well. The conclusions pupils draw from what they read will depend in large measure on their backgrounds, experiences, and knowledge about a topic.

To help pupils draw conclusions about what they read, the teacher's questioning is key. Teachers can encourage children to think about character

6.7 Putting Ideas to Work
Drawing Conclusions

Reading (or listening) with understanding involves making an ongoing series of conclusions. As children read Bernard Waber's *Ira Sleeps Over*, for example, they can draw conclusions about Ira's relationship with his mother, his father, his sister, his friend Reggie, and his teddy bear. Pupils can also draw conclusions about Ira's uneasiness, his bravado, and his return home to get Tah Tah when he realizes that Reggie sleeps with a teddy bear, too.

Humor requires the ability to draw conclusions. As students read books of jokes and riddles, they can explain the point of the humor in the language.

In mystery stories—for example, simple detective books like Marjorie Weinman Sharmat's *Nate the Great* series, David A. Adler's *Cam Jansen* or *Fourth Floor Twins* series, and Donald J. Sobol's *Encyclopedia Brown* mysteries—the need to draw conclusions is built in. Pupils can trace the step-by-step clues that enable these junior sleuths to solve the mystery every time.

traits and conclude how characters may act in other situations. ("What might Homer Price say to Soup Vinson if the two characters met?") Questions asked during reading ("What do you think might happen next? Why?") and after reading ("Was your prediction correct? Why?") lead pupils to draw conclusions based on the evidence they encounter in stories.

Cause-effect relationships are related to conclusions. A cause-effect relationship is an association between an outcome and the conditions that caused the outcome to happen. Cause-effect relationships are present in virtually anything a child reads in the classroom.

Cause-effect elements in text are frequently indicated by signal words and phrases such as *because, so, since, thus, as a result of, therefore*, and the like. Even when these signal words are not part of the story, however, children can learn to understand that one event occurs as a result or consequence of another. Some cause-effect relationships are stated directly, and others are implied.

In literature-based programs, cause-effect relationships can be an instructional focus from the very early stages of emerging literacy. Young children can identify the causes of the three pigs' problems or the reasons why Hansel and Gretel were sent away or how they managed to escape. From the beginning stages of learning to read, almost any story presents cause-effect relationships that can be explored and developed through instruction.

Ongoing discussion and questioning engage pupils in looking for cause-effect relationships as they read. In guided reading, postreading discussion, and dialogue in literature groups, *why* questions are the most effective for helping children understand these relationships. Questions should relate to the text so that students can cite evidence of the relationship between events.

6.8 Putting Ideas to Work
Cause-Effect Relationships

Cause-effect relationships can be part of a discussion on why characters behave as they do. For Maurice Sendak's modern classic *Where the Wild Things Are*, for example, the teacher can draw cause circles and effect circles with elements like:

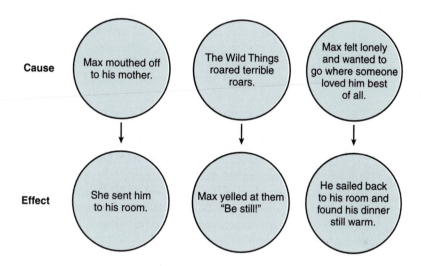

Children can match the related causes and effects of these actions.

One instructional device for focusing on multiple causes and effects is a chart with two columns headed *Causes* and *Effects,* and with appropriate items listed under each heading. For example, we can develop such a chart using Laura Jaffe Numeroff's *If You Give a Mouse a Cookie*, a story that children (and most adults) genuinely enjoy:

Causes	Effects
You give a Mouse a cookie.	He'll want a glass of milk.
You give him a glass of milk.	He'll want a straw.
He notices his hair needs cutting.	You give him a scissors.
He needs to take a nap.	He'll want a blanket and a pillow.
etc.	etc.

Children also need to become aware of multiple cause-effect relationships and causal chains. In multiple cause-effect relationships, several effects may result from a single cause. In causal chains, one event causes another, which in turn causes another, and so on in a chain reaction. Consider the series of causes and effects in Gene Zion's delightfully funny *Harry by the Sea*. The dog is hot so he goes into the water; when he goes into the water, he gets covered by seaweed; when people see him covered by seaweed, they think he is a sea monster; because they think he is a sea monster, they become frightened; because they become frightened, . . . and so on.

Teachers can highlight cause-effect relationships in both narrative and expository text. In narrative stories, these relationships can be the link between what the characters are like and what they do, between setting and action, between people and their surroundings. In understanding causes and effects, the reader understands the crucial question *why?*

Integrating instruction in comprehension is important. The comprehension factors we described—identifying main ideas and details, determining sequence, drawing conclusions, and identifying cause-effect relationships—are not separate, discrete, individual skills. They are closely integrated elements that children can think about as they strive for general understanding. Taken together, they enhance the students' ability to make meaning and add a dimension to their understanding and appreciation of literature.

Although all these factors are closely linked, conventional reading instructional programs list, treat, and teach them as largely separate entities—supplying a practice book on cause-effect relationships, a stack of worksheets on sequencing, some exercises on main ideas. With trade books, all these components of comprehension are closely integrated and interwoven as elements of a single—albeit complex—entity.

Using literature to help children develop these aspects of reasoning while reading offers particular advantages. In conventional reading programs, these elements are typically developed with paragraph-length selections. A worksheet or skills exercise book usually includes unrelated individual paragraphs on main ideas or sequencing or cause-effect relationships. These programs usually test these elements with paragraph-length segments of print, too. Standardized tests of reading comprehension typically contain paragraphs or very short selections, followed by questions to assess particular comprehension components *(What's the best title for this story?).*

The ultimate aim of reading is not understanding at the paragraph level, however. Although comprehending the meanings of paragraphs is indeed important, the real payoff in reading comes when children can understand total selections. Using trade books enables children to develop and practice comprehension within this broader focus.

Levels of Thinking.   One way to view comprehension is to consider what levels of thinking are involved in reading comprehension. This is an attempt to analyze comprehension according to a taxonomy or classification scheme of the mental operations involved in understanding what one reads. Several taxonomies attempt to describe such a hierarchy. Among the best known are:

Bloom (1956)	Sanders (1966)	Barrett (1974)	Guilford (1985)
Evaluation	Evaluation	Appreciation	Evaluation
Synthesis	Synthesis	Evaluation	Divergent
Analysis	Analysis	Inference	Production
Application	Application	Literal	Convergent
Comprehension	Interpretation	recognition or	Production
Knowledge	Translation	recall	Memory
	Memory		Cognition

6.9 Putting Ideas to Work
Bloom's Taxonomy

*B*loom's taxonomy is widely used to develop reading comprehension questions at various cognitive levels. Bloom's categories progress in a hierarchical fashion from low-level thinking (Knowledge) to higher-level mental operations (Analysis, Synthesis, and Evaluation). The following questions at different levels are based on Lois Lowry's Newbery-award winner, *The Giver*, the provocative story of a 12-year-old-boy who escapes from his perfectly ordered futuristic world:

> *Knowledge*—Who selected Jonas to become the receiver in training?
> *Comprehension* —Why was Jonas selected to receive special training?
> *Application*—In what ways is your world similar to the one Jonas lives in?
> *Analysis*—What were the real reasons Jonas took Gabe and escaped into the night?
> *Synthesis*—Keeping in mind all you know about Jonas, how would you describe his character?
> *Evaluation*—In what ways is *The Giver* a work of science fiction?

Very often, higher-level questions are open-ended, with no right or wrong answers.

These taxonomies differ in purpose. Bloom's, by far the most popular in schools, is a classification scheme for writing educational objectives. Sanders's list was produced as a criterion for formulating and judging instructional questions. Guilford's model was an attempt to account for our intellectual structure. Barrett's taxonomy was designed to describe the reading comprehension component in a published basal-reading program; it was presented in a professional text about teaching reading. The models also differ in detail, with different labels attached to different levels of thinking. Components of these taxonomies have been adapted, renamed, and applied in different ways in relation to reading comprehension.

When applied to reading instruction, level of thinking is often related to understanding at the literal, inferential, and critical-creative levels. Literal comprehension involves the ability to understand information and ideas specifically expressed in text. Inferential comprehension involves the ability to infer, analyze, and question information and ideas not explicitly stated. Critical-creative comprehension demands that readers move beyond the text in applying higher mental processes to more universal ideas drawn from what they read.

Literal comprehension consists of "reading the lines" and involves the most basic level of understanding—the recognition and recall of information explicitly stated in text. This level of comprehension has been described as "text explicit" because the information is directly stated in the text.

In literal comprehension, there is an important distinction between recognition and recall of information. Recognition requires the reader to locate a piece of information they are seeking; recall requires the reader to remember that information after reading it. Recognition is usually easier than recall. (That is why good readers read the questions before they read the paragraphs in a silent reading test.) Whether the task involves recognition or recall, comprehension at this level demands that the reader understand information that is found directly in the text.

Literal understanding may involve different *types* of comprehension; that is, it may involve the recognition of a main idea contained in a topic sentence or the identification of a directly explained cause-effect relationship. No matter what aspect of reasoning is involved, the reader can respond to literal-level questions by referring directly to information contained in the text.

Some reading tasks require primary reliance on literal comprehension. Pupils need to understand what is happening in a story before they can draw inferences or react mentally or emotionally to the story. Good readers, however, quickly move on to higher levels of thinking while reading.

Inferential or *interpretative comprehension*, "reading between the lines," requires the reader to understand facts or ideas the text does not directly state. Inferences are reasoned assumptions about information implied in a text. Making inferences requires the reader to supply information the author does not provide directly. Comprehension at this level is *text implicit*; that is, the information is not stated directly but is implied. Since no text is totally explicit, readers make inferences virtually every time they interact with a piece of print.

In a classroom setting, children use their background knowledge and experience to help them understand text-implicit information. For example, in reading Bernard Waber's *Ira Sleeps Over* (the story of the little boy who wants to take his teddy bear when sleeping over at a friend's house), children use their backgrounds to infer how Ira felt when his sister warned him, "Reggie will laugh," and how Ira felt when he discovered that his friend Reggie slept with a teddy bear, too. Readers play an active role in inferential comprehension as they combine the information in the text with their knowledge of the world.

Making inferences is an ongoing part of the comprehension process. As they read, children make inferences about a number of things—the details of the story setting, causes or effects of actions, time elements, motivations and emotions of characters, solutions to problems, and so forth. Pupils will not always make inferences spontaneously or automatically, however. Teacher direction can stimulate their ability to infer meaning and supply information not directly stated in text. Research has shown that students can improve their inferential comprehension through strategies such as cloze exercises, teacher-pupil interviews, questions requiring inferential understanding, background discussions that foster predictions, and self-monitoring procedures (Johnson and Johnson, 1988). Through careful suggestions and well-chosen questions, teachers guide pupils to develop the ability to "read between the lines" and understand what the author implies in a text.

Critical-creative comprehension, the third and highest level of thinking, involves "reading beyond the lines" to react or respond to what one has

6.10 Putting Ideas to Work
Developing Critical Thinking

Critical thinking does not occur on a set schedule. Opportunities abound for critical reading each time children read. Evidence shows that even children reading picture books can develop critical thinking skills, not only in the cognitive area but also in aesthetic awareness (Kiefer, 1984).

Primary grade pupils can:

> relate their own experiences to the events in Russell Hoban's *A Bargain for Frances*, in which Frances is the victim of an unfair trade;
>
> make judgments about justice and fairness when reading Bill Peet's *Big Bad Bruce*, a story about a bear who was a bully before he was cut down to size (literally and figuratively!);
>
> judge the actions of the characters in Eve Bunting's *Smoky Night*, a story based on the Los Angeles riot in the early 1990s.

As their growing reading abilities lead to greater independence, pupils can:

> compare details of frontier life as described in the many books of Laura Ingalls Wilder with those Patricia MacLachlan describes in *Sarah, Plain and Tall*.
>
> sort out reality and fantasy—which events could have happened and which are plainly impossible—from books like *Stone Fox* by John Reynolds Gardiner or *From the Mixed-Up Files of Mrs. Basil E. Frankweiler* by E. L. Konigsburg.
>
> relate their own experiences to Stacy as she comes to grips with her cultural identity in Laurence Yep's *Thief of Hearts*.

Children can also relate to the experiences of characters like Beverly Cleary's lovable *Ellen Tebbits* or Jean Lowery Nixon's character Margaret Ledoux in *Maggie, Too*.

In addition to the many planned and spontaneous opportunities that arise every day in the classroom as children encounter literature, professionally designed instructional strategies can help pupils engage in critical thinking about what they read. For example, *Diological-Thinking Reading Lesson (D-TRL)* was specifically designed to promote critical thinking during reading (Commeyras, 1993). Diological thinking involves the serious consideration of competing points of view. The strategy encourages students to try to identify reasons to support alternative conclusions regarding a story theme or issue. Through discussion, students offer more than one point of view on a story, react to other points of view, consider alternatives, and make critical judgments. In this four-step process, (1) the teacher poses a critical question and two points of view related to the question, (2) students identify reasons to support both points of view, (3) students discuss the reasons, and (4) children draw conclusions based on their discussion.

read. The ability to think critically and creatively about the text is the ultimate stage in the reading process.

It is not easy to make hard and fast distinctions between critical and creative reading. Critical comprehension may be viewed as the logical, analytical processing of what one reads: evaluating, analyzing, synthesizing, and prioritizing ideas, for example. It involves clarifying and assessing the reasonableness of ideas. Creative thinking involves fluency, flexibility, versatility, originality, and elaboration of ideas generated in connection with reading. In the actual reading-thinking process, however, sharp lines disappear quickly as one tries to identify or classify the higher mental processes involved.

The distinction between critical and creative comprehension can be expressed in another way: critical reading involves a logical, cognitive reaction; creative reading involves a more emotional reaction. In critical reading, you react with your head; in creative reading, you react with your heart. Creative comprehension is evidenced by a tear in one's eye or a lump in one's throat as Billy buries his two faithful hound dogs near the end of Wilson Rawls's heartwarming story *Where the Red Fern Grows*, or of Robert Munsch's *Love You Forever*.

This type of emotional response to text may, in fact, be the highest form of reading comprehension. At the creative reading level, the reader not only recognizes what the characters are doing but also infers the significance of their actions. The reader is reading so well that he or she actually understands how the character feels and shares in the character's joy, sorrow, love, or disappointment. When the reader becomes one with the character, he or she truly comprehends a story.

Students engage in critical comprehension as they form judgments about what they have read. These mental operations include evaluating the adequacy or validity of the material, judging the appropriateness or acceptability of the text, comparing different sources of information, weighing the value of ideas in light of previous experience, and otherwise thinking about the facts and ideas they have read. Critical reading is an active mental process.

Several components of critical reading have long received specific attention in classroom reading programs. These components include distinguishing between fact and opinion, seeing the difference between real and make-believe, and detecting propaganda in print. Combs (1996) states that the critical reader must have the ability to decide "What is of value, what is accurate, and what is worthy of retaining for future use" (p. 27). All these components are essential to the intelligent use of reading in a free society.

A literature-based program can effectively help students develop and practice critical reading. In selecting and reading trade books, for example, pupils can determine the primary purpose of the text: to entertain, to inform, or to persuade. Although some books are more singular in intent, others have all three purposes. Asking children to talk about the purpose of a book like Hardie Gramatky's classic *Little Toot* gives them a chance to practice critical thinking in connection with reading from the beginning. Some children's books—like Evaline Ness's *Sam, Bangs, and Moonshine* and Chris Van Allsburg's *Polar Express*—are written specifically around a critical-creative reading theme.

Critical thinking is not unique to reading, of course. It is important in all areas of the curriculum. Watching television commercials to detect propaganda or to separate reality and fantasy are valuable critical listening exercises. But since reading is so essential to learning and reaches into all areas of school life, critical thinking finds its home in reading from the very early stages.

6.11 Putting Ideas to Work

Question-Answer Relationships

*R*aphael (1982, 1986) suggests a strategy for teaching pupils to explicitly analyze the tasks comprehension questions demand prior to answering them. She calls this technique Question-Answer Relationships (QAR). Consistent with the interactive model of reading comprehension, QAR gives students a way to figure out whether answers can be drawn from information in the text or from the reader's own background knowledge.

The two primary question categories that Raphael uses are (1) *In the Book*, and (2) *In My Head*. The first category includes questions designated as:

> *Right There,* literal, text-explicit responses that can be found right in the reading material itself; and
> *Think and Search* (or *Putting It Together*), responses that can be found in the text but are not contained in a single sentence or paragraph; readers need to put ideas together to find the answers.

The *In My Head* QAR category includes:

> *On My Own,* responses in which the reader needs to use prior knowledge or experience to find the answer; and
> *The Author and You,* responses that are not in the text; readers need to determine how what the author tells them fits with what they already know.

Raphael suggests a series of lessons in which pupils learn to use QAR. Instruction includes feedback, progress from shorter to longer segments of text, building independence from group to individual activities, and transitioning from easier to more difficult response tasks.

Most of the research on QAR has focused on fourth grade and above, but the technique can be adapted for use with children in the lower grades. QAR has also proven effective in helping pupils answer questions based on expository reading material.

Once the teacher focuses on the importance of critical-creative reading in literature-based reading instruction, opportunities to engage children in higher-level thinking as they read will suggest themselves aplenty. "Instructional strategies to promote the development and use of good critical and creative thinking are most effective when they involve students in forms of thinking that they will use again and again in their lives. This is best done by infusing the teaching of critical and creative thinking into regular classroom instruction" (Massachusetts Department of Education, 1988; p. 7). The teacher need not manufacture opportunities to stimulate critical and creative thinking. Prereading activities like brainstorming ideas about the possible content of a story, sharing information related to the topic, focusing on the relationships among ideas, forming hypotheses, and setting purposes related to critical-creative thought set the stage for critical thinking while reading.

6.12 Putting Ideas to Work
Junior Great Books

One way to directly use literature to develop critical reading and thinking skills in the elementary grades is through the Junior Great Books program. This program aims to help pupils understand and think critically about good books. Under the direction of a trained leader, students discuss the language and ideas in stories that range from Margery Williams's *The Velveteen Rabbit* and Marcia Brown's *Stone Soup* in the early grades to Paula Fox's *Maurice's Room* and works by Langston Hughes in the upper elementary grades. Discussion focuses on interpretation of meaning, support for ideas from the text, questioning, and shared inquiry that requires opinion and interpretation in response—all essential elements of comprehension at the highest levels.

The Great Books Foundation offers staff development sessions for teachers. More information about the program is available from The Great Books Foundation, 40 East Huron Street, Chicago, IL 60611.

Ongoing dialogue can lead children to evaluate what they read, to confirm hypotheses, and to refine information during reading. Follow-up questions can ask children to make judgments about what they have read, to apply, to extend, to evaluate, and to stimulate their thinking beyond the text. These types of activities engage children in reading as a critical thinking activity.

Schemata

Schema theory is a means of explaining how humans organize and store information. *Schemata* (the plural form of *schema*) are mental structures or conceptual systems for arranging information inside our heads—the mental "slots" or connected webs in which we organize and store knowledge.

Schema theory is a theory about knowledge, how it is organized, and how it is used. According to this theory, humans organize knowledge or information into units called schemata. In addition to the knowledge itself, these "packets of data" contain information about how to use the knowledge and about the network of relationships among various schemata. In other words, our schemata consist of all our associated knowledge and expectations. As such, they are critical building blocks children use to bring meaning to the literature they read.

Readers approach text with lots of information about their world. They use this knowledge, along with the information in the text itself, to construct meaning, connecting new knowledge they find in text to the knowledge they already have. A body of research evidence indicates that students' comprehension improves greatly, especially at the inferential level, when teachers draw relationships between their background knowledge and the content of the text they're reading (Pearson and Fielding, 1991).

Reading comprehension and schemata are reciprocally related. People acquire their schemata through experiences. This background—the picture in their heads of a particular topic—influences their understanding as they read about that topic. At the same time, reading a story can broaden one's background and provide vicarious experiences that will alter or enrich one's schemata. As children read, they integrate new material into what they already know. For example, Betsy Byars's witty and touching *The Animal, the Vegetable, and John D. Jones* is a story about two sisters who look forward to spending a seaside vacation with their divorced father, only to have their father show up with his new girlfriend and her son. On the one hand, pupils who have spent a vacation at the shore, and/or children who have had to unwillingly share the attention of a divorced parent, will comprehend this story in a different way from those who have not had these experiences. On the other hand, students who do not have a well-defined seaside-vacation schema or a schema concerning unwillingly sharing a single parent will be able to develop insights (new schemata) by reading the book. "Trade books offer opportunities for building richly elaborated schemata that go considerably beyond those offered in most school books" (Wilson, Anderson, and Fielding, 1986; p. 6).

Schemata are absolutely essential to inferential comprehension because what a person reads "between the lines" depends almost wholly on his or her background and expectations. Anderson and Pearson (1984) provide the following illustration. If you read that the governor christened a ship last Saturday, what do you think she used for the christening? And if you read that at the same time last Saturday the vicar was christening a child, what do you think he used for the christening? Your ability to make inferences, to infer champagne in one case and water in the other, is attributable to the fact that you have a christening schema in your head. Within that schema are two subschemata—a ship-christening subschema and a child-christening subschema. This shows how schemata form a scaffolding for understanding what we read.

Obviously, language is an important part of our schemata, too. The linguistic labels pupils attach to items of background knowledge and to the associations they make between concepts affect their comprehension as they expand these concepts through reading. *Indian in the Cupboard* is a popular story written by a British author (Lynne Reid Banks) about a uniquely American topic (cowboys and Indians). Most upper-elementary students have the background to understand the story, but some of the British expressions—a Matchbox *lorry* (truck), the *dustbins* (garbage cans) out in back, or the gate that keeps the *infants* (first and second graders) in the schoolyard—cause American readers to pause. The unfamiliar language does not, however, appear so frequently as to prevent comprehension.

What are some of the implications of schema theory for helping children better comprehend what they read in literature-based programs? Schema theory emphasizes the importance of activating prior knowledge; to do so, the teacher can employ prereading strategies that encourage pupils to use their own experiences to predict characters' problems and actions in the stories they read. Wide reading builds prior experience. So do media presentations. Pupils

6.13 Putting Ideas to Work
Activating Prior Knowledge

Activating prior knowledge to link what children are about to read to what they already know as an aid to comprehension is normally part of prereading discussion in any reading lesson. For example, prior to a basal reading lesson on *Bumps in the Night* (an Arnold Lobel story about unfounded fears that appear in a popular basal series), the teacher reads Dick Gackenbach's *Harry and the Terrible Whatzit*, a story with the same theme, and children share some of their unfounded fears.

Formal strategies have also been developed to help pupils use their schemata to improve comprehension; for example:

PreReading Plan (PReP) is designed to give children opportunities to think about what they know about a topic before reading. Developed by Langer (1981), the strategy involves two steps. In step one, pupils engage in a discussion about key concepts in a story, brainstorming for an initial association, reflecting on that association, and extending information related to the concept. In the second step, the teacher analyzes pupil responses to determine how their existing understandings can prepare them for understanding new text and to see which students may need extra help in comprehension. PReP is a direct way to prepare pupils to comprehend a selection by using the knowledge they already have.

Anticipation guides are designed to activate students' knowledge before reading, while at the same time providing a guide as they read. The teacher prepares a number of written statements about the key concepts in a story; the group discusses the statements, and then pupils read to determine whether the story verifies the statements.

Text previews both build prior knowledge and provide an organizational framework for comprehension. The text preview may contain a brief synopsis and purpose-setting questions. The children discuss the preview before reading. Although they are time-consuming to construct, text previews have proved to be effective aids to comprehension (Graves, Cooke, and LaBerge, 1983). These and other prereading strategies have the same intent: to help pupils think about what they already know in relation to a story so that they will more effectively build on this knowledge through reading.

who have read Laura Ingalls Wilder's *Little House in the Big Woods* will likely be better able to comprehend *Little House on the Prairie, Farmer Boy,* and Wilder's other books because of their familiarity with the background information in the series. A built-in element of motivation is present, too, when a reader has "met" and grown to care about the characters in a series.

Seeing videos, movies, or filmstrips of *Little House* or any other book will also build the students' schemata by providing background knowledge that will enhance understanding. Presenting videos and books in combination can be an excellent exercise in critical reading as well. After pupils have read (or listened to) a book like Marie McSwigan's exciting adventure story *Snow Treasure,* and then seen the movie based on the book, they can make critical comparisons between the print and movie versions of the story. More often than not, children come to the same conclusion that many adult readers do: "The movie was good, but I liked the book a lot better."

Perhaps the ultimate schema-building device is direct, real-life experience. For many stories, this is impossible, since topics are often removed in time and space from children's experiences. Finding a story based on an experience that children have had, however, greatly improves the chances that students will comprehend that story. For example, children in Boston who take the "Make Way For Ducklings Tour" follow the path that Mr. and Mrs. Mallard and their ducklings followed from the Charles River Basin to the Duck Pond on the Boston Common. These children will certainly be able to read Robert McCloskey's *Make Way for Ducklings* with greater understanding and enjoyment.

Schema theory indicates that children who have gaps in their knowledge about a topic may have trouble comprehending what they read about that topic. This suggests how important it is for the teacher to fill in some of the information gaps before reading. Within the context of schema theory, reading comprehension might be likened to a jigsaw puzzle. All the information must fit into place without forcing—all the important slots must contain information, and the completed picture must make sense (Anderson and Pearson, 1984). A missing piece that the teacher provides may be the key to a complete understanding of the entire "puzzle."

Reading comprehension is affected by what we already know. Helping children to build on their schemata as they read text is an effective way to help them comprehend what they read in school.

Metacognition

An aspect of reading comprehension that deserves significant attention is metacognition. The term *metacognition* means "an awareness and knowledge

6.14 Putting Ideas to Work
The Metacomprehension Strategy Index

Schmitt (1990) has developed a 25-item questionnaire to assess children's awareness of metacognitive activity before, during, and after they read. This instrument, called the Metacomprehension Strategy Index (MSI), is designed to measure strategies for comprehending narrative text. Based on the premises that metacognition is characteristic of good readers and that metacomprehensive strategies can be taught, the MSI provides teachers with a way to assess pupils' awareness of prereading, reading, and postreading metacomprehension strategies.

Even if it is not used as an assessment instrument, the MSI can be a useful guide to the metacognitive strategies teachers can help students develop in reading narrative prose. The complete questionnaire appears in the March 1990 issue of *The Reading Teacher.*

of one's mental processes such that one can monitor, regulate, and direct them to a desired end." When applied to reading, it involves "knowing when what one is reading makes sense by monitoring and controlling one's own comprehension" (Harris and Hodges, 1995; p. 153). *Metacomprehension,* a closely related term, means an awareness of, and control over, one's understanding. Very simply, it is the awareness of what is going on inside your head as you read. "The key words associated with metacognition reveal its emphasis: awareness, monitoring, control, and evaluation" (Pearson, 1985b; p. 15).

Metacognition makes reading an active mental process. It begins with a basic awareness that reading is an activity that demands cognitive involvement, not just decoding. This may seem obvious, but poor readers tend to focus primarily (sometimes exclusively) on the decoding dimensions as they read. Taking metacognition into account in the classroom encourages pupils to develop a sensitivity to the demands of reading for meaning.

At a basic level, metacognition makes a person aware of whether he or she is comprehending. Good readers consistently monitor their own reading activity. They adapt strategies to fit the types of questions asked. When they realize they are not extracting meaning from a text, they take appropriate action; that is, they slow down, spend more time on difficult parts, reread sections, or work harder to achieve meaning. Poor readers do not apply these strategies. They tend not to "self-monitor their comprehension or try to repair miscomprehension. By not becoming actively involved in the reading process, they fail to understand its interactive nature and passively accept their failure" (Garcia, Pearson, and Jiminez, l994; p. 14).

How can teachers influence the metacognitive activity that goes on inside students' heads? Studies have tried to determine how well children monitor their reading by determining the degree of confidence they have in their responses to reading, monitoring their self-corrections of the miscues they make in oral reading, examining their performance on cloze tests

6.15 Putting Ideas to Work
Developing Metacognition

*P*upils learn to comprehend better when teachers help them learn how, why, and when to perform problem-solving tasks necessary to fully understand text.

Metacognition can become a regular part of instruction in reading comprehension through a variety of formal and informal activities, including:

Questioning.   Questions might focus on thought processes and not just answers; that is, the teacher can follow up questions such as "Where did the pirates hide the gold?" with questions such as "How do you know?" These types of questions help pupils become aware of their line of reasoning and thought processes.

Teacher Modeling.   Teachers can provide students with their own predictions and hypotheses before and during reading, explaining their own line of reasoning and verbalizing their thoughts as they read. This modeling should be genuine; children are quick to see through predictable behavior when the teacher always knows the right answers.

Role Playing and Peer Teaching.   Children can role play as teachers in helping groups of classmates deal with words and construct meaning from text. When students have the responsibility of teaching others, they must consider how to help their peers think as they read.

Pupil-Generated Questioning.   Students can generate questions about a book or a section of book. The teacher should make sure their questions focus on higher levels of thinking, since children tend to select trivial items in an attempt to "trick" peers.

Rating Answers.   After pupils have answered questions about a story, they can rate how confident they are in the accuracy of their answers. This confidence rating can help students become more aware of what they know and do not know as a result of reading; part of metacognition is being aware of what one needs to know.

Writing Instruction.   Learning to write paragraphs and longer stories according to certain organizational patterns helps pupils gain metacognitive awareness of these patterns as they appear in print.

The purpose of these activities is to help children think and to help them monitor their thinking as they read.

(which demand a total sense of a passage), and studying their eye movements and measuring their eye-voice span while they read. Teachers can also encourage pupils to "think out loud" about their reading by participating in discussions. This is part of the teacher-pupil dialogue that characterizes good questioning.

Brown (1980) identifies reading strategies related to metacognition as "any deliberate planful control of activities that give birth to comprehension (including): 1. clarifying the purposes of reading . . . ; 2. identifying aspects of a message that are important; 3. allocating attention so that concentration can be focused on the major content area rather than trivia; 4. monitoring ongoing activities to determine whether comprehension is occurring; 5. engaging in review and self-interrogation to determine if goals are being achieved; 6. taking corrective action (when appropriate); 7. recovering from disruptions and distractions" (p. 456).

Metacognition is complex, but helping children develop metacognitive awareness and strategies is important. Research indicates that when teachers overtly instruct poor readers in these strategies, they achieve spectacular results (Marazano et al., 1987). Pupils learn to comprehend better when teachers help them learn how, why, and when to perform the problem-solving tasks that will give them a full understanding of the literature they encounter in the classroom.

Other Reader-Based Factors

Other elements "behind the reader's eye" can affect a child's comprehension of narrative text.

Motivation is an important factor. Comprehension is an active mental process; students must care enough about reading and learning to make an effort to search for the essence of what they are reading and commit it to memory. To motivate students, teachers must provide reading materials the pupils are interested in. One of the advantages of using literature extensively in the process of teaching reading is that most children are motivated to read these stories.

State of mind or emotional condition affects comprehension as well. Have you ever tried to read while waiting for an important phone call, or tried to study while preoccupied with a personal problem? Comprehension demands attention. The child who worries that the class bully will be waiting to beat him up at recess or who is concerned she has just lost her best friend will have trouble understanding the text in a reading lesson.

A host of other factors can have an impact on comprehension—physical condition, level of comfort, time of day, modality preference, personal style, and environmental factors, to name a few. Carbo, Dunn, and Dunn (1986) identified these and other elements as variables in the comprehension process for individual children. In short, much that a child brings to the printed page will affect what he or she takes away. These factors vary as much as human nature itself.

Context

Along with text-based and reader-based factors, social context can affect reading comprehension. Reading occurs in a particular context. The comprehension demands of reading for sheer enjoyment differ from those of reading in preparation for later discussion or sharing in a literature circle, or reading within the more directed context of an instructional group.

Many of the factors involved in organizing and managing a classroom program—providing time for reading, creating opportunities to talk and to write about books, making displays that document book work and author study, supplying a variety of trade books, and conducting frequent read-aloud sessions—create the context that literature-based instruction occurs in. Galda (1988) suggests the need for classroom conditions that produce "a community of readers," a secure environment in which pupils have time to read and to respond to what they read in a variety of ways.

The Role of Teacher Questioning

The types of questions a teacher asks have an enormous effect on how students develop comprehension. Questioning creates a teacher-pupil dialogue about text. The teacher's questions not only foster and guide the pupils' understanding; they also model the types of questions children need to learn to formulate on their own as they read.

Questions are useful before, during, and after reading. Prereading questions focus on setting the purposes for reading a particular text, predicting, and relating the text to prior knowledge. Questions during reading help guide comprehension and highlight the elements essential to a full understanding and appreciation of the story. Questions following reading stimulate student discussion and critical-creative thinking.

Prereading questions can set both general and specific purposes; this is important because children who read with a purpose comprehend better than those who do not (Blanton, Wood, and Moorman, 1990). Generally, prereading questions draw on a child's background, connect prior knowledge to the story, and focus children's thinking on the theme or main idea of the story. Specific questions give children something to look for while they read. For example, before children read Byrd Baylor's *Amigo*, the touching story of a boy who adopts a prairie dog because his impoverished family cannot afford the pet he so desperately wants, general questions can set the tone for reading, questions like "Have you ever had a pet?" and "What might you do if you wanted a pet but couldn't have one?" More specific questions or directions such as "As you read the first few pages, see if you can discover the boy's problem and what his mother suggests," offer children an immediate purpose as they begin to read the book.

Questions during reading focus pupils' attention on the major elements of the story. Again, with *Amigo*, questions like "What did Francisco's mother suggest? What do you think he will do? What problems do you think he might have?" give children a continuing purpose for reading and help them engage actively in understanding what they read. Questions that help pupils integrate the major elements of a story are best because such questions have been shown to improve comprehension and help create more useful schemata.

Postreading questions can stimulate discussion on critical elements ("How likely is it that a boy could train a prairie dog to become a pet, as Francisco did?") and creative thinking ("What else do you think Francisco might have done?"). These questions are most effective when they relate directly to prereading activities and questions.

Questions may be either instructional or evaluative. Questioning is, in fact, a generic instructional strategy for comprehension (Strother, 1989). Instructional questions help pupils improve comprehension by guiding their reading and by helping them develop effective reading strategies. Evaluative questions, which have traditionally dominated reading lessons, assess the amount and type of comprehension that has taken place.

6.16 Putting Ideas to Work
InQuest and ReQuest

Given the importance of questioning in promoting reading comprehension, several strategies have been proposed to help pupils improve their own questioning techniques. Two of these strategies are known as InQuest and ReQuest.

Investigative Questioning Procedures (InQuest) is a creative idea that encourages young readers to interact with text. This technique, developed by Shoop (1986), can be used in reading instructional groups. The group stops reading at a crucial point in a story; one pupil assumes the role of a major character, and others become on-the-scene investigative reporters who query the character about story events. The emphasis in InQuest is to develop children's high-level questioning.

Reciprocal Questioning (ReQuest) is a well-researched strategy suggested by Manzo (1969). In ReQuest, teachers and students read silently and then take turns asking each other questions about the material. The teacher's role is to model good questioning techniques and to provide feedback on children's questions. Although the strategy is easily adaptable to group reading instruction, Manzo suggests working initially with individuals and focusing on specific types of questions.

A variety of questions at the literal, inferential, and critical-creative levels help promote breadth and depth of reading comprehension. Literal questions are fairly easy to formulate and identify; the answers to these questions appear in the text. The distinction between inferential and critical-creative questions is not as sharp. In general, inferential questions involve connections between pieces of evidence in the text: in Harry Allard's *Miss Nelson Is Missing*, for example, "How do you know Miss Nelson and Miss Swamp are the same person?" would serve as an inferential question. Critical-creative questions require that students extend beyond the text—forming judgments, applying information, generating emotional responses, making decisions, and otherwise using their heads and hearts in responding to what they read.

The kinds of questions teachers ask can help shape the way pupils respond to what they read. Questions can generate both aesthetic and efferent responses (Rosenblatt, 1982). Questions that stimulate an *efferent* response focus on the *information* a pupil can carry away from reading. Questions that stimulate an *aesthetic* response ask how the reader *feels* in response to a story. Questions designed to set the purpose for reading or to stimulate postreading discussion influence both how students view and how they respond to the literature they read. When we ask efferent questions such as "What were the children's names?" "Why did Sarah travel west?" and "What did you learn about life on the prairie?" about *Sarah, Plain and Tall,* pupils may come away with the impression that this book is merely a vehicle for a comprehension check. When our questions focus on aesthetic responses, children see the book as a piece of literature to enjoy, as well as a story to try to understand.

6.17 Putting Ideas to Work
Rules of Thumb for Reading Comprehension

*F*rom the Center for the Study of Reading (Pearson, Roehler, Dole, and Duffy, 1990) come the following rules of thumb about how to teach reading comprehension, and what to teach:

> *We need a few well-taught, well-learned strategies*—a handful of key strategies that children learn well.
>
> *Reading develops as a process of emerging expertise,* and is not best learned as a set of isolated skills picked up along an assembly line.
>
> *Good reading strategies are as adaptable as they are intentional;* they change according to the reader's perception of the text, the task, the purpose, and the consequences of reading.
>
> *Good reading instruction is as adaptable as it is intentional;* teachers adjust objectives in light of pupils' needs.
>
> *Good reading instruction depends upon the creation of an environment that continually portrays the usefulness and value of reading.*
>
> *Good reading instruction involves opportunities for students to activate their prior knowledge.*
>
> *Good reading instruction involves careful scaffolding* that allows students to use a strategy while they gradually gain control of it.
>
> *Good reading instruction involves the development of broad conceptual understandings about reading,* and about how, when, and where to use strategies.
>
> *Both reading comprehension and comprehension instruction are highly interactive and reciprocal.* Teachers and students provide one another with demonstrations of how to build, share, and revise models of meaning, both of the texts they read and the instruction they are trying to render sensible.

Adapted from *Developing Expertise: Reading Comprehension: What Should Be Taught?* by D. Pearson, L. Roehler, M. Dole, and A Duffy. Technical Report No. 512. Used with permission of the Center for the Study of Reading, University of Illinois at Champaign, Urbana.

The pattern of questioning teachers use is very important. Klein (1988) makes a distinction between questioning *strategies, techniques,* and *activities*— three terms often used interchangeably in reading instruction. *Strategy* refers to the overall plan of the lesson; strategy questions are designed to meet the objective or goal that the teacher sets. For example, the teacher might select a predict-test-conclude strategy. Prereading questions would call upon students to predict; questions during reading would help them test their predictions; and postreading questions would encourage them to draw conclusions. *Techniques,* which are more specific than strategies, give the teacher a particular line of questioning to use. For example, if he or she had decided on the predict-test-conclude strategy, the teacher might choose the technique of asking comparison-contrast questions. *Activities* are the particular format the teacher uses to carry out the overall strategy—debate, dialogue, or discussion, for example. While predict-test-conclude is not the only strategy Klein describes, this idea is easily adaptable to literature-based instruction in the elementary grades.

6.18 Putting Ideas to Work
Putting It All Together

*T*eachers use their professional skills, knowledge, and ingenuity to design strategies that will help children get the most from the books they are reading. To do so, they need to sort through a myriad of factors that affect pupils' understanding.

The following ideas suggest how to apply the interactive view of comprehension to help children understand Miska Miles's beautiful and touching *Annie and the Old One*. This is the story of a young Navajo girl's realization, denial, and final acceptance of the impending death of the grandmother she loves so much.

Text-Based Factors

Readability.   Based on text analysis, the teacher would recognize this book as a story written for the upper primary level.

Structure.   The story has a narrative structure and focuses on the central plot element of a young girl's conflict with herself.

Content.   The setting is a Navajo community; the characters are family members—a relationship most children know well.

Reader-Based Features

Language Background.   The teacher might start by constructing a semantic map for grandmother, including expressions such as "gnarled" and "a web of wrinkles," which are used to describe the old woman in the book. (This semantic map would also activate pupils' schemata.) The teacher would also introduce the technical vocabulary words *hogan* and *mesa*.

Schemata.   To activate prior knowledge, the group might examine the illustration on the cover of the book. Prereading discussion might focus on what pupils already know about Native Americans. To provide information important to comprehending this story, the teacher could highlight the patriarchal/matriarchal role grandparents play in some societies (like the Navajo society portrayed in this story).

Cognitive Processing and Metacognition.   Using a predict-test-conclude questioning strategy, the teacher might identify the central problem ("This is a story about a young girl who finds out that her grandmother will soon

A vital objective of teacher questioning as part of the reading program is to encourage children to learn to generate their own questions as they read. Capable readers direct their own reading. They formulate hypotheses, anticipate what might lie ahead, test their predictions, refine and restructure their understanding, and actively process information as they read. Strategies that help children pose their own questions have long-term effects on comprehension and on successful decision making. Techniques such as initiating a pupil-directed dialogue in literature study groups, analyzing the question-answer relationship (see Putting Ideas to work 6.11), and providing paired practice in formulating questions all help pupils to become adept at raising questions as they read.

Teachers need to exercise caution, however, when asking children questions in literature-based reading instruction. Teachers sometimes ask so many die"), frame questions related to this problem ("How do you think the girl in the story might react? How would you react?"), and help students formulate hypotheses related to the problem ("What do you think she might do?"). This type of prereading activity provides an advanced organizer that sets a purpose for reading.

Questions and discussion during reading can help pupils reformulate or modify hypotheses. The questioning technique can focus on cause-effect relationships, identifying the multiple causes and effects of Annie's actions. Questions may focus on other elements as well—main ideas (inferring the nature of Annie's relationship with the Old One based on the details of their actions), sequencing (ordering the plans Annie designed to forestall her grandmother's death), or comparison/contrast (riding the school bus versus the old tribal lifestyle). Guide questions should also direct the children's attention to key segments of text ("When the new rug is taken from the loom, I will go to Mother Earth"). Obviously, a limited number of questions should be asked during reading so as not to disrupt reading or diminish the pupils' enjoyment of the story.

Follow-up discussion can focus on critical and creative thinking—summarizing key ideas, testing conclusions based on the hypotheses made before reading, judging the appropriateness of Annie's actions, tracing the metacognitive connections children employed to identify the relationships between causes and effects in the story, relating the story to the students' own experiences, generating additional questions that the story suggests, or relating this story to other stories the children have read.

Potential follow-up ideas for oral and written expression are legion—summarizing the story; rewriting (or retelling) it from another point of view, such as Annie's or the Old One's; orally reading key passages; extending into writing letters to older people in nursing homes; examining the connotations of the various terms we use to describe old people (from "Golden Agers" to "Old Fogies"); dramatizing parts of the story—whatever the teacher or students can imagine.

These suggestions are by no means exhaustive. What the teacher does will depend on what he or she hopes to achieve (whether stimulating critical thinking or just providing enjoyment), the nature of the class (pupils in the rural Southwest will likely understand the setting better than those in a coastal New England town), and the spontaneous opportunities that arise as pupils read. These ideas are merely a few of the possibe instructional activities that might enhance children's reading comprehension, extending their understanding beyond the lines of print on a page.

questions that children lose interest in reading. Having to answer a dozen "motivating" questions when one is anxious to get started, stopping at the end of every page to answer interminable questions that interrupt the flow of the story, and having to account for every scrap of information in the book after one has finished reading it defeats many of the purposes of literature-based instruction and quenches the enjoyment it is designed to foster.

Possibilities for comprehension-related teaching activities are virtually limitless, so judicious choice is important. Children's literature offers untold opportunities for affective rewards; that is one of the primary advantages of literature-based instruction. Prereading activities that help pupils interact with text more effectively, reading activities that guide them toward greater understanding of what they read, and postreading activities that help them become critical readers are vital to effective instruction. When the list of instructional activities dulls the enjoyment of reading, however, it is time to reexamine the program.

The teacher may be the starting point for reading comprehension, but the children are the finishing points. Research suggests that an instructional model "that begins with a fairly heavy reliance on the teacher and builds toward student independence and ownership and that includes demonstrations of how to perform the skill is superior to a model that emphasizes practice, assessment, and more practice" (Pearson, 1985b; p. 24). The same research reports, "Explicit instruction associated with guided practice, lots of opportunity to practice and apply strategies independently, as well as attention to monitoring the application of such strategies seems to help students perform better on a variety of comprehension measures" (Pearson, 1985b; p. 26).

Summary and Conclusions

Some teachers make no distinction between the terms *reading* and *reading comprehension* because without comprehension, reading does not really occur in the fullest sense. Understanding is at the heart of the reading process.

Comprehension is a complex phenomenon that takes place in the mind of the reader. To comprehend written text, decoding, psycholinguistics, and information processing must come into play. A constellation of factors that extend far beyond any specific reading act and that involve many different kinds of knowledge influence comprehension.

Comprehension requires active mental involvement on the part of the reader. Understanding forms in the reader's mind based on the information contained in the text. Reading comprehension is thus dependent on factors in the text (the level, structure, and content of the narrative), as well as factors that the reader brings to the text (language background, cognitive processing, schemata, and metacognitive awareness). To help pupils comprehend the literature they read, teachers must take these factors into account as part of the instructional process.

Comprehension is not "taught" as other aspects of reading are typically taught; that is, one cannot teach comprehension as one might teach vocabulary ("*Censorship* means the suppression of objectionable features on moral, political, or military grounds"), decoding principles ("When two vowels go walking, the first one does the talking"), or study skills ("When trying to find a word in the dictionary, consult the guide words at the top of the page"). Teachers can, however, foster, promote, stimulate, and aid reading comprehension. They do so by offering pupils direct help in using reading strategies, prior knowledge, and thinking abilities to build meaning from text. They model qualities that lead pupils to greater degrees of independence. Teachers face an ongoing job of improving children's comprehension as part of reading instruction.

Discussion Questions and Activities

1. Review the diagram of the interactive model of comprehension in Putting Ideas to Work 6.1. Research one of the text- or reader-based features in this model. What additional information can you find to extend the content of this chapter?
2. Reflect on your own reading of this chapter. What text-based features helped or hindered your understanding? How did your own schemata and metacognitive awareness affect your comprehension of what you read?

3. Select a picture book or easy-to-read trade book. Describe how you might use this book to develop children's competency in recognizing main ideas or determining cause-effect relationships. Develop questions at all levels related to the book you select.

4. Construct a story map or other graphic device for the plot of a children's trade book you are familiar with. Make a list of ways you might use this story map in a classroom.

5. Examine the comprehension section of the scope and sequence chart in a basal reading program. After noting one or two of the comprehension components listed, check the lesson plan in the teacher's edition to see how the program develops these components.

School-Based Assignments

1. Select a trade book you might use for instructional purposes in your classroom. Describe how the backgrounds of the students might influence the way you would approach comprehension.

2. Observe a reading lesson designed to improve comprehension. What does the teacher do beforehand to activate prior knowledge? What types of questions does the teacher ask during reading? What kind of follow-up questions does he or she ask? Take special note of the pupils' activities and reactions during the lesson. Make a list of things you might do differently if you were teaching this lesson.

3. Review the strategies suggested in the Putting Ideas to Work sections of this chapter. Design a lesson centered on one or two of these ideas and test the lesson with a small group of pupils.

4. Talk to a group of children about a story they read as part of a reading lesson, or about a book they read independently. Try to determine how aware they are of their strategies for building meaning as they read. What might you do to help them improve their understanding?

5. Plan and teach a reading lesson to a group of pupils, emphasizing comprehension. Have a peer or colleague observe your lesson and provide feedback.

Children's Trade Books Cited in This Chapter

Adler, David A. (1980–1988). *Cam Jansen Mysteries.* (13 titles). New York: Penguin.
Adler, David A. (1985–1988). *Fourth Floor Twins.* (9 titles). New York: Penguin.
Allard, Harry. (1979). *Bumps in the Night.* New York: Bantam.
Allard, Harry. (1977). *Miss Nelson Is Missing.* Boston: Houghton Mifflin.
Atwater, Florence and Atwater, Richard. (1938). *Mr. Popper's Penguins.* Boston: Little, Brown.
Banks, Lynne Reid. (1985). *The Indian in the Cupboard.* New York: Doubleday
Baylor, Byrd. (1963). *Amigo.* New York: Collier.
Blume, Judy. (1978). *Freckle Juice.* New York: Dell.
Bonsall, Crosby. (1973). *Mine's the Best.* New York: Harper & Row.
Brown, Marcia. (1947). *Stone Soup.* New York: Scribner.
Bunting, Eve. (1994). *Smoky Night.* San Diego: Harcourt Brace.
Burnford, Sheila. (1960). *Incredible Journey.* Boston: Little, Brown.
Byars, Betsy. (1982). *The Animal, the Vegetable, and John D. Jones.* New York: Dell.
Catling, Patrick Skene. (1986). *John Midas in the Dreamtime.* New York: Morrow.
Cleary, Beverly. (1951). *Ellen Tebbits.* New York: Dell.

Cleary, Beverly. (1965). *The Mouse and the Motorcycle*. New York: Morrow.

Emberley, Barbara. (1967). *Drummer Hoff*. Englewood Cliffs, NJ: Simon & Schuster.

Fox, Paula. (1988). *Maurice's Room*. New York: Macmillan.

Gackenbach, Dick. (1979). *Harry and the Terrible Whatzit*. Boston: Houghton Mifflin.

Gardiner, John Reynolds. (1980). *Stone Fox*. New York: Harper & Row.

George, Jean Craighead. (1988). *My Side of the Mountain*. New York: Dutton.

Gramatky, Hardie. (1939). *Little Toot*. New York: Putnam.

Hall, Donald. (1979). *The Ox-Cart Man*. New York: Penguin.

Hoban, Russell. (1970). *A Bargain for Frances*. New York: Harper & Row.

Hutchins, Pat. (1972). *Good Night, Owl!* New York: Macmillan.

Konigsburg, E. L. (1967). *From the Mixed-Up Files of Mrs. Basil E. Frankweiler*. New York: Atheneum.

Kuskin, Karla. (1982). *The Philharmonic Gets Dressed*. New York: Harper and Row.

Lobel, Arnold. (1962). *Frog and Toad Are Friends*. New York: Harper & Row.

Lobel, Arnold. (1984). *Bumps in the Night*. New York: Bantam.

Lowry, Lois. (1993). *The Giver*. Boston: Houghton Mifflin.

MacLachlan, Patricia. (1985). *Sarah, Plain and Tall*. New York: Harper & Row.

McCloskey, Robert. (1941). *Make Way for Ducklings*. New York: Viking.

McSwigan, Marie. (1986). *Snow Treasure*. New York: Scholastic.

Miles, Miska. (1971). *Annie and the Old One*. Boston: Little, Brown.

Munsch, Robert. (1986). *Love You Forever*. Willowdale, ON: Firefly Books.

Munsch, Robert. (1983). *Mortimer*. Toronto: Annick Press.

Ness, Evaline. (1966). *Sam, Bangs, and Moonshine*. New York: Henry Holt.

Nixon, Jean Lowery. (1985). *Maggie, Too*. New York: Dell.

Numeroff, Laura Jaffe. (1985). *If You Give a Mouse a Cookie*. New York: Harper & Row.

Parrish, Peggy. (1963). *Amelia Bedelia*. New York: Harper & Row.

Peet, Bill. (1982). *Big Bad Bruce*. Boston: Houghton Mifflin.

Rawls, Wilson. (1961). *Where the Red Fern Grows*. New York: Doubleday.

Robinson, Barbara. (1972). *The Best Christmas Pageant Ever*. New York: Avon.

Sendak, Maurice. (1963). *Where the Wild Things Are*. New York: Harper & Row.

Seuss, Dr. (Theodore Geisel). (1960). *Green Eggs and Ham*. New York: Random House.

Sharmat, Marjorie Weinman. (1977–1989). *Nate the Great*. (11 titles). New York: Putnam.

Sobol, Donald. (1967–1984). *Encyclopedia Brown Mysteries*. (18 titles). New York: Bantam.

Van Allsburg, Chris. (1985). *Polar Express*. Boston: Houghton Mifflin.

Voigt, Cynthia. (1982). *Dicey's Song*. New York: Fawcett.

Waber, Bernard. (1972). *Ira Sleeps Over*. Boston: Houghton Mifflin.

Wilder, Laura Ingalls. (1953). *Farmer Boy*. New York: Harper & Row.

Wilder, Laura Ingalls. (1953). *Little House in the Big Woods*. New York: Harper & Row.

Wilder, Laura Ingalls. (1953). *Little House on the Prairie*. New York: Harper & Row.

Williams, Margery. (1984). *The Velveteen Rabbit*. New York: Doubleday.

Yep, Lawrence. (1995). *Thief of Hearts*. New York: HarperCollins.

Zion, Gene. (1965). *Harry by the Sea*. New York: Harper & Row.

References

Adams, M. J. (1990). *Beginning to Read: Thinking and Learning about Print*. Cambridge, MA: M.I.T. Press.

Anderson, R., and Pearson, D. (1984). A Schema Theoretic View of Basic Processes in Reading Comprehension. In D. Pearson, ed., *Handbook of Reading Research*. New York: Longmans.

Barrett, T. T. (1974). Taxonomy of Reading Comprehension. In R. C. Smith and T. C. Barrett, eds., *Teaching Reading in the Middle Grades*. Reading, MA: Addison-Wesley.

Beach, W., and Hynds, S. (1991). Research on Response to Literature. In R. Barr, M. Kamil, P. Mosenthal, and P. D. Pearson, eds., *Handbook of Reading Research, Vol. 2*. New York: Longmans.

Blanton, W. E., Wood, K. D., and Moorman, G. B. (1990). The Role of Purpose in Reading Instruction. *The Reading Teacher* 43:486–493.

Bloom, B. S. (1956). *Taxonomy of Educational Objectives*. New York: Longmans.

Brown, A. (1980). Metacognitive Development in Reading. In R. J. Spiro, B. C. Bruce, and W. F. Brewer, eds., *Theoretical Issues in Reading Comprehension*. Hillsdale, NJ: Erlbaum.

Carbo, M., Dunn, R., and Dunn, K. (1986). *Teaching Students to Read through Their Individual Learning Styles*. Englewood Cliffs, NJ: Prentice-Hall.

Combs, M. (1996). *Developing Competent Readers and Writers in the Primary Grades*. Englewood Cliffs, NJ: Prentice-Hall.

Commeyras, M. (1993). Promoting Critical Thinking through Dialogical Thinking of Reading Lessons. *The Reading Teacher* 46:486–494.

Devine, T. G. (1986). *Teaching Reading Comprehension: From Theory to Practice*. Boston: Allyn & Bacon.

Fowler, G. L. (1982). Developing Comprehension Skills in Primary Students through the Use of Story Frames. *The Reading Teacher* 36:176–179.

Galda, L. (1988). Readers, Texts, and Contexts: A Response-Based View of Literature in the Classroom. *The New Advocate* 1:92–102.

Garcia, G. E., Pearson, P. D., and Jiminez, R. T. (1994). *The At-Risk Situation: A Synthesis of Reading Research*. Urbana-Champaign: University of Illinois Center for the Study of Reading.

Graves, M. F., Cooke, C. L., and LaBerge, M. J. (1983). Effects of Previewing Difficult Short Stories on Low-Ability Junior High School Students' Comprehension, Recall, and Attitudes. *Reading Research Quarterly* 18:262–276.

Guilford, J. P. (1985). The Structure-of-Intellect Model. In B. B. Wolman, ed., *Handbook of Intelligence*. New York: Wiley.

Harris, T. L., and Hodges, R. E., eds. (1995). *The Literacy Dictionary: The Vocabulary of Reading and Writing*. Newark, DE: International Reading Association.

Johnson, D. D., and Johnson, B. V. (1988). Making Inferences. *Massachusetts Primer* 17:4–17.

Kiefer, B. (1984). *Thinking, Language and Reading: Children's Responses to Picture Books*. Champaign, IL: ERIC Clearinghouse on Language Arts. EJ253–869.

Klein, M. L. (1988). *Teaching Reading Comprehension and Vocabulary: A Guide for Teachers*. Englewood Cliffs, NJ: Prentice-Hall.

Langer, J. A. (1981). From Theory to Practice: A Prereading Plan. *Journal of Reading* 25:2.

Manzo, A. V. (1969). The ReQuest Procedure. *Journal of Reading* 2:123–126.

Marazano, R. J., Hagerty, P. J., Valencia, S. W., and DiStefano, P. P. (1987). *Reading Diagnosis and Instruction*. Englewood Cliffs, NJ: Prentice-Hall.

Massachusetts Department of Education. (1988). *Reading and Thinking: A New Framework for Comprehension*. Boston: Massachusetts Department of Education.

Pearson, P. D. (1985a). Changing the Face of Comprehension Instruction. *The Reading Teacher* 38:724–738.

Pearson, P. D. (1985b). *The Comprehension Revolution: A Twenty-Year History of Process and Practice Related to Reading Comprehension*. Reading Education Report No. 57. Urbana-Champaign: University of Illinois Center for the Study of Reading.

Pearson, P. D., and Fielding, L. (1991). Comprehension Instruction. In R. Barr, M. L. Kamil, P. Mosenthal, and P. D. Pearson, eds., *Handbook of Reading Research, Vol. II.* New York: Longmans.

Pearson, P. D., Roehler, L. R., Dole, J. A., and Duffy, G. G. (1990). *Developing Expertise in Reading Comprehension: What Should Be Taught? How Should It Be Taught?* Champaign: University of Illinois Center for the Study of Reading.

Raphael, T. E. (1982). Question-Answering Strategies for Children. *The Reading Teacher* 36:186–190.

Raphael, T. E. (1986). Teaching Question-Answer Relationships, Revisited. *The Reading Teacher* 39:516–523.

Rosenblatt, L. M. (1978). *The Reader, the Text, the Poem.* Carbondale: University of Southern Illinois Press.

Rosenblatt, L. M. (1982). The Literary Transaction: Evocation and Response. *Theory into Practice* 21:268–277.

Rosenblatt, L. M. (1989). Writing and Reading: The Transactional Theory. In J. M. Mason, ed., *Reading and Writing Connections.* Boston: Allyn & Bacon.

Rosenshine, B. V. (1980). Skill Hierarchies in Reading Comprehension. In R. J. Spiro, B. C. Bruce, and W. F. Brewer, eds., *Theoretical Issues in Reading Comprehension.* Hillsdale, NJ: Erlbaum.

Sanders, N. M. (1966). *Classroom Questions.* New York: Harper & Row.

Schmitt, M. C. (1990). A Questionnaire to Measure Children's Awareness of Strategic Reading Processes. *The Reading Teacher* 43:454–461.

Shoop, M. (1986). InQuest: A Listening and Reading Comprehension Strategy. *The Reading Teacher* 39:670–674.

Strother, D. B. (1989). Developing Thinking Skills through Questioning. *Phi Delta Kappan* 71:324–327.

Wilson, P. T., Anderson, R. C., and Fielding, L. G. (1986). *Children's Book Reading Habits: A New Criterion for Literacy.* Reading Education Report No. 63. Champaign-Urbana: University of Illinois Center for the Study of Reading.

*R*eading and Writing across the Curriculum: Comprehending Expository Text

© Chris Boylan/Unicorn Stock Photos

Chapter 7 Outline

Features

Key Concepts in This Chapter

Nonfiction trade books are essential to literature-based reading programs. These informational books can be used hand-in-hand with textbooks to help pupils read and understand expository text.

Expository text places demands on readers that narrative text does not. Since most reading instructional materials are narrative, children need special help in learning to comprehend expository writing.

Text-based features of expository writing—the readability level of the material, structural patterns, and the nature of the material—affect how well students understand informational trade books and textbooks.

Since the purpose of expository text is to present information, reader-based features—language background, cognitive processing, schemata, and metacognition—also apply to informational trade books and textbooks in particular ways.

Introduction

R eading and writing are more than separate school subjects. They are integral parts of all areas of the curriculum. Learning is the major purpose of schooling, and reading is a major means of learning.

As adults, we learn much of what we know through reading. Scientists acquire scientific knowledge through print; in fact, the American Association for the Advancement of Science (1989) has long identified communication as a basic scientific process. Learning in social studies relies no less heavily on communication skills. The Standards of the National Council of Teachers of Mathematics (1989) also places a heavy emphasis on communication—especially reading and writing—in learning math. Reading and writing play an integral role in every part of the curriculum.

Trade Books and Textbooks

Literature-based reading involves much more than stories and poems; it includes literary nonfiction as well. Literature-based programs make extensive use of informational trade books for two purposes: to help pupils acquire information and to help develop their reading abilities. "The integration of both fiction and nonfiction helps children experience two ways of knowing literature" (Crook and Lehman, 1991; p. 35).

For a long time, textbooks have been the primary vehicles for conveying information in print to students, and reading to learn was an important part of instruction in content areas of the curriculum. Although textbooks are still used in literature-based programs, they are supplemented—and in some cases replaced—by nonfiction trade books and fictional works that help students learn content. A wealth of fine expository reading material is available for Pre-K through grade 6 and beyond. Both trade books and textbooks can help pupils develop the unique strategies required to read and comprehend expository text.

Expository Text

Most reading material that children encounter early in their school lives is narrative—it tells a story. Young children use language for another reason, however; they use it to acquire information and to make sense of their world. The presentation of information is the primary function of expository text that children encounter both in and out of the classroom.

Expository text is written to explain, describe, and inform. This type of writing conveys facts, clarifies concepts, or presents arguments. Pupils encounter expository text in science, social studies, and other content-area textbooks. They also encounter expository text in informational trade books, including biographies, concept books, and other forms of nonfiction.

Expository text requires the same comprehension processes as narrative text. Children often enjoy reading informational material as much as they do fiction. Strategies involved in comprehending narrative text apply to expository text as well. However, the qualities of expository text demand its own emphasis in the classroom (and its own chapter in this book).

Much expository text has narrative features. "Story" elements are found in scientific accounts of how the earth's crust was formed or in historical accounts of how a nation was born. Children often can respond to these narrative features with all the interest and excitement they express in reading fiction; however, not all expository text contains narrative features, and the major purpose of expository writing is still presenting information.

Pupils generally find expository text more difficult to comprehend than narrative text (Mason and Au, 1990). Expository text does not typically follow the narrative story structure children are familiar with. Expository writing tends to be more dense and is often loaded with terms and concepts unfamiliar to children. Expository text should be an integral part of literature-based reading instruction to help pupils develop techniques for comprehending this type of text. Reading is best taught in a purposeful, authentic context, and reading about school subjects is a very functional purpose for reading. Reading competency develops through, not apart from, reading informational material.

Textbooks

In most classrooms, textbooks have conventionally been the major sources of printed material in content areas of the curriculum. Textbooks cover the subject matter children are expected to learn. As such, these resources are integral to the instructional process.

Textbooks have distinct advantages as learning tools. They concentrate and organize material to assist student learning. They provide resources for acquiring skills and understanding in mathematics, science, social studies, art, and other subjects. Textbooks serve as references to expand on information a student first acquires from a picture book or novel. When well-chosen and well-used, textbooks can be valuable devices for teaching pupils how to read.

At the same time, however, an overreliance on textbooks causes problems. Because any single textbook is likely to be beyond the reading ability of some children, the book may cause some frustrating reading experiences. A survey of the best-selling science textbooks revealed a range of reading levels from first through tenth grade within the same textbook (Wood and Wood, 1988). The amount of information presented and the format it is presented in often make textbooks difficult for many pupils. Moreover, textbooks often lack coherence and assume unrealistic levels of background knowledge—"features that have been given the label 'inconsiderateness' " (McKeown, Beck, and North, 1993). This is why trade books are becoming more widely used tools to teach content areas.

Trade Books

Trade books offer some compelling advantages as supplements to textbooks. Even for children at the beginning stages of learning to read, picture books provide opportunities "for deepening literary and aesthetic responses as well as for broadening their understandings of social and cultural worlds" (Kiefer, 1988; p. 260). Trade books can capture pupils' interest more quickly and often present information in a more interesting manner. Trade books on various topics also come in a range of reading levels. They offer unique opportunities to develop critical thinking skills, and they add a breadth and depth of up-to-date information. Furthermore, while most textbooks focus on lower-level thinking skills, trade books often stimulate higher-level critical and creative thinking.

Trade books enrich the curriculum. While textbooks contain essential information, trade books can expand understanding and provide a deeper dimension of learning about a subject. Many textbooks provide a collection of facts only vaguely related to one another. Informational trade books and novels can tie these facts together and put them into perspective for students. In studying the Civil War, for example, pupils can learn from informational books like Russell Freedman's *Lincoln: A Photobiography* and Delia Ray's *Behind the Blue and Gray: The Soldier's Life in the Civil War*. Fictional works can further broaden and deepen their understanding. In *Across Five Aprils*, for example, Irene Hunt tells the story of the Civil War through the eyes of a young boy, recounting how that terrible war affected his family. Paul Fleischman presents the points of view of several characters from both North and South in *Bull Run*. These accounts not only contain historically accurate information but also provide insight on to how the war affected the lives of many individuals.

Johnson and Ebert (1992) describe how teachers can organize history units around children's trade books to give pupils a better sense of the past and an opportunity to share the joy and despair of historical figures. They provide suggestions for a variety of cooperative learning group projects, whole-class response activities, small group and individual projects, writing, critical thinking, problem solving, and a full range of activities that help pupils use trade books to experience what Johnson and Ebert call "time travel." They report that with the use of literature, motivation is higher, knowledge is wider, and history comes alive in the minds of students.

Trade books can be easily adapted to the range of reading levels typically found in an elementary classroom. While a single textbook may be well above or far below the reading level of many pupils, it is usually possible to find trade books on curriculum topics that match the reading levels of individual pupils. Easy-to-read informational trade books can help build the conceptual background that will enable less capable readers to more easily understand what they read in a text.

Using trade books to teach content is an effective way to promote, as well as to teach, reading. "The greatest benefit of using literature across the curriculum is that meaningful reading is taking place all day long in a variety of settings and with a variety of texts. . . . Literature used across the curriculum extends and enriches the life of the classroom and the attitudes, knowledge, and understandings of the students who work there" (Chatton, 1989; p. 69).

Chatton (1989) identifies other values and functions of literature across the curriculum. Literature can raise questions about various topics and, at the same time, provide answers to these questions. It helps children make connections among subjects, avoiding the fragmentation that can occur when learning isolated facts. Literature can also enhance pupils' problem-solving abilities and foster their critical thinking and decision-making skills. Smith and Johnson (1994) call literature "the lens through which content is

7.1 Putting Ideas to Work
Models for Using Literature in Content Areas

Smith and Johnson (1994) suggest three models for using literature to teach content-related curriculum topics. These models are:

1. The *Single-Discipline Literature Model*, in which the teacher selects a single trade book or set of texts that examine a theme from multiple perspectives. A number of reading and writing activities are centered around the book(s).
2. The *Interdisciplinary Literature Model*, in which the theme is extended into two or more subject areas. Reading and writing activities related to the theme are planned for science, math, social studies, and other subjects.
3. The *Integrative Literature Model*, in which the theme breaks the boundaries of subject matter and extends into critical thinking, problem solving, social action, and other areas of learning and development.

viewed" (p. 198). Duthie (1994) demonstrated how studying informational trade books at the first grade level leads children to understand and appreciate informational text as a literary genre.

Finally, literature entertains. It is fun. Books like those in Laura Ingalls Wilder's *Little House* series not only give children a sense of what it was like to live at a particular time and place in American history, but they also tell authentic stories appropriate to any time and place where human beings live. Even books written specifically to inform—such as Aliki's *Mummies Made in Egypt*—can often be enormously entertaining in their own right.

Book Clusters or Text Sets

Book clusters or text sets are collections of fiction and nonfiction trade books related to a topic students are studying in the classroom. These collections can be put together for a full range of curriculum topics. A primary grade science unit on weather might make use of a reading center featuring factual books like Franklyn M. Branley's *Sunshine Makes the Seasons*, fictional books like Marie Hall Ets's *Gilberto and the Wind*, and a book of poems such as Jack Prelutsky's *Rainy Rainy Saturday.* But "literature across the curriculum does not mean forcing connections. (It means) recognizing that some pieces of literature have a strong background of fact and provide a unique human perspective on historical, scientific, and technological subjects" (Huck, Hepler, and Hickman; 1987, p. 617).

Fact and fantasy need to be balanced in using book clusters. When studying about bears, for example, pupils can use such nonfiction trade books as *The Baby Bears* by Sonja Bullatz and Angelo Lomeo or *Bears* by Mark Rosenthal, along with books like Bill Peet's delightfully humorous fantasy

Big Bad Bruce, Paul Galdone's version of the popular fairy tale *The Three Bears,* or Robert McCloskey's popular story *Blueberries for Sal.* In mixing fact and fiction, however, it is necessary to help children separate reality and fantasy, an important critical-reading component. Separating fact from fiction is not difficult when comparing books like Louis Slobodkin's *The Three-Seated Space Ship*, a madcap story about children who blast off with their grandmother into outer space, with Suzanne Lord and Jolie Epstein's *A Day In Space*, a photographic account of a day on a NASA space shuttle. Separating what may have happened (fiction) with what really happened (fact) may require more critical consideration when reading and discussing a book like Esther Forbes's *Johnny Tremain*.

Informational trade books can be important tools from the beginning stages of learning to read. In preschool and kindergarten, a rich variety of high-quality nonfiction picture books can be used to stimulate language, generate interest in books, and meet the other needs of an emergent literacy program. Informational books can be shared at story time, can be enjoyed by pupils independently, can be the basis of early writing and art projects, and can be used to expand children's horizons by increasing their store of knowledge about the world.

Throughout the grades, trade books related directly to curriculum topics abound. In science, there are books on the life cycle of humans and animals, books explaining how the world functions, and experiment and activity books that emphasize the scientific process. In social studies, biographies of famous people, documents and journals, photographic essays, and historical fiction bring learning to life. In math there are counting books that vary in complexity from simply enumerating objects to introducing number concepts and problem solving, along with higher-level books that explain a variety of sophisticated number concepts. In areas of general interest, there are plenty of craft and how-to books, sports stories, books of trivia, and a plethora of informational trade books on topics that range from photography to aeronautics, from choosing careers to understanding human emotions. Each can help pupils acquire information while developing reading competency in the elementary grades.

How does the teacher use expository text to help pupils build reading competency and confidence? The same text- and reader-based factors involved in the interactive model of reading comprehension apply to expository text as to narrative text, but in different ways. As with narrative text, readers use features of the expository text itself to construct meaning in their own minds. Reading comprehension depends on the level of the text, the structure of the text, the content of the material, and other textual features. Meaning is also dependent on the reader's language background, cognitive processing, schemata, and metacognitive awareness. The interaction of text-based and reader-based features enables the reader to comprehend expository text.

7.2 Putting Ideas to Work
Book Clusters

*B*efore beginning units on curriculum-related topics, teachers often assemble collections of fiction and nonfiction books clustered around a unit topic. For example, the following is the beginning of a primary grade cluster on the topic of flight. It contains a combination of easy-to-read books and more challenging titles for more capable readers.

This cluster of trade books provides a focus for study and recreational reading during the unit. The school librarian can suggest additional references.

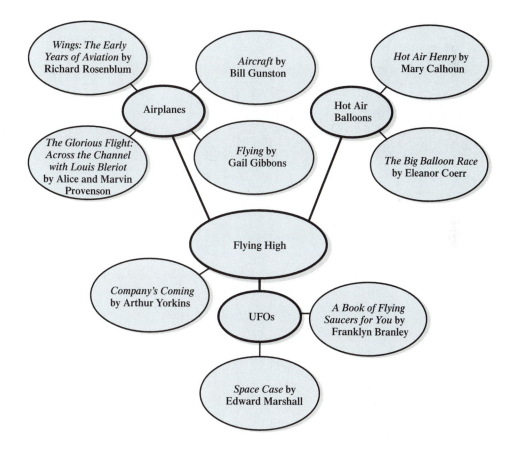

Crook and Lehman (1991) have described and demonstrated the extent to which book clusters can be built around a curriculum concept.

Continued on next page.

From P. R. Crook and B. A. Lehman (1991), "Themes for Two Voices: Children's Fiction and Nonfiction as 'Whole Literature'," *Language Arts* 68:37. Copyright © 1991 by the National Council of Teachers of English. Reprinted with permission.

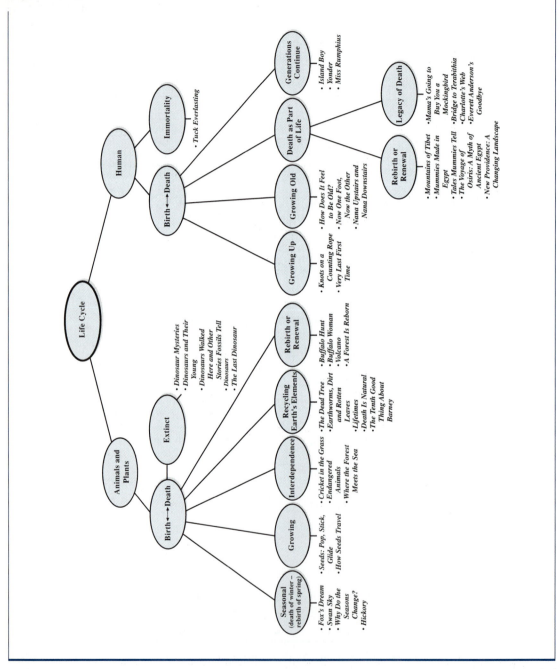

Life Cycle

Human

Immortality
- *Tuck Everlasting*

Birth ↔ Death

Generations Continue
- *Island Boy*
- *Yonder*
- *Miss Rumphius*

Death as Part of Life

Growing Up
- *Knots on a Counting Rope*
- *Very Last First Time*

Growing Old
- *How Does It Feel to Be Old?*
- *Now One Foot, Now the Other*
- *Nana Upstairs and Nana Downstairs*

Rebirth or Renewal
- *Mountains of Tibet*
- *Mummies Made in Egypt*
- *Tales Mummies Tell*
- *The Voyage of Osiris: A Myth of Ancient Egypt*
- *New Providence: A Changing Landscape*

Legacy of Death
- *Mama's Going to Buy You a Mockingbird*
- *Bridge to Terabithia*
- *Charlotte's Web*
- *Everett Anderson's Goodbye*

Animals and Plants

Extinct
- *Dinosaur Mysteries*
- *Dinosaurs and Their Young*
- *Dinosaurs Walked Here and Other Stories Fossils Tell*
- *Dinosaurs*
- *The Last Dinosaur*

Birth ↔ Death

Seasonal (death of winter – rebirth of spring)
- *Fox's Dream*
- *Swan Sky*
- *Why Do the Seasons Change?*
- *Hickory*

Growing
- *Seeds: Pop, Stick, Glide*
- *How Seeds Travel*

Interdependence
- *Cricket in the Grass*
- *Endangered Animals*
- *Where the Forest Meets the Sea*

Recycling (Earth's Elements)
- *The Dead Tree*
- *Earthworms, Dirt and Rotten Leaves*
- *Lifetimes*
- *Death Is Natural*
- *The Tenth Good Thing About Barney*

Rebirth or Renewal
- *Buffalo Hunt*
- *Buffalo Woman*
- *Volcano*
- *A Forest Is Reborn*

7.3 Putting Ideas to Work
A Checklist for Choosing Nonfiction Trade Books

Sudol and King (1996) have designed the following checklist for choosing nonfiction trade books. They designed the list for "busy classroom teachers who need a quick and efficient method for reviewing and evaluating trade books, and who, like us, have limited funds" (p. 422).

A Checklist for Evaluating Nonfiction Trade Books

Theme: _____   Price: _____

Author: _____   Call no.: _____

Title: _____

Publisher and date: _____

Series: _____   ISBN: _____

Total score: _____   Recommend: _____   For whom? _____

3 = meets all or most criteria   2 = meets some criteria   1 = meets few criteria

Check all that apply, or write NA if not applicable. Then select an overall score for each category.

_____ **Accuracy**
   information about author expertise/experience given
   information about photo credits given
   references cited throughout text or bibliography provided
   information is current and accurate

_____ **Organization and layout**

table of contents	chapter and section headings	summaries
index	glossary	charts
graphs	maps	illustrations

   predominant pattern of organization: cause and effect, comparison/contrast, problem/solution, time order, description

_____ **Cohesion of ideas**
   major ideas are logically connected throughout text
   sentence level ideas are logically connected to each other (i.e., do not require reader to make a lot of inferences)
   respects reader's probable background knowledge
   appropriate conceptual load
   avoids irrelevant details
   provides good model of expository writing

_____ **Specialized vocabulary**
   defined as it is introduced
   defined in pictures, captions, labels, or clarified visually
   defined in glossary

_____ **Reader interest**
   has aesthetic appeal
   has colorful illustrations or photos
   users appropriate format (i.e., page and print size)
   has positive role models with respect to gender and ethnicity
   activities and/or experiments within the text are motivating

Annotation:

Text-Based Features

Both expository and narrative text have certain features—level of difficulty, structural patterns, content, and design elements. These features differ in the respective classes of text, however. The readability level of expository text used for instructional purposes in the classroom tends to be on the high side of students' grade placement. Organizational patterns of expository text vary greatly from those of narrative text. Content is different, too: while narrative text may be loaded with information, it is written primarily to tell a story and not to present facts and concepts. The design and illustrations in expository text play a more essential role. Teachers need to take these text features into account in using expository text to teach reading.

Readability

An important early step in teaching reading with expository text is to determine the relationship between the level of the material and the pupil's reading ability. The easiest and most obvious way to do this is to have the child read a portion of the text before using it as a teaching vehicle. Since this is not always possible, teachers commonly use readability measures.

As was briefly described in the previous chapter, readability is an estimate of the ease with which someone can read and understand a written selection. Readability measures are used to predict how relatively easy or difficult a text is to read.

The method commonly used for estimating reading level is a readability formula, a statistically based, predictive device designed to determine level of difficulty. Typically, these formulas focus on measurable aspects of the language used in a piece of print. Most formulas rely primarily on word length (judged by the number of syllables or letters per word) and sentence length. Although some formulas also employ word lists, the number of affixes in a segment of text, or other factors in computing a readability score, most formulas still rely on word length and sentence length. Using several short samples of text, the formula is applied to produce a grade score or index indicating the expected readability or difficulty level of the material.

Readability figures are usually expressed as grade level equivalents, since grade level is the "coin of the realm" in our educational numbering system. Thus, depending on the particular formula, a trade book or a chapter in a textbook might be said to be at a "low third-grade readability level" or at a "9.8 readability level." (See Putting Ideas to Work 7.4.)

Although readability formulas have been used for some time as a convenient way to compute readability, they provide very imperfect measures of text difficulty. "For a large number of readers with varying abilities, and for large numbers of texts with varying sentence and word lengths, formulas can be used to make fairly successful predictions. But for more specific cases, they become less and less sensitive to special features of texts and readers"

7.4 Putting Ideas to Work

Fry Readability Graph

Originally developed by Edward Fry in the 1960s, the Fry Readability Graph provides a quick way to determine the estimated readability level of text. To use the graph:

1. Randomly select three sample passages of 100 words each. Do not count proper nouns, numbers, and abbreviations.
2. Count the number of sentences in each sample; round the length of the last sentence to the nearest one-tenth.
3. Count the total number of syllables in each passage.
4. Plot the average sentence length and average number of syllables on the graph.
5. The area where the dot is plotted indicates the approximate grade level.

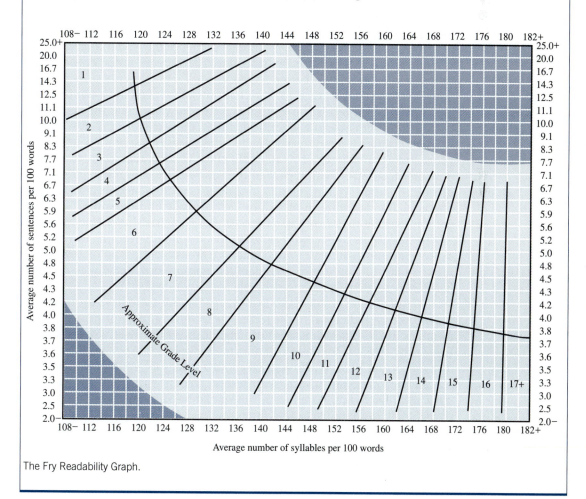

The Fry Readability Graph.

Fry, E. (1977). Fry's Readability Graph: Clarification, Validity, and Extension to Level 17. Journal of Reading, December 1977, p. 249.

(Davidson, 1985). Formulas are not sensitive to the factors that most strongly influence how well readers will comprehend what they read.

Readability formulas take language factors into account, but they consider only measurable aspects of language. Thus, words are "weighted" by number of letters or syllables. Formulas generally do not consider how familiar or common a word might be, so a five-syllable familiar word like *electricity* would compute as much more difficult than the phonetically regular but less familiar, monosyllabic word *erg*. Similarly, because it is easy to count the number of words in a sentence, sentence length or number of sentences per sample passage is used to determine readability—without regard for sentence complexity, concept density, or literary style in a sentence. Sentence form is typically more important than sentence length in making a sentence more or less easy to understand.

Readability formulas fail to account for what the text does not explicitly express, implied material that is often crucial to understanding. Nor do these formulas account for the constellation of factors that readers bring to a piece of print—their familiarity with the material, their interest or motivation, their experiences and expectations. And since the reader's contribution is so important to the comprehension of text, any measure that does not take the reader into account is bound to be flawed.

Perhaps more dangerous than the problems inherent in the formulas themselves, however, is the way in which educators view the concept of readability—with absolute, uncritical faith in the accuracy of scores. Despite repeated cautions, many teachers and administrators accept scores at face value, not as an *estimate* of relative difficulty. Overconfidence in readability measures has had a great impact on the nature of texts used in content areas of the curriculum. Writing quality in textbooks is often sacrificed on the altar of readability, resulting in oversimplified, choppy and unnatural language patterns written to conform to a formula. Research has shown that altering a text to "reduce its difficulty" according to a readability formula can actually make a text more difficult to understand (Davidson and Kantor, 1982). Trying too hard to conform to a readability measure can sometimes do more harm than good in producing readable and accurate text.

Despite their problems, however, readability formulas can help provide a general indication of the *relative difficulty* of a piece of print. Though formulas are by no means absolute, they can yield a relative high or low readability estimate for a piece of information-related text.

Vacca and Vacca (1996) suggest another means for judging readability—a readability checklist. Checklists take into account such elements as *understandability* (including vocabulary, conceptual background, and presentation of material), *usability* (including organizational aids found in the text), and *interestability* (including attractive illustrations and motivating activities). Although they are useful for examining curriculum-related reading materials, these checklists provide only general and subjective measures of how appropriate a book might be for a particular pupil.

Teachers need to be aware of the general readability level of a selection of expository text before using it to help pupils learn to read. Curriculum area textbooks, especially at the middle school level, are sometimes selected for content, with little regard for readability. In other words, teachers might adopt a seventh-grade science textbook because it does a particularly good job of presenting the concepts and information contained in the science curriculum even though it is not geared to the reading ability of the average seventh grader. Those responsible for selecting textbooks are becoming more sensitive to readability issues, but many classrooms still have textbooks that are very difficult for students to read.

At the beginning of the year, it makes sense for teachers to administer a cloze test to establish readability levels before using a basal class textbook in science or social studies. This measure takes only a short time to administer and correct, yet it can give the teacher an immediate overall indication of how appropriate the textbook is for the pupils. This type of cloze exercise does not necessarily validate the publisher's readability figure, but it does indicate the match between the writing level of the text and the reading level of a group of students.

Even if the textbook proves to be beyond the readability level of most students, it is unlikely that the teacher will be able to abandon the use of the text altogether. After administering a cloze test, however, teachers will know how heavily they can rely on the textbook as a source of independent assignments. Cloze also provides teachers with a thumbnail indication of which children are likely to have the most problems with the textbook, so that the teacher can adjust instruction for them and/or use alternative sources of print to introduce the same content. With that awareness, the teacher can also help pupils develop devices called graphic organizers (described later in this chapter) to help them comprehend and recall text content.

An awareness of readability is also important as teachers set up displays of trade books on spiders, on the Westward Movement, or on any other curriculum-related topic. Trade books at different reading levels in these displays can provide reading material that matches the varying reading levels in a typical classroom.

Text Structure

All text has structure. Structure is the organization of the ideas, events, facts, and other content presented in a passage. Text structure connects the materials in a passage in logical fashion. Recognizing the organization of text is a key to reading comprehension, and, therefore, making pupils aware of text structure is an important task when teaching them to read expository text.

The linear structure of narrative text suggests ways to make children aware of narrative text structure. Expository text is structured or organized differently. Informational trade books and content textbooks are written primarily to inform. They relate ideas in a different manner. Good readers learn to look for these relationships.

7.5 Putting Ideas to Work

Using Cloze for Readability

Cloze is a measure of readability that takes the reader into account. Cloze procedures help pupils use context to determine the pronunciation and meaning of unknown words. Cloze exercises can also help determine the readability of a book in relationship to a student's reading level.

W. Taylor (1953) proposed cloze as a means of measuring readability, and John Bormuth (1966, 1968) further developed and applied it to education. Cloze exercises allow readers to use their syntactical and semantic awareness, along with their knowledge of content, to indicate an understanding of what they read.

The directions for constructing, administering, and scoring a cloze test are:

1. Select a passage of about 250–275 words. Obviously, a shorter selection would be used for primary-grade, easy-to-read informational books.
2. Leaving the first sentence intact, delete every fifth word until you have left 50 blanks. The final sentence in the passage should be left intact. In the primary grades, the deletion of every tenth (rather than every fifth word) is often recommended.
3. After explaining the purpose and nature of the exercise, ask pupils to complete the exercise independently, filling in one word per blank. There is no time limit to the exercise.
4. In scoring, accept only the exact word that was deleted from the text. *Synonyms should not be counted* since performance criteria were established on the basis of exact word replacements. Incorrectly spelled words are acceptable (as long as they approximate the deleted word). Each correct response is multiplied by 2 to obtain a cloze score.
5. A score of 45–60 percent indicates that the material is at the pupils' instructional level; that is, the material may be challenging to the reader, but can be understood with help and guidance. A score higher than 60 percent indicates that the material is suitable for independent reading; a score of less than 45 percent indicates that the material may be too difficult.

Two points are important to keep in mind regarding cloze as a measure of readability. The first relates to children's familiarity with the whole idea of cloze. The more familiar pupils are with cloze and the more practiced they are with the procedure, the more reliable the readability measure will be. This suggests the need to practice cloze exercises before using the technique to measure readability of printed material.

The second point relates to accepting only exact replacements (not synonyms) as correct responses. This may seem rather harsh; however, accepting synonyms as correct responses can "muddy the water" in arriving at a readability measure. Moreover, the pupil is not unfairly punished, since a score of less than 50 percent still indicates an acceptable readability level for instructional materials. On the other hand, when using cloze to teach the use of context clues, synonyms should not be prohibited; in fact, using words with similar meanings should be encouraged!

Cloze is an appropriate device for judging the relationship between a reader and a piece of print. The procedure is useful because it takes the reader's background and content schemata into account. Besides, instead of relying on a predictive formula, cloze gives the teacher a measure of children's performance in attempting to understand the text they will actually read. Cloze passages can also be designed with trade books to determine how well a particular book might match a child's reading ability.

Patterns of Expository Text.   Four patterns of organization are common in expository text: enumeration, time order, comparison-contrast, and cause-effect. Other labels are sometimes used for these patterns of organization, and additional patterns (such as problem-solution or persuasive) have been identified as well. But teaching pupils these four patterns will give them a solid start in identifying text structure as an aid to comprehension.

In *enumeration*, the most common pattern of textbook organization, the text lists information about a topic. This pattern relates closely to the reading comprehension component of main ideas and details. The text enumerates main topics, then defines, explains, and expands them with related details.

Example from Textbook

Rocks look different. They are different colors. Some are shiny. Some are dull. Rocks feel different. Some are rough. Some are smooth.

From *Holt Science*. (1984). New York: Holt, Rinehart, and Winston.

Example from Trade Book

The biggest shark is the whale shark. It is longer than a bus. The whale shark has three thousand teeth. But it will never bite you. It eats only tiny shrimp and fish. The whale shark is very gentle. A diver can even hitch a ride on its back.

From Cole, Joanna. (1986). *Hungry, Hungry Sharks.* New York: Random House.

Time order relates to sequence. Facts or events are arranged according to the order in which they occur, or steps are described in the order in which they are to be followed.

Example from Textbook

Do you know how to make bread? Making one loaf of bread is similar to the way a baking factory makes many loaves. At a large factory, the flour is mixed with water and yeast. The three items are mixed together to make dough. Milk, salt, and more flour and water may be added. The dough is put in a warm room. The heat sets off an action in the yeast that makes the dough rise to a larger size. Finally the dough is formed into loaves and put into pans. At last, it is baked.

From *Our Regions*. (1983). New York: Holt, Rinehart, and Winston, p. 166.

Example from Trade Book

In the morning, the wind still blew. Waves rolled across Matinicus Rock. Abbie blew out each light. She trimmed each wick. She cleaned each lamp. She put in more oil. Then she went to breakfast. Then, at last, she went to bed.

From Roop, Peter and Connie. (1985). *Keep the Lights Burning, Abbie.* Minneapolis: Carolrhoda Books.

Comparison-contrast, as the name suggests, involves organizing text by identifying how the facts or ideas in a text are alike and different.

Example from Textbook

The environment of a valley is different from the environment of a mountain top. In a valley, summer days are warm. Squirrels chatter in the tall trees. Birds sing. On the top of a mountain, the air is cold. Even in summer, there is often snow on the ground. Strong winds blow. A mountain top has a cold climate.

From *Communities Large and Small.* (1987). Lexington, MA: D.C. Heath.

Example from Trade Book

A great variety of animals inhabit the earth. Like plants, their bodies are composed of cells. Unlike plants, however, these cells are not held together by rigid cell walls, but are soft and flexible. Again, unlike plants, animals cannot manufacture their own food. Instead, they are dependent on plants and other animals for nourishment.

From Grillone, Lisa, and Gennaro, Joseph. (1978). *Small Worlds Close Up.* New York: Crown.

Cause-effect organization builds on the premise that ideas or events come about as a result of certain causes, and it explores the relationship between the causes and the events. Sometimes, this organizational pattern takes the problem-solution form, showing the development of a problem and its solution in a cause-effect relationship.

Example from Textbook

Alcohol slows down the nervous system. The nervous system controls the whole body. Too much alcohol makes people lose control over their bodies. It makes them clumsy and unable to walk in a straight line. The alcohol can make them see things as a blur. They cannot tell how far away things are. They may crash into things when they try to walk.

From *HBJ Health.* (1987). New York: Harcourt Brace Jovanovich, p. 177.

Example from Trade Book

The earth spins around, or rotates, once in twenty-four hours. That's why we have day and night. When we are on the sun side of the earth, there is daylight. As the earth rotates, we turn away from the sun. There is sunset and the night.

From Branley, Franklyn. (1985). *Sunshine Makes the Seasons.* New York: Harper and Row.

Finding the text pattern in expository writing is not always easy. Facts are not as neatly presented, nor text as tightly organized, as in the preceding samples. Chapters are often complex, and authors may use different organizational patterns to express the relationships among their ideas. Nevertheless, an overall pattern usually emerges in good expository writing. Students' awareness of text structure improves their comprehension of expository text.

7.6 Putting Ideas to Work

How to Make Pupils Aware of Text Structure

Pupils can be made aware of expository text structure through:

Language experience activities, as the teacher constructs dictated group stories according to specific expository text patterns (Kinney, 1985) and as pupils write their own Big Books on content-related topics (Snowball, 1989).

Teacher questioning, as teachers ask questions during lessons involving expository text. For example, when a paragraph follows a comparison-contrast pattern, the teacher might ask students to identify the ideas or concepts compared, the basis on which the comparisons are made, and how the items are alike and different.

Signal words, which call attention to specific words and phrases that are a natural part of certain organizational patterns; for example: *enumeration*—most important, for example, in sum, furthermore; *time order*—first, second, next, then, finally, before, after, later; *comparison-contrast*—however, but, on the other hand, nevertheless, rather, although, likewise; *cause-effect*—because, therefore, as a result, consequently, so that, hence. The process is not as simple as merely looking for these words as an absolute indication of a particular text pattern. These signal words are function words that fit many different organizational patterns; and of course, a passage may have no explicit signal words at all. This is when pupils need to use inferential comprehension to determine the relationships among ideas in a paragraph or selection.

Diagrams or maps of expository text, which make use of different graphic organizers for different text patterns. Constructing diagrams based on text structure has a dual function. First, graphic organizers help children recognize text structure as an aid in understanding what they read; diagrams provide a representation of the way ideas are arranged in relationship to one another. At the same time, these maps require close attention to content that may be important for pupils to learn.

Writing, since awareness of text pattern is also important as children begin writing expository text. In their written answers to questions, their essays, and their reports on curriculum-related topics, pupils can apply their knowledge of expository text patterns to organize their own writing. McGee and Richgels (1985) have documented the effectiveness of using graphic organizers as children write their own expository text passages.

Content

Content is a text-based feature of paramount importance in comprehending expository text. Informational trade books and textbooks are used to teach reading in content areas of the curriculum: social studies, science, mathematics, and the arts. Helping pupils learn to understand this material is at the heart of the reading instructional process.

The abilities needed to read content from various areas of the curriculum are essentially the same as those needed to read any other material, which is why expository text can be used for reading instruction. However, comprehension in different subject areas often demands that the reader adapt his or her approach to the content.

7.7 Putting Ideas to Work
Trade Books for Social Studies

Social studies is a broad field, and trade books are available on virtually any aspect of the subject. For example, a full range of trade books can be found on:

American history—from picture books like Tomie de Paola's *An Early American Christmas* and Donald Hall's *The Ox-Cart Man*, through the range of Jean Fritz's popular children's books (such as *Where do You Think You're Going, Christopher Columbus?)*, to books for the upper grades such as Elizabeth George Speare's *The Witch of Blackbird Pond* and Esther Forbes's classic *Johnny Tremain*.

World history—from picture books such as Aliki's brilliantly illustrated *A Medieval Feast* to Marguerite de Angeli's *The Door in the Wall*.

Geography—books that inject a human dimension into learning about landforms, from picture books like William Kurelek's *A Prairie Boy's Winter* to Jean Fritz's *Around the World in a Hundred Years: From Henry the Navigator to Magellan* to Jean Craighead George's detailed description of the Arctic tundra in *Julie of the Wolves*.

World culture—from books such as Jean Rogers's account of an Eskimo child in *The Runaway Mittens* to John Steptoe's retelling of the African tale *Mufaro's Beautiful Daughters* to *Home Is Where Your Family Is*, a story by Katie Kavanaugh about a girl who moves from Poland to the United States.

These titles represent only a tiny fraction of trade books on topics related to various areas of social studies. The list of available books is almost endless, with quality books published every year. Trade book titles to use in teaching social studies can be found in Laughlin and Kardaleff's *Literature-Based Social Studies: Children's Books and Activities to Enrich the K–5 Curriculum* (1991). The April/May edition of the journal *Social Education* contains an annotated bibliography of notable children's trade books in social studies published in the previous year.

Social studies text is generally closer in nature and structure to the narrative style pupils are familiar with. However, social studies textbooks are designed primarily as sources of information, and they often condense important facts and ideas that are difficult for many students. Words and concepts may be obscure, and children do not always see the relevance of the information. Teaching social studies content builds pupils' schemata and supports comprehension; at the same time, reading is a powerful way to help pupils acquire information and develop understanding in social studies.

Trade books show pupils relationships among facts and ideas, and they provide human insights no textbook can match. Trade books focus on the human side of social studies. On the topic of Japan, for example, textbooks typically present essential facts about physical and cultural features related to population, land forms, cities, imports, exports, and the like. But teachers can enhance the study of Japan with books such as Eleanor Coerr's *Sadako and the Thousand Paper Cranes*, the moving story of a terminally ill child who practices the Japanese art of origami; Ina Freeman's *How My*

7.8 Putting Ideas to Work

I-Charts for Critical Thinking

*H*offman (1992) suggests that teachers use Inquiry Charts (I-Charts) to nurture critical thinking strategies in the classroom. The I-Chart procedure involves the following three phases:

1. *Planning,* which includes identifying a topic (the voyage of Columbus, for example, or the Civil War), formulating questions related to this topic, constructing the chart with questions along the top and sources of information down the left-hand side, and gathering informational materials (trade books, magazine articles, textbooks, encyclopedias, and the like).
2. *Interacting,* which includes assessing and recording students' prior knowledge on the topic, adding interesting facts and new questions to the questions pupils have already formulated, and recording on the chart information gleaned from various sources. The I-Chart needs to be large enough that children can fit their responses in the cells.
3. *Integrating and evaluating,* which involves writing summary statements for each question, comparing these summary statements to prior knowledge statements, researching questions that remain unanswered, and reporting the results of this research to the class. The I-Chart provides a practical framework for promoting children's critical thinking about what they read in the classroom.

Parents Learned to Eat, a personal account of the courtship of the author's American father and Japanese mother; Taro Yashima's sensitive picture storybook, *Crow Boy,* a hauntingly illustrated story about a lonely boy in a Japanese country school; and Pearl Buck's *The Big Wave,* a traditional tale about peasant life in Japanese villages. Each of these books allows children to gain a glimpse of different aspects of Japanese art, values, and way of life. Trade books enrich understanding by presenting the soul of a culture, not just facts about a country.

Social studies content demands critical reading, especially the separation of fact and opinion, recognition of an author's bias, and the identification of propaganda techniques. Children can expand their horizons by comparing what is in their textbooks with what they read in trade books. Comparisons of trade books such as Jean Fritz's factual *What's the Big Idea, Ben Franklin?* with Robert Lawson's more fanciful *Ben and Me* can be both interesting and enjoyable. Determining Mildred Taylor's point of view in *Roll of Thunder, Hear My Cry;* discussing Irene Hunt's impression of the Civil War in *Across Five Aprils;* comparing Jane Yolen's story of Christopher Columbus told through the eyes of a native child in *Encounter* with Jean Fritz's more conventional version in *Where Do You Think You're Going, Christopher Columbus?*—all can help pupils generate insights and engage in critical thinking. These skills will serve them well for a lifetime in reading about social studies.

Science text is loaded with information. The number of new and difficult concepts presented and the complexity of the interrelationships between them can present problems for many children. Technical vocabulary can be a formidable obstacle to understanding, as well. Newport (1990) noted that pupils meet more technical and specialized vocabulary in science textbooks than they meet in a beginning foreign language text. Adjusting instruction in light of these issues can aid comprehension.

As in any content area, reading in science promotes both literacy and scientific learning. "Merging literacy and science processes through literacy-based instruction allows students to broaden their application of the processes in both areas" (Casteel and Isom, 1994; p. 544), producing learners more knowledgeable in science and more proficient in reading. Interesting parallels appear between science processes (questioning, hypothesizing, gathering and organizing data, drawing conclusions, analyzing and reporting) and literacy processes (setting purposes, predicting, organizing ideas, constructing and composing, evaluating, and communicating).

The very nature of scientific text requires a teacher to adjust his or her approach. Some material demands slow and careful reading, as when pupils read the steps to follow in an experiment in their science textbooks or in science-related trade books such as Simon Seymour's interesting *The Paper Airplane Book*. Other science material can involve more rapid reading, as when students read background information in a trade book about a curriculum topic, such as *Ducks Don't Get Wet* by Augusta Goldin or *Salamanders* by Emery and Durga Bernhard. Pupils need to recognize differences in science reading materials, too, as when they read Eric Carle's colorfully illustrated account of *The Tiny Seed* versus the more detailed and factual account presented by Claire Merrill in *A Seed Is a Promise*.

Fictional trade books have sometimes been used to extend awareness in science. For example, William Steig's *Doctor DeSoto*, the story of a mouse-dentist, has been used to encourage children's interest in dental hygiene. In making these leaps from fact to fiction, teachers need to be aware of anthropomorphism, the technique of ascribing human characteristics to nonhuman creatures. Even in the very early grades, pupils can learn to separate fact and fiction by comparing books such as Steven Kroll's *The Biggest Pumpkin Ever*, the story of two bands of mice who take care of a pumpkin (one by day and one by night) with Douglas Florian's simple, predictable book *Vegetable Garden* or with Dorothy Hinshaw Patent's *Where Food Comes From*, which give children a clear, matter-of-fact look at where we get our food. Pupils need to learn that even though anthropomorphism is an effective literary technique, it is hardly scientific.

An interesting way to integrate science and reading is to use some of Jerry Pallotta's sophisticated alphabet books, which provide a wealth of scientific information.

Poetry provides another means of using literature to help pupils develop insights into science. Poetry and science have more in common than first meets the eye. Science aims to explain the world around us. A poem

7.9 Putting Ideas to Work
Trade Books for Science

As in the case of social studies, there is no shortage of trade books on topics that are part of the science curriculum in the elementary grades. Trade books in science include those that contain straight informational material and those that are fictional but have a strong basis in fact and contain scientifically accurate material.

Informational books that have proved popular and useful in the elementary classroom include such titles as David Macaulay's fascinating (to adults as well as children) *The Way Things Work;* Joanna Cole's *Cars and How They Go;* books from Franklyn M. Branley's Let's-Read-and-Find-Out Series, such as *The Sky Is Full of Stars,* and *Sunshine Makes the Seasons;* books about nature like Dorothy Hinshaw Patent's *The American Alligator;* and Simon Seymour's books that take pupils on scientific expeditions above the earth (*Galaxies*), across the earth (*Deserts*), under the earth (*Earthquakes*), and many points in between.

Information-based books of fiction include titles such as *Fireflies!,* Julie Brinckloe's first-person account of a boy's chase after these fascinating insects; *If You Are a Hunter of Fossils,* Byrd Baylor's almost lyrical account of searching for fossils; *Old Yeller,* Fred Gipson's moving story of a boy and his dog that also helps children learn about wildlife in the southwest and the transmission of contagious diseases in the ecosystem.

A number of resource books relate literature to science. *Keepers of the Earth* by Michael J. Caduto and Joseph Bruchac provides a marvelous integration of literature and interesting science experiments. A valuable reference guide to the full range of science topics in children's literature is *Science and Technology in Fact and Fiction: A Guide to Children's Books* by DayAnn M. Kennedy, Stella S. Spangler, and Mary Ann Vanderwerf (1990). Also, resource books such as *Science through Children's Literature: An Integrated Approach* by Carol M. and John W. Butzow (1989) provide suggestions on how to use children's literature as part of science.

As with social studies, the list of available informational trade books in science is extensive. The March issue of the journal *Science and Children* lists outstanding children's trade books in science published during the previous year.

also attempts to interpret the world, using metaphorical images to describe natural phenomena. Although science is more factual and objective and poetry more lyrical and imaginative, poetry can produce insights into science, and vice versa. Poems can help children understand scientific concepts and writing poetry can help them demonstrate their understanding.

Mathematics presents unique problems for many students. The writing in math textbooks is generally more difficult to read than text in other content areas (Harris and Sipay, 1985). By its nature, mathematics requires slow and careful reading of short segments of text, since this text is concise and intense. Reading in math involves dealing with two different symbol systems—word symbols and number symbols—and comprehension involves the ability to move fluidly from one set of symbols to the other.

Trade books provide a supplemental means of introducing and exploring mathematical concepts. "In children's literature, mathematics is viewed as

7.10 Putting Ideas to Work
Integrating Literature and Science

Robb (1989) describes how literature and science can be effectively integrated in the elementary grades.

While reading Jean Craighead George's *Julie of the Wolves*, Robb's sixth grade class discovered that Julie's experiences with wolves did not match their own stereotyped views of "the big bad wolf." The children read everything they could get their hands on about wolves, and their discussion of the topic dominated even their lunchtime conversations.

As a result, Robb planned a unit that would combine literature with a naturalist's view of the world. Using more of George's novels and other sources, the pupils read, wrote response journals, recorded information, discussed what they had learned, and extended their reading beyond what Robb had originally assigned. Groups studied and shared poems about nature, researched and wrote reports on a range of related topics, and bound their writing into a class journal. They wrote letters to the Environmental Protection Agency and discussed how they could effect change.

Robb discovered that the issues raised during her literature/science unit "can touch the inner spirits of children and draw them to reading, discussion, research, writing, and positive action" (p. 810).

a process, not merely an event; it is part of a larger experience and can only be understood in its total context" (Whitin, Mills, and O'Keefe, 1990; p. 69).

Reading mathematical word problems can be especially difficult. Students typically have more problems reading and understanding what to do in these problems than in performing simple mathematical operations. Various methods of attack or solution strategies for word problems have been suggested by Polya (1945), Earp (1970), and Forgan and Mangrum (1989). These techniques differ from one another in detail, but they usually involve five steps:

1. Read first to visualize the problem and get a general idea of what needs to be done.
2. Reread more slowly, noting specific information that is provided and separating extraneous material.
3. Reread a third time to determine what operations need to be done.
4. Do the mathematical computation needed to solve the problem.
5. Reread a final time to check the reasonableness of the solution.

The relationship between mathematics and literacy extends beyond reading. Kleiman and Kleiman (1992) have demonstrated how pupils can write creative word problems in mathematics based on literature they have enjoyed. Children's literature and other curriculum content areas overlap in the elementary grades.

7.11 Putting Ideas to Work
Trade Books for Mathematics

*D*ifferent types of trade books can help children develop important mathematical concepts.

Counting books, such as Mitsumasa Anno's well-known *Anno's Counting Book* and Tana Hoban's alphabet-and-number book *26 Letters and 99 Cents* are among the hundreds of counting books available. Some, such as Peter Sis's brilliantly colorful *Going Up*, present ordinal numbers.

Concept books, such as David M. Schwartz's two works *If You Made A Million* and *How Much Is a Million?*, help pupils grasp mathematical concepts with text and illustration.

Storybooks sometimes illustrate mathematical concepts and operations in a narrative context, as do Pat Hutchins's humorous *The Doorbell Rang*, which is based on the idea of sharing cookies (division); Judith Viorst's delightful *Alexander, Who Used to Be Rich Last Sunday*, in which a boy sees his money disappear (subtraction); and David Birch's *The King's Chessboard*, in which a wise man wants a grain of rice to be doubled each day for as many days as there are squares on a chessboard (multiplication and geometric progression).

Art deals primarily with nonprint media, yet this curriculum area certainly involves visual processing. Even very young children use terms such as *color, line,* and *shape* in directed discussion about the illustrations in picture books. Expository text related to art often requires students to follow directions and engage in critical reading. Trade books in art—such as John J. Reiss's simple *Shapes*, James F. Seidman and Grace Mintoyne's *Shopping Cart Art*, or Bija LeTord's *A Blue Butterfly: A Story of Claude Monet*—can provide enrichment and background for expanding interest in this area. Art can also be used to introduce such books as Wendy Kesselman's warm and touching *Emma*, the story of an elderly woman living in a city apartment who overcomes her loneliness when she begins painting.

Music involves a special type of reading in its own right, as students learn to interpret the special symbol system of musical notation. To process text in this curriculum area, students must master technical and specialized vocabulary and understand appropriate critical concepts. Music also offers opportunities for background and interest reading with such trade books as Karen Ackerman's Caldecott Award-winning *Song and Dance Man*, a brilliantly illustrated account of an old vaudeville performer; *The Philharmonic Gets Dressed*, Karla Kuskin's amusing account of musicians getting dressed for a performance, or Vy Higginsen's *Mama, I Want to Sing* with background on the origins of gospel music. Trade books with musical themes can help pupils explore the world of music while providing another avenue for reading. Children's books that are

7.12 Putting Ideas to Work

Eleven Questions on Math-Related Trade Books

Schiro (1996) has developed a comprehensive set of criteria for evaluating children's trade books that contain mathematical ideas. The following eleven questions have been adapted from Schiro's criteria:

1. Correctness: Is the math in the book correct and accurate?
2. Effectiveness: Is the math presented effectively?
3. Worthiness: Is the math worthy of being learned?
4. Visibility: Is the math visible to the reader?
5. Attitude: Does the book present an appropriate view of math?
6. Appropriateness: Is the math intellectually and developmentally appropriate for its audience?
7. Involvement: Does the book involve the reader in math?
8. Understandability: Does the book provide the reader with the information needed to do the math?
9. Unity: Do the story and the math complement each other?
10. Transferability: Is the math presented in a way that will help the reader apply, transfer, and generalize it?
11. Usefulness: How much time, effort, and money are needed to help a child benefit from the math presented in the book?

set to music—Maurice Sendak's *Chicken Soup with Rice*, for example, or John Langstaff's *Frog Went a-Courtin'*—can provide a delightfully integrated, musical classroom experience.

Drama and dance can be integrated with literature as children pantomime or dramatize the actions while the teacher reads a story like *Shadow*, the African folk tale translated and brilliantly illustrated by Marcia Brown, or they can learn through books like *Anna Pavlova: Genius of Dance* by Ellen Levine. Sebesta (1987) provides a wealth of practical suggestions for enriching the humanities and reading curricula through interviews, dance, art, writing, drama, and a range of other activities based on children's trade books.

Physical education typically does not involve much expository text processing, but a variety of how-to books are available on virtually any sport pupils are interested in. Children are also often drawn to the biographies of famous athletes—the relatively easy *Wonder Women of Sports* by Betty Millsaps Jones, for example, or biographies written at a higher readability level such as *Babe Didrickson, Athlete of the Century* by R. R. Knudson. They can also learn from books like David Kristy's *Couberton's Olympics: How the Games Began*. Moreover, physical education teachers can have a powerful influence in recommending trade books, particularly for reluctant readers.

There is no part of the school curriculum in which reading does not play a part. Although comprehension in each area depends on a child's overall reading competency and his or her ability to reconstruct meaning, children

have to make adjustments from carefully reading the terse text of a mathematical word problem to reading a descriptive account in a book of historical fiction for enrichment and enjoyment. Text in each of these areas, however, can be used to teach reading across the curriculum. Learning to read and reading to learn are part of the same process.

Thematic units cross traditional curriculum boundaries and offer students an opportunity to study literature and content in an interdisciplinary context, a trend that is becoming more and more popular even in high schools. Thematic units center around a particular theme or central topic: for example, space exploration, pets, rain forests, or the lives of the Plains Indians. While language arts remains the focal point, these units reach into math, science, social studies, and other curriculum areas.

Salinger (1996) describes thematic units in this way: "The idea of integrating the curricular areas rather than thinking of them as distinct separate subjects is based on the constructivist view of learning. . . . Knowledge and skills in the real world are rarely fragmented. People use language arts skills, math skills, and knowledge from other content areas in integrated ways as they confront real-life problems" (p. 36). Lauritzen and Jaeger (1994) describe the integrated model as that which "coalesces disciplines and marshals them as ways of thinking for solving authentic human dilemmas" (p. 564).

Raphael and Hiebert (1996) summarize the advantages of an integrated curriculum. An interdisciplinary approach can be less intimidating to students, since learning can be made more explicit. It is more relevant to life outside the classroom, more efficient in developing multiple skills and areas of knowledge at once, and potentially more motivating for students.

Topics or ideas for thematic units can come from students, the teacher, or from the district's curriculum guides. Themes need to be coherent and allow students to make connections through literature. The teacher can gather book clusters of narrative and informational trade books related to the theme. Often, computer programs and videotapes are also included.

As pupils encounter the literature in the unit, they engage in a variety of large- and small-group activities related to math, science, social studies, art, and other curriculum areas. Students gather information through independent research and cooperative learning activities. In literature circles, they read and discuss books related to the theme. Writer's workshops focus on research reports and stories on thematic topics. Read-aloud selections focus on the theme as well.

An integral part of a thematic unit is helping children see the interconnections among seemingly unrelated facts and ideas. Teachers can make a web to illustrate these relationships. "The inclination to 'discover connections' is at the heart of all thematically organized instruction" (Lipson et al., 1993; p. 253).

As the unit progresses, the teacher monitors student progress, not only in reading and writing, but in content knowledge as well. Observations, conferences, and work samples indicate the children's progress. The unit concludes with a culminating activity. Pupils plan a class display, a public presentation, or some other activity that ties together the concepts from the unit and demonstrates their learning.

Integrated units provide opportunities to promote genuinely meaningful teaching and learning, while at the same time keeping literature at the core of the curriculum.

Other Text-Based Features

In narrative text, design and illustration are text-based features that can enhance understanding. In expository text, these features are even more important for helping pupils comprehend. Headings and subheadings highlight important information and provide "road signs" for pupils as they read. Illustrative material such as maps, charts, graphs, and diagrams are essential tools for presenting information to reinforce or extend the content of the text. Students need to learn how to understand the information in these devices in order to expand their knowledge and extend their reading ability.

Design.   All textbooks and some informational trade books contain:

> *a table of contents*, a chronological summary of content, presented at the beginning of the book;
>
> *an index*, a systematic topical guide to content, presented at the end of the book; and
>
> *a glossary*, a mini-dictionary of the pronunciations and definitions of technical and potentially difficult words used in the text.

7.13 Putting Ideas to Work
Thematic Unit: Quilts

Laurie Zacarese, a third grade teacher, and Millie Gort, a bilingual teacher, both work at the South Lawrence Elementary School in Lawrence, Massachusetts. Zacarese and Gort collaborated on a thematic unit related to the topic of quilts. After finishing a thematic unit on Native Americans, they moved in a historical progression to a study of the pioneers. They raided the library for a collection of books on quilts, including:

> *The Quilt Block History of Pioneer Days* by Mary Cobb
> *Luka's Quilt* by Georgia Guback
> *Sweet Clara and the Freedom Quilt* by Deborah Hopkins
> *The Boy and the Quilt* by Shirley Kurtz
> *Eight Hands Round: A Patchwork Alphabet* by Ann Whitford Paul
> *The Josephina Story Quilt* by Eleanor Coerr
> *The Keeping Quilt* by Patricia Polacco
> *The Quilt Story* by Tony Johnson
> *The Quilt* by Ann Jonas
> *Sam Johnson and the Blue Ribbon Quilt* by Lisa Campbell Ernst
> *The Patchwork Quilt* by Valerie Flournoy
> *The Mountains Quilt* by Nancy Willard

When both English and Spanish editions of the books were available, the teachers used them. Resources also included computer programs: *Tesselmania,* which children used to learn the geometry of making quilts, and *The Oregon Trail,* which helped children relive the experiences of the early pioneers.

The unit began with a videotape on pioneer life; children compared their lives in an urban environment with those of the pioneers. The discussion turned to the need for self-reliance and moved to the necessity of producing goods that the early settlers could not buy, including quilts.

As books were read aloud and/or shared in instructional settings, they became the focus of learning activities in language arts and content areas. For example, *Sweet Clara and the Freedom Quilt,* a story about a quilt that showed slaves the route to freedom, led to a lively discussion of slavery and how the Underground Railroad served as an escape route to freedom prior to and during the Civil War. *The Keeping Quilt,* the story of a quilt created by four successive generations of an immigrant family, took this culturally and linguistically diverse group of children into a discussion of their own family backgrounds and values.

Language arts activities focused both on reading/writing skills and strategies and on content. After reading *The Quilt Story,* pupils made Venn diagrams comparing the two families in the story. *The Patchwork Quilt* introduced sequencing (with the arrangement of sentence strips from the story), story frames (focusing on comprehension), and journal entries about special memories that children had of their own families (writing). For *The Josephina Story Quilt,* activities included writing about places that children would like to travel to, including reasons for their choices, a "feelings chart" in which pupils talked about Faith's emotions in the story (vocabulary), and predictions on what would follow in successive chapters.

Continued on next page.

Math focused primarily on geometry, with the study of shapes and size and measurement. Children learned about geometric figures—triangles, squares, and rectangles—as they studied and created patchwork designs. They learned how to compute the area of a rectangle. They also sorted, classified, and measured the pieces of paper and cloth they used. Folding provided a mini-lesson on fractions.

Social studies extended into the study of pioneer life. Using *The Josephina Story Quilt* and the computer program *The Oregon Trail*, children did a K–W–L exercise (see Putting Ideas to Work 7.18, p. 289) with what they knew about traveling in a covered wagon, what they wanted to know, and what they had learned as a result of their reading. They made a comparison chart (with a time line) on modes of transportation, past and present. They also developed map skills by tracing famous trails (the Wilderness Road, the Cumberland Gap, and so on) that early pioneers followed moving west.

In science, the children had a chance to experience pioneer life through a lab that involved dying pieces of fabric. Students boiled fruits and vegetables (spinach, cranberries, tea, and so forth) and placed pieces of cloth inside different vials of dye. Children learned about evaporation as they charted how long it took for the cloths to dry, and then the patches were put together to make a naturally dyed quilt.

Art involved the creation of a quilt display with pieces of cloth, colorful oaktag, and wallpaper pieces patched together. Music included songs from pioneer times and a discussion of the place music had in the lives of the early settlers in the West.

The culminating activity was a display of the quilts the children had made, and a pioneer day parents and other classes were invited to. The children learned about differences in lifestyles (then and now), the expansion and development of our nation, family traditions, and the development of the American culture.

As these two gifted teachers shared their unit and other units they developed, they made an interesting observation: working together involved their own cooperative learning as professionals. They had twice as much to offer their students because their efforts were combined.

Used with permission of Laurie Zacarese and Millie Gort.

Recognizing the purpose of each feature can aid students in understanding expository text. Teachers can help children learn to effectively use these features through both planned and spontaneous activities in the reading instructional program. For example, when distributing textbooks, the teacher can explain the nature and function of these features. Instead of the usual direction, "Open your books to page 48," a teacher can say, "Open your books to the chapter on transportation," thus directing students to the table of contents. In a small group reading lesson with a social studies book, asking a question such as, "Who can most quickly find the pages with information on forestry products?" will help children discover that the index is an efficient tool for quickly locating information on specific topics. As individual pupils encounter difficult technical words in the science text, they can learn to use the glossary to look up vocabulary. In short, teachers need to be aware of the many opportunities they have to weave these elements into instruction in content area reading.

Knowledge acquired from maps and globes is important to comprehending expository text in social studies and other subjects.
© James L. Shaffer

Individual chapters in textbooks and some informational trade books frequently include elements such as:

introductory statements that provide an overview of the chapter content;

introductory questions that provide a purpose for reading;

headings and subheadings that divide the chapter into logical units and indicate text organization;

guide questions that highlight important concepts in specific segments of text; and

summary statements that recap the major points presented in the chapter.

Because each of these elements can enhance children's comprehension by providing clues to text organization, pupils need to become adept in using them. As in teaching about the parts of a book, the first instructional step is to make students aware of these features. Teachers should point out these chapter elements and discuss their purposes and uses.

Graphic Materials. Expository writing often includes a variety of illustrations, maps, tables, charts, graphs, diagrams, and cartoons. Even though these devices are information-laden, students often ignore them because they do not know how to interpret them.

Pictures and illustrations, the most widely used of all graphic aids, appear in virtually all children's books. In early narrative picture books, illustrations are integrated with print to tell the story directly and are at least as important—if not more important—than text. As the amount of print increases, illustrations become more incidental. Yet pictures remain important in helping a young reader capture in his or her mind's eye the images that words convey. In expository writing, illustrations build students' background knowledge and help develop and clarify concepts. Teachers can examine and discuss them as they help pupils learn ideas presented in text.

Maps appear frequently, especially in social studies textbooks. Teachers sometimes take maps for granted, assuming children will use them as learning resources. But map reading should be taught with the same perspective as text reading: that is, students need to learn to decode map symbols, to interpret the literal meaning of maps, and to use maps to make inferences, draw conclusions, and think critically about the information presented.

Since maps represent the earth's physical features, pupils need to be aware of the distortions that occur when the spherical shape of the globe is flattened into a two-dimensional map. Computer programs are especially effective in presenting this concept.

In learning about maps and how to use them, children need to understand the nature and purpose of:

> *map projections* (Mercator versus polar versus Peter's projections) and the effects these projections have on the size and shape of the geographic features represented;
>
> *types of maps* (physical maps, political maps, population maps, product maps, climate maps, and the like) and the kind of information each type contains;
>
> *legends*, with keys to the symbols that cartographers use to represent various features; and
>
> *scales and location*, with the use of grids and keys to indicate various distances and directions.

Just as decoding sound–letter relationships and interpreting print is essential for constructing meaning from text, so decoding symbols and interpreting information is essential for comprehending maps. And just as the skilled text reader moves beyond text, skilled map readers develop critical thinking skills as they use these graphic aids.

In addition to some outstanding CD-ROM presentations, informational trade books about maps and globes can be effectively used in the classroom. For example, Jack Knowlton's *Maps and Globes* provides a historical account of map making, as well as information about the types of maps typically found in books. Harvey Weiss's *Maps: Getting from Here to There* is an instructional account of maps and their purposes.

Graphs constitute another important source of information in curriculum-related reading materials. Students receive direct instruction in making and interpreting graphs in math, but teachers should also focus on graph reading as pupils encounter these devices in expository text.

Students need to understand the nature and purpose of various types of graphs:

> *line graphs*, which are familiar to most children, and which show relationships among various types of data with a simple line;
>
> *bar graphs*, which compare items using solid vertical and horizontal bars;

7.14 Putting Ideas to Work
Graphic Information Lesson

Reinking (1986) suggests a strategy called a Graphic Information Lesson (GIL). This strategy was designed for occasional postreading use to help students interpret and use graphic information in relation to text information. The three stages of a Graphic Information Lesson are:

1. *Determining graphic information.* After reading the text, the teacher leads a discussion on the information found in graphic aids, focusing on higher-level thinking skills. With the help of teacher modeling, pupils learn to determine whether graphic information is supplemental, redundant, or complementary to text.
2. *Integrating and synthesizing.* The teacher introduces *pseudographs*, graphic displays of information related to, but not contained in, the text. Children decide how accurate the pseudographs are, based on information in the text.
3. *Reinforcing and applying.* Students engage in a variety of activities, from constructing their own pseudographs to selecting graphs that are most important to text.

pictographs, which present information through simple representative pictures or drawings; and

circle or pie graphs, in which proportionate parts of a whole are represented as a "slice" or percentage of a 360° circle.

In addition to providing interactive graphing programs that pupils can use, teachers can spontaneously instruct children in graph reading as they encounter graphs in their texts. Skillful, purposeful questions can lead pupils from literally "reading" the information to making inferences about the data to exercising the critical thinking skills of application and prediction based on the data.

Tables, charts and diagrams are other graphic devices that typically appear in curriculum-related reading material. Like graphs, charts systematically arrange information, often using pictures to show relationships among sets of facts or ideas. Tables are organized presentations of raw data in rows and columns. Diagrams are drawings that pictorially illustrate the order of concepts or steps in a process. Children can use spread sheets on computer programs such as *Clarisworks* to create charts and tables for class reports and presentations. All of these graphic devices support text and provide visual summaries of information presented in print.

Tables, charts, and diagrams condense information and require careful reading. As students encounter these graphic devices in expository text, teachers can discuss the information presented and formulate questions that will lead pupils to interpret the information accurately and with meaning.

Since graphic devices contain large amounts of information, it is imperative that teachers and children pay attention to these devices when reading expository text in the elementary classroom. Graphic devices are too important to be ignored. Because maps, charts, graphs, tables, and diagrams will become more important as learning aids in middle and high school, and because these devices will remain potential sources of information in the reading material that pupils will encounter as adults, it makes sense to develop their awareness and skill in using graphic aids in expository text early in their school lives.

Reader-Based Features

As with narrative text, what is "behind the eye" of the reader has an enormous impact on the reader's comprehension of expository text. Major reader-based features include language background, cognitive processing, schemata, and metacognitive awareness.

Language Background

Children's understanding of language has a huge impact on their ability to comprehend expository text. The same elements in language that affect understanding of narrative text—the ability to decode, knowledge of word meaning, comprehension of paragraphs, and understanding total selections— impact comprehension of expository text.

Decoding. The ability to recognize or figure out the meaning of unknown words in print is essential to all reading. Informational trade books and textbooks can be used to help students develop and apply effective decoding strategies.

Structural analysis—the ability to identify unknown words by analyzing their prefixes, suffixes, and roots—can be especially important in content materials. The structure of a word often indicates its definition: the meaning of *dioxide* (two oxygen atoms), for example, can be determined from the meaning of the prefix *di-* (two) and the root *-oxide* (oxygen). A word that illustrates structural analysis nicely, and one that children enjoy, is the longest word in the English language:

pneumonoultramicroscopicsilicovolcanocontiosis

This is "a lung disease caused by breathing extremely fine siliceous dust particles," and its meaning becomes apparent when one examines the meaning of each structural element:

> *pneumono*—having to do with the lungs
>
> *ultra*—very
>
> *micro/scopic*—tiny
>
> *silico*—containing silicon
>
> *volcano*—floating in air as dust from a volcano
>
> *conti/osis*—diseased condition

This type of exercise not only builds on students' fascination with unusual words, it also effectively demonstrates how structural analysis can be used to attack some of the seemingly formidable terminology they may encounter in text.

Word Knowledge. The strong link between vocabulary knowledge and comprehension has been well documented. Vocabulary development in content areas is doubly important. Not only does word knowledge contribute to understanding in reading, but words represent the concepts and ideas that are at the heart of content areas of the curriculum.

Apart from the general store of words pupils need for all their communications activities, two types of vocabulary are uniquely important to learning in content areas: technical words and specialized words.

Technical vocabulary consists of words unique to a particular subject. When, for example, was the last time you heard the word *iambic* used outside an English classroom, or *longitude* used other than in reference to maps? Each area of the curriculum has its own core of technical words, and mastering these words is important in comprehending expository text in that area.

Specialized words are words that have a generally common meaning but that take on specialized meaning in a particular content area. Most people pay bills; legislatures pass bills; ducks have bills. With specialized words, pupils need to adjust their understanding of the word according to its use in context.

Since specialized vocabulary takes on a special meaning depending on the content being studied, multiple-meaning word exercises are a natural part of teaching students to read expository text. Activities such as the following, which focuses on "map words," give children practice in assimilating multiple meanings:

Can you think of a word that means:

to slide or ride down a hill on a sled	(*coast*)	a strip of land next to the sea
land drained by a river	(*basin*)	a bowl for containing liquid
a strip of leather worn around the waist	(*belt*)	a region with a similar type of vegetation or climate
a large break or fracture in a rock formation	(*fault*)	a defect in a person or thing

Exercises like these stimulate pupils to focus on the specific meanings of words in relation to content. These activities can also extend children's awareness of words, leading them from specialized meanings to other meanings: a *gulf* (between two people), to *harbor* (a fugitive), a *tidal wave* (of public opinion).

As they teach vocabulary in content areas, teachers can help students build their conceptual backgrounds while reinforcing word meanings. This demonstrates the reciprocal relationship between developing reading competency and acquiring information. Vocabulary activities can

7.15 Putting Ideas to Work
Teaching Content Words

*B*uilding word meaning with expository text involves sound techniques included in any vocabulary instruction. In a language-rich classroom, vocabulary from content areas will be part of ongoing word work—part of word alerts, semantic study, and other activities that help build word meaning. As expository text is used for instructional purposes, word work will include technical and specific terms that relate to specific subject areas. Activities focusing on words might include:

Word sorts, in which pupils sort out words related to particular topics ("Separate the following into *Weather Words* and *Plant Words*: humid, erosion, algae, barometer, cell, chlorophyll, horizon, seed, stem, moisture . . .").

Analogies, with terms related to curriculum areas (biology:humans :: zoology:[animals] astronaut:space:: aquanaut:[water]).

Synonyms and antonyms, although many technical terms do not have specific synonyms. Knowledge of terms (and concepts) such as *barter* can be enhanced with a synonym search (*trade, exchange, convey, swap*) or an antonym activity (*keep, retain, hold*).

Categorizing, in which students determine relationships among technical terms:

Circle the word that best describes the other words:

(Social Studies)	dictator	king	president	ruler	czar
(Science)	dog	whale	mammal	bat	horse
(Art)	color	red	fuchsia	purple	mauve

Direct teaching is often appropriate, given the relationship between words and concepts. It is important to give students opportunities to use words in different contexts following direct teaching and dictionary work.

Graphic organizers, similar in nature and purpose to semantic maps, which show words connected to ideas and related concepts.

build children's schemata before they study a chapter in a science book for a guided reading activity, or can help them review and reinforce important concepts after they read.

Sentences. Just as understanding the sentence is essential to comprehending narrative text, it is equally important in comprehending expository text. Sentences are the key language units for conveying meaning in prose.

Most sentences in expository text are packed full of information. As part of reading instruction using expository material, teachers need to focus on sentence understanding by asking children to:

identify topic, summary, and other key sentences in paragraphs;

restate the meaning of important sentences in their own words;

explain relationships in sentence parts that express meaning;

break longer sentences apart and combine the parts in new ways;

identify technical and specialized vocabulary and write them in new sentences.

These reading and writing activities reinforce both information acquisition and sentence mastery as part of comprehending expository text.

Paragraphs.   As in narrative text, paragraphs are groups of sentences related to a central idea. In well-written expository text, the idea or main point of a paragraph is clear and focused. Helping pupils learn text structure is an integral part of instruction in paragraph comprehension. Simple graphic organizers such as the following can help children understand the structure of paragraphs in expository text:

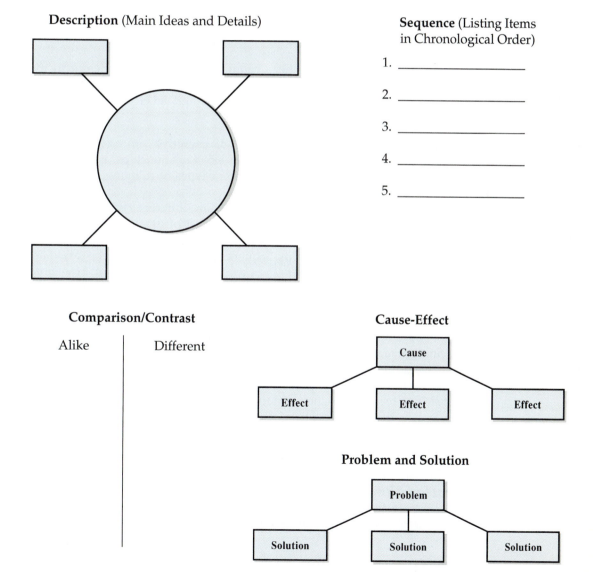

Description (Main Ideas and Details)

Sequence (Listing Items in Chronological Order)

1. _____

2. _____

3. _____

4. _____

5. _____

Comparison/Contrast

Alike | Different

Cause-Effect

Cause

Effect | Effect | Effect

Problem and Solution

Problem

Solution | Solution | Solution

Focusing on organizational patterns in this way increases pupils' comprehension and recall of what they read in paragraphs.

Selections. Understanding words, sentences, and paragraphs leads students to comprehend larger selections of expository text—chapters in content area textbooks and entire informational trade books. Sound teaching practices—setting purposes for reading, guiding reading through a variety of multilevel questions, and directing postreading discussions on the information acquired in reading—help build pupils' understanding of larger segments of expository text.

A child's language background at all levels—from word knowledge and basic decoding skills to understanding the meaning of large segments of expository text—profoundly affects reading comprehension. While building language background at these various levels, the teacher is teaching reading and content concurrently, helping students learn to read and read to learn at the same time.

Cognitive Processing

Cognitive processing is another "behind the eye" factor inherent in the comprehension process. In reading informational material, pupils apply their thinking to expository text. Both type and level of thinking affect comprehension.

Type of Thinking. This dimension of cognitive processing involves reading for main ideas and details, cause–effect relationships, and sequence, among others. Children use these different types of thinking to recognize text structure in informational material.

Different types of expository text require different types of thinking. Reading a word problem in mathematics, a set of directions for a science experiment, or instructions for an art project require careful, deliberate reading to follow a sequence of steps. Sequence is also important in historical fiction such as Alice Dalgliesh's *The Courage of Sarah Noble,* but in a more general and less deliberate way. A textbook chapter on urban and rural life suggests a specific focus on comparison and contrast. Most textbooks and informational trade books suggest a focus on more than one type of thinking. For example, a full range of thinking can apply in reading Oz Charles's fascinating, factual account *How Does Soda Get into the Bottle?*

Deciding which type of cognitive processing is most appropriate for a piece of expository text is part of the process of using informational material in teaching reading. Teachers can focus on various types of thinking in reading lessons that use expository text, teaching them in purpose-setting and schema building in prereading activities, making them part of the questions to guide the reading, and including them in postreading discussions and exercises designed to reinforce and extend content presented in text.

Level of Thinking. Literal, inferential, and critical-creative levels of thinking are as vital (if not more important) in comprehending expository text as in understanding narrative text.

7.16 Putting Ideas to Work

Herringbone Technique

*T*he Herringbone Technique is a strategy used to help pupils organize and recall information presented in large segments of expository text. The technique focuses on six essential comprehension questions: Who? What? When? Where? Why? and How? Information is arranged in this format:

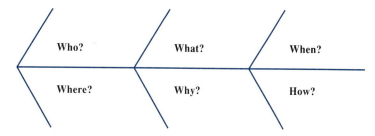

The Herringbone format can be introduced on a chart or an overhead projector. Teachers can direct groups of pupils through the process as part of guided reading instruction using textbook chapters or informational trade books. Follow-up discussions can focus on student responses and extend into sentence and paragraph writing activities.

Teachers direct pupils to exercise certain levels of thinking largely through the questions they ask. Questions that are part of guided reading lessons—before, during, and after reading—can help students reach toward higher levels of thinking. Strategies such as Question-Answer Relationships, teacher modeling, study guides (see Putting Ideas to Work 7.17), and other techniques help children develop the habit of independently questioning as they read on their own.

Schemata

Schemata—the conceptual organizational structures of a child's knowledge background—provide an important foundation for understanding the material in expository text. Reading activates existing knowledge as we integrate newly acquired information with what we already know, so lack of existing knowledge can be a formidable obstacle to reading comprehension.

Vacca and Vacca (1996) identify three schema-related problems that can interfere with understanding in reading:

schema availability, in which children lack the relevant background knowledge and information needed to comprehend a text;

schema selection, failure to bring background knowledge to bear as they read; and

schema maintenance, in which pupils are not aware or skilled enough to recognize shifts in schema during reading.

7.17 Putting Ideas to Work
Study Guides

*S*tudy guides can address both the type and level of thinking a child employs while reading. Study guides provide pupils with a "road map" that will guide them through important segments of expository text by focusing their attention on major ideas.

Preparation.   Teachers first decide which parts of an informational trade book or a chapter in a textbook they want children to concentrate on. They then decide which type and aspect of thinking they want to emphasize.

Construction.   Teachers formulate questions centered on the particular information or ideas they want to emphasize and that are directed at the type and level of thinking they want students to use.

Use.   Study guides should be used in the context of well-planned reading lessons. Prereading should include vocabulary activity and schema building. Teachers explain the purpose of the guides, which pupils can use independently or cooperatively as they read. Postreading discussion should focus on student responses to questions and directions in the guide.

Schema theory suggests the importance of assessing background knowledge before reading. Readers bring a reservoir of experiences to the printed page. If the information in the text aligns with these experiences, comprehension is enhanced. If not, comprehension is not as easy. Determining what children already know about a topic and setting purposes that help determine what they can acquire from text (that is, to determine how their schemata may be altered) are important prereading activities in content-related reading lessons.

To address students' schemata as part of reading instruction, the teacher must teach reading and content at the same time. As teachers help pupils acquire and organize the background information that leads to better reading comprehension, they simultaneously help pupils learn material that is normally part of the school curriculum.

Building a knowledge background is essential to comprehension. Knowledge is acquired in a variety of ways: through reading, through direct experience, through dramatized or vicarious experience, through audio-visual presentations, or through discussions and related verbal interactions. Background knowledge acquired through these various means will support comprehension when the student later reads about a topic.

Humans learn best through direct experience; we build schemata by dealing directly with the world around us. In studying a unit on the Florida Everglades, for example, pupils who have lived in or visited the Everglades will have a richer schema about that subject. Children who have watched a movie or visited a model of the Everglades in a science museum will also have a more concrete basis of understanding. While it is obviously not possible for teachers to provide direct or vicarious experiences for everything pupils are

7.18 Putting Ideas to Work

K–W–L

Designed by Ogle (1986, 1992), K–W–L is a structured teaching technique for helping pupils access prior knowledge as they read expository text. K–W–L involves three steps:

K—Assessing What I Know.   This step involves brainstorming and categorizing ideas related to the topic of an expository reading selection. The teacher notes students' ideas on the chalkboard or on a chart.

W—What Do I Want to Learn?   Based on what children already know, the teacher poses questions on what they might want to learn. Pupils then read the selection.

L—What I Learned.   As students finish reading, they note what they learned about a topic and list questions that still need to be addressed.

Variations and adaptations of K–W–L have been suggested; for example, K–W–H–L (the *H* being "How Will I Learn What I Want To Know") and K–W–S–L (the *S* being "What I Still Need to Learn"). No matter what adaptations one makes, the basic technique has proven to be an effective strategy for reading and understanding expository text.

expected to study, it is possible to use classroom discussions and other activities to provide some prior knowledge about a topic before children read about it. Prior knowledge will support their reading comprehension.

Building knowledge is one of the functions of trade books in the content areas. A collection of attractive books about a topic will provide students with a supply of information that will build their schemata to support their comprehension as they read.

Metacognition

Metacognition—the awareness of and control over one's mental functioning—is another "behind the eye" factor crucial to reading comprehension. Metacognition involves thinking while reading. It includes not only pupils' abilities to think about the content contained in text, but also about the processes they use to understand the ideas the author is expressing and their ability to use this knowledge to monitor their own reading.

Children's ability to monitor their own reading is an important part of metacognition. Experienced readers know when they are running into trouble understanding text, and they know what to do about it. In this respect, reading might be compared to driving. When everything is going smoothly, the process of reading (and driving) is fairly automatic for the experienced and skilled practitioner. But when problems develop, the reader (or driver) must attend more closely to the process itself. A good reader attends to problems that are blocking his or her attempts to build meaning from text and develops strategies to overcome those problems.

7.19 Putting Ideas to Work
Purpose, Classification, and Response

Mary Lou Hess (1991), a teacher in an inner-city elementary school, describes a three-step strategy she developed to help her pupils comprehend nonfiction material. The strategy involves:

Developing a purpose.   Students brainstorm to raise questions about what type of information may be in their reading material. They write their questions on paper and then read to find answers, giving a purpose for reading.

Classifying.   Children sort their questions into categories and generate their own text. With animals, for example, categories might include *habitat, food,* and *appearance.* After pupils read and take notes, they work in pairs to cut out and sort facts. These classification activities increase their nonfiction comprehension by making them aware of text structure.

Responding through talk.   Students are given opportunities to talk about the information they are collecting, since exchanging information helps them incorporate new learning into their existing mental framework. By talking about the information they have gained, students explain facts to peers, raise questions that involve rereading to verify or adjust understandings, and gain ownership of the new information.

"It became clear to me," Hess wrote, "that having a purpose, classifying, and talking worked simultaneously to increase my students' ability to comprehend nonfiction. . . . Pupils used these strategies to become more proficient, independent readers" (p. 231).

How can teachers begin to promote this metacognitive awareness as part of reading instruction? With informational reading materials, teachers can use:

> *metacognitive discussions* before reading assignments to develop an awareness of the reading task and how best to handle it;
>
> *schema-building activities* that arouse children's awareness of what they might expect to learn;
>
> *teacher modeling,* demonstrating their own reading behaviors in reading segments of expository text. Baumann, Jones, and Seifert-Kessell (1993) describe how teacher modeling can be used in think-alouds to help children acquire the ability to monitor their own thinking during reading;
>
> *careful questioning,* focused not only on content but also on process (*What does the author say were three reasons for the American Civil War? How do you know? Where did you find the answer to that question? What language does the author use to express this view? Do you think the author might give other reasons later on?*)

With a constant classroom focus on metacognitive activity while reading, pupils are apt to begin to apply these learning strategies themselves as they read. "The key to metacognition is moving from teacher-directed to student-directed reading activities, a shift from teacher-developed questions to student-developed questions, questions that students ask *themselves* during the act of reading" (Dupuis et al., 1989; p. 55).

This type of prereading and postreading discussion related to metacognitive processing is not entirely new or revolutionary. It has long been a part of directed or guided reading lessons that skilled teachers have carried out. Metacognition adds the dimension of helping children look at the act of reading, as well as the content being read, during these discussion/questioning procedures.

Motivation

The level of interest or motivation that children bring to reading can have a powerful effect on their comprehension of expository reading material. Pupils who are especially interested in a particular topic will usually extend themselves or "read beyond their level" in reading about that topic. Conversely, students with no special interest will approach reading with less enthusiasm and less concentration than they may need to understand what they read.

Interest and motivation belong to the affective domain of reading, the area that is often the most difficult to develop and to measure. As they read informational materials, children's attitudes will depend on their interest in reading itself, their interest in the subject matter, and the way the content is presented.

Although textbook writers often assume that pupils want to learn about the subject of their writing, teachers recognize this assumption is not necessarily valid. Even students who are capable and enthusiastic readers of narrative material are not always interested in reading assignments related to school subjects. At this point, it is important for teachers to inject some of the motivational spark needed to fire students' interest by making the material personal and meaningful through trade books.

Both intrinsic and extrinsic motivation are at work in a classroom. Extrinsic motivation involves rewards and punishments—fear of poor grades, for example, or the chance to use free classroom time to work on a favorite computer activity. By contrast, intrinsic motivation involves a child's internal interest and success in dealing with a particular topic. Books pupils choose to read for fun—such as a book by their favorite author or material they select for Sustained Silent Reading—have an intrinsic motivational element built in.

Motivation can be built into the instructional techniques for content area reading lessons, as suggested earlier. For example, selecting trade books at the children's reading level gives pupils a better shot at success and is likely to improve motivation. Showing students how to succeed in a textbook reading assignment is motivational. Schema-building activities that help forge a link between content and the pupils' real-world needs can spark interest. Allowing pupils to make choices from lists of topics or to generate personal choices for curriculum reports provides motivation. Finally, although it is a cliché, enthusiasm is catching; teachers who are enthusiastic about the topics under study in content areas will likely generate interest and motivation among their pupils.

Summary and Conclusions

In school as in life, reading fulfills two major functions: to entertain and to inform. Just as children are entertained through narrative materials, they are informed through the expository text they encounter throughout their early school years. Teachers should use nonfiction trade books in content and reading instruction from the emergent literacy stage throughout the school years.

Each part of the school curriculum requires reading competency. Reading is a vehicle for learning in all school subjects; at the same time, curriculum-related materials help develop reading and writing competency. Expository text fuses the learning-to-read and reading-to-learn functions of literacy.

Children's trade books are effective and appealing sources of information for reading and learning in today's classrooms. Informational trade books are available on virtually all curriculum topics. Students can use them apart from or in conjunction with textbooks.

Comprehension occurs as a result of the interaction between factors "in front of the reader's eye" (text-based factors) and factors "behind the reader's eye" (reader-based factors). Textbook readability levels often tend to be high in relation to pupils' grade placements. In addition, the content of each curriculum area involves its own unique demands in understanding text. Because maps, charts, diagrams, and other graphic aids are especially important to expository writing, these devices require a specific instructional focus.

Reader-based features include language background, cognitive processing, schemata, metacognitive awareness, and motivation. Understanding successively larger units of language is necessary for comprehension. Technical and specific vocabulary require particular attention. Teaching pupils to comprehend expository material also involves questioning that focuses on both the types and levels of thinking students are using. Because pupils often lack the schemata needed to understand curriculum topics, building background information is vital as well, and developing metacognitive awareness can help children meet the particular demands of reading expository text. Finally, both extrinsic and intrinsic factors can stimulate children's interest in reading in the content areas.

Discussion Questions and Activities

1. Using a third or fourth grade social studies or science textbook, select a topic and locate several trade books on the subject. (Or locate some of the informational trade books listed in *Science and Children* or *Social Education*.) What are some of the differences you notice between the two sources? List the advantages and disadvantages of using trade books versus a textbook as an instructional tool for reading.
2. Research the topic of readability. Using a software package, compute the readability of a piece of expository text designed for use in the elementary grades. What conclusions can you draw? (Another option: Do a readability measure on this textbook and send the author the results!)

3. Examine a sample of expository writing with an eye to text structure. Design a graphic organizer that you might use to make students aware of this structural pattern in text.
4. Prepare a reading lesson using an informational trade book. What might you do to build pupils' schemata before reading? List the questions you would use to guide reading. What postreading strategies or activities would you use?
5. As part of a group project, plan a thematic unit. Decide on a topic, locate informational and narrative trade books (along with computer programs and videotapes) related to the theme, and plan a list of activities. Don't forget to make adjustments for children with varying abilities.

School-Based Assignments

1. Interview a small group of pupils about their favorite curriculum topic. Then find a trade book related to one of those topics. Share the book with the group, noting the instructional adjustments you would need to make in order to use the book to teach reading.
2. Examine the teacher's edition of a mathematics, science, or social studies textbook your classroom uses. What suggestions does the text make for helping pupils develop word knowledge with the material in the text? What provisions does it make for using the book to teach reading?
3. Select an expository selection from a basal reader. Locate informational trade books or magazine articles on the topic of the basal selection. Describe how you might use these materials to extend the basal reading experience. Try out your ideas with a small group.
4. Using the components of the interactive model of reading comprehension as a framework for your observations, observe a supervising teacher or colleague as he or she teaches a reading lesson using an expository text selection. Note how the teacher prepares the students, and the types of guided instruction he or she provides during reading and postreading activities. Pay particular attention to the pupils. In your log or journal, make a record of your observations, including what you might have done differently.
5. Observe a teacher presenting a thematic unit in a classroom. What is the topic or major idea in the unit? What connections did the class make among all curriculum areas? How are reading and writing integrated into the unit?

Children's Trade Books Cited in This Chapter

Ackerman, Karen. (1988). *Song and Dance Man.* New York: Knopf.
Anno, Mitsumasa. (1977). *Anno's Counting Book.* New York: Putnam.
Aliki. (1979). *Mummies Made in Egypt.* New York: Crowell.
Aliki. (1983). *A Medieval Feast.* New York: HarperCollins.
Baylor, Byrd. (1980). *If You Are a Hunter of Fossils.* New York: Atheneum.
Bernhard, Emery and Durga. (1995). *Salamanders.* New York: Holiday House.
Birch, David. (1988). *The King's Chessboard.* New York: Dial.
Branley, Franklyn. (1981). *The Sky Is Full of Stars.* New York: Harper & Row.
Branley, Franklyn. (1985). *Sunshine Makes the Seasons.* New York: Harper & Row.
Brinckloe, Julie. (1985). *Fireflies!* New York: Macmillan.
Brown, Marcia. (1982). *Shadow.* New York: Macmillan.
Buck, Pearl. (1986). *The Big Wave.* New York: Harper & Row.
Bullatz, Sonja, and Lomeo, Angelo. (1983). *The Baby Bears.* New York: Golden Books.

Caduto, Michael J., and Bruchac, Joseph. (1988). *Keepers of the Earth*. Golden, CO: Fulcrum.
Carle, Eric. (1986). *The Tiny Seed*. New York: Scholastic.
Charles, Oz. (1988). *How Does Soda Get into the Bottle?* New York: Simon & Schuster.
Cobb, Mary. (1995). *The Quilt Block History of Pioneer Days*. Brookfield, CT: Millbrook.
Coerr, Eleanor. (1977). *Sadako and the Thousand Paper Cranes*. New York: Putnam.
Coerr, Eleanor. (1986). *The Josephina Story Quilt*. New York: HarperCollins.
Cole, Joanna. (1983). *Cars and How They Go*. New York: Harper & Row.
Cole, Joanna. (1986). *Hungry, Hungry Sharks*. New York: Random House.
Dalgliesh, Alice. (1954). *The Courage of Sarah Noble*. New York: Scribner.
de Angeli, Marguerite. (1949). *The Door in the Wall*. New York: Doubleday.
de Paola, Tomie. (1987). *An Early American Christmas*. New York: Holiday House.
Ernst, Lisa C. (1983). *Sam Johnson and the Blue Ribbon Quilt*. New York: Lothrup.
Ets, Marie Hall. (1963). *Gilberto and the Wind*. New York: Viking.
Fleischman, Paul. (1993). *Bull Run*. New York: HarperCollins.
Florian, Douglas. (1991). *Vegetable Garden*. Orlando: Harcourt Brace Jovanovich.
Flournoy, Valerie. (1985). *The Patchwork Quilt*. New York: Dial.
Forbes, Esther. (1945). *Johnny Tremain*. Boston: Houghton Mifflin.
Freedman, Russell. (1987). *Lincoln: A Photobiography*. New York: Clarion.
Freeman, Ina. (1984). *How My Parents Learned to Eat*. Boston: Houghton Mifflin.
Fritz, Jean. (1976). *What's the Big Idea, Ben Franklin?* New York: Coward-McCann.
Fritz, Jean. (1980). *Where Do You Think You're Going, Christopher Columbus?* New York: Putnam.
Fritz, Jean. (1994). *Around the World in a Hundred Years: From Henry the Navigator to Magellan*. New York: Putnam.
Galdone, Paul. (1977). *The Three Bears*. New York: Scholastic.
George, Jean Craighead. (1972). *Julie of the Wolves*. New York: Harper & Row.
Gipson, Fred. (1956). *Old Yeller*. New York: Harper & Row.
Goldin, Augusta. (1965). *Ducks Don't Get Wet*. New York: Crowell.
Grillone, Lisa, and Gennaro, Joseph. (1978). *Small Worlds Close Up*. New York: Crown.
Guback, Georgia. (1994). *Luka's Quilt*. New York: Greenwillow.
Hall, Donald. (1979). *The Ox-Cart Man*. New York: Penguin.
Higginsen, Vy. (1995). *Mama, I Want to Sing*. New York: Scholastic.
Hoban, Tana. (1987). *26 Letters and 99 Cents*. New York: Greenwillow.
Hopkins, Deborah. (1995). *Sweet Clara and the Freedom Quilt*. New York: Random House.
Hunt, Irene. (1964). *Across Five Aprils*. Chicago: Follett.
Hutchins, Pat. (1986). *The Doorbell Rang*. New York: Greenwillow.
Johnson, Tony. (1992). *The Quilt Story*. New York: Putnam.
Jonas, Ann. (1984). *The Quilt*. New York: Greenwillow.
Jones, Betty M. (1981). *Wonder Women of Sports*. New York: Random House.
Kavanaugh, Katie. (1994). *Home Is Where Your Family Is*. Chatham, NJ: Raintree.
Kesselman, Wendy. (1980). *Emma*. New York: Doubleday.
Knowlton, Jack. (1985). *Maps and Globes*. New York: Harper & Row.
Knudson, R. R. (1985). *Babe Didrickson: Athlete of the Century*. New York: Viking.
Kristy, David. (1995). *Coubertin's Olympics: How the Games Began*. New York: Lerner.
Kroll, Steven. (1986). *The Biggest Pumpkin Ever*. New York: Scholastic.
Kurelek, William. (1973). *A Prairie Boy's Winter*. Boston: Houghton Mifflin.
Kurtz, Shirley. (1991).*The Boy and the Quilt*. Intercourse, PA: Good Books.
Kuskin, Karla. (1982). *The Philharmonic Gets Dressed*. New York: Harper & Row.
Langstaff, John. (1955). *Frog Went a-Courtin'*. New York: Harcourt Brace.
Lawson, Robert. (1951). *Ben and Me*. Boston: Little, Brown.
LeTord, Bija. (1995). *A Blue Butterfly: A Story of Claude Monet*. New York: Doubleday.
Levine, Ellen. (1995). *Anna Pavlova: Genius of Dance*. New York: Scholastic.
Lord, Suzanne, and Epstein, Jolie. (1986). *A Day in Space*. New York: Scholastic.

Macaulay, David. (1988). *The Way Things Work*. Boston: Houghton Mifflin.

McCloskey, Robert. (1963). *Blueberries for Sal*. New York: Viking.

Merrill, Claire. (1973). *A Seed Is a Promise*. New York: Scholastic.

Patent, Dorothy Hinshaw. (1991). *Where Food Comes From*. New York: Holiday House.

Patent, Dorothy Hinshaw. (1995). *The American Alligator*. New York: Clarion.

Paul, Ann Whitford. (1991). *Eight Hands Round: A Patchwork Alphabet*. New York: HarperCollins.

Peet, Bill. (1982). *Big Bad Bruce*. Boston: Houghton Mifflin.

Polacco, Patricia. (1993). *The Keeping Quilt*. Columbus, OH: Variety.

Prelutsky, Jack. (1980). *Rainy, Rainy Saturday*. New York: Greenwillow.

Ray, Delia. (1991). *Behind the Blue and Gray: The Soldier's Life in the Civil War*. New York: Lodestar.

Reiss, John J. (1974). *Shapes*. New York: Macmillan.

Rogers, Jean. (1988). *The Runaway Mittens*. New York: Greenwillow.

Roop, Peter, and Roop, Connie. (1985). *Keep the Lights Burning, Abbie*. Minneapolis: Carolrhoda Books.

Rosenthal, Mark. (1983). *Bears*. Chicago: Children's Press.

Schwartz, David M. (1987). *How Much Is a Million?* New York: Lothrup.

Schwartz, David M. (1989). *If You Made a Million*. New York: Lothrup.

Seidman, James F., and Mintoyne, Grace. (1970). *Shopping Cart Art*. New York: Macmillan.

Sendak, Maurice. (1962). *Chicken Soup with Rice*. New York: Harper & Row.

Seymour, Simon. (1971). *The Paper Airplane Book*. New York: Penguin.

Seymour, Simon. (1988). *Galaxies*. New York: Morrow.

Seymour, Simon. (1990). *Deserts*. New York: Morrow.

Seymour, Simon. (1991). *Earthquakes*. New York: Morrow.

Sis, Peter. (1989). *Going Up*. New York: Greenwillow.

Slobodkin, Louis. (1962). *The Three-Seated Space Ship*. New York: Macmillan.

Speare, Elizabeth George. (1958). *The Witch of Blackbird Pond*. New York: Dell.

Steig, William. (1982). *Doctor DeSoto*. New York: Farrar, Straus & Giroux.

Steptoe, John. (1987). *Mufaro's Beautiful Daughters: An African Tale*. New York: Lothrup.

Taylor, Mildred. (1976). *Roll of Thunder, Hear My Cry*. New York: Dial.

Viorst, Judith. (1978). *Alexander, Who Used to Be Rich Last Sunday*. New York: Macmillan.

Weiss, Harvey. (1991). *Maps: Getting from Here to There*. Boston: Houghton Mifflin.

Willard, Nancy. (1987). *The Mountains Quilt*. San Antonio, TX: Harcourt Brace.

Yashima, Taro. (1955). *Crow Boy*. New York: Viking.

Yolen, Jane. (1992). *Encounter*. San Antonio, TX: Harcourt Brace.

Children's Books Cited in Putting Ideas to Work 7.2

Aliki. (1979). *Mummies Made in Egypt*. New York: Harper & Row.

Andrews, Jan. (1986) *.Very Last First Time*. New York: Macmillan.

Babbitt, Natalie. (1976). *Tuck Everlasting*. New York: Farrar, Straus & Giroux.

Baker, Jeannie. (1988). *Where the Forest Meets the Sea*. New York: Greenwillow.

Bender, Lionel. (1988). *Volcano!* New York: Franklin Watts.

Branley, Franklyn. (1973). *A Book of Flying Saucers for You*. New York: Crowell.

Brown, Palmer. (1978). *Hickory*. New York: Harper & Row.

Calhoun, Mary. (1981). *Hot Air Henry*. New York: Morrow.

Clifton, Lucille. (1988). *Everett Anderson's Goodbye*. New York: Henry Holt.

Codrington, Kenneth deBurgh. (1959). *Cricket in the Grass*. London: Faber and Faber.

Coerr, Eleanor. (1981). *The Big Balloon Race*. New York: Harper & Row.

Cooney, Barbara. (1985). *Miss Rumphius*. New York: Viking.

Cooney, Barbara. (1988). *Island Boy*. New York: Viking Kestrel.

de Paola, Tomie. (1978). *Nana Upstairs and Nana Downstairs.* New York: Puffin.

de Paola, Tomie. (1981). *Now One Foot, Now the Other.* New York: Putnam.

Elting, Mary, and Goodman, Ann. (1980). *Dinosaur Mysteries.* New York: Putnam.

Farber, Norma. (1985). *How Does It Feel to be Old ?* Illustrated by Trina S. Hyman. New York: Dutton.

Freedman, Russell. (1983). *Dinosaurs and Their Young.* New York: Holiday House.

Freedman, Russell. (1988). *Buffalo Hunt.* New York: Holiday House.

Gerstein, Mordicai. (1987). *Mountains of Tibet.* New York: Harper & Row.

Gibbons, Gail. (1966). *Flying.* New York: Holiday House.

Gibbons, Gail. (1987). *Dinosaurs.* New York: Holiday House.

Goble, Paul. (1984). *Buffalo Woman.* New York: Bradbury.

Gunston, Bill. (1986). *Aircraft.* New York: Watts.

Johnson, Tony. (1988). *Yonder.* New York: Dial.

Lauber, Patricia. (1985). *Tales Mummies Tell.* New York: Crowell.

Lauber, Patricia. (1987). *Dinosaurs Walked Here and Other Stories Fossils Tell.* New York: Bradbury.

Lauber, Patricia, and Wexler, Jerome. (1987). *Seeds: Pop, Stick, Glide.* New York: Crown.

Little, Jean. (1986). *Mama's Going to Buy You a Mocking Bird.* New York: Penguin.

Marshall, Edward. (1982). *Space Case.* New York: Dial.

Martin, Bill Jr., and Archambault, John. (1987). *Knots on a Counting Rope.* New York: Henry Holt.

McLaughlin, Molly. (1986). *Earthworms, Dirt and Rotten Leaves: An Exploration in Ecology.* New York: Macmillan.

Murphy, Jim. (1988). *The Last Dinosaur.* New York: Scholastic.

Newton, James. (1982). *A Forest Is Reborn.* New York: Harper & Row.

Overbeck, Cynthia. (1982). *How Seeds Travel.* Minneapolis: Lerner.

Paterson, Katherine. (1977). *Bridge to Terabithia.* New York: Harper & Row.

Penny, Malcom. (1988). *Endangered Animals.* New York: Watts.

Pringle, Laurence. (1977). *Death Is Natural.* New York: Macmillan.

Provensen, Alice, and Provensen, Marvin. (1983). *The Glorious Flight: Across the Channel with Louis Bleriot.* New York: Viking.

Rosenblum, Richard. (1980). *Wings: The Early Years of Aviation.* New York: Four Winds Press.

Tejima, Keizaburo. (1987). *Fox's Dream.* New York: Putnam.

Tejima, Keizaburo. (1988). *Swan Sky.* New York: Putnam.

Tresselt, Alvin. (1972). *The Dead Tree.* New York: Parents Magazine Press.

Tscharner, Renata von, and Fleming, Ronald L. (1987). *New Providence: A Changing Landscape.* San Diego: Harcourt Brace.

Viorst, Judith. (1971). *The Tenth Good Thing about Barney.* New York: Atheneum.

White, E. B. (1952). *Charlotte's Web.* New York: Harper & Row.

Whitfield, Philip, and Pope, Joyce. (1987). *Why Do the Seasons Change?* New York: Penguin.

Yorkins, Arthur. (1988). *Company's Coming.* New York: Crown.

References

American Association for the Advancement of Science (1989). *Science for All Americans: Project 2061.* Washington, D.C.: AASA.

Baumann, J. F., Jones, L. A., and Seifert-Kessell, N. (1993). Using Think Alouds to Enhance Children's Comprehension Monitoring Abilities. *The Reading Teacher* 47:184–193.

Bormuth, J. R. (1966). Readability: A New Approach. *Reading Research Quarterly* 1:79–132.

Bormuth, J. R. (1968). The Cloze Readability Procedure. *Elementary English* 45:429–436.

Butzow, C. M., and Butzow, J. W. (1989). *Science through Children's Literature: An Integrated Approach.* Englewood, CO: Teacher Ideas Press.

Casteel, C. P., and Isom, B. A. (1994). Reciprocal Processes in Science and Literacy Learning. *The Reading Teacher* 47:538–545.

Chatton, B. (1989). Using Literature Across the Curriculum. In J. Hickman and B. Cullinan, eds., *Children's Literature in the Classroom: Weaving Charlotte's Web*. Needham, MA: Christopher Gordon Publishers.

Crook, P. R., and Lehman, B. A. (1991). Themes for Two Voices: Children's Fiction and Nonfiction as "Whole Literature." *Language Arts* 68:34–41.

Davidson, A. (1985). *Readability—The Situation Today*. Technical Report No. 359. Champaign: University of Illinois Center for the Study of Reading.

Davidson, A., and Kantor, R. N. (1982). On the Failure of Readability Formulas to Define Readable Texts: A Case Study from Adaptations. *Reading Research Quarterly* 17:187–209.

Dupuis, M. M., Lee, J. W., Badiali, B. J., and Askov, E. N. (1989). *Teaching Reading and Writing in the Content Areas*. Glenview, IL: Scott, Foresman.

Duthie, C. (1994). Nonfiction: Genre Study for the Primary Classroom. *Language Arts* 71:588–595.

Earp, N. W. (1970). Procedures for Teaching Reading in Mathematics. *Arithmetic Teacher* 17:575–579.

Forgan, H. W., and Mangrum, C. T. (1989). *Teaching Content Area Reading Skills* (4th ed.). Columbus, OH: Merrill.

Fry, E. (1977). Fry's Readability Graph: Clarification, Validity, and Extension to Level 17. *Journal of Reading* 21:242.

Gere, A. A. (ed.) (1985). *Roots in the Sawdust: Writing to Learn across the Disciplines*. Urbana, IL: National Council of Teachers of English.

Harris, A. J., and Sipay, E. R. (1985). *How to Increase Reading Ability* (8th ed.). New York: Longmans.

Hess, M. L. (1991). Understanding Nonfiction: Purposes, Classification, Responses. *Language Arts* 68:228–232.

Hoffman, J. V. (1992). Critical Reading/Thinking Across the Curriculum: Using I-Charts to Support Learning. *Language Arts* 69:121–127.

Huck, C., Hepler, S., and Hickman, J. (1987). *Children's Literature in the Elementary School* (4th ed.). New York: Holt, Rinehart & Winston.

Johnson, N. M., and Ebert, M. J. (1992). Time Travel Is Possible: Historical Fiction and Biography—Passport to the Past. *The Reading Teacher* 45:488–495.

Kennedy, D., Spangler, S., and Vanderwerf, M. (1990). *Science and Technology in Fact and Fiction: A Guide to Children's Books*. New York: Bowker.

Kiefer, B. (1988). Picture Books as Contexts for Literacy, Aesthetic, and Real World Understandings. *Language Arts* 65:260–271.

Kinney, M. A. (1985). A Language Experience Approach to Teaching Expository Text Structure. *The Reading Teacher* 39:854–856.

Kleiman, M., and Kleiman, G. W. (1992). Life Among the Giants: Writing, Mathematics, and Exploring Gulliver's World. *Language Arts* 69:128–136.

Laughlin, M., and Kardaleff, P. (1991). *Literature-Based Social Studies: Children's Books and Activities to Enrich the K-5 Curriculum*. Phoenix: Oryx Press.

Lauritzen, C., and Jaeger, M. (1994). Education Within a Transdisciplinary Curriculum. *Language Arts* 71: 581–597.

Lipson, M. Y., Valencia, S. W., Wixon, K. E., and Peters, C. W. (1993). Integration and Thematic Teaching: Integration to Improve Teaching and Learning. *Language Arts* 70:252–263.

Mason, J. M., and Au, K. H. (1990). *Reading Instruction for Today* (2nd ed.). Glenview, IL: Scott Foresman.

McGee, L. A., and Richgels, D. J. (1985). Teaching Expository Text Structure to Elementary Students. *The Reading Teacher* 39:739–748.

McKeown, M. G., Beck, I. L., and North, M. J. (1993). Grappling with Text Ideas: Questioning the Author. *The Reading Teacher* 46:560–566.

National Council of Teachers of Mathematics. (1989). *Curriculum and Evaluation Standards for School Mathematics*. Reston, VA: NCTM.

Newport, J. F. (1990). What Is Wrong with Science Textbooks? *National Elementary Principal* 69:22–24.

Ogle, D. (1986). K–W–L: A Teaching Model That Develops Active Reading of Expository Text. *The Reading Teacher* 39:564–570.

Ogle, D. (1992) K–W–L in Action: Secondary Teachers Find Applications that Work. In E. K. Dishner, J. E. Readance, and D. W. Moore, eds., *Reading in the Content Areas* (3rd ed.). Dubuque: Kendall-Hunt.

Polya, G. (1945). *How to Solve It*. Princeton, NJ: Princeton University Press.

Raphael, T. E., and Hiebert, E. H. (1996). *Creating an Integrated Approach to Literacy Instruction*. Fort Worth: Harcourt Brace.

Reinking, D. (1986). Integrating Graphic Aids into Content Area Instruction: The Graphic Information Lesson. *Journal of Reading* 30:146–151.

Robb, L. (1989). Books in the Classroom. *The Horn Book Magazine* 65:808–810.

Salinger, T. S. (1996). *Literacy for Young Children* (2nd ed.). Englewood Cliffs, NJ: Prentice Hall.

Schiro, M. (1996). *Integrating Children's Literature and Mathematics in the Classroom*. New York: Teachers College Press.

Sebastia, S. L. (1987). Enriching the Arts and Humanities through Children's Books. In B. E. Cullinan, ed., *Children's Literature in the Reading Program*. Newark, DE: International Reading Association.

Smith, J. L., and Johnson, H. (1994). Models for Implementing Literature in Content Studies. *The Reading Teacher* 48:198–209.

Snowball, D. (1989). Classroom Big Books: Links Between Reading and Writing Nonfiction. *The Reading Teacher* 43:267.

Sudol, P., and King, C. M. (1996). A Checklist for Choosing Trade Books. *The Reading Teacher* 49:422–424.

Taylor, W. (1953). Cloze Procedure: A New Tool for Measuring Readability. *Journalism Quarterly* 30:415–433.

Vacca, R. T., and Vacca, J. L. (1996). *Content Area Reading* (5th ed.). New York: HarperCollins.

Whitin, D. J., Mills, H., and O'Keefe, T. (1990). *Living and Learning Mathematics*. Portsmouth, NH: Heinemann.

Wood, T. L., and Wood, W. (1988). Assessing Potential Difficulties in Comprehending Fourth Grade Science Textbooks. *Science Education* 72:561–574.

*T*he Role of the Library in a Literature-Based Reading Program

© Chromo Sohm/Sohm/Unicorn Stock Photos

Chapter 8 Outline

Key Concepts in This Chapter

The library or media/resources center is an essential support to a classroom literature-based reading program.

In addition to supplying books for information and pleasure, the library provides additional reading resources for children to use, including the reference materials, newspapers, magazines, and technology that supplement informational trade books in a balanced reading program.

The "information superhighway" passes through the library as well, bringing CD-ROMs and online services to students.

As children increase in reading competency and independence, the rate at which they read may be a concern. Rate, however, depends on a child's comprehension and on his or her flexibility in adapting to different purposes for reading.

Introduction

Although children's literature is at the heart of a classroom reading program, and trade books are essential to literacy instruction, pupils also need to learn to use materials that extend beyond the normal diet of reading materials in the classroom. These materials include print and electronic reference tools, newspapers and magazines, and other sources of information typically found in the school library or media center.

Teachers and Librarians

In a literature-based reading program, students will be familiar with the library or resources center. The library is central to a school that values literature and uses it as an integral part of literacy instruction. During story hours, children travel to the library to enjoy stories an upper-grade pupil, a parent volunteer, or the librarian shares. For those who love literature, libraries are very special places.

The school librarian or media/resource center coordinator is an important member of the instructional team in literature-based programs. As the resident expert on books, the librarian is in a unique position to have an important impact on reading. The key to maximizing this impact is to foster

8.1 Putting Ideas to Work
Children's Trade Books on Using the Library

Some simply written, informative children's trade books on using libraries are available, including:

Carol Green's *I Can Be a Librarian*
Patricia Fujimoto's *Libraries*
Claire McInerney's *Find It! The Inside Story at Your Library*
Cherry Gilcrest's *A Visit to the Library*
Anne Rockwell's *I Like the Library*

The school or public librarian may suggest some additional titles as well. Although these books introduce library services, explain how to use the library, and/or tell about the role of the librarian, they are no substitute for firsthand experiences in the library.

cooperation between the classroom teacher and the librarian. Although they have different jobs, teachers and librarians have similar goals—to help children develop the ability and the inclination to read. An active, trusting relationship is essential to ensure that both professionals meet these goals (Dales, 1990).

Librarians, who must keep up-to-the-minute on new books, can recommend newly published trade books students and teachers can use for different purposes in the classroom—an especially good book for a read-aloud, just the right reference on snakes, a newly published book that would be perfect for third graders to listen to on a rainy day. Some librarians compile lists of new acquisitions to circulate to teachers and parents. Librarians (including public librarians in some communities) can also prepare collections of books that a teacher can check out for weeks at a time to supplement the classroom library or to support a thematic unit.

At times, the teacher and the librarian may be able to co-teach aspects of the reading program. "Connections between library and classroom programs have a new sense of urgency as more teachers move to literature-based and whole language learning where trade books (i.e., library books) are integral to literacy experiences" (Hiebert, Mervar, and Person, 1990). Classes typically make weekly visits to the library for story time or for instruction in how to utilize various library resources. Instead of dropping the class at the library door and heading for the teachers' lounge (however tempting or well-deserved that respite might be), the teacher can coordinate efforts with the librarian to provide a double dose of instruction. All of the following activities combine the resources of teacher and librarian:

1. The librarian reads a book during story time; the teacher follows up with classroom enrichment activities related to the book.

The librarian can play an important part in introducing young children to literature with the help of technology.
© James L. Shaffer

2. The classroom teacher begins a thematic unit with preplanning help from the librarian; the librarian gears instruction in library use directly to the unit theme.

3. The librarian introduces one book in a series during story time—Michael Bond's *A Bear Called Paddington* in the primary grades, for example, or T. M. Murphy's *The Secrets of Belltown* in the upper elementary grades; the classroom teacher continues with other books in the series.

4. The librarian introduces a reading-related component during library time—for example, the metaphorical riddles in Brian Swann's strikingly illustrated *A Basketful of White Eggs*; the teacher continues the direct instructional focus by asking pupils to write and illustrate their own riddles.

5. The librarian shares with children the CD-ROM presentation of Mercer Mayer's *Just Grandma and Me*, a delightful account of a day in the life of a critter and his grandmother, with each page of the book coming alive on the computer screen; back in the classroom, the teacher follows up with other books by Mercer Mayer, other books about grandparents, and/or has children work with other interactive disks containing popular stories.

6. The librarian plans a display of children's reviews and commentaries about books; the teacher plans a reading-writing activity to produce the materials needed for the display.

7. The librarian shares a book based on a song, such as John Langstaff's *Frog Went a-Courtin'*; the music teacher uses this song in class. The key to this collaboration is planning.

The primary responsibility for the reading program rests with the teacher in the classroom. But most librarians are more than happy to provide all the help and support they can. Teachers who involve librarians add an incredibly enriched dimension to their classroom reading programs.

To become literate citizens, pupils must learn the nature and purpose of print and nonprint reference tools that include:

atlases, books and disks of maps and other geographic information;

almanacs, annual references containing up-to-date information on an incredible range of topics;

other reference sources, such as books about children's authors or reference books about specific topics such as Reginald Bragomer, Jr., and David Fisher's *What's What: A Visual Glossary of the Physical World* (Maplewood, NJ: Hammond, 1981), which contains illustrations and descriptions of physical objects from an *aba* to a *zipper.*

It is reasonable to expect that dictionaries, an atlas, an almanac, and perhaps a set of encyclopedias will be available in the classroom for immediate use, but the library or media center usually houses a larger collection of reference tools.

Learning to Use Reference Tools

Libraries contain mountains of printed and electronic information on vast arrays of topics. Finding their way through the labyrinth of informational material can be a daunting task for some pupils.

Finding information requires children to develop skills in two areas: knowing where to look for what they need to know, and using strategies to dig out the information. Pupils need at least a rudimentary knowledge of how the library classifies and arranges fiction and nonfiction, how to gain access to available resources, and how to use the print or electronic access system in the library or resource center.

How can students learn to use the library effectively? Too often, instruction in using the library consists of early-in-the-year visits that bombard children with information ranging from library protocol to the difference between the Dewey Decimal and the Library of Congress cataloging systems. Even if pupils pay attention during these visits, too much information is presented at one time to make any practical sense.

Children can learn to use library resources through authentic opportunities that bring them into contact with what the library has to offer. For example:

> as they engage in searches for information based on thematic units they are studying in the classroom;
>
> as older students provide instructional sessions for younger ones on how to use reference tools;
>
> as they search out answers to questions of interest that arise on the playground, over lunch, or in the classroom.

Ultimately, pupils learn how to use the library as they seek information on topics of interest related to their school work or their lives.

Children need special skills to find their way through the maze of material on the information superhighway. Instead of encouraging students to "surf the Net" for information, teachers are helping students learn to "mine the Net"; that is, to turn to the World Wide Web with specific goals in mind and navigate through the vast array of information to dig out specific topics.

Just as literature-based reading instruction aims to develop a lifelong interest in reading, the attitudes and strategies children develop in using research tools for informational purposes will be beneficial throughout a pupil's life. Every time we use the phone book to find the number of the closest pizza parlor or use a database to prepare a term paper for a college course, we use the capabilities we developed as we learned to read for information.

Organizing Information

Once children have located information in nonfiction trade books, in reference books, or in electronic reference materials, they may need to extract what they read and to organize it in an efficient and usable way. This means they need to develop strategies for taking notes and for arranging the information in some systematic format.

Notetaking involves making brief written records of ideas and facts gathered from printed (and other) sources of information. Research indicates that "notetaking has great potential as a studying aid, for it allows the student to record a reworked (and perhaps more deeply processed) version of text" (Anderson and Armbruster, 1984; p. 666).

Effective notetaking is based on a range of comprehension components, including recognizing main ideas and details, separating relevant from irrelevant information, and summarizing. To take effective notes, pupils need to recognize essential information in informational trade books and other sources of expository text and to make a brief written record of this information for later use.

Some pupils equate notetaking with copying word-for-word from an encyclopedia or other reference source. More often than not, students copy verbatim when the reference sources they are expected to use are too difficult; in addition, pupils often do not have the prerequisite strategies to extract essential ideas from text. When they do find it necessary to copy, the teacher should make sure students understand the principles and practices of giving credit.

Notetaking is most effective when children do it with a specific purpose, and when the information they seek meets authentic interests or needs. Once students have gathered all the information they need, they must organize it so they can remember it and/or present it to others.

Organizing information into a systematic format enables pupils to better use the information they have gathered. Organizing begins with recognizing expository text structure and comprehending the relationships among ideas.

The conventional outline format of numbers and letters to indicate main and subordinate ideas is the most common means of organizing information. But devices such as story maps for narrative text and graphic organizers such as the Herringbone Technique for expository text provide other ways to express the relationships among ideas. Children can look at graphic devices such as chapter subheads in nonfiction trade books and textbooks as examples of how to organize material systematically.

Pupils can become aware of organizing strategies through direct and incidental instruction in a literature-based reading program. For example, they can learn strategies

as they are introduced to the table of contents in a nonfiction trade book they are using in the classroom;

as they learn about text structure during classroom reading and writing activities;

as they organize their class schedules at the beginning of the school day;

as they prepare curriculum-related written reports as part of thematic units.

Obviously, reading expository text does not always mean children will have to take notes and organize information in a systematic form. At times, pupils will read trade books to find specific information without needing to copy it down, or they will simply browse through reference materials in search of information on sports, careers, music, or other topics of interest. When they do need to take notes and organize information, however, research strategies can help them.

Newspapers and Magazines

While students will often seek information in informational trade books and school texts, they can also find up-to-the-minute information in newspapers and magazines. Online computer services update and expand these resources on a daily basis. Websites give students access to information updated nearly by the minute. Newspapers and magazines provide a full range of narrative and expository text that teachers can use effectively in the classroom to help pupils develop reading competency.

Newspapers

Over the years, the daily newspaper has proved to be a practical tool in teaching reading. Teachers from kindergarten through the high school level have developed thousands of ideas using the newspaper to provide a full range of reading and writing activities, while at the same time helping pupils acquire information related to all areas of the curriculum. The newspaper, which has been called "the thinking child's textbook," can be no less valuable in literature-based programs.

Newspapers offer a unique advantage: they contain many different kinds of texts in a single source. Newspapers feature news to inform, editorials to persuade, reviews to promote critical thinking, features to enrich, comics to entertain, puzzles to stimulate language development, and advertisements to convince. Calling them "indispensable in the teaching of language arts," du Boulay (1988) identifies other valuable features newspapers bring to the classroom:

They provide purposeful, relevant information.

They are associated with life beyond the classroom.

They are inexpensive and easy to obtain.

They provide interesting examples of narrative and nonnarrative text.

8.3 Putting Ideas to Work
Ten Ways to Use the Newspaper

Specific reading and writing activities using the newspaper are virtually limitless. The ten activities suggested here can easily be expanded a hundredfold.

1. Using "the 5 Ws and an H" format of news stories (who, what, when, where, why, and how), students can rewrite accounts of their favorite episodes in trade books or write their own narrative accounts of events in their lives.
2. Children can match headlines to stories (main idea), write headlines based on stories, or write stories based on headlines.
3. Pupils can read editorials or letters to the editor to determine reasons for the writer's thinking. They can also write their own letters to the editor based on a classroom discussion of current issues, or they can write an editorial-style review of a book they have read.
4. Students can examine display and classified ads with an eye to vocabulary and propaganda techniques, then create advertisements for trade books they have enjoyed.
5. Children can rearrange the frames of comic strips or design their own comic strips based on their favorite story characters.
6. Pupils can search through back issues of newspapers to research items of interest from local or state history.
7. Children can interview community members who are experts on specific topics and write up the interview as a news story. As an alternative, they can write stories based on real or imagined interviews with real authors.
8. Pupils can examine book reviews from their local papers and use them as models for submitting their own reviews of new books.
9. Students can develop word banks related to specific topics in newspaper sections (politics, finance, travel, or sports, for example).
10. Pupils can produce their own classroom newspaper featuring school or neighborhood news, editorials on local policies, advertisements for school events, book reviews, and samples of their original writing.

These ten suggestions relate to language arts. The newspaper can also be used in math, social studies, science, and other areas of the curriculum.

The American Newspaper Publishers Association Foundation (Box 17407, Dulles International Airport, Washington, DC 20041) and The Newspaper Center (11600 Sunrise Valley Dr., Reston, VA 22091) have a wealth of suggestions for using the newspaper to develop literacy. Most local newspapers also provide information and material for classroom use.

In sum, newspapers provide a resource for integrating language instruction across the broad spectrum of the curriculum.

Conrad (1989) points out that the newspaper is an authentic and functional medium for reading and language instruction in the whole language classroom. The newspaper provides interesting examples of narrative and nonnarrative text and offers an integrated approach to teaching reading and writing. Newspapers contain information related to thematic units. They also provide current, relevant information on a variety of curriculum-related topics, along with background information teachers can use to activate prior knowledge and help pupils build meaning as they read. Newspaper stories sometimes contain theme, plot, character traits, and other qualities common in literature. In short, the newspaper addresses real issues that affect children's lives and that reflect their culture and environment.

Beyond its general value as an essential source of information in a democratic society, the newspaper can be used for a variety of specific purposes in the reading/writing program, including:

letter recognition, word recognition, and oral language development with younger pupils;

critical thinking, propaganda, and verbal problem solving in the upper elementary grades;

research skills for students at all levels seeking information on specific subjects;

writing, as the news is used as a writing model to forge the reading-writing connection (Kossack, Kane, and Fine, 1987).

In the final analysis, the newspaper is more than a daily teaching tool for reading and writing. It is a vehicle for the dissemination of information and the expression of opinion in a democratic society. Even when reading instruction is centered largely on literature, it makes good sense to give pupils a headstart in developing a skilled and critical approach to reading the newspaper.

Magazines

Another potentially valuable set of reading materials in the library or school media center are magazines, including:

Junior Scholastic (50 W. 44th Street, New York, NY 10036)

World (National Geographic Society, Washington, DC 20036)

Ranger Rick (National Wildlife Federation, 8925 Leesburg Pike, Vienna, VA 22184)

These and other similar publications provide a wealth of interesting and valuable material that children can enjoy and, at the same time, use for instructional purposes.

Magazines offer unique advantages as supplements to trade books in literature-based reading programs. Selections are manageably short. Content typically focuses on topics of current interest. Articles can provide a springboard for further reading about high-interest topics. The writing provides a model for teachers to use in writing lessons. And magazines often appeal to more reluctant readers.

Magazines provide material that supplements literature-based instruction. When multiple copies of the same magazine are available for a classroom reading lesson, articles can be used in reading groups much as trade books and textbooks are. For example, after hearing a Chinese legend about how

8.4 Putting Ideas to Work
Magazines That Publish Children's Writing

*P*ublication is the consummation of the writing act, and publishing one's writing in a national magazine is the ultimate in publication. A number of national magazines accept stories, poems, letters, essays, plays, and other products written by elementary school pupils. A short list of these magazines includes:

Boys' Life (1325 Walnut Hill Lane, Irving, TX 75602)
Children's Digest (P.O. Box 567, Indianapolis, IN 46206)
Highlights for Children (803 Church Street, Honesdale, PA 18431)
Jack and Jill (P.O. Box 567, Indianapolis, IN 46206)
Kids Magazine (P.O. Box 3041, Grand Central Station, New York, NY 10017)
Scholastic Magazines (50 W. 44th Street, New York, NY 10036)
Young World (P.O. Box 567, Indianapolis, IN 46206)

pandas got their black and white fur, the class can share informational magazine articles about pandas. With a balance between literature and magazine articles, students have opportunities to enjoy relevant samples of both narrative and expository text.

Adults fall into three reading categories: book readers, nonbook readers, and nonreaders. Many adults, even those who do not frequently read books, devour daily newspapers and regularly read such magazines as *Time, Good Housekeeping, Popular Mechanics, Business Week,* and other publications that seem to overpopulate newsstands. Using magazines as reading instructional tools in a literature-based program gives children a headstart in learning to use this material critically and well.

Reading Rate and Reading Efficiency

As pupils learn to read widely and as the volume of their reading increases, rate of reading may become a concern. When enjoying a good piece of literature, the speed at which one reads is less important than comprehension and enjoyment (unless the rate is inordinately slow). As the volume of text to be read increases, however, rate becomes important since students need to read fast enough to keep up.

Speed alone—the number of words read per minute—is not of primary importance. More important by far are comprehension and the flexibility to adjust rate to the nature of the text and one's purpose for reading it.

Comprehension

Reading quickly may be important at times, but comprehension is vital all the time. Rapid reading is of little use if pupils do not understand what they are reading. Reading for speed alone suggests the old line, "I took a speed reading course and read *War and Peace* in 20 minutes. It's about Russia." Comprehension involves more than rate; it involves all the text- and reader-based factors that are part of interactive comprehension.

Flexibility

Students need to learn to adjust their reading rate according to purpose. Usually, children realize they read at a different speed when reading a favorite novel, for example, than they do when reading a difficult word problem in math. The ability to adjust reading rate to the nature of the material is a metacognitive competency, an awareness that can be developed early in a pupil's reading life. In group reading lessons in the classroom, teacher and children can discuss how best to approach a text selection before they begin to read it, deciding whether quick perusal, careful reading, or a combination of both may be best.

Two types of rapid reading are sometimes useful in reading informational trade books and other types of expository text: skimming and scanning. Both are special types of rapid reading.

Skimming means reading to pick up the main idea or to get a very general overview of text. When readers skim, they make a superficial survey in order to form an overall impression of a trade book or other reading material.

Scanning means reading rapidly to find a specific piece of information, as when we look for a name in a telephone book or when pupils quickly locate an item in an index.

In a reading instructional setting, teachers can introduce skimming by asking pupils to:

survey a few pages in a trade book to see whether the story is appealing or appropriate for independent reading;

quickly find the main idea of a passage in a nonfiction trade book or textbook;

look quickly over a newspaper article and match it with an appropriate headline;

quickly glance through a selection to see if it might be a useful source of information for a theme unit.

Scanning can be introduced as pupils try to find a topic in an index or find a specific piece of information such as a name or a date in a chapter. The teacher can prepare a list of factual questions and assign children to quickly find the answers as a prereading or postreading activity.

Beyond the elementary grades, audacious (some say outrageous) "speed reading" programs claim they can "triple your reading speed or double your money back." Although certain techniques and devices can help people speed up their reading pace, the same principles apply to adults in speed reading programs as to children: how fast a person reads depends on the nature of the material and the person's purpose for reading it.

8.5 Putting Ideas to Work
Selective Reading Guide

*F*or upper elementary pupils, Cunningham and Shablak (1975) suggest using Selective Reading Guides to encourage flexibility and comprehension in reading expository text. Assuming that not all content is of equal significance in content area textbooks, the teacher previews chapters to determine which ideas are particularly important and which are not.

In a reading group, the teacher then guides pupils through the chapter with directions such as, "Look at the heading on page 100. Read this paragraph about pioneer life slowly and carefully"; or "On pages 101 and 102 is a story about a pioneer family. It is interesting but not especially important. Read it quickly and move on to page 103."

This type of guided reading relates to purpose setting and questioning—parts of every well-developed reading lesson focusing on content. The teacher can tape record the guided instructions so pupils can work independently.

Summary and Conclusions

In a literature-based reading program, pupils will encounter both fact and fiction in the trade books they read. They will also extend their reading for information into reference books, newspapers and magazines, and other types of reading materials they will continue to encounter throughout their lives. Given the flood of information children will face as they enter high school and adulthood during the 21st century, early encounters with this type of print are important.

Through story hours and other literature-related activities, students can learn to see the library as a treasured place from their early school years. With graduated instruction, pupils can become aware that the library is a rich source of reference materials that they can use to find information on virtually any topic. Learning to use these references effectively and efficiently is part of literacy instruction in the elementary grades.

Along with library reference tools, newspapers and magazines are learning tools that can be used for literacy development. These current sources of information can be used in an incredible variety of ways to develop reading, writing, thinking skills, and knowledge to supplement the use of literature in teaching reading.

As young readers gain competency and independence in reading, the volume of printed material they are expected to read usually increases, suggesting the need to increase reading rate. Although teachers can introduce rapid reading strategies such as skimming and scanning in the elementary grades, a child's reading rate must adjust in light of the nature of the material, the reader's purpose for reading it, and the need to comprehend.

Discussion Questions and Activities

1. When preparing for a research assignment for one of your college courses, make a list of strategies you need to complete the assignment. (Don't take anything for granted; you need, for example, to understand the concept of alphabetical order.) With the help of a librarian, fully explore the range of resources available to you in researching your topic.

2. Discuss how research tools have changed since you were in elementary school. Look at some of the CD-ROMs and other research tools in your Curriculum Resource Center, or browse the Net for information on a particular topic of interest (children's literature, for example). How do you think these advances in technology will influence the assignments you make as a teacher?
3. Examine your local or national newspaper or children's magazine. Make a list of the activities you could plan to use this material to teach reading and writing in the classroom or resource room.
4. How important is reading rate to you? With a classmate, compare how you adjust your reading speed according to the different types of reading you do throughout the day—for example, reading the newspaper, the lunch menu in the cafeteria, or course material in preparation for a test. How does your reading rate differ from that of someone just learning to read?

School-Based Assignments

1. Observe a science or social studies lesson or talk to pupils about a topic they are particularly interested in. Then visit the school library or media center and/or the local public library to locate trade books, reference books, or computerized reference tools on the topic. Prepare a list of resources you might use in your classroom.
2. In the school library or media center, locate a magazine written for elementary pupils, and select (perhaps with the help of some children) an article that would appeal to the grade level you are interested in. Design a directed reading lesson using the article. If possible, try the lesson with a small group of students.
3. What technological tools are available in your school to help students with research? How do pupils at different grade levels use these tools?
4. How quickly do the children in your classroom read? Give a small group of pupils a brief timed test and check their comprehension. Make a list of suggestions to help them improve their reading rate.

Children's Trade Books Cited in This Chapter

Bond, Michael. (1960). *A Bear Called Paddington*. Boston: Houghton Mifflin.
Fujimoto, Patricia. (1984). *Libraries*. Chicago: Children's Press.
Gilcrest, Cherry. (1985). *A Visit to the Library*. New York: Cambridge University Press.
Green, Carol. (1988). *I Can Be a Librarian*. Chicago: Children's Press.
Langstaff, John. (1955). *Frog Went a-Courtin'*. New York: Harcourt Brace.
Mayer, Mercer. (1985). *Just Grandma and Me*. New York: Western.
McInerney, Claire. (1989). *Find It! The Inside Story at Your Library*. Minneapolis: Lerner.
Murphy, T. M. (1996). *The Secrets of Belltown*. Parsippany, N.J.: Silver Burdett Press.
Rockwell, Anne. (1977). *I Like the Library*. New York: Dutton.
Swann, Brian. (1988). *A Basketful of White Eggs*. New York: Orchard Books.

References

Anderson, T. H., and Armbruster, B. B. (1984). Studying. In P. D. Pearson, ed., *Handbook of Reading Research*. New York: Longmans.

Conrad, S. (1989). Newspaper in the Whole Language Classroom. In *A Whole Language Primer*. Quincy, MA: The Patriot Ledger.

Cunningham, D., and Shablak, S. L. (1975). Selective Reading Guide-o-Rama: The Content Teacher's Best Friend. *Journal of Reading* 18:380–382.

Dales, B. (1990). Trusting Relationships Between Teachers and Librarians. *Language Arts* 67:732–734.

du Boulay, G. (1988). Newspapers: Text for Non-Narrative and Narrative Reading and Writing. *Australian Journal of Reading* 11:206–210.

Hiebert, E. H., Mervar, K. B., and Person, D. (1990). Research Directions: Children's Selection of Trade Books in Libraries and Classrooms. *Language Arts* 67:758–763.

International Reading Association and National Council of Teachers of English. (1996). *Standards for the English Language Arts*. Newark, DE and Urbana, IL: IRA and NCTE.

Kossack, S., Kane, S., and Fine, J. (1987). Use the News: The Reading–Writing Connection. *Journal of Reading* 30:730–732.

*S*haring Literature through Oral Reading

© Tony Freeman/PhotoEdit

Chapter 9 Outline

Features

Key Concepts in This Chapter

For centuries, oral reading has been part of education, and it is still practiced widely in elementary schools today. Sharing stories by reading aloud is one of the cornerstones of a literature-based program.

Expression and fluency are essential qualities of oral reading; these qualities enable the reader to convey meaning to listeners.

Reading aloud to pupils opens the world of literature to them. It stimulates their imaginations and enhances their language background.

Helping children become skilled oral readers means using techniques other than the round-robin reading many classrooms traditionally carry on.

Introduction

Oral reading has enjoyed a position of prominence in formal education for a very long time. The ancient Greeks and Romans thought of reading exclusively as an oral process. To many ancient learners, the lines of writing represented "rivers of speech" and the nature of reading was "to recapture the actual speech, the sounds, the author's actual words. . . . To get the full benefit of what the reader read, he had to read aloud" (Mathews, 1966; p. 12).

In the centuries that followed, this view of reading as an oral activity persisted. Throughout the Middle Ages and the Renaissance, and during the Industrial Revolution in England and the Colonial period in America, people considered silent reading a peculiar habit, and the instructional emphasis remained on reading aloud. In fact, in the New World, reading was equated with "elocutionary delivery" from the first years of education. Teachers taught reading mainly for the purpose of "exercising the organs of speech" and for providing practice in "just and distinct articulation." The goal of developing eloquent oral reading overshadowed the goals of comprehension or enjoyment. Oral reading was taught as a social skill because the few who knew how to read were expected to read the Bible and other books aloud to others (Smith, 1965).

During the first quarter of the 20th century, the educational emphasis shifted from oral reading to silent reading. In 1917, Edward Thorndike published a classic study indicating that proficient oral reading did not always involve comprehension (Langer and Allington, 1992). The pendulum swung from reading for articulation to reading for meaning. As educators and psychologists developed standardized reading achievement tests, comprehension became a primary concern. Proficient silent reading replaced oral reading as the aim of instruction in the classroom.

Although reading instruction continues to emphasize silent reading, oral reading is still part of reading instruction in the elementary school. When people recall their early experiences in learning to read, most remember reading aloud in front of classmates—and being embarrassed by it—as one of their most frequent and vivid memories (Savage, 1978). Oral reading is not just for practice; sound instruction in oral reading can influence children's development as readers (Reutzel, Hollingsworth, and Eldredge, 1994).

Reading aloud is one of the basic characteristics of literature-based instruction. "Reading aloud gives teachers the opportunity to open up the world of literature to students who may not discover it on their own" (Peterson and Eeds, 1990; p. 9). In literature-based classrooms, oral reading involves both (1) reading aloud *to* pupils for the purpose of sharing literature, while modeling mature, effective reading behaviors; and (2) reading aloud *by* pupils to teach them to use effective reading strategies and to read as a way to communicate to others. Besides, one way to observe the underlying processes that children use to construct meaning in text is to listen while they read aloud, so oral reading is a valuable diagnostic tool as well.

"Read with Expression"

Oral reading involves more than just standing in front of others trying to say all the words correctly. The goal of all reading—silent and oral—is comprehension. Research has shown that there is a significant relationship between

9.1 Putting Ideas to Work

The Suprasegmental Phoneme System

*T*he suprasegmental phoneme system consists of three elements: pitch, stress, and juncture.

Pitch is the level of the voice as one speaks or reads aloud. There are four levels of pitch in American English: /1/ the level the voice falls to at the end of a statement, /2/ the normal pitch level, /3/ the level the voice rises to at the end of most questions, and /4/ the level saved to express extreme surprise or shock.

Stress is the relative force of articulation, or loudness, we make sounds with. American English defines four degrees of stress: /´/ primary, /ˆ/ secondary, /`/ tertiary, and /˘/ weak.

Juncture is the transition between one speech sound and the next in a stream of speech. Included here are internal junctures /+/, which represent pauses within sentences, and terminal junctures— /↓/ (falling) and /↑/ (rising)—which represent end-sentence pauses.

These sound features operate closely together to produce an "overlay" that gives total meaning to the language one speaks or reads aloud.

accurate oral reading and reading comprehension (Pinnell et al., 1995). Oral reading requires that the reader not only comprehend an author's message but also communicate that message to others. One derives and communicates meaning to others through expressive, fluent oral reading.

Expression

Teachers and parents have long urged children to "read with expression." But what makes for expression in oral reading? How does expression come into play as pupils render lines of print into their spoken equivalents?

Expression in oral reading comes from the same elements that make up intonation in speech—the three elements of what is known as the suprasegmental phoneme system of any language: pitch, stress, and juncture (see Putting Ideas to Work 9.1).

Expression and Meaning. Speakers use intonation to convey total meaning in speech; readers use expression to convey total meaning in oral reading. A reciprocal relationship exists between expression and meaning. On the one hand, children must fully grasp the total meaning of a passage to be able to read the passage with appropriate expression. Struggling with individual words distracts them from the larger meaning in text and results in the word-by-word performance characteristic of young or immature readers. On the other hand, expression allows the reader to transmit full meaning to others.

Holdaway (1972) explores the relationship between expression and meaning and illustrates the role expression plays in conveying full meaning with the sentence *He was a little boy*. Taken out of context, this sentence likely would be read with a normal intonation pattern. But in the larger context of

Poor Herman! He wasn't a bear. He was a little boy.

the expression would change to convey the full meaning. "These sentences have not been read until the appropriate intonation patterns have been perceived" (Holdaway 1972; p. 98).

In the extreme, expression in oral reading—the way in which a reader reads a passage—alters meaning drastically. Consider the conflicting interpretations possible with the following segment of print (referring to Putting Ideas to Work 9.1 to interpret the numbers and symbols):

a woman without her man is lost

If one interprets the meaning of this line of print as, "A woman is lost without a man," the sentence would be written

A woman without her man is lost.

We would read this with a normal intonation pattern:

If, on the other hand, one interprets the meaning as, "A man is lost without a woman," the sentence would be written

A woman—without her, man is lost.

We would read this with an intonation pattern like the following:

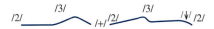

The two interpretations of this line of print are diametrically different. In the first, the woman is lost without the man. In the second, the man is lost without the woman. The meanings do not reside in the language, but rather in the way the language is expressed. The difference well illustrates the old cliché, "It's not what he said, but how he said it!"

Punctuation. From the preceding example, you probably see the important role that punctuation and other graphic devices (such as capital letters, italics, and boldface print) play in writing and in oral reading. End-sentence punctuation marks (periods, question marks, and exclamation points) indicate not only sentence function but also the sound of the voice in reading. Internal punctuation (commas, colons, semicolons, dashes, ellipsis points) indicate the expression shifts that occur within sentences. Punctuation, of course, represents only the most obvious intonational elements. A relationship exists between punctuation and the suprasegmental phonemes, but just as with the relationship between letters and sounds, the correspondence is far from perfect.

The suprasegmental phoneme system in English, as in any language, is quite complex. Children learn to use it very early in speech as part of the language acquisition process. When they come to school, they learn how the system applies to reading aloud.

Fluency, Accuracy, and Rate

Oral reading instruction must focus on the three interrelated elements of fluency, accuracy, and rate, as well as on comprehension (a given in any reading activity).

Fluency is the ability to read aloud smoothly and easily. It involves the ability to read in phrases or meaningful thought units while adhering to the text structure the author has used, along with using the elements of expression described in the previous section.

"Developing oral reading fluency, while not the only goal of reading instruction, has the potential to help readers develop more resonant understandings of text" (Slater and Allington, 1991; p. 145). Researchers disagree on whether fluency is a prerequisite or a by-product of reading ability (Lipson and Lang, l991). Whether the cause or the effect of good reading, fluency improves as young readers use predictable books with familiar text, perform repeated readings, and pay direct attention to the qualities of skilled oral reading.

Accuracy is another quality of effective oral reading. Accuracy involves efficient word recognition and a high level of automaticity in identifying words. Pupils who do not recognize the words they encounter and who cannot easily decode these words will often "bump along," reading in a word-by-word manner. Skilled readers, on the other hand, can identify words easily and quickly. This is one reason for the strong relationship between fluent, accurate oral reading and good overall reading ability.

There is, however, an irony in helping children achieve fluency via word identification. Teachers often try to improve fluency by focusing on letters, sounds, and words in isolation "in the mistaken belief that more attention to this area will result in improved (oral) reading" (Allington, 1983; p. 557). Merely learning to recognize words quickly does not automatically produce fluent oral reading. While comprehension is certainly dependent on recognizing the meaning of individual words, the evolving meaning of the passage can often provide clues to the pronunciations and meanings of unfamiliar words.

Rate is another factor in reading aloud. Skilled oral readers read at a natural, comfortable story pace, one that allows the reader to make connections among ideas in the text. When reading is too slow, these connections are often difficult to make. The natural pace for reading aloud is the rate at which the reader can comprehend meaning and convey it to others.

To help children develop oral reading ability, teachers need to use strategies that focus specifically on the elements of good oral reading. They can use such techniques as modeling, repeated reading, and phrase marking to help pupils become more competent at reading aloud.

9.2 Putting Ideas to Work
Suggestions for Reading Aloud

Sloan and Latham (1981) offer some direct, practical advice on techniques for reading aloud to children:

1. Define new words as you introduce a story or after reading it, but let context carry the meaning during the reading.
2. Let the pupils know a little about the author—this information makes the story more interesting and may lead students to read other works by the author.
3. Group children so they can see you easily.
4. Read with feeling that comes from a genuine enthusiasm for the story.
5. Hold the book so that the students can see your facial expressions.
6. If you use gestures, make them slight.
7. Summarize long descriptive passages to give the story "more vitality and movement as a read-aloud tale."
8. Maintain eye contact to personalize reading and to keep the audience involved.
9. Stop at interesting places to heighten the excitement for the next episode.
10. Use ongoing evaluation, keeping the dialogue related to pupils' interests.

Modeling.   Sharing stories by reading aloud every day is one of the essential characteristics of a literature-based reading program. When the teacher reads aloud to pupils, he or she models fluent oral reading. Studies show that when the teacher reads the first hundred or so words as a selection is introduced to a reading group, the students' fluency improves and their oral reading errors decrease in number (Smith, 1979).

Repeated Reading.   This simple rehearsal strategy allows children to practice reading the same passage several times. Evidence shows that when pupils have a chance to preview text silently before reading it aloud, and when they have opportunities to read the material more than once, fluency, accuracy, and speed in oral reading improve (Dowhower, 1989). Repeated reading also has a positive impact on comprehension. Passages should be relatively brief (50–100 words) and appropriate for the child's reading ability. Students can sometimes engage in repeated reading with a partner as a cooperative learning activity; at other times, they can reread a passage independently (Samuels, 1979).

Marking Phrases.   Fluent readers put words together in meaningful phrases. When the teacher lightly marks phrases in oral reading material, pupils learn to read the words in "meaningful chunks." The use of phrase marking helps children develop an efficient eye-voice span—the distance the eye is ahead of the voice—that contributes to both expression and fluency in oral reading.

Reading Aloud to Pupils

Reading aloud to pupils is an important part of teaching children how to
read and is one of the distinguishing characteristics of a literature-based
reading program. As Peterson and Eeds (1990) point out:

> These are the goals of reading aloud with the total group:
> To make the language of word artists a part of students' lives.
> To make students aware of the delight which can be found in literature.
> To help students discover and entertain all genres and styles of writing (such
> as poetry, nonfiction, fantasy and science fiction, folk and fairytale, realistic
> stories, satire, classics, picture books) they might never discover on their own.
> To develop community through building a common literary history.
> To provide a forum for the making and sharing of connections which have
> been inspired by reading.
> To provide an opportunity for you to help build children's awareness of
> literary elements. (p. 49)[1]

Children first experience the world of literature as they listen to stories,
and sharing literature through oral reading continues to be an essential part
of literacy instruction throughout the grades.

Advantages of Reading Aloud

Reading aloud to pupils has a number of distinct advantages. It is one way
to share literature with pupils, literature that some children might otherwise
never enjoy. Reading aloud stimulates children's imaginations and allows
them to engage in experiences vicariously. Hearing a good story read well

---

[1]Excerpted from GRAND CONVERSATIONS: LITERATURE GROUPS IN ACTION by Ralph
Peterson and Maryann Eeds. Copyright © 1990 by R. Peterson M. Eeds. Reprinted by permission of
Scholastic, Inc.

has an enormously positive effect on students' language and reading development. Reading to pupils is a powerful device for stimulating vocabulary growth, since the story introduces new words and uses them in meaningful contexts (Elley, 1989). Careful questioning can focus on the many dimensions of comprehension as well. A shared reading experience can trigger group discussion, as when a class examines prejudice after hearing Theodore Taylor's *The Cay*, a book in which a young white boy and an old black man develop a warm friendship. But for all of its instructional benefits, the primary purpose of reading aloud to children is enjoyment. Reading aloud can ignite a child's desire to read on his or her own.

By the time they begin preschool or kindergarten, some children have discovered the pleasure of being read to at home or in other child-care settings. These pupils will arrive in the classroom already having escaped Mr. McGregor's garden with Peter Rabbit, having been to the ball with Cinderella, and having sailed away for a year and a day with the Owl and the Pussycat in their beautiful pea green boat. Other children are not so lucky. But since teachers have little or no direct control over the experiences their pupils have with books at home, it becomes the teacher's job to make sure that story time is a regular and important part of life in the classroom.

Conditions and Techniques for Reading Aloud

A teacher does not need to be an Academy Award nominee to read aloud to pupils, but sharing books does take some good oral reading skills. Preparation is important. If possible, the teacher should preview stories to note the points of high suspense (a good place to terminate a daily oral reading period) or to mark long passages that are less essential to the story and that are likely to tax the children's collective attention span. Preparation also enables teachers to spot words or incidents in the story that may prove embarrassing or otherwise unfortunate to one of the pupils—a cruel nickname that might be pinned on a child, for example, or an incident that might reflect a child's unhappy home experience.

A comfortable environment enhances oral reading. The primary purpose of story time is enjoyment, so students should sit where they can listen comfortably. Pupils should have a chance to see the illustrations that are essential to the story. In continuing stories, the teacher can set the tone by asking the class to briefly recall what happened in the previous episode or to predict what might happen next. These introductions should be brief, however, so that they do not take away from the enjoyment of the listeners.

Not every child will enjoy every story a teacher reads, but pupils owe it to each other not to ruin story time for the rest of the group. Art supplies can keep uninterested pupils quietly engaged, but more often than not, these children will become involved in the story as it progresses. A large number of disinterested pupils suggests that the book was an inappropriate choice. If this is the case, teachers should not hesitate to abandon a book and select another. Lack of success in arousing interest is not necessarily a sign that a book is not well written or that it should be abandoned forever.

For a number of reasons, a well-written book that meets one teacher's purposes in one classroom may not be a good choice for reading aloud in another classroom.

Reading should be slow enough for students to savor the language and to visualize the settings and actions. Slow reading is especially important during suspenseful parts, with changes in tone during dialogue (assuming the teacher is comfortable doing so). Tone, volume, and expression ought to convey humor, mystery, sadness, and other moods the story creates. And the reader should keep the story moving without long interruptions from pupils' anecdotes or questions. If the story lends itself to discussion, the class can talk after reading, as long as the discussion does not turn into a quiz.

Barrentine (1996) suggests interactive read-alouds in which children are encouraged to interact verbally with the text, peers, and the teacher during oral reading. Teachers ask questions that enhance meaning construction for pupils and use oral reading to show how the voice makes sense of text.

Selecting Books for Reading Aloud

Selecting books for reading aloud is a practical concern. Selections will vary according to classroom demographics—the age, grade level, interests, and backgrounds of the pupils. A good rule of thumb to follow in selecting books is this: Any book that teachers and students can enjoy together is a good book to read aloud.

In the very early grades, picture books are most appropriate, favorites like Bernard Waber's *Ira Sleeps Over* or Robert McCloskey's *Make Way for Ducklings*. Picture books need not be limited to the beginning reading stages, however; upper grade students—even "upper grade" college students and experienced teachers—enjoy hearing picture books read aloud during classes or in-service sessions. These books are often shared as part of instructional sessions with Big Books. Reading aloud to (or with) students using Big Books can have a more direct instructional focus.

From short picture books, teachers can move on to chapter books, including old favorites like *The Littles* by John Peterson, Michael Bond's *Paddington Bear*, A. A. Milne's *Winnie-the-Pooh*, and Betty MacDonald's *Mrs. Piggle Wiggle*. Reading books like these to primary grade children enables them to enjoy the language and the stories before they are able to read the books independently. Moreover, it whets their appetite for more of the delightful experiences literature provides.

The range of read-aloud selections for pupils in the middle grades is nearly as great as the field of children's literature itself. Read-aloud selections can range from old favorites like Norton Juster's *The Phantom Tollbooth* and John Steinbeck's *The Red Pony* to titles like Stephen Manes's *Be a Perfect Person in Just Three Days* and Phyllis Reynolds Naylor's *Shiloh*.

Obviously, teachers' choices will depend on grade level, but it is difficult (and often dangerous) to pinpoint a specific grade level to a particular book. Although the background and schemata of a primary grade child may not allow him or her to fully comprehend such realistic fiction as Katherine

9.3 Putting Ideas to Work
Good Books to Read Aloud

Pupils need to hear many types of books read aloud:

humorous books, like Thomas Rockwell's *How to Eat Fried Worms*, Dick King-Smith's *Ace, the Very Important Pig*, and William Steig's *Grown-ups Get to Do All the Driving;*

improbable stories, like Oliver Butterworth's *The Enormous Egg* and Deborah and James Howe's *Bunnicula;*

mysteries, like E. L. Konigsburg's *From the Mixed-Up Files of Mrs. Basil E. Frankweiler* or Bill Brittain's *The Wish Giver;*

fantasies, like Roald Dahl's *Charlie and the Chocolate Factory* or Robert O'Brien's *Mrs. Frisby and the Rats of NIMH;* J. R. R. Tolkien's *The Hobbit*, and C. S. Lewis's *The Lion, the Witch, and the Wardrobe;*

sad books, like Doris Smith's *A Taste of Blackberries* or Wilson Rawls's *Where the Red Fern Grows;*

adventure books, like John Gardiner's *Stone Fox*, Armstrong Sperry's *Call It Courage*, or Lois Lowry's *Number the Stars;*

curriculum-related books, such as Alice Dalgliesh's *The Courage of Sarah Noble* or James and Christopher Collier's *My Brother Sam Is Dead;*

biographies, such as Donald Sobol's *The Wright Brothers at Kitty Hawk*, Carl Sandburg's *Abe Lincoln Grows Up*, and Peter Burchard's *Charlotte Forten: A Black Teacher in the Civil War;*

animal stories, like Sheila Burnford's *The Incredible Journey* and Jim Kjelgaard's *Big Red;*

historical tales, such as Marguerite de Angeli's *The Door in the Wall* and Elizabeth George Speare's *The Sign of the Beaver;*

science fiction, such as Madeleine L'Engle's *A Wrinkle in Time* and Margaret Bechard's *Star Hatching;*

classics, such as Robert Louis Stevenson's *Treasure Island* or Mark Twain's *Tom Sawyer* (teachers often find they have to do a bit of "editing" or explain some of the content and language of these classics to modern-day pupils);

recently published books that have become popular, such as Sid Fleischman's *The Whipping Boy*, Jerry Spinelli's *Maniac McGee*, and Lois Lowry's *The Giver.*

There is no limit to possible read-aloud titles in the classroom! Selections for reading aloud to students appear in books like Jim Trelease's popular *The New Read-Aloud Handbook* (1989) and Eden Ross Lipson's *Parent's Guide to the Best Books for Children* (1991). Good textbooks about children's literature often include lists of read-aloud books as well.

A list of read-aloud books passed from one year's teacher to the next will give a running record of what a class has heard read, although favorite books can certainly be repeated.

Patterson's *The Great Gilly Hopkins* or Betsy Byars's *The Pinballs*, books like E. B. White's *Charlotte's Web* or Patricia MacLachlan's *Sarah, Plain and Tall* have proved popular with pupils at different grade levels. And the myths contained in books like Virginia Hamilton's *In the Beginning: Creation Stories from Around the World* make marvelous read-alouds across the grades.

9.4 Putting Ideas to Work
Oral Recitation Lesson

*H*offman (1985, cited in Reutzel, Hollingsworth and Eldredge, 1994) details an effective three-step procedure for oral reading practice.

In the first phase, the teacher introduces the story, reads it to the pupils as they follow, and discusses the story—including vocabulary and story structure—with the group.

In the second phase, the teacher reviews the story and models oral reading. Students read parts of the story and the teacher makes assignments for the next day.

In the final phase, the teacher begins reading the story, and students read their assigned parts

When a teacher introduces an author to a class by reading the author's book aloud, children often want to read (or hear) more selections from the same author. For example, after hearing Robert Newton Peck's very funny story *Soup*, pupils will likely search out Peck's follow-up books featuring the same puckish character, *Soup and Me* and *Soup for President*.

The read-aloud fare need not be limited to storybooks, of course. Poetry—from the humor of Edward Lear and Shel Silverstein, to the rhythm of David McCord and Robert Louis Stevenson, to the beauty of Aileen Fisher and Eleanor Farjeon—ought to be a staple in the read-aloud diet. Poetry anthologies, with poems for different occasions, can be kept at the teacher's fingertips to be used at a moment's notice. Reading poetry aloud to pupils is especially important because children need to hear poetry read well to learn to enjoy its beauty and understand its significance. Other selections of print—interesting items in newspapers, magazine articles, jokes and riddles, and the like—often are appropriate for reading aloud to students as well.

In a literature-based reading program, reading aloud to pupils is much more than a "time filler" or a "fun activity to break up the day." It is not an extra. Reading to pupils helps them make a favorable connection between the stories they hear and the stories they read themselves. It is also a way to inject literature directly into the lifeblood of reading instruction, a means of creating an awareness and love of books. As such, reading aloud to students is an integral component of literature-based classroom reading instruction.

Reading Aloud by Pupils

Adults engage primarily in silent reading. Children in classrooms spend a significant amount of time reading aloud. Oral reading is an important part of classroom instructional programs. Along with being an effective way to share literature, oral reading helps build reading competency.

Differences Between Oral and Silent Reading

Reading aloud and reading silently both involve the interpretation of printed messages, but there are important differences between the two. Silent reading involves one-to-one communication between a writer and a reader; oral reading involves one-to-many communication as the reader conveys the author's message to an audience. Silent reading is rapid; oral reading is slower because it takes longer to articulate the speech sounds. In oral reading, the reader must accurately pronounce each word; thus, he or she relies heavily on graphophonic cues. In silent reading, the reader can use context to guess at certain words. Silent reading aims primarily at comprehension. Although comprehension is also important in reading aloud, the related demands of oral reading sometimes get in the way of understanding and recalling what one reads.

These differences notwithstanding, teachers often judge a pupil's reading competency by his or her oral reading performance. Students are "good readers" if they can smoothly read a passage from their basal readers; conversely, pupils who do not read aloud well are labeled "poor readers," irrespective of their ability to comprehend what they read. Some teachers consider oral reading a simple and straightforward way of checking on pupil progress.

The assumption that good oral reading strategies automatically transfer to silent reading is not necessarily valid. Although oral and silent reading are indeed related, and though competent readers usually read well both orally and silently, oral reading is not simply an outward manifestation of silent reading ability. Oral reading relies heavily on facility in word recognition; overall reading competency, by contrast, is defined primarily in terms of comprehension. When one considers the relatively limited amount of time that people spend reading aloud as adults, the time children sometimes spend reading aloud in the classroom seems disproportionate. Competency in oral reading is important during adulthood when, for example, reading the minutes of a meeting, reading an announcement or a report to colleagues, sharing a snippet of print with family or friends, or reading to one's children, but the values of oral reading in the classroom sometimes extend beyond these functional situations.

Teachers use oral reading both as a diagnostic and as an instructional tool. In the learning-to-read stage, for example, reading aloud is important in making the transition from word-by-word reading to the natural flow that indicates comprehension of text. Reading the predictable text in Big Books is itself an important way of helping young children learn to read. If children are to realize the full value of oral reading, however, the practice needs to be conducted in a manner consistent with the purposes of oral reading. In other words, *what teachers do* must be consistent with *why they do it*.

Round-Robin Reading

The technique traditionally used for classroom oral reading instruction and practice is the "round-robin" method, described by Austin and Morrison (1963) as:

Around the circle	**'Round the circle**
Or up the row	Out of the text
You read orally	You read aloud
'Til I say, "Whoa!"	'Til I say, "Next."[2]

Just about anyone who has gone to school is familiar with round-robin reading. One child begins reading at a designated point in the text while all the others (supposedly) follow along and monitor their classmate's reading. After a paragraph or two, the teacher calls on the next pupil, and so on until all have had a chance, until they reach the end of the passage, or until the bell rings (whichever comes first).

Memories of this type of oral reading are unpleasant for most people. They remember the dread of waiting to be called on, making mistakes in front of classmates, or drawing laughter as they read. Adults recall furtively looking ahead in anticipation of being called on to read, only to be chided by the teacher for failing to "keep the place."

Despite the wide popularity of the practice, research suggests "that the practice of round-robin reading is suspect. [Researchers] conclude that its use in the classroom is not defensible if comprehension is the goal" (Tierney, Readence, and Dishner, 1995; p. 464).

When one considers the different instructional purposes of oral reading—diagnosing reading needs, developing expression, listening, providing auditory feedback, interacting with others—it is obvious that round-robin reading falls short in many respects. Diagnosis is an individual process, and many readers feel embarrassed about having to expose their oral reading ability (or lack thereof) in a reading group. Expression is best developed in other settings. Round-robin reading can actually hamper listening, because following the lines of print and looking ahead to see one's passage to read can be a distraction instead of an aid to listening.

In short, "in terms of listening and meaning-making, this strategy is a disaster. The children are being reinforced for tuning out," not listening in (Sloan and Latham, 1981; p. 135). Because the practice of round-robin oral reading fails to meet the legitimate purposes of reading aloud, teachers need to explore and practice other alternatives in the literature-based classroom.

Alternatives to Round-Robin Reading

A number of practical alternatives using trade books can replace round-robin oral reading. Some of these alternatives include purposeful oral

[2]Reprinted with permission of Macmillan Publishing Co. from *The First R:* The Harvard Report on Reading in the Elementary Schools by Mary C. Austin and Coleman Morrison. Copyright © 1963 by Macmillan Publishing Company.

9.5 Putting Ideas to Work
One-Liners

An especially effective group activity for helping students develop the oral reading skills involves "one-liners." The teacher selects lines spoken by the characters from a popular children's trade book. For example, the following is a brief sample selected from *The BGF* by Roald Dahl:

> *Don't be sad.*
> *Do you like vegetables?*
> *You mustn't feel bad about it.*
> *Giants is everywhere around.*
> *Aren't you really a little mixed up?*
> *Let's go back inside.*
> *I cannot help thinking about your poor mother and father.*

For oral reading practice, pairs of pupils read the lines with differing interpretations. For example:

> **Don't be sad.** Read pleadingly. Read as a command.
> **Let's go back inside.** Read eagerly. Read reluctantly.
> **I can't help thinking about your poor mother and father.** Read casually. Read sadly.

Using lines like these for practice in interpreting print allows children to focus directly on the elements of expression—pitch, stress, and juncture—that make oral reading effective. Teachers can choose books matched to the reading levels and interests of pupils, or the students themselves can create these exercises based on books they have read and enjoyed.

reading in groups, reading aloud in individual conferences, paired practice, echo reading, audience reading, choral reading, and reading plays and scripts. Each of these activities offers students the opportunity to share literature with those around them.

Group Oral Reading. Children can practice oral reading in instructional groups with trade books as the vehicles of instruction; however, instead of circling the group round-robin fashion, pupils can read selections of text for specific purposes. For example, a teacher could ask a student to "Read the sentence that proves that Keith was happy in his new home." Pupils can share parts of stories that show how characters felt, descriptive passages related to settings, segments that summarize points of conflict, or other passages that are essential to the story. Students can also read with a focus on affective response, as when they share selections that strike them as especially beautiful, fascinating, humorous, or otherwise noteworthy. Pippi Longstocking's very creative account of "schools in Argentina" in Astrid Lindgren's *Pippi Longstocking* is one such selection.

Individual Conferences.   In addition to group work, one-to-one pupil-teacher conferences provide an appropriate setting for working on oral reading. Individual conferences are certainly the most appropriate time to determine the strategies children rely on as they read. Conferences also provide opportunities for valuable one-to-one instructional sessions—teachers can offer direct instruction on strategies using trade books. In this less threatening situation, the teacher can help the pupil use context to construct meaning and explore different ways to attack unfamiliar words (Taylor and Nosbush, 1983). One-to-one sessions are also opportunities for individual discussion and feedback on a child's response to literature.

The tape recorder is a handy device to use during these oral reading conferences. Tape recordings give a pupil direct feedback on his or her oral reading performance. Individual tapes for each student supply a cumulative record of growth throughout the school year, and teachers can discuss these recorded assessments of pupil progress with parents during conferences. Tapes also allow the teacher to review a child's performance several times.

Conferences offer opportunities for personal conversations about books. The conference can be the time when the teacher introduces a book that he or she suspects would be ideal for a particular pupil, to discuss the stories students have been reading, to ask critical-level questions, and to otherwise interact with students concerning literature.

Individual conferences are part of the personalized activity that makes teaching a special profession. Conferences fill a range of functions, not the least of which is the development of oral reading skills.

Paired Practice.   As its name suggests, paired reading takes place when two pupils take turns reading aloud. Both are given material consistent with their reading levels and seated side by side so that each can visually follow what the other is reading. One child reads while the other listens, following along in the text. After ten minutes or so, their roles change. As pupils finish reading, they retell each other what they have just read. Retelling monitors comprehension without using specific questions based on text. Research has shown that paired reading can be very effective in improving children's oral reading (Topping and Lindsay, 1992; Rekrut, 1994).

Paired reading is another dimension of cooperative learning. More fluent readers become models, and less fluent readers practice oral reading in an atmosphere more relaxed than the typical reading group. Teachers can monitor oral reading as pupils read in pairs.

Echo and Shadow Reading.   The practices of echo and shadow reading are related to paired reading. In shadow reading, the teacher, aide, or other competent reader, rather than a peer, models oral reading. The teacher sits slightly behind the student, and both read in unison, with the student attempting to read along as quickly and accurately as possible. At the outset, the teacher reads slightly louder and faster than the pupil, although the pupil eventually takes the lead. In echo reading, the teacher (or aide) reads a

section and the student "echoes" the reading. The purpose of either technique is to help the child achieve a fluent reading pattern.

Audience Reading.   Communicating written messages to a large group of people for a specific purpose is the essence of oral reading. Reading to an audience for the purpose of information or entertainment can give pupils practice in oral reading for authentic purposes in the classroom.

A very practical application of audience reading occurs when older students read stories to groups of younger children. Teachers can arrange, for example, for third graders to read to groups of kindergarten children. The teacher helps the older pupils select appropriate books and prepare the stories. Even the slowest reader in a class can participate by reading a relatively easy book to a lower-grade student. Upper-grade students can also make tape recordings of favorite books to use in primary classrooms. This type of pupil-pupil reading provides models for younger children and gives older children the opportunity to practice effective oral reading skills for a real purpose.

There are plenty of planned and spontaneous opportunities to practice audience reading in the classroom. Teachers can appoint a student each week to read the announcements that frequently arrive at the classroom door. An upper-grade class can read the morning announcements over the school's public address system. (In some schools where literature is especially valued, a very brief book report is part of these morning announcements.) Teachers can appoint a child to read something at the opening of class each day—a poem, a quote for the day, or the daily weather forecast, for example. Pupils practice audience reading when they read their own writing to the class or when they read short excerpts from books they are reporting on. In short, teachers can be on the lookout for the many opportunities that arise to give children a chance to practice their oral reading in front of classmates.

9.6 Putting Ideas to Work
Radio Reading

Searfoss (1975) recommends radio reading as an alternative to conventional round-robin reading in the classroom. The primary instructional goal of this strategy is comprehension rather than word-perfect reading. The four steps in the process are:

1. *Getting started.* This involves selecting material to be read aloud (short informational pieces from newspapers or magazines or brief narrative passages are appropriate) and explaining the ground rules to students.
2. *Communicating the message.* The reader reads; the audience listens. Since the reader's job is to convey information, the reader can change particular words, insert new words, and omit or substitute words as warranted.
3. *Checking for understanding.* The audience briefly discusses content as a check on comprehension. If the meaning is clear, the reader is free to continue. Otherwise, the role of the radio reader rotates to another member of the group.
4. *Clarifying unclear messages.* If audience discussion indicates that the reader has not conveyed meaning accurately, the reader returns to the text and reads the parts needed for audience understanding. Prompting and correcting have no place in radio reading. When readers make errors in reading aloud, listeners need to listen skillfully enough to adjust to the meaning.

Content areas of the curriculum provide occasions for reading nonfiction material to an audience as well. With prior practice, pupils read aloud selections from informational trade books as classmates listen for the ideas and information contained in the passages. This type of oral reading practice provides another way to extend literacy into all areas of the curriculum.

Choral Reading.   Related to the oral language activity of choral speaking, choral reading involves the group rendition of a text—a poem or story passage, for example. In choral reading, everybody reads the same material aloud together. Group oral reading is good for shy children; the experience and the support of reading aloud as part of a group bolsters their reading confidence. The practice provides an effective way to help children develop interpretation and meaning while sharing books such as Bill Martin, Jr., and John Archambault's popular *Chicka Chicka Boom Boom* or Glen Rounds's version of the old favorite *I Know an Old Lady Who Swallowed a Fly.*

Choral reading can be either rehearsed or spontaneous. When it is rehearsed, students receive the material ahead of time, discuss its meaning, and decide how they can read it to reflect their interpretation. They can plan different arrangements: *antiphonal*, with two groups of readers balanced against each other reading alternative segments; *refrain*, involving a solo voice for some lines and groups responding in refrain; *cumulative*, adding or reducing the number of readers for successive parts of the text; or *unison*,

Dramatizing parts of a favorite story is an effective way of bringing literature alive in the classroom.
© Elizabeth Crews/The Image Works

reading an entire selection together. These formal choral reading presentations require the careful selection of material and some preparation time.

Spontaneous choral reading requires less preparation. Occasionally the teacher might say, "Let's all read the poem we've been talking about," or "I want you all to read that final paragraph aloud together, because it sums up nicely the main points the author is trying to make." Books such as Nadine Bernard Wescott's adaptation of the delightful old song *The Lady with the Alligator Purse* or Paul Fleischman's *A Joyful Noise: Poems for Two Voices* provide enjoyable choral reading experiences.

Reading Plays and Scripts. No material is better suited for oral reading in the classroom than plays. In contrast to narrative and expository text, plays are specifically written to be performed or read aloud, and therefore they are ideal for developing and practicing oral reading skills. In a literature-based program, this activity introduces another literary genre—drama—into the reading program. And finally, reading plays directly addresses the affective dimension of reading instruction—pupils love to read them.

Reader's theatre is a technique that teachers can use in having children read plays and scripts. Wolfe (1993) describes how children involved in reader's theatre learn to critically examine the labels often given to them—at risk, learning disabled, or low achiever.

Reader's theatre productions can be relatively simple (as when students read their parts seated on chairs or stools in a "stage" area) or fairly elaborate (as when upper-grade groups stage a program in which they read Mother Goose rhymes or fairy tales to kindergartners, complete with lollipops and balloons). Presenting literature as a simple reader's theatre production is a motivational device for pupils, as well as an opportunity to practice oral reading in an authentic setting.

Students can often adapt popular children's trade books to be read aloud in dramatic form. For example, the writing style in *The Pinballs*, Betsy Byars's moving account of three foster children, lends itself to a three-part

9.7 Putting Ideas to Work

Play Week

A play week is a five-day period devoted to drama and oral reading. In preparation, the teacher selects plays appropriate for classroom use. On Monday, different groups of children receive copies of the plays; plays are matched to groups according to reading level and number of characters. Pupils select (or are assigned) roles and begin reviewing their respective parts. The teacher introduces vocabulary as needed and discusses meaning with students. On Tuesday, pupils continue to practice reading their play together. The last three days of the week are performance days, as the children stage their plays as readers theatre: they read, not memorize and recite, their lines to an audience. Each group might want to use some simple props: "May we borrow your briefcase?" (Yes). "Can I bring in my brother's hunting knife?" (No!).

Play weeks take a little extra planning on the teacher's part. The teacher must locate, review, and select plays. He or she must match the number of characters in each play to the number of children in each group, although adjustments are usually not hard to make. The teacher must also match the reading level of the play to that of the pupils who will perform it, and the whole process must be closely monitored. But when the teacher sees the enjoyment and the enthusiasm that play weeks generate, and when the pupils begin asking for another play week on the Monday morning after the first one, the rewards are well worth the effort.

oral reading performance. The style in which other books are written—for example, Bill Martin, Jr., and John Archambault's *Knots on a Counting Rope,* a story told in an exchange of dialogue between a Navaho grandfather and his blind grandson; Crosby Bonsall's *Mine's the Best,* a simply written exchange between two boys; and Angela Johnson's *Tell Me a Story, Mama,* a mother-and-child conversation that can be read in two parts—adapts well to paired oral reading. As they enjoy other books, students can be alert to books they could share through paired dramatic reading.

There is no shortage of opportunities for pupils to share literature through oral reading. The range of activities teachers use should reflect the variety of purposes they have in bringing literature into the reading program and in helping pupils improve oral reading competency.

Summary and Conclusions

Most elementary classrooms place much emphasis on oral reading, and most teachers spend a significant amount of their time listening to students read aloud. Although oral reading has a number of functions, "the main emphasis is on cognitive learning; hearing reading is not mainly for social interaction or for maintaining individual contact with a child as a means of 'individualized teaching.' Its purpose should be to show children how to use all the cueing systems available to them through positive reinforcement" (Arnold, 1982; p. 81).

Oral reading continues to be an essential part of literature-based reading instruction throughout the grades. In addition to its diagnostic and instructional value, it is an effective vehicle for sharing literature in the community of readers.

The teacher-pupil interaction that typically characterizes shared oral reading provides the teacher with many rich opportunities to teach. During oral reading, teachers can demonstrate and discuss how to use appropriate strategies to process text. They can encourage students to analyze and discuss various dimensions of meaning. The purposes that teachers establish and the questions that they ask help pupils develop the reflective approach characteristic of thoughtful, critical readers. Aside from direct instruction, stories shared through oral reading provide enjoyment and serve as a springboard to additional reading.

Reading aloud is a valuable instructional activity. It can extend beyond the ritual of public performance and into a variety of functional educational experiences. When teachers view oral reading in this way, teachers and pupils have a purpose for reading out loud.

Discussion Questions and Activities

1. It is extremely important to read to children in the home during the emergent literacy stage. Research some of the material on reading aloud to young children, and prepare a document you could share with parents on the importance of reading aloud with their children.
2. Recall your own school experiences. What role did oral reading play? How did you react to reading aloud in the classroom? What do you see as the advantages and disadvantages of oral reading?
3. Examine a lesson in the teacher's edition of a basal reading series. What suggestions does it provide for reading the story orally? How might you adapt or expand the lesson to include oral reading as part of your instructional focus?
4. Select a trade book and develop a lesson plan (or series of plans) using this book to help students develop oral reading fluency. Use some of the techniques suggested in the chapter in your plan (echo reading, paired practice, or one-liners, for example).
5. Make an audio or videotape of your performance as you read a ten-minute segment of a children's book. Have a classmate listen to or view the tape and offer suggestions on how you might improve your delivery.

School-Based Assignments

1. After interviewing teachers from different grade levels make a list of ten books that are popular read-aloud titles. Familiarize yourself with these books.
2. Observe a classroom, noting how much time pupils spend reading aloud during a typical school day. What procedures or strategies does the teacher use in oral reading? Write one or two alternative strategies you might use if you were in charge of the classroom.
3. Brainstorm a list of alternatives to round-robin oral reading in addition to those this chapter suggests. Test some of these alternatives with a small group of students in a classroom.
4. Using the techniques suggested in Putting Ideas to Work 9.2, read a story aloud to a group of pupils. Videotape your performance or have a colleague observe you and provide feedback on your reading.
5. Observe a child reading aloud in a one-to-one setting and, if possible, make an audio or videotape recording of his or her performance. What strategies would you suggest to help this student improve his or her oral reading?

Bechard, Margaret. (1995). *Star Hatching*. New York: Viking.

Bond, Michael. (1973). *Paddington Bear*. New York: Random House.

Bonsall, Crosby. (1973). *Mine's the Best*. New York: Harper & Row.

Brittain, Bill. (1983). *The Wish Giver*. New York: Harper & Row.

Burchard, Peter. (1995). *Charlotte Forten: A Black Teacher in the Civil War*. New York: Crown.

Burnford, Sheila. (1960). *Incredible Journey*. Boston: Little, Brown.

Butterworth, Oliver. (1956). *The Enormous Egg*. Boston: Little, Brown.

Byars, Betsy. (1977). *The Pinballs*. New York: Harper & Row.

Collier, James, and Collier, Christopher. (1974). *My Brother Sam Is Dead*. New York: Four Winds Press.

Dahl, Roald. (1983). *Charlie and the Chocolate Factory*. New York: Penguin.

Dahl, Roald. (1989). *The BGF*. New York: Penguin.

Dalgliesh, Alice. (1954). *The Courage of Sarah Noble*. New York: Scribner.

de Angeli, Marguerite. (1949). *The Door in the Wall*. New York: Doubleday.

Fleischman, Paul. (1988). *A Joyful Noise: Poems for Two Voices*. New York: Harper & Row.

Fleischman, Sid. (1986). *The Whipping Boy*. New York: Greenwillow.

Gardiner, John Reynolds. (1980). *Stone Fox*. New York: Harper & Row.

Hamilton, Virginia. (1988). *In the Beginning: Creation Stories from Around the World*. New York: Harcourt Brace.

Howe, Deborah, and Howe, James. (1979). *Bunnicula*. New York: Atheneum.

Johnson, Angela. (1989). *Tell Me a Story, Mama*. New York: Orchard Books.

Juster, Norton. (1961). *The Phantom Tollbooth*. New York: Random House.

King-Smith, Dick. (1990). *Ace, the Very Important Pig*. New York: Crown.

Kjelgaard, Jim. (1956). *Big Red*. New York: Holiday House.

Konigsburg, E. L. (1967). *From the Mixed-Up Files of Mrs. Basil E. Frankweiler*. New York: Atheneum.

L'Engle, Madeleine. (1962). *A Wrinkle in Time*. New York: Farrar, Straus & Giroux.

Lewis, C. S. (1961). *The Lion, the Witch, and the Wardrobe*. New York: Macmillan.

Lindgren, Astrid. (1950). *Pippi Longstocking*. New York: Viking.

Lowry, Lois. (1989). *Number the Stars*. Boston: Houghton Mifflin.

Lowry, Lois. (1994). *The Giver*. Boston: Houghton Mifflin.

MacDonald, Betty. (1957). *Mrs. Piggle Wiggle*. New York: Harper & Row.

MacLachlan, Patricia. (1985). *Sarah, Plain and Tall*. New York: Harper & Row.

Manes, Stephen. (1982). *Be a Perfect Person in Just Three Days*. New York: Bantam.

Martin, Bill Jr., and Archambault, John. (1987). *Knots on a Counting Rope*. New York: Henry Holt.

Martin, Bill Jr., and Archambault, John. (1989). *Chicka, Chicka, Boom, Boom*. New York: Simon & Schuster.

McCloskey, Robert. (1941). *Make Way for Ducklings*. New York: Viking.

Milne, A. A. (1926). *Winnie-the-Pooh*. New York: Dutton.

Naylor, Phyllis R. (1991). *Shiloh*. New York: Macmillan.

O'Brien, Robert. (1971). *Mrs. Frisby and the Rats of NIMH*. New York: Macmillan.

Paterson, Katherine. (1978). *The Great Gilly Hopkins*. New York: Harper & Row.

Peck, Robert Newton. (1974). *Soup*. New York: Knopf.

Peck, Robert Newton. (1975). *Soup and Me*. New York: Knopf.

Peck, Robert Newton. (1978). *Soup for President*. New York: Knopf.

Peterson, John. (1967). *The Littles*. New York: Scholastic.

Rawls, Wilson. (1961). *Where the Red Fern Grows*. New York: Doubleday.

Rockwell, Thomas. (1973). *How to Eat Fried Worms*. New York: Franklin Watts.

Rounds, Glen O. (1991). *I Know an Old Woman Who Swallowed a Fly*. New York: Holiday House.

Sandburg, Carl. (1954). *Abe Lincoln Grows Up.* New York: Harcourt Brace.
Smith, Doris Buchanan. (1973). *A Taste of Blackberries.* New York: Crowell.
Sobol, Donald J. (1961). *The Wright Brothers at Kitty Hawk.* New York: Scholastic.
Speare, Elizabeth George. (1983). *The Sign of the Beaver.* Boston: Houghton Mifflin.
Sperry, Armstrong. (1940). *Call It Courage.* New York: Macmillan.
Spinelli, Jerry. (1990). *Maniac Magee.* Boston: Little, Brown.
Steig, William. (1995). *Grown-ups Get to Do All the Driving.* New York: HarperCollins.
Steinbeck, John. (1986). *The Red Pony.* New York: Viking.
Stevenson, Robert Louis. (1972). *Treasure Island.* New York: Scholastic. (Other editions available.)
Taylor, Theodore. (1969). *The Cay.* New York: Doubleday.
Tolkien, J. R. R. (1938). *The Hobbit.* Boston: Houghton Mifflin.
Twain, Mark. (1982). *Tom Sawyer.* New York: Simon & Schuster. (Other editions available.)
Waber, Bernard. (1972). *Ira Sleeps Over.* Boston: Houghton Mifflin.
Wescott, Nadine Bernard. (1988). *The Lady with the Alligator Purse.* Boston: Little, Brown.
White, E. B. (1952). *Charlotte's Web.* New York: Harper & Row.

References

Allington, R. L. (1983). Fluency: The Neglected Reading Goal. *The Reading Teacher* 36:556–561.
Arnold, H. (1982). *Listening to Children Read.* London: United Kingdom Reading Association.
Austin, M., and Morrison, C. (1963). *The First R.* New York: Macmillan.
Barrentine, S. J. (1996). Engaging with Reading Through Interactive Read-Alouds. *The Reading Teacher* 50:36–43.
Dowhower, S. L. (1989). Repeated Reading: Research into Practice. *The Reading Teacher* 42:502–507.
Elley, W. (1989). Vocabulary Acquisition from Listening to Stories. *Reading Research Quarterly* 24:174–187.
Hoffman, J. V. (1985). *The Oral Recitation Lesson: A Teacher's Guide.* Austin, TX: Academic Resource Consultants.
Holdaway, D. (1972). *Independence in Reading.* Auckland, New Zealand: Ashton-Scholastic.
Langer, J. A., and Allington, R. L. (1992). Curriculum Research in Writing and Reading. In P. W. Jackson, ed., *Handbook of Research on Curriculum.* New York: Macmillan.
Lipson, E. R. (1991). *Parent's Guide to the Best Books for Children.* New York: Random House.
Lipson, L. Y., and Lang, L. B. (1991). Not as Easy as It Seems: Some Unresolved Questions about Fluency. *Theory into Practice* 30:218–225.
Mathews, M. M. (1966). *Teaching to Read: Historically Considered.* Chicago: University of Chicago Press.
Peterson, R., and Eeds, M. (1990). *Grand Conversations: Literature Groups in Action.* New York: Scholastic.
Pinnell, G. S., Pikulski, J. J., Wixon, K. K., Campbell, J. R., Gough, P. B., and Beatty, A. S. (1995). *Listening to Children Read Aloud.* Washington, DC: U.S. Department of Education.
Rekrut, M. D. (1994). Peer and Cross-Age Tutoring: The Lessons of Research. *Journal of Reading* 37:356–362.
Reutzel, D. R., Hollingsworth, P. M., and Eldredge, J. L. (1994). Oral Reading Instruction: The Impact on Student Reading Development. *Reading Research Quarterly* 29:41–62.

Samuels, S. J. (1979). The Method of Repeated Reading. *The Reading Teacher* 32:403–408.

Savage, J. F. (1978). What Do You Remember about Learning to Read? *New England Reading Association Journal* 13:6–10.

Searfoss, L. W. (1975). Radio Reading. *The Reading Teacher* 29:295–296.

Slater, F. Z., and Allington, R. L. (1991). Fluency and Understanding of Texts. *Theory into Practice* 30:143–148.

Sloan, P., and Latham, R. (1981). *Teaching Reading Is . . .* Melbourne: Thomas Nelson.

Smith, D. D. (1979). The Improvement of Children's Oral Reading Through the Use of Teacher Modeling. *Journal of Learning Disabilities* 12:39–42.

Smith, N. B. (1965). *American Reading Instruction*. Newark, DE: International Reading Association.

Taylor, B. M., and Nosbush, L. (1983). Oral Reading for Meaning: A Technique for Improving Word Identification Skills. *The Reading Teacher* 37:234–237.

Tierney, R. J., Readence, J. E., and Dishner, E. K. (1995). *Reading Strategies and Practices: A Compendium* (4th ed.). Boston: Allyn & Bacon.

Topping, K., and Lindsay, G. A. (1992). The Structure and Development of the Paired Reading Technique. *Journal of Research in Reading* 15:120–136.

Trelease, J. (1989). *The New Read-Aloud Handbook* (2nd ed.). New York: Penguin.

Wolfe, S. A. (1993). What's in a Name? Labels and Literacy in Reader's Theatre. *The Reading Teacher* 46:540–545.

*R*eading-Writing Connections

© James L. Shaffer

Chapter 10 Outline

Features

Key Concepts in This Chapter

Reading and writing are closely related. Both are active, meaning-making processes that require common areas of knowledge. Literature is the glue that holds the reading-writing connection.

Literature generates a response in readers. When this response takes the form of writing, opportunities arise to help pupils develop competence in the many aspects of written language.

Most teachers follow a process-writing model of instruction. Process writing involves a series of stages or steps that writers follow: making a series of prewriting decisions, writing a first draft, and engaging in a series of postwriting activities that lead to publication.

Literature can serve as the focus for classroom writing instruction—the "glue" that forges the reading-writing connection.

Introduction

One of the direct effects of the whole language movement in schools all over the English-speaking world has been an emphasis on the close connection between reading and writing. The closer integration of reading and writing has been called "the single most important change in language instruction" today (Pearson, 1985).

In traditional language arts programs, writing instruction followed reading instruction. Not only were reading and writing taught separately, but even the various components of writing were separated. Spelling, hand-writing, grammar, punctuation, capitalization—each "owned" a separate part of the school program. Separate curriculum guides, separate textbook series, and occasionally different teachers taught each of these areas. The net effect of this practice was skill-and-drill exercises on grammar, punctuation, spelling, and other mechanical aspects of writing, with little time devoted to producing continuous, connected, and meaningful text.

Reading and writing were largely compartmentalized as two separate entities, with little instructional relationship between the two. The words children learned in spelling differed from the vocabulary in the basal reader. The phonics taught during reading was rarely viewed as an aid to spelling. Teachers taught paragraph-writing techniques with little attention to how these techniques could lead to better reading comprehension. In short, programs operated in considerable isolation.

In classrooms today, reading and writing are more closely linked. "A growing body of research has demonstrated that reading and writing are closely related and that both processes can be learned better in connection with each other rather than in isolation" (Noyce and Christie, 1989; p. 3). This close relationship has a lot to do with how we teach both reading and writing in the classroom. Writing during the early years has been called a "natural gateway to literacy" (Jensen, 1993).

What do reading-writing connections have to do with literature-based reading instruction? The link between reading and writing can be forged whether one uses basal readers, trade books, or the print on cereal boxes to teach children how to read. Literature, however, forges more powerful reading-writing connections by providing a generous source of ideas and a focus for writing. Moreover, reading real books by real people, and letting pupils produce purposeful written products that others take seriously, add authenticity to teaching reading and writing simultaneously.

Reading-Writing Relationships

Reading and writing are related in a number of ways. Building on these relationships is the key to literacy development in the classroom.

Reading and writing both deal with written language. Reading involves the intake of ideas through print; writing, the output of ideas through print. Literacy is defined as the ability to read and write. In addition to being related aspects of language, reading and writing are connected through meaning and through instructional activities in the classroom.

The Meaning Connection

Meaning is central to both reading and writing. Making meaning is at the core of the reading-writing connection. Writers construct meaning as they select words and craft language structures that will convey on paper (or on the side of a wall or in some other medium) this meaning to others. Readers construct meaning as they use their knowledge of language and their schemata to mentally shape their own versions of the author's intended message. Reading and writing are essentially similar meaning construction processes. The reader's goal is similar to the writer's; that is, to represent meaning in a comprehensible, coherent framework.

Awareness of the meaning element in both reading and writing develops simultaneously in young children. Instead of the first-reading-then-writing view that prevailed in early childhood education for such a long time, the concept of emergent literacy encourages the development of both aspects of literacy together.

Both reading and writing are cognitive activities, and the thinking processes involved in both are closely connected. Hittleman (1988; p. 28) identifies the thinking processes that connect the two: "The act of composing text allows students to learn how texts work. They learn how to organize information, how to present ideas clearly and without ambiguity, how to establish purposes for communicating, and how to address their writing to particular audiences. The current thinking and research on the integration of reading and writing programs support this conclusion." Reading and writing both involve critical thinking. Teaching pupils to write and read simultaneously has proven to be a very effective way to develop children's critical thinking abilities, better than teaching either activity alone (Tierney et al., 1989).

Reading and writing are both active, thinking operations. Competent readers and writers approach texts in similar ways. Both set goals and mobilize prior knowledge. Both make certain assumptions about their respective audiences. Both tentatively construct meaning, monitor their efforts, and revise according to how well they are meeting their goals.

Rubin and Hansen (1984) identify five areas of knowledge that both have in common:

1. *Information knowledge,* including topical knowledge and grammatical background. This is what both readers and writers use to construct text. "Information that is gained in reading is one possible source of content for writing" (Rubin and Hansen, 1984; p. 6).
2. *Structural knowledge,* which includes the organizational patterns writers use when they write and readers recognize when they read.

"Writers produce text with structures; readers use these structures when they construct meaning" (Rubin and Hansen, 1984; p. 7).

3. *Transactional knowledge,* an awareness of writing as a medium of communication between author and reader.
4. *Aesthetic knowledge,* or knowledge of aesthetic devices such as style or topics that generate appeal.
5. *Process knowledge,* an awareness of the elements common to both reading and writing.

Meaning, then, is a crucial element in reading-writing connections. Readers construct meaning from text. Writers construct meaning as they build language structures to convey their thoughts and ideas in written form.

The Language Connection

In addition to having a meaning connection, reading and writing are connected through language. As they write about literature, students develop competencies in both reading and writing. Evidence suggests that students who write about what they read comprehend better (Kelly, 1990). At the same time, when children write about books, they learn to process successive units of language. Research shows that both reading and writing draw from the same pool of cognitive and linguistic understandings (Moore, 1995). They help children develop skills in the following areas:

Encoding/decoding words. Writing requires that pupils attend to the details of words. The sound-symbol relationships students must know to decode unfamiliar words as they read are the same ones they need to know in order to spell the words they write. Pupils need to know that the letter *b* represents the phoneme /b/ in sounding out the unfamiliar word *baboon;* they need the same knowledge to write a story about a *balloon.*

Writing sentences. Sentence construction is essential to both reading and writing. Effective writing is characterized by well-constructed sentences. At the same time, an understanding of sentence construction is essential to reading comprehension. In fact, the ability to match sentences with similar meanings has been used as a measure of children's reading comprehension (Simons, 1971; Brown, Hammill, and Wiederholt, 1986).

Developing paragraphs. In paragraphs, reading and writing are related in terms of structure and organization. Writers produce text with structure; readers who understand those structures better comprehend what they read. Pupils apply their knowledge of structural patterns both as they read and as they write.

Writing longer selections. Children learn about story structure as they deal with literature. They become aware that a well-constructed story has a beginning, a middle, and an end, and that stories revolve around a conflict or a problem. As they develop sophistication, they become aware of the roles character and setting play. They see how description and dialogue are used to tell stories. As they become aware of these elements in the stories they read, pupils also become more sensitive to these elements in the stories they write.

Reading and writing are not only two sides of the same coin of written language, they are aspects of learning that can develop simultaneously as children use literature in the classroom.

The Instructional Connection

Reading and writing are related instructionally as well; teaching one necessarily involves teaching the other. Shanahan (1988) suggests seven instructional principles based on research about the connection between reading and writing:

1. *Reading and writing both need to be taught.* Although closely related, they are independent enough to merit direct, daily, separate attention in the classroom.
2. *Both should be introduced from the earliest years.* Since reading ability is not a prerequisite for writing development, writing can be one focus of instruction from the early stages of a child's school (or preschool) life.
3. *The relationships between reading and writing need to be emphasized in different ways at different stages of a pupil's development.* At the very early stages, the decoding-encoding connections may deserve stress; later, cognitive connections—linking the meaning-making processes in both—may need emphasis.
4. *Reading-writing connections must be made explicit.* The transfer of knowledge between reading and writing is not automatic; teachers need to focus specifically on the relationship to heighten pupils' awareness of it.
5. *Content and process relationships should be emphasized.* Knowing what to do and how to do it are important in both reading and writing. For example, whether reading or writing, pupils need to know whether meaning is clear, and if not, how to take action.
6. *Communicative aspects of reading and writing should be stressed.* Reading and writing forge a communicative connection between a reader and an author. This connection should be stressed through author awareness activities and other programs.
7. *Reading and writing should be taught in meaningful contexts.* Children should practice both for a variety of purposes in the classroom.

These, then, are the major connections between reading and writing: both are meaning-making processes that involve language; both involve common understandings essential to processing print; and both can be taught concurrently in the classroom. "Reading and writing need to be viewed as supportive and interactive processes whereby what is learned from reading can be used when writing, and what is learned by writing can foster an appreciation for authorship and reading" (Kolczynski, 1989; p. 76).

Writing cements this reader-writer relationship. "Research advancing this perspective has suggested that reading, like writing, is composition, that both writing and reading involve 'transactions' between a reader and a text, that an awareness of the author-reader relationship is central to both reading

and writing, and that the writing process includes reading. This view recognizes the central fact of reading and writing—they are instances of communication between people" (Rubin and Hansen, 1984; p. 4).

Responding to Literature

Literature typically generates a response, and often, that response is emotional. Young children show delight by clapping their hands to the rhythm of language and repeating the request, "Read it again!" Children's literature can also evoke an emotional response in adults. Many mature adults get misty-eyed when they read Robert Munsch's simple *Love You Forever* or Tomie de Paola's *Now One Foot, Now the Other,* two children's stories about the relationship between young people and older people. Few refrain from shedding a tear when Leslie dies in Katherine Patterson's *Bridge to Terabithia* or when they learn the fate of the animals at the end of Wilson Rawls's *Where the Red Fern Grows.* The fact that authors can make us care so much about what we read is evidence of the power and value of literature in classroom reading programs.

Reader response is an essential component of literature-based reading. Reader response theory is based on the notion that a transaction occurs between a reader and a text. Rosenblatt (1982) distinguishes between *efferent* responses and *aesthetic* responses. Efferent responses focus on knowledge or information taken away from a text; aesthetic responses focus more on an emotional reaction. "Any reading event falls somewhere on the continuum between the aesthetic and the efferent poles" (Rosenblatt, 1982; p. 269), and elements of both aesthetic and efferent response may arise in any encounter with print. Although a reader's response may be primarily aesthetic when Charlotte the spider dies in E. B. White's *Charlotte's Web,* readers also come away with knowledge about spiders and pigs and the type of man Farmer Zukerman was. Similarly, readers carry away information about how fossils are created in Byrd Baylor and Peter Parnall's *If You Are a Hunter of Fossils,* but the poetic nature of the language evokes an aesthetic response as well.

Literary response is not a simple, singular process. It depends on a constellation of factors, including readers' "cognitive abilities, their stance toward reading, personality orientations, social-cognitive competencies, knowledge of literature, and language conventions" (Beach and Hynds, 1991; p. 480). All these factors influence how readers infuse meaning into text as part of the comprehension process. Classroom responses to literature are an integral part of literacy development. They include oral language responses, artistic responses, and written language responses.

Responding Orally

Pupils can respond to literature through a variety of oral language activities in the classroom. Oral language competency is the foundation for literacy. Classroom oral language activities help develop the thinking, vocabulary, audience awareness, listening, and fluent expression essential to effective communication.

Talking about books is a natural response among children. Focusing that talk on books in the classroom—from class discussions on shared literature to "grand conversations" in smaller literature circles—stimulates children's interest in literature as well as provides opportunities to develop oral language skills.

Responding Artistically

Another common response to literature in the elementary grades is art. Pupils produce a variety of artistic products from simple illustrations to detailed dioramas in response to books they have read and enjoyed. Teachers engage pupils in using a variety of media—from paints and crayons to fabric and metal—to produce artistic products in response to literature. As they dictate or write summary captions for their artwork, students move toward the common response of writing.

Some teachers have also helped children respond musically. The class may select a musical selection to accompany a scene or chapter.

Responding in Writing

The written response to literature forms the foundation of the reading-writing connection in a literature-based program. Pupils can respond to literature through various forms of writing, from personal-response journals that reflect spontaneous feelings (Karolides, 1992) to more detached forms of responses such as reports or letters. Each written response offers children the opportunity to develop skills in reading and writing at the same time.

10.1 Putting Ideas to Work
Oral Language Responses to Literature

Oral responses to literature can take many forms in the classroom. The possibilities include:

Storytelling.   Pupils can take turns retelling different parts of a serial folktale such as *Why Mosquitoes Buzz in People's Ears,* an African tale retold by Verna Aardema; or they might retell another aspect of a familiar fairy tale, as Teresa Celsi did in *The Fourth Little Pig,* an easy-to-read account of how the three little pigs encounter the fourth little pig (their sister), who tells her brothers to get a life, or as Alexander Wolf (actually author Jon Scieszka) did in *The True Story of the Three Little Pigs.*

Creative dramatics.   Students can act out old favorites like *The Three Billygoats Gruff* or improvise stories like Nonnie Hogrogian's *One Fine Day,* an ideal story for dramatization about a fox who goes on a prolonged search to get his amputated tail sewn back on. Dramatic activities can include puppetry, as children create characters with simple puppets from sticks, paper bags, or socks.

Discussion.   Groups can engage in critical thinking and problem solving by discussing the fairness of Thelma's actions in Russell Hoban's *A Bargain for Frances* or the racial prejudice that the Logan family encounters in Mildred Taylor's *Roll of Thunder, Hear My Cry.*

Dialogue.   Referring to teachers as "curators of literature," Eeds and Peterson (1991) suggest ways teachers can focus pupils' attention on literary elements (structure, character, time and place, point of view, mood, and symbolism) through dialogue, as students share their reactions in literature study groups. Eeds and Peterson also describe the literary insights children develop as they talk about such books as John Gardiner's *Stone Fox,* Frances Hodgson Burnett's *The Secret Garden,* and Allan Eckert's *Incident at Hawk's Hill.*

Oral reports.   Pupils can report orally on informational trade books they have found especially interesting, such as Robert Quackenbush's *Oh, What an Awful Mess!,* the biographical account of how Charles Goodyear invented rubber, or R. R. Knudson's biography *Babe Didrickson, Athlete of the Century.*

Choral speaking.   Students can select poems that lend themselves especially well to large group recitation— poems with dialogue and contrasts in mood, question-and-answer poetry ("Who has seen the wind?"), ballads, and poems with humor and repeated language ("I know an old woman who swallowed a fly").

Opportunities for oral language experiences with books are virtually limitless: songs, puppets, finger plays, sharing, news time, readers' theatre adaptations of favorite stories, and other activities are all appropriate for responding orally to literature.

Literature response journals or literature logs allow students to generate written responses to books from a personal perspective. A journal is a personal invitation to pupils to think and write about what they have read. Salinger (1996) describes literature logs as "records of [children's] thinking about their reading and their questions and observations during reading" (p. 277).

Literature response journals or logs are personal forms of writing. In the early stages, the teacher can model a log entry on a chart. Prompts can be open-ended or structured ("Tell how you felt when you read the part of *Sylvester and the Magic Pebble* when Sylvester's parents could not find him.").

10.2 Putting Ideas to Work
Pupils Respond to Books

*T*he following pieces of writing show two samples of pupils' responses to books. They are not intended to set standards for judging other children's responses; they are simply examples.

Sometimes responses can be intensely personal. After reading stories about teddy bears—*Corduroy; Ira Sleeps Over; Hi Bears, Bye Bears;* and others—Juanita wrote the following in her journal:

> The bear stories made me think of Fuzz. Fuzz is my stuffed bear. He's precshous to me because my dad gave him tome before he moved to Huston. He is two feet tall and has fluffy gray hair. When I am full of sad, Fuzz understands. When no one is home, I think of my dad and hug Fuzz.

Continued on next page.

Formats can be open, double entry (with quotes on the left side of the page and space for a reaction on the right side), or any other form that fits the class's needs. The one rule is that the task should not be so overwhelming that it interferes with the child's enjoyment of the literature.

Response journals or logs not only give children a way to express personal thoughts about a book; they also involve pupils in constructing meaning through reading and writing, encourage critical thinking, and move students beyond writing mere summaries of their reading. Sometimes, these journals consist of thoughts about and reactions to the events and characters children encounter as they read. At other times, they are learning logs that apply across the curriculum. At all times, they record in writing a child's reaction to what he or she has read.

A considerable body of research has grown around the theory and practice of literature response journals. Kelly (1990) describes a program that used personal response very effectively with third graders to add "a substantive element to the literature program." Building on the work of Bleich (1987) and Petrosky (1982), the teacher supplied three prompts: (1) "What did you notice

At other times, responses are more objective. Jon was part of a literature group reading survival tales. Here's his response to *Hatchet* by Gary Paulsen:

Hatchet

Nov. 8

More trouble for Brian! A storm blew across the lake and recked his shelter. He'll build a new one.

I admire Brian. He's brave and smart because he can figure out how to live alone in the woods.

In the end, I think he will be saved. Like the kid in ~~the~~ My Side of the Mountain, someone will come along and save him.

in the story?" (2) "How did the story make you feel? "and (3) "What does the story remind you of in your own life?" (p. 466). These prompts provide a framework for discussion and writing. After they practiced group responses orally, the third graders moved on to respond through writing. As they practiced, their written responses increased in length and fluency and showed greater depth of understanding and higher levels of comprehension.

Tomkins (1990) suggests a similar plan for generating pupil responses to literature. Each day, the teacher reads a chapter of a popular book to the class. Students spend ten minutes writing an entry about the chapter in a log or journal. Their entries are personal responses; that is, instead of summarizing the chapter, the children write about their favorite characters, how the story relates to their own lives, how it makes them feel, or how they might change the events in the story. Their writing thus involves them in the story.

Wollman-Bonilla and Werchadlo (1995) describe literature response journals in first grade. After teachers modeled responses to books they had read aloud, the children began to generate and share their own responses. As their reading independence grew, so did the length and variety of the responses the children wrote. In the first grade classroom, the interconnections among reading, writing, discussing, and thinking became apparent, and children engaged more deeply with literature through their response journals.

Smith (1995) demonstrated the positive impact reader response journals reflected when African American children responded to literature that closely mirrored their own cultural frame of reference—that is, stories and poems by and about African Americans.

Working with upper elementary grade pupils, Hancock (1993) explored the ways students can respond to literature in journals. These include: *personal meaning making* (monitoring understanding, making inferences, making and validating predictions, and expressing wonder); *character and plot involvement* (character interaction and assessment, as well as involvement in the story plot), and *literary evaluation* (critical response).

Literature response journals can take many forms, but they lead children in the same direction—toward a greater involvement in literature.

Buddy journals are a related form of personal response to literature. Bromley (1989) cited three important reasons for making connections between reading and writing: "First, we know that reading and writing develop simultaneously. Second, reading and writing reinforce each other. Third, through reading and writing, language is used for communication" (p. 122). Bromley goes on to describe buddy journals as one way to connect reading and writing. As the name suggests, a buddy journal is a written diary or log that pairs of pupils share with each other. By exchanging journals, pupils carry on a real and meaningful "written conversation." The writing is functional, the activity is interactive, and the feedback is immediate. Frequently, teachers respond to what students write in their buddy or dialogue journals. When books are the basis for the students' exchange of ideas, literature cements the reading-writing connection.

10.3 Putting Ideas to Work
Guidelines for Literature Response Journals

*H*ancock (1993) suggests several guidelines for encouraging a variety of responses to literature, "to awaken the reader to possible outlets for exploring literature through response" (p. 471).

The first five points set the environment for the response:

Feel free to write your innermost feelings, opinions, thoughts, likes and dislikes. This is your journal.

Take time to write down anything you are thinking as you read.

Don't worry about the accuracy of spelling and mechanics in the journal.

Record the page number you were reading when you wrote your response. You might want to look back to verify your thoughts.

One side only of your spiral notebook paper, please.

The next five points suggest response options:

Relate the book to your own experiences and share similar moments from your life or from books you have read in the past.

Ask questions while reading to help you make sense of the characters and the unraveling plot.

Make predictions about what you think will happen as the plot unfolds. Validate or change these predictions as you proceed.

Talk to the characters as you begin to know them.

Praise or criticize the book, the author, or the literary style.

The final point invites the writer to discover or develop additional avenues of response.

There is no limit to the types of responses you may write. Your honesty in capturing your thoughts throughout the book is your most valuable contribution to the journal. These guidelines are meant to trigger, not limit, what you write.

Guidelines from Hancock, Marjorie R. (1993, March) Exploring and extending personal response through literary journals. *The Reading Teacher*, 46:466–474. Reprinted with permission of Marjorie R. Hancock and the International Reading Association. All rights reserved.

Writing in the literature-rich classroom flourishes when the emphasis is on responding to trade books. Phillips (1989) compared the writing of two groups of students, one exposed to a rich diet of literature and one that had progressed through a conventional basal reading program. After analyzing 1,200 samples of the children's writing, she concluded the literature group "was much more sophisticated in this writing as evidenced in the increasing complexity in vocabulary and sentence structure. The length, fluency and literary quality of the literature class's writing flourished" (p. 1).

Such dramatic results are hardly surprising. Children tend to mimic language they see and hear. If skill development materials are the only language models they are exposed to, pupils will likely write by controlling their vocabularies, maintaining simplistic sentence structure, and repeating ideas. When they are frequently exposed to high-quality writing, however, and when adults and peers take them seriously as authors, children become more meaningful and sophisticated in written expression. Words that pupils encounter in their reading appear in their writing over and over again.

One way to promote the reading-writing connection is to let pupils learn about what famous authors were like as children. Some delightful autobiographical accounts of well-known children's authors describe the early experiences that shaped their lives as authors. Through activities that promote author awareness, students begin to see the connection between everyday experiences and stories produced by people like Roald Dahl, Beverly Cleary, and other authors they know and love.

In using literature (or any other topic) to develop children's writing abilities, schools today almost universally utilize a model called process writing. Process writing involves a series of steps or stages, and literature has its place at every point along the way.

Process Writing

Process writing is a theory, along with a set of instructional practices based on the theory, about teaching pupils how to write. Instead of focusing primarily on written products—stories, poems, reports, letters, and other pieces of writing children produce—the instructional focus is on the writing process, the steps writers follow as they produce a written product. "The idea of writing as a process arrived on the educational scene in the mid-1960s. Its swift and almost universal acceptance marked it as a 'paradigm shift,' a new way of understanding, which at once rendered traditional 'product-centered composition teaching' as obsolete" (Walshe, 1988; p. 212).

The writing process starts long before the teacher says, "Take out your pencils and papers," and goes beyond the inevitable "The End" children pen with a flair of finality as they conclude their writing. Process writing involves all the thoughts and activities that occur from the time the writer makes the decision to write until the time when the final product is completed. Generally, the process is divided into four stages: (l) prewriting, (2) drafting, (3) editing/revising, and (4) publishing.

Prewriting

Prewriting is the first stage of the writing process. This planning and organizational stage consists of a series of decisions—decisions about why to write, what to write about, which aspect of the topic to focus on, who the audience will be, and which approach to take.

In many instances, a child decides to write because the teacher says, "Take out your pencils" (or the professor says, "Term projects are due next Tuesday"). Classroom writing should meet the range of authentic purposes for literacy—it should be at times social, imaginative, informative, and persuasive. Literature can be the springboard for many writing experiences; ideas from literature often motivate children to write. After enjoying the best of their

10.4 Putting Ideas to Work

"I Don't Have Nothin' to Write About"

The common complaint "I don't have nothin' to write about" can often be overcome by invoking some of the imaginative stories so frequently found in children's books. For example, the teacher could suggest that a student write a story based on the outrageous improbability of the actions of such animals as:

the cat who wreaks havoc in Dr. Seuss's widely known and greatly loved *The Cat in the Hat*;

the bear who wakes the little boy in the middle of the night and asks the boy to remove his sore tooth in David McPhail's delightful fantasy *The Bear's Toothache*;

the exotic animals who invade the girl's home in Mercer Mayer's wonderful *What Do You Do with a Kangaroo?*; and

the jungle animals who appear in the living room of Judy and Peter's home as the children play the intriguing board game in Chris Van Allsburg's *Jumanji*.

These stories provide children with a springboard for developing story ideas—the children can imagine animals in improbable situations and write stories around their ideas.

literary heritage, pupils often want to engage in telling stories themselves. The key is the spark of motivation that turns "have to" into "want to."

Literature provides models as well as motivation. In the beginning stages of writing, models of form can be important, even essential. In using literature to provide models, a prewriting discussion might focus on reproduction versus innovation—that is, the extent to which students should initiate the models versus the extent to which they should move out on their own. Children exposed to fairy tales and fantasy in the very early grades begin to include sophisticated writing features in their own writing (Phillips, 1989). Upper elementary students who have been exposed to stories about Paul Bunyan and Mike Fink are ready to write their own tall tales, replete with the exaggeration and humor they find in the models. Models are essential for writing poetry, especially for poems like limericks and haiku, which adhere more strictly to form than many other types of poetry.

Finding something to write about is an early step in the prewriting process. Children's lives are full of experiences and their heads are full of dreams, but they often need to be convinced that their lives are an appropriate topic for their writing. Prewriting includes opportunities to brainstorm about ideas for stories, with a specific focus on the vocabulary that is necessary to write the story. When pupils are familiar with literature, they often realize that wonderful stories can be generated from everyday ideas, events, and feelings. Reading a book like Beverly Cleary's *Dear Mr. Henshaw* or Patricia Reilly Giff's *The Beast in Ms. Rooney's Room* can give students the sense that their ordinary home or school experiences are indeed worthy subjects for written work.

Trade books also show pupils how to approach a topic, which aspects to include, and how to focus on detail in relating incidents from their lives. The writer's focus on detail is like the photographer's angle when using a camera. The photographer must decide whether to take a picture of the entire castle or a close-up of a gargoyle under the eaves. The author must decide whether to write about a larger experience ("What I Did on Summer Vacation") or on only one aspect of that experience ("The Day I Pitched for the Mets"). Trade books can help students learn to apply this sense of focus to their writing. Very few of us haven't dreamed of taking to the air and flying above our neighborhoods. Pupils can see how Peter Spier treated this fantasy in *Bored—Nothing to Do*.

Deciding on form is another prewriting decision; often the same topic might work in a narrative story, an expository text, a poem, a personal letter, an advertisement, or another form of written response. *Dear Mr. Henshaw*, for example, is a story told from personal letters, and many of Shel Silverstein's poems tell stories as well.

Identifying an audience is another important prewriting decision. "The purpose of writing is not to arrange ink on paper, to provide a mirror for the author's thoughts, but to carry ideas and information from the mind of one person into the mind of another" (Murray, 1968; p. 3). Determining the audience helps define the appropriate tone, form, and style. In responding to a book, for example, pupils can write a journal entry about how the book made them feel, a recommendation for the book in a letter to a pen pal, a concise and factual "index card" review for classmates to use in deciding whether to read the book, or a story about a character or episode to be displayed in the school corridor for all to read. The possibilities vary enormously.

Prewriting also includes incubation time, a time to allow children's ideas to jell and take shape. In some ways, the entire prewriting stage is a time for mental and verbal gestation. During this stage of the writing process, pupils can discuss with both teacher and peers the focuses, formats, and voices open to them, and they can organize their ideas into a meaningful structure.

The prewriting steps cannot be reduced to any predetermined order, or to a recipe that will include a cup of motivation, a pound of critical analysis, a pinch of brainstorming, and ten minutes of conferencing with the teacher. Prewriting activities depend on the nature of the writing activity, the grade and ability levels of the writers, the goals of the teacher, and many other factors. What is important is that prewriting be a part of the classroom writing process.

Writing

Writing is the second stage of the process, the time when pupils commit their ideas to paper. After making some prewriting decisions on what they want to say and how they want to say it, children now practice using the tools of the writer's trade. In their writing, their ideas take form. Details are reduced to words, key points to phrases. Thoughts are forged into sentences,

Literature cements the reading-writing connection as children respond in writing to stories and poems they read.
© James L. Shaffer

and sentences are gathered into paragraphs. The act of composing is going on. Atwell (1987) suggests ways to promote the reading-writing connection in the writing workshop, since students look at what they have written from a reader's point of view, and she suggests some practical ways to promote this concept.

Writing time is a busy time. The classroom takes on a workshop atmosphere. Not all children sit quietly to write. While some are still fiddling with ideas and deciding on form, others are busily engaged in the writing act itself. The teacher is an active participant in the workshop environment. This is not the time to straighten out the lunch and picture money, correct the math homework, or tidy up the desk. Rather, the teacher is a mobile and visibly available observer and consultant, an adult audience who provides reaction, a resource to advise one pupil on the choice of a word and another on the organization of a paragraph, a coach to provide a few words of encouragement here and a little prodding there, a referee to adjudicate conflicting peer responses, a diagnostician to give instruction on specific areas of writing when individual students need a little extra help. What the teacher encounters during this time often suggests areas of widespread instructional need—problems with punctuation, run-on sentences, subject-predicate agreement, or other troublesome aspects that might be addressed in large or small group instruction.

In addition to offering an opportunity to confer with individual students, the writing time provides teachers with an opportunity to do a little writing themselves. "There is nothing better for increasing awareness of the true artistry in words than attempting the process yourself" (Eeds and Peterson, 1991; p. 175). Teacher modeling has a powerful influence on pupil

10.5 Putting Ideas to Work
Invented Spelling

When children write in first-draft form, they often use *invented spelling,* attempting to spell a new word according to the way it sounds. Parents (and some teachers) sometimes raise questions about this practice, but children go through predictable developmental stages on their way to competency in conventional spelling. They progress through:

> *Random spelling,* stringing random letters and pseudoletters together in an attempt to create a message, often with no phonemic resemblance to conventional orthography (*NTXQ* for "I love you").
>
> *Prephonemic* or *early phonemic spelling,* when the child shows a primitive awareness of the alphabetic principle and may represent words with one or two letters (*LV* for "I love you," or *I wnt to my fatrsant dirdy* for "I went to my father's aunt's birthday").
>
> *Phonetic spelling,* when children begin to match letters more directly to sounds, often by letter name (*SAVNRG* for "Save energy").
>
> *Transitional spelling,* when children begin to use the conventional spelling system, to show awareness of standard print, and to spell some words correctly (*Thay saled away on the bote* for "They sailed away on the boat").
>
> *Conventional spelling,* when the child applies standard orthographic rules consistently (although only a very fortunate few achieve the rules, just as very few achieve absolute happiness).

Weaver (1988) documents these stages of invented spelling with abundant examples of children's work.

Invented spelling is a normal part of children's language development and certainly part of the reading-writing connection. It is a powerful indicator of early literacy awareness. A child's attempt to "spell words like they sound" indicates a developing awareness of the phoneme-grapheme relationships in our language, just as "sounding out words" does in reading.

behavior. When teachers write, they can discuss their own development as writers in group conferences.

It should be clear from the outset that in their written responses to literature, as in all their classroom writing, students first write in first-draft form. Rare and talented indeed is the writer—whether a Pulitzer Prize winner, a young child, or an undergraduate student—who can take pen in hand and produce a polished product on the first attempt. The first version should be a draft that allows pupils to experiment with putting meaning on paper.

If students and teachers understand that every writing experience starts with a first draft, they don't need to worry about spelling, word usage, punctuation, handwriting, and other mechanical matters of form at the beginning. The first draft is a starting point. The best advice that teachers can give pupils during this writing phase is to get their ideas down on paper. "For now, write your story so that you can read it to an audience. If you can't spell a word, write it down the way it sounds and we can get it right later on."

10.6 Putting Ideas to Work
Research on Good Instructional Practices

Applebee and his colleagues (1993) identify a number of conditions that contribute to success in learning to write. These include:

a school environment that values writing and reinforces high standards of achievement;

writing assignments that range over a wide variety of genres and topics;

an instructional environment that introduces students to the strategies accomplished writers draw upon to further their own writing (for example, planning, drafting, and revising strategies);

writing assignments that encourage sustained involvement over a period of time, allowing multiple drafts and time for reflection and revision;

ongoing response to and evaluation of works-in-progress, often through a writing partner or small group;

a shift in emphasis in grading and evaluation from correctness in form toward quality of thought and ability to sustain and elaborate an argument or point of view.

Collectively, these conditions are often referred to as "process-oriented instruction" or "process writing." (pp. 120–121)

Source: *NAEP 1992 Writing Report Card* by A. N. Applebee, Langer, J. A., Mullis, I. S., Lathem, A. S. and Gentele, A. S. (1993) Washington, DC: U.S. Department of Education.

Correctness in writing is important, however, because it contributes to the ultimate effectiveness of written communication. Teachers and pupils can address mechanics as children revisit their writing during the editing/revising stage, because review and revision are integral components of the writing process.

Editing and Revising

Editing and revising are important parts of writing. Editing involves proof-reading and working to ensure that all words are spelled correctly, all sentences are complete and begin with capital letters and end with proper punctuation marks, and that the writing is mechanically sound. The editing phase is more than a search for errors; it is a chance to help children develop an *attitude* of independent self-appraisal. A major aim is to help pupils take responsibility for shaping their writing into an effective form.

Revising focuses on meaning and clarity, with an eye to interesting word choice, sentence variety and linguistic complexity, paragraph organization, clarity of ideas, and sensitivity to form and content that contribute to overall effectiveness in writing.

Revising takes place during reading, too, though we may not often realize it. As good readers read, they "examine their developing interpretations and view the model they build as draft-like in quality" (Tierney and Pearson, 1983; p. 576). The more serious the reader or writer is, the more thoughtful the reading is likely to be. If you jot a note to your roommates to tell them you have gone shopping, you probably do not need to carefully draft or revise. Nor would you pause to ponder over a similar note from one of them. But if you were reading a serious letter from a loved one or preparing a piece of important work you know you will be judged on, you would most likely reflect on the writing and develop an interpretation that might require several revisions over time. Fitzgerald (1989) explains that the revision stage of the writing process is closely related to critical reading because both draw on similar thinking processes. Throughout the writing process, writers cast a critical eye on what they are writing. At the revision stage, authors examine what they have written in comparison to the anticipated expectations of their readers; that is, they judge the "fit" between what they have written and what they expect their readers to understand. This careful examination of text is the essence of critical reading.

Part of the editing/revising stage of the writing process involves writer's conferences. As time allows, the teacher meets with individual pupils to discuss their writing. The teacher's role is not primarily to find errors, but to show how the young writer can make improvements and to identify problems in such a way that pupils see they can overcome them. Graves (1983) and Calkins (1986) have effectively detailed the role the teacher can play in the conference.

Effective writing conferences focus on the writing process as well as on the product. The teacher talks about where the child got his or her ideas, decided on how to approach the topic, selected the language, and might go about editing. In addition to these process-oriented issues, the conference also focuses on mechanics such as ensuring complete sentences, checking over spelling, and reviewing grammatical structure.

Peer conferences are also appropriate, as students discuss each other's writing with partners or in small groups. With demonstration, modeling, discussion, and guided practice, pupils become adept at helping each other in postwriting activities. In the safe and supportive atmosphere of the classroom writing workshop, they can let each other know whether their writing successfully entertains, informs, or convinces (depending on its purpose), and they can suggest improvements. When children read and react to each other's writing, they become more aware of what makes their own writing more effective. The link between reading and writing is forged as pupils read each other's writing with an eye to constructing meaning in text.

Fitzgerald (1989) suggests that group conferences on student writing can help children become better critical readers and writers. In a supportive and trusting environment, small groups of pupils take turns reading their writing aloud. To stimulate discussion, the teacher asks questions: "What was the piece about? What do you like about it? Do you have any comments, questions, or suggestions for the author?" Students then revise their writing based on the feedback they receive in these conferences.

Feedback and comments need to be constructive and positive. Children can learn to ask questions such as "What other words might you use?"

10.7 Putting Ideas to Work

Using the Word Processor

*I*f the computer has influenced one area of classroom literacy instruction more than others, that area is writing. Word processing is especially useful in the postwriting stage of the writing process.

Word processing programs have proven to be effective instructional tools in teaching writing. Bragert-Drowns (1993) reviewed 32 research studies that compared students who used word processing in writing versus those who didn't. Based on this research, he concluded that word processing improved the quality and length of what they wrote. Similarly, the nation's *Writing Report Card* (Applebee et al., 1993) reported great differences in word processing availability in the top-performing schools versus the lowest-performing schools: "Computers were less likely to be available at all for writing instruction in the bottom-performing schools" (p. 11). The relationship between writing proficiency and the computer changed through the grades. In grade 4, poorer students most often used computers; by twelfth grade, higher-achieving students were using the computer much more for writing.

Most students are motivated when using computers. Once they have mastered basic keyboard skills, they often find typing easier than using pens and paper. The computer aids every part of the writing process: brainstorming and listing ideas at the prewriting stage, composing first drafts at the writing stage, and editing and revising at the postwriting stage. The writer can use programs to guide proofreading; he or she can also quickly correct spelling, especially with the aid of a spellchecker; substitute more colorful words for their less interesting counterparts; easily revise by adding words or combining sentences; and move whole blocks of print effortlessly. Conferencing, peer editing, and revising become relatively painless when pupils work with their writing on a screen.

With word processors, students make more revisions and produce neater, more error-free text. By easing mechanical difficulties in editing and revising, word processing allows the writer to attend to higher-order decisions.

Beyond revision, computers also allow children to print their writing so that their stories, poems, letters, and reports take on a more professional appearance. Sophisticated programs allow students to create stories with elaborate graphics, including video segments. Computers can promote the communicative aspects of writing as well—students can send their writing to readers across town or around the country.

Scores of user-friendly word processing programs are available for young writers. Since this field is developing at an astounding speed, more are sure to follow.

rather than make comments such as "That's a dumb word to use!" Teachers can model this constructive approach, always sans red pen.

Based on feedback and revision, pupils produce a final draft. Rewriting has conventionally been viewed as punishment, the price one must pay for carelessness or stupidity (or both) in one's attempts at writing. Revising demands a price, all right, but it is a price worth paying for effectiveness in written expression. Rewriting is not evidence of failure, but a way to achieve a greater measure of success in writing.

Publishing

Publishing is the culmination of the writing process. In conventional writing instruction, writing assignments were typically written for an audience of

10.8 Putting Ideas to Work
Revising, Editing, and Proofreading Checklist

	Sentences	YES	NO
R	Is each sentence a complete thought that makes sense?		
	Are my words lively, colorful, and interesting?		
E	Does each sentence begin with a capital letter?		
	Does it end with the correct punctuation mark?		
	Are all the words spelled correctly?		
	Paragraphs		
R	Does the topic sentence state the main idea of my paragraph?		
	Do the supporting sentences tell about the topic sentence?		
	Does my paragraph have a clincher sentence?		
	Do all the sentences flow in a logical or sensible order?		
	Did I use different kinds of sentences in my paragraph?		
	Is there only one main idea in my paragraph?		
E	Did I indent at the beginning of my paragraph?		
	Is my paragraph neatly written and easy to read?		
	Writing Selections		
R	Does my writing selection have an interesting title?		
	Does it contain words that paint a clear picture for my readers?		
	Does my writing selection have enough action?		
	Have I included all the details that I want to include?		
E	Can I answer YES to all the EDITING questions for the sentences and paragraphs in my writing selection?		
P	**Proofreading Sentences, Paragraphs, and Writing Selections**		
	Have I marked all corrections carefully?		

R = Revising   **E** = Editing   **P** = Proofreading

Publication of children's writing is the culmination of the writing process.
© James L. Shaffer

one (the teacher), primarily as a vehicle for correction. Writing, however, is a communication activity, and the circle of communication is not complete until the intended audience reads the writing. Publication involves finding readers, "not 'pretend readers' but the real kind who will show interest in writing and let the writer know what they think" (Walshe, 1988; p. 213).

A number of options are available for publishing student writing. A simple and rather intimate form of publication occurs when pupils read each other's writing as part of a classroom community of writers, or when they post their work on the classroom bulletin board for classmates and visitors to read. Publication extends beyond the classroom when children post their stories in the school lobby or cafeteria, reproduce their writing in a class newspaper, or take it home for parents and others to read. Teachers can also make arrangements to have pupils record their stories on cassette tapes to use in listening centers, or to make videotapes of children as they read their stories. Sharing stories in any of these ways is an example of writing for communication.

More formal publication takes place when pupils gather their writing into class books. "For many children, book publishing is the most exciting part of the literature program. Frequently, the first reading that some children do is their own published story, so being an author makes as much of an impact on the child as being a reader" (Routman, 1988; p. 110). In the very early grades, before children have developed much independent writing competency, teachers, parent volunteers, student teachers, or pupils from upper grades can transcribe children's stories, which the original authors can then illustrate. As independent writing skills develop, children can use their own final drafts. Others can help them tape their illustrated stories in laminated covers, mount them in heavy cardboard covered by wallpaper, stitch them by hand or with a sewing machine, or otherwise bind them in a sturdy enough form to withstand repeated handling by elementary students.

It is important to give student-written books and other writing status as literature. This level of respect solidifies the reading-writing connection in

10.9 Putting Ideas to Work
The Author's Chair

*T*he author's chair is a concept or device Donald Graves and Jane Hansen (1982) suggest. In the classroom, the teacher designates a special chair as "The Author's Chair." The teacher sits in this chair while reading to children, and pupils have the honor of sitting in it as they read their writing to classmates. Students read their stories aloud, just as the teacher reads the works of famous authors. Thus, children gain a sense of themselves as authors and a feeling of genuine worth about their writing.

pupils' minds and encourages them to take themselves seriously as authors, as producers as well as consumers of stories. This perception can be a powerful motivation and an ego-enhancing dimension of a classroom literacy program.

Opportunities also exist for publishing children's writing more widely. The "Kids as Authors" competition was established in 1986 to encourage children to write. Winning books are commercially published. Information about Kids as Authors can be obtained from 801 94th Ave. No., St. Petersberg, FL 33702. Also, children can publish their work on the World Wide Web on websites such as KidPub (http://www:en-garde.com/kidpub). This site features stories written by children (along with great ideas for language arts teachers).

This, then, is the writing process— the steps of prewriting, writing, editing/revising, and publishing. The specifics of the stages and steps will vary from activity to activity, from grade to grade, from classroom to classroom, and from child to child within any classroom. Some pupils will be able to skip over various steps along the way—those who arrive in the classroom with a keen sense of story, with facile expressional skills, with easy mastery of the mechanics of writing. For most students, however, writing competency grows as they follow the steps professional writers take.

DeGroff (1989) describes how literature can "support the process that takes writers from topic selection to a final model form." Using Ezra Jack Keats's popular story *The Snowy Day*, she shows how pupils can shape the events of a perfectly ordinary day into a story topic. Discussion can focus on why the author chose to include some incidents and not others, the tone of the writing, and the author's choice of words—all the prewriting decisions writers make.

DeGroff describes how discussion can help students see how they draft meaning as they read in much the same way that authors draft meaning as they write. She also describes how literature discussions can provide a model for writers' conferences between teachers and pupils in process writing. "During literature discussion we want students to notice how respondents comment and question but respect writer's ownership of their

10.10 Putting Ideas to Work
Decisions in the Writing Process

Whether writing an imaginative story in the third grade or writing a term paper for a course in teaching reading, the writing process consists of four steps or stages, each of which involves a series of decisions.

Stages	Decisions
Prewriting	Stimulus for writing—*Why am I writing this?* Finding a topic—*What will I write about?* Focus on detail—*What aspect of the topic will I emphasize?* Deciding on form—*Will I write a story or a poem?* Deciding on audience—*Who will read what I write?*
Writing	Drafting—*What ideas and details will I include?* Vocabulary—*What words will I use to express actions and feelings?* Sentences—*How can I write so others will be interested and entertained?*
Editing/Revising	Sentences—*Do my sentences make sense? Are they clear? Do they begin with capitals and end with periods?* Paragraphs—*Do they have topic sentences? Are they too long? Do I have enough details?* Selection—*Does it have an interesting title? Did I include exciting action and interesting details?*
Publishing	Personal—*Will it be a diary or journal for me only?* Intimate—*Will it be shared with only select people such as parents or classmates?* Public—*Will it be posted on a bulletin board or published in a class book?*

work. . . . We do not tell Ezra Jack Keats that he must change his book. We simply comment and raise questions that reflect our understanding and response" (p. 118).

Using Keats's story, DeGroff explains how readers and writers revise as they encounter new information in text, consider alternative word choices, and examine how the author might have written the story differently. Pupils also examine the editorial decisions Keats must have made about *A Snowy Day:* size, shape, title, illustration, and design of the book. Examining works of children's literature in this way opens students' eyes to the options they can exercise in their own writing activities. The idea can be extended if children discuss how the story could have changed

if the story had taken place on a sunny day in the summer;

if the main character had been a girl instead of a boy; or

if the setting had been the country instead of the city.

Discussing stories in this way opens children's eyes to wider possibilities in their writing. It also encourages critical reading and an awareness of story structure elements in literature.

Each stage of the writing process involves the reading-writing connection. Wide reading gives students impressive models and helps them generate ideas they can use as topics during the prewriting stage. The act of writing itself involves pupils in constructing meaning in text, which is essential to both composing and comprehending. Editing and revising alert them to the language qualities that will make them keener processors of print. Publishing what they have written gives children a sense of authorship that influences them as readers.

Written Products Based on Literature

The writing process results in written products, which can include imaginative stories, informational reports, journals and logs, friendly letters, various types of poetry, scripts and dialogues, and other forms of writing. Each of these products can relate directly to literature in the classroom.

Stories

Story writing is stimulated by the narratives pupils encounter in the world of children's literature. They can create their own witches and goblins, heroes and villains, friends and foes based on the characters they find in books. They can create their own versions of favorite stories, create new endings, write sequels, or produce a variety of imaginative tales and realistic accounts of their own lives. An awareness of narrative story structure—how problems develop in stories and how these problems are solved—provides a structural dimension that children's writing often lacks.

Reports

Written reports provide students with opportunities to develop expository writing, and informational trade books are essential in gathering content for these reports. As part of a thematic unit on dinosaurs, for example, written reports might include information found in such nonfiction trade books as:

Aliki's *My Visit to the Dinosaurs*

Franklyn Branley's *What Happened to the Dinosaur?*

Kathy Lasky's *Dinosaur Dig*

Patricia Lauber's *News About Dinosaurs*

Bernard Most's *If the Dinosaurs Came Back*

Peter Zallinger's *Dinosaurs*

Using trade books to research thematic topics creates a direct link in the reading-writing connection. Children can build expository text into a report by organizing their writing according to the text structure in the informational books. This helps cement the connection.

10.11 Putting Ideas to Work
Using Big Books as Writing Models

*B*ig books can be used in virtually thousands of ways to stimulate written language activities in the classroom. Some teachers have used the predictable and repeated language patterns found in many Big Books as the basis for writing activities. For example:

1. The language patterns in Pat Hutchins's *Good Night, Owl* can be repeated in writing Halloween stories (*The skeleton shook—rattle, rattle—and Ghost tried to sleep*), science stories about winter animals (*The rabbit hopped—hop, hop—and Bear tried to sleep*), or in stories focused on another primary grade theme or topic.
2. The patterned language in Bill Martin Jr.'s, *Brown Bear, Brown Bear, What Do You See?* can be the model for end-of-the-month summaries of activities: *Grade 1, grade 1, what did we do? In January, we celebrated Julie's and Juan's birthdays, we took a field trip to the bakery, we had an assembly on safety*, and so on.

Sometimes a fictional story that pupils read can stimulate their interest in a topic enough to lead them to research and report on it further. Robb (1989) tells about a fifth grade class that developed "an all-consuming curiosity about wolves and their environment" after reading Jean Craighead George's *Julie of the Wolves.* The pupils spent a year researching the topics of animal behavior and the environment after the literature had sparked their interest.

Letters

Writing letters is an authentic language and social skill, and writing letters to favorite authors has long been a classroom practice. Some authors ask for letters from their young readers and make an honest attempt to respond. Others do not. When an author does respond to a class letter, the children's excitement is usually high, and another link in the reading-writing connection is established. Even when the class receives an apologetic "We're sorry, but the author is too busy writing a new book to respond" reaction from a publisher, at least their letters generate an authentic response.

Prewriting activities for letters to authors should include a discussion about the number and types of questions that are appropriate (with cautions about questions like "How much money do you make?" and about outlandish requests such as "Please use my name in your next book"). This type of discussion centers on the social aspects of using language.

Literature suggests other opportunities for imaginative letter-writing activities. Children can write notes of condolence to Beatrix Potter's beloved *The Tale of Peter Rabbit* or letters to Alexander (from Judith Viorst's *Alexander and the Terrible, Horrible, No Good, Very Bad Day*) telling him about *their* very bad days. They can also write letters and notes unrelated to literature.

10.12 Putting Ideas to Work
Literature-Based Writing

*T*he idea of writing a friendly letter to an author illustrates the difference between a literature-based and a more conventional approach to language teaching in the classroom. Teaching the form and protocol of writing friendly letters and business letters is typically part of the elementary school curriculum, and lessons on letter writing are normally included in most language arts textbook series. In conventional programs, these lessons are the starting point and focus in teaching this important writing skill.

With literature-based instruction, children's books are the starting point for this aspect of the language arts curriculum. The children respond to the literature or raise questions about it as a result of their reading, and this stimulates them to want to know how to write a letter to the author.

The content of the letter-writing lesson is basically the same in either approach. The purpose of and motivation for writing, however, differ dramatically in the literature-based approach.

Teachers and students have plenty of opportunities to write thank-you notes to class guests, get-well messages to classmates who are absent for prolonged periods, letters of appreciation to the school secretary, and letters to pen pals across the miles or to senior citizens across town.

Another form of letter writing occurs when pupils exchange letters about the books that they have read through a classroom mailbox. This type of activity is an extension of buddy journals; the added dimension is that children are expected to follow the conventional letter form—heading, salutation, body, and closing, all punctuated appropriately.

To provide an even deeper dimension of learning about letter writing, Beverly Cleary's warm and sensitive, award-winning *Dear Mr. Henshaw* can show how a whole story may be told through a series of personal letters, as can Rosa Guy's *The Ups and Downs of Carl Davis III.*

Poems

Writing poetry is another popular and important writing activity in the literature-based classroom. Children exposed to the full range of lyric, descriptive, narrative, humorous, fanciful, and free-verse poems will likely want to respond to literature in poetic form. Although conventional elements of rhythm and rhyme have enormous appeal to children, teachers need to focus on meaning as their pupils write poems.

Some forms of poetry necessarily start with direct modeling. To learn the forms of limericks or haiku, for example, students must be exposed to models of these poems in books such as John Ciardi's collection of absurd limericks, *The Hopeful Trout and Other Limericks,* or one of Ann Atwood's beautiful collections of haiku such as *Fly with the Wind, Flow with the Water.* After exposure to the forms of these structured poems, pupils will be able to produce some versions of their own.

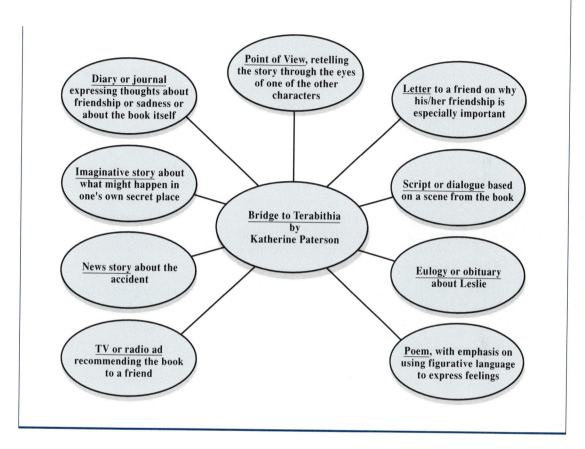

When writing less structured forms of poetry, children need considerable freedom in putting their thoughts, ideas, emotions, and images into poetic form.

Scripts and Dialogues

Scripts and dialogues provide opportunities to integrate reading, writing, and speaking, as pupils produce and stage their own versions of stories. Many stories like Arnold Lobel's *Frog and Toad Are Friends* and Bill Martin, Jr. and John Archambault's *Knots on a Counting Rope* provide dialogue models for students to follow as they write. Wordless books provide ideal opportunities for pupils at any level to produce dialogue; supplying words for the old woman in Tomie de Paola's popular *Pancakes for Breakfast* or lines for the various characters in Martha Alexander's *Bobo's Dream* allows children to cement the reading-writing connection by creating written expressions of meaning.

Journals and Logs

Response journals, logs, and other personal written responses to literature, described earlier in this chapter, are an integral and regular part of literature-based instruction. These personal forms of writing provide an ongoing record of stories, poems, and other materials pupils have experienced, along with their responses to this literature. Students may recall their own struggles with cursive handwriting in response to Beverly Cleary's *Muggie Maggie* or tell why they find Susan Pearson's *Well, I Never!* so funny. Unlike other forms of writing produced in response to literature, journals take a personal perspective. More detached responses take the form of book reports.

Book Reports

A common form of writing in response to literature is, of course, the good old book report. Given the emphasis on reader response in the literature-based classroom, many consider the conventional book report outdated. Traditionally, book reports were occasional assignments, apparently given to make sure students had read the books they were supposed to read. When reading is an everyday classroom experience and when responding to literature is a regular part of language instruction, book reports become overwhelming to children. They can do reports in many personal and creative ways, including:

index card reports—two-sentence summary and response statements written to recommend (or not recommend) the book to others;

character reports—written through the eyes of one of the book's characters, sometimes delivered in costume as an oral report to the class;

author reports—written as an interview with the author, perhaps delivered as a press conference with classmates asking questions about the book;

advertisements—written as print, radio, or television ads for the book, with an emphasis on using propaganda techniques as a critical thinking activity as well;

letters—written to actually send to the author or to exchange with classmates through a classroom mailbox;

posters—in the form of a baseball card for a sports hero, for example, or a "Wanted, Dead or Alive" poster for the character in a mystery book;

news reports—recalling part of a book through a TV, radio, or newspaper report;

taped readings—in which pupils tape record sections of a story for others to enjoy.

illustrations from the story, with appropriate captions;

book covers or jackets—with illustration and information about both the book and the author;

10.14 Putting Ideas to Work

Children's Trade Books about Writing

A number of children's trade books deal directly with the subjects of writing and publishing. A small sampling includes:

Aliki's, *How a Book Is Made.* Using simple language and lively illustrations, the author explains the steps of the book-publishing process and the roles of the people involved.

Sandy Asher's *Where Do You Get Your Ideas?* This book is about developing ideas for stories and poems. Well-known authors like Marjorie Weinman Sharmat, Patricia Reilly Giff, and Lois Lowry explain where they find inspiration.

Marion Dane Bauer's *What's Your Story? A Young Person's Guide to Writing Fiction.* This book provides instruction and advice for aspiring writers in the upper elementary grades.

Carol Lea Benjamin's *Writing for Kids.* This book provides advice and ideas about many aspects of writing.

Sylvia Cassedy's *In Your Own Words: A Beginner's Guide to Writing.* The author provides ideas for writing poetry and plays in this book for ages 10 and up.

Gillian Chapman and Pam Robson's *Making Books: A Step-by-Step Guide to Your Own Publishing* and *Making Shaped Books.* These two books emphasize bookmaking as a craft activity.

Eileen Christelow's *What Do Authors Do?* Through humorous fiction, the author describes what writers do.

Louise Colligan's *Scholastic's A+ Junior Guide to Good Writing.* More appropriate for upper grade students, this guide emphasizes process writing, with how-to's related to narrative and expository text.

Vivian Dubrovin's *Write Your Own Story.* This is a practical guide on writing for children in the upper elementary grades.

Norton Juster's *A Surfeit of Similes.* This book contains just what the title suggests, by the author of *The Phantom Tollbooth.*

Julia C. Mahon's *First Book of Creative Writing.* This is a direct and specific guide with lots of ideas for writing.

report cards—giving a grade and comment about some aspect of the character in the story (honesty, resourcefulness, or humor, for example);

conversations—between characters from different books; and

puppets—made from socks, sticks, or coffee cans to reflect characters from the book.

Book reports can take other forms as well. In a classroom full of literature, there will be no shortage of creative ideas teachers can suggest and students can use to respond to and report on their reading.

Even in a literature-based reading program, not all the writing children do will be about the books they have read. They will write about their personal experiences, both real and imagined; they will write about the most interesting characters they have ever met, and what they hope to do when they become adults; they will write letters to the residents of nursing homes nearby and pen pals far away; they will write about the ideas that fill their heads and the emotions that fill their hearts.

Literature, however, does provide a fruitful source of topics and rich language models for writing. Using a process writing model, children can produce an infinite variety of poems, stories, reports, letters, advertisements, essays, biographies, scripts, and other written products in response to the literature they read. Literature supplies the force that forges the reading-writing connection.

The professional literature is full of practical ideas on how to make the reading-writing connection through literature in the classroom (Tway, 1985; Criscuolo, 1988; Noyce and Christie, 1989; Mason, 1989). Creative teachers find numerous other ways to make this important connection, including giving pupils a chance to participate in planning literature-based writing activities. Children have original ideas, and when they are given responsibility for planning writing activities, they feel a heightened sense of ownership over the final product.

Summary and Conclusions

Three basic premises underlie the reading-writing connection: (1) an integral connection exists between the process of learning to read and the process of learning to write; (2) children can develop competency in both areas simultaneously; and (3) the development of one can have a powerful influence on the development of the other. Literature provides an ideal vehicle for forging the reading-writing connection, since the books and other materials pupils read strongly influence their writing.

Process writing is a movement that has dramatically changed the way schools teach writing. The writing process includes a prewriting stage that involves making a series of decisions, a writing stage in which the writer produces a draft, a postwriting stage that involves editing and revision, and finally publication of a finished product. Literature can support each step in the process, from helping children generate ideas and explore forms through publishing their writing.

The written products pupils produce can take a variety of forms, from imaginative stories and informational reports to personal expressions of emotion through poetry. All of these forms are possible written responses to the literature students read in and outside of school.

The most obvious link between reading and writing lies in decoding and encoding words. However, as Adams (1990) explains:

> . . . just as there is more to reading than word recognition, there is more to writing than spelling, and there is far more to the reading-writing connection than just reciprocal exercise with individual words. . . .
>
> As children become authors, as they struggle to express, refine, and reach audiences through their own writing, they actively come to grips with the most important reading insights of all.
>
> Through writing, children learn that text is not preordained or immutable truth. It is human voice. . . . Children learn that the purpose of text is not to be read but to be understood. They learn that text does not contain meaning but is meaningful only to the extent that it is understood by its reader.

They learn that different readers respond differently to the same text. They also learn that sometimes understanding comes only through hard work even for the best readers. They learn that cogent writing may depend on consulting other sources, inviting the insight that cogent reading may do this, too.

They learn that text is written about an underlying organization, inviting the insight that it may be productively read in that way too.

They learn, in short, that reading is about thinking, and that lesson is critical. (pp. 404–405).[*]

And that is the basis of the reading-writing connection!

Discussion Questions and Activities

1. After doing additional reading and research, make a list of ways in which reading and writing are related and how literature cements this relationship.
2. Think of the last writing assignment you had to do—a research report or term paper for a class you are taking, for example. Trace the process you followed in writing the paper, from your prewriting decision of choosing (or being assigned) a topic to the final product.
3. Using a children's trade book you know well, plan a process writing lesson you could use in the classroom. Be sure to include prewriting activities, ideas for the writing workshop, and provisions for editing and publication.
4. Select a children's trade book you especially enjoy. Using the model suggested in Putting Ideas to Work 10.13, design a writing web for this book.
5. Recall your own writing experiences from elementary school. Compare these early experiences to the ideas this chapter presents.

School-Based Assignments

1. Examine a sample of pupils' writing in your school placement. What can you tell about the students' writing abilities and instructional needs based on what you observe? How might you address these needs in a class lesson?
2. Work with a small group of children to develop part of a writing lesson or to design a writing web (see Putting Ideas to Work 10.13) based on a trade book that they have read or that you have read to them.
3. After reading a book chapter to a class, plan a lesson in which pupils write literature response journals or logs. Remind the children they should react to the story rather than merely retell what happened. Select one or two of the responses and plan conferences with the authors.
4. Visit an elementary classroom. What written evidence indicates that literature is alive and well in that classroom? Are students' written responses to literature displayed around the room? If you were the teacher, what activities would you plan to involve pupils in literature-based writing encounters?
5. Select a children's trade book and discuss it with children following the model in DeGroff's discussion of A Snowy Day (see pp. 364–366).

[*]From M. J. Adams, *Beginning to Read: Thinking and Learning about Print.* Cambridge, MA: MIT Press. Reprinted with permission.

Aardema, Verna. (1975). *Why Mosquitoes Buzz in People's Ears: A West African Folk Tale.* New York: Dial.

Alexander, Martha. (1970). *Bobo's Dream.* New York: Dial.

Aliki. (1985). *My Visit to the Dinosaurs.* New York: Crowell.

Aliki. (1988). *How a Book Is Made.* New York: Harper & Row.

Asher, Sandy. (1987). *Where Do You Get Your Ideas?* New York: Walker.

Atwood, Ann. (1979). *Fly with the Wind, Flow with the Water.* New York: Scribner.

Bauer, Marion. (1992). *What's Your Story? A Young Person's Guide to Writing Fiction.* New York: Clarion.

Baylor, Byrd, and Parnall, Peter. (1980). *If You Are a Hunter of Fossils.* New York: Atheneum.

Benjamin, Carol Lea. (1985). *Writing for Kids.* New York: Harper & Row.

Branley, Franklyn. (1989). *What Happened to the Dinosaurs?* New York: Crowell.

Burnett, Frances Hodgson. (1989). *The Secret Garden.* New York: Dell.

Cassedy, Sylvia. (1979). *In Your Own Words: A Beginner's Guide to Writing.* Garden City, NJ: Doubleday.

Celsi, Teresa. (1992). *The Fourth Little Pig.* Austin, TX: Raintree Steck-Vaughn.

Chapman, G., and Robson, P. (1991). *Making Books: A Step-by-Step Guide to Your Own Publishing.* Brookfield, CT: Millbrook.

Chapman, G., and Robson, P. (1995). *Making Shaped Books.* Brookfield, CT: Millbrook.

Christelow, E. (1995). *What Do Authors Do?* Boston: Clarion.

Ciardi, John. (1989). *The Hopeful Trout and Other Limericks.* Boston: Houghton Mifflin.

Cleary, Beverly. (1983). *Dear Mr. Henshaw.* New York: Morrow.

Cleary, Beverly. (1991). *Muggie Maggie.* New York: Morrow.

Colligan, Louise. (1988). *Scholastic's A+ Junior Guide to Good Writing.* New York: Scholastic.

de Paola, Tomie. (1978). *Pancakes for Breakfast.* New York: Harcourt Brace.

de Paola, Tomie. (1981). *Now One Foot, Now the Other.* New York: Putnam.

Dubrovin, Vivian. (1984). *Write Your Own Story.* New York: Franklin Watts.

Eckert, Allan. (1971). *Incident at Hawk's Hill.* Boston: Little, Brown.

Freeman, Don. (1968). *Corduroy.* New York: Viking.

Gardiner, John Reynolds. (1980). *Stone Fox.* New York: Harper & Row.

George, Jean Craighead. (1972). *Julie of the Wolves.* New York: Harper & Row.

Giff, Patricia Reilly. (1984). *The Beast in Ms. Rooney's Room.* New York: Dell.

Guy, Rosa. (1989). *The Ups and Downs of Carl Davis III.* New York: Delacourte.

Hoban, Russell. (1970). *A Bargain for Frances.* New York: Harper & Row.

Hogrogian, Nonnie. (1971). *One Fine Day.* New York: Macmillan.

Hutchins, Pat. (1972). *Good Night, Owl!* New York: Macmillan.

Juster, Norton. (1989). *A Surfeit of Similes.* New York: Morrow.

Keats, Ezra Jack. (1962). *The Snowy Day.* New York: Penguin.

Knudson, R. R. (1985). *Babe Didrickson, Athlete of the Century.* New York: Viking.

Lasky, Kathy. (1990). *Dinosaur Dig.* New York: Morrow.

Lauber, Patricia. (1989). *News about Dinosaurs.* New York: Bradbury.

Lobel, Arnold. (1970). *Frog and Toad Are Friends.* New York: Harper & Row.

Mahon, Julia C. (1968). *First Book of Creative Writing.* New York: Franklin Watts.

Martin, Bill, Jr. (1983). *Brown Bear, Brown Bear, What Do You See?* New York: Henry Holt.

Martin, Bill Jr., and Archambault, John. (1987). *Knots on a Counting Rope.* New York: Henry Holt .

Mayer, Mercer. (1987).*What Do You Do with a Kangaroo?* New York: Scholastic.

McPhail, David. (1972). *The Bear's Toothache.* Boston: Little, Brown.

Most, Bernard. (1978). *If the Dinosaurs Came Back.* New York: Harcourt Brace Jovanovich.

Munsch, Robert. (1986). *Love You Forever.* Willowdale, ON: Firefly Books.

Paterson, Katherine. (1977). *Bridge to Terabithia.* New York: Harper & Row.

Paulsen, Gary. (1987). *Hatchet*. New York: Macmillan.

Pearson, Susan. (1991). *Well, I Never!* New York: Simon & Schuster.

Potter, Beatrix. (1992). *The Tale of Peter Rabbit*. New York: Random House.

Quackenbush, Robert. (1980). *Oh, What an Awful Mess!* Englewood Cliffs, NJ: Prentice-Hall.

Rawls, Wilson. (1961). *Where the Red Fern Grows*. New York: Doubleday.

Seuss, Dr. (Theodore Geisel). (1957). *The Cat in the Hat*. New York: Random House.

Spier, Peter. (1978). *Bored—Nothing To Do*. New York: Doubleday.

Steig, William. (1969). *Sylvester and the Magic Pebble*. New York: Simon & Schuster.

Taylor, Mildred. (1976). *Roll of Thunder, Hear My Cry*. New York: Dial.

Van Allsburg, Chris. (1981). *Jumanji*. Boston: Houghton Mifflin.

Viorst, Judith. (1972). *Alexander and the Terrible, Horrible, No Good, Very Bad Day*. New York: Atheneum.

Waber, Bernard. (1973). *Ira Sleeps Over*. Boston: Houghton Mifflin.

White, E. B. (1952). *Charlotte's Web*. New York: Harper & Row.

Wolf, Alexander (Jon Scieska, pseud.). (1989). *The True Story of the Three Little Pigs*. New York: Penguin.

Yektai, Niki. (1991). *Hi Bears, Bye Bears*. New York: Orchard.

Zallinger, Peter. (1988). *Dinosaurs*. New York: Random House.

References

Adams, M. J. (1990). *Beginning to Read: Thinking and Learning about Print*. Cambridge, MA: MIT Press.

Applebee, A. N., Langer, J. A., Mullis, I. V. S., Latham, A. S., and Gentile, L. A. (1993). *NAEP 1992 Writing Report Card*. Washington, DC: U. S. Department of Education.

Atwell, N. (1987). *In the Middle: Writing, Reading, and Learning with Adolescents*. Portsmouth, NH: Heinemann.

Bragert-Drowns, R. L. (1993). The Word Processer as an Instructional Tool: A Meta-Analysis of Word Processing in Writing Instruction. *Review of Educational Research* 63:69–93.

Beach, R., and Hynds, S. (1991). Research on Response to Literature. In R. Barr, M. L. Kamill, P. Mosenthal, and P. D. Pearson, eds., *Handbook on Reading Research, Vol. 2*. New York: Longman.

Bleich, D. (1987). *Subjective Criticism*. Baltimore: John Hopkins University Press.

Bromley, K. D. (1989). Buddy Journals Make the Reading-Writing Connection. *The Reading Teacher* 43:122–129.

Brown, V. L., Hammill, D. D., and Wiederholt, J. L. (1986). *Test of Reading Comprehension*. Austin, TX: Pro-Ed.

Calkins, L. M. (1986). *The Art of Teaching Writing*. Portsmouth, NH: Heinemann.

Criscuolo, N. P. (1988). Twelve Practical Ways to Make the Reading/Writing Connection. *The New England Reading Association Journal* 24:30–32.

DeGroff, L-J. (1989). Developing Writing Processes with Children's Literature. *The New Advocate* 2:115–123.

Eeds, M., and Peterson, R. (1991). Teacher as Curator: Learning to Teach about Literature. *The Reading Teacher* 45:118–126.

Fitzgerald, J. (1989). Enhancing Two Related Thought Processes: Revision in Writing and Critical Reading. *The Reading Teacher* 43:42–48.

Graves, D. H. (1983). *Writing: Teachers and Children at Work*. Portsmouth, NH: Heinemann.

Graves, D. H., and Hansen, J. (1982). The Author's Chair. *Language Arts* 60:176–183.

Hancock, M. R. (1993). Exploring and Extending Personal Response Through Literature Journals. *The Reading Teacher* 46:466–474.

Hittleman, D. R. (1988). *Developmental Reading, K–8: Teaching from a Whole-Language Perspective* (3rd ed.). Columbus, OH: Merrill.

Jensen, J. M. (1993). What Do We Know About the Writing of Elementary School Children? *Language Arts* 70:290–294.

Karolides, N. J. (ed.) (1992). *Reader Response in the Classroom: Evoking and Interpreting Meaning in Literature.* New York: Longman.

Kelly, P. R. (1990). Guiding Young Students' Responses to Literature. *The Reading Teacher* 43:464–470.

Kolczynski, R. G. (1989). Reading Leads to Writing. In J. W. Stewig and S. L. Sebesta, eds., *Using Literature in the Elementary Classroom.* Urbana, Ill.: National Council of Teachers of English.

Mason, J. M. (ed.) (1989). *Reading and Writing Connections.* Boston: Allyn & Bacon.

Moore, S. R. (1995). Questions for Research into Reading-Writing Relationships and Text Structure Knowledge. *Language Arts* 72:598–606.

Murray, D. M. (1968). *A Writer Teaches Writing.* Boston: Houghton Mifflin.

Noyce, R. M., and Christie, J. F. (1989). *Integrating Reading and Writing Instruction in Grades K–8.* Boston: Allyn & Bacon.

Pearson, P. D. (1985). Changing the Face of Reading Comprehension Instruction. *The Reading Teacher* 38:724–728.

Petrosky, A. R. (1982). From Story to Essay: Reading and Writing. *College Composition and Communication* 33:19–36.

Phillips, L. M. (1989). *Using Children's Literature to Foster Written Language Development.* Technical Report No. 446. Champaign: University of Illinois at Urbana–Champaign Center for the Study of Reading.

Robb, L. (1989). Books in the Classroom. *The Horn Book* 65:808–810.

Rosenblatt, L. M. (1982). The Literary Transaction: Evocation and Response. *Theory Into Practice* 21:268–277.

Routman, R. (1988). *Transitions from Literature to Literacy.* Portsmouth, NH: Heinemann.

Rubin, A., and Hansen, J. (1984). *Reading and Writing: How Are the First Two 'R's' Related?* Reading Education Report No. 51. Champaign: University of Illinois at Urbana–Champaign Center for the Study of Reading.

Salinger, T. S. (1996). *Literacy for Young Children* (2nd ed.). Columbus, OH: Merrill.

Shanahan, T. (1988). The Reading-Writing Relationship: Seven Instructional Principles. *The Reading Teacher* 41:636–647.

Simons, H. D. (1971). Reading Comprehension: The Need for a New Perspective. *Reading Research Quarterly* 7:340–361.

Smith, E. B. (1995). Anchored in Our Literature: Students Responding to African American Literature. *Language Arts* 72:571–574.

Tierney, R. J., and Pearson, P. D. (1983). Toward a Composing Model of Reading. *Language Arts* 60:568–580.

Tierney, R. J., Soter, A., O'Flahoran, J. F., and McGinley, T. (1989). The Effects of Reading and Writing upon Thinking Critically. *Reading Research Quarterly* 24:134–173.

Tomkins, G. E. (1990). *Teaching Writing: Balancing Process and Product.* Columbus, OH: Merrill.

Tway, E. (1985). *Writing Is Reading: 26 Ways to Connect.* Urbana, IL: National Council of Teachers of English.

Walshe, R. D. (1988). Questions Teachers Ask about Teaching Writing K–12. In R. D. Walshe and P. March, eds., *Teaching Writing K–12.* Melbourne, Australia: Dellastar.

Weaver, C. (1988). *Reading Process and Practice: From Sociopsycholinguistics to Whole Language.* Portsmouth, NH: Heinemann.

Wollman-Bonilla, J. E., and Werchadlo, B. (1995). Literature Response Journals in a First-Grade Classroom. *Language Arts* 72:562–570.

The Learning Spectrum: Using Literature with Exceptional Learners

© James L. Shaffer

Chapter 11 Outline

Features

Key Concepts in This Chapter

A full range of abilities are found among pupils in any classroom; using literature helps meet this range of literacy needs in specific ways.

Because of learning problems, some children experience greater-than-normal difficulty in acquiring literacy. Literature-based reading instruction can meet the needs of these pupils.

Some children display attitude and behavior problems that prevent them from learning to read. For these students, trade books can be vehicles both for reading instruction and for reflecting some of their emotional experiences to themselves and to others.

Gifted learners can use literature in a variety of ways to extend their learning and enhance classroom literacy instruction.

Introduction

All children are different. Not all learn at the same rate or in the same way; individual differences in the classroom are a fact of life. Most children arrive at school with physical, emotional, and cognitive abilities that will allow them to learn to read with regular instruction. Others arrive with fewer—or more—of the characteristics needed to achieve success in gaining literacy.

In any classroom, teachers encounter a wide spectrum of learners. At one end of the spectrum are those whose cognitive or neurological characteristics create barriers in learning to read. The range also includes physically challenged pupils whose orthopedic or sensory handicaps impede the learning process or limit full participation in classroom programs, as well as students who have attitude or behavior problems that affect their ability to learn to read. At the other end of the spectrum are gifted children who learn to read easily, or arrive at school able to read.

Children with similar challenges may even exhibit different degrees of problems that affect their ability to learn to read. "At the mild end of the continuum, the behavioral and educational differences (among groups) are blurred at best. . . . In fact, the overlap of underachievement and social/emotional problem behavior commonly found in mild and moderate learning disabled and emotionally disturbed students makes differentiating between the two groups sometimes little more than the flip of a diagnostic coin. With respect to reading behaviors, similar difficulties occur" (McCoy and Prehm, 1987; pp. 256–257).

Students who are atypical in one dimension of learning may be very typical in other aspects of learning and of life. For example, a pupil may be highly talented in reading but not so gifted in math. Or a child who has a learning disability that makes reading inordinately difficult may be an especially gifted artist. In such cases, the key is to help the child use his or her areas of strength to develop interest and competency in reading.

Children with different learning abilities need high-quality instruction, but it need not differ substantially from the instruction in a high-quality classroom reading program. Some children may need extra technological support and need certain aspects of the reading instructional program adjusted to meet special learning needs. But no matter what their learning characteristics, all pupils need instruction that stresses meaning from the very beginning, provides direct instruction in reading strategies, integrates reading and writing, extends reading into content areas of the curriculum, and that is permeated with fine literature—in short, a program that teaches effective reading and writing strategies and teaches them well.

Mainstreaming and Inclusion: The Heterogeneous Classroom

Exceptional children have always been part of society. At first, society kept children with special problems excluded from schools and hidden away at home. Through the late 1800s and into the 20th century, special educational institutions were established for children with more severe and obvious needs—schools for the blind, for example, or for the severely mentally retarded. Later, public schools set up separate classrooms for pupils charac-terized as special-needs learners; classes for the emotionally disturbed, for example, or resource rooms for children with learning disabilities. Even those not classified as learners with special needs but who had trouble learn-ing to read received out-of-class remedial instruction in what Allington (1994) has called "a second system of education." These pull-out programs drew criticism for failing to integrate the pupil's in-class and out-of-class reading instruction and for labeling children.

As experts in medicine, psychology, and education have learned more about the unique characteristics of exceptional children, and as society has become more aware of the importance of addressing the needs of all learn-ers, the practice of integrating students with special learning needs into reg-ular school settings has developed. In 1975, Congress passed Public Law 94–142 to ensure that all children, whatever their needs, receive a free, appropri-ate education from the ages of 3 to 21. In 1992 this law was updated and renamed the Individuals with Disabilities Education Act (IDEA). This legis-lation stipulates that learners with special needs must be educated "in the least restrictive environment"; that is, to the extent possible, these children must take part in the normal school life all children experience.

Federal and state laws related to children with special needs led to the widespread practices of *mainstreaming* and *inclusion* of pupils with special needs in regular classrooms. Mainstreamed students spend part or all of the school day in a regular classroom and then pull out as needed for special services. These children may be in the regular classroom for certain sub-jects—perhaps art or social studies—but may receive other instruction—in reading and writing, for example—in separate settings within the school.

Under the Regular Education Initiative (REI), a movement developed to include all children with special needs in regular classrooms on a full-time basis, with appropriate support services in the classroom. Inclusion pre-sumes that children with special needs belong with their peers all the time (Roach, 1995). "Under inclusion, regular education is expected to change in significant ways so that all or most of the individual student's special needs are met in the context of the regular classroom" (Terman et al., 1996; p. 17).

Mainstreaming and inclusion have had an impact on reading instruc-tion. Teachers are both enriched and challenged by the need to provide read-ing instruction for children all along the learning spectrum—for those well equipped to learn and those who are less so, for those tuned into reading and those who are not, for those who learn easily and those who don't.

While the Regular Education Initiative has its critics (Smelter, et al., 1994; Kauffman, et al., 1995; Zigmond et al., 1995), it also has supporters who point to its successes (Taylor, 1982; Lipsky and Gartner, 1992; Stevens and Slavin, 1995). Inclusion is important for special-needs children. Not only do these pupils benefit both socially and academically by interacting with their peers, but the lives of these peers are also enriched when they interact with children with different needs.

However, placement in a regular classroom is not the crucial element in the success of children with learning problems. Instruction is. "There is no

11.1 Putting Ideas to Work

Ten Guidelines for Including Students with Disabilities

Michael F. Giangreco (1996) provides the following ten recommendations for successfully including students with disabilities into the regular classroom:

1. *Get a little help from your friends.* Look to other professionals in the school for support and suggestions.
2. *Welcome the student in your classroom.* Demonstrate with your actions that the student is a valuable member of the class.
3. *Be the teacher of all students.* Merely "hosting" the student doesn't work very well.
4. *Make sure everyone belongs to the classroom community.* Disabled students should take part in all class assignments and activities.
5. *Clarify shared expectations with team members.* Determine what the learning priorities and expected outcomes are.
6. *Adapt activities to the student's needs.* All children need successful experiences in the classroom.
7. *Provide active and participatory learning experiences.* Activity-based learning is often well adapted to the needs of the disabled student.
8. *Adapt classroom arrangements, materials, and strategies.* Be willing to initiate alternate teaching methods or classroom adaptations as necessary.
9. *Make sure support services help.* Work closely with members of the student's support team.
10. *Evaluate your teaching.* Reflect to make sure that your teaching makes a real difference in the lives of students.

Excerpted from Giangreco, M. F. (1996) "What Do I Do Now? A Teacher's Guide to Including Students with Disabilities. *Educational Leadership.* 53:56–59. Reprinted with permission of the author.

compelling evidence that placement is the critical factor in student academic or social success; the classroom environment and quality of instruction have more impact than placement per se on the success of students with disabilities" (Hocutt, 1996; p. 97). Placement alone will not eliminate any child's learning problems. Children may overcome their learning disabilities, however, if they receive direct teaching of reading and writing, experience cooperative learning, engage in peer tutoring, acquire effective skills and strategies, and participate in other activities, with literature at the heart of the instructional process. "One of the most effective ways to reduce the number of children who will ultimately need remedial services is to provide the best possible classroom instruction in the first place" (Slavin and Madden, 1989; p. 9).

Students with Learning Difficulties

Children struggle in learning to read and write for a variety of reasons, including:

> *Cognitive Developmental Delay* —The child's intellectual ability or learning capacity is not at the expected level for his or her age; a child with cognitive delay was conventionally called a slow learner.

11.2 Putting Ideas to Work
Reading Recovery

Reading recovery is an early intervention program used with young children who are experiencing reading problems. Designed by New Zealand educator Marie M. Clay, the program aims to reach first graders who are having difficulty learning to read in the hope that early intervention will help them succeed before they fall into a pattern of failure.

The program provides children with one-to-one lessons with highly trained tutors for 30 minutes each day. Pupils are selected based on teacher recommendation and a diagnostic survey that measures the child's knowledge of letters and words, concepts about print, writing, and text reading. The tutoring is provided in addition to instruction in the regular classroom.

Although tutoring sessions differ depending on the teacher and the needs of the child, each Reading Recovery lesson normally consists of:

1. *Reading familiar books.* The child reads trade books that he or she has enjoyed before. The teacher observes and assesses the child as he or she reads these familiar stories.
2. *Assessing reading strategies.* The child reads a book that was new to him or her the previous day. The teacher keeps a running record of the child's reading behavior to determine the strategies the child uses while reading. This also provides an ongoing record of the child's progress.
3. *Writing messages and stories.* The child composes and writes a daily message, with assistance from the teacher as needed. The teacher copies this message and uses it in various ways for instruction. Teacher and student also spend time working with letters and decoding strategies.
4. *Reading new books.* The teacher introduces the child to a new book that the child will read the next day. Child and teacher discuss the book and set the stage for meaning before reading.

Reading Recovery is a literature-based reading program for problem readers. The program uses trade books with natural language rather than controlled vocabulary in the instructional process. The program has become extremely popular, and reported results have been generally positive (Wasik and Slavin, 1993; Pinnell et al., 1994; Pikulski, l994; Shanahan and Barr, 1995; and Spiegel, 1995).

A full description of the diagnostic and instructional procedures involved in Reading Recovery is featured in *Reading Recovery: A Guidebook for Teachers in Training* by Marie M. Clay (1993).

Learning Disability—The child has difficulty understanding or using language, and this difficulty cannot be attributed to sensory, cognitive, emotional, environmental, or economic disadvantage. Learning disabilities are sometimes called dyslexia, minimal brain damage, or perceptual disorder.

Attention-Deficit Hyperactivity Disorder (ADHD)—The child is exceptionally inattentive, impulsive, and hyperactive.

Speech and Language Disorders—The child has articulation difficulties, sometimes along with problems in comprehending, word finding, or other language tasks.

Sensory or Physical Disabilities—The child has hearing or visual impairments, or perhaps has other orthopedic difficulties.

11.3 Putting Ideas to Work
Success for All

Another early intervention program that uses children's literature is Success for All. Designed by Slavin and his colleagues (1996) for use in innercity schools, Success for All is an all-school program that places an early emphasis on reading.

Like Reading Recovery, Success for All is an early intervention program that involves one-on-one tutoring with first graders in an attempt to head off reading problems before they interfere with the child's school success. Unlike Reading Recovery, however, Success for All is a more comprehensive school restructuring plan that extends throughout the elementary grades. It promotes cooperative learning, homogeneous grouping for reading instruction, and family support teams that get parents involved.

In daily 20-minute periods of tutoring during first grade, Success for All places a heavy emphasis on decoding, the systematic presentation of phonics, and reading from meaningful text. Tutoring sessions involve reading a story that the child has encountered previously in tutoring or in reading class; conducting short, intensive drills on letter sounds; and reading shared stories. Tutoring sessions also emphasize comprehension exercises, oral reading for fluency, and writing activities. First graders may receive the tutoring all year long and sometimes even into second grade.

Success for All is closely integrated with the child's classroom reading program. Tutors work on the same elements taught during classroom instruction. Research on the program (Wasik and Slavin, 1993; Slavin et al., 1994) shows it has helped children reach a measure of success in reading achievement. The program also provides a Spanish reading curriculum for grades 1–5.

When a student has more than one of these conditions, learning problems can be exacerbated considerably. Although not all children with learning problems have the same disorders, the manifestation of their problems is often similar. In reviewing research related to reading, Kirk, Kliebhan, and Lerner intermingled research findings related to slow learners and pupils with learning disabilities because "the characteristics, learning patterns, and diagnostic and teaching procedures for these two groups of children overlap to a great extent. The research findings for one group have obvious implications for the other" (Kirk, Kliebhan, and Lerner, 1978; p. 198).

The majority—as many as 80 percent—of students with learning problems have their primary deficit in reading. For many pupils, learning problems first become apparent as the child tries to learn to read. During the preschool years, the child's development may have been normal—sometimes even advanced—in every way. Not until reading instruction begins do his or her learning problems begin to show up. Since their problems so directly impact their ability to learn to read and write, literacy instruction is vital in helping these children address their problems.

Pupils with learning difficulties need to learn to use the same skills and strategies good readers use. They need to decode unfamiliar words and figure out meaning from context. They need to draw on their schemata to construct meaning from what they read. They need to monitor their own

11.4 Putting Ideas to Work
First Steps

Another literacy program that attempts to address reading problems early in a child's school life is First Steps. Developed in Australia, the program focuses on children's development as readers and writers and matches instruction to their individual characteristics. The program includes components for reading, writing, spelling, and oral language.

Teachers determine a child's phase of development by observing his or her literacy behavior. In reading, for example, five phases extend from Role Play Reading (in which the child shows interest in print and reading-like behavior) to Independent Reading (in which the child is aware of strategies he or she employs in purposeful reading activities). Teaching techniques are matched to children at each phase. In the early stage, for example, the teacher presents print in natural and meaningful contexts, rereading favorite stories and sharing Big Books. At the later stages, the teacher introduces critical reading and higher-level thinking activities. First Steps is geared toward teaching practices rather than a particular set of instructional materials. Most schools adopt the program on a school-wide basis.

Most of the research on First Steps has been conducted in Australia (Rees, 1994). While it is published in Australia, the program is available in this country through Heinemann Books.

comprehension as they proceed through text, and they need to apply comprehension strategies as they read informational materials. Finally, they need lots and lots of literature.

McCoy and Prehm (1987) emphasize the importance of direct instruction, time on task, and classroom management techniques in teaching children with learning problems how to read. In direct instruction, the teacher sets specific objectives, aims at helping pupils generalize, carefully sequences lessons, uses familiar examples to build comprehension, and allows students plenty of practice to apply what they have learned. The teacher must also pay particular attention to time on task, concentrating on reading-related activities at an appropriate level of difficulty. Classroom management considerations include providing enough instructional time for reading, finding different levels of reading material on the same topic, giving children the extra attention they need, and involving them in a variety of instructional groups.

Obviously, one way to deal with the issue of learning problems is to address these problems early in the child's school career. This is the goal of intervention programs such as Reading Recovery (see Putting Ideas to Work 11.2) and Success for All (Putting Ideas to Work 11.3). In a review of research related to programs offered to pupils in danger of failing, Slavin and Madden (1989) concluded that effective programs are comprehensive, intensive, and adapted to the student's individual needs; in other words, these programs have the same qualities that define effective instruction for problem learners in the classroom.

Teaching Strategies

Although it is important to pay attention to vocabulary and decoding strategies, improving comprehension is the goal in teaching reading. A variety of techniques have proved effective in helping less capable readers improve their reading comprehension through the use of trade books.

Decoding Strategies.   The ability to decode unknown words is no less important for the problem reader than for the capable reader; in fact, it may be more important. Research has shown that phonemic awareness is a predictor of reading success, so focusing on this early in the child's school career is important. The longer a child goes without identification and intervention, the more difficult the task of remediation will be. That's why programs like Reading Recovery (Putting Ideas to Work 11.2) are geared to the very early grades.

A number of highly structured intensive phonics programs are used with children with reading problems, among them the Orton-Gillingham method, Wilson Reading Systems, Won-Way Phonics, Project READ, and others. Each of these focus heavily on the synthetic approach to phonics; that is, the child learns letter-sound combinations in isolation and blends them into larger units.

Children with reading problems certainly need greater-than-average attention to help them master decoding strategies, but the real goal of reading—comprehension—should remain strong. While word skills have proven important in a direct and balanced instructional program, trade books and authentic reading materials are also important for reading success (Fawcett, 1995; Morris, Ervin, and Conrad, 1996).

The teacher needs to reinforce these skills and help the pupil apply decoding strategies as one method of identifying unfamiliar words when reading authentic text. The word identification techniques taught to all students need to be constantly reinforced with the problem reader. Fluent and automatic processing of words is essential to comprehension.

Semantic Mapping.   In their work with students having reading disabilities, some of whom attended special classes, Sinatra, Stahl-Gemake, and Berg (1984) found semantic mapping to be an effective means of improving reading comprehension. A semantic map—a graphic representation of the relationships among words, ideas, or events in text—is a cognitive strategy that helps children comprehend what they read. Teachers can present maps before reading a text, or they can help pupils construct a map as they read a selection of narrative or expository text.

Scaffolding.   Providing support to help learners bridge the gap between what they know and what they need to know has been suggested as an effective technique for helping pupils with reading problems (Graves and Graves, 1994; Graves, Graves, and Braaten, 1996). For poor readers, scaffolding involves prereading activities such as preteaching vocabulary and concepts, activating background knowledge, and suggesting strategies children can use while reading. During the lesson, scaffolding might involve guided reading or reading to the pupils. In using a chapter book for reading lessons, for example, the teacher can read the first chapter (and perhaps several succeeding chapters) aloud to the students, either directly or on tape. For informational trade books, study guides can be provided. Post-reading scaffolding activities might include a directed discussion on the book's content and on comprehension strategies, along with a variety of writing and other activities related to the story. While scaffolding is appropriate for all students, differentiated scaffolding is important for pupils who experience difficulties while reading.

Direct Instruction on Comprehension Components.

Explicit instruction on essential elements is appropriate with a literature-based approach. By focusing directly and specifically on causal relationships in stories, Varnhagen and Goldman (1986) helped a group of extremely slow learners improve their ability to identify and understand the relationships among ideas and events in text. The children reinforced this understanding by writing stories that emphasized the relationships among episodes in the original stories. This focus could extend to other components of comprehension as well.

Pogrow (1990) used a program called HOTS (Higher Order Thinking Skills) to help high-risk students improve reading comprehension. HOTS is based on the premise that a fundamental problem with poor readers is that they do not understand "understanding"; that is, they lack the metacognitive strategies involved in linking new information to the knowledge they already have. Pogrow developed a program that focuses on higher-level thinking processes and consciously applies metacognitive strategies to problem solving, making inferences, generalizing ideas, and synthesizing information. These strategies replace the traditional drills that characterize instruction for poor readers. The HOTS program uses questioning strategies extensively, engaging pupils in conversations that sound like Socratic dialogue. By modeling the problem-solving process through questioning and dialogue, teachers show children how to tackle new concepts by building on what they already know. The HOTS program has produced very positive effects with high-risk pupils, leading to the conclusion that "a thinking skills program can improve achievement as much as a good remedial approach—and probably a great deal more" (Pogrow, 1990; p. 391).

Davey (1983) has identified aspects of cognitive processing that good readers have and poor readers lack: the abilities to make predictions, visualize, build on prior knowledge, self-monitor, and self-correct. She proposes that poor readers can acquire these competencies through modeling and practice, and she suggests using "Think Alouds" that help slow learners

11.5 Putting Ideas to Work

Leo the Late Bloomer: A Lesson for Children with Reading Problems

*I*n any heterogeneous group, adjustments must be made for children with reading problems. Using Robert Kraus's *Leo the Late Bloomer,* the story of a tiger who has trouble learning to do things (a trade book which may itself be an encouraging message for some children with reading problems), one teacher developed the following group lesson for her first grade class:

> *Prereading*—To connect the story to their previous experiences, the teacher asked the children to think about things they were once not able to do but now could do. Children's suggestions included tying their shoes, swimming, skating, walking to school alone, and so on.
>
> The teacher wrote the title of the book on the chalkboard and pointed to each word as the class read it aloud. She called special attention to the long *a* in *Late* and the *oo* in *Bloomer,* phonetic elements she had taught earlier.
>
> The class talked about the picture on the cover of the story and discussed how the look on Leo's face indicated he might be feeling. The teacher asked the children what questions the picture raised in their minds.
>
> The group discussed the meaning of the word *bloom* and the derivative *bloomer.*
>
> The teacher asked the class to read the story to find out what Leo's problem was and how he solved it.
>
> *Reading*—The teacher began reading the story to the group. She read the first several pages, and when she came to the line, "And, he never said a word," she asked the group what they thought might happen next.
>
> The teacher then divided the group into three subgroups. One subgroup went off in pairs to read the story to each other independently and to practice reading the dialogue in readers theatre fashion. Another subgroup went to the listening station to follow the lines of print as they heard the story read aloud on a tape recorder. Children with reading problems stayed with the teacher for directed instruction.
>
> The teacher continued reading the story aloud, asking children to supply the words she knew they could read on their own. They briefly discussed the meaning of the word *patience.*
>
> When they came to the last page, they practiced reading the final line "I made it!" in different tones—with relief, triumph, or surprise. Children retold the story in the group.
>
> *Postreading*—For decoding practice, the teacher wrote the words *late* and *bloom* on separate charts, and asked children to supply other words with the *-ate* and *-oom* rhymes.
>
> The group then went to the listening station to hear the story read again on tape, while the teacher met with each of the other two subgroups.
>
> Children drew pictures and wrote sentences describing their own "What I couldn't do before/What I can do now" experiences.
>
> Later, the teacher gathered the group for a shared reading experience and for additional practice with the decoding elements in *late* and *bloom.* Children then shared what they had written and drawn in response to the story.

approach reading more strategically, systematically, and thoughtfully. The steps in the Think-Aloud Process are:

1. As pupils follow silently in a text, the teacher makes predictions, discusses visual impressions, comments on prior knowledge, and verbalizes the mental processes the teacher uses while reading.
2. After modeling experiences, students read aloud in pairs, following the same procedures.
3. Children then move to independent practice and integrate the Think-Aloud procedures into other classroom reading experiences.

Hahn (1985) found that remedial readers benefited from instruction in strategic behaviors that help to comprehend text better. Pupils learned to use the following text strategies: "(a) asking themselves questions while reading expository text, (b) practicing recall of these same texts, and (c) learning how to write text-based and reader-based questions" (Hahn, 1985; p. 73). Metacognitive activities such as self-questioning and recalling or reviewing what they had read helped slow learners understand and remember more.

All of these techniques—a focus on metacognition, HOTS, Think Alouds, strategy training, and others—help poor readers apply the strategies good readers use.

Reading to Younger Pupils. For pupils who are reading at levels well below their peers in the regular classroom, reading a trade book other children consider "too easy" or "a baby book" can be embarrassing. But students can read these books to children in the lower grades in a cross-grade cooperative activity. This provides a motivational dimension to learning.

Modeling Techniques. Modeling techniques can help poor readers achieve fluency and learn to connect spoken language with its written equivalent.

In *neurological impress,* the teacher sits near the student and reads aloud while pointing to the word being read. The pupil attempts to read along with the teacher as quickly and accurately as possible. Over time, the teacher decreases speed and volume so the student can gradually take the lead.

In *taped reading,* a child reads along silently with a recorded text. Many trade books popular with pupils at a particular grade level will be written above the reading level of the less able readers in the class. Students can use the listening center to listen to tapes as they follow the text that other pupils in the class are reading. Following the lines of a story while listening to a tape produces double benefits: it helps establish the speech-print connection in the child's mind, and exposure to the book allows the pupil to engage in literature discussions and other reading-related activities with classmates.

In *repeated reading,* a pupil reads a passage aloud to the teacher and then listens to a tape recording of the passage to practice fluency. This technique is recommended for children whose word recognition abilities match the reading level of the text.

11.6 Putting Ideas to Work
Working with Multiple Intelligences

*H*oward Gardner (1993, 1995) has proposed a theory of multiple intelligences, suggesting that humans have many ways to solve problems and learn what they need to know and do. The seven intelligences that Gardner identifies are:

> *Verbal/Linguistic*—responsible for, and awakened by, language.
> *Logical/Mathematical*—associated with numbers, reasoning, and calculations.
> *Visual/Spatial*—dealing with the visual arts.
> *Musical/Rhythmic*—recognizing and using rhythm and tonal patterns.
> *Bodily/Kinesthetic*—using the whole body in learning.
> *Interpersonal*—having social understanding and working well with others.
> *Intrapersonal*—knowledge of the internal aspects of self.

Gardner's theory suggests that teachers must consciously activate children's multiple intelligences by injecting their lessons with strategies and activities to build upon the multiple strengths children have. Fran Jacobs and Amy Johnson, two teachers from the Beacon Hill School in Seattle, Washington, describe how they apply multiple intelligences to lessons with bilingual first graders and other young children with reading problems, using the popular fairy tale *The Three Billygoats Gruff.*

> *Verbal/Linguistic*—The teacher writes key sentences on story strips, and children read them.
> *Logical/Mathematical*—The teacher reads an alternative version of the story, and children create Venn diagrams based on the two versions.
> *Visual/Spatial*—As the teacher first reads the story aloud, he or she asks the children to visualize the action. At intervals, the teacher stops and children draw story scenes on folded pieces of paper. (This activity led to a concept book on small, medium, and large.)
> *Musical/Rhythmic*—Children chant part of the story, emphasizing the rhythm of the language.
> *Bodily/Kinesthetic*—Children act out the story in creative dramatics.
> *Interpersonal*—Children read the story with a tutor or a buddy.
> *Intrapersonal*—The teacher guides a discussion not only on what happened in the story, but on how it relates to the children's lives.

These seven intelligences are not discrete. At times, one merges into another. For example, the language activity of reading story strips to others is an interpersonal activity as well.

Ms. Jacobs writes, "What we have found is that our children develop a connectedness to our stories when we do these lessons. By the time they get the text to read, it is an old friend. Our struggling readers, for this one story and at this one moment in time, are fluent readers."

Used with permission of Frances S. Jacobs.

Cross-grade tutoring—with older pupils reading to younger ones—has proved to be an effective technique for promoting literacy.
© David M. Grossman/ Photo Researchers, Inc.

In each of these procedures, literature is a direct part of reading instruction for the student with learning disabilities. But the techniques and strategies suggested here are not intended only for children with reading problems. A solid classroom reading program will address the needs of both good and poor readers. These sometimes overlooked techniques have proved effective in improving the reading development of the less able reader.

Holistic Reading. Reading instruction programs for pupils with reading problems sometimes overemphasize isolated skill development, stressing worksheets and other materials that can discourage extensive reading. Poor readers need explicit instruction in reading strategies, but this instruction should be tied to authentic reading experiences rather than to practice exercises removed from the connected discourse of a good story. For poor readers, as for any reader, the purposeful application and integration of skills and strategies in reading for meaning are more important than the mastery of the skills themselves.

Recently, educators have tended to approach reading instruction for children with learning disabilities in a more holistic manner. "Contemporary approaches to teaching learning disabled students and remedial learners tend to focus directly on the academic area in which the student is having difficulty. Thus, if a student has reading difficulties, instruction focuses on working with sound/letter relationships, word recognition, and/or reading texts as opposed to teaching an underlying ability like perceptual skills" (Rhodes and Dudley-Marling, 1988; p. 7). In approaching instruction for pupils with learning disabilities (and other children with reading problems), a four-step sequence is suggested:

1. *Developing summary statements* based on specific observations of what the child does as a reader and a writer. For example, "When Vladimir encounters an unfamiliar word, he relies exclusively on graphophonic

cues to identify the word" or "Aphrodite's independent writing rarely exceeds one or two sentences."

2. *Develop learner objectives* based directly on observed needs, statements that reflect what the teacher hopes the student will accomplish. For example, "Vladimir will begin to examine context clues to identify words he does not recognize in print" or "Aphrodite will begin to produce longer independent writing passages."

3. *Develop teaching goals* that state specifically what the teacher will do to help pupils achieve these objectives. For example, "The teacher will use cloze passages to introduce Vladimir to the use of context clues" or "In writing conferences, the teacher will encourage Aphrodite to elaborate on one idea in her writing."

4. *Conduct ongoing evaluation,* close monitoring and careful record keeping that enables the teacher to reexamine and revise goals in light of the child's daily reading and writing performance.

With this more holistic approach, the focus is directly on reading and writing rather than on an underlying perceptual disorder that influences literacy development. The teacher using holistic practices delivers explicit instruction on reading strategies, but he or she does so within the context of authentic stories rather than skills-based exercises.

Classroom Accommodations. Appropriate classroom accommodations often need to be made in light of the problems children have. A child with ADHD, for example, may need to be seated in a particular place in the classroom and may need a structured regimen of instructional activities.

Obviously, accommodations are necessary when a child has sensory or physical handicaps. Children with visual problems may need advantageous seating, optical aids such as enhanced computer screens, a class buddy to provide visual assistance, time adjustments for assignments, and large-print books. Consultation with a resource teacher will be important. Hearing-impaired pupils may need amplification devices like hearing aids, a classroom buddy, and visual reinforcement for vocabulary and other instructional components. Hearing-impaired students especially profit from the natural language in good literature as part of reading instruction. McCoy and Prehm (1987) question the contrived language found in conventional basal readers as the most effective tool for teaching children who have difficulty hearing. These authors suggest that appropriate language levels and reasonable phonetic emphasis are the cornerstones of a suitable reading program. Vocabulary development with semantic mapping, the use of contextual analysis, effective word attack, and monitoring of comprehension are all effective techniques as well.

Working in conjunction with the resource specialist, the classroom teacher can make accommodations for physically challenged pupils; for example, children with severe motor problems may need wheelchairs, special typewriters, separate desks or workspaces, or other adaptive equipment; students whose neuromuscular problems make speech difficult may

Technology enables students who are visually impaired to participate more fully in literature-based instruction.
© Rhoda Sidney/PhotoEdit

need a system of nonverbal communication; pupils with motor coordination problems may need some sort of physical support for holding books.

Technical advances in computers and other communications devices hold enormous promise for facilitating the learning of multihandicapped pupils. Erickson and Koppenhaver (1995), for example, describe a reading program that was successful for severely disabled pupils. But even as advances are made, teachers need patience, sensitivity to the frustration the child may often feel, willingness to give the child time to produce a response, and a knack for using whatever works to promote the pupil's learning.

Beyond instructional adjustments and classroom accommodations for reading, it is important that children with handicaps be accepted and treated as part of the class. This means including these pupils in all activities, applying the same rules for appropriate behavior, integrating them into the social life of the classroom, and encouraging independence. Teachers need to be sensitive to the fact that some children with handicaps prefer to be inconspicuous so as not to appear different at an age when conformity is important, and that many nonhandicapped pupils shy away from those who are disabled. Teachers need to apply a measure of support and TLC in making the student with handicaps as much a part of the life of the classroom as possible. Full participation and social integration are the goals.

Literature for Pupils with Learning Difficulties

Reading strategies are integrated and applied through reading trade books. Children who don't learn well need exposure to literature, just as all children do. Through literature, students who are less able readers learn that reading can be a pleasure, not always a chore.

11.7 Putting Ideas to Work
Books about Children with Sensory and Physical Handicaps

A number of trade books that feature children with handicaps as main characters are available for use in the classroom. A small sampling of these books includes:

> Ada B. Litchfield's *A Cane in Her Hand,* the story of how a visually impaired child adjusts to feeling different.
>
> Bill Martin, Jr., and John Archambault's *Knots on a Counting Rope,* the story of a blind American Indian child, told in an interesting narrative style.
>
> Edith Fisher Hunter's *Child of the Silent Night,* a simply written, moving biography of Laura Bridgeman, a child whose illness left her both blind and deaf.
>
> Ivan Southall's *Let the Balloon Go,* an Australian book about a boy with cerebral palsy and his mother's reluctance to let him experiment with his own capabilities.
>
> Eleanor Spence's *October Child,* a courageous story that reveals the effects an autistic child has on his family.
>
> Patricia MacLachlan's *Through Grandpa's Eyes,* which tells how a young boy sees the world around him differently because of his grandfather's blindness.
>
> Theodore Taylor's *The Cay,* a survival tale about a boy who learns to use his other senses when he loses the ability to see.

These are not just books about exceptional children; they are compelling stories that happen to center on children with handicaps. Betsy Byars did not win the coveted Newbery Award for her *Summer of the Swans* because the book was about a girl's relationship with her severely retarded brother; she won the award because of the quality of the book as a piece of children's literature.

Portraying Persons with Disabilities: An Annotated Bibliography of FICTION for Children and Teenagers by Debra E. J. Robertson and *Portraying Persons with Disabilities: An Annotated Bibliography of NONFICTION for Children and Teenagers* by Joan Brest Friedberg, et al. are two annotated bibliographies that list books about individuals with special needs.

Gentile and McMillan (1990) identify some of the values of using literature to help less capable readers make sense out of print. Literature "provides them with the means to apply skills contextually, using rich material that educates and entertains. Moreover, good literature is knowledge-based and furnishes these students with a broad range of historical, geographical, political, scientific, mathematic, religious, biographical, and literary information. It stirs wonderment and imagination, facilitates these students' understanding of themselves and others and the world in which they live, and offers them a sense of identity or control that can empower the spirit and motivate them to express their thoughts and feelings" (Gentile and McMillan, 1990; p. 389). In short, literature has the same power for at-risk students as it does for other learners inside and outside of school. Schumaker and Schumaker (1988) describe how a project based on Eleanor

11.8 Putting Ideas to Work

Using Literature with Learning Disabled Pupils

---

*F*ollowing are some of the reflections and reactions of Carol J. Fuhler (1990), a junior high school teacher of learning-disabled students:

> I teach a literature-based reading program to a group of learning-disabled boys who revel in the absence of worksheets and tests. Two of them showed a three-year growth in reading this year while another improved a year and a half. For students who used to dislike and distrust books, that's exciting.
>
> My students have taught me that daily reading, even for a mere ten minutes, is a special time spent sharing a good book together.
>
> I believe that based on hearing a variety of stories read well, students are better able to build their own sense of story, to improve linguistic development, and eventually, to foster enthusiasm and a growing love of reading on their own.
>
> I have found that essential reading skills can be taught through a literature-based curriculum in a subtle, efficient manner within the context of the material each child is actively reading.

Coerr's *Sadako and the Thousand Paper Cranes* brought a group of upper-grade remedial readers out of the academic shadows and into the spotlight, and identify the advantages of using trade books for reading instruction with slow learners. By reading real books, these pupils realized that reading and writing are not just school subjects—they bring empowerment in the real world. Literature revitalizes the reading experience for slow learners, communicates acceptance and recognition of them as readers, and introduces great authors to children who might not otherwise encounter them. Children who are remedial readers in the upper elementary grades need literature most of all. "Literature offers neutral ground, free of classroom competition, grouping and grades. It emphasizes the worth of remedial activity. It . . . enhances the child's self-concept and reduces the isolation of the struggling student. Finally, it has the look, sound, and rhythm of language as used by masters, unlike the artificial language constructs of workbooks and the anonymous voices of textbooks" (Schumaker and Schumaker, 1988; pp. 547–548).

Instructional materials must be adjusted to a poor reader's reading level; however, this adjustment often means that at-risk pupils end up reading books obviously easier than the books their classmates are reading. The unfortunate consequence can be merciless comments such as "Jack is reading baby books," or "I read that book two years ago!" To provide authentic reading experiences with lower-level materials in the regular classroom, the teacher can:

arrange to have upper-grade pupils read easier books aloud to children in the lower grades;

11.9 Putting Ideas to Work
The "Curious George" Strategy

Richek and McTague (1988) suggest a literature-based remedial approach that they call "The Curious George Strategy for Students with Reading Problems." The strategy involves carefully planned, small group reading lessons using trade books in series, such as H. A. and Margaret Rey's series about the mischievous monkey, Curious George, Norman Bridwell's imaginative Clifford, the big red dog, and Gene Zion's engaging pooch Harry. (Since vocabulary and language patterns are consistent throughout the series, children find successive books in a series progressively easier to read.)

As a first step, the teacher introduces the book and reads it aloud. Pupils are invited to assist by reading the predictable words. Teacher and students make word cards from the vocabulary in the story. This procedure is repeated with successive sections of each book until the entire book has been read. At that point, students dictate their own versions of the story. This same strategy is carried out with successive books in the series.

Richek and McTague report that the technique generates enthusiasm and a willingness to read more independently. Other activities emerge from the strategy—sentence building with word cards, shared reading with pupil-initiated discussion, and an abundance of writing activities.

Beyond the excitement that the strategy generates among otherwise reluctant readers, statistical data support the success of the program. Students in the Curious George group performed significantly better than children in a control group in tests of oral reading and comprehension. The informal observations of teachers and parents reaffirmed the success of the strategy.

With highly motivating books such as Curious George, remedial readers can read well above their expected level of achievement.

set up author groups, in which students read different books by an author who has written at different difficulty levels;

provide supplementary instructional support that will allow the less able readers to handle books a little above their expected levels; and

plan whole group and cooperative learning projects in which poorer readers carry out meaningful assignments in line with their abilities.

When children have learning difficulties, teachers typically emphasize skills in helping them learn to read and write. But being literate goes beyond having literacy skills such as the ability to sound out words or to identify main ideas or topic sentences. "The sense of being literate derives from the ability to exhibit *literate behaviors*" (Heath, 1991; p. 3). Literature affords all children the opportunity to be part of a literate community.

In the final analysis, children with reading problems profit from high-quality, innovative instruction, as all pupils do. And like all children, they deserve to read literature as part of that instruction. "A literature-based approach . . . becomes a program of prevention rather than remediation. Even our low-ability readers benefit from an understanding of good literature" (Routman, 1988; p. 18).

Through cooperative learning activities, all children—including those with special needs—can take part in literature-based reading and writing instruction.

© James L. Shaffer

Writing

Since learning problems often affect writing as much as reading, students with learning disablities often need special attention when it comes to writing. These students typically have ideas for writing, but the process of getting words and ideas on paper in an interesting, organized manner may require extra effort and guidance.

Children with learning disabilities need to follow the steps in the writing process more slowly and intensively than their peers. At the prewriting stage, special-needs pupils included in the regular classroom may benefit from the use of imagery. "The children lie on the floor and close their eyes, except for children who are deaf, and the teacher tells an imagery-evoking story starter . . . imagery and relaxation are critical for breaking through the negative feelings that most [special-needs] students have about writing" (Twiss, 1995; p. 67). At the writing stage, teachers need to provide support and encourage the use of invented spelling. Students should clearly understand that they produce first drafts they can revise later on. Conferencing is important at the postwriting stage; peer conferencing and team proofreading can be a beneficial cooperative learning experience.

The mechanics of writing can be especially problematic for children with learning problems. Handwriting is often virtually unintelligible. Spelling can be a particular problem; such children frequently reverse letter order and may have trouble remembering how to spell familiar words. For pupils with learning problems, the word processor is a godsend. It eliminates handwriting difficulties; the grammar- and spell-check functions provide essential assistance; and even the process of keyboarding helps students learn to encode language.

11.10 Putting Ideas to Work

Literature as Part of Language Therapy

Since reading is a language activity, speech and language problems can seriously impede the process of learning to read, and language therapy is frequently part of the instructional program for pupils with learning disabilities. Literature can be an integral part of this instructional component, as one speech and language pathologist explains:

> I utilize literature during language therapy sessions in lieu of traditional picture cards that depict action verbs, spatial relations, and story sequences. Individualized Educational Plans written for pupils with language delays or disorders typically contain goals and objectives aimed at improving their verb tense usage, their understanding of spatial relations, story sequence skills, pronoun usage, and vocabulary development. Literature can be used to integrate and reinforce all of these skills and make instruction more motivating and memorable. The rhythm, rhyme, humor, and repetition in a good children's story can capture a pupil's attention far better than a stack of picture cards monotonously flipped to produce a desired response. Besides, quality literature is rich with language and linguistic forms.
>
> Stories can be used in a variety of ways. Using a Big Book, for example, past tense verbs can be hidden using self-sticking memo sheets. As pupils hear the story retold, they supply the missing verbs. Correct responses are rewarded. This cloze procedure can be adapted to be used with auxiliary verbs, prepositional phrases, pronouns, and selected vocabulary items. Having pupils predict what happens next or asking them to explain what happened before an event in a story are effective scaffolding techniques aimed at strengthening storytelling or narrative discourse capabilities.
>
> Any book containing good language is a good book to use. I love books by Chris Van Allsburg—*The Stranger, Jumanji, The Garden of Abdul Gasazi, The Wreck of the Zephyr.* I also like poetry, books like Jack Prelutsky's *New Kid on the Block* and Shel Silverstein's *Where the Sidewalk Ends* and *A Light in the Attic.* I've also used *Lon Po Po* by Ed Young and *What Do You Do with a Kangaroo?* by Mercer Mayer. In any quality children's book, one can find language to work with.
>
> Reading is enjoyable! Apart from addressing specific language needs, literature in language therapy sessions can provide a motivating and pleasurable experience for both the pupils and the speech pathologist.

Used with permission of Jacalyn R. Costello, CCC-SP Speech/Language Pathologist.

Teachers can make adjustments for children with learning difficulties for written language activities in the classroom. Pupils can dictate into a tape recorder or directly to a scribe to achieve writing fluency. Dialogue journals, response journals, and other types of personal writing may also help the student.

In short, the child with learning disabilities needs every support possible in classroom writing activities.

11.11 Putting Ideas to Work
Literature-Based Reading for Students with Emotional Handicaps

D'Alissandro (1990) describes how she initiated a literature-based reading program in a self-contained classroom of children with emotional handicaps. Many of these pupils had other disabilities that compounded their difficulty in learning to read. As an alternative to the conventional basal reading and language experience approaches, the teacher focused her reading program on novels at varying reading levels—books such as Aesop's *City Mouse–Country Mouse*, Judy Blume's popular *Tales of a Fourth Grade Nothing*, and E. B. White's classic *Charlotte's Web*.

Pupils sat in groups for 40 minutes. Everyone—including the teacher—read aloud. The story became the focus of discussion, additional reading, and other related activities for concept building.

Results were extremely positive. The children's word identification improved significantly, even though they spent very little time in direct instruction on word attack. Standardized test scores rose. Interests and attitudes improved demonstrably. Pupils gained in their ability to sustain interest and comprehend while reading. But for these children with emotional problems, "the full integration of the program takes place when the experiences gained from the readings are attached to personal experiences and become meaningful insights" (D'Alissandro, 1990; p. 292).

The program was a success, and the success was long-lasting.

Pupils with Attitude and Behavior Problems

No learning is ever devoid of emotion. Attitude and behavior, the emotional or affective dimensions of learning, can directly influence the process of learning to read. Children's self-concepts, the relationships they maintain with others, the attitudes they bring to school, and the process of learning to read itself will have a strong impact on their learning experiences.

Trying to determine how emotional issues and reading problems are related is analogous to asking the question "Which came first, the chicken or the egg?" On the one hand, fear or a low self-image will likely cause problems in learning to read. At the same time, failure may cause frustration, embarrassment, hostility, and a range of emotions that can be marks of personality problems. Success breeds confidence, which leads to continuing success in reading. No matter which is cause and which is effect, attitude and learning to read are inseparable.

Teaching Techniques

Instructional techniques suggested for students with problems in attitude and behavior often relate more to behavior management strategies than to strategies for processing print. These techniques include:

using language experience activities (often based on stories that teachers read aloud) as vehicles for reading acquisition;

using the lyrics of popular songs or the scripts of television shows as motivational devices;

employing a structured behavior modification program that identifies acceptable behaviors, defines conditions for learning, and rewards success;

contracting, or setting up a pupil-teacher agreement for the completion of reading-related tasks;

making charts that document progress or record short-term growth in learning or behavior patterns;

role playing to help pupils discover how their behavior affects others;

adjusting assignments to accommodate for the shorter-than-usual attention spans of some students.

In short, quality reading instruction must provide plenty of successful learning experiences and encouragement to reinforce both learning and behavior. One reading technique that has proved successful with students with attitude and behavior problems is bibliotherapy.

Bibliotherapy

Books often contribute to more than the academic development of emotionally troubled children; books can contribute to their personal and emotional development as well. Skilled teachers sometimes use trade books to help pupils deal with some of their personal problems or the strong feelings they may experience as a result of events in their lives. This process is known as bibliotherapy.

Bibliotherapy is a dynamic interaction between a person and a piece of literature, an interaction that helps the person satisfy emotional needs or find solutions to personal problems. Bibliotherapy is one way to help pupils work through some of their personal, social, and affective problems and to promote mental health through literature. "Using bibliotherapy may be one way to help a child think about the situation in a new or more positive way, or simply validate the many feelings that the child may be experiencing" (Dialessi and Burns, 1994; p. 20).

The process of using books to help children identify and deal with personal problems includes three steps:

1. Universalization and identification, as pupils discover they are not the only ones with a particular problem;
2. Catharsis, as students identify with the characters and share their feelings; and
3. Insight, as students become aware of the motivations and behavior of story characters and develop a realistic view of themselves and their problems.

Through bibliotherapy, pupils meet book characters with problems similar to their own. By identifying with the problems of these characters, young readers may develop insights into their own problems. They may see how book characters cope with problems and relate the solutions to their own lives. Students often transfer the insights they develop into how characters solve problems in stories to their own worlds. They thus gain knowledge about themselves and insights into their own behaviors. A child from a special education class, for example, frightened other children away with his overly aggressive behavior on the playground. When his teacher read Margaret Howell's *The Lonely Dragon,* the story of a friendly dragon who frightened children away because he breathed smoke and fire when he became excited, the child began to realize the effect his excited behavior was having on others.

Over the years, researchers have shown that books shape pupils' attitudes and influence their behavior (Kimmel, 1970; Sullivan, 1987; Schumaker and Schumaker, 1988). Bibliotherapy can be a successful dimension of reading instruction for children with emotional problems.

Although bibliotherapy attempts to promote emotional health through literature, books do not stand alone in helping pupils find solutions to problems. Bibliotherapy requires the careful guidance of teachers in story selection and in interpretation. Follow-up questions and discussions, retelling and role playing, writing and art projects will highlight and reinforce the positive therapeutic effects of a book.

Gifted and Talented Pupils

At the other end of the learning spectrum are gifted and talented students, children who add another dimension to the classroom reading program. Who are the gifted and talented?

Defining Gifted and Talented

The traditional standard for designating a child "gifted" was his or her score on an IQ test; however, giftedness and academic talent extend beyond the single criterion of cognitive ability and into the area of creativity.

Not all gifted learners are the same, but they share certain characteristics that influence their literacy development. They learn quickly. They consistently read two or more years above their grade level. Many enter school already able to read, and they continue to make rapid progress in reading. They are usually very interested in reading and writing. They have larger-than-average vocabularies, owing largely to their wider-than-average reading. They have excellent recall, persistent curiosity, and the ability to grapple with complex ideas. They are quick to understand relationships, facile with abstract concepts, and creative in making jumps in abstract thinking and problem solving. They have the gifts of higher intellectual ability and academic aptitude.

11.12 Putting Ideas to Work
Children's Books on "Tender Topics"

Authors of books for children and young adults often deal with sensitive issues in their writing. They broach such tender topics as death, divorce, and family problems with skill and insight. Here is a small sampling of books that deal with some of these issues:

Death

> Lucille Clifton's *Everett Anderson's Goodbye,* in which a young boy struggles through stages of the grief process over his father's death.
> Judith Viorst's *The Tenth Good Thing about Barney,* a picture book that deals sensitively with a child's grief over the death of his pet.
> Jane Rush Thomas's *Saying Good-bye to Grandma,* a story about a seven-year-old who attends her grandmother's funeral and comes to grips with many of the traditions surrounding death.
> Doris Buchanan Smith's *A Taste of Blackberries,* a story about the shock and grief of a boy who witnesses the accidental death of his friend.
> Katherine Patterson's *Bridge to Terabithia,* the moving story of a young boy who has to deal with the death of his best friend.
> Mary Kate Jordan's *Losing Uncle Tim,* a story about an uncle who dies from AIDS.

Realignment of Family Structures

> Helen S. Rogers's *Morris and His Brave Lion,* the story of a small boy who receives a stuffed lion from his father before the father leaves home.
> Beverly Cleary's *Dear Mr. Henshaw,* a boy's insightful reflections on some of the emotions involved when parents divorce.
> Betsy Byars's *The Animal, the Vegetable, and John D. Jones,* the story of two sisters who have to share their annual vacation with their father's new girlfriend and her son.
> Barbara Williams's *Mitzi's Honeymoon with Nana Potts,* an amusing account of a girl who is sent to stay with her new stepfather's mother while her own mother goes on a honeymoon.
> Patricia MacLachlan's *Journey,* a poignant story in which a mother leaves her son and daughter at their grandparents' house and the family has to cope with abandonment.
> Jill Krementz's *How It Feels When Parents Divorce,* a nonfiction book with real-life stories about children dealing with divorce.

Abuse

> Jeanette Caines's *Chilly Stomach,* a simply written story about a child's reaction to an overly friendly uncle.
> Linda Barr's *I Won't Let Them Hurt You,* the story of a babysitter who learns that the child in her care is being physically abused.
> Betsy Byars's *The Pinballs,* in which three foster children learn that they can take control of their lives.
> Carolyn Coman's *What Jamie Saw,* the story of a boy, his mother, and baby sister who are trying to escape an abusive relationship.

Continued on next page.

Homelessness

Eve Bunting's *Fly Away Home,* the touching story of a boy and his father who live in an airport because "the airport is better than the streets."

Karen Ackerman's *The Leaves in October,* a portrayal of how children grow up quickly in a homeless shelter.

Vicki Grove's *The Fastest Friend in the West,* an upper-grade book in which a friendship leads to insights into the problems of homelessness.

Jerry Spinelli's *Maniac Magee,* an upper-level book about an adolescent who uses his unique talents to overcome the problems of living on his own.

These books sometimes trouble adults, since they can contain strong stuff about painful life experiences. With careful guidance, however, many of these books can help pupils to cope with similar problems in their own lives.

The titles in this list make up only a fraction of the books that might be used for bibliotherapy. For additional titles, annotated by problem area, check the American Guidance Council's *The Bookfinder,* or *Books to Help Children Cope with Separation and Loss: An Annotated Bibliography* by Rudman et al.

Like all children, gifted students come in all shapes and sizes. Not all excel in reading. Some may be talented in athletics or art, some may be brilliant in mathematics. Those who have above-average talent in reading and writing are the ones we are concerned with in this chapter.

Often, gifted pupils receive larger assignments rather than more challenging and enriching assignments. ("Now that you've learned the names of all the U.S presidents, memorize the names of their vice presidents.") More is not necessarily better, however. A curriculum for the gifted and talented should offer something other than the normal fare. These children need some different kinds of reading experiences consistent with their abilities. "Appropriate, differentiated reading programs are essential for the academic growth of highly capable readers and for the preservation of their desire to learn" (Dooley, 1993; p. 547).

Challenging Reading

Because gifted and talented students usually do not demand the same degree of attention as pupils with problems, they often get lost in the larger educational landscape. Classroom programs that stress enrichment and acceleration can meet the needs of these very bright pupils in the regular classroom. *Books for the Gifted Child* by Paula Hauser and Gail A. Nelson is a two-volume bibliographic reference of fiction and nonfiction titles that are

11.13 Putting Ideas to Work
How to Recognize and Promote Talent

Feldhusen (1996) suggests the following six strategies teachers might use to recognize and develop talent in their pupils:

1. *Commit yourself to the role of talent scout.* Be alert to signs of talent in four areas—academic/intellectual, artistic, vocational/technical, and interpersonal/social.
2. *Structure some learning activities* that give students particularly good opportunities to demonstrate their talent potential.
3. *Recognize and reinforce signs of talent through praise.*
4. *Help students who have shown signs of talent* in a particular area to set learning goals in that area.
5. *Locate resources* to help foster students' talents.
6. *Share your observations* of budding talent with students' parents, and enlist the parents in the efforts to identify and nurture their children's talents.

particularly appropriate for academically talented children. Using quality literature, the teacher can plan such activities as:

deep reading in areas of interest from different sources; for example, reading not only biographies of famous people but books about their eras of history;

extended reading beyond the curriculum into areas of personal interest;

focusing on the author's craft, exploring how authors achieve their intended purposes;

problem solving, examining two or three versions of the same story, or reading to find answers to questions consistent with the reader's own needs, purposes, and interests;

inquiry reading, long-term reading projects in which pupils select their topics, do extensive reading and research, and communicate their findings to others (Cassidy, 1981);

critical reading, in-depth higher mental processing with the help of reading guides (Savage, 1983; Dooley, 1993);

Junior Great Books, a program that enriches the reading diet and promotes the discussion and critical thinking many gifted pupils thrive on;

writing, with stories, poems, and responses to literature that elaborate on ideas and show a depth of critical and creative reaction.

In short, gifted and talented students should have the freedom to expand beyond the bounds of narrow curriculum requirements and engage in reading and writing activities that encourage exploration and invention.

Literature plays an especially important role in reading for gifted and talented pupils. A literature-based program provides the breadth and depth of stories needed to challenge the abilities of exceptionally bright and creative children. Trade books offer an attractive alternative to more routine instructional materials and allow these students to explore the worlds of fantasy and reality consistent with their abilities.

Certain notable prodigies notwithstanding, pupils who are remarkably gifted in factors related to reading are often no different from their peers in their physical, social, and emotional development. Thus, young students who may be capable of reading a story several years above their grade placement may not possess the schemata or enjoy the social maturity that would allow them to comprehend or appreciate the story at the level the teacher might expect.

As in any learning situation, the teacher is the key to planning reading programs for gifted and talented students in the regular classroom. What Nelson and Cleland wrote almost 30 years ago is no less true today: "It is the teacher who sets the environment which inspires or destroys self-confidence, encourages or suppresses interests, develops or neglects abilities, fosters or banishes creativity, stimulates or discourages critical thinking, and facilitates or frustrates achievement" (Nelson and Cleland, 1971; p. 47). And these words will remain true as long as teachers and pupils work together in schools.

The Teacher on the Team

More often than not, specialists provide help and support services for children at the extreme ends of the learning spectrum. Special services available in many schools include:

remedial reading instruction, intensive programs for children reading below grade level or expected achievement level;

Title I programs, federally funded programs for extra services, including reading and language instruction and greater parent involvement;

resource room programs, where special teachers and tutors work with students diagnosed as learning disabled;

speech and language therapy for pupils with articulation problems and other language difficulties;

guidance and counseling for children who need special services in the affective dimensions of learning and life; and

special programs for gifted and talented learners that offer challenges these pupils might not experience in the classroom.

11.14 Putting Ideas to Work
Individualized Educational Programs

*T*he federal Individuals with Disabilities Education Act (IDEA) of 1992, as well as the earlier version of P.L. 94-142, mandates that every child receiving special education services must have an Individualized Educational Program (IEP). Developed by a multidisciplinary team that includes teachers, other professionals, and the child's parents, the IEP includes both academic and behavior goals for the child and specifies the special services the child will receive to help him or her achieve those goals.

Since children with special needs are now often included in regular classrooms, IEPs need to reflect the components of the classroom reading program. This includes an appropriate emphasis on literature. While the team leader—usually a school psychologist or special educator—has the primary responsibility for developing the plan, the professional with the most familiarity with the classroom reading program—the classroom teacher—needs to have major input into the IEP.

Because IEPs emphasize measurable objectives, they have tended to be very skills oriented, with isolated objectives set for mastery of sight words, decoding elements, and lower-level comprehension components. The main goal of reading, however, is the ability to apply these skills in encounters with authentic, meaningful language.

In addition to learning objectives such as *Mila will pronounce words containing the short* a *sound with 80 percent accuracy*, IEPs should contain objectives such as *Mila will independently read (or will retell the story)* The Cat in the Hat *with 80 percent accuracy*. Trade books, along with isolated worksheets, ought to be part of the special materials the IEP lists. The IEP should also specify the role the resource specialist will play in the classroom to help the special needs child interact with these books.

Under the Regular Education Initiative, the specialist involved in providing support services works directly with the special-needs learner in the classroom. Sometimes, however, these services are provided through "pull-out" programs offered outside the regular classroom. With all the coming and going in the classroom, however, it is important that students who need extra help do not miss regularly scheduled reading instruction. And it is vital that these children not miss recess, art, or other activities they especially enjoy.

When children receive special services, the classroom teacher becomes part of a professional team providing reading instruction. The teacher shares responsibility with other professionals to meet individual learning needs more fully. In reality, however, "a common pattern in the public schools is that one or two 'specialists,' usually including a school psychologist, see the child briefly, hold a meeting at which the child's teacher says little, and produce a report" (Bateman, 1992; p. 33).

The Regular Education Initiative has created a new partnership between classroom teachers and special educators. As a member of a multidisciplinary team, the classroom teacher must become a full participant in the decision-making process. The teacher should not be intimidated by the extra credentials or areas of expertise that many learning specialists have.

He or she must have a loud voice in planning reading instruction for the child. The teacher must also be involved in preparing the child's Individual Educational Plan, since much of this plan will be implemented in the classroom. In short, the teacher needs to be a champion who will speak and act on behalf of the child.

To make maximum use of available services, communication and coordination are crucial. Classroom teachers need to be aware of any services the pupil may be receiving in special programs outside the classroom and how their own classroom instruction can extend and reinforce these services. Based on their observations of children with special needs in classroom settings, they may need to suggest leads for specialists to follow. This two-way communication is absolutely vital to the reading instruction of children who need help.

In many ways, classroom teachers are the stars of multidisciplinary teams, since they are the central force in the education of the child. While successful performance in the one-to-one setting of a special program can be important, the ultimate payoff comes when the student succeeds in the everyday environment of the classroom. This is why teachers need to assume a central role in planning reading instruction for the atypical learner.

Summary and Conclusions

Helping all pupils achieve their full potential is a major aim of education in any society. All teachers face a challenge: achieving this goal in the face of the diverse needs and characteristics of the students in their classrooms.

Most children acquire the ability to read and write with normal instruction. For others, achieving literacy is more difficult. Educators have many names for this group—remedial readers, learning-disabled pupils, slow learners, underachievers, dyslexics, handicapped learners, and at-risk students, to name a few. What schools do not have is an easy solution to the problems these children encounter in acquiring literacy.

An essential beginning to meeting the needs of the full range of students in the classroom is to see all students as learners. The next step is to provide quality instruction—by selecting appropriate trade books and other instructional materials, building language, developing schemata, setting purposes, making pupils aware of their active involvement in the reading process, extending reading into the many facets of their lives both in and out of school, saturating instruction with literature; in short, doing well what we already know how to do. "America will become a nation of readers when verified practices of the best teachers in the best schools can be introduced throughout the country" (Anderson et al., 1985; p. 120).

The final step in meeting the reading instructional needs of all pupils is to make adjustments for each student's unique learning needs—adjusting the level and pace of instruction for children who learn more slowly, adapting presentations for pupils who have difficulty processing information, building a backlog of successful experiences with reading in an attempt to turn around negative attitudes and behaviors, making physical adjustments to accommodate students' physical disabilities, allowing gifted children the freedom and flexibility to develop to their full potential. In making these efforts, the classroom teacher can expect the direct assistance and support of other professionals who work with special-needs learners.

A Massachusetts law requiring special education for all children is based on the premise that:

a. all children are normal,
b. all children are different,
c. the differences in children are normal (Audette, 1974).

Taking these normal differences into account is what makes reading instruction a fine art and a precise science.

Discussion Questions and Activities

1. From the special education section of the library, read a reference on reading instruction for special-needs learners. What special provisions or programs does the reference suggest?
2. What do you think are the advantages and disadvantages of having specialists work with exceptional learners in the classroom rather than removing these pupils for special services?
3. Examine the research to identify the specific characteristics of children with attitude and behavior problems. Describe how these characteristics might affect a child's ability to learn to read and write.
4. Someone has suggested that classroom teachers should "get out of the light" of gifted and talented children and let them develop to their maximum potential on their own. What do you think of this idea? How can teachers promote this maximum development in the classroom?
5. Based on what you learned from this chapter, from your own school experiences, and from other sources you may have consulted, make a list of the five most important considerations in dealing with the wide spectrum of children you might expect to encounter in a classroom. Compare your list to lists that other students compiled. Then make a "master list" of suggestions for the class.

School-Based Assignments

1. In your field-based setting, identify a student who might be termed an exceptional learner. Observe the pupil during reading instruction. What types of adjustments or accommodations have been made to meet his or her needs? What other adaptations would you recommend on the basis of what you observe?
2. Interview teachers in your school about their response to the Regular Educational Initiative, which promotes the inclusion of children with special needs in the regular classroom. Summarize their opinions and compare them to your own.
3. Find a book on one of the "Tender Topics" identified in Putting Ideas to Work 11.12, or find other titles related to these topics. Select and share one of these books with a group of pupils. Note their reactions and responses to the story.
4. Interview two or three students with reading problems in your school. What are their perceptions of reading? How do they feel about the instruction they receive? Based on what you find out, what recommendations would you make to the teacher or principal?
5. Based on what you have read and what you see in schools, what are the three most challenging problems you anticipate in teaching reading to the entire spectrum of learners in the classroom? How can you prepare yourself to meet these challenges?

Ackerman, Karen. (1991). *The Leaves in October.* New York: Atheneum.

Aesop. (1970). *City Mouse–Country Mouse and Two More Mouse Tales.* New York: Scholastic.

Barr, Linda. (1988). *I Won't Let Them Hurt You.* Worthington, OH: Willowisp Press.

Blume, Judy. (1972). *Tales of a Fourth Grade Nothing.* New York: Dutton.

Bunting, Eve. (1991). *Fly Away Home.* New York: Clarion.

Byars, Betsy. (1970). *Summer of the Swans.* New York: Viking.

Byars, Betsy. (1977). *The Pinballs.* New York: Harper & Row.

Byars, Betsy. (1983). *The Animal, the Vegetable, and John D. Jones.* New York: Dellacourt.

Caines, Jeanette. (1986). *Chilly Stomach.* New York: Harper & Row.

Cleary, Beverly. (1983). *Dear Mr. Henshaw.* New York: Morrow.

Clifton, Lucille. (1983). *Everett Anderson's Goodbye.* New York: Henry Holt.

Coerr, Eleanor. (1977). *Sadako and the Thousand Paper Cranes.* New York: Putnam.

Coman, Carolyn. (1995). *What Jamie Saw.* Arden, NC: Front Street.

Grove, Vicki. (1991). *The Fastest Friend in the West.* New York: Putnam.

Howell, Margaret. (1972). *The Lonely Dragon.* London: Longman.

Hunter, Edith Fisher. (1963). *Child of the Silent Night.* New York: Dell.

Jordan, Mary Kate. (1989). *Losing Uncle Tim.* Morton Grove, IL: Albert Whitman.

Kraus, Robert. (l971). *Leo the Late Bloomer.* New York: Simon & Schuster.

Krementz, Jill. (1988). *How It Feels When Parents Divorce.* New York: Knopf.

Litchfield, Ada B. (1977). *A Cane in Her Hand.* Morton Grove, IL: Albert Whitman.

MacLachlan, Patricia. (1983). *Through Grandpa's Eyes.* New York: HarperCollins.

MacLachlan, Patricia. (1991). *Journey.* New York: Dellacourt.

Martin, Bill Jr., and Archambault, John. (1987). *Knots on a Counting Rope.* New York: Henry Holt.

Mayer, Mercer. (1987). *What Do You Do with a Kangaroo?* New York: Scholastic.

Paterson, Katherine. (1977). *Bridge to Terabithia.* New York: Harper & Row.

Prelutsky, Jack. (1984). *New Kid on the Block.* New York: Greenwillow.

Rogers, Helen. (1975). *Morris and His Brave Lion.* New York: McGraw-Hill.

Silverstein, Shel. (1974). *Where the Sidewalk Ends.* New York: Harper & Row.

Silverstein, Shel. (1981). *A Light in the Attic.* New York: Harper & Row.

Smith, Doris Buchanan. (1973). *A Taste of Blackberries.* New York: Crowell.

Southall, Ivan. (1968). *Let the Balloon Go.* New York: St. Martin.

Spence, Eleanor. (1976). *October Child.* London: Oxford University Press.

Spinelli, Jerry. (1990). *Maniac Magee.* Boston: Little, Brown.

Taylor, Theodore. (1989). *The Cay.* New York: Doubleday.

Thomas, Jane Rush. (1988). *Saying Good-bye to Grandma.* Boston: Houghton Mifflin.

Van Allsburg, Chris. (1979). *The Garden of Abdul Gasazi.* Boston: Houghton Mifflin.

Van Allsburg, Chris. (1981). *Jumanji.* Boston: Houghton Mifflin.

Van Allsburg, Chris. (1983). *The Wreck of the Zephyr.* Boston: Houghton Mifflin.

Van Allsburg, Chris. (1986). *The Stranger.* Boston: Houghton Mifflin.

Viorst, Judith. (1971). *The Tenth Good Thing About Barney.* New York: Atheneum.

White, E. B. (1952). *Charlotte's Web.* New York: Harper & Row.

Williams, Barbara. (1983). *Mitzi's Honeymoon with Nana Potts.* New York: Dell.

Young, Ed. (1989). *Lon Po Po: A Red-Riding Hood Story from China.* New York: Putnam.

References

Allington, R. L. (1994). Reducing the Risk: Integrated Language Arts in Restructured Elementary Schools. In *Integrated Language Arts: Controversy to Consensus.* Boston: Allyn & Bacon.

Anderson, R. C., Hiebert, E. H., Scott, J. A., and Wilkinson, I. A. G. (1985). *Becoming a Nation of Readers: Report of the Commission on Reading*. Washington, DC: National Institute of Education.

Audette, R. (1974). Concept Paper. In *Core Evaluation Manual*. Bedford, MA: Institute for Educational Services.

Bateman, B. (1992). Learning Disabilities: The Changing Landscape. *Journal of Learning Disabilities* 25:29–36.

Cassidy, J. (1981). Inquiry Reading for the Gifted. *The Reading Teacher* 35:17–21.

Clay, M. M. (1993). *Reading Recovery: A Guidebook for Teachers in Training*. Portsmouth, NH: Heinemann.

D'Alissandro, M. (1990). Accomodating Emotionally Handicapped Children Through a Literature-Based Reading Program. *The Reading Teacher* 44:288–293.

Davey, B. (1983). Think-Aloud—Modeling the Cognitive Processes of Reading Comprehension. *Journal of Reading* 27:44–47.

Dialessi, J., and Burns, J. (1994). About Dying and Divorce: How Can a Book Console a Child? *The New England Reading Association Journal* 30:17–23.

Dooley, C. (1993). The Challenge: Meeting the Needs of Gifted Readers. *The Reading Teacher* 46:546–551.

Erickson, K. A., and Koppenhaver, D. A. (1995). Developing a Literacy Program for Children with Severe Disabilities. *The Reading Teacher* 48:676–684.

Fawcett, G. (1995). Beth Starts Like Brown Bear! *Phi Delta Kappan* 75:721–722.

Feldhusen, J. F. (1996). How to Identify and Develop Special Talents. *Educational Leadership* 53:66–69.

Friedberg, J. B., Mullins, J. B., and Sukiennik, A. W. (1992). *Portraying Persons with Disabilities: An Annotated Bibliography of NONFICTION for Children and Teenagers*. New Providence, NJ: Bowker.

Fuhler, C. J. (1990). Let's Move Toward Literature-Based Reading Instruction. *The Reading Teacher* 43:312–316.

Gardner, H. (1993). *Frames of Mind: The Theory of Multiple Intelligences* (2nd ed.). New York: Basic Books.

Gardner, H. (1995). Reflections on Multiple Intelligences: Myths and Messages. *Phi Delta Kappan* 77:200–209.

Gentile, L. M., and McMillan, M. M. (1990). Literacy Through Literature: Motivating At-Risk Students to Read and Write. *Journal of Reading, Writing, and Learning Disabilities* 6:383–393.

Giangreco, M. C. (1996). What Do I Do Now? A Teacher's Guide to Including Students with Disabilities. *Educational Leadership* 53:56–59.

Graves, M. F., and Graves B. B. (1994). *Scaffolding Reading Experiences: Designs for Student Success*. Boston: Allyn & Bacon.

Graves, M. F., Graves, B. B., and Braaten, S. (1996). Scaffolded Reading Experiences for Inclusive Classes. *Educational Leadership* 53:14–16.

Hahn, A. L. (1985). Teaching Remedial Students to Be Strategic Readers and Better Comprehenders. *The Reading Teacher* 39:72–77.

Hauser, P., and Nelson, G. (1988). *Books for the Gifted Child*. New Providence, NJ: Bowker.

Heath, S. B. (1991). The Sense of Being Literature: Historical and Cross-Cultural Features. In R. Barr, et al., eds., *Handbook of Reading Research, Volume II*, New York: Longman.

Hocutt, A. M. (1996). Effectiveness of Special Education: Is Placement a Factor? In *Special Education for Students with Disabilities*. Los Altos, CA: Center for the Future of Children, The Davis and Lucile Packard Foundation.

Kauffman, J. M., Lloyd, J. W., Baker, J., and Riedel, T. M. (1995). Inclusion for All Students with Emotional or Behavioral Disorders? Let's Think Again. *Phi Delta Kappan* 76:542–546.

Kimmel, E. (1970). Can Children's Books Change Children's Values? *Educational Leadership* 28:209–211.

Kirk, S. A., Kliebhan, J. M., and Lerner, J. W. (1978). *Teaching Reading to Slow and Disabled Learners*. Boston: Houghton Mifflin.

Lipsky, D. K., and Gartner, A. (1992). Achieving Full Inclusion: Placing the Student at the Center of School Reform. In W. Stainback and S. Stainback, eds., *Controversial Issues Confronting Special Education: Divergent Perspectives*. Boston: Allyn & Bacon.

McCoy, K. M., and Prehm, H. J. (1987). *Teaching Mainstreamed Students: Methods and Techniques*. Denver: Love Publishing.

Morris, D., Ervin, C., and Conrad, K. (1996). A Case Study of Middle School Reading Disability. *The Reading Teacher* 49:368–377.

Nelson, J. B., and Cleland, D. L. (1971). The Role of the Teacher of Gifted and Creative Children. In P. A. Witty, ed., *Reading for the Gifted and the Creative Student*. Newark, DE: International Reading Association.

Pikulski, J. J. (1994). Preventing Reading Failure: A Review of Five Effective Programs. *The Reading Teacher* 48:30–39.

Pinnell, G. S., Lyons, C. A., DeFord, D. E., Bryk, A. S., and Seltzer, M. (1994). Comparing Instructional Models for the Literacy Education of High-Risk First Graders. *Reading Research Quarterly* 29:9–40.

Pogrow, S. (1990). The Effects of Intellectually Challenging At-Risk Elementary Students: Findings from the HOTS Program. *Phi Delta Kappan* 71:389–397.

Rees, D. (1994). *Reading: Developmental Continuum*. Melbourne: Longman Australia.

Rhodes, L. K., and Dudley-Marling, C. (1988). *Readers and Writers with a Difference: A Holistic Approach to Teaching Learning Disabled and Remedial Students*. Portsmouth, NH: Heinemann.

Richek, M. A., and McTague, B. K. (1988). The "Curious George" Strategy for Students with Reading Problems. *The Reading Teacher* 42:220–226.

Roach V. (1995). Supporting Inclusion: Beyond the Rhetoric. *Phi Delta Kappan* 76: 295–299.

Robertson, D. (1992). *Portraying Persons with Disabilities: An Annotated Bibliography of FICTION for Children and Teenagers*. New Providence, NJ: Bowker.

Routman, R. (1988). *Transitions: From Literature to Literacy*. Portsmouth, NH: Heinemann.

Rudman, M. K., Gagne, K. D., and Bernstein, J. E., eds. (1994). *Books to Help Children Cope with Separation and Loss: An Annotated Bibliography* (4th ed.). New Providence, NJ: Bowker.

Savage, J. F. (1983). Reading Guides: Effective Tools for Teaching the Gifted. *Roeper Review* 5:9–11.

Schumaker, M. P., and Schumaker, R. C. (1988). 3,000 Paper Cranes: Children's Literature for Remedial Readers. *The Reading Teacher* 46:544–548.

Shanahan, T., and Barr, R. (1995). Reading Recovery: An Independent Evaluation of the Effects of an Early Instructional Intervention for At-Risk Learners. *Reading Research Quarterly* 30:958–996.

Sinatra, R. C., Stahl-Gemake, J., and Berg, D. N. (1984). Improving Reading Comprehension of Disabled Readers Through Semantic Mapping. *The Reading Teacher* 38:22–29.

Slavin, R. E., and Madden, N. A. (1989). What Words for Students At Risk: A Research Synthesis. *Educational Leadership* 46:4–13.

Slavin, R. E., Madden, N. A., Dolan, L. J., Wasik, B. A., Ross, S. M., and Smith, L. J. (1994). Whenever and Wherever We Choose: The Replication of Success for All. *Phi Delta Kappan* 75:639–647.

Slavin, R. E., Madden, N. A., Darwest, N. L., Dolan, L. J., and Wasik, B. A. (1996). *Every Child, Every School: Success for All*. Newbury Park, CA: Corwin.

Smelter, R. W., Rasch, B. W., and Yudewitz, G. J. (1994). Thinking of Inclusion for All Special Needs Students? Better Think Again. *Phi Delta Kappan* 75:35–38.

Spiegel, D. L. (1995). A Comparison of Traditional Remedial Programs and Reading Recovery: Guidelines for Success of All Programs. *The Reading Teacher* 49:86–96.

Stevens, R. J., and Slavin, R. E. (1995). The Cooperative Elementary School: Effects on Students' Achievement, Attitudes and Social Relations. *American Educational Research Journal* 32:321–351.

Sullivan, J. (1987). Read-Aloud Sessions: Tackling Sensitive Issues Through Literature. *The Reading Teacher* 41:874–878.

Taylor, S. J. (1982). From Segregation to Integration: Strategies for Integrating Severely Handicapped Students in Normal School and Community Settings. *TASH Journal* 8:42–49.

Terman, D. L., Larner, M. B., Stevenson, C. S., and Behrman, R. E. (1996). Special Education for Students with Disabilities: Analysis and Recommendations. *Special Education for Students with Disabilities*. Los Altos, CA: Center for the Future of Children, The Davis and Lucile Packard Foundation.

Twiss, L. L. (1995). Inclusion of Children with Disabilities in Elementary School Classrooms. *The Reading Teacher* 49:66–68.

U.S. Department of Education (1991). *Report to the 13th Congress on the Implementation of the Education of the Handicapped Act*. Washington, DC: U.S. Department of Education.

Varnhagen, C. K., and Goldman, S. R. (1986). Improving Comprehension: Causal Relations Instruction for Learning Handicapped Learners. *The Reading Teacher* 39:896–904.

Wasik, B. A., and Slavin, R. E. (1993). Preventing Early Reading Failure with One-to-One Tutoring: A Review of Five Programs. *Reading Research Quarterly* 28:179–199.

Zigmond, N., Jenkins, J., Fuchs, L. S., Deno, S., Fuchs, D., Baker, J. N., Jenkins, L., and Couthino, M. (1995). Special Education in Restructured Schools: Findings from Three Multi-year Studies. *Phi Delta Kappan* 76:531–540.

Using Multicultural Literature: Working with Diverse Learners

© James L. Shaffer

Chapter 12 Outline

Features

12.1 **AHANA**
12.2 **Empty Glass or Full Basket?**
12.3 **Integrating Multicultural Literature into the Curriculum**
12.4 **Cinderella or Yeh-Shen?**
12.5 **A Multicultural Sampler**
12.6 **Teaching Multicultural Literature**
12.7 **Dialects**
12.8 **Dialect in Print**
12.9 **Children's Books with an African American Perspective**
12.10 **Principles of Second Language Learning**
12.11 **Literature from a Latino Perspective**
12.12 **Children's Literature and Second Language Learning**

Key Concepts in This Chapter

Culture, language, and literacy are closely related. Multicultural literature brings all three elements together.

All languages are a collection of dialects. Pupils who speak a nonstandard dialect may need instructional adjustments as they learn to read and write in the standard language of print.

Children whose first language is not English may need special provisions to help them learn to read and write in English. Once again, literature plays an important part in their reading instruction.

Multicultural literature is not intended solely for linguistically and culturally diverse students; it is an important part of reading and writing instruction for all children.

Introduction

T oday's educational scene is increasingly becoming a multicultural mosaic. The percentage of children in schools who are culturally and linguistically different from the majority—mostly African American, Hispanic, Asian, and

12.1 Putting Ideas to Work
AHANA

*T*he term *AHANA* is used in this chapter in place of the more conventional term *minority*. Coined in 1979 by two undergraduate students at Boston College, AHANA is an acronym for African American, Hispanic, Asian, and Native American. The term is used increasingly on U.S. campuses.

AHANA is used in this text because it gets away from the pejorative connotations that often surround the word *minority*. Reflecting on what the world might be like for African Americans in the year 2035, comedian, actor, and author Bill Cosby said, "The word *minority* has connotations of weakness, lesser value, self-doubt, tentativeness, and powerlessness" (Cosby, 1990; p. 61). The use of the alternative term AHANA avoids these impressions. Moreover, when one walks into a school in which 40 percent of the pupils are African American, 30 percent Latino, 20 percent Asian, and 5 percent Native American, these children hardly constitute a "minority" of the population in that school. AHANA again seems a more fitting term.

Native American, or AHANA pupils (see Putting Ideas to Work 12.1)—is rising dramatically. In 1990, AHANA students made up one-third of total public school enrollment; by the end of the century, these students will constitute almost half of the school population. In many areas today, AHANA children constitute a substantial majority in the schools (Lara, 1994).

As education moves into the 21st century, schools need to be increasingly aware of the needs of AHANA pupils. These students bring diverse backgrounds, experiences, perspectives, and skills to their education. They also bring cultures and languages that affect the ease with which they learn to read and write standard English. Although educators need to respect and value each pupil's cultural and linguistic heritage, schools are required to teach all children to read and write in standard English.

Traditionally, schools often have trouble meeting the needs of AHANA pupils. Their scores on achievement tests are generally lower and their dropout rates are higher. Race and ethnicity are not direct causes of these educational problems, however. "Familial poverty is more directly related to school failure than racial, ethnic, and linguistic diversity. . . . Little note is made of the fact that roughly 40 percent of all African American families are in the middle class and that, academically, these children outperform poor children regardless of ethnicity" (Allington, 1994; p. 195).

A number of metaphors have been used to describe the diversity of American society—the traditional "melting pot," where cultural differences meld into a single social entity; a salad bowl, with each cultural group maintaining its identity while contributing to the overall taste and texture of the salad; a quilt, with different pieces maintaining their uniqueness while combining to produce a beautiful whole. Whatever metaphor one uses, teachers have a responsibility to educate children to live in an increasingly diverse society, regardless of the cultural backgrounds or language patterns of their pupils.

Multicultural literature plays an important role in children's classroom experiences. Books that reflect diverse cultural groups, along with stories and poems written by authors from different backgrounds, are vital to literature-based reading instruction. Quality multicultural literature contributes to the literacy development of all students, those who are members of AHANA groups and those who are not.

Cultural Dimensions of Literacy

Edward Tylor's famous definition of culture is "that complex whole which includes knowledge, belief, art, morals, law, customs, and any other capabilities and habits acquired by [any human] as a member of society" (Tylor, 1929; p. 1). Culture has also been described as "the prism through which members of a group see the world and create 'shared meanings' " (Bowman, 1989; p. 118). In the technological world today's children inhabit, literacy is certainly part of the complex cultural whole they are expected to acquire. Cultural issues therefore need to be part of the language arts curriculum.

Culture plays a part in learning to read. Although some reading-related issues are more culturally determined than others—for example, the common research finding that girls read better than boys in the primary grades is true in only a handful of countries, including the United States and England—culture determines much about a people's lifestyles and values. Literacy itself is one of the values in our culture, as well as a purveyor of other values.

Literature has a special place in the cultural life of any people. Stories passed down from one generation to the next reflect the values that a group of people treasure—bravery, honesty, integrity, cunning, respect for elders, or wisdom. In American literature, for example, the Paul Bunyan stories reflect the strength, confidence, and ingenuity the pioneers needed to open the rugged American wilderness. This is one reason why literature has long been part of education and why it is assuming a more important role in today's elementary school.

AHANA students bring to school a set of experiences not always reflected in the curriculum (see Putting Ideas to Work 12.2). Their schemata are built from these experiences, so it is important to have books available that reflect experiences familiar to them. AHANA pupils need to see their world reflected in trade books as they learn to read. In the words of a white middle-class mother who had adopted a young Korean orphan, "I want picture books in which my son can at least see faces that look like his own."

Values of Multicultural Literature in the Classroom

Through the 1950s, children's trade books sometimes stereotyped, but more often ignored, AHANA cultures. With the increased social consciousness the civil rights movement helped generate in the 1960s, a body of multicultural

12.2 Putting Ideas to Work

Empty Glass or Full Basket?

*I*n the September 1990 issue of *Teacher Magazine*, Robert Lake, a member of the Seneca and Cherokee Indian tribes, wrote an open letter regarding the education of his son, Wind-Wolf. With poignancy, the father wonders why, at the age of five, his child must be labeled a "slow learner."

The letter goes on to describe how difficult it is for Wind-Wolf to adjust to a new cultural environment that demands learning new ideas. Lake writes of all the science, social studies, music, math, and language that his son has learned as part of his upbringing in a Native American culture, and the father pleads for an educational experience that will help his son maintain pride in his cultural heritage while at the same time develop the skills necessary to succeed in the wider society.

"My son Wind-Wolf," the letter concludes, "is not an empty glass coming into your class to be filled. He is a full basket coming into a different environment and society with something special to share. Please let him share his knowledge, heritage, and culture with you and his peers."

literature—books that authentically reflect non-Western cultures, with characters and experiences other than those from mainstream America—began to emerge. While the percentage of books about people of color is relatively small—estimated at between 1 and 2 percent in 1992 (Bishop, 1992)—an ever-growing body of multicultural literature is becoming available for classroom use.

Multicultural literature has been defined as "literature by and about people who are members of groups considered to be outside the socio-political mainstream of the United States . . . [including] fiction set in countries where people of color are in the majority and informational books about these countries" (Bishop, 1992; p. 39, 40). Diamond and Moore (1995) define multicultural literature as "literature that focuses on specific cultures by highlighting and celebrating their cultural and historical perspectives, traditions, and heritages, language and dialects, and experiences and lifestyles . . . [including] literature of diverse cultures outside the United States, from which the people of color in this nation claim ancestral heritage" (p. 43).

Multicultural literature contains special value for all children. These books help all pupils better understand themselves and others, experience the literary heritage of different cultures, and discover values that connect present and past. Multicultural literature can also help students expand their understanding of geography and history, and it can broaden their awareness of social issues and literary techniques (Norton, 1990). Further, literature from other lands is a powerful medium for developing the concept of increasing global interdependence (Diaakiw, 1990).

Emphasizing the importance of using children's books with a multicultural perspective in the classroom, Bishop (1987) identifies three values of literature in a multicultural society: (1) literature can show how people are

Multicultural literature is becoming more and more important in reflecting the multicultural landscape of today's schools.
© Stuart Spates

connected with common human experiences; (2) books can help pupils understand the unique differences that make cultural groups distinctive; and (3) literature can help children understand "the effects of social issues and forces on the lives of ordinary individuals" (Bishop, 1987; p. 60).

Multicultural literature is appropriate for all children, not just those who are culturally and linguistically distinct. It does, however, offer special value to AHANA pupils by affirming their cultural identities. Students from diverse cultural groups feel pride in their heritage when they see their culture reflected in the books they read. They respond more positively when they relate to the events and characters in a story. Moreover, the reading and writing of children from diverse backgrounds often seems to improve with the use of multicultural literature (Harris, 1992; Au, 1993). Books that reflect their cultures may provide students with inspiration and confidence to write from their own unique point of view.

The values of multicultural literature, however, extend to all children. "For minority and immigrant children, these books can be a mirror, reflecting and validating familiar cultures and experiences. For mainstream children, these books can be a window, revealing a multicultural vista that juxtaposes the familiar and the less familiar" (Cox and Galda, 1990; p. 582).

Beyond raising a child's awareness of his or her own or other cultures, literature can lead pupils to a deep understanding and even action over issues of social concern. "Textbooks touch the mind with sanitary descriptions of events: stories, told from the points of view of persons who lived through the events, have the power to touch the hearts of readers and move them to the type of action that characterizes the highest level of multicultural study. . . . Multicultural learning achieves its pinnacle when students are inspired to challenge and act upon their beliefs and values about people who are different from them or from the mainstream" (Rasinski and Padak, 1990; pp. 579–580).

12.3 Putting Ideas to Work

Integrating Multicultural Literature into the Curriculum

*B*anks (1989) has identified four approaches to integrating ethnic content into the curriculum:

1. *The Contributions Approach* focuses on heroes, holidays, and discrete cultural elements; for example, pupils read about the life of Dr. Martin Luther King, Jr., or observe a period such as Black History Month.
2. *The Ethnic Additive Approach* adds ethnic content and issues to the curriculum without changing its basic structure—studying the internment of Japanese-Americans as part of the study of World War II, for example.
3. *The Transformation Approach* changes the basic structure of the curriculum by having students view concepts or themes from diverse ethnic perspectives; pupils examine the Westward Movement, for example, through the eyes of Native Americans.
4. *The Social Action Approach* includes all the aspects of the Transformation Approach and adds the element of decision making on social issues; students reflect on the way their values relate to the diversity in their culture.

Rasinski and Padak (1990) suggest four ways to use children's literature in accordance with Banks's four approaches:

1. In the *Contributions Approach,* children encounter the lives of famous people through biographies or the customs of different cultures through trade books.
2. In the *Ethnic Additive Approach,* students read and discuss books such as Mildred Taylor's *Roll of Thunder, Hear My Cry,* the story of the prejudice a black family experiences in the rural South, when they study the region; or they read Byrd Baylor's *Amigo,* the story of an impoverished Latino child who adopts a prairie dog, in a unit on pets.
3. In the *Transformation Approach,* pupils might compare accounts of the American Revolution by reading two books: Esther Forbes's *Johnny Tremain,* the story of a heroic young boy closely involved in the Revolution, and James and Christopher Collier's *War Comes to Willy Freeman,* the story of a newly emancipated black female who witnesses the death of her father in battle with the British and then finds that the Redcoats have kidnapped her mother.
4. In the *Social Action Approach,* children might read about the treatment of Japanese-Americans in Yoshiko Uchida's *Journey to Topaz* and *Journey Home.* They then might further explore the issue of sanctioned bigotry and decide what they would do in similar circumstances.

Types of Multicultural Trade Books

Multicultural literature encompasses the full range of literary genres—picture storybooks, folktales and traditional stories, realistic fiction, biographies and informational books, and poetry.

Picture Books.   Books that reflect diverse cultures can begin with ABC and counting books. Muriel Feelings's *Jambo Means Hello: A Swahili Alphabet Book* not only introduces Swahili words but also cultural aspects of life in

African villages where Swahili is spoken. John Agard's *The Calypso Alphabet* does the same with a Caribbean flavor, as does Idalia Rosario's *Idalia's Project ABC* with a Latino flavor. Feelings's *Moja Means One: A Swahili Counting Book* extends the multicultural concept to numbers.

Primary grade teachers have access to an extensive selection of multicultural picture storybooks, beginning reading books, and trade books for children beginning to achieve independence in reading. Books reflecting a multicultural focus should be a regular and normal part of literature-based instruction—books such as Ann Grifalconi's *Osa's Pride* and Tololwa M. Mullel's *The Orphan Boy*, both stories that reflect African traditions; Sally Scott's *The Magic Horse*, a tale from Persia; Junko Marimoto's *Mouse's Marriage*, a simply written story with illustrations that reflect Japanese customs, and Allan Say's Caldecott Award-winning *Grandfather's Journey*, about his grandfather's connections with his native Japan; Paul Goble's *Her Seven Brothers* and Peggy Parrish's *Good Hunting, Blue Sky*, books that reflect the cultures of different Native American groups; Edna O'Brien's *Tales for the Telling*, a book of Irish stories; Lina Mao Wall's *Judge Rabbit and the Tree Spirit*, a folktale from Cambodia; Ann Tompert's *Grandfather Tang's Story*, a story rooted in the ancient Chinese tradition; and Jeanne M. Lee's *Ba-Nam*, a story about the culture of Vietnam.

These books and others suggested in this chapter reflect only a small fraction of the multicultural literature available for use in the primary grades. These early-level trade books reflect the broader multicultural mosaic found in so many elementary classrooms. All pupils can enjoy using them in learning to read and write.

Folktales and Traditional Literature. Folk literature addresses universal themes that transcend cultural boundaries and appeal to people of different backgrounds; folktales are grounded in particular cultures. These stories reflect the values and traditions of the people who tell them. Folk literature reveals the heart and soul of a people. Since it springs from the oral tradition, this type of literature also lends itself especially well to reading aloud, storytelling, dramatization, and other language activities.

Fairy tales and legends add to the multicultural fabric of the classroom. African folk literature is reflected in such books as *Abiyoyo*, Pete Seeger's adaptation of the South African lullaby and folk story of a trickster-turned-hero who made a monster disappear; Verna Aardema's retelling of the West African story *Why Mosquitoes Buzz in People's Ears*; or Veronique Tadjo's *Lord of the Dance: An African Retelling*. Folk literature stories like these give African-American pupils a keen awareness of the antiquity and richness of their culture.

Similarly, Gerald McDermott's *Arrow to the Sun* is a strikingly illustrated folk story from the Pueblo Indians. Paul Goble's *The Gift of the Sacred Dog* and other stories reflect the traditions of the Plains Indians, while Diane Hoyt-Goldsmith's *Pueblo Storyteller* offers information about Indians of the Southwest. Each story stems from the deep roots of Native American culture.

12.4 Putting Ideas to Work
Cinderella or Yeh-Shen?

*A*ll young children delight in familiar fairy tales; they can enrich their experiences by comparing tales that they know with equivalent fairy tales from other lands. For example, after reading a traditional version of *Cinderella*, the teacher can share stories with the Cinderella theme that come from other cultures:

> *Yeh-Shen: A Cinderella Story from China* by Louie Ai-Ling
> *The Korean Cinderella* by Shirley Climo
> *The Egyptian Cinderella* by Shirley Climo
> *The Rough-Faced Girl* by Rafe Martin
> *Mufaro's Beautiful Daughter: An African Tale* by John Steptoe
> *The Brocaded Slipper and Other Vietnamese Tales* by Lynette Vuong
> *Princess Furball* by Charlotte Huck

These variations of a popular story show the cross-cultural nature of traditional themes and the universality of folk literature.

Ed Young's *Lon Po Po: A Red-Riding Hood Story from China* is a Caldecott winner that tells the age-old story of the cunning of the wolf, with an interesting cultural twist. Mats Rehnman's *The Clay Flute* is a Persian variation of the fairy tale about the Frog Prince. *Vasilissa the Beautiful* by Elizabeth Winthrop is a Russian folktale (illustrated by Soviet artist Alexander Koshkin) with a Cinderella and Hansel and Gretel theme. Each of these versions of favorite stories reflects the unique cultural perspective of the country where the story is told.

Chinese Mother Goose Rhymes, edited by Robert Wyndham, is a collection of Chinese nursery rhymes and ballads for children. This volume illustrates the universal nature of the language, content, and themes of children's poetry across cultures.

Using well-known stories and poems like these broadens pupils' views of the world, enhances their understanding, and heightens their appreciation of other cultures and literary traditions.

Books such as Tom Birdseye's *A Song of the Stars*, Dianne Snyder's version of the Japanese trickster tale *The Boy of the Three-Year Nap*, and Lawrence Yep's *The Rainbow People*, a collection of traditional tales carried by Chinese workers who came to America in the 1800s, represent Asian folk legends retold in children's literature.

Folk literature might also include religious themes such as John Bierhorst's translation of *The Spirit Child*, an intriguing Aztec story of the Nativity, or Adele Gera's anthology *My Grandmother's Stories: A Collection of Jewish Folk Tales*. Students can develop critical reading skills as they compare Tomie de Paola's version of the Italian folktale *The Legend of Old Befana* with Ruth Robbins's award-winning adaptation of the Russian folktale *Baboushka and the Three Kings*, both stories about the January 6 gift-giving tradition. These stories, in dealing with religious themes, reflect the ethnic and religious diversity of our society.

Although the United States cannot boast the antiquity of other cultures, it has its own folk tradition. Beyond the Paul Bunyan, Pecos Bill, and

Johnny Appleseed stories, pupils can enjoy books such as *The Diane Goode Book of American Folk Tales and Songs*, Ann Durell's collection of traditional literature from various ethnic groups (blacks, Pueblo Indians, Hispanics) and regions (Appalachia, New England) of the United States.

Realistic Fiction. Students in the middle grades devour realistic fiction, and this genre is especially important as they develop independence as readers. In reflecting AHANA cultures, realistic fiction should be just that—*realistic*. Teachers should be especially wary of books that present cultural groups in a stereotyped manner. Historically, some trade books for children perpetuated negative images; contemporary literature tends to avoid stereotyping.

Among the plethora of realistic fiction books written for middle-grade pupils, a number focus on the experiences of AHANA cultures. African American characters appear in different settings, from the farm in Virginia Hamilton's *Zeeley* to the ghetto in Paula Fox's *How Many Miles to Babylon*? Latino characters populate books like Nicholasa Mohr's *Felita*, a story about hatred in a city neighborhood, and Joseph Krumgold's *And Now Miguel*, a story that takes place on a New Mexico sheep farm. In realistic fiction featuring Native Americans, the theme often focuses on the conflict between traditional and contemporary values that young characters face, as in Virginia Driving Hawk Sneve's *Jimmy Yellow Hawk*. Linda Crew's *Children of the River* allows readers to experience the cultural clash between contemporary American society and traditional Cambodian values.

Multiethnic realistic fiction contains the same universal conflicts and themes contained in all contemporary realistic fiction. No matter what their ethnic backgrounds, children face conflicts within themselves, with adults and peers, with nature, and with society in the process of becoming an adult in today's world.

Biographies and Informational Books. Multicultural literature for children is full of biographical and autobiographical accounts of famous and not-so-famous people. These books range from easy reading books such as *Ragtime Trumpie*, Alan Schroeder's account of the childhood of black entertainer Josephine Baker, to longer books like Beth Bao Lord's autobiographical account of a Chinese child's adjustment to living in a new land, *In the Year of the Boar and Jackie Robinson*. These books reveal a personal dimension to growing up in another culture.

Informational books also provide descriptions of the customs and traditions of AHANA cultures. *Lion Dancer: Ernie Wan's Chinese New Year* by Kate Waters and Madeleine Slovenz-Low is an informative and entertaining account of ancient Chinese customs, and Joan Hewett's *Hector Lives in the United States Now: The Story of a Mexican-American Child* gives a realistic description of the life of one Hispanic family living in the United States. Books like these, which are often illustrated with photographs, promote cultural awareness as well as help children learn to read.

For pupils who have recently arrived from foreign lands (and for those whose ancestors arrived a long time ago), William Jay Jacobs's factual

account of *Ellis Island: New Hope in a New Land* gives a sense of both the history and the personal emotion of arriving in a new land; so does Veronica Lawlor's *I Was Dreaming to Come to America: Memories from the Ellis Island Oral History Project*. A fictional but nonetheless realistic account of more recent immigration is Eve Bunting's *How Many Days to America? A Thanksgiving Story*, the story of a group of political refugees who come to the United States as "boat people." A whole "Coming to America" series of children's trade books is available, with such titles as *The Chinese-American Experience* by Dana Ying-Hul Wu and Jeffrey Dao-Shend Tung, and *The Irish American Experience* by Seamus Cavan.

Poetry. Poems also provide literature for children from a multicultural perspective—Virginia Driving Hawk Sneve's *Dancing Teepees* is a collection of the poetry of American Indian youth, for example, and John Agard and Grace Nichols's *No Hickory, No Dickory, No Dock: Caribbean Nursery Rhymes* is a collection of original and traditional rhymes from that part of the world.

While many trade books reflect the values and experiences of one particular cultural group, some books include a mix of different groups in their stories. Eve Bunting's *Smoky Night*, an award-winning book based on the Los Angeles riots of the early 1990s, is about the experience of getting along with others, no matter what one's background or ethnicity. In Juanita Havill's *Jamaica and Brianna*, two friends—one African American and one Asian American—discover the bumps and smooth spots of friendship. And Jama Kim Rattigan's *Dumpling Soup* is a story about a truly multicultural family whose members are Japanese, Korean, Hawaiian, and Caucasian.

A full range of ethnic literature can enrich the reading program in any classroom. When children's cultures are reflected in trade books, the stories strengthen self-concepts, deepening their sense of pride in their cultural identity. At the same time, quality literature featuring characters and settings that reflect diverse cultural populations can lead *all* students to better understand different cultures, while giving them reading material with genuine appeal.

12.5 Putting Ideas to Work
A Multicultural Sampler

As the cultural diversity of our society increases, so does the need for books that reflect that cultural diversity. The following is a tiny sampling of the range of children's trade books available about various AHANA groups. (Separate samplings of trade books dealing with African American and Latino cultures will be presented later in this chapter.) The total inventory of trade books with a multicultural focus is far too extensive to list here; the following are only a handful of titles appropriate for use in a literature-based reading program.

Native American

Primary Grades

> *The Legend of Bluebonnet*, retold by Tomie de Paola, a beautifully illustrated version of a Comanche tale.
> *Hawk, I'm Your Brother* by Byrd Baylor, describing the kinship between a young boy and a hawk.
> *Eagle Boy: A Traditional Navajo Legend* by Gerald Hausman, one of the author's many books of Native American stories.

Intermediate Grades

> *Annie and the Old One* by Miska Miles, a story about the love between a girl and her grandmother, told against a backdrop of contemporary Navajo life.
> *Knots on a Counting Rope* by Bill Martin, Jr., and John Archambault, a beautifully told tale in which a boy learns about his name and his heritage.
> *Fox Song* by Joseph Bruchac, in which a modern child reflects on his rich heritage.

Upper Grades

> *The Sign of the Beaver* by Elizabeth George Speare, a popular story about a Native American boy who teaches a friend both survival skills and values.
> *Owl's Song* by Janet Hale, in which a young boy faces loneliness and prejudice as he searches for his identity as a Native American and as an American.
> *The Navajos* by Virginia Driving Hawk Sneve, one of a series of informational books about the "first Americans."

Japanese

Primary Grades

> *Anna in Charge* by Yoriko Tsutsui, a simple, contemporary picture story about an older and a younger sister.
> *Crow Boy* by Taro Yashima, a haunting story about a boy rejected by his peers at school, with striking illustrations.
> *A Stranger in the Mirror* by Allan Say, in which a young Asian boy reflects (figuratively and literally) on what he sees.

Intermediate Grades

> *The Big Wave* by Pearl Buck, a compelling story of human tragedy and friendship, in which a famous writer tells about a culture she understands well.
> *The Bracelet* by Yoshiko Uchida, a personal story about the heartbreak of Japanese internment during World War II.

Upper Grades

Sadako and the Thousand Paper Cranes by Eleanor Coerr, the popular story about a girl who develops leukemia as a result of the Hiroshima bombing.

Journey to Topaz by Yoshiko Uchida, another moving story of the internment of Japanese-Americans in World War II.

Chinese

Primary Grades

The Magic Leaf by Winifred Morris, a picture book that reflects many aspects of the culture.

Tikki, Tikki, Tembo retold by Arlene Mosel, a humorous folktale that children (and adults) delight in repeating.

The Empty Pot by Demi, a delicately illustrated story about an ancient Chinese emperor in search of a successor.

Intermediate Grades

In the Year of the Boar and Jackie Robinson by Beth Bao Lord, the story of a girl who finds friends in Brooklyn after the hardship of immigration.

The Chinese Word for Horse and Other Stories by John Lewis, a book that contains information about the Chinese writing system and Chinese culture.

Upper Grades

Dragonwings by Laurence Yep, a compelling story with strong characters that reflect Chinese cultural values and ways of life.

Angel Island Prisoner by Helen Chetin, the story of the struggles of brave and wise Chinese immigrant women.

Ribbons by Laurence Yep, a contemporary story about the arrival of a grandmother from Hong Kong.

Native Americans, Chinese, and Japanese children are not the only cultural groups represented in today's classroom. Irish, Russians, Italians, and other ethnic groups have added to the richness of our culture, and trade books based on the traditions of these groups are also available. Trade books with many cultural perspectives need to be included in a child's reading diet, books such as:

Aekyung's Dream by Min Paek and *Chi-Hoon: A Korean Girl* by Patricia McMahon, stories of the experiences of young Korean girls in the United States.

The Golden Carp and Other Romantic Tales from Vietnam by Lynette Dyer Vuong, containing six traditional tales retold and brilliantly illustrated.

Angel Child, Dragon Child by Michele M. Suart, in which a Vietnamese child relies on her mother's gift of a silver matchbox to help her cope with the prejudice she encounters as a new pupil in school.

There are literally thousands of books with a multicultural perspective available for use in the elementary reading program. Updated lists of multicultural trade books are available regularly from the Children's Book Council, 568 Broadway, Suite 404, New York, NY 10012, and from the Council on Interracial Books for Children, 1841 Broadway, Room 608, New York, NY 10023. Also, the National Council of Teachers of English has begun to publish *Kaleidoscope*, an annotated list of multicultural literature for grades K–8.

12.6 Putting Ideas to Work
Teaching Multicultural Literature

Norton (1990) details a sequence for the study of multicultural literature as part of the language arts curriculum in the upper elementary grades. The model includes five steps or phases:

Phase 1 begins with literature that comes from the oral tradition. The class shares and discusses folktales, fables, myths, and legends of a group of people (such as Native Americans or African Americans). Pupils develop their own storytelling activities that reflect the literature they have been reading.

Phase 2 narrows the focus to the literature of a specific group—one or two Native American people, for example, or African American folk literature from the slave era. Students develop critical awareness as they search for deeper cultural values reflected in the stories they read.

Phase 3 takes pupils into other areas of literature—for example, into informational books on the history of the culture being studied, or biographies of people from the culture. Pupils extend their critical analysis by comparing the values and beliefs expressed in folk literature with those reflected in the biographies they read, or by judging the authenticity of the information presented.

Phase 4 involves historical fiction, as children "read, analyze, and evaluate historical fiction according to their authenticity of setting, credibility of conflict, believability of characterization, authenticity of traditional beliefs expressed by characters, and appropriateness of themes and authors' styles" (Norton, 1990; p. 34).

Phase 5 moves into contemporary poetry, fiction, and biography, as students search for continuity from one type of writing to another and as they compare literature written by members of cultural groups with literature written by others. In this final phase, pupils also trace the cultural threads across genres.

Norton provides extensive examples of books and activities for the study of Native American cultures, with suggestions for using her model in the study of African American and Latino literature as well.

Dialect Speakers

Dialect is a fact of language. All languages have dialects, and all native speakers of any language speak some dialect of that language. In fact, a language may be defined as a collection of dialects that are mutually understandable to a group of native speakers.

There are two types of dialects: regional and social. Within these categories, dialects differ from each other in three respects: phonology, vocabulary, and syntax.

Regional Dialect

Regional dialect, as the name indicates, is a dialect peculiar to speakers living in the same geographic area. The area may be relatively large (like the state of Maine) or relatively small (like the lower east side of Manhattan Island); yet natives of these areas share the same general speech features.

12.7 Putting Ideas to Work
Dialects

Dialect is not an "inferior brand" of language. All languages have dialects; all native speakers speak them.

Dialects can be either

REGIONAL
or
SOCIAL

Dialects differ in

PHONOLOGY
VOCABULARY
SYNTAX

Social Dialect

Social dialects exist within every geographic region. A social dialect distinguishes people from different social strata or levels of society.

Regional and social dialects differ from each other in three ways:

Phonologically, with clearly marked sound differences distinguishing one dialect from another; Bostonians pronounce words like *car* and *yard* "cah" and "yahd."

Lexically, with different words used to name the same object or action from one dialect to the next; a sandwich on an Italian roll, for example, is called a *submarine* (or *sub*), *hoagie, hero, grinder, torpedo,* or *po'boy* in various parts of the United States.

Syntactically, with certain grammatical forms characterizing one dialect or another. "How be you?" is a greeting in some regional dialects, while "He be here" is a syntactical feature of some social dialects.

This type of linguistic diversity is part of the fascination of language.

Standard English

Out of the linguistic pluralism that characterizes any language emerges a form of language described as "standard." *Standard English* is speech free of the variations that characterize regional and social dialects. It has been called the language of public life because it generally includes the language conventions that govern public communications across geographic, social, ethnic, and other lines. Broadcasters use standard language forms as they deliver the national network news each evening.

Standard English has long been the language taught in schools, just as it is the language used in business, government, and all other aspects of public life. Schools are rightly expected to teach Standard English. But in so doing, they sometimes perpetuate a negative view of dialect, a notion that some dialects are inferior language forms. Dialects are *different* language forms, but they are not *deficient* language forms. They are not ineffective approximations of Standard English, but rather systematic language forms that speakers use to meet the full range of daily communication needs. They are as effective as Standard English for expressing complex thoughts. Rather than being inferior versions of the standard form, dialects are fully developed language systems that differ in systematic ways from Standard English.

Schools have sometimes attempted to replace children's dialects with Standard English; however, schools often fail to realize how closely dialect is tied to cultural identity. Language is part of culture. It is intimately tied to the family customs and values that are part of the child's cultural identity. To denigrate children's language is to denigrate part of their very being. Although Standard English should be used and taught in the classroom, dialects must be recognized and respected for what they mean, what they do, and what they are.

What does all this discussion about dialect have to do with teaching reading and writing with literature? As a group, dialect speakers—whether African American youngsters from the inner city, Native American children from reservations, or white pupils from impoverished rural areas—tend not to score as well on reading measures as their mainstream, middle-class counterparts (Garcia et al., 1994). Complicating factors such as nutrition, home background, educational level of parents, and economic factors compound the educational problems of these children. But their dialect affects their learning as well, since language is a factor in learning to read. This is especially true of African American pupils in many innercity schools today. However, as Delpit (1995) points out, while dialect is intimately connected to community and personal identity, standard English is the language of economic success, and children have the right to expect to learn this language form in schools.

Black English or Ebonics

The dialect spoken by many African Americans has come to be known as Ebonics (from *ebony* and *phonics*). Not all blacks speak Ebonics. Yet a large number of African American speakers share this dialect variation of American English. Sometimes known as Black English Vernacular (BEV), this dialect variation has been thoroughly defined and described (Dillard, 1972; Burling, 1973; Smitherman, 1981). A dialect with Creole origins, Black English Vernacular is as rich and fully formed as any dialect in our language.

As with any dialect, Ebonics has its own unique phonological features (for example, dropping a sound in a consonant cluster at the end of a word, so that *desk* may be pronounced *"des"*), vocabulary items (*hood* to

12.8 Putting Ideas to Work
Dialect in Print

*D*ialect is unique to spoken language. No matter how many ways the word in pronounced—*cah, caw, cour, cayr*—it is still written *c-a-r*. In using multicultural literature in the classroom, teachers need to be aware of *eye dialect*.

Eye dialect is writing that portrays unique phonological, lexical, and syntactic features of dialect in print. For example, Mark Twain depicted the dialect of the slave Jim in *The Adventures of Huckleberry Finn* ("We're safe, Huck. I jis knows it!"), and Theodore Taylor did the same with the language of the old Virgin Islander Timothy in *The Cay* ("Many schooner go by dis way, 'an dis also be d'ship track to Jamaica an' on,").

Authors of contemporary children's stories sometimes use eye dialect to reflect characters' spoken language as well. For example, John Steptoe's *Daddy Is a Monster . . . Sometimes* contains lines such as "Daddy, you ain't gonna knock me out 'cause I'm gonna give you a knuckle sandwich," and "He be real nice and read you a story, but then—when the story be over and he kiss you good-night and cut off the lights, he start to do it again." The grandmother in Valerie Flournoy's warm and touching book *The Patchwork Quilt* says, "Stuff? This ain't stuff. These little pieces gonna make me a quilt," and "A year ain't that long, honey. Makin' the quilt gonna be a joy."

The use of eye dialect in stories written for children is controversial. Reflecting a reasonable representation of colloquial speech patterns can add an element of authenticity and enjoyment to a story, but it can also stereotype dialect speakers and offend readers—black and white alike. In children's books that use eye dialect, language ought not to be the only matter of concern; the quality and appeal of the story are more important considerations.

mean "neighborhood"), or grammatical features (use of the verb *be* to distinguish between a state or condition that is permanent—"My brother be sick"—or only temporary—"My brother sick" (today, but he should be better tomorrow). It is important to remember that these variations are systematic, that not all features are characteristic of the language of all African American speakers, and that many of these features are common among white speakers as well.

To teach reading to pupils who speak Black English dialect, teachers need to maintain a high level of respect for the children and their language background, realizing that their dialect is a bona fide communication system that meets their needs outside the classroom. Teachers also need to watch for points of conflict between the standard language of print and the natural language the student brings into the classroom. For example, the vowel phonemes in words such as *pen* and *pin* sound the same in some dialects, so insisting that the young child "hear the difference in the sounds" during phonemic awareness exercises may be futile. Similarly, when a dialect speaker pronounces the word *ten* for tent, insisting that the pupil repeat the word "until he says it right" is inappropriate.

Barnitz (1980) suggests five implications dialects have for teaching reading:

1. Using the home dialect in oral reading is natural.
2. Because dialects differ in their homonym pairs, the use of context must be encouraged.
3. Because dialects and languages vary in the contrasts made by native speakers, auditory discrimination test items must be interpreted cautiously.
4. Phonological differences exist across dialects. The nature of phonics generalizations may vary.
5. Communication of meaning is part of all dialects. Reading instruction should emphasize meaning by incorporating all the language arts and the cultural background of the child.

Children should not be penalized for reading in their own dialect, even when apparent discrepancies occur between the language of the text and the language of the pupil (as when the child reads *asked* as "axed," for example, or reads "they was" instead of *they were*). Allowing dialect speakers to render print in their natural language is not only instructionally sound; it is good common sense. Few of us read *Charlie and the Chocolate Factory* or *James and the Giant Peach* with a British accent, even though Roald Dahl, the Englishman who wrote these delightful stories, spoke with a British accent. Similarly, it makes sense to allow children who speak Black English dialects to read stories in their natural language patterns. As pupils read, teachers should be aware of which miscues are dialect-related and which result from inaccurate processing of text. Deriving enjoyment and meaning from the stories remains paramount.

Children's Literature with an African American Perspective.
Literature-based reading demands the use of books that reflect African American cultural experiences. All children should read these books, no matter what the color of their skin or ethnic background. Children's trade books by and about African Americans stimulate cross-cultural awareness as part of the classroom reading program.

Sims (1982) studied children's literature from an African American perspective and classified books by the following orientations:

1. *Socially conscious literature*—books that raise the social awareness of nonblack readers about such issues as prejudice. Books like Beverly Naidoo's *Journey to Jo'burg* or *Chain of Fire*, for example, tell stories about young black South Africans against a background of apartheid.
2. *Melting pot literature*—books that stress the universality of human experiences such as friendship, family relations, and everyday life. The characters that Ezra Jack Keats creates in *Peter's Chair*, for example, are African American, but their race is incidental to the concerns Peter expresses about the imminent arrival of a new baby and his father's sensitive reassurances.

3. *Culturally conscious literature*—books that celebrate the unique quality of the black experience, the traditions that are part of growing up as part of a distinct cultural group. For example, Mildred Taylor's books—*Roll of Thunder, Hear My Cry; Let the Circle Be Unbroken; Song of the Trees;* and *The Road to Memphis*—are all heartwarming and often heartrending stories about growing up as an African American in the segregated South of the 1930s and 40s.

Each of these categories provides a perspective on African American culture to enhance the reading program in the classroom.

Literature in the Reading Program.
In addition to having a representative sample of books with an African American perspective in the classroom library and sharing these books regularly with children, books reflecting African American culture can be systematically incorporated into the classroom reading program through:

Thematic units. As children study families, friendship, nutrition, and other topics, books by African American authors about their own experiences can be part of the unit. In the upper grades, a literature group can study prejudice and segregation, reading books by authors like Mildred Taylor and Beverly Naidoo. These books present not only the facts of segregation, but human accounts of how prejudice affects people.

Author study. Author study can focus on African American authors such as Faith Ringgold in the lower grades and Virginia Hamilton or Eloise Greenfield in the upper grades. As with any author study, children should read and enjoy the books of these writers.

Genre study. Multicultural literature should be part of any genre study. Biographies of African Americans, folktales and legends from Africa and the Caribbean, the work of African American poets—all should be included as children explore different types of literature. Young and Ferguson (1995) describe how trickster tales can be used in the classroom, with African, African American, and Caribbean tricksters (as well as those from other cultures) effectively incorporated.

Walker-Dalhouse (1992) has demonstrated the effectiveness of reading aloud books in which the major character is African American (Virginia Hamilton's *Zeeley,* for example, or Bette Greene's *Phillip Hall Likes Me, I Reckon Maybe*) and using these books to discuss ethnicity.

Dialect variation is a natural sociolinguistic phenomenon between regional areas and social classes. Teachers not only need to take dialects into account in teaching children how to read, they also need to recognize these dialects as legitimate language systems that form part of a child's culture. Teachers need to accept and understand children's dialects in literature-based reading programs.

12.9 Putting Ideas to Work
Children's Books with an African American Perspective

Classroom libraries need to be amply supplied with trade books that provide an African American perspective. These include such books as:

Primary Grades

Grandpa's Face by Eloise Greenfield, a beautiful story of intergenerational love and respect in an extended family.

Tar Beach and *Aunt Harriet's Underground Railroad in the Sky*, both by Faith Ringgold, fantasies in which Cassie enjoys flying over the city and countryside.

The Black Snowman by Phil Mendez, an intriguing tale that connects the present with the past as a black snowman helps a boy discover the beauty of his heritage.

Aunt Flossie's Hats (and Crab Cakes Later) by Elizabeth Fitzgerald Howard, about the relationship two girls maintain with their 98-year-old aunt.

Caribbean culture is reflected in books like Phyllis Gershator's *Rata, Pata, Scata, Fata: A Caribbean Story* or Frane Lessac's *My Little Island*.

Intermediate Grades

Sister by Eloise Greenfield, a strong personal account of growing up black.

The Faithful Friend by Robert San Souci, the retelling of a traditional tale from the French West Indies.

The Hundred Penny Box by Sharon Bell Mathis, a tender story about a young boy's compassion and sensitivity toward his 100-year-old great-great-aunt.

Uncle Jed's Barbershop by Margaree King Mitchell, the story of a close-knit family set in the segregated South of the 1920s.

Upper Grades

Roll of Thunder, Hear My Cry by Mildred Taylor, the powerful story of a black family growing up in the rural segregated South, winner of the Newbery Award as the most notable contribution to children's literature in 1977.

Finding Buck McHenry by Alfred Slote, a baseball story about the old "Negro League" with a commentary about discrimination.

Sounder by William Armstrong, the popular story of a young boy's experience with prejudice and security.

For Reading Aloud

The People Could Fly: American Black Folktales by Virginia Hamilton, a critically acclaimed collection of African American folk literature that reflects the richness of black culture.

Listen, Children by Dorothy Strickland, a collection of poems, short stories, and plays that can be read aloud or acted out.

Again, lists of other titles reflecting an African American perspective are available from the Interracial Council of Children's Books.

Students Whose First Language Is Not English

For many pupils, the process of becoming literate is influenced by the fact that English is not their first or native language. These may be the children of immigrants from Mexico or other Latin American countries, from the Philippines or Southeast Asia, from newly democratized nations in Eastern Europe, or from other nations whose citizens seek the hope of a better life in the United States. With their varied backgrounds, these children contribute to the rich multicultural mosaic of today's educational scene, and demographic projections indicate that their numbers will continue to grow into the next century.

Apart from the fact that their first language is not English, these students constitute a very diverse group. Some are bilingual, more comfortable in their native language but able to communicate adequately in English. Others need to learn English as a second or foreign language. Some are able to speak and understand the language used in their homes, but cannot read it. Others have had the benefit of an excellent education before immigrating and will be fully literate in their first language. Levels of language competency vary widely among bilingual or ESL (English as a Second Language), also known as LEP (Limited English Proficiency), pupils, but all will likely have a limited ability to use English, which will influence how well they learn to read and write.

Educators have long debated how best to provide instruction for children whose native language is not English. Three types of programs are currently in vogue:

Transitional bilingual education. In this—by far the most common— approach, students receive instruction in ESL and are taught academic subjects in their native language until they become proficient enough in English to succeed in an English-only environment.

Structured immersion programs. In these programs, students receive all instruction in English, although their teachers typically speak and understand the students' language.

Developmental bilingual programs. In this approach, students with limited English proficiency are placed in the same classroom with native English speakers, and each group is expected to learn the other's language. Instruction is provided in both languages in a two-way enrichment approach.

Whichever model is used, several features are important in helping pupils from non-English-speaking homes learn to read and write in English.

Reading Instruction

Reading instruction for bilingual and ESL pupils begins with a heavy emphasis on speaking and listening. Nonnative speakers need a strong background in oral language to build word meanings and sentence patterns

12.10 Putting Ideas to Work
Principles of Second Language Learning

*S*ummarizing a wealth of research on ESL teaching, Early (1990) suggests the following principles of second-language learning:

1. ESL learning should build on the experiences and language children bring to school. Teachers should encourage pupils to use their first language as a means of developing proficiency in English.
2. Learning a language means learning to use that language for a range of purposes and functions. This takes many years, so expecting quick and full-fledged competence is unrealistic.
3. Integrating language teaching with subject areas of the curriculum is a promising procedure in developing language, thought, and academic knowledge.
4. Integrated activities hold more promise than isolated exercises in teaching English as a second language.
5. Although verbal language is the major means of communication, students also communicate through drawing and other forms of meaning-making.
6. Parent participation is especially important both to school achievement and to the social growth of ESL students.

Early describes thematic units that integrate content and language as particularly effective tools for developing language competency and promoting academic learning at the same time. Trade books are an integral part of the process.

that will support comprehension in reading. This instruction should be provided in meaningful context rather than with lists of isolated words or pronunciation drills. Language develops in a learning environment in which students feel free to express their thoughts without fear of ridicule and/or constant correction. As is true with first language acquisition, children acquire a second language through use, not by studying rules: "Attempts to teach children the rules of language do not result in second language competence" (Zarrillo, 1994; p. 9). In other words, children learn English by using it to communicate.

Even as print is introduced, the emphasis on oral language remains. In postreading discussions, lack of oral language fluency may prevent ESL or LEP students from demonstrating what they have understood, so teachers need to build on their ideas by elaborating on their oral responses. This occurs, in part, through a range of book-related activities typically carried out in literature-based instruction.

Ernst and Richard (1995) picture a classroom where "literacy carves pathways to meaningful conversation among second language learners" (p. 320). They describe a program where reading, writing, and speaking activities have a thematic focus; where a shared classroom culture exists; where reading aloud occurs daily; and where children write and publish often, in an environment that emphasizes what children *have* rather than what they *lack*.

Instruction in oral language involves helping students become familiar with the sound system of American English. The pronunciation system that LEP pupils bring to school is apt to differ from the sound system native speakers use. Different languages have different sound systems (which is why a nonnative speaker of any language has "an accent"). Spanish, for example, does not have the /sh/ phoneme (the initial sound in *sheep*), so Latino students may pronounce the word *sheep* as "*cheep.*" This has obvious implications for the phonemic awareness that is so important in early reading achievement.

Phonetic elements of English should not be taught as isolated exercises, however. Sounds are contained in words, and the best practice in English pronunciation takes place in the context of meaningful discourse. For the LEP pupil, good reading does not equal perfect pronunciation. The same principle applies to nonnative speakers as to dialect speakers; that is, pupils should render text into their natural language patterns. Meaning is more important than the exact form used to express it. For LEP pupils, accents are a normal part of speaking and reading.

Word knowledge is essential to all reading and writing. Since English may not be the language spoken in the ESL pupils' homes and neighborhoods, their English word knowledge will likely not be as wide or as deep as that of children who come from English-speaking environments. Especially in the early years, concept books are useful in helping students to attach word labels to objects and experiences, and to build vocabulary as schemata they can use in learning to read. The semantic webs, word alerts, and other vocabulary-building activities important for all pupils in the classroom are particularly important to the LEP pupil. Just as reading provides English-speaking children with vocabulary extension, LEP or ESL reading is a primary means of vocabulary growth. "Second-language readers have been shown to gain significant word knowledge simply from reading, and increasing a second-language student's volume of reading has been found to produce significant gains in vocabulary knowledge and other aspects of linguistic proficiency" (Nagy, 1995; p. 16).

Syntax is also important to the pupil's knowledge of language. LEP students need to acquire language patterns that convey meaning. Instruction must extend beyond the narrow grammatical focus of proper usage (such as avoiding expressions like *ain't* and double negatives) to understanding the underlying grammatical relationships that convey meaning in connected discourse. This requires exposure to a variety of language patterns in trade books and in oral language exercises, and an examination of how the same idea can be expressed in a number of ways.

Sutton (1989) identifies four critical areas that help LEP students become more proficient readers of English:

> *building word recognition,* with word meanings presented in the context of functional, integrated language activities;

experiencing language competence, with language used for real communication (such as constructing daily messages, role playing, planning classroom activities, and the like);

expanding conceptual frameworks, starting with reading material that is culturally familiar and helping students develop a framework for dealing with unfamiliar text;

introducing strategies, showing pupils how to develop the strategies all good readers use to construct meaning from text.

Farnan, Flood, and Lapp (1994) identify research-based instructional strategies that they recommend teachers use with ESL or LEP students. These include integrating reading and writing, semantic mapping, summarizing, and writing dialogue journals, among others. These techniques have proven effective in helping all children learn to read and write. Throughout the process, the researchers stress, teachers can put quality literature to good use to help ESL students develop literacy in English.

Literature in the Reading Program

Literature is a vehicle for fostering the language competency of the LEP student. Good trade books expose children to meaningful units of text, while providing interesting material to share and discuss. "ESL programs that emphasize skills and workbook activities can deprive these young learners of the richly supportive context offered by good children's books" (Allen, 1989; p. 58).

The concentrated instruction given bilingual and ESL pupils often is more effective with trade books than with a stack of cards or isolated drills. Many of the same techniques that work in language therapy for children with special needs also work with ESL students. Not only do trade books provide interesting material to help students develop competency in English, these books also provide a multicultural dimension to the classroom reading program.

Allen (1989) points out how literature can support the many dimensions of language development for bilingual and ESL pupils. A trade book provides children with "a large, cohesive, uninterrupted chunk of language." Predictable and patterned stories with repeated refrains are especially appropriate for younger LEP students, since these books allow pupils to function quickly as readers of English text. Stories are made comprehensible by illustrations, by repeated language patterns, and by predictable story structure. Good literature also provides children with models for developing their writing proficiency in English.

Informational trade books support second language learners in content areas of the curriculum. These books often provide a more readable alternative to content area textbooks, and they convey an enormous amount of information with the combination of illustration and text.

12.11 Putting Ideas to Work
Literature from a Latino Perspective

Children's trade books written from a Latino perspective are important to classroom reading programs. Although Spanish-speaking children share a common language, their cultural traditions can be very diverse. Respective groups of Latino pupils trace their traditions to Cuba, Puerto Rico, Mexico, and other Latin American nations, and teachers need to be sensitive to the range of literature that reflects these varied cultural traditions.

A sample of books that reflect Latino experiences and can be used in the classroom include:

Primary Grades

Isla by Arthur Dorros, a celebration of the imaginations of Rosalba and her grandmother.
Hello, Amigos! by Tricia Brown, a photographic exploration of a day in the life of a young Latino boy.
Gilberto and the Wind by Marie Hall Ets, a picture book that fits into science as well.

Intermediate Grades

Jo, Flo, and Yolanda by Carol de Poix, the story of three sisters who look alike but behave differently.
Cesar Chavez by Ruth Faucher, a biography that relates the story of this leader's childhood.
Beneath the Stone: A Mexican Zapotec Tale by Bernard Wolf, in which the reader sees the customs and family life in a Mexican village through the eyes of a young boy.

Upper Grades

The House on Mango Street by Sandra Cisneros, the story of a young girl's experiences with family, friends, and the neighborhood.
Felita by Nicholasa Mohr, which describes the prejudice and isolation a girl feels when her family moves to a "better" neighborhood.
Local News by Gary Soto, stories about growing up in a Mexican American neighborhood in California.

As is true with African American and other multiethnic literature, the Council on Interracial Books for Children can suggest additional titles.

Pupils with limited English proficiency can use trade books in a number of ways. For example, they can learn through:

Shared stories. Children's language power grows as they participate in conversations and informal discussions about familiar stories shared in group settings. Small group settings are more advantageous for LEP pupils, since they have more occasions to speak and feel more comfortable. "Books can do more than provide an input of vocabulary and structure. They give pupils something to talk about by providing a very special kind of shared experience" (Allen, 1989; p. 59).

Read Alouds. Hearing good stories read well exposes children to literary language and helps them become familiar with narrative text structure. When the teacher reads good stories often and well, it helps

12.12 Putting Ideas to Work
Children's Literature and Second Language Learning

The effectiveness of using an infusion of literature in reading programs for students whose first language is not English has been clearly demonstrated.

To test the hypothesis that repeated exposure to high-interest, illustrated storybooks produces rapid second-language learning, Elley and Mangubhai (1983) placed hundreds of high-interest trade books written in English into classrooms in rural schools in the South Pacific island nation of Fiji. The researchers then determined the effect this "book flood" had on the general language competence of the pupils, for whom English was a second language.

The trade books were used in teacher-directed, shared reading sessions followed by book-related activities, and in daily periods of sustained silent reading. Results showed that the children exposed to literature progressed dramatically in reading and in listening comprehension, demonstrating the role literature can play in helping pupils learn English as a second language.

In the United States, Roser, Hoffman, and Farest (1990) conducted a study in which children's literature was infused into a traditional language arts program serving primarily limited-English-speaking children from economically disadvantaged environments. The project involved introducing literature units (including trade books on focused topics) into kindergarten, first, and second grade classrooms in which over 80 percent of the pupils were Latino. Books were shared, enjoyed, and discussed; children talked, drew, and wrote in response to stories; trade books became the focus of formal reading lessons. In short, literature became an integral part of the reading program.

The results? Very positive! Student scores increased on both the standardized reading achievement test administered in the district and on the state test of basic skills. Teachers developed insights and teaching techniques they did not have before. "Our results indicate that a literature-based program can be implemented successfully in schools that serve at-risk students. Further, there is every indication that these students respond to such a program in the same positive ways as any student would—with enthusiasm for books, with willingness to share ideas, and with growth in language and literacy" (Roser, Hoffman, and Farest, 1990; p. 559).

LEP pupils develop vocabulary and grammatical patterns, not to mention a sense of story structure and enjoyment.

Filmstrips and story boards. For bilingual and ESL pupils, visual referents are sometimes important clues to unfamiliar vocabulary and concepts. Illustrations in picture books can provide a focus for discussion, language, and concept building as well.

Songs and chants. Students can share their own cultural backgrounds with teachers and peers by sharing the songs and chants they know. If the teacher writes the words on a chart, the whole group can learn them. A good trade book in this regard for Latino pupils is Lulu Delacre's *Arroz con Leche: Popular Songs and Rhymes from Latin America,* a bilingual collection of traditional folk songs and rhymes from Mexico, Puerto Rico, and Argentina.

Repetition and patterns. Repetitious poetry and predictable pattern books such as Pat Hutchins's *Good Night, Owl* provide pupils with printed text they can easily learn to read independently through repetition. This builds their confidence in their ability to handle the text on their own.

Choral reading. Using the works of such favorite children's poets as Shel Silverstein and Jack Prelutsky, McCauley and McCauley (1992) have demonstrated that choral reading is a highly effective technique for promoting language learning and reading success for children whose first language is not English.

Bilingual texts. Books with parallel versions in two languages—such as Rebecca Emberley's English/Spanish books *Taking a Walk/Cammandro* and *My Home/Mi Casa*—allow Latino children to build vocabulary and concepts by matching the Spanish text to the English. These bilingual texts not only promote second language learning; they provide an indication that the pupil's native language and culture are valued in the classroom. Stories such as Alberto Blanco's *The Desert Mermaid/La sirena del desierto* or Harriet Rohmer and Mary Anchondo's Aztec legend *How We Came to the Fifth World/Como vinimos al quinto mundo* contain good stories that reflect cultural traditions as well. Trade books in Spanish, such as *Flecha al Sol*, the Spanish edition of Gerald McDermott's *Arrow to the Sun*, allow Spanish-speaking children to enjoy classic literature in their native tongue.

Figurative language. LEP pupils usually need special help with idiomatic expressions and figures of speech, since they often interpret the meaning of expressions such as "It's raining cats and dogs" in a literal sense. Peggy Parish's *Amelia Bedelia* books provide a wealth of material in this area. Pupils can illustrate their own figures of speech and write original sentences illustrating the meaning of idiomatic expressions.

Technology. Technology also plays a role in the instructional program for children whose native language is not English. Interactive storybooks on CD-ROM offer LEP children the same advantages they offer other children, while they also provide the additional support the non-English-speaking child might need. Pupils with limited ability in English can follow the lines as they listen to a recorded or taped version of a story such as Arthur Dorros's *Radio Man*, an upbeat tale about migrant farm workers in the west. Using software programs such as *Multicultural Links* (see Diamond and Moore, 1995), students can tap into stories and informational books related to a country or culture, as well as find a wealth of information (and even listen to national anthems) from all parts of the world.

As students whose dominant language is one other than English begin to achieve more independence in dealing with print, trade books are still essential for the development of their reading competency. "To help students to begin to read on their own, teachers will want to find comprehensible materials, such as picture books with illustrations that directly support the text, and stories with predictable patterns and repetitive language. Well-written, high-interest literature provides a better basis for reading instruction than materials written in a simpler but stilted fashion" (Au, 1993; p. 149). Trade books directly related to the child's ethnic or cultural background have a built-in element of interest. Pupils often have the schemata to comprehend books they can relate to.

There are no mystical, magical techniques for helping bilingual and ESL students learn to read with literature. Making sure that there is a sound basis of language and understanding; providing a variety of multicultural trade books; using pupils' own backgrounds to build understanding; being aware of points at which a child's language and experience may create problems in understanding; providing well-planned direct instruction in applying effective reading strategies—these are the best procedures for teaching reading to children whose first language is not English.

As they develop language competence and reading ability, ESL and bilingual pupils need to be writing, since the reading-writing connection is no less important to these children than to those whose native language is English. ESL pupils develop writing ability through process writing activities, dialogue journals, and other techniques that have proved effective for all students (Hudelson, 1987).

Multicultural literature can be a powerful force in enhancing literacy and in leading to personal empowerment for all children.

Cooperative Teaching

In the belief that "two heads are better than one," bilingual resource specialists and classroom teachers need to work closely together to support the success of the ESL child in the classroom. Whether children are grouped in transitional classes, in structured immersion programs, or in developmental bilingual groups, a close, cooperative relationship between the classroom teacher and the bilingual specialist is essential.

As is the case with resource specialists who work with special-needs children, coordination and communication are vital. Since resource specialists for ESL pupils often speak the pupil's first language, these specialists can provide valuable information about children's family backgrounds, cultural backgrounds, and native language—information that the teacher can use in planning a successful reading program in the classroom.

Resource specialists can also provide effective contact with the home, since parent involvement is important in the literacy development of the ESL pupil. For a variety of cultural and linguistic reasons, parents of ESL and bilingual students are sometimes reluctant to approach the school as full partners in their children's education. Yet because family values reinforce school expectations, "interpreting the school's agenda for parents is one of the most important tasks teachers face" (Bowman, 1989).

Teachers need to communicate with parents regarding their child's progress and let them know what parents can do to promote literacy in the home. The resource specialist is vital in translating notices into the parents' home language. Bilingual texts such as Rebecca Emberley's *My Day/Mi Dia* and *Let's Go/Vamos* can bridge the gap between the classroom and the Latino home environment.

Parent involvement is important for reasons more directly related to literacy. When English is not the native language spoken at home, children lose opportunities for language development and schema building that support success in learning to read. That is why many partnership programs invite parents and children to work cooperatively in reading and related language-instructional activities (Quintero and Huerta-Macias, 1990).

Summary and Conclusions

North America has always been considered an ethnic and cultural melange, a place where people from many nations, languages, and cultures come together as "one nation under God." It is in this context that schools are educating pupils to form the society of the 21st century, and multicultural children's literature needs to be part of that education.

Multicultural literature opens windows of understanding and sharpens children's appreciation of their place in a diverse society. Literature that reflects different multicultural perspectives allows racially and ethnically diverse pupils to feel proud of their rich cultural heritage while encouraging all students to recognize the literary diversity of our society.

The language that children bring to school affects how they learn to read and write. Pupils arrive in the classroom with different regional and social varieties of speech, and teachers need to take these dialects into account in teaching children how to read. Some aspects of instruction may need to be adjusted in light of the phonological, lexical, and syntactical features of a child's dialect; the strategies used to create meaning in printed text remain the same for all pupils.

When the language that students bring to the classroom is not English, further adjustments are required. Instruction in reading and writing English must be firmly rooted in oral language competency. The emphasis in literacy instruction remains on understanding and appreciating print.

No matter what the child's language—be it a dialect of English or a language other than English—that language is rooted in the child's cultural roots and traditions. These traditions are tied to, and illustrated by, the literature that is part of that culture. Multicultural literature is valuable for all students. It constitutes meaningful material essential to reading instruction in today's elementary school.

Discussion Questions and Activities

1. Select several books by a well-respected AHANA author of children's literature—Virginia Hamilton, John Steptoe, Virginia Driving Hawk Sneve, or Lawrence Yep, for example. Find some background information on the author. What special qualities do the works have that reflect the author's understanding of his or her culture?

2. Do a little sociolinguistic research. Using a linguistic atlas or other reference tool, investigate the speech patterns of the language used in your area. How are these language patterns manifested in the language of your friends and fellow students?

3. Prepare a reading lesson plan based on a trade book with a multicultural focus. What type of adjustments might you have to make if you were teaching this lesson to a group of innercity or rural dialect speakers, or to a group of children with limited English proficiency?

4. Compile a list of trade books you might use in planning a program like the one featured in Putting Ideas to Work 12.6. Suggest one or two ways you might use different books at each phase. Compare your list of books and your ideas with those your classmates compile.

5. In a group, respond to the following discussion question: If you were teaching in a mostly white, middle-class community, why would it be important to have a strong focus on multicultural literature in your reading program? Take notes on your group's discussion and the conclusions you reach.

School-Based Assignments

1. Interview a teacher on how he or she views language differences in his or her classroom. What adjustments does the teacher think are necessary for pupils who speak a nonstandard dialect or who speak English as a second language?

2. Take a look at the classroom library with an eye to its selection of multicultural books. How many books are available with a multicultural perspective? How do these books reflect various cultures?

3. Select a children's trade book appropriate to your grade level, one that has a distinct multicultural focus or flavor. Share the book with a group of students either by reading it to them or by using it in a directed reading activity. Determine whether the children notice the multicultural elements in the story and note their reaction. What type of activity, beyond reading and writing, would be appropriate to focus on the diversity this book reflects?

4. Multicultural literature has an important place in thematic units in social studies. Select a social studies topic that is part of the curriculum in your

school. Make a list of children's trade books you could use in this unit, along with one or two activities for each book.

5. Since they come from the oral tradition, ethnic folktales typically have qualities that make them appealing to storytellers. With the help of the librarian (if necessary), select a piece of folk literature and work with a small group of students in preparing to share it orally with a younger class.

Children's Trade Books Cited in This Chapter

Aardema, Verna. (1975). *Why Mosquitoes Buzz in People's Ears: A West African Folk Tale*. New York: Dial.

Agard, John. (1989). *The Calypso Alphabet*. New York: Henry Holt.

Agard, John, and Nichols, Grace. (1994). *No Hickory, No Dickory, No Dock: Caribbean Nursery Rhymes*. New York: Candlewick.

Ai-Ling, Louie. (1982). *Yeh-Shen: A Cinderella Story from China*. New York: Philomel.

Armstrong, William. (1969). *Sounder*. New York: Harper & Row.

Baylor, Byrd. (1976). *Hawk, I'm Your Brother*. New York: Macmillan.

Baylor, Byrd. (1989). *Amigo*. New York: Macmillan.

Bierhorst, John. (1984). *The Spirit Child*. New York: Morrow.

Birdseye, Tom A. (1990). *A Song of the Stars*. New York: Holiday House.

Blanco, Alberto. (1992). *The Desert Mermaid/La sirena del desierto*. San Francisco: The Children's Press.

Brown, Tricia. (1986). *Hello, Amigos!* New York: Henry Holt.

Bruchac, Joseph. (1993). *Fox Song*. New York: Putnam.

Buck, Pearl. (1986). *The Big Wave*. New York: Harper & Row.

Bunting, Eve. (1988). *How Many Days to America? A Thanksgiving Story*. New York: Clarion.

Bunting, Eve. (1994). *Smoky Night*. New York: Harcourt Brace.

Cavan, Seamus. (1993). *The Irish-American Experience*. Brookfield, CT: Millbrook.

Chetin, Helen. (1982). *Angel Island Prisoner*. Berkeley, CA: New Seed Press.

Cisneros, Sandra. (1989). *The House on Mango Street*. Houston: Arte Publico.

Climo, Shirley. (1989). *The Egyptian Cinderella*. New York: Harper & Row.

Climo, Shirley. (1993). *The Korean Cinderella*. New York: HarperCollins.

Coerr, Eleanor. (1977). *Sadako and the Thousand Paper Cranes*. New York: Dell.

Collier, James, and Collier, Christopher. (1983). *War Comes to Willy Freeman*. New York: Putnam.

Crew, Linda. (1989). *Children of the River*. New York: Dell

Dahl, Roald. (1962). *James and the Giant Peach*. New York: Knopf.

Dahl, Roald. (1977). *Charlie and the Chocolate Factory*. New York: Bantam.

Delacre, Lulu. (1989). *Arroz con Leche: Popular Songs and Rhymes from Latin America*. New York: Scholastic.

Demi. (1991). *The Empty Pot*. New York: Holt.

de Paola, Tomie. (1980). *The Legend of Old Befana*. New York: Harcourt.

de Paola, Tomie. (1983). *The Legend of Bluebonnet*. New York: Putnam.

de Poix, Carol. (1979). *Jo, Flo, and Yolanda*. Carrboro, NC: Lollipop Power.

Dorros, Arthur. (1993). *Radio Man*. New York: HarperCollins.

Dorros, Arthur. (1996). *Isla*. New York: Dutton.

Durrel, Ann. (1989). *The Dianne Goode Book of American Folk Tales and Songs*. New York: Dutton.

Emberley, Rebecca. (1990). *Taking a Walk/Cammandro*. Boston: Little, Brown.

Emberley, Rebecca. (1993). *Let's Go/Vamos*. Boston: Little, Brown.

Emberley, Rebecca. (1993). *My Day/Mi Dia*. Boston: Little, Brown.

Emberley, Rebecca. (1993). *My Home/Mi Casa*. Boston: Little, Brown.

Ets, Marie Hall. (1978). *Gilberto and the Wind*. New York: Puffin.

Faucher, Ruth. (1988). *Cesar Chavez*. New York: Harper & Row.

Feelings, Muriel. (1971). *Moja Means One: A Swahili Counting Book*. New York: Dial.

Feelings, Muriel. (1974). *Jambo Means Hello: A Swahili Alphabet Book*. New York: Dial.

Flournoy, Valerie. (1985). *The Patchwork Quilt*. New York: Dial.

Forbes, Esther. (1969). *Johnny Tremain*. New York: Dell.

Fox, Paula. (1967). *How Many Miles to Babylon?* New York: White.

Gera, Adele. (1990). *My Grandmother's Stories: A Collection of Jewish Folk Tales*. New York: Knopf.

Gershator, Phyllis. (1994). *Rata, Pata, Scata, Fata: A Caribbean Story*. Boston: Little, Brown.

Goble, Paul. (1980). *The Gift of the Sacred Dog*. New York: Bradbury.

Goble, Paul. (1989). *Her Seven Brothers*. New York: Bradbury.

Greene, Bette. (1974). *Philip Hall Likes Me, I Reckon Maybe*. New York: Dial.

Greenfield, Eloise. (1974). *Sister*. New York: Crowell.

Greenfield, Eloise. (1988). *Grandpa's Face*. New York: Philomel.

Grifalconi, Ann. (1990). *Osa's Pride*. Boston: Little, Brown.

Hale, Janet. (1976). *Owl's Song*. New York: Avon.

Hamilton, Virginia. (1967). *Zeeley*. New York: Macmillan.

Hamilton, Virginia. (1985). *The People Could Fly: American Black Folktales*. New York: Knopf.

Hausman, Gerald. (1996). *Eagle Boy: A Traditional Navajo Legend*. New York: HarperCollins.

Havill, Juanita. (1993). *Jamaica and Brianna*. Boston: Houghton Mifflin.

Hewett, Joan. (1990). *Hector Lives in the United States Now: The Story of a Mexican-American Child*. New York: Lippincott.

Howard, Elizabeth Fitzgerald. (1991). *Aunt Flossie's Hats (and Crab Cakes Later)*. Boston: Houghton Mifflin.

Hoyt-Goldsmith, Diane. (1991). *Pueblo Storyteller*. New York: Holiday House.

Huck, Charlotte. (1989). *Princess Furball*. New York: Greenwillow.

Hutchins, Pat. (1972). *Good Night, Owl*. New York: Macmillan.

Jacobs, William Jay. (1990). *Ellis Island: New Hope in a New Land*. New York: Scribner.

Keats, Ezra Jack. (1967). *Peter's Chair*. New York: Harper & Row.

Krumgold, Joseph. (1953). *And Now Miguel*. New York: Crowell.

Lawlor, Veronica. (1995). *I Was Dreaming to Come to America: Memories from the Ellis Island Oral History Project*. New York: Viking.

Lee, Jeanne, M. (1987). *Ba-Nam*. New York: Henry Holt.

Lessac, Frane. (1985). *My Little Island*. New York: HarperCollins.

Lewis, John. (1980). *The Chinese Word for Horse and Other Stories*. New York: Schocken Books.

Lord, Beth Bao. (1984). *In the Year of the Boar and Jackie Robinson*. New York: Harper & Row.

Martin, Bill Jr., and Archambault, John. (1987). *Knots on a Counting Rope*. New York: Henry Holt.

Martin, Rafe. (1992). *The Rough-Faced Girl*. New York: Putnam.

Mathis, Sharon Bell. (1975). *The Hundred Penny Box*. New York: Viking.

McDermott, Gerald. (1974). *Arrow to the Sun*. New York: Viking.

McDermott, Gerald. (1991). *Flecha al Sol*. New York: Viking.

McMahon, Patricia. (1993). *Chi-Hoon: A Korean Girl*. Honesdale, PA: Boyds Mills Press.

Mendez, Phil. (1989). *The Black Snowman*. New York: Scholastic.

Miles, Miska. (1971). *Annie and the Old One*. Boston: Little, Brown.

Mitchell, Margaree K. (1993). *Uncle Jed's Barbershop*. New York: Simon & Schuster.

Mohr, Nicholasa. (1979). *Felita*. New York: Dial.

Morimoto, Junko. (1986). *Mouse's Marriage*. New York: Viking Kestrel.

Morris, Winnifred. (1987). *The Magic Leaf*. New York: Atheneum.

Mosel, Arlene. (1968). *Tikki, Tikki, Tembo*. New York: Henry Holt.

Mullel, Tololwa M. (1990). *The Orphan Boy*. New York: Clarion.

Naidoo, Beverly. (1985). *Journey to Jo'burg*. New York: Lippincott.

Naidoo, Beverly. (1989). *Chain of Fire*, New York: HarperCollins.

O'Brien, Edna. (1988). *Tales for the Telling*. New York: Penguin.

Paek, Min. (1988). *Aekyung's Dream*. San Francisco: The Children's Book Press.

Parrish, Peggy. (1989). *Good Hunting, Blue Sky*. New York: Random House.

Parrish, Peggy. (1992). *Amelia Bedelia*. New York: HarperCollins.

Rattigan, Jama Kim. (1990). *Dumpling Soup*. Boston: Little, Brown.

Rehnman, Mats. (1989). *The Clay Flute*. New York: Farrar, Straus & Giroux.

Ringgold, Faith. (1991). *Tar Beach*. New York: Crown.

Ringgold, Faith. (1992). *Aunt Harriet's Underground Railroad in the Sky*. New York: Crown.

Robbins, Ruth. (1990). *Baboushka and the Three Kings*. Boston: Houghton Mifflin.

Rohmer, Harriet, and Anchondo, Mary. (1988). *How We Came to the Fifth World/ Como vinimos al quinto mundo*. San Francisco: The Children's Book Press.

Rosario, Idalia. (1987). *Idalia's Project ABC*. New York: Henry Holt.

San Souci, Robert. (1995). *The Faithful Friend*. New York: Simon & Schuster.

Say, Allan. (1993). *Grandfather's Journey*. Boston: Houghton Mifflin.

Say, Allan. (1995). *A Stranger in the Mirror*. Boston: Houghton Mifflin.

Schroeder, Alan. (1989). *Ragtime Trumpie*. Boston: Little, Brown.

Scott, Sally. (1988). *The Magic Horse*. New York: Morrow.

Seeger, Pete. (1986). *Abiyoyo*. New York: Macmillan.

Slote, Alfred. (1991). *Finding Buck McHenry*. New York: HarperCollins.

Sneve, Virginia Driving Hawk (1972). *Jimmy Yellow Hawk*. New York: Holiday House.

Sneve, Virginia Driving Hawk (1989). *Dancing Teepees: Poems of American Indian Youth*. New York: Holiday House.

Sneve, Virginia Driving Hawk (1993). *The Navajos*. New York: Holiday House.

Snyder, Dianne. (1988). *The Boy of the Three-Year Nap*. Boston: Houghton Mifflin.

Soto, Gary. (1993). *Local News*. Orlando: Harcourt Brace.

Speare, Elizabeth George. (1983). *The Sign of the Beaver*. Boston: Houghton Mifflin.

Steptoe, John. (1980). *Daddy Is a Monster . . . Sometimes*. New York: Lippincott.

Steptoe, John. (1987). *Mufaro's Beautiful Daughter: An African Tale*. New York: Lothrup.

Strickland, Dorothy. (1986). *Listen, Children*. New York: Bantam.

Suart, Michele M. (1983). *Angel Child, Dragon Child*. Milwaukee: Raintree.

Tadjo, Veronique. (1989). *Lord of the Dance: An African Retelling*. New York: HarperCollins.

Taylor, Mildred. (1975). *Song of the Trees*. New York: Dial.

Taylor, Mildred. (1976). *Roll of Thunder, Hear My Cry*. New York: Dial.

Taylor, Mildred. (1981). *Let the Circle Be Unbroken*. New York: Dial.

Taylor, Mildred. (1990). *The Road to Memphis*. New York: Dial.

Taylor, Theodore. (1989). *The Cay*. New York: Doubleday.

Tompert, Ann. (1990). *Grandfather Tang's Story*. New York: Crown.

Tsutsui, Yoriko. (1989). *Anna in Charge*. New York: Viking Kestrel.

Twain, Mark. (1986). *The Adventures of Huckleberry Finn*. New York: Viking. (Other editions available.)

Uchida, Yoshiko. (1971). *Journey to Topaz*. New York: Scribner.

Uchida, Yoshiko. (1982). *Journey Home*. New York: Macmillan.

Uchida, Yoshiko. (1993). *The Bracelet*. New York: Putnam.

Vuong, Lynette. (1992). *The Brocaded Slipper and Other Vietnamese Tales*. New York: HarperCollins.

Vuong, Lynette. (1993). *The Golden Carp and Other Romantic Tales from Vietnam*. New York: Lothrup.

Wall, Lina Mao. (1991). *Judge Rabbit and the Tree Spirit*. San Francisco: The Children's Book Press.

Waters, Kate, and Slovenz-Low, Madeleine. (1990). *Lion Dancer: Ernie Wan's Chinese New Year*. New York: Scholastic.

Winthrop, Elizabeth. (1991). *Vasilissa the Beautiful*. New York: HarperCollins.

Wolf, Bernard. (1994). *Beneath the Stone: A Mexican Zapotec Tale*. New York: Orchard Books.

Wu, Dana Y., and Tung, Jeffrey D. (1993). *The Chinese-American Experience*. Brookfield, CT: Millbrook.

Wyndham, Robert, ed. (1968). *Chinese Mother Goose Rhymes*. New York: Philomel.

Yashima, Taro. (1955). *Crow Boy*. New York: Viking.

Yep, Laurence. (1985). *Dragonwings*. New York: Harper & Row.

Yep, Laurence. (1989). *The Rainbow People*. New York: Harper & Row.

Yep, Laurence. (1996). *Ribbons*. New York: Harper & Row.

Young, Ed. (1989). *Lon Po Po: A Red-Riding Hood Story from China*. New York: Philomel.

References

Allen, V. G. (1989). Literature as Support to Language Acquisition. In P. Rigg and V. G. Allen, eds., *When They Don't All Speak English: Integrating the ESL Student into the Regular Classroom.* Urbana, IL: National Council of Teachers of English.

Allington, R. L. (1994). Reducing the Risk: Integrated Language Arts in Reconstructed Elementary Schools. In L. M. Morrow, J. K. Smith, and L. C. Wilkinson, eds., *Integrated Language Arts: Controversy to Consensus.* Boston: Allyn & Bacon.

Au, K. H. (1993). *Literacy Instruction in Multicultural Settings*. Fort Worth: Harcourt Brace Jovanovich.

Banks, J. A. (1989). Integrating the Curriculum with Ethnic Content: Approaches and Guidelines. In J. A. Banks and C. A. McGee Banks, eds., *Multicultural Education: Issues and Perspectives.* Boston: Allyn & Bacon.

Barnitz, J. G. (1980). Black English and Other Dialects: Sociolinguistic Implications for Reading Instruction. *The Reading Teacher* 33:779–786.

Bishop, R. S. (1987). Extending Multicultural Understanding Through Children's Books. In B. Cullinan, ed., *Children's Literature in the Reading Program.* Newark, DE: International Reading Association.

Bishop, R. S. (1992). Multicultural Literature for Children: Making Informed Choices. In Violet J. Harris, ed., *Teaching Multicultural Literature in Grades K–8.* Norwood, MA: Christopher Gordon Publishers.

Bowman, B. T. (1989). Educating Language-Minority Children: Challenges and Opportunities. *Phi Delta Kappan* 71:118–120.

Burling, R. (1973). *English in Black and White*. New York: Holt, Rinehart & Winston.

Cosby, B. (1990). 45 Years from Today. *Ebony* 46:61.

Cox, S., and Galda, L. (1990). Multicultural Literature: Mirrors and Windows on a Global Community. *The Reading Teacher* 43:582–589.

Delpit, L. (1995). *Other People's Children: Cultural Conflict in the Classroom.* New York: The New Press.

Diaakiw, J. Y. (1990). Children's Literature and Global Education: Understanding the Developing World. *The Reading Teacher* 44:296–300.

Diamond, B. J., and Moore, M. A. (1995). *Multicultural Literacy: Mirroring the Reality of the Classroom.* New York: Longman.

Dillard, J. L. (1972). *Black English*. New York: Random House.

Early, M. (1990). Enabling First and Second Language Learners in the Classroom. *Language Arts* 67:567–575.

Elley, W. R., and Mangubhai, F. (1983). The Impact of Reading on Second Language Learning. *Reading Research Quarterly* 19:53–67.

Ernst, G., and Richard, K. J. (1995). Reading and Writing Pathways to Conversation in the ESL Classroom. *The Reading Teacher* 48:320–326.

Farnan, N., Flood, J., and Lapp, D. (1994). Comprehending Through Reading and Writing: Six Research-Based Instructional Strategies. In K. Spangenbert-Urbschat and R. Prichard, eds., *Kids Come in All Languages: Reading Instruction for ESL Students*. Newark, DE: International Reading Association.

Garcia, G. E., Pearson, P. D., and Jimenez, R. T. (1994). *The At-Risk Situation: A Synthesis of Reading Research*. Champaign: University of Illinois at Urbana-Champaign Center for the Study of Reading.

Harris, V. J. (1992). *Teaching Multicultural Literature in Grades K–8*. Norwood, MA: Christopher Gordon Publishers.

Hudelson, S. (1987). The Role of Native Language Literacy in the Education of Language-Minority Children. *Language Arts* 64:827–841.

Lake, R. (1990). An Indian Father's Plea. *Teacher Magazine* 2:48–53.

Lara, J. (1994). Demographic Overview: Changes in Student Enrollment in American Schools. In K. Spangenbert-Urbschat and R. Prichard, eds., *Kids Come in All Languages: Reading Instruction for ESL Students*. Newark, DE: International Reading Association.

McCauley, J. K., and McCauley, D. S. (1992). Using Choral Reading to Promote Language Learning for ESL Students. *The Reading Teacher* 45:526–537.

Nagy, W. E. (1995). *On the Role of Context in First- and Second-Language Vocabulary Learning*. Technical Report No. 627. Champaign: University of Illinois at Urbana-Champaign Center for the Study of Reading.

Norton, D. E. (1990). Teaching Multicultural Literature in the Reading Curriculum. *The Reading Teacher* 44:28–40.

Quintero, R., and Huerta-Macias, A. (1990). All in the Family: Bilingualism and Biliteracy. *The Reading Teacher* 44:306–312.

Rasinski, T. V., and Padak, N. D. (1990). Multicultural Learning Through Children's Literature. *Language Arts* 67:576–580.

Roser, N. L., Hoffman, J. V., and Farest, C. (1990). Language, Literature, and At-Risk Children. *The Reading Teacher* 43:554–559.

Sims, R. (1982). *Shadow and Substance: Afro-American Experiences in Contemporary Children's Fiction*. Urbana, IL: National Council of Teachers of English.

Smitherman, G., ed. (1981). *Black English and the Education of Black Children and Youth*. Detroit: Center for Black Studies, Wayne State University.

Sutton, C. (1989). Helping the Nonnative English Speaker with Reading. *The Reading Teacher* 4:684–688.

Tylor, E. B. (1929). *Primitive Cultures* (5th ed.). London: J. Murray.

Walker-Dalhouse, D. (1992). Using African-American Literature to Increase Ethnic Understanding. *The Reading Teacher* 45:416–422.

Young, T. A., and Ferguson, P. M. (1995). From Anansi to Zomo: Trickster Tales in the Classroom. *The Reading Teacher* 48:490–503.

Zarrillo, J. (1994). *Multicultural Literature, Multicultural Teaching: Units for the Elementary Grades*. Fort Worth: Harcourt Brace.

Assessing Literacy Development

© James L. Shaffer

Chapter 13 Outline

Features

13.1 **Dimensions of Assessment**
13.2 **New Views of Reading Assessment**
13.3 **"The Nation's Report Card"**
13.4 **Assessing Attitudes Toward Reading**
13.5 **Assessment of Emergent Literacy**
13.6 **Multiple Options for Alternative Assessment**
13.7 **Comprehension Matrix and Profile**
13.8 **Sample Checklist/Rating Scale**
13.9 **Literature Reading Behavior Inventory**
13.10 **Informal Reading Inventories**
13.11 **Using Trade Books as "Benchmark" Measures**
13.12 **Using the Tape Recorder**

Key Concepts in This Chapter

Literacy assessment has many purposes; a variety of tools and techniques are needed to achieve these different purposes in a literature-based program.

Formal reading tests have been used for a long time in schools. These norm-referenced instruments were designed both to measure individual pupil progress and to assess the effectiveness of reading programs.

Alternative assessment involves gathering classroom performance measures to provide an ongoing indication of students' reading and writing abilities, along with the processes they use.

Portfolio assessment involves compiling multiple measures to monitor and record a child's progress in becoming literate.

Introduction

Assessment of learning is a major concern for anyone involved in education—teachers, administrators, parents, pupils, school boards, state legislators, and the general public. Everyone is anxious to know, "How are we doing?" This is no less true of literature-based instruction than of more conventional reading programs.

Because of this widespread concern, testing is a pervasive part of schooling. For a long time, standardized testing dominated the educational landscape. It has been estimated that 105 million standardized tests are administered every year—an average of 2.4 tests per student per year, and this is a conservative estimate (Neill and Medina, 1989). Moreover, the amount of testing we do seems to be increasing (Haney and Madaus, 1989). Schools have a heavy philosophical and financial investment in formal testing.

Testing seems to impact reading more than any other curriculum area. Because reading is so close to the heart of the educational process, and because success in school is so closely related to literacy development, everyone is interested in the results of reading tests. Reports on local achievement test performance make the front page of the newspaper, and important educational decisions are based on reported test results.

Assessment, however, extends well beyond the narrow concept of testing. Although the terms *testing, assessment, measurement,* and *evaluation* are often used interchangeably, these processes differ. *Evaluation* refers to the process of gathering information to see how well pupils have achieved objectives. *Testing* is the technology we use to gather this data, and *measurement* is the process of quantifying the data. *Assessment* is a broad term that includes both gathering and using this information to improve instruction. Part of assessment is diagnosis, or the process of determining a student's strengths and weaknesses for the purpose of planning instruction. These terms are related, to be sure, and arguments arise over their definitions. The main point is, however, that assessment has many dimensions and many purposes in literacy programs.

When we use literature to teach students to read and write, it is important to maintain a broad perspective on assessment. Formal tests are only one (some say distorted) part of assessment. While large-scale testing catches the public's attention, the assessments that really count are those that have a daily impact on students' learning and self-concepts.

Reasons for Assessment

Why does so much testing go on in schools? The reasons for assessment include:

> *to provide accountability to the public* for the money it spends on schooling—to let the taxpayers know they are getting a return on their educational investment;

> *to gather information that tells parents* how much learning has taken place, to indicate how well their children are progressing, and to compare the performances of various groups;

> *to gather data that helps teachers* assess instructional outcomes and to indicate how they can better meet pupils' needs and interests.

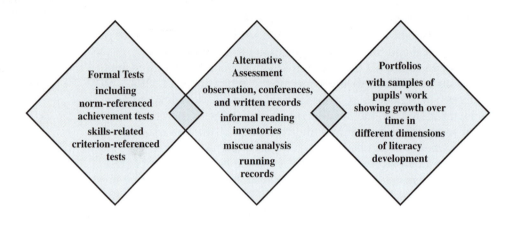

To achieve these purposes, we need different types of assessment tools and procedures. For decades, education has relied heavily on a variety of formal instruments—norm-referenced reading tests to measure levels of achievement, criterion-referenced tests to determine mastery of specific skills, diagnostic instruments to indicate pupils' strengths and weaknesses, basal reading tests to monitor learning from the reading series, and other formal measures designed to determine the amount and/or kind of learning that has taken place. Beyond these formal measures, teachers have long used their own informal observations and record-keeping systems to keep track of children's progress. More recently, educators have developed and used alternative assessment procedures, and portfolios have become an important part of student reading and writing assessment. Each of these elements constitutes a part of the total picture in assessing pupils' progress and problems in learning to read.

A General Perspective

Before examining the specifics of formal, informal, and portfolio dimensions of assessment, we need to examine the whole process of assessment from a general perspective. Any view of assessment needs to consider three points:

1. Assessment extends beyond testing; it is a continuous part of learning.
2. The more abstract an element is, the more difficult it is to measure with confidence.
3. The face of reading assessment is continuing to change dramatically.

13.2 Putting Ideas to Work

New Views of Reading Assessment

Valencia and Pearson (1987) identify a "litany of conflicts" between new views of reading and conventional practices in reading assessment.

A Set of Contrasts Between New Views of Reading and Current Practices in Assessing Reading

New views of the reading process tell us that . . .	Yet when we assess reading comprehension, we . . .
prior knowledge is an important determinant of reading comprehension.	mask any relationship between prior knowledge and reading comprehension by using lots of short passages on lots of topics.
a complete story or text has structural and topical integrity.	use short texts that seldom approximate the structural and topical integrity of authentic text.
inference is an essential part of the process of comprehending units as small as sentences.	rely on literal comprehension test items.
the diversity in individual prior knowledge as well as the varied causal relations in human experiences invite many possible inferences to fit a text or question.	use multiple choice items with only one correct answer, even when many of the responses might, under certain conditions, be plausible.
the ability to vary reading strategies to fit the text and the situation is one hallmark of an expert reader.	seldom assess how and when students vary the strategies they use during normal reading, studying, or when the going gets tough.
the ability to synthesize information from various parts of the text and from different texts is one hallmark of an expert reader.	rarely go beyond finding the main ideas of an isolated paragraph or passage.
the ability to ask good questions of text, as well as to answer them, is one hallmark of an expert reader.	seldom ask students to create or select questions about a selection they have just read.
all aspects of a reader's experience, including habits that arise from school and home, influence reading comprehension.	rarely view information on reading habits and attitudes as being as important as information about performance.
reading involves the orchestration of many skills that complement one another in a variety of ways.	use tests that fragment reading into isolated skills and report the student's performance on each.
skilled readers are fluent; their word identification is sufficiently automatic to allow them to apply most cognitive resources to comprehension.	rarely consider fluency as an index of skilled reading.
learning from text involves the restructuring, application, and flexible use of knowledge in new situations.	often ask readers to respond to the text's declarative knowledge rather than to apply it to other tasks.

From Sheila W. Valencia and P. David Pearson. (1987, April) Reading Assessment: A Time for Change. *The Reading Teacher* 40 (8):726–732. Copyright © 1987 International Reading Association, Newark DE. Reprinted with permission of Sheila Valencia and the International Reading Association. All rights reserved.

Assessment Is Part of Learning. Assessment extends beyond the narrow concept of "testing" to become an integral element in the total instructional process. It is the beginning and end of the learning cycle that reflects good teaching; that is, teachers assess in order to set goals and objectives for lessons, design instruction to meet these goals and objectives, and assess again to determine whether the goals have been met. Assessment also helps teachers reflect on their teaching and students to reflect on their learning.

Formal tests are administered only periodically; assessment takes place each day. It happens before the teacher recommends a trade book to a student for independent reading, and as the teacher solicits the child's reaction to the story. It goes on in reading groups as the teacher tries to find out what pupils already know about a topic before they read and later as he or she guides postreading questions and discussion. It is an inherent part of instructional strategies as InQuest, ReQuest and K-W-L. In short, assessment is an integral part of the teaching-learning process.

Tests in themselves will not improve teaching. Tests measure learning outcomes; they will improve learning outcomes only when they lead to improved instruction. "Collecting data about students is an empty exercise unless the information is used to plan instruction" (McKenna and Kear, 1990; p. 627).

The More Abstract an Element Is, the More Difficult It Is to Measure. Assessment involves measurement. Standardized tests and other assessment tools are educational yardsticks that quantify reading development. But we cannot measure reading ability with the same precision and confidence that we have when we measure physical qualities. It is far more difficult to measure a pupil's intelligence or reading ability with absolute accuracy than his or her height or weight, and it is more difficult still to measure the affective dimensions of learning.

Current models of assessment measure not only product—whether the child is reading at a 3.4 grade level, for example, or whether the child has mastered all the short vowel sounds—but also the processes the child uses in learning. The best way to measure reading and writing is to have the child read and write, not fill in bubbles on an "objective" multiple-choice test. Literacy assessment tries to get at the abstract qualities that make a learner literate.

The Face of Reading Assessment Is Changing Dramatically.
Research on the nature of the reading process has affected reading instruction, and assessment theory and practice is starting to catch up with these changes. Although some newly developed reading assessment instruments are beginning to reflect the findings of recent reading research (Peters and Wixon, 1989; Tierney, Carter, and Desai, 1991), many conventional standardized measures of reading achievement still look the same as they did in the 1920s.

As our view of reading has shifted from mastery of a discrete set of separate skills to the reader's more dynamic interaction in constructing meaning from text, assessment dimensions have been changing to reflect that view. Since literacy development is seen as a multifaceted process, assessment is taking on a multidimensional focus, and as constructivist approaches have influenced classroom instruction, new assessment tools have advanced to the forefront. "The assessment of reading seems best described as being in a state of *transition*" (Pikulski, 1989; p. 80).

What will these changes mean as schools move into the 21st century? A different approach to reading demands a different approach to assessment. Reliance on a single standardized measure of reading ability is giving way to alternative forms of assessment. "Performance assessment has become an essential ingredient in a complete school assessment program" (Stiggins, 1995; p. 239). Tests have begun to include alternative modes of response. The focus is shifting to pupils' everyday performance as a viable alternative to standardized measurement tools. Interest in assessment methods is drawing closer to classroom practice. Assessment has become less test-centered and more teacher- and pupil-centered.

Literature-based reading instruction lends itself especially well to this changing view of assessment. Teachers who use literature as the centerpiece of their reading instructional programs do not abandon the components of conventional programs. Instead, using trade books as instructional tools, they make reading an authentic encounter with text. As enjoyment and meaning are the primary goals of instruction, these elements are the primary concerns in assessment.

As these trends develop, classroom teachers will continue to interpret the results of formal measures, engage in informal assessment processes, and compile portfolios to assess the reading and literacy development of their pupils.

Formal Assessment

Formal measures of reading that schools commonly use include standardized reading achievement tests and skill-development tests, including criterion-referenced tests and tests of specific components related to literacy.

Standardized Reading Achievement Tests

Most college students are very familiar with standardized reading achievement tests because they have had years of experience answering such questions as "What's the best title for this story?" These are the test batteries pupils typically take once a year from grade K–12, the familiar timed tests in a multiple-choice format. American education has traditionally relied on these tools to monitor students' progress in reading; to compare, rank, and sort pupils; and to pass judgment on the quality of education our schools provide.

Each of the words that describe these measurement tools tells about the instruments themselves:

13.3 Putting Ideas to Work
"The Nation's Report Card"

*T*he National Assessment of Educational Progress (NAEP) is a national testing program designed to monitor the achievement of American students in reading and other subjects. A congressionally mandated project conducted at present by the Educational Testing Service, the program assesses work samples from students in grades 4, 8, and 12 and charts their performance over time. The results produce a kind of national "satellite photo" of the nation's level of reading proficiency, a broad picture of the educational achievement of the nation as a whole. NAEP also gathers information about student reading attitudes and behaviors.

What are the results of the most recent NAEP testing? *The NAEP 1992 Reading Report Card* (Mullis, Campbell, and Farstrup, 1993) indicates that even though national gains in reading proficiency were not dramatic, trends are generally positive. The overall picture shows a nation of pupils reading better now than in the past, albeit only slightly better. AHANA (African American, Hispanic, Asian, and Native American) children have made particularly impressive gains according to recent test results.

With regard to attitudes and experiences in reading, pupils of all ages were more aware of reading in content areas of the curriculum. And although many students do not read frequently or highly value reading as an activity, older pupils reported reading more today than their counterparts did in the early 1970s. Not surprisingly, the data indicate that children who read the most display the highest reading proficiency.

What about writing? Students in grades 4, 8, and 12 were asked to produce samples of informative, persuasive, and narrative writing. *The NAEP 1992 Writing Report Card* (Applebee et al., 1993) reports that "taken as a whole, the results show that given time and familiarity with the topic, the best students can write relatively effective informative and narrative pieces. Even the best students continue, however, to have difficulty with writing tasks that require them to muster arguments and evidence in persuasive writing" (p. 2). And the gap between the most and least proficient writers was considerable.

Writing proficiency was higher for students who had more types of reading material in the home—indicating the link between reading and writing. Also, at all grade levels, those who watched the most television had significantly lower writing proficiency.

Standardized. These reading achievement tests are designed for use on a national basis. Test items are specified, procedures for administering the tests are carefully controlled, and rules are enforced so that comparable measures are obtained from students in different areas and under different circumstances. Just as measuring devices for weight and height are standardized with consistent units of measurement, so are formal measuring devices for reading achievement.

Reading. Standardized tests measure reading achievement in terms of discrete skills. They contain separate sections for vocabulary (or word meaning) and comprehension. Some have additional sections as well—for example, sections on decoding or on reading speed. Performance levels on these separate sections are combined in an attempt to provide a measure of overall reading ability.

Achievement. Achievement indicates the amount of information a student has gained or the level of proficiency he or she has attained. Standardized reading achievement tests are *norm-referenced* measures; that is, test results are determined by comparing the child's performance to others in a sample selected to represent a national cross-section of students. In other words, pupils' performances are judged by how their scores compare to a large, representative group of students at the same age and grade level. Achievement test scores thus indicate a child's relative standing in the general school population.

Tests. A *test* is defined as "a set of systematic tasks or questions yielding responses that may be quantified so performance can be interpreted" (Harris and Hodges, 1995; p. 254). The test items students respond to reflect their purported levels of achievement in these norm-referenced tests.

While their basic purpose and format remains the same, standardized reading achievement tests have undergone some changes as researchers in the field of literacy instruction and assessment have made new discoveries. To reflect the literature-based focus of most reading instruction programs, standardized tests now contain original stories and articles written by children's authors. They include more examples of narrative writing and an occasional poem. The tests also contain some open-ended assessment items in addition to multiple-choice items that have just one correct answer. Some tests attempt to evaluate reading processes with items designed to tap metacognition and the child's conscious use of reading strategies.

Standardized tests are written by experts in the fields of reading and measurement and are published by commercial publishing companies independent of particular instructional programs. They report figures to provide statistical validity and reliability. For a long time, they were "the coin of the realm" in reporting the results of reading assessment, used in virtually every school system in the land. While schools today rely less heavily on formal measures, these tests are so ingrained in our educational system that they will likely remain so for the near future.

Those who favor the use of standardized reading achievement tests view them as objective instruments, "national yardsticks" that provide a way to measure the reading levels of children from diverse geographical, ethnic, social, economic, and demographic backgrounds. Standardized tests are easily administered and scored. They provide uniform standards that supposedly avoid the variations inherent in subjective judgments. They allow schools to gage how their students are doing in comparison to students nationwide.

At the same time, a whirlwind of criticism continues to surround standardized reading achievement tests. Critics say these tests are product-oriented and ignore important elements in the reading process; they use only indirect indicators of learning; they reduce reading response to one single correct answer; they tend to focus on isolated bits of information; and they place students in the role of passive learners (Silvernail, 1992). In addition, "there is normally considerable waste of time in standardized group tests because able children spend the most time on items that are too easy, and less able readers spend the most time on items that are too difficult" (Johnson, 1984; p. 156).

13.4 Putting Ideas to Work
Assessing Attitudes toward Reading

*B*ecause developing a positive attitude toward reading is a major goal of any classroom program—especially one that values and uses literature—measuring a child's attitude toward reading should be an important part of assessment. Attitude toward reading has a lot to do with a pupil's reading performance, yet most performance measures ignore it. Instruments that do try to measure the affective dimensions of reading include the following:

The Elementary Reading Attitude Survey (McKenna and Kear, 1990) determines how children feel about reading and learning to read. The instrument has 20 items designed to gather information about students' recreational and academic reading with brief and simply worded questions. The four-point response mode is interesting; pupils indicate their response to each question by circling one of four drawings of the popular cartoon cat Garfield, each with a pose and facial expression that convey an emotion between delight and disgust.

The Reader Self-Perception Scale (Henk and Melnick, 1995) is a tool designed for the upper elementary grades, with a general item that asks students to think about their reading ability and 32 other items focusing on how they see themselves as readers.

The Motivation to Read Profile (Gambrell et al., 1996) consists of two parts: (1) a reading survey that measures the child's self-concept as a reader and his or her perception of the value of reading, and (2) a conversational interview between teacher and student that provides individual information.

The three measures, along with directions for administering each and details regarding the technical aspects of their development, appear in the following issues of *The Reading Teacher*:

The Elementary Reading Attitude Survey (May 1990)
The Reader Self-Perception Scale (March 1995)
The Motivation to Read Profile (April 1996)

Reading extends well beyond the realm of what standardized reading achievement tests can measure. These tests may take a pupil's "reading pulse," but pulse is only one factor in a person's overall health. As new assessment procedures are developed in light of what we know about reading, and as the concept of assessment extends beyond mere testing, schools are breaking away from the bondage of standardized achievement tests and broadening their horizons on reading assessment.

Whatever their form and however they report results—as grade-level measurements, standard score, percentile, or level of proficiency—the purpose of achievement tests is the same: to indicate "how well" a student reads. The test samples reading behavior and reports an overall score that sorts and ranks students according to a norm. While analyzing the results of various parts of a reading achievement battery can produce information about sub-areas of reading development, skill-development tests try to produce more specific information.

Skill-Development Tests

As their name indicates, reading skill-development tests are designed to measure a pupil's progress in developing particular reading skills. These assessment tools include criterion-referenced measures and formal instruments that focus on particular aspects of reading.

Criterion-Referenced Tests. Criterion-referenced tests are formal measures designed to assess students' progress in specific skills—for example, phonics, vocabulary, or different dimensions of reading comprehension. Rather than compare a pupil's performance to others, criterion-referenced tests focus on the child's ability to reach a certain level of performance. Norm-referenced measures are designed to indicate how a child compares with others in a sample group; criterion-referenced tests yield results in terms of specific performance standards.

Sometimes called "mastery tests," criterion-referenced tests get their name from the idea that the pupil needs to attain a certain score as a criterion for mastery. Because criterion-referenced tests are less concerned with whether the student reads better or worse than other pupils, the tests provide less global measures and are closely related to the view of reading as a skill-development process.

Although criterion-referenced tests appear to be more objective evaluation measures, these tests have earned their share of criticism. Critics complain that they sample only a small slice of behavior that may or may not accurately reflect a child's true capacity. One lucky guess on a criterion-referenced test can mean the difference between "mastery" and "nonmastery." They are based on the view that learning to read involves learning a series of isolated skills, arbitrarily sequenced and largely unrelated to one another.

For teachers who emphasize the skills dimension of reading, criterion-referenced tests are useful measures. In literature-based reading instruction, they are rarely, if ever, used.

While some criterion-referenced tests take small samples to evaluate many different skills, other skills tests are diagnostic measures which attempt to provide in-depth and detailed information in areas related to reading.

Basal reading programs also have testing components. Given the skills orientation of traditional basals, these tests are typically criterion-referenced, skills-mastery tests. Most literature-based series have maintained a separate instrument to assess discrete skills (knowledge of phonics, for example, or the ability to see cause-effect relationships). However, more recent programs also include other assessment tools such as theme tests that focus on comprehension, placement tests, information inventories geared to the series, observation forms, checklists, writing samples to evaluate children's writing, and folders for children's portfolios.

Standardized Skills Tests. Standardized skills tests concentrate on particular components of reading competency. These tests include the following:

The *Test of Reading Comprehension* (Brown, Hammill, and Wiederholt, 1986) measures comprehension in reading, with subtests on word meaning, paragraph meaning, sentence matching, sequencing, and comprehension of content-related materials.

The *Peabody Picture Vocabulary Test* (Dunn and Dunn, 1981) is a test that requires pupils to name objects in pictures to measure vocabulary.

The *Test of Written Language* (Hammill and Larsen, 1988) is a comprehensive measure of written language that assesses both stylistic features (syntactic maturity, logical sentences, thematic maturity, and so on) and mechanical aspects (spelling, vocabulary, and so forth) of writing.

The *Woodcock-Johnson Psycho-Educational Battery, Revised* (Woodcock and Johnson, 1991) is a comprehensive battery designed to measure cognitive functioning and academic achievement, with a reading subtest that includes tests of letter and word identification, along with passage comprehension.

These tests, and others like them, focus in depth on particular aspects of literacy. They are normally administered to one child at a time by specialists qualified to administer the test and interpret the results. Usually, these tests are reserved for pupils who experience greater-than-average difficulty in learning to read. *Buros 12th Mental Measurements Yearbook* (Close, Conoley, and Impara, 1995) reviews such tests regularly.

The ammunition in the arsenal of reading assessment is extensive and impressive. Formal measuring devices exist for virtually every aspect of a child's development as a reader. But in a literature-based reading program, the on-the-spot performance assessment the teacher does in the classroom is far more valuable for guiding the instruction of a child learning to read. "The best possible assessment of reading would seem to occur when teachers observe and interact with students as they read authentic texts for genuine purposes" (Valencia and Pearson, 1987; p. 728).

Alternative Assessment

Teachers typically do not need batteries of formal standardized reading tests to evaluate their students' progress and problems in learning to read. A test is a one-shot event that may or may not reflect what a pupil knows or can do. Alternative assessment—defined as "assessment other than standardized tests to achieve direct, 'authentic' assessment of student performance on important learning tasks" (Harris and Hodges, 1995)—involves a variety of classroom-based procedures designed to indicate student performance in reading and writing on a day-to-day basis.

Ideally, alternative assessment is also *authentic*. There are many definitions and perceptions of what authentic assessment is. Valencia, Hiebert, and Afflerbach (1994) define it as "assessment activities that represent literacy behavior of the community and workplace, and that reflect the actual learning and instructional activities of the classroom and out-of-school worlds" (p. 11). Authentic assessment is not a measure of a child's ability to perform isolated, decontextualized tasks. Rather, assessment data are

13.5 Putting Ideas to Work
Assessment of Emergent Literacy

*F*or many years, schools assessed kindergartners and beginning readers with standardized norm-referenced reading readiness tests. These tests consisted of items designed to measure the child's competency in such areas as visual discrimination, auditory discrimination, alphabet knowledge, visual motor ability, and beginning word recognition, all considered indicators of the child's reading readiness. Some school standardized achievement tests still measure knowledge of letter names and sounds, word recognition, and listening comprehension.

As the concept of emergent literacy took hold, early assessment began to focus more on the young child's awareness of print and ability to deal with it in a more functional context. Clay (1993) has developed a widely used measure that assesses a child's letter identification, concepts about print, simple word recognition, and beginning reading skills. Clay's instrument is widely used as a diagnostic measure in many emergent literacy programs.

Assessment in the early years needs to be an ongoing process that focuses on a broad range of skills and knowledge reflecting various dimensions of early literacy development. Fisher (1989) has developed a three-phase, systematic assessment framework for kindergartners:

Beginning of Year Assessment involves interviewing each child, observing reading and writing behaviors, and assessing letter recognition.
Ongoing Assessment requires monthly recordings of observations of literacy-related activities in a wide range of contexts.
End of Year Assessment involves an interview focusing on what children can tell about themselves as readers and writers, a review of assessment records compiled throughout the year, and a measure of letter-sound knowledge.

gathered as the child engages in real literacy events that have meaning in and out of their classroom lives. This includes their encounters with literature, since trade books represent authentic (as opposed to controlled) text that children read for authentic purposes.

Goodman (1978) uses the term *kid watching* to describe this type of in-class alternative assessment. Information gathered as a result of kid watching provides a basis for the instructional decisions teachers make as part of literature-based reading. The teacher's role is vital. Speaking of the teacher as evaluator, Johnson (1987) says, "The most fundamental goal of all educational evaluation is optimal instruction for all children and evaluation practices are legitimate only to the extent that they serve this goal" (p. 744). Since most classroom decision making takes place on a moment-to-moment or day-to-day basis, and since the teacher is the one making these decisions, the ongoing assessment the teacher conducts is a key element in the assessment process.

Rather than being "The Great Administrator of Tests," the teacher can take an active, dynamic role in the assessment process in a literature-based

13.6 Putting Ideas to Work

Multiple Options for Alternative Assessment

*I*f literature is used for instruction, it makes sense to use literature for assessment purposes as well. Since literature does not easily lend itself to standardized measures, teachers need to devise alternative strategies.

Several alternative assessment procedures might be used after children have read *Alexander and the Terrible, Horrible, No Good, Very Bad Day*, a delightful story by Judith Viorst about a young boy who has a day when nothing seems to go right:

Recall—Rather than focusing on insignificant details with low-level questions such as "What number did Alexander forget?" or "What was the dentist's name?" the teacher can assess factual recall by asking pupils to construct a graphic organizer similar to the following:

Think about the many things that made Alexander's day "terrible, horrible, no good, and very bad." List at least three things that happened to Alexander before, during, and after school.

Before School	During School	After School
_____	_____	_____
_____	_____	_____
_____	_____	_____
_____	_____	_____
_____	_____	_____

Cloze—The teacher can use cloze exercises in which every tenth word is deleted to see how well children can reconstruct the meaning of the story. Remember, a 45 percent accuracy rate on a cloze exercise represents adequate comprehension.

Retelling—Retelling can serve the same purpose. The focus can be on recalling events in order and/or on the child's interpretation of Alexander's emotions or responses to the events.

program. Teachers select assessment tools or techniques to match the pupil behaviors they want to sample. Standardized evaluation measures put the responsibility for assessment on the instrument itself; classroom-based evaluation measures empower teachers and students and place assessment at the heart of the instructional process.

Authentic assessment in the classroom happens all the time as students learn to read and write. As teachers help students probe and expand the meanings of new words, as they engage in discussion to determine a child's level of comprehension, as they conference with a student about a piece of writing, they are informally assessing progress. Alternative assessment involves cloze exercises, story maps, and other devices teachers use for instructional purposes. It includes listening to what pupils say about reading and writing in their "grand conversations" in literature groups, learning how children believe reading and writing fits into their lives, hav-

Nonverbal Response—Pupils might arrange three or four pictures from the story in sequence or act out Alexander's responses to certain events. This type of nonverbal response may be especially appropriate for children with language problems.

Vocabulary—The teacher can test to see whether the child understands selected word meanings in context:

In the following sentence, what does the word *invisible* mean?
   *The teacher did not like my picture of the **invisible** castle; she could not see it on the page.*

To assess metacognition, the teacher can ask the child to explain how he or she determined the meaning of the word.

Scaffolded Questioning—Questions can build from literal ("What happened at breakfast?") to interpretative ("How did Alexander feel when he found out he had lost his best friend?") to critical/creating comprehension ("How might Alexander have responded differently to Nick when he called Alexander a crybaby?").

Open-Ended Response—The teacher can pose questions or arrange activities that encourage a free response rather than a directed response and divergent rather than convergent thinking. For example: "Make a list of things that might have made Alexander's day more pleasant."

Hands-On Response—Pupils can make a poster advertising the book to classmates.

Writing—The teacher can assign a writing activity such as a dialogue journal entry (focusing on comprehension and response) or an index card report (focusing on quality and accuracy of writing). Students might also write their own versions of the story: *Yolanda and the Wonderful, Terrific, Marvelous, Very Good Day.*

These assessment procedures are neither discrete nor mutually exclusive, and lots of other assessment activities can be designed. Several require open-ended responses and many may require writing. All, however, give the teacher options for assessing how well a child comprehended and enjoyed the story. For some stories, alternative assessment can spill over into math, social studies, and science.

ing them talk about the metacognitive strategies they use—thus adding self-evaluation to the assessment process as well.

Alternative assessment is closely aligned with the curriculum. In addition to taking advantage of the many incidental occasions that arise as part of instruction, a teacher can employ many specific assessment techniques to evaluate children's reading performance in the classroom, including observation checklists, rating forms, and anecdotal records; informal reading inventories; miscue analysis; and running records.

Observation

Observing children as they read is not only a powerful method of gathering data, it is essential to forming a complete picture of a pupil's literacy development. Through observation, teachers can determine children's reading

behaviors within their normal context, not in a strained and artificial testing situation.

Observation involves more than passively watching pupils as they read. It involves active involvement in gathering data and making judgments based on this information. Several structured strategies for observation have proved effective.

In *Reciprocal Teaching* (Palinscar, 1984), teachers observe children as they engage in an interactive dialogue about what they have read, focusing on their ability to predict, question, and critically evaluate.

In *Interactive Assessment* (Paratore and Indrisano, 1987), the teacher explains the purpose of assessment and guides the student through a series of assessment/instructional steps. This strategy integrates teaching practices into an assessment model.

In *Think Alouds* (Alvermann, 1984), pupils tell what they are thinking as they read to indicate their ongoing processing of text.

In *Book Discussions* (Paradis et al., 1991), teachers use a combination of comprehension matrices, anecdotal records, journals and logs, tape recordings, and other devices to record discussions and determine how well students understand what they read.

In *Retelling* (Irwin and Mitchell, 1983), students recall as much as they can about what they have read. Assessment is based on the thoroughness of their recall, with five levels of richness ranging from good to poor. Not only is retelling an assessment technique, it's also a means of helping good and poor readers improve their comprehension (Gambrell et al., 1991).

All these techniques—Reciprocal Teaching, Interactive Assessment, Think Alouds, Book Discussions, and Retelling—are effective classroom strategies in literature-based programs; all can be used as students read trade books. The activities are authentic because they involve pupils reading real books for real purposes. Assessment derives from the classroom program, not from an outside test. The strategies are based "on the assumption that the 'human-as-instrument' is as effective and valued as the 'test-as-instrument' when assessing "human behaviors" (Cambourne and Turbill, 1990; p. 340). Each strategy focuses on the reading process and not on the production of a single answer. Each integrates instruction with assessment.

Although a teacher can observe and assess a child's literacy development any time that child reads or writes, *conferences* are especially important to classroom assessment. Conferences occur when teachers meet pupils for assessment purposes. They can be conducted individually, when the teacher meets a student one-to-one to talk about a trade book the student may be reading; or they can include several pupils at once, as when the teacher participates in a literature study group. They can be scheduled sessions with structured questions and activities designed for evaluation and diagnosis; or they can be casual encounters as teachers discuss the books students are enjoying.

Different types of conferences have different purposes. Intense, individual attention is needed to observe the strategies a child uses when he or she encounters challenging material, or when the teacher wants to determine a student's reading level or the amount of progress that student has made. More casual conferences can elicit children's responses to what they are reading and how their attitudes are being shaped. Although they differ in nature and intent, all conferences can provide valuable information that teachers can use to assess pupils' progress and problems.

Checklists. Observation can be supported, focused, and organized through a checklist. A checklist is a simple Yes/No indication of whether a characteristic or behavior is present . "Checklists are used . . . to keep the observer focused, to provide a method of recording observations that requires a minimum of writing, and to provide consistency from one observation to the next" (Cockrum and Castillo, 1991; p. 76). The purpose of a checklist is not to indicate whether or not a child "measures up." Rather, the checklist provides a profile of qualities and characteristics that suggest goals for future instruction. Moreover, they serve as record-keeping devices that show growth from month to month or term to term in a school year, and from year to year in a student's school life.

Rating Scales. Rating scales are similar to checklists, but they assign degrees or frequencies to measure reading behaviors. The scale can be numerical (*1 to 5*) or qualitative (*none of the time, some of the time, most of the time, all the time*). Sometimes, qualitative scales require the teacher to make a value judgment (*excellent, good, fair, poor*) based on observation.

As tools of classroom-based assessment, checklists and rating scales can focus on many dimensions of reading, from a pupil's ability to apply decoding strategies to his or her understanding of the literary elements in a story. They can be customized according to a child's level of literacy development, according to the dimensions of literacy the child engages in, and according to aims that the teacher has in an instructional program. The sample in Putting Ideas to Work 13.8 is merely one example of the thousands of checklists a teacher could choose from for performance-based assessment.

13.7 Putting Ideas to Work
Comprehension Matrix and Profile

Wood (1988) suggests several recording devices for observations in reading groups or in individual conferences. The Group Comprehension Matrix allows the teacher to focus on the performance of a whole group or on the performance of individuals within the group. The Individual Comprehension Profile is designed to assess how students handle different types of reading.

The group matrix and individual profile can be used with a variety of reading materials—trade books, basal stories, content area textbooks, or other reading material. Both are designed "to assess the student in the act of comprehending while the teacher is in the act of teaching," and both view assessment "as a dynamic ongoing process," not as a one-shot task.

Group Comprehension Matrix

Story *The Mandarin and the Magician*   Date *October 14th*

Genre: Narrative (realistic, (fantasy))   Grade *4th*
        Poetry
        Plays
        Exposition

* *New student - Oct. 1st*

	Kelly	Ryan*	Marti	Tonya	Jason	David	Teresa
Makes predictions about story	S	+	—	S	—	+	—
Participates in the discussion	S	+	S	S	—	+	S
Answers questions on all levels	—	+	S	S	S	+	S
Determines word meanings through context	—	+	—	—	—	S	—
Reads smoothly and fluently	+	+	+	S	—	+	S
Can retell selection using own words	S	+	+	S	S	S	—
Comprehends after silent reading	N	N	N	N	N	N	N
Can read "between the lines"	—	S	S	—	—	S	—
Possesses broad background knowledge	S	S	—	—	—	S	—

Comments: *The students had much difficulty comprehending the story until I provided much more background information. Their predictions were not as accurate and abundant as usual—largely due to their lack of knowledge of Chinese dynasties. Jason remains very quiet unless asked specific questions. He is much more responsive one-to-one. While his recall is good, his oral reading is very choppy. Teresa is always willing to volunteer any answers although her recall is on the literal level. Ryan may need to move up another level—will test individually.*

Often	+	Words to review:
Sometimes	S	*dynasty*
Seldom	—	*Mandarin*
Not observed	N	*queue*

From Wood, Karen D. (1988, January). Techniques for Assessing Students' Potential for Learning. *The Reading Teacher*, 41 (4):440–447.

Individual Comprehension Profile

Name __Eric Matthews__   Date __September 3__   Grade __3__

	Reading type		Genre					Recall mode			Degree of guidance			Overall compr. (1 = none, 2 = some, 3 = most, 4 = all)	Comments
	Oral	Silent	Poetry	Plays	Realistic fiction	Fantasy	Nonfiction	Free recall	Probed recall	Infer, predict	Background knowl.	Preteaching vocab.	Assist during rdg.		
Level 2_2 p. 41	✓				✓			✓	✓		–	–	–	3	A little choppy at first, then very fluent with accurate recall
Level 2_2 p. 76	✓			✓				✓	✓	✓	–	–	–	4	Very fluent reading and retelling
Level 2_2 p. 168		✓					✓	✓	✓	✓	–	–	–	4	Needs no assistance – has control over word recognition and comprehension
Level 3_1 p. 101	✓				✓			✓	✓	✓	–	–	–	2	Some fluency problems & sketchy recall (e.g., misread "trail" for "trial," "beautiful" for "body")
Level 3_1 p. 96	✓					✓		✓	✓	✓	✓	✓	–	3	With help, recall is improved; can predict and infer (e.g., Why do you think....)
Level 3_1 p. 66		✓					✓	✓	✓	✓	✓	✓	✓	4	Had difficulty recognizing "ambulance" – "emergency." Defined "Red Cross" & "swerved." This helped!
Level 3_1 p. 119		✓					✓	✓	✓	✓	✓	✓	✓	4	Tried with and without guidance. Comprehension is improved with help.

Overall assessment: Eric's comprehension while reading silently seems better than while reading orally. Can retell in own words at level 3, but gives more detail when probed or prompted. With assistance, seems to benefit from instruction in this material.

Appropriate placement level __3_1__

Anecdotal Records. Written records provide evidence of how pupils are growing as readers and writers. Because they document student performance and achievement as it occurs, anecdotal records are part of the complete assessment picture in the literature-based classroom.

Keeping daily records of observations provides an ongoing classroom assessment. These anecdotal records include observations about materials children are reading, how well they are progressing, how they use reading and writing skills, how they are responding to literacy activities, and unique notations about literacy events that occur in the classroom. These notes can be kept in a loose-leaf notebook, with pages devoted to individual students and a section for general reflections. Anecdotal notes document the kid-watching and related activities that are an integral part of classroom assessment.

Anecdotal records provide more than a record of children's growth as learners; they also give reflective teachers information to consider in evaluating their own classroom performance. Often these records become part of the journals that more and more teachers are beginning to maintain.

The records students keep in response to their reading—literature journals and logs—can provide valuable data on their development as readers and writers. In literature-based programs, pupils keep logs listing books they have read and notations of their responses to these books. These notations can reveal the child's depth of understanding or awareness of literary elements. Building on the reading-writing connection, children can react to what they read in more detail in written responses such as buddy journals, exchanges with teachers (Atwell, 1987), and other forms of writing. These responses are potential gold mines of information that can contribute to classroom-based assessment.

Like every dimension of assessment, observation has its advantages and disadvantages. On the positive side, observation is tailored to the individual child, the text, and the teacher's instructional purposes. The teacher focuses on the processes pupils use as they read; thus, the focus extends beyond seeing the child find the right answer itself to finding out how he or she arrives at answers based on the reading materials. The results provide immediate feedback that the teacher can use to plan the next step in instruction. Observation empowers the teacher as the ultimate decision maker in teaching children how to read and write, bringing the teacher's professionalism one notch higher.

The down side of classroom-based assessment is lack of objectivity. Two teachers interpret a pupil's response or performance differently. Observation is also labor-intensive and time-consuming.

Validity and reliability are other concerns. People tend to have more faith in numbers than in qualitative judgments. Cambourne and Turbill (1990) argue that traditional criteria of "scientific rigor" cannot be applied to informal assessment techniques; but they suggest that qualities of credibility, transferability, dependability, and confirmability be built into classroom assessment to safeguard the trustworthiness of the conclusions the teacher derives. Most parents will accept a teacher's observation of progress even without the reinforcement of test results (Aiex, 1988), especially when the results are documented by the child's work (Linek, 1991).

13.8 Putting Ideas to Work
Sample Checklist/Rating Scale

Early to Beginning Stages

Name _____

Dates

	1st	2nd	3rd	4th

Indicators of Developing Control and Comprehension

Code: M = Most of the time   S = Sometimes   N = Not yet

Talking and Listening	Code				Comments
—Communicates with others about own activities					
—Explains ideas clearly					
—Uses expanded vocabulary related to classroom activities					
—Communicates in a group setting					
—Repeats nursery rhymes, chants, poems, etc.					
—Responds to and talks about stories					
—Sings songs					
—Dictates stories, personal messages					
—Listens attentively to class activity					
—Listens and responds in community talk					
—Talks about reading and writing					

Reading					
—Displays interest in books					
—Chooses to spend time with books					
—Asks for rereading of favorite stories					
—Anticipates and joins in on repetitive phrases					
—Displays sense of story					
—Understands environmental print					
—Possesses knowledge about letters					
—Pretend or memory reads					
—Recognizes some words					
—Focuses on deriving meaning from text					

Continued on next page.

From Church, J. C. (1991). Record Keeping in Whole Language Classrooms. In Bill Harp, ed., *Assessment and Evaluation in Whole Language Programs*. © 1991 by Christopher Gordon Publishers, Inc., Norwood MA. Reprinted with permission of Christopher Gordon Publishers, Inc.

13.8 Putting Ideas to Work—Continued
Sample Checklist/Rating Scale

Writing		Code			Comments
—Displays interest in print					
—Pretend writes and attaches meaning					
—Spends time writing					
—Attaches print to art work and other work					
—Understands a variety of purposes and kinds of writing					
—Uses inventive spelling • random letters					
• some representative letters					
• phonetic spelling					
• correct spelling of high-frequency words					
—Writes on own for personal communication					
—Patterns writing after literary structures					
Indicators of Attitudes and Social Behaviors					
—Is willing to be challenged					
—Is productive and involved during work periods					
—Expresses enjoyment as a result of hard work and achievement					
—Cooperates with others					
—Contributes to group work					
—Displays sensitivity and respect for others					
—Learns from watching others					
Indicators of Thinking Skills					
—Articulates ideas clearly					
—Generates solutions and ideas to solve problems					
—Considers suitable resources					
—Differentiates between relevant and nonrelevant information					
—Considers other points of view					
—Spends time reading, writing, constructing, researching, reflecting, etc.					
—Talks about information discovered					
—Explains, shows, or helps others to understand learning					
—Asks worthwhile questions					
—Plans, organizes, and carries through on tasks					
—Understands not all problems have simple solutions					

13.9 Putting Ideas to Work
Literature Reading Behavior Inventory

*I*n a literature-based reading program, trade books are the vehicles for many of the teacher's informal assessment activities. Gail Heald-Taylor (1987) has designed an inventory to guide teachers in evaluating the reading development of young children who learn to read with literature.

The behaviors are not listed sequentially, so teachers should not expect children to acquire these behaviors in a neat, linear fashion.

Literature Reading Behavior Inventory

Book Awareness	Beginning	Secure	Date
The child: • listens to stories • shares reading with others (unison reading) • begins looking at books as a self-initiated activity • holds the book right side up • turns pages in sequence from right to left, front to back • examines pictures in book • enjoys having stories read to him or her			
Comprehension	**Beginning**	**Secure**	**Date**
The child: • recalls the main idea of the story • recalls details from the story • can name events in the story • understands cause and effect in the story • predicts			
Readinglike Behavior	**Beginning**	**Secure**	**Date**
The child: • attempts to read the selection (oral response may or may not reflect the exact text or pictures) • attempts to read using pictures as the cue to story line • attempts to read by retelling a remembered text (attends to memory and pictures) • attempts to read by matching the retelling to particular pages (page matching using pictures and memory as clues)			
Directionality	**Beginning**	**Secure**	**Date**
The child: • consistently turns pages from right to left • recognizes where print begins on a page • recognizes where print ends on a page • begins to move his/her eyes and finger left to right across the print while attempting to read (finger does not stop at individual words)			

Continued on next page.

13.9 Putting Ideas to Work—Continued

Literature Reading Behavior Inventory

	Beginning	Secure	Date
• develops awareness of line directionality (child's finger moves left to right across line of print and then moves to the far left of the page and down to track the next line of print)			

Print and Word Awareness	**Beginning**	**Secure**	**Date**

The child:
• begins to point to clumps of letters and assign an oral response (oral response may not accurately match the text)
• begins to accurately word match:
  ✓ beginning of sentences
  ✓ names of people and things
  ✓ end of sentences
• remembers holistically—uses memory, picture, and text to recall the story line
• accurately word matches a repetitive pattern in the story
• tracks (word points) to find a specific word
• word points according to oral language syllables
• recognizes common words in stories
• integrates many strategies to get meaning (picture clues, memory, tracking, word recognition, context, and syntax)
• begins to accurately word match familiar literature pattern books (uses picture clues, memory, word recognition, context, and syntax)
• begins to self-correct for meaning			

Use of Cueing Systems	**Beginning**	**Secure**	**Date**
The child: • uses memory, picture clues, tracking, syntax, and semantic systems well • becomes aware of letter and sound symbol relationships • recognizes letter names in familiar words • talks about his or her own reading behaviors ("That's 'dog.' I know because it begins like my name—David.") • begins to use the phonetic cueing system with familiar materials • integrates picture, memory, tracking, syntax, semantics, and phonetics to read familiar material • uses a variety of cueing systems to read new material			

Texts	**Beginning**	**Secure**	**Date**
The child: • reads familiar predictable texts • reads unfamiliar pattern texts • reads unfamiliar texts (without pattern) • reads factual texts (functional, fantasy) • chooses to read for enjoyment			

Informal Reading Inventories

Another form of alternative assessment that teachers have used for a long time is the Informal Reading Inventory (IRI). An IRI consists of series of sequentially graded paragraphs that increase in difficulty from primer to sixth-grade level or beyond, along with a set of questions based on the material. The inventory is a performance-based measure that determines a child's reading level through actual reading rather than by filling in a set of bubbles on the answer sheet of a standardized test.

The reading levels that informal reading inventories determine are designated as *independent, instructional,* and *frustration.* Criteria for determining these levels are:

> *Independent*—96 to 100 percent accuracy in word recognition; 90 percent accuracy in comprehension; good reading behaviors. This means that pupils make no more than one to four oral reading errors in every 100 words in a passage, can understand most of what they read, and show no signs of physical inefficiency (like finger pointing or head movement) or unusual anxiety when reading.

> *Instructional*—93 to 95 percent accuracy in word recognition; 75 percent accuracy in comprehension; adequate reading behaviors. In other words, children at this level make no more than five to seven mistakes per 100 words, understand at least three-quarters of what they read, and show little evidence of inefficiency or nervousness as they read.

> *Frustration*—90 percent or less in word recognition; 50 percent or less in comprehension; poor reading behaviors. Material at this level is considered too difficult for students to handle, even with support and help from the teacher.

Administering the inventory is an individual enterprise. Students read words on a graded word list to determine their beginning point for reading. The teacher asks the pupil to begin reading at an appropriate entry point, usually a grade level or two below the pupil's reading level. The child then reads paragraphs at higher and lower levels until the teacher determines which levels of reading material constitute the student's independent, instructional, and frustration levels.

As the child reads, the teacher marks areas that indicate word recognition difficulties—insertions of extra words, omissions of words or word parts, substitutions, mispronunciations, or words pronounced by the examiner. After the reading, the student is asked specific questions based on the content of the passages. The teacher computes the scores and determines the independent, instructional, and frustration levels based on these scores. Johnson, Kress, and Pikulski (1987) provide more detailed information about constructing and administering informal reading inventories.

Teachers do not need to formally administer an informal reading inventory, however, to achieve the purposes the IRI was designed to accomplish. The teacher can use IRI guidelines as an "ear" for listening to students read

13.10 Putting Ideas to Work
Informal Reading Inventories

Although teachers are frequently encouraged to construct their own informal inventories for use in their classrooms, a number of commercially produced IRIs are available in the marketplace. Among the most popular are:

> *Classroom Reading Inventory* (8th ed.) by Nicholas J. Silvaroli. Dubuque, IA: Brown & Benchmark Publishers, 1997.
>
> *Informal Reading Inventory: Preprimer to Twelfth Grade* (4th ed.) by Paul C. Burns and Betty D. Roe. Boston: Houghton Mifflin, 1993.
>
> *Group Assessment in Reading: Classroom Teacher's Handbook* by Edna W. Warncke and Dorothy A. Shipman. Englewood Cliffs, NJ: Prentice-Hall, 1984.
>
> *Flynt-Cooter Reading Inventory for the Classroom* by E. Sutton Flynt and Robert Cooter, Jr. Scottsdale, AZ: Gorsuch Scarisbrick Publishers, 1993.
>
> *Analytical Reading Inventory* (2nd ed.) by Mary Lynn Woods and Alden J. Moe. Columbus, OH: Merrill Publishing, 1985.
>
> *Basic Reading Inventory* by J. Johns. Dubuque, IA: Kendall-Hunt, 1985.
>
> *Bader Reading and Language Inventory* (2nd ed.) by Lois A. Bader and Katherine Wiesendanger. New York: Macmillan, 1994.
>
> *Qualitative Reading Inventory* by Lauren Leslie and Joanne Caldwell. Glenview, IL: Scott Foresman, 1990.
>
> *Informal Reading-Thinking Inventory* by Anthony V. Manzo, Ula C. Manzo, and Michael E. Mckenna. Fort Worth: Harcourt Brace, 1995.

aloud, noting the type of oral reading practices students seem to need assistance with. Even if the inventory itself is not used as a diagnostic device, the guidelines provide a benchmark for listening to pupils' oral reading.

The IRI is a functional diagnostic tool that assesses student performance by observing actual reading. IRIs provide an authentic reading assessment because they require the student to actually perform the task they are measuring. Results can be used to match pupils to appropriate reading material. In helping a student to select a trade book, for example, the teacher can use the criteria for the independent or instructional levels to determine whether the child can read the book independently at home or would benefit from the support of a reading group.

There are legitimate criticisms regarding the theory and use of the IRI, however. Some consider the criteria for determining reading levels too arbitrary, rigid, and high. The procedure relies extensively on oral reading performance, although most inventories provide a parallel set of passages for silent reading as well. One paragraph per grade provides only a narrow sample of reading behavior. Children's performances on informal inventories may not reflect their ability to deal with other printed material (expository text in content areas, for example). Their performances can also be inconsistent; a child can do well in reading a passage at one level, completely bog down at the next level, and read well at the level above that. Students' interest in what they read may influence their performance. Many factors can cause inconsistent performance, and this inconsistency makes it difficult for the teacher to determine which passages represent the pupil's independent, instructional, or frustration levels of reading.

A serious concern that frequently crops up regarding informal reading inventories relates to their emphasis on word skills as a means of assessing reading ability. Word skills are heavily emphasized in an IRI. Word recognition is balanced equally with comprehension, yet extracting meaning is far more important in reading than merely saying the words.

Instead of relying solely on IRI criteria in listening to students read aloud for diagnostic purposes, teachers can gain much information about reading performance by combining observations, IRIs, and miscue analysis.

Miscue Analysis

Miscue analysis takes the assessment process a step further than the IRI. A "miscue" is an oral reading response that does not match the text on the page. It is an inaccuracy in oral reading that many would traditionally call an error or a mistake.

Kenneth Goodman (1965, 1969) introduced the term *miscue* into the professional literature in the 1960s to replace the terms *error* or *mistake* in describing a reader's departure from printed text. The intent in using the term *miscue* was to remove the negative connotations associated with error and to get away from the idea that all departures from print indicate weaknesses or problems in reading. Listening to oral reading with an ear to miscues involves noting which cueing system may have led the reader away from the exact reading of the words on the page.

Miscue analysis requires that the teacher not only note that the pupil did not read exactly what is printed in the text, but also examine the type of departure the student made while reading orally. The three major categories of miscues are:

Semantic—a miscue based on word meaning; the child might substitute a word with the same meaning as the word in the text:

Example: That apple pie ~~certainly~~ tasted good.

Syntactic—a miscue in which the student's departure from print corresponds to an equivalent grammatical form:

Example: "I am going home right now," Linda said.

Graphophonic—a miscue based on sound-symbol similarities in the text:

$$\text{horse}$$
Example: The children saw a ~~house~~ in the field.

Miscue analysis helps the teacher develop more insight into the reading process by looking at the *nature* of a departure from text rather than just noting the fact that the student misread a word or a phrase. For example, suppose the sentence in a passage is: *The children went to the beach to go swimming.* Adam reads, "The *chicken* went to the beach to go swimming," and Beth reads, "The *kids* went to the beach to go swimming." With an IRI, both errors would simply count as "substitutions," yet the nature of the miscues is very different. Adam is depending on graphophonic cues and largely ignoring context. On the other hand, Beth is virtually ignoring graphophonic cues and is relying primarily on meaning-based context. Sometimes a substitution might be a calculated response rather than a random guess at a word. Miscue analysis involves a qualitative rather than quantitative look at a child's oral reading.

Conducting miscue analysis, like administering an IRI, is an individual enterprise. Unlike an IRI, however, miscue analysis uses a longer passage that is complete in itself: one or two chapters from a trade book, an entire basal reading story, a chapter from a content text, or an article from a magazine. Reading is thus based on the holistic context of a selection with larger meaning than a paragraph or two would typically contain. The level of the material is usually about a year above the child's reading grade level, challenging enough to promote miscues but not so difficult as to be frustrating. The intent of miscue analysis is not to locate a particular reading level; rather, it is to determine the types of language cueing systems the pupil is using while reading. The content can be familiar to the reader, but the child should not have already read the particular passage.

As the student reads, the teacher marks the miscues, codes each according to its type (semantic, syntactic, or graphophonic), notes whether the child self-corrects, notes whether the miscue fits the context of the passage, and records whether the miscue preserves the meaning of the text. The teacher does not count miscues resulting directly from dialect—reading *creek* as "crick," for example, or reading "they was" when the text says *they were.* Following the reading, the student recounts what he or she just read as a check on comprehension.

Hittleman (1988), Weaver (1988), and Watson and Henson (1991) provide more complete directions for formally analyzing miscues during oral reading.

Even without the formal procedures, miscue analysis provides a focus for listening to students read aloud. Analyzing miscues enables the teacher to listen to oral reading with a fine-tuned ear. The teacher can gain information about the strategies pupils use while reading—whether they use context and language cues, or whether they rely on other strategies as they read.

Less proficient readers tend to rely heavily on graphophonic cues (sounding out) and less on semantic and syntactic cues in reading words they do not recognize. This suggests the kind of instruction that might be appropriate for a child who makes such miscues.

The miscues pupils make can also indicate how they process meaning as they read aloud. Some miscues obstruct meaning; others preserve the essential meaning of text. Sometimes a child who miscues in one part of the text will make a second miscue to preserve meaning. For example, look at the two miscues in the following sentence:

Jack took an apple *and* wrapped *it* in paper.

Technically, these insertions could be counted as two errors, but the second insertion indicates the child is comprehending. After the reader inserted the word *and*, the second insertion (*it*) became necessary to preserve the meaning and syntactic structure of the sentence. That is why the term *miscue* gets away from all the negative connotations of *mistake*. Miscues indicating a departure from meaning are the ones we should attend to closely and quickly.

Of course, miscue analysis is only one indication of a pupil's ability to derive meaning; other techniques such as retelling and postquestioning also reveal level of comprehension. For example, this miscue changed the meaning of a text:

When the boat docked, the sailors were waiting to ̶g̶o̶ on shore.

Yet, when recounting what he had read, the child who omitted the expression *to go* was able to tell exactly where the sailors were waiting (and why). Some students can fracture oral reading and still manage to comprehend much of what they read. These are the children who suffer when teachers judge reading competency on the basis of oral reading alone.

Miscue analysis involves more than the simple tabulation of mistakes. It is a complex process that examines reading performance to determine the psycholinguistic processing that goes on as a student reads. Although it can be complex and time-consuming, miscue analysis is invaluable in revealing the type of strategies pupils use while reading, thus providing information essential to instructional planning. It carries reading diagnosis beyond recording "faults" to be remediated and on to strategies the teacher can use to help children improve reading competency.

Miscue analysis requires skill, expertise, and confidence from the teacher. It also demands knowledge of the reading process, so that the teacher can make accurate judgments about pupils' responses to print. Some would argue that readers should produce verbatim what is on a page of print and that no deviation from print should be excused or "rationalized." These concerns notwithstanding, miscue analysis provides a powerful tool

13.11 Putting Ideas to Work
Using Trade Books as "Benchmark" Measures

When literature is an important part of instruction, trade books need to be an important part of assessment. The Whole Language Council of the Milwaukee Public Schools (1990) has developed an assessment guide that puts literature at the heart of the assessment process.

The Council designates certain popular trade books as benchmark books at different grade levels. They usually choose two or three books per grade; for example:

Grade 2—*Frog and Toad Together* by Arnold Lobel
Grade 4—*Sarah, Plain and Tall* by Patricia MacLachlan
Grade 5—*James and the Giant Peach* by Roald Dahl

Students are expected to read most of the book independently. A section of the book is designated for assessment purposes—the story "The Dream" in *Frog and Toad Together,* for example, or the two final chapters of *Sarah, Plain and Tall.* The teacher asks six or more verification questions on the designated section, all focusing on comprehension. Student responses determine whether the book is at each pupil's independent, instructional, or frustration level. The Council's guide contains instructions and forms for other assessment techniques as well.

for analyzing oral reading performance and assessing a child's problems and progress in learning to read.

Goodman (1996) has taken the process of miscue analysis a step further with Reflective Miscue Analysis (RMA), a process that invites students to reflect on their own reading behaviors. After reading, the teacher asks questions such as, "How did you figure that out?" or "What led you to believe that?" RMA involves pupils themselves in the assessment process.

Running Records

Closely related to miscue analysis are running records. A running record is an ongoing assessment of the reading behaviors a child uses during authentic reading experiences. As the child reads orally, the teacher places a checkmark above every word pronounced correctly and marks the departures the child makes from the text. Following the reading, responses are coded. The teacher identifies one or two instructional points and the child's instructional material is adjusted based on his or her performance.

Running records are an integral part of the Reading Recovery program. Clay (1993) fully describes the procedures for keeping running records.

Running records are qualitative measures that reveal immediately useful diagnostic information about the child. Although they represent a sample of reading behaviors that may or may not reveal a complete and accurate picture, they do provide an alternative assessment teachers can use on the spot. They also constitute an assessment device closely related to the instructional process.

13.12 Putting Ideas to Work
Using the Tape Recorder

*I*n assessment activities involving oral reading, a tape recorder can be useful. Tape recording relieves much of the pressure and anxiety (and curiosity, too) that pupils experience when they watch the teacher make mysterious marks as they read. It also frees the teacher to direct full attention to the child and alleviates the problem of trying to record the reading of a student who reads rapidly. The tape recording gives the teacher a chance to listen and reflect on the reading several times outside the typically distracting atmosphere of the busy classroom.

While listening to the tapes, however, teachers should give an ear to their own performance as well. "Until a teacher listens to herself in action, she may not realize that she has become predominantly a 'prompter' or a 'sound-it-outer' or an over-zealous 'corrector' " (Arnold, 1982; p. 37). Assessment is most useful when it leads to improvements in instruction. Teachers can listen to their responses during oral reading to determine whether they are helping students make use of the full range of cues available, cues both in the text and "behind the reader's eye."

Alternative assessment—including teacher observation, informal inventories, miscue analysis, running records, and other planned and incidental procedures teachers follow—is an essential dimension of reading instruction. Even though policy makers and the general public frequently put their faith in the single measure of a standardized test, the day-to-day assessment that goes on in the classroom gives direction to the reading instructional process.

Portfolios

One widely used form of alternative assessment is the portfolio. Portfolios are cumulative collections of material that demonstrate students' literacy development. Just as artists use portfolios to showcase their artistic ability, pupils use portfolios to demonstrate their growth and competency in reading and writing. More revealing than a single grade, score, or checklist, portfolios contain a combination of items that can be used for short- and long-term assessment. They are dynamic, ever-growing showcases of the child's literacy achievements.

Tierney, Readence, and Dishner (1995) point out that portfolios are meant "to engage students in a form of self-assessment of their improvement, efforts, and achievement . . . to engage students, often in partnership with teachers and parents, in periodical evaluations and goal setting; and to serve as a vehicle whereby teachers or other interested parties can pursue a process for collecting, analyzing, and developing plans or interpretations from a range of primary artifacts of students' work and explorations" (p. 480).

Valencia (1990) has identified four theoretical cornerstones underlying the concept of portfolio assessment: (1) good assessment comes from a

In preparing portfolios, students and teachers need to collaborate to select work that reflects the child's development as a reader and a writer.

© James L. Shaffer

variety of literacy experiences that pupils engage in within the classroom; (2) assessment should be continuous to chronicle ongoing development; (3) assessment should be multidimensional, reflecting the multifaceted nature of literacy development; and (4) assessment should include "active, collaborative reflection by both teacher and students" (p. 330). A portfolio gets away from a single, one-dimensional performance measure—a standardized reading achievement test score or a simple letter grade—to indicate how well a child is doing in reading and writing. It measures growth over time; it is not a single sample of performance on a given day.

What Do Portfolios Contain?

Portfolios are not merely work folders. The contents are chosen selectively to show growth over time. Each work sample is dated so that teachers, parents, and child know when the work was performed.

There is no prescribed list of contents for pupils' assessment portfolios. The collections should contain a variety of materials that reflect the student's developing competency in reading and related language areas. A portfolio might contain:

> *samples of the students' work*—original stories at various stages of completion, story maps or exercises the child has worked on, reading logs or other written responses to literature, additional writing samples, and other examples of work that reflects achievement and growth;
>
> *the teacher's observational notes*—the results of interviews about books the child has read, checklists or anecdotal notes;
>
> *test scores*—from norm-referenced or criterion-referenced tests the student might have taken;

audio (and perhaps video) tapes of the child's reading performance;

lists of trade books the student has read independently, along with responses to these books;

photos of projects and displays the child has created;

pupil-generated computer disks or CD-ROMs related to literacy learning;

self-assessment indicators, personalized statements from the student to enhance both the teacher's and the parent's understanding. "The instrument can be a written report by the child describing strengths and weaknesses . . . or a series of answers to questions [such as]: 1. How well do you think you do in reading? 2. What do you do when you try to read a hard word? 3. How do you select your own reading material?" (Flood and Lapp, 1989; p. 513). Self-evaluation comments can be placed on three-by-five-inch index cards. These cards can also include a list of objectives for the next assessment period, mutually generated by teacher and student.

Some of the work samples in a portfolio might include "captions," brief teacher comments as to why the sample was included and what it demonstrates about that particular pupil and his or her achievements. Some portfolios also include written comments from parents and others who review the material.

A portfolio summary sheet is often useful to organize the material in the folder. This summary sheet provides a guide for administrators and others who have neither the time nor the need to review the contents in great detail. The summary sheet is also useful to pass along to next year's teacher.

A portfolio ought not be a potpourri of every piece of work that a child has completed in a school term. Just as an artist selects the pieces of art that show his or her artistic development—not every piece he or she ever created—so pupils should choose work samples that reflect their development as readers and writers. The portfolio might, for example, contain a spontaneous writing sample done in September with a similar sample from December, or a tape recording of a passage read in January and the same passage read in March. The key is to choose material that will clearly reflect the student's growth—a collection of work not so extensive as to be unmanageable, but large enough to provide valid evidence of progress. A two-part question might guide the selection process: "Why am I including this material, and for whom is it intended?"

Portfolios are typically packaged in expandable file folders and kept in an accessible place in the classroom. Sometimes, teachers keep different portfolios for different subjects—a social studies or science portfolio, for example. At other times, different portfolios might be appropriate for different purposes; for example, the principal would view a portfolio differently than the child's parent. Anyone with access to a portfolio should keep its contents confidential, although pupils often share their portfolios with friends.

Student input on what goes into a portfolio is important. Traditionally, children have been "targets" of assessment; with input, they are participants in the assessment process. Pupils should have opportunities to select their best work or work that is especially important to them. A collaborative teacher-student effort in selecting portfolio samples focuses attention on student effort and achievement. It allows children to more fully understand the teacher's expectations in the area of literacy. At the same time, collaboration allows the teacher to gain insight into the students—how they perceive themselves as learners and how they understand the metacognitive dimensions of learning to read and write. Student ownership is an important goal.

Collaboration also gives pupils a voice in the assessment process. "Portfolios have the advantage of self-reflection and examination of growth over time, aspects of learning rarely captured in standardized tests or even in the newer once-a-year performance tasks" (Valencia, Hiebert, and Afflerbach, 1994; p. 290). Collaboration takes the sole responsibility for assessment off the teacher's shoulders and enables students to develop confidence in their ability to evaluate their learning and set their own goals (Levi, 1990). It helps make pupils realize that assessment should not always come from the outside, that they need to take a measure of personal responsibility, and that they have a stake in achieving and assessing the quality of their own work.

How Are Portfolios Used?

Portfolios are both assessment tools and learning devices. They need to be reviewed fairly frequently to add new material and remove older samples, thus encouraging the integration of assessment and instruction.

Portfolios are especially valuable during parent conferences. Instead of handing parents a simple grade or a single standardized test score as an indication of all the work their children have done, portfolios provide parents with a more complete picture of their children's efforts and accomplishments. They also validate the instructional decisions the teacher has made and provide tangible evidence of what the pupil has done.

Portfolios are no less valuable in meetings with administrators. Samples of work reflect students' achievement and learning far better than a printout of test scores. They let the principal know what is going on in the classroom. They provide the principal with details of how the teacher is implementing the curriculum, information that any administrator can use with constituencies outside the school.

Portfolios are a dimension of teacher assessment as well; teachers use these devices to look at their own professional development. A set of pupil portfolios reflects the variety of an enriched classroom instructional program. "The result is not a score on a teachers' exam. Instead, it is a reflection of a sample of work [that] offers a humane, useful and generative portrait of development—one that a teacher, like a student, can learn from long after the isolated moment of assessment" (Wolf, 1989; p. 39).

Portfolio assessment involves work, and portfolio effectiveness is "tied partially to how the portfolio process is implemented and the students' developing abilities to pursue self-analysis and trace their development" (Tierney, Readence, and Dishner, 1995; p. 492). Portfolios can be messy, and putting them together takes a lot more effort than relying on a single measure to reflect the effort of a teacher and students for all the work they did during a year or term. Although the process is time-consuming, the effort is worth it because portfolios reflect so many variables involved in learning to read and write. Besides, portfolios reflect an attitude toward assessment. "Portfolios reflect a philosophy that demands that we view assessment as an integral part of our instruction, providing a process for teachers and students to use to guide learning" (Valencia, 1990; p. 340).

Summary and Conclusions

Accountability is a catchword in education. Schools are expected to answer to elected officials, parents, taxpayers, and policy makers to justify their efforts in terms of cost-effectiveness and student progress. The progress they are held accountable for is most often judged by test scores. Norm-referenced measures have for a long time been the primary means of assessing individual pupils, schools, districts, states, and even our nation as a whole. Legislators and school boards make decisions based on how well students perform on standardized tests. Thus, these tests take on a larger-than-life specter for many teachers.

The general public puts great faith in these tests, not realizing that these instruments are imperfect measures that do not always accurately reflect what is inside a child's head or heart. When classroom instruction is tailored to the test—when the teacher "teaches to the test" by focusing narrowly on test items and content—then the tail is wagging the dog.

Formal tests are only one part of assessment. Standardized achievement tests can generate data to indicate trends, but they are generally inappropriate for judging the performance of individual pupils. Instead, we need a repertoire of alternative, authentic assessment strategies teachers can use in the classroom, including teacher observations, student interviews, informal inventories, analysis of miscues and students' responses to print, and running records—all assessment techniques that guide instruction. In answer to the question "How can teachers monitor a student's progress in literature-based programs without skills workbooks or tests to grade?" Aiex (1988) suggests writing samples, checklists, observation, and other informal devices. These informal measures will not make formalized tests go away; they are simply different yardsticks for measuring pupil progress. But alternative assessment has gained impetus as views on literacy have changed, along with the methods of assessment related to these views.

Portfolios containing samples of student work have become popular in classrooms, both as a means of assessment and as a showcase of progress in reading and writing skills. The writing samples, tape recordings, and other work a portfolio contains are tangible evidence of progress on the road to reading and writing competency.

Students are complex human beings. Reading and writing are complex human behaviors. A full range of tools and techniques is necessary to create an accurate and effective picture of how literacy learning takes place.

1. What do you remember about standardized reading achievement testing? Make a list of your most vivid recollections about these tests. As a teacher, what special provisions would you make for administering these tests to your class? Why would you make these provisions?
2. Take a position—pro or con—on formal norm-referenced and criterion-referenced testing. Be prepared to defend your opinion. How does your position relate to your view of the reading process?
3. Prepare a brief explanation of authentic assessment techniques that you might give parents of the children in your class. Explain why you might use these techniques as part of your assessment of their children. Explain how the information you would gather relates to the assessment information gained from formal tests.
4. Describe the changing role of the teacher that newer assessment approaches define. In other words, how will you be a different consumer and producer of assessment data than your teachers were when you were in elementary school?
5. Prepare your own teaching portfolio. Include lesson plans you have developed, teaching materials you have created, notes and journals you may have kept about your educational experiences, a videotaped excerpt of a lesson you have taught, and other materials that show your developing professionalism as a teacher. Get ready to use this portfolio in job interviews.

School-Based Assignments

1. Examine a formal test used in your classroom—a standardized norm-referenced achievement test, a test that is part of your basal program, or a criterion-referenced skills test. What components of reading does the test assess? Interview your cooperating teacher about how he or she uses the results of the test. How might you use the results differently?
2. Using a selection from a basal reading textbook or a trade book, conduct an informal reading inventory or a miscue analysis with a student in your classroom. Find out whether the material is at the child's independent, instructional, or frustration level. What language coding systems does the child appear to use when dealing with text? Write a brief account of your experience.
3. Assess your students' attitudes toward reading. Include attitudes toward both academic and recreational reading. Based on pupil responses, what instructional activities might you plan?
4. How are assessment results used in your classroom? List all the assessment devices and activities that the teacher uses, and explain how he or she uses the results of these assessment activities to plan instruction for pupils.
5. Working with one or two students, begin to build a portfolio, or review the contents of the students' portfolios if they are already used in the classroom. What types of materials are included? How do these materials show the students' growth in reading and writing?

Children's Trade Books Cited in This Chapter

Dahl, Roald. (1962). *James and the Giant Peach*. New York: Knopf.
Lobel, Arnold. (1972). *Frog and Toad Together*. New York: Harper & Row.
MacLachlan, Patricia. (1985). *Sarah, Plain and Tall*. New York: Harper & Row.
Viorst, Judith. (1972). *Alexander and the Terrible, Horrible, No Good, Very Bad Day*. New York: Macmillan.

Aiex, N. K. (1988). Literature-Based Reading Instruction. *The Reading Teacher* 41:458–461.

Alvermann, D. (1984). Second Graders' Strategic Preferences While Reading Basal Stories. *Journal of Educational Research* 77:184–189.

Applebee, A. N., Langer, J. A., Mullis, I. V. A., Latham, A. S., and Gentile, C. A. (1993). *The NAEP 1992 Writing Report Card*. Washington, DC: U.S. Dept. of Education.

Arnold, H. (1982). *Listening to Children Read*. London: United Kingdom Reading Association.

Atwell, N. (1987). *In the Middle: Writing, Reading, and Learning with Adolescents*. Portsmouth, NH: Heinemann.

Brown, V. L., Hammill, D. D., and Wiederholt, J. L. (1986). *Test of Reading Comprehension*. Austin, TX: Pro-Ed.

Cambourne, B., and Turbill, J. (1990). Assessment on Whole-Language Classrooms: Theory into Practice. *The Elementary School Journal* 90:338–349.

Clay, M. M. (1993). *An Observation Survey of Early Literacy Achievement*. Portsmouth, NH: Heinemann.

Close, J., Conoley, J. C., and Impara, J. C. (1995). *Buros Twelfth Mental Measurements Yearbook*. Lincoln, NE: University of Nebraska, Buros Institute of Mental Measurement.

Cockrum, W. A., and Castillo, M. (1991). Whole Language Assessment and Evaluation Strategies. In Bill Harp, ed., *Assessment and Evaluation in Whole Language Programs*. Norwood, MA: Christopher Gordon Publishers.

Dunn, L. M., and Dunn, L. M. (1981). *Peabody Picture Vocabulary Test*. Pines, MN: American Guidance Service.

Fisher, B. (1989). Assessing Emergent and Initial Readers. *Teaching K–8* 20:56–58.

Flood, J., and Lapp, D. (1989). Reporting Reading Progress: A Comparison Portfolio for Parents. *The Reading Teacher* 42:508–514.

Gambrell, L. B., Koskinen, P. S., and Kapinus, B. A. (1991). Retelling and the Reading Comprehension of Proficient and Less Proficient Readers. *Journal of Educational Research* 84:356–362.

Gambrell, L. B., Palmer, B. M., Codling, R. M., and Mazzone, S. A. (1996). Assessing Motivation to Read. *The Reading Teacher* 49:518–533.

Goodman, K. (1965). A Linguistic Study of Cues and Miscues in Reading. *Elementary English* 42:639–643.

Goodman, K. (1969). Analysis of Reading Miscues: Applied Psycholinguistics. *Reading Research Quarterly* 5:126–135.

Goodman, Y. M. (1978). Kid-Watching: An Alternative to Testing. *National Elementary School Principal* 57:41–45.

Goodman, Y. (1996). Revaluing Readers while Readers Revalue Themselves: Retrospective Miscue Analysis. *The Reading Teacher* 49:600–609.

Hammill, D. D., and Larsen, S. C. (1988). *Test of Written Language*. Austin, TX: Pro-Ed.

Haney, W., and Madaus G. (1989). Searching for Alternatives to Standardized Tests: Whys, Whats, and Whithers. *Phi Delta Kappan* 70:683–687.

Harris, T. L., and Hodges R. E., eds. (1995). *The Literacy Dictionary: The Vocabulary of Reading and Writing*. Newark, DE: International Reading Association.

Heald-Taylor, B. G. (1987). Predictable Literature Selections and Activities for Language Arts Instruction. *The Reading Teacher* 41:6–12.

Henk, W. A., and Melnick, S. A. (1995). The Reader Self-Perception Scale (RSPS): A New Tool for Measuring How Children Feel About Themselves as Readers. *The Reading Teacher* 48:470–481.

Hittleman, D. (1988). *Developmental Reading, K–8: Teaching from a Whole-Language Perspective* (3rd ed.). Columbus, OH: Merrill.

Irwin, P. A., and Mitchell, J. N. (1983). A Procedure for Assessing the Richness of Retellings. *Journal of Reading* 26: 391–396.

Johnson, M., Kress, R., and Pikulski, J. (1987). *Informal Reading Inventories* (2nd ed.). Newark, DE: International Reading Association.

Johnson, P. (1984). Assessment in Reading. In P. D. Pearson, ed., *Handbook of Reading Research*. New York: Longman.

Johnson, P. (1987). Teachers as Evaluation Experts. *The Reading Teacher* 41:744–748.

Levi, R. (1990). Assessment and Educational Vision: Engaging Learners and Parents. *Language Arts* 67:267–274.

Linek, W. M. (1991). Grading and Evaluation Techniques for Whole Language Teachers. *Language Arts* 68:125–132.

McKenna, M. C., and Kear, D. J. (1990). Measuring Attitude Toward Reading: A New Tool for Teachers. *The Reading Teacher* 43:626–639.

Mullis, I. V. S., Campbell, J. R., and Farstrup, A. (1993). *The NAEP 1992 Reading Report Card*. Washington, DC: U.S. Dept. of Education.

Neill, D. M., and Medina, N. J. (1989). Standardized Testing: Harmful to Educational Health. *Phi Delta Kappan* 70:688–697.

Palinscar, A. S. (1984). The Quest for Meaning from Expository Text: A Teacher-Guided Journey. In G. G. Duffy, L. R. Roehler, and J. Mason, eds., *Comprehension Instruction*. New York: Longman.

Paradis, E., Chatton, B., Boswell, A., Smith, M., and Yovich, S. (1991). Accountability: Assessing Comprehension During Literature Discussions. *The Reading Teacher* 45:8–17.

Paratore, J. R., and Indrisano, R. (1987). Intervention Assessment of Reading Comprehension. *The Reading Teacher* 41:778–783.

Peters, C. W., and Wixon, K. K. (1989). Smart New Reading Tests Are Coming. *Learning 89* 17:43–44, 53.

Pikulski, J. J. (1989). The Assessment of Reading: A Time for Change? *The Reading Teacher* 43:80–81.

Silvernail, D. L. (1992). Alternative Forms of Student Assessment: Establishing their Validity. *Journal of Maine Education* 8:27–31.

Stiggins, R. J. (1995). Literacy Assessment for the 21st Century. *Phi Delta Kapan* 77: 238–249.

Tierney, R. J., Carter, M. A., and Desai, L. E. (1991). *Portfolios in the Reading-Writing Classroom*. Norwood, MA: Christopher-Gordon Publishers.

Tierney, R. J., Readence, J. E., and Dishner, E. K. (1995). *Reading Strategies and Practices: A Compendium*. Boston: Allyn & Bacon.

Valencia, S. (1990). A Portfolio Approach to Classroom Reading Assessment: The Whys, Whats, and Hows. *The Reading Teacher* 43:338–340.

Valencia, S., and Pearson, P. D. (1987). Reading Assessment: Time for a Change. *The Reading Teacher* 41:726–732.

Valencia, S. W., Hiebert, E. H., and Afflerbach, P. P. (1994). Definitions and Perspectives. In S. W. Valencia, E. H. Hiebert, and P. P. Afflerbach, eds., *Authentic Reading Assessment: Practices and Possibilities*. Newark, DE: International Reading Association.

Watson, D., and Henson, J. (1991). Reading Evaluation—Miscue Analysis. In Bill Harp, ed., *Assessment and Evaluation in Whole Language Programs*. Norwood, MA: Christopher-Gordon Publishers.

Weaver, C. (1988). *Reading Process and Practice*. Portsmouth, NH: Heinemann.

Whole Language Council, Milwaukee Public Schools. (1990). *Whole Language Assessment Guide*. Milwaukee: Milwaukee Public Schools.

Wolf, D. P. (1989). Portfolio Assessment: Sampling Students' Work. *Educational Leadership* 36:35–40.

Wood, K. D. (1988). Techniques for Assessing Students' Potential for Learning. *The Reading Teacher* 41:440–447.

Woodcock, R. W., and Johnson, M. B. (1991). *Woodcock-Johnson Psycho-Educational Battery* (rev. ed.). Allen, TX: DLM/Teaching Resources.

Appendix

Award-Winning Literature

The Caldecott Medal and Honor Awards

The Caldecott Medal, first awarded in 1938, is presented annually to the illustrator of the most distinguished picture book published in the United States. The award is named after Randolph Caldecott, a British illustrator, and is given by the Children's Services Division of the American Library Association.

1938 **Medal:** *Animals of the Bible* by Helen Dean Fish, illustrated by Dorothy P. Lathrop—Frederick A. Stokes
Honor Books: *Seven Simeons: A Russian Tale* by Boris Artzybasheff—Viking; *Four and Twenty Blackbirds: Nursery Rhymes of Yesterday Recalled for Children of Today* by Helen Dean Fish, illustrated by Robert Lawson—Frederick A. Stokes

1939 **Medal:** *Mel Li* by Thomas Handforth—Doubleday, Doran
Honor Books: *The Forest Pool* by Laura Adams Armer—Longmans Green; *Wee Gillis* by Munro Leaf, illustrated by Robert Lawson—Viking; *Snow White and the Seven Dwarfs* by Wanda Gag—Coward-McCann; *Barkis* by Clare Newberry—Harper and Brothers; *Andy and the Lion: A Tale of Kindness Remembered or the Power of Gratitude* by James Daugherty—Viking

1940 **Medal:** *Abraham Lincoln* by Ingrid and Edgar Parin D'Aulaire—Doubleday Doran
Honor Books: *Cock-a-Doodle Doo: The Story of a Little Red Rooster* by Berta and Elmer Hader—Macmillan; *Madeline* by Ludwig Bemelmans—Simon & Schuster; *The Ageless Story* by Lauren Ford—Dodd Mead

1941 **Medal:** *They Were Strong and Good* by Robert Lawson—Viking
Honor Book: *April's Kittens* by Clare Newberry—Harper and Brothers

1942 **Medal:** *Make Way for Ducklings* by Robert McCloskey—Viking
Honor Books: *An American ABC* by Maud and Miska Petersham—Macmillan; *In My Mother's House* by Ann Nolan Clark, illustrated by Velino Herrera—Viking; *Paddle-to-the-Sea* by Holling C. Holling—Houghton Mifflin; *Nothing at All* by Wanda Gag—Coward-McCann

1943 **Medal:** *The Little House* by Virginia Lee Burton—Houghton Mifflin
Honor Books: *Dash and Dart* by Mary and Conrad Buff—Viking; *Marshmallow* by Clare Newberry—Harper and Brothers

1944 **Medal:** *Many Moons* by James Thurber, illustrated by Louis Slobodkin—Harcourt Brace
Honor Books: *Small Rain: Verses from the Bible* selected by Jessie Orton Jones, illustrated by Elizabeth Orton Jones—Viking; *Pierre Pigeon* by Lee Kingman, illustrated by Arnold E. Bare—Houghton Mifflin; *The Mighty Hunter* by Berta and Elmer Hader—Macmillan; *A Child's Good Night Book* by Margaret Wise Brown, illustrated by Jean Charlot—W. R. Scott; *Good-Luck Horse* by Chih-Yi Chan, illustrated by Plato Chan—Whittlesey

1945 **Medal:** *Prayer for a Child* by Rachel Field, illustrated by Elizabeth Orton Jones—Macmillan
Honor Books: *Mother Goose: Seventy-Seven Verses with Pictures* illustrated by Tasha Tudor—Henry Z. Walck; *In the Forest* by Marie Hall Ets—Viking; *Yonie Wondernose* by Marguerite de Angeli—Doubleday; *The Christmas Anna Angel* by Ruth Sawyer, illustrated by Kate Seredy—Viking

1946 **Medal:** *The Rooster Crows* (traditional Mother Goose), illustrated by Maud and Miska Petersham—Macmillan
Honor Books: *Little Lost Lamb* by Golden MacDonald, illustrated by Leonard Weisgard—Doubleday; *Sing Mother Goose* by Opal Wheeler, illustrated by Marjorie Torrey—E. P. Dutton; *My Mother is the Most Beautiful Woman in the World* by Becky Reyher, illustrated by Ruth Gannett—Howell, Soskin; *You Can Write Chinese* by Kurt Wiese—Viking

1947 **Medal:** *The Little Island* by Golden MacDonald, illustrated by Lenord Weisgard—Doubleday
Honor Books: *Rain Drop Splash* by Alvin Tresselt, illustrated by Leonard Weisgard—Lothrop, Lee & Shepard; *Boats on the River* by Marjorie Flack, illustrated by Jay Hyde Barnum—Viking; *Timothy Turtle* by Al Graham, illustrated by Tony Palazzo—Robert Welch; *Pedro, the Angel of Olvera Street* by Leo Politi—Charles Scribner's Sons; *Sing in Praise: A Collection of the Best-Loved Hymns* by Opal Wheeler, illustrated by Marjorie Torrey—E. P. Dutton

1948 **Medal:** *White Snow, Bright Snow* by Alvin Tresselt, illustrated by Roger Duvoisin—Lothrop, Lee & Shepard
Honor Books: *Stone Soup: An Old Tale* by Marcia Brown—Charles Scribner's Sons; *McElligot's Pool* by Dr. Seuss—Random House; *Bambino the Clown*

by George Schreiber—Viking; *Roger and the Fox* by Lavinia Davis, illustrated by Hildegard Woodward—Doubleday; *Song of Robin Hood* edited by Anne Malcolmson, illustrated by Virginia Lee Burton—Houghton Mifflin

1949 **Medal:** *The Big Snow* by Betta and Elmer Hader—Macmillan
Honor Books: *Blueberries for Sal* by Robert McCloskey—Viking; *All Around the Town* by Phyllis McGinley, illustrated by Helen Stone—J. B. Lippincott; *Juanita* by Leo Politi—Charles Scribner's Sons; *Fish in the Air* by Kurt Wiese—Viking

1950 **Medal:** *Song of the Swallows* by Leo Politi—Charles Scribner's Sons
Honor Books: *America's Ethan Allen* by Stewart Holbrook, illustrated by Lynd Ward—Houghton Mifflin; *The Wild Birthday Cake* by Lavinia Davis, illustrated by Hildegard Woodward—Doubleday; *The Happy Day* by Ruth Krauss, illustrated by Marc Simont—Harper and Brothers; *Bartholomew and the Oobleck* by Dr. Seuss—Random House; *Henry Fisherman* by Marcia Brown—Charles Scribner's Sons

1951 **Medal:** *The Egg Tree* by Katherine Milhous—Charles Scribner's Sons
Honor Books: *Dick Whittington and His Cat* by Marcia Brown—Charles Scribner's Sons; *The Two Reds* by William Lipkind, illustrated by Nicholas Mordvinoff—Harcourt; *If I Ran the Zoo* by Dr. Seuss—Random House; *The Most Wonderful Doll in the World* by Phyllis McGinley, illustrated by Helen Stone—J. B. Lippincott; *T-Bone, The Baby Sitter* by Clare Newberry—Harper and Brothers

1952 **Medal:** *Finders Keepers* by William Lipkind, illustrated by Nicholas Mordvinoff—Harcourt
Honor Books: *Mr. T. W. Anthony Wood: The Story of a Cat and a Dog and a Mouse* by Marie Hall Ets—Viking; *Skipper John's Cook* by Marcia Brown—Charles Scribner's Sons; *All Falling Down* by Gene Zion, illustrated by Margaret Bloy Graham—Harper and Brothers; *Bear Party* by William Pene du Bois—Viking; *Feather Mountain* by Elizabeth Olds—Houghton Mifflin

1953 **Medal:** *The Biggest Bear* by Lynd Ward—Houghton Mifflin
Honor Books: *Puss in Boots* by Charles Perrault, illustrated and translated by Marcia Brown—Charles Scribner's Sons; *One Morning in Maine* by Robert McCloskey—Viking; *Ape in a Cape: An Alphabet of Odd Animals* by Fritz Eichenbert—Harcourt; *The Storm Book* by Charlotte Zolotow, illustrated by Margaret Bloy Graham—Harper and Brothers; *Five Little Monkeys* by Juliet Kepes—Houghton Mifflin

1954 **Medal:** *Madeline's Rescue* by Ludwig Bemelmans—Viking
Honor Books: *Journey Cake, Ho!* by Ruth Sawyer, illustrated by Robert McCloskey—Viking; *When Will the World Be Mine?* by Miriam Schlein, illustrated by Jean Charlot—W. R. Scott; *The Steadfast Tin Soldier* by Hans Christian Andersen, translated by M. R. James, illustrated by Marcia Brown—Charles Scribner's Sons; *A Very Special House* by Ruth Krauss, illustrated by Maurice Sendak—Harper and Brothers; *Green Eyes* by Abe Birnbaum—Capitol

1955 **Medal:** *Cinderella, or the Little Glass Slipper* by Charles Perrault, translated and illustrated by Marcia Brown—Charles Scribner's Sons
Honor Books: *Book of Nursery and Mother Goose Rhymes* illustrated by Marguerite de Angeli—Doubleday; *Wheel on the Chimney* by Margaret Wise Brown, illustrated by Tibor Gergely—J. B. Lippincott; *The Thanksgiving Story* by Alice Dalgliesh, illustrated by Helen Sewell—Charles Scribner's Sons

1956 **Medal:** *Frog Went A-Courtin* edited by John Langstaff, illustrated by Feodor Rojankovsky—Harcourt
Honor Books: *Play with Me* by Marie Hall Ets—Viking; *Crow Boy* by Taro Yashima—Viking

1957 **Medal:** *A Tree Is Nice* by Janice May Udry—illustrated by Marc Simont—Harper and Brothers
Honor Books: *Mr. Penny's Race Horse* by Marie Hall Ets—Viking; *1 Is One* by Tasha Tudor—Henry A. Walck; *Anatole* by Eve Titus, illustrated by Paul Galdone—Whittlesey; *Gillespie and the Guards* by Benjamin Elkin, illustrated by James Daugherty—Viking; *Lion* by William Pene du Bois—Viking

1958 **Medal:** *Time of Wonder* by Robert McCloskey—Viking
Honor Books: *Fly High, Fly Low* by Don Freeman—Viking; *Anatole and the Cat* by Eve Titus, illustrated by Paul Galdone—Whittlesey

1959 **Medal:** *Chanticleer and the Fox* adapted from Chaucer by Barbara Cooney—Thomas Y. Crowell
Honor Books: *The House that Jack Built: A Picture Book in Two Languages* by Antonio Frasconi—Harcourt Brace; *What Do You Say, Dear?* by Sesyle Joslin, illustrated by Maurice Sendak—W. R. Scott; *Umbrella* by Taro Yashima—Viking

1960 **Medal:** *Nine Days to Christmas* by Marie Hall Ets and Aurora Labastida, illustrated by Marie Hall Ets—Viking
Honor Books: *Houses from the Sea* by Alice E. Goudey, illustrated by Adrienne Adams—Charles Scribner's Sons; *The Moon Jumpers* by Janice May Udry, illustrated by Maurice Sendak—Harper and Brothers

1961 **Medal:** *Baboushka and the Three Kings* by Ruth Robbins, illustrated by Nicolas Sidjak—Parnassus Imprints
Honor Book: *Inch by Inch* by Leo Lionni—Obolensky

1962 **Medal:** *Once a Mouse . . .* by Marcia Brown—
Charles Scribner's Sons
Honor Books: *The Fox Went Out on a Chilly Night:
An Old Song* by Peter Spier—Doubleday; *Little
Bear's Visit* by Else Holmelund Minarik, illustrated
by Maurice Sendak—Harper and Brothers; *The
Day We Saw the Sun Come Up* by Alice E. Goudey,
illustrated by Adrienne Adams—Charles Scribner's
Sons

1963 **Medal:** *The Snowy Day* by Ezra Jack Keats—Viking
Honor Books: *The Sun Is a Golden Earring* by
Natalia M. Belting, illustrated by Bernarda
Bryson—Holt, Rinehart & Winston; *Mr. Rabbit and
the Lovely Present* by Charlotte Zolotow, illustrated
by Maurice Sendak—Harper & Row

1964 **Medal:** *Where the Wild Things Are* by Maurice
Sendak—Harper & Row
Honor Books: *Swimmy* by Leo Lionni—Pantheon;
All in the Morning Early by Sorche Nic Leodhas,
illustrated by Evaline Ness—Holt, Rinehart &
Winston; *Mother Goose and Nursery Rhymes*
illustrated by Philip Reed—Atheneum

1965 **Medal:** *May I Bring a Friend?* by Beatrice Schenk de
Regniers, illustrated by Beni Montresor—Atheneum
Honor Books: *Rain Makes Applesauce* by Julian
Scheer, illustrated by Marvin Bileck—Holiday
House; *The Wave* by Margaret Hodges, illustrated
by Blair Lent—Houghton Mifflin; *A Pocketful of
Crickets* by Rebecca Caudill, illustrated by Evaline
Ness—Holt, Rinehart & Winston

1966 **Medal:** *Always Room for One More* by Sorche Nic
Leodhas, illustrated by Nonny Hogrogian—Holt,
Rinehart & Winston
Honor Books: *Hide and Seek Fog* by Alvin Tresselt,
illustrated by Roger Duvoisin—Viking; *Tom Tit Tot*
by Evaline Ness—Charles Scribner's Sons

1967 **Medal:** *Sam, Bangs & Moonshine* by Evaline Ness—
Holt, Rinehart & Winston
Honor Book: *One Wide River to Cross* by Barbara
Emberley, illustrated by Ed Emberley—Prentice-Hall

1968 **Medal:** *Drummer Hoff* by Barbara Emberley,
illustrated by Ed Emberley—Prentice-Hall
Honor Books: *Frederick* by Leo Lionni—Pantheon;
Seashore Story by Taro Yashima—Viking; *The
Emperor and the Kite* by Jane Yolen, illustrated by
Ed Young—World

1969 **Medal:** *The Fool of the World and the Flying Ship* by
Arthur Ransom, illustrated by Uri Shulevitz—
Farrar, Straus & Giroux
Honor Book: *Why the Sun and the Moon Live in the
Sky: An African Folktale* by Elphinstone Dayrell,
illustrated by Blair Lent—Houghton Mifflin

1970 **Medal:** *Sylvester and the Magic Pebble* by William
Steig—Windmill/Simon & Schuster

Honor Books: *Goggles!* by Ezra Jack Keats—
Macmillan; *Alexander and the Wind-Up Mouse* by
Leo Lionni—Pantheon; *Pop Corn and Ma Goodness*
by Edna Mitchell Preston, illustrated by Robert
Andrew Parker—Viking; *Thy Friend, Obadiah* by
Brinton Turkle—Viking; *The Judge: An Untrue Tale*
by Harve Zemach, illustrated by Margot Zemach—
Farrar, Straus & Giroux

1971 **Medal:** *A Story, a Story* by Gail E. Haley—Atheneum
Honor Books: *The Angry Moon* by William Sleator,
illustrated by Blair Lent—Little, Brown; *Frog and
Toad Are Friends* by Arnold Lobel—Harper & Row;
In the Night Kitchen by Maurice Sendak—Harper &
Row

1972 **Medal:** *One Fine Day* by Nonny Hogrogian—
Macmillan
Honor Books: *If All the Seas Were One Sea* by Janina
Domanska—Macmillan; *Moja Means One: A Swahili
Counting Book* by Muriel Feelings, illustrated by
Tom Feelings—Dial; *Hildilid's Night* by Cheli Duran
Ryan, illustrated by Arnold Lobel—Macmillan

1973 **Medal:** *The Funny Little Woman* by Arlene Mosel,
illustrated by Blair Lent—E. P. Dutton
Honor Books: *Anansi the Spider: A Tale from the
Ashanti* adapted and illustrated by Gerald
McDermott—Holt, Rinehart & Winston; *Hosie's
Alphabet* by Hosea, Tobias, and Lisa Baskin,
illustrated by Leonard Baskin—Viking; *Snow White
and the Seven Dwarfs* translated by Randall Jarrell,
illustrated by Nancy Ekholm Burkert—Farrar,
Straus & Giroux; *When Clay Sings* by Byrd Baylor,
illustrated by Tom Bahti—Charles Scribner's Sons

1974 **Medal:** *Duffy and the Devil* by Harve Zemach,
illustrated by Margot Zemach—Farrar, Straus &
Giroux
Honor Books: *Three Jovial Huntsmen* by Susan
Jeffers—Bradbury; *Cathedral: The Story of Its
Construction* by David Macaulay—Houghton
Mifflin

1975 **Medal:** *Arrow to the Sun* adapted and illustrated by
Gerald McDermott—Viking
Honor Books: *Jambo Means Hello: A Swahili
Alphabet Book* by Muriel Feelings, illustrated by
Tom Feelings—Dial

1976 **Medal:** *Why Mosquitoes Buzz in People's Ears* by
Verna Aardema, illustrated by Leo and Diane
Dillon—Dial
Honor Books: *The Desert Is Theirs* by Byrd Baylor,
illustrated by Peter Parnall—Charles Scribner's
Sons; *Strega Nona*, retold and illustrated by Tomie
de Paola—Prentice-Hall

1977 **Medal:** *Ashanti to Zulu: African Traditions* by
Margaret Musgrove, illustrated by Leo and Diane
Dillon—Dial
Honor Books: *The Amazing Bone* by William
Steig— Farrar, Straus & Giroux; *The Contest*, retold

and illustrated by Nonny Hogrogrian—Greenwillow; *Fish for Supper* by M. B. Goffstein—Dial; *The Golem: A Jewish Legend* by Beverly Brodsky—McDermott; *Hawk, I'm Your Brother* by Byrd Baylor, illustrated by Peter Parnall—Charles Scribner's Sons

1978 **Medal:** *Noah's Ark* by Peter Spier—Doubleday
Honor Books: *Castle* by David Macaulay—Houghton Mifflin; *It Could Always Be Worse* retold and illustrated by Margot Zemach—Farrar, Straus & Giroux

1979 **Medal:** *The Girl Who Loved Wild Horses* by Paul Goble—Bradbury
Honor Books: *Freight Train* by Donald Crews—Greenwillow; *The Way to Start a Day* by Byrd Baylor, illustrated by Peter Parnall—Charles Scribner's Sons

1980 **Medal:** *Ox-Cart Man* by Donald Hall, illustrated by Barbara Cooney—Viking
Honor Books: *Ben's Trumpet* by Rachel Isadora—Greenwillow; *The Treasure* by Uri Shulevitz—Farrar, Straus & Giroux; *The Garden of Abdul Gasazi* by Chris Van Allsburg—Houghton Mifflin

1981 **Medal:** *Fables* by Arnold Lobel—Harper & Row
Honor Books: *The Bremen-Town Musicians* by Ilse Plume—Doubleday; *The Grey Lady and the Strawberry Snatcher* by Molly Bang—Four Winds; *Mice Twice* by Joseph Low—Atheneum; *Truck* by Donald Crews—Greenwillow

1982 **Medal:** *Jumanji* by Chris Van Allsburg—Houghton Mifflin
Honor Books: *A Visit to William Blake's Inn: Poems for Innocent and Experienced Travelers* by Nancy Willard, illustrated by Alice and Martin Provensen—Harcourt Brace Jovanovich; *Where the Buffaloes Begin* by Olaf Baker, illustrated by Stephen Gammell—F. Warne; *On Market Street* by Arnold Lobel, illustrated by Anita Lobel—Greenwillow; *Outside Over There* by Maurice Sendak—Harper & Row

1983 **Medal:** *Shadow* by Blaise Cendrars, illustrated by Marcia Brown—Charles Scribner's Sons
Honor Books: *When I Was Young in the Mountains* by Cynthia Rylant, illustrated by Diane Goode—E. P. Dutton; *A Chair for My Mother* by Vera B. Williams—Morrow

1984 **Medal:** *The Glorious Flight: Across the Channel with Louis Bleriot, July 25, 1909* by Alice and Martin Provensen—Viking
Honor Books: *Ten, Nine, Eight* by Molly Bang—Greenwillow; *Little Red Riding Hood* retold and illustrated by Trina Schart Hyman—Holiday House

1985 **Medal:** *St. George and the Dragon* by Margaret Hodges, illustrated by Trina Schart Hyman—Little, Brown
Honor Books: *Hansel and Gretel* retold by Rika Lesser, illustrated by Paul O. Zelinsky—Dodd; *Have You Seen My Duckling?* by Nancy Tafuri—

Greenwillow; *The Story of Jumping Mouse* by John Steptoe—Lothrop, Lee & Shepard

1986 **Medal:** *The Polar Express* by Chris Van Allsburg—Houghton Mifflin
Honor Books: *King Bidgood's in the Bathtub* by Audrey Wood, illustrated by Don Wood—Harcourt Brace Jovanovich; *The Relatives Came* by Cynthia Rylant, illustrated by Stephen Gammell—Bradbury

1987 **Medal:** *Hey, All* by Arthur Yorinks, illustrated by Richard Egielski—Farrar, Straus & Giroux
Honor Books: *Alphabatics* by Suse MacDonald—Bradbury; *Rumpelstiltskin* retold and illustrated by Paul O. Zelinsky—E. P. Dutton; *The Village of Round and Square Houses* by Ann Grifalconi—Little, Brown

1988 **Medal:** *Owl Moon* by Jane Yolen, illustrated by John Schoenherr—Philomel
Honor Book: *Mufaro's Beautiful Daughters: An African Tale* by John Steptoe—Lothrop, Lee & Shepard

1989 **Medal:** *Song and Dance Man* by Karen Ackerman, illustrated by Stephen Gammell—Alfred A. Knopf
Honor Books: *The Boy of the Three-Year Nap* by Dianne Snyder, illustrated by Allen Say—Houghton Mifflin; *Free Fall* by David Wiesner—Lothrop, Lee & Shepard; *Goldilocks* retold and illustrated by James Marshall—Dial; *Mirandy and Brother Wind* by Patricia C. McKissack, illustrated by Jerry Pinkney—Alfred A. Knopf

1990 **Medal:** *Lon Po Po: A Red-Riding Hood Story from China* by Ed Young—Philomel
Honor Books: *Bill Peet: An Autobiography* by Bill Peet—Houghton Mifflin; *Color Zoo* by Lois Ehlert—J. B. Lippincott; *Hershel and the Hanukkah Goblins* by Eric Kimmel, illustrated by Trina Schart Hyman—Holiday House; *The Talking Eggs* by Robert D. San Souci, illustrated by Jerry Pinkey—Dial

1991 **Medal:** *Black and White* by David Macaulay—Houghton Mifflin
Honor Books: *"More More More," Said the Baby: Three Love Stories* by Vera B. Williams—Greenwillow; *Puss in Boots* by Charles Perrault, translated by Malcolm Arthur, illustrated by Fred Marcellino—Farrar, Straus & Giroux

1992 **Medal:** *Tuesday* by David Weisner—Clarion
Honor Book: *Tar Beach* by Faith Ringold—Crown

1993 **Medal:** *Mirette on the High Wire* by Emily Arnold McCully—G. P. Putnam's Sons
Honor Books: *Stinky Cheese Man and Other Fairly Stupid Tales* by Jon Scieska, illustrated by Lane Smith—Viking; *Working Cotton* by Sherley Anne Williams, illustrated by Carol Byard—Harcourt Brace; *Seven Blind Mice* by Ed Young—Philomel

1994 **Medal:** *Grandfather's Journey* by Allen Say—Houghton Mifflin

Honor Books: *Peppe the Lamplighter* by Elisa Baron, illustrated by Ted Lewin—Lothrop, Lee & Shepard; *In the Small, Small Pond* by Denise Fleming—Henry Holt; *Owen* by Kevin Henkes—Greenwillow; *Raven: A Trickster Tale from the Pacific Northwest* by Gerald McDermott—Harcourt Brace; *Yo! Yes?* by Chris Raschka—Orchard

1995 **Medal:** *Smoky Night* by Eve Bunting, illustrated by David Diaz—Harcourt Brace
Honor Books: *John Henry* by Julius Lester, illustrated by Jerry Pickney—Dial; *Swamp Angel* by Paul Zelinsky, illustrated by Anne Issacs—E. P. Dutton; *Time Flies* by Eric Rohmann—Crown

1996 **Medal:** *Officer Buckle and Gloria* by Peggy Ratham—Putnam
Honor Books: *Alphabet City* by Stephen T. Johnson—Viking; *Zin! Zin! Zin! A Violin* by Lloyd Moss, illustrated by Marjorie Priceman—Simon and Schuster; *The Faithful Friend* by Robert San Souci, illustrated by Brian Pinkney—Simon and Schuster; *Tops and Bottoms* by Janet Stevens—Harcourt Brace

1997 **Medal:** *Golem* by David Wisniewski—Clarion
Honor Books: *The Graphic Alphabet* edited by Neal Porter, illustrated by David Pelletier—Orchard; *Hush! A Thai Lullaby* by Minfong Ho, illustrated by Holly Meade—Orchard; *The Paperboy* illustrated by Dav Pilkey—Orchard; *Starry Messenger* by Peter Sis—Farrar, Straus & Giroux

The Newbery Medal and Honor Awards

First presented in 1922, the Newbery Medal is awarded for the most distinguished contribution to children's literature published in the United States. The award is named after John Newbery, the first English publisher of books for children. It is given by the Children's Services Division of the American Library Association.

1922 **Medal:** *The Story of Mankind* by Hendrik Willem van Loon—Boni & Liveright
Honor Books: *The Great Quest* by Charles Hawes—Little, Brown; *Cedric the Forester* by Bernard Marshall—Appleton; *The Old Tobacco Shop: A True Account of What Befell a Little Boy in Search of Adventure* by William Bowen—Macmillan; *The Golden Fleece and the Heroes Who Lived Before Achilles* by Padraic Colum—Macmillan; *Windy Hill* by Cornelia Meigs—Macmillan

1923 **Medal:** *The Voyages of Doctor Dolittle* by Hugh Lofting—Frederick A. Stokes

1924 **Medal:** *The Dark Frigate* by Charles Hawes—Atlantic Monthly Press

1925 **Medal:** *Tales from Silver Lands* by Charles Finger—Doubleday, Page

Honor Books: *Nicholas: A Manhattan Christmas Story* by Anne Carroll Moore—G. P. Putnams' Sons; *Dream Coach* by Anne Parrish—Macmillan

1926 **Medal:** *Shen of the Sea* by Arthur Bowie Chrisman—E. P. Dutton
Honor Book: *Voyagers* by Padraic Colum—Macmillan

1927 **Medal:** *Smoky, the Cowhorse* by Will James—Charles Scribner's Sons

1928 **Medal:** *Gayneck, the Story of a Pigeon* by Dhan Gopal Mukerji—E. P. Dutton
Honor Books: *The Wonder Smith and His Son: A Tale from the Golden Childhood of the World* by Ella Young—Longmans, Green; *Downright Dencey* by Caroline Snedeker—Doubleday

1929 **Medal:** *The Trumpeter of Krakow* by Eric P. Kelly—Macmillan
Honor Books: *Pigtail of Ah Lee Ben Loo* by John Bennett—Longmans, Green; *Millions of Cats* by Wanda Gag—Coward-McCann; *The Boy Who Was* by Grace Hallock—E. P. Dutton; *Clearing Weather* by Cornelia Meigs—Little, Brown; *Runaway Papoose* by Grace Moon—Doubleday, Doran; *Tod of the Fens* by Elinor Whitney—Macmillan

1930 **Medal:** *Hitty, Her First Hundred Years* by Rachel Field—Macmillan
Honor Books: *Daughter of the Seine: The Life of Madame Roland* by Jeanette Eaton—Harper and Brothers; *Pran of Albania* by Elizabeth Miller—Doubleday, Doran; *Jumping-Off Place* by Marian Hurd McNeely—Longmans, Green; *Tangle-Coated Horse and Other Tales: Episodes from the Fionn Saga* by Ella Young—Longmans, Green; *Vaino: A Boy of New England* by Julia Davis Adams—E. P. Dutton; *Little Blacknose* by Hildegarde Swift—Harcourt

1931 **Medal:** *The Cat Who Went to Heaven* by Elizabeth Coatsworth—Macmillan
Honor Books: *Floating Island* by Anne Parrish—Harper and Brothers; *The Dark Star of Itza: The Story of a Pagan Princess* by Alida Malkus—Harcourt; *Queer Person* by Ralph Hubbard—Doubleday, Doran; *Mountains Are Free* by Julia Davis Adams—E. P. Dutton; *Spice and the Devil's Cave* by Agnes Hewes—Alfred A. Knopf; *Meggy Macintosh* by Elizabeth Janet Gray—Doubleday, Doran; *Garram the Hunter: The Boy of the Hill Tribes* by Herbert Best—Doubleday, Doran; *Ood-Le-Uk the Wanderer* by Alice Lide and Margaret Johansen—Little, Brown

1932 **Medal:** *Waterless Mountain* by Laura Adams Armer—Longmans, Green
Honor Books: *The Fairy Circus* by Dorothy P. Lathrop—Macmillan; *Calico Bush* by Rachel Field—Macmillan; *Boy of the South Seas* by Eunice Tietjens—Coward-McCann; *Out of the Flame* by Eloise Lownsbery—Longmans, Green; *Jane's Island* by Marjorie Allee—Houghton Mifflin; *Truce of the*

Wolf and Other Tales of Old Italy by Mary Gould Davis—Harcourt

1933 **Medal:** *Young Fu of the Upper Yangtze* by Elizabeth Foreman Lewis—John C. Winston
Honor Books: *Swift Rivers* by Cornelia Meigs—Little, Brown; *The Railroad to Freedom: A Story of the Civil War* by Hildegarde Swift—Harcourt Brace; *Children of the Soil: A Story of Scandinavia* by Nora Burglon—Doubleday, Doran

1934 **Medal:** *Invincible Louisa: The Story of the Author of 'Little Women'* by Cornelia Meigs—Little, Brown
Honor Books: *The Forgotten Daughter* by Caroline Snedeker—Doubleday, Doran; *Swords of Steel* by Elsie Singmaster—Houghton Mifflin; *ABC Bunny* by Wanda Gag—Coward-McCann; *Winged Girl of Knossos* by Erik Berry—Appleton-Century; *New Land* by Sarah Schmidt—R. M. McBride; *Big Tree of Bunlahy: Stories of My Own Countryside* by Padraic Colum—Macmillan; *Glory of the Seas* by Agnes Hewes—Alfred A. Knopf; *Apprentice of Florence* by Ann Kyle—Houghton Mifflin

1935 **Medal:** *Dobry* by Monica Shannon—Viking
Honor Books: *Pageant of Chinese History* by Elizabeth Seeger—Longmans, Green; *Davy Crockett* by Constance Rourke—Harcourt Brace; *Day on Skates: The Story of a Dutch Picnic* by Hilda Van Stockum—Harper

1936 **Medal:** *Caddie Woodlawn* by Carol Ryrie Brink—Macmillan
Honor Books: *Honk, the Moose* by Phil Stong—Dodd, Mead; *The Good Master* by Kate Seredy—Viking; *Young Walter Scott* by Elizabeth Janet Gray—Viking; *All Sail Set: A Romance of the Flying Cloud* by Armstrong Sperry—John C. Winston

1937 **Medal:** *Roller Skates* by Ruth Sawyer—Viking
Honor Books: *Phoebe Fairchild: Her Book* by Lois Lenski—Frederick A. Stokes; *Whistler's Van* by Idwal Jones—Viking; *Golden Basket* by Ludwig Bemelmans—Viking; *Winterbound* by Margery Bianco—Viking; *Audubon* by Constance Rourke—Harcourt Brace; *The Codfish Musket* by Agnes Hewes—Doubleday, Doran

1938 **Medal:** *The White Stag* by Kate Seredy—Viking
Honor Books: *Pecos Bill* by James Cloyd Bowman—Little, Brown; *Bright Island* by Mabel Robinson—Random House; *On the Banks of Plum Creek* by Laura Ingalls Wilder—Harper and Brothers

1939 **Medal:** *Thimble Summer* by Elizabeth Enright—Holt, Rinehart & Winston
Honor Books: *Nino* by Valenti Angelo—Viking; *Mr. Popper's Penguins* by Richard and Florence Atwater—Little, Brown; *"Hello the Boat!"* by Phyllis Crawford—Henry Holt; *Leader by Destiny: George Washington, Man and Patriot* by Jeanette Eaton—Harcourt Brace; *Penn* by Elizabeth Janet Gray—Viking

1940 **Medal:** *Daniel Boone* by James Daugherty—Viking
Honor Books: *The Singing Tree* by Kate Seredy—Viking; *Runner of the Mountain Tops: The Life of Louis Agassiz* by Mabel Robinson—Random House; *By the Shores of Silver Lake* by Laura Ingalls Wilder—Harper and Brothers; *Boy with a Pack* by Stephen W. Meader—Harcourt Brace

1941 **Medal:** *Call It Courage* by Armstrong Sperry—Macmillan
Honor Books: *Blue Willow* by Doris Gates—Viking; *Young Mac of Fort Vancouver* by Mary Jane Carr—Thomas Y. Crowell; *The Long Winter* by Laura Ingalls Wilder—Harper and Brothers; *Nansen* by Anna Gertrude Hall—Viking

1942 **Medal:** *The Matchlock Gun* by Walter D. Edmonds—Dodd, Mead
Honor Books: *Little Town on the Prairie* by Laura Ingalls Wilder—Harper and Brothers; *George Washington's World* by Genevieve Foster—Charles Scribner's Sons; *Indian Captive: The Story of Mary Jemison* by Lois Lenski—Frederick A. Stokes; *Down Ryton Water* by Eva Roe Gaggin—Viking

1943 **Medal:** *Adam of the Road* by Elizabeth Janet Gray—Viking
Honor Books: *The Middle Moffat* by Eleanor Estes—Harcourt Brace; *Have You Seen Tom Thumb?* by Mabel Leigh Hunt—Frederick A. Stokes

1944 **Medal:** *Johnny Tremain* by Esther Forbes—Houghton Mifflin
Honor Books: *The Happy Golden Years* by Laura Ingalls Wilder—Harper and Brothers; *Fog Magic* by Julia Sauer—Viking; *Rufus M.* by Eleanor Estes—Harcourt Brace; *Mountain Born* by Elizabeth Yates—Coward-McCann

1945 **Medal:** *Rabbit Hill* by Robert Lawson—Viking
Honor Books: *The Hundred Dresses* by Eleanor Estes—Harcourt Brace; *The Silver Pencil* by Alice Dalgliesh—Charles Scribner's Sons; *Abraham Lincoln's World* by Genevieve Foster—Charles Scribner's Sons; *Lone Journey: The Life of Roger Williams* by Jeanette Eaton—Harcourt Brace

1946 **Medal:** *Strawberry Girl* by Lois Lenski—J. B. Lippincott
Honor Books: *Justin Morgan Had a Horse* by Marguerite Henry—Wilcox & Follett; *The Moved-Outers* by Florence Crannell Means—Houghton Mifflin; *Bhimsa, the Dancing Bear* by Christine Weston—Charles Scribner's Sons; *New Found World* by Katherine Shippen—Viking

1947 **Medal:** *Miss Hickory* by Carolyn Sherwin Bailey—Viking
Honor Books: *Wonderful Year* by Nancy Barnes—J. Messner; *Big Tree* by Mary and Conrad Buff—Viking; *The Heavenly Tenants* by William Maxwell—Harper and Brothers; *The Avion My Uncle Flew* by Cyrus Fisher—Appleton-Century; *The Hidden Treasure of Glaston* by Eleanore Jewett—Viking

1948 **Medal:** *The Twenty-One Balloons* by William Pene du Bois—Viking
Honor Books: *Pancakes-Paris* by Claire Huchet Bishop—Viking; *Le Lun, Lad of Courage* by Carolyn Treffinger—Abingdon-Cokesbury; *The Quaint and Curious Quest of Johnny Longfoot* by Catherine Besterman—Bobbs Merrill; *The Cowtail Switch and Other West African Stories* by Harold Courlander—Henry Holt; *Misty of Chincoteague* by Marguerite Henry—Rand McNally

1949 **Medal:** *King of the Wind* by Marguerite Henry—Rand McNally
Honor Books: *Seabird* by Holling C. Holling—Houghton Mifflin; *Daughter of the Mountains* by Louis Rankin—Viking; *My Father's Dragon* by Ruth S. Gannett—Random House; *Story of the Negro* by Arna Bontemps—Alfred A. Knopf

1950 **Medal:** *The Door in the Wall* by Marguerite de Angeli—Doubleday
Honor Books: *Tree of Freedom* by Rebecca Caudill—Viking; *The Blue Cat of Castle Town* by Catherine Cobletz—Longmans, Green; *Kildee House* by Rutherford Montgomery—Doubleday; *George Washington* by Genevieve Foster—Charles Scribner's Sons; *Song of the Pines: A Story of Norwegian Lumbering in Wisconsin* by Walter and Marion Havighurst—John C. Winston

1951 **Medal:** *Amos Fortune, Free Man* by Elizabeth Yates—E. P. Dutton
Honor Books: *Better Known as Johnny Appleseed* by Mabel Leigh Hunt—J. B. Lippincott; *Gandhi, Fighter Without a Sword* by Jeanette Eaton—Morrow; *Abraham Lincoln, Friend of the People* by Clara Ingram Judson—Wilcox & Follett; *The Story of Appleby Capple* by Anne Parrish—Harper

1952 **Medal:** *Ginger Pye* by Eleanor Estes—Harcourt Brace
Honor Books: *Americans Before Columbus* by Elizabeth Baity—Viking; *Minn of the Mississippi* by Holling C. Holling—Houghton Mifflin; *The Defender* by Nicholas Kalashnikoff—Charles Scribner's Sons; *The Light at Tern Rock* by Julia Sauer—Viking; *The Apple and the Arrow* by Mary and Conrad Buff—Houghton Mifflin

1953 **Medal:** *Secret of the Andes* by Ann Nolan Clark—Viking
Honor Books: *Charlotte's Web* by E. B. White—Harper; *Moccasin Trail* by Eloise McGraw—Coward-McCann; *Red Sails to Capri* by Ann Weil—Viking; *The Bears on Hemlock Mountain* by Alice Dalgliesh—Charles Scribner's Sons; *Birthdays of Freedom, Vol. 1* by Genevieve Foster—Charles Scribner's Sons

1954 **Medal:** *And Now Miguel* by Joseph Krumgold—Thomas Y. Crowell
Honor Books: *All Alone* by Claire Huchet Bishop—Viking; *Shadrach* by Meindert DeJong—Harper; *Hurry Home, Candy* by Meindert DeJong—Harper; *Theodore Roosevelt, Fighting Patriot* by Clara Ingram Judson—Follett; *Magic Maize* by Mary and Conrad Buff—Houghton Mifflin

1955 **Medal:** *The Wheel on the School* by Meindert DeJong—Harper
Honor Books: *The Courage of Sarah Noble* by Alice Dalgliesh—Charles Scribner's Sons; *Banner in the Sky* by James Ullman—J. B. Lippincott

1956 **Medal:** *Carry on, Mr. Bowditch* by Jean Lee Latham—Houghton Mifflin
Honor Books: *The Secret River* by Marjorie Kinnan Rawlings—Charles Scribner's Sons; *The Golden Name Day* by Jennie Lindquist—Harper; *Men, Microscopes, and Living Things* by Katherine Shippen—Viking

1957 **Medal:** *Miracles on Maple Hill* by Virginia Sorensen—Harcourt Brace
Honor Books: *Old Yeller* by Fred Gipson—Harper; *The House of Sixty Fathers* by Meindert DeJong—Harper; *Mr. Justice Holmes* by Clara Ingram Judson—Follett; *The Corn Grows Ripe* by Dorothy Rhoads—Viking; *Black Fox of Lorne* by Marguerite de Angeli—Doubleday

1958 **Medal:** *Rifles for Watie* by Harold Keith—Thomas Y. Crowell
Honor Books: *The Horsecatcher* by Mari Sandoz—Westminister; *Gone-Away Lake* by Elizabeth Enright—Harcourt Brace; *The Great Wheel* by Robert Lawson—Viking; *Tom Paine, Freedom's Apostle* by Leo Gurko—Thomas Y. Crowell

1959 **Medal:** *The Witch of Blackbird Pond* by Elizabeth George Speare—Houghton Mifflin
Honor Books: *The Family Under the Bridge* by Natalie Savage Carlson—Harper; *Along Came a Dog* by Meindert DeJong—Harper; *Chucaro: Wild Pony of the Pampa* by Francis Kalnay—Harcourt Brace; *The Perilous Road* by William O. Steele—Harcourt Brace

1960 **Medal:** *Onion John* by Joseph Krumgold—Thomas Y. Crowell
Honor Books: *My Side of the Mountain* by Jean Craighead George—E. P. Dutton; *America is Born* by Gerald W. Johnson—Morrow; *The Gammage Cup* by Carol Kendall—Harcourt Brace

1961 **Medal:** *Island of the Blue Dolphins* by Scott O'Dell—Houghton Mifflin
Honor Books: *America Moves Forward* by Gerald W. Johnson—Morrow; *Old Ramon* by Jack Schaefer—Houghton Mifflin; *The Cricket in Times Square* by George Selden—Farrar, Straus & Giroux

1962 **Medal:** *The Bronze Bow* by Elizabeth George Speare—Houghton Mifflin
Honor Books: *Frontier Living* by Edwin Tunis—World; *The Golden Goblet* by Eloise McCraw—Coward-McCann; *Belling the Tiger* by Mary Stolz—Harper

1963 **Medal:** *A Wrinkle in Time* by Madeleine L'Engle—Farrar, Straus & Giroux
Honor Books: *Thistle and Thyme: Tales and Legends from Scotland* by Sorche Nic Leodhas—Holt, Rinehart & Winston; *Men of Athens* by Olivia Coolidge—Houghton Mifflin

1964 **Medal:** *It's Like This, Cat* by Emily Cheney Neville—Harper & Row
Honor Books: *Rascal* by Sterling North—E. P. Dutton; *The Loner* by Ester Wier—D. McKay

1965 **Medal:** *Shadow of a Bull* by Maia Wojciechowska—Atheneum
Honor Book: *Across Five Aprils* by Irene Hunt—Follett

1966 **Medal:** *I, Juan de Pareja* by Elizabeth Borton de Trevino—Farrar, Straus & Giroux
Honor Books: *The Black Cauldron* by Lloyd Alexander—Holt, Rinehart & Winston; *The Animal Family* by Randall Jarrell—Pantheon; *The Noonday Friends* by Mary Stolz—Harper & Row

1967 **Medal:** *Up a Road Slowly* by Irene Hunt—Follett
Honor Books: *The King's Fifth* by Scott O'Dell—Houghton Mifflin; *Zlateh the Goat and Other Stories* by Isaac Bashevis Singer—Harper & Row; *The Jazz Man* by Mary H. Weik—Atheneum

1968 **Medal:** *From the Mixed-Up Files of Mrs. Basil E. Frankweiler* by E. L. Konigsburg—Atheneum
Honor Books: *Jennifer, Hecate, Macbeth, William McKinley, and Me, Elizabeth* by E. L. Konigsburg—Atheneum; *The Black Pearl* by Scott O'Dell—Houghton Mifflin; *The Fearsome Inn* by Isaac Bashevis Singer—Charles Scribner's Sons; *The Egypt Game* by Zilpha Keatley Snyder—Atheneum

1969 **Medal:** *The High King* by Lloyd Alexander—Holt, Rinehart & Winston
Honor Books: *To Be a Slave* by Julius Lester—Dial; *When Shlemiel Went to Warsaw and Other Stories* by Isaac Bashevis Singer—Farrar, Straus & Giroux

1970 **Medal:** *Sounder* by William H. Armstrong—Harper & Row
Honor Books: *Our Eddie* by Sulamith Ish-Kishor—Pantheon; *The Many Ways of Seeing: An Introduction to the Pleasures of Art* by Janet Gaylord Moore—World; *Journey Outside* by Mary Q. Steele—Viking

1971 **Medal:** *Summer of the Swans* by Betsy Byars—Atheneum
Honor Books: *Kneeknock Rise* by Natalie Babbitt—Farrar, Straus & Giroux; *Enchantress from the Stars* by Sylvia Louise Engdahl—Atheneum; *Sing Down the Moon* by Scott O'Dell—Houghton Mifflin

1972 **Medal:** *Mrs. Frisby and the Rats of NIMH* by Robert C. O'Brien—Atheneum
Honor Books: *Incident at Hawk's Hill* by Allan W. Eckert—Little, Brown; *The Planet of Junior Brown* by Virginia Hamilton—Macmillan; *The Tombs of Atuan* by Ursula K. LeGuin—Atheneum; *Annie and the Old One* by Miska Miles—Little, Brown; *The Headless Cupid* by Zilpha Keatley Snyder—Atheneum

1973 **Medal:** *Julie of the Wolves* by Jean Craighead George—Harper & Row
Honor Books: *Frog and Toad Together* by Arnold Lobel—Harper & Row; *The Upstairs Room* by Johanna Reiss—Thomas Y. Crowell; *The Witches of Worm* by Zilpha Keatley Snyder—Atheneum

1974 **Medal:** *The Slave Dancer* by Paula Fox—Bradbury
Honor Book: *The Dark is Rising* by Susan Cooper—Atheneum

1975 **Medal:** *M. C. Higgins, the Great* by Virginia Hamilton—Simon & Schuster
Honor Books: *Figgs & Phantoms* by Ellen Raskin—E. P. Dutton; *My Brother Sam is Dead* by James Lincoln Collier and Christopher Collier—Four Winds; *The Perilous Gard* by Elizabeth Marie Pope—Houghton Mifflin; *Philip Hall Likes Me, I Reckon Maybe* by Bette Greene—Dial

1976 **Medal:** *The Grey King* by Susan Cooper—Atheneum
Honor Books: *The Hundred Penny Box* by Sharon Bell Mathis—Viking; *Dragonwings* by Laurence Yep—Harper & Row

1977 **Medal:** *Roll of Thunder, Hear My Cry* by Mildred D. Taylor—Dial
Honor Books: *Abel's Island* by William Steig—Farrar, Straus & Giroux; *A String in the Harp* by Nancy Bond—Atheneum

1978 **Medal:** *Bridge to Terabithia* by Katherine Paterson—Thomas Y. Crowell
Honor Books: *Ramona and Her Father* by Beverly Cleary—Morrow; *Anpao: An American Indian Odyssey* by Jamake Highwater—J. B. Lippincott

1979 **Medal:** *The Westing Game* by Ellen Raskin—E. P. Dutton
Honor Book: *The Great Gilly Hopkins* by Katherine Paterson—Thomas Y. Crowell

1980 **Medal:** *A Gathering of Days: A New England Girl's Journal 1830–32* by Joan Blos—Charles Scribner's Sons
Honor Book: *The Road from Home: The Story of an Armenian Girl* by David Kherdian—Morrow

1981 **Medal:** *Jacob Have I Loved* by Katherine Paterson—Thomas Y. Crowell
Honor Books: *The Fledgling* by Jane Langton—Harper & Row; *A Ring of Endless Light* by Madeleine L'Engle—Farrar, Straus & Giroux

1982 **Medal:** *A Visit to William Blake's Inn: Poems for Innocent and Experienced Travelers* by Nancy Willard—Harcourt Brace Jovanovich
Honor Books: *Ramona Quimby, Age 8* by Beverly Cleary—Morrow; *Upon the Head of the Goat: A Childhood in Hungary, 1939–1944* by Aranka Siegal—Farrar, Straus & Giroux

1983 **Medal:** *Dicey's Song* by Cynthia Voigt—Atheneum
Honor Books: *Blue Sword* by Robin McKinley—Greenwillow; *Doctor DeSoto* by William Steig—Farrar, Straus & Giroux; *Graven Images* by Paul Fleischman—Harper & Row; *Homesick: My Own Story* by Jean Fritz—Putnam; *Sweet Whisper, Brother Rush* by Virginia Hamilton—Philomel

1984 **Medal:** *Dear Mr. Henshaw* by Beverly Cleary—Morrow
Honor Books: *The Sign of the Beaver* by Elizabeth George Speare—Houghton Mifflin; *A Solitary Blue* by Cynthia Voigt—Atheneum; *The Wish Giver* by Bill Brittain—Harper & Row; *Sugaring Time* by Kathryn Lasky—Macmillan

1985 **Medal:** *The Hero and the Crown* by Robin McKinley—Greenwillow
Honor Books: *Like Jake and Me* by Mavis Jukes—Alfred A. Knopf; *The Moves Make the Man* by Bruce Brooks—Harper & Row; *One-Eyed Cat* by Paula Fox—Bradbury

1986 **Medal:** *Sarah, Plain and Tall* by Patricia MacLachlan—Harper & Row
Honor Books: *Commodore Perry in the Land of the Shogun* by Rhoda Blumberg—Lothrop, Lee & Shepard; *Dogsong* by Gary Paulsen—Bradbury

1987 **Medal:** *The Whipping Boy* by Sid Fleischman—Greenwillow
Honor Books: *A Fine White Dust* by Cynthia Rylant—Bradbury; *On My Honor* by Marion Dane Bauer—Clarion; *Volcano: The Eruption and Healing of Mount St. Helens* by Patricia Lauber—Bradbury

1988 **Medal:** *Lincoln: A Photobiography* by Russell Freedman—Clarion
Honor Books: *After the Rain* by Norma Fox Mazer—Morrow; *Hatchet* by Gary Paulsen—Bradbury

1989 **Medal:** *Joyful Noise: Poems for Two Voices* by Paul Fleischman—Harper & Row
Honor Books: *In the Beginning: Creation Stories from Around the World* by Virginia Hamilton—Harcourt Brace Jovanovich; *Scorpions* by Walter Dean Myers—Harper & Row

1990 **Medal:** *Number the Stars* by Lois Lowry—Houghton Mifflin

Honor Books: *Afternoon of the Elves* by Janet Taylor Lisle—Orchard; *Shabanu, Daughter of the Wind* by Susan Fisher Staples—Alfred A. Knopf; *The Winter Room* by Gary Paulsen—Orchard

1991 **Medal:** *Maniac Magee* by Jerry Spinelli—Little, Brown
Honor Book: *The True Confessions of Charlotte Doyle* by Avi—Orchard

1992 **Medal:** *Shiloh* by Phyllis Reynolds Naylor—Atheneum
Honor Books: *Nothing but the Truth* by Avi—Orchard; *Wright Brothers* by Russell Freedman—Holiday House

1993 **Medal:** *Missing May* by Cynthia Rylant—Orchard
Honor Books: *What Hearts* by Bruce Brooks—HarperCollins; *Dark Thirty: Southern Tales of the Supernatural* by Patricia C. McKissack—Alfred A. Knopf; *Somewhere in the Darkness* by Walter Dean Myers—Scholastic

1994 **Medal:** *The Giver* by Lois Lowry—Houghton Mifflin
Honor Books: *Crazy Lady!* by Jane Leslie Conly—HarperCollins; *Dragon's Gate* by Laurence Yep—HarperCollins; *Eleanor Roosevelt: A Life of Discovery* by Russell Freedman—Clarion

1995 **Medal:** *Walk Two Moons* by Sharon Creech—HarperCollins
Honor Books: *Catherine, Called Birdy* by Karen Cushman—Clarion; *The Ear, the Eye, and the Arm* by Nancy Farmer—Orchard

1996 **Medal:** *The Midwife's Apprentice* by Karen Cushman—Clarion
Honor Books: *What Jamie Saw* by Carolyn Coman—Front Street; *The Watsons Go to Birmingham—1963* by Christopher Paul Curtis—Dellacourt; *Yolanda's Genius* by Carol Fenner—Margaret K. McElderry Books; *The Great Fire* by Jim Murphy—Scholastic

1997 **Medal:** *The View from Saturday* by E. L. Konigsburg—Atheneum
Honor Books: *A Girl Named Disaster* by Nancy Farmer—Orchard; *Belle Prater's Boy* by Ruth White—Farrar; Straus & Giroux; *Moorchild* by Eloise McGraw—Simon & Schuster; *The Thief* by Megan Whalen Turner—Greenwillow

Index

Richgels, D. J., 119, 136, 267
Rickelman, R. J., 84
Ringgold, F., 39, 431, 432
Roach, V., 380
Road, 431
Road to Memphis, The (Taylor), 431
Roar and More (Kuskin), 137
Robb, L., 272, 367
Robbins, R., 421
Robertson, D. E. J., 393
Robins, J., 186, 187
Robinson, B., 46, 210
Robson, P., 371
Rockwell, A., 123, 301
Rockwell, H., 122, 123
Rockwell, T., 46, 327
Roe, B. D., 474
Roehler, L. R., 241
Rogers, H. S., 401
Rogers, J., 268
Rohmer, H., 439
Roll of Thunder, Hear My Cry (Taylor), 269, 349, 419, 431, 432
Roll Over! (Gerstein), 187
Roop, C., 265
Roop, P., 265
Rootabaga Stories (Sandburg), 7
Rosa Parks (Greenfield), 48
Rosario, I., 420
Rosenblatt, L. M., 204, 205, 240, 347, 348
Rosenblum, R., 257
Rosenshine, B. V., 91, 217
Rosenthal, M., 255
Roser, N. L., 438
Rosie's Walk (Hutchins), 39, 128, 175, 185
Roskos, K., 77, 144
Rough-Faced Girl, The (Martin), 40, 421
Round-robin reading, 330
Rounds, G. O., 41, 334
Routman, R., 81, 91, 363, 395
Rubin, A., 344, 345, 347
Rudenga, E. A., 76
Rudman, M. K., 402
Runaway Mittens, The (Rogers), 268
Running records, 478–479

S

Sadako and the Thousand Paper Cranes (Coerr), 268, 394, 425
Salamanders (Bernhard and Bernhard), 270
Salinger, T. S., 120, 275, 349
Sam, Bangs, and Moonshine (Ness), 56, 219, 221, 230
Sampson, M., 24
Samuels, S. J., 323
San Souci, R., 40, 432
Sandburg, C., 7, 219, 327
Sanders, N. M., 226, 227

Sarah, Plain and Tall (MacLachlan), 179, 229, 240, 327, 478
Savage, J. F., 17, 80, 319, 403
Saxby, M., 35, 54
Say, A., 24, 420, 424
Saying Good-bye to Grandma (Thomas), 401
Scaffolded Questioning, for reading assessment, 463
Scaffolding, 385
and problem readers, 385–386
Scanning, 312
Schade, S., 137
Scharer, P. L., 17
Schedule. *See* Time-elements
Schemata, 112–114
and comprehension, 232–235
and comprehension of expository text, 287–289
Schiller, A., 167
Schiro, M., 274
Schmidt, K., 186
Schmitt, M. C., 236
Scholastic Magazines, 311
Scholastic's A+ Junior Guide to Good Writing (Colligan), 371
Schroeder, A., 422
Schumaker, M. P., 92, 393, 394, 400
Schumaker, R. C., 393, 394, 400
Schumaker, R. L., 92
Schwartz, D. M., 273
Science and Children (journal), 271
Science and Technology in Fact and Fiction: A Guide to Children's Books (Kennedy, Spangler, Vanderwerf), 271
Science fiction, elements of, 44–45
Science through Children's Literature: An Integrated Approach (Butzow and Butzow), 271
Science, trade books for, 270–271
Scieszka, J., 57, 349
Scott, S., 420
Scripts, writing of, 369
Searfoss, L. W., 334
Sebesta, S. L., 56, 274
Secret Garden, The (Burnett), 349
Secrets of Belltown, The (Murphy), 302
Seed Is a Promise, A (Merrill), 270
Seeger, P., 420
Segal, E., 82
Segal, L., 187
Seidman, J. F., 273
Seifert-Kessell, N., 290
Selective Reading Guides, 313
Self-selection of materials, 9
Seligman, I., 187
Semantic context clues, 176–178
Semantic mapping, 163–165
and problem readers, 385
Semantic study, 167

Sendak, M., 7, 14, 38, 52, 61, 129, 130, 135, 138, 225, 274
Sentences, and comprehension, 214, 284–285
Sequence, comprehension of, 222–223
Setting, 51–52
Seven Blind Mice (Young), 143
Seven Little Ducks (Friskey), 187
Seymour, S., 48, 75, 270, 271
Shablak, S. L., 313
Shadow (Brown), 274
Shadow reading, 332
Shanahan, T., 346, 382
Shannon, P., 19, 20, 81
Shapes (Reiss), 123, 273
Sharke, K., 94
Sharmat, M. W., 165, 224, 371
Sharp, R. M., 87
Sharp, V. F., 87
Shaw, N., 138
Shecter, B., 186
Sheep on a Ship (Shaw), 138
Sheila Rae, the Brave (Henkes), 186
Shiloh (Naylor), 326
Shipman, D. A., 474
Shoes (Winthrop), 138
Shoop, M., 240
Shopping Cart Art (Seidman and Mintoyne), 273
Showers, P., 138
Shulevitz, U., 187
Sight words, 171–176
listing for beginning readers, 173–174
personal words as, 175
selecting vocabulary, 171–172
teaching of, 172–176
Sign of the Beaver, The (George), 424
Sign of the Beaver, The (Speare), 327
Silent reading, 329
Silvaroli, N. J., 474
Silvernail, D. L., 457
Silverstein, S., 50, 51, 138, 219, 328, 356, 397, 439
Simons, H. D., 345
Sims, R., 430
Sinatra, R. C., 385
Sing a Song of Popcorn (de Regniers, Moore, White, Carr), 137
Sing a Song of Popcorn: Every Child's Book of Poems (de Regniers), 50
Sing Down the Moon (O'Dell), 47
Single-Discipline Literature Model, 255
Sipay, E. R., 271
Sis, P., 273
Sister (Greenfield), 432
Six Sleepy Sheep (Gordon), 137
Skimming, 312
Sky Is Full of Stars, The (Branley), 271
Slake's Limbo (Holman), 95